A Book About Colab
(and Related Activities)

Poster front:
Various artists. Images from *A Book About Colab
(and Related Activities)*. New York: Printed Matter,
2024.

Poster back:
Cara Perlman. *Fingerpaint Portraits*, 1981.
Fingerpaint on paper, 56.5 × 41 cm each.
Courtesy of Cara Perlman.

Cover:
Albert DiMartino. *Colab meeting*.
B/W photograph, 9 × 12.5 cm.
Courtesy of ABC No Rio Book Archive.

Inside cover:
Colab logos by Tom Otterness and Becky Howland.

A Book About Colab (and Related Activities)

Published subsequent to
A Show About Colab (and Related Activities)

at Printed Matter
October 15–November 30, 2011

Including artwork, text, photo documentation,
documents and ephemera by:

Charlie Ahearn
John Ahearn
Patti Astor
Beth B and Scott B
Andy Baird
Liza Béar
Glenn Branca
Andrea Callard
Robert Cooney
Ellen Cooper
Mitch Corber
Diego Cortez
Peter Cramer
Jody Culkin
Jimmy DeSana
Fritz Demmer
Jane Dickson
Albert DiMartino
Stefan Eins
Brigitte Engler
Bradley Eros
Erotic Psyche
  (Bradley Eros
  and Aline Mare)
Barbara Ess
Peter Fend
Coleen Fitzgibbon
Matthew Geller
Mike Glier
Bobby G
  (Robert Goldman)
Ilona Granet

Julie Harrison
John Hogan
Jenny Holzer
Becky Howland
Tod Jorgensen
Lisa Kahane
Francene Keery
Christof Kohlhöfer
Justen Ladda
Sherrie Levine
Joe Lewis
Karen Luna
Aline Mare
Michael McClard
Jorge Mendez
Ann Messner
Dick Miller
Eric Mitchell
Peter Moennig
Terry Mohre
Alan Moore
John Morton
Peter Nadin
Beverly Naidus
James Nares
Joseph Nechvatal
Ocean Earth
  Construction and
  Development (OECD)
Offices of Fend,
  Fitzgibbon, Holzer,
  Nadin, Prince & Winters

Tom Otterness
Carol Parkinson
Cara Perlman
Marcia Resnick
Judy Rifka
Ulli Rimkus
Walter "Mike" Robinson
Tim Rollins & K.O.S.
Christy Rupp
David Schmidlapp
Jane Sherrry
Terise Slotkin
Kiki Smith
Lindzee Smith
Wolfgang Staehle
Jolie Stahl
Betsy Sussler
Seth Tillet
Daryl Turner
Sophie VDT
Franz Vila
Tom Warren
Jack Waters
Sally White
Reese Williams
Robin Winters
Steven Wright
X & Y
  (Coleen Fitzgibbon
  and Robin Winters)

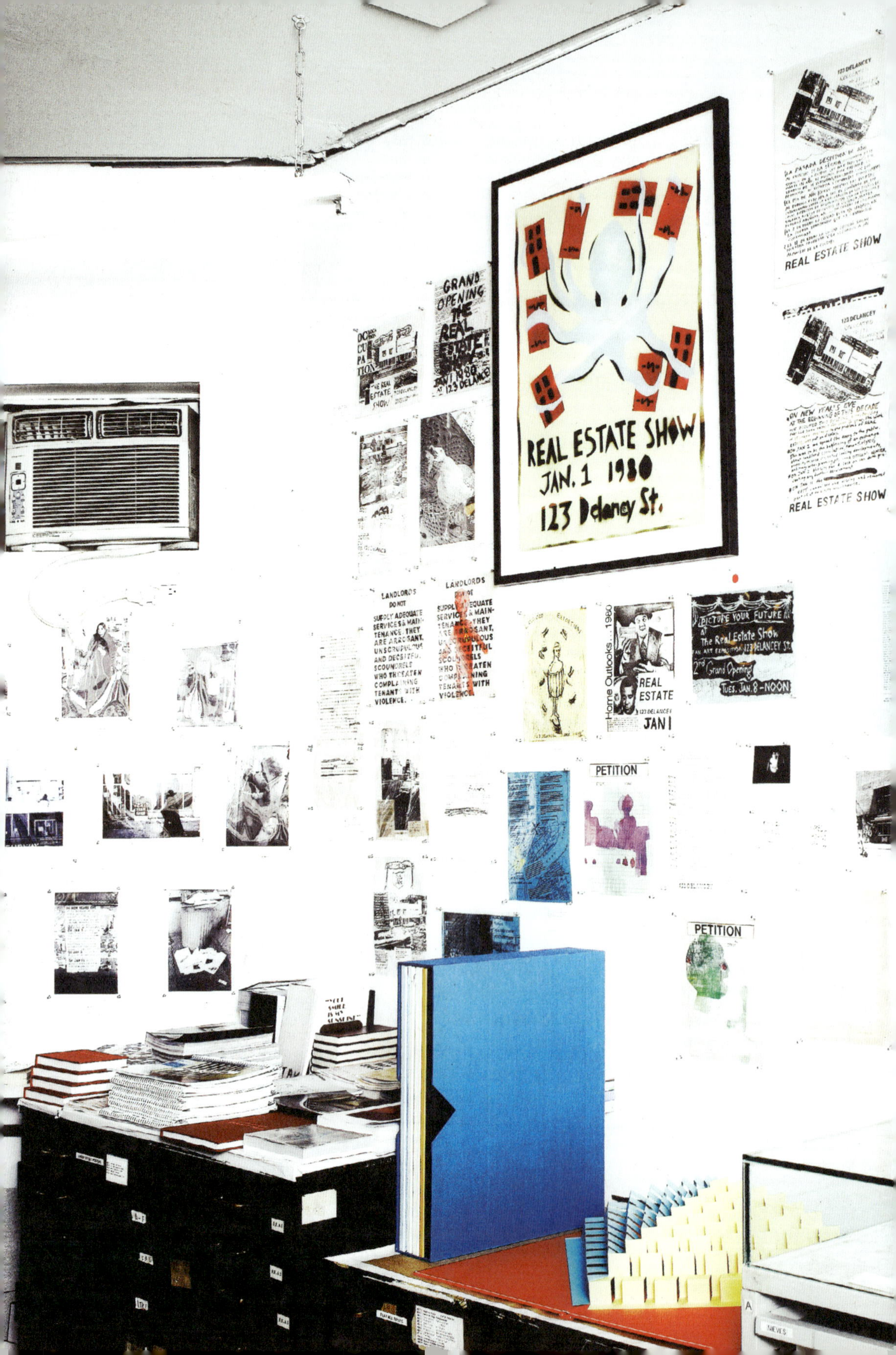

REAL ESTATE SHOW
JAN. 1 1980
123 Delancy St.
GRAND OPENING THE REAL ESTATE SHOW JAN 1980 123 DELANCEY
OCCUPATION
REAL ESTATE SHOW
REAL ESTATE SHOW
LANDLORDS DO NOT SUPPLY ADEQUATE SERVICES & MAINTENANCE. THEY ARE ARROGANT, UNSCRUPULOUS AND DECEITFUL SCOUNDRELS WHO THREATEN COMPLAINING TENANTS WITH VIOLENCE.
LANDLORDS DO NOT SUPPLY ADEQUATE SERVICES & MAINTENANCE. THEY ARE ARROGANT, UNSCRUPULOUS AND DECEITFUL SCOUNDRELS WHO THREATEN COMPLAINING TENANTS WITH VIOLENCE.
Home Outlooks...1980
REAL ESTATE
JAN 1
PICTURE YOUR FUTURE at The Real Estate Show 123 DELANCEY ST.
2nd Grand Opening
TUES. JAN. 8 - NOON
PETITION
PETITION

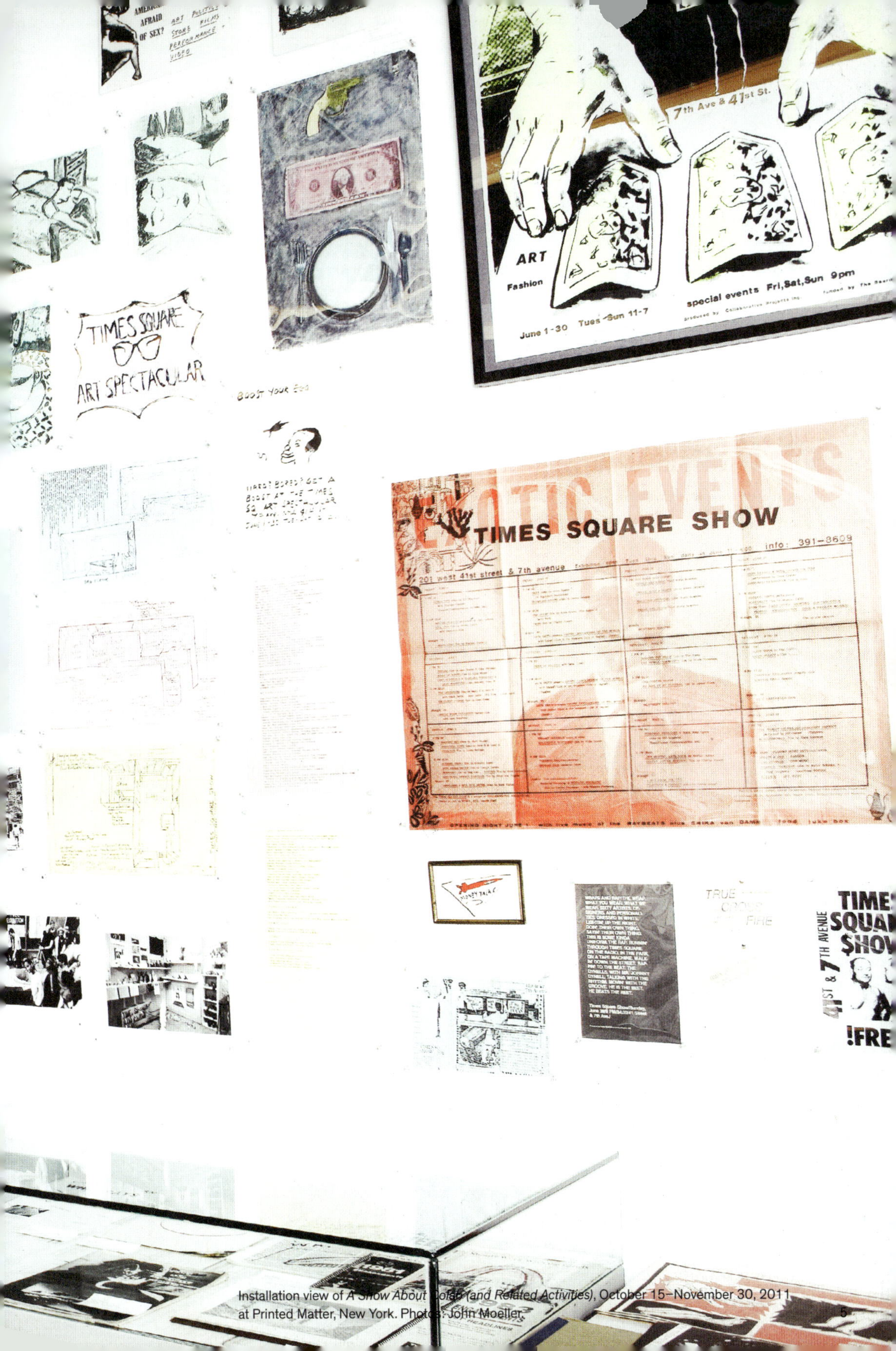

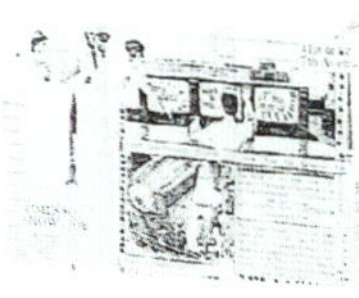

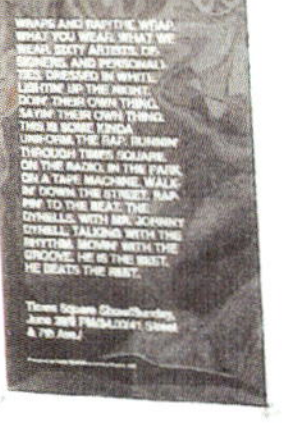

Installation view of *A Show About Colab (and Related Activities)*, October 15–November 30, 2011 at Printed Matter, New York. Photos: John Moeller.

WIN   LOSE
TRY
YOUR LUCK

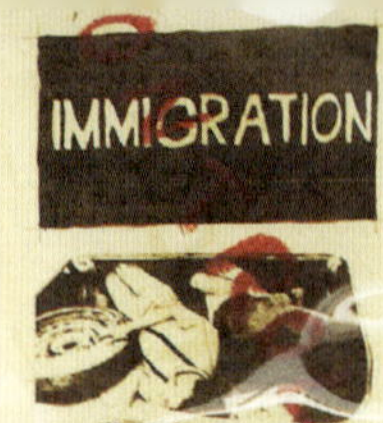

IMMIGRATION

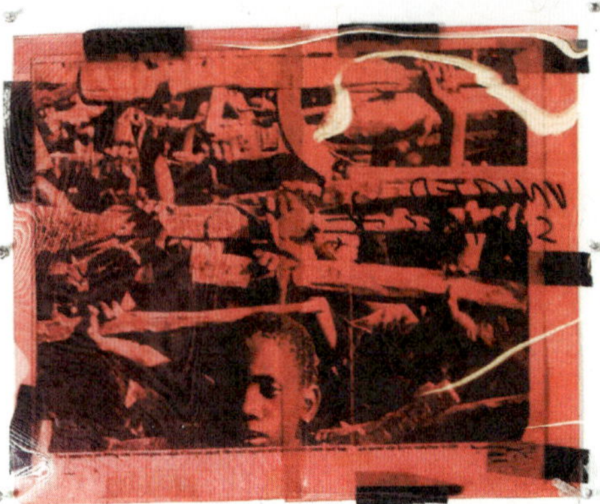

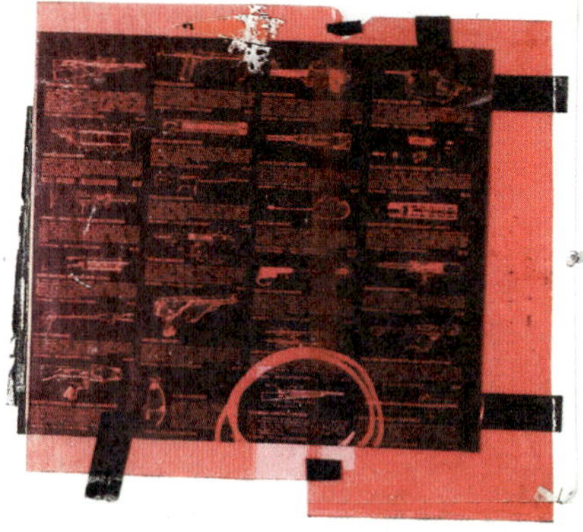

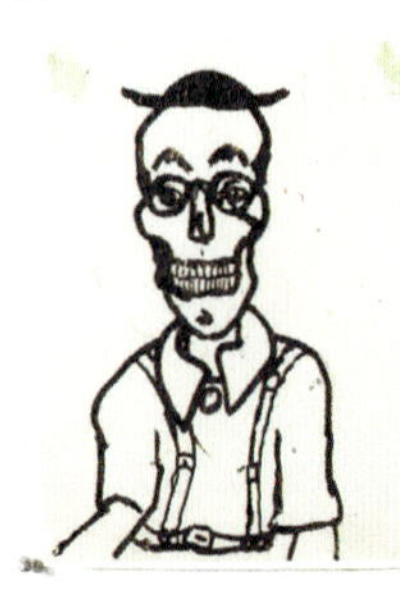

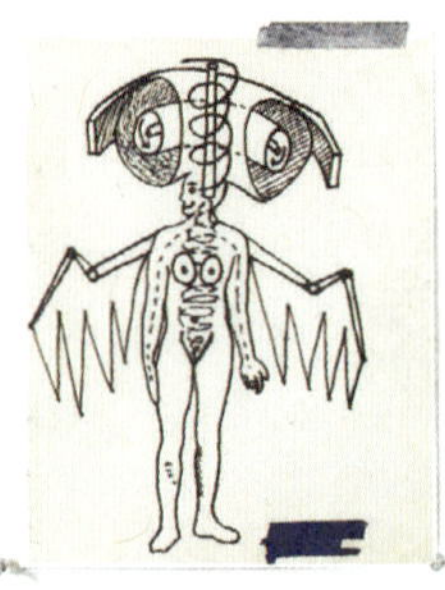

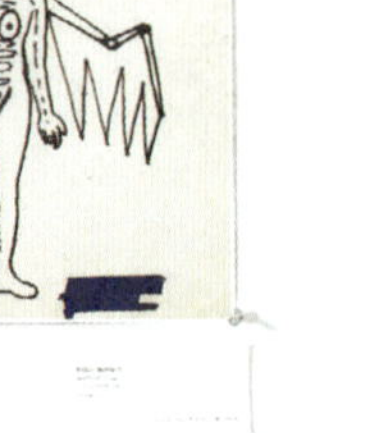

MUTUAL FUNDS!

SA

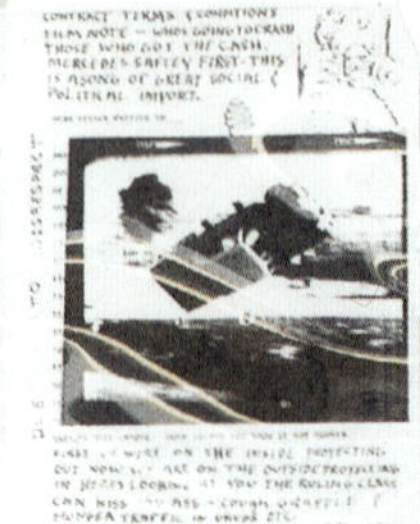

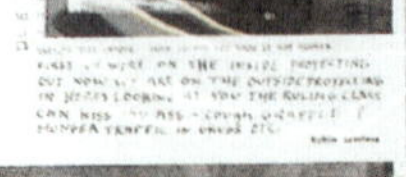

RECIEVE
SEND

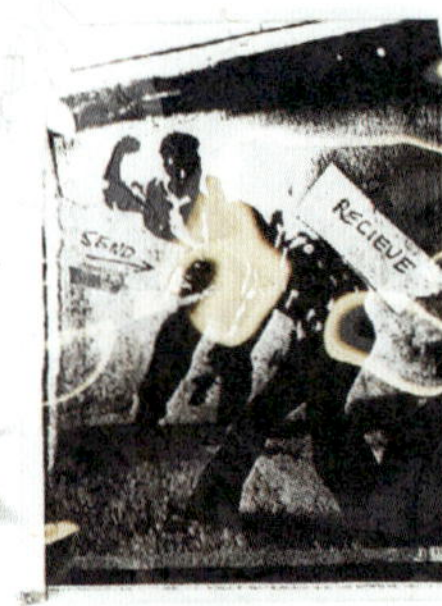

ASS

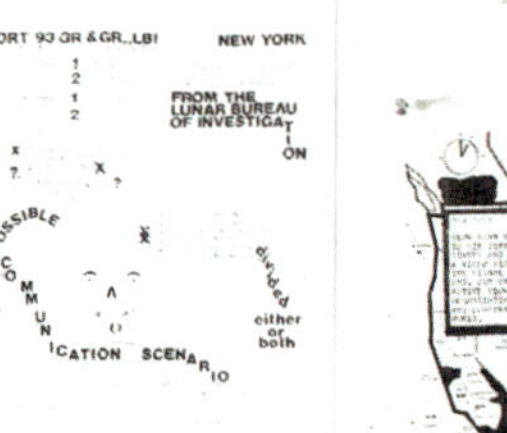

Q.PORT 93 QR & GR. LBI   NEW YORK
1   2
1   2
2
X   FROM THE
?   X   X   LUNAR BUREAU
A POSSIBLE   OF INVESTIGAT   ON
  C   X
  O   X   divided
  M   either
  M   or
  U   both
  N
  I
  CATION SCENARIO
ity
oblique

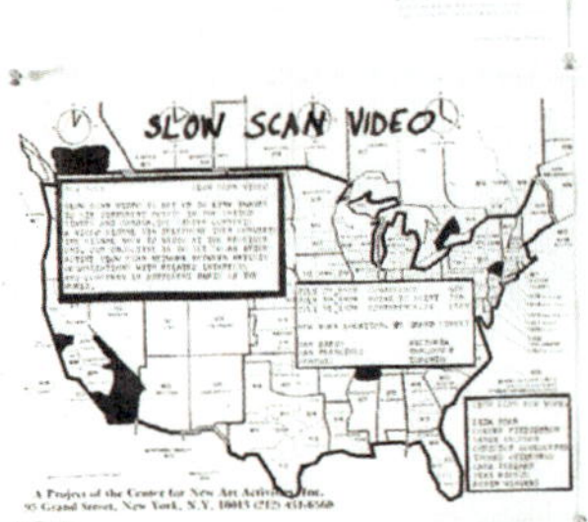

SLOW SCAN VIDEO
A Project of the Center for New Art Activities, Inc.
95 Grand Street, New York, N.Y. 10013 (212) 431-4360

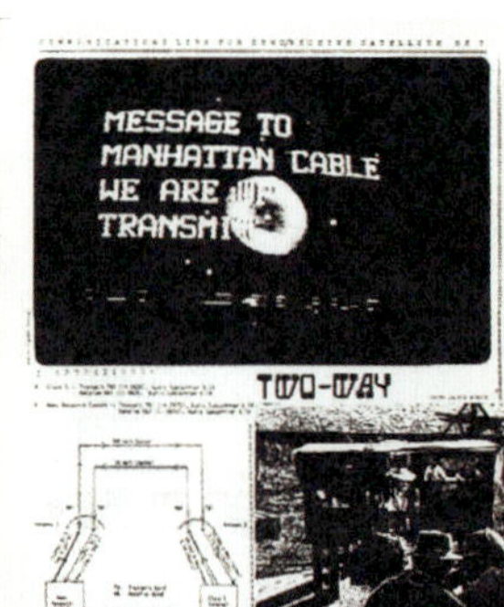

MESSAGE TO
MANHATTAN CABLE
WE ARE
TRANSMI
TWO-WAY

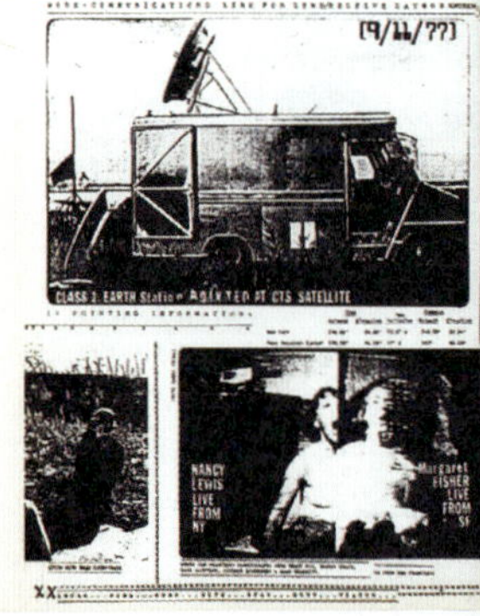

[9/16/??]
CLASS 3 EARTH STATION BUILT TO FIT CTS SATELLITE
NANCY
LEWIS
LIVE
FROM
NY
MARGARET
FISHER
LIVE
FROM

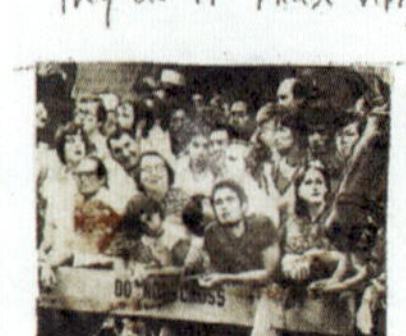

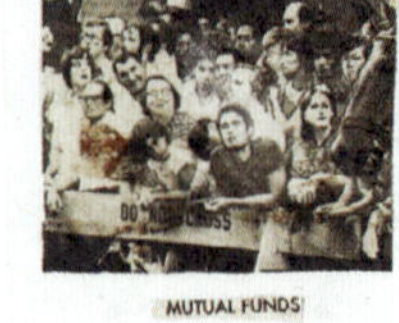

there once was a little village where
all the people lived happy and
productive lives how did
they DO it phase reply

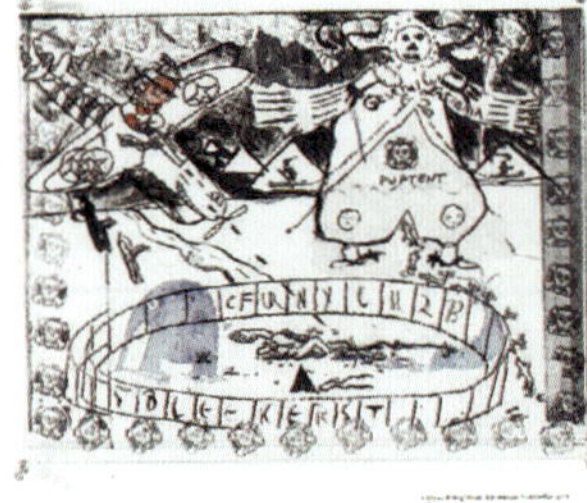

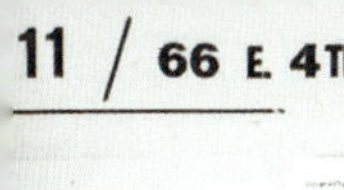

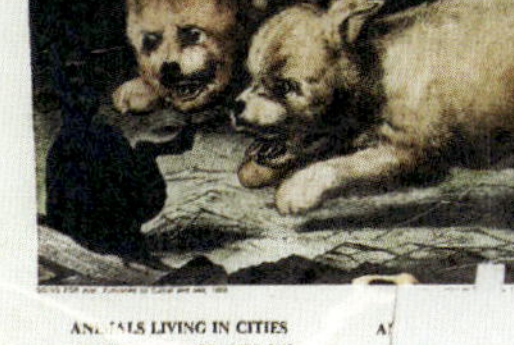

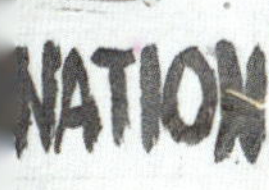

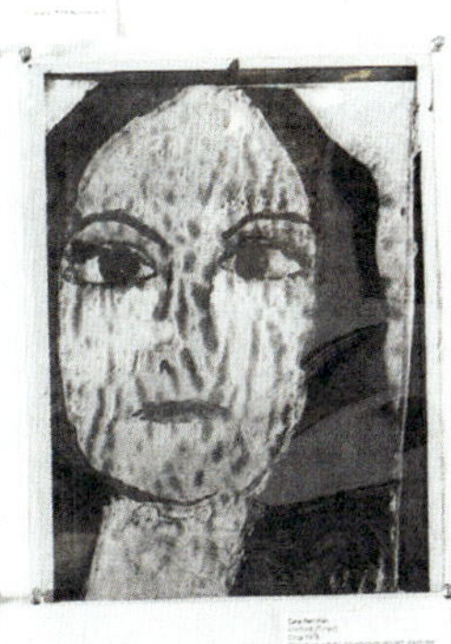

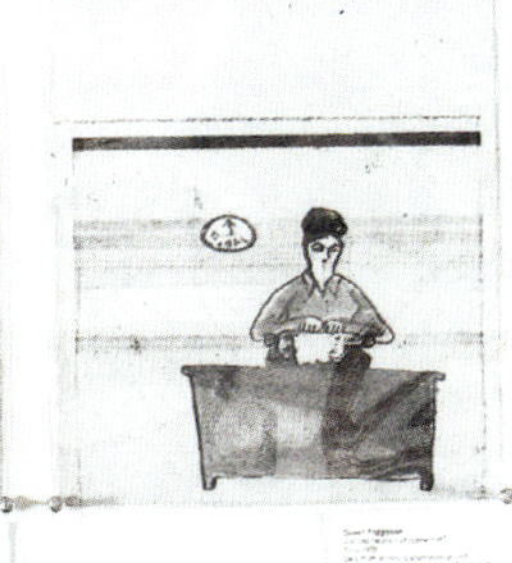

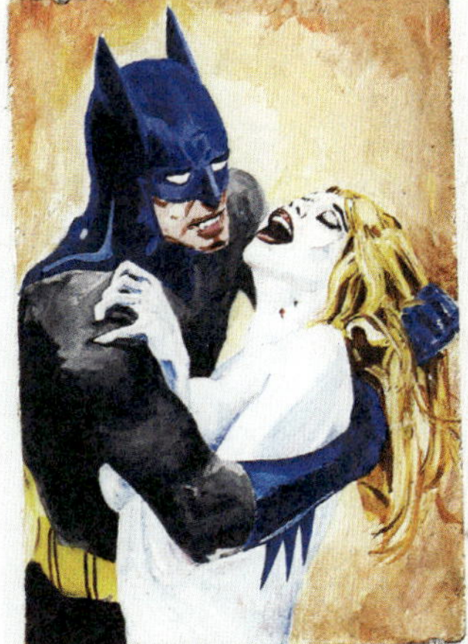

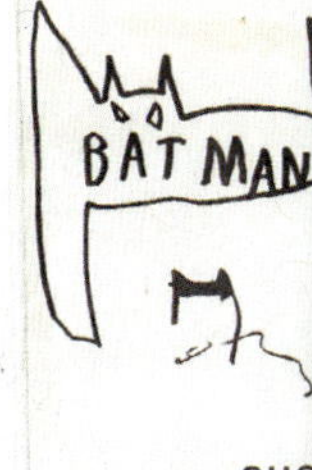

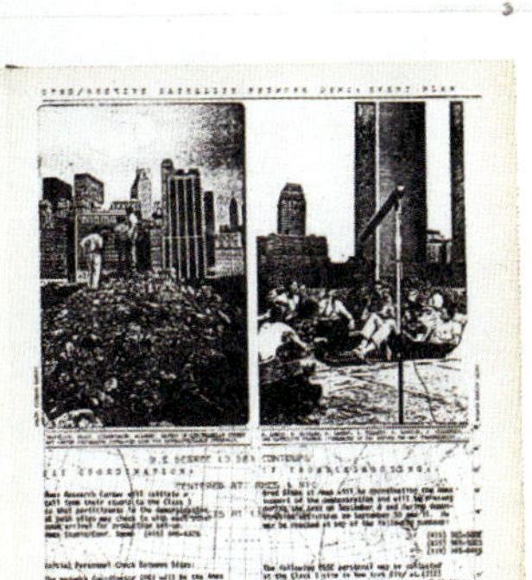

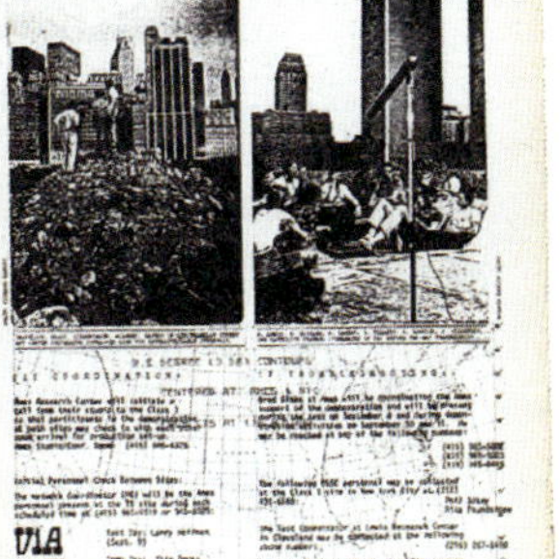

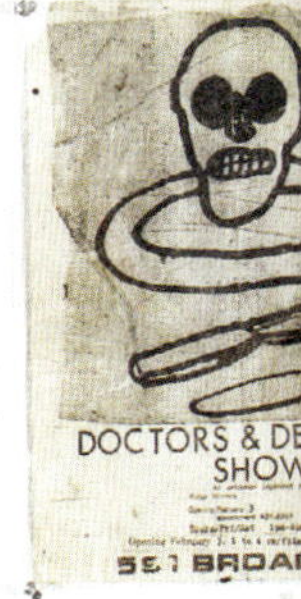

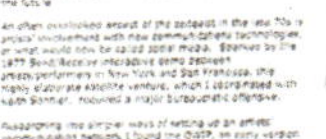

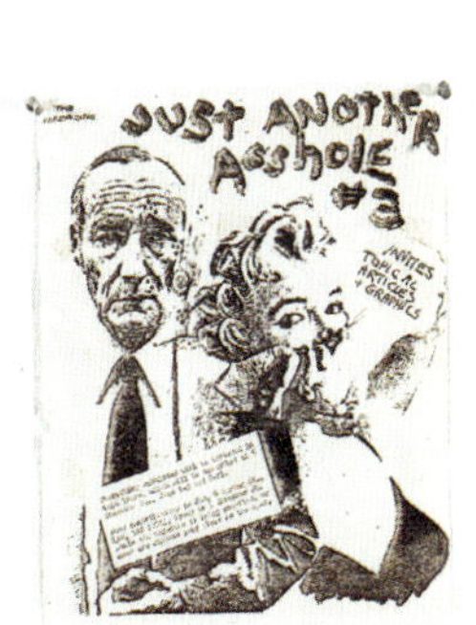

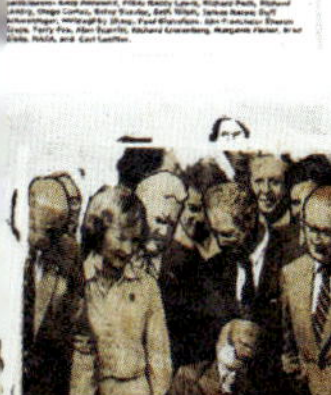

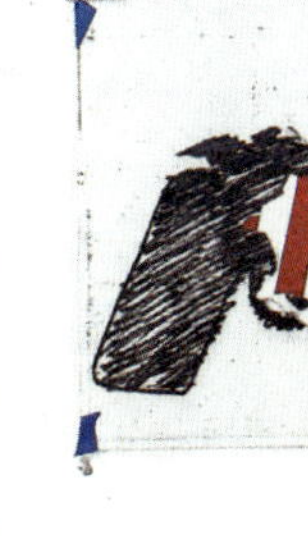

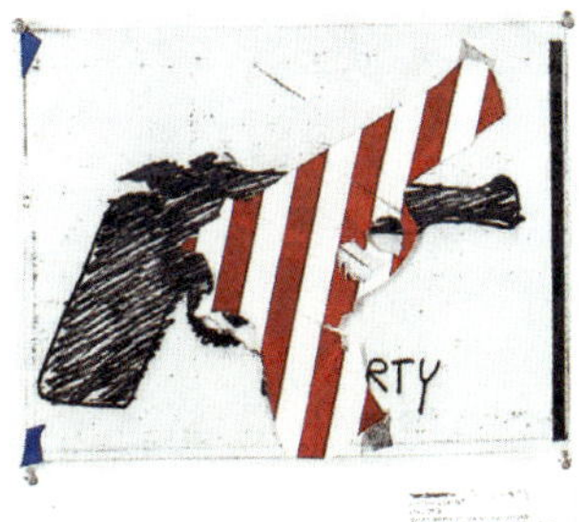

Installation view of *A Show About Colab (and Related Activities)*, October 15–November 30, 2011 at Printed Matter, New York. Photos: John Moeller.

Looking back more than 35 years, Collaborative Projects certainly sounds like a grand success. It took over a vacant city building on Delancey Street in 1980 to mount the *The Real Estate Show*, and was subsequently given the Lower East Side storefront that became ABC No Rio. Later that year, it mounted *The Times Square Show* in a former massage parlor at 7th Avenue and 41st Street, which the *Village Voice* called "the first avant-garde art show of the 1980s." It put on a variety of other exhibitions, and was affiliated with Fashion Moda, run by Stefan Eins and Joe Lewis in the South Bronx. It had a film division—the New Cinema—that operated a movie theater on St Marks Place, and a video division that had a public access cable TV show called Potato Wolf. It put together a yearly holiday gift shop, first on Broome Street, then at Gladstone Gallery, Tilton Gallery and still later at White Columns and Printed Matter.

All together, Colab involved maybe 50 artists or more, helping them make their individual marks and providing a context within which they could work. It's funny to remember, a third of a century later, how random it all felt at the time. We tended to approach serious matters with a fractured nonchalance. It all seemed so simple then, and appears so amazing now. Tom Otterness and John Ahearn talked a slum landlord into letting us use his derelict building in Times Square. Bobby G, Alan Moore and Becky Howland met with city bureaucrats on the Lower East Side and got them to turn over the keys to a city-owned tenement on Rivington Street. We convinced the New York State Council on the Arts and the National Endowment for the Arts to give us thousands and thousands of dollars.

We were a gang of young artists who had nothing to lose, and as a result we had the power to accomplish anything that we could think of.

—Walter Robinson

**Out of the art world &
onto the streets**

—Tom Otterness

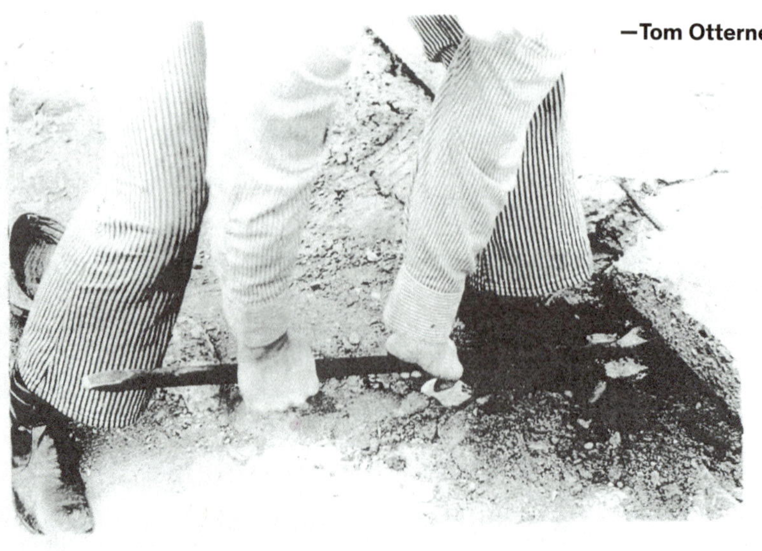

Stefan Eins. *Crowbar*, 1974. Photocopy, 28 × 21.5 cm. Flyer for exhibition
Crowbars and Pulleys at 3 Mercer Street Store. Courtesy of Stefan Eins.

A Book About Colab (and Related Activities)

This publication has been conceived as a book version of the exhibition *A Show About Colab (and Related Activities)* that I put together at Printed Matter in October of 2011, and which surveyed the projects and activities of the artists' group Collaborative Projects, Inc (aka Colab), as well as a wide range of related and overlapping art undertakings. The exhibition material was made up of a broad compilation of ephemera, documents, publications, artworks, and other items that were generously lent from the personal collections of over 35 participants, collaborators and witnesses. On the occasion of bringing all of this together under one roof, the suggestion came from a number of directions that a book should be compiled from all the material. And here, finally, after four years of incubation, it is!

Active from the late 1970s through the mid 80s, Colab was a highly energetic, creative and productive gathering of mostly young downtown artists in New York City. While Colab was initially formed to take advantage of funding sources designed for organizations supporting new art, many group members were also motivated by specifically democratic ideas about artists' collectivity and self-representation. Colab's organizational structure emulated its own creative processes as inclusive, collaborative and broadly accessible, with an open membership and rotating officers. Composed only of artists, Colab advocated a form of cultural activism that was purely artist-driven, sidestepping existing institutions via their own scrappy DIY efforts—the artists did the fundraising, scouted out the exhibition spaces, curated the shows, did their own PR, and created their own critical discourse. They responded to the political themes and predicaments of their time—the recessions of the 1970s; the Reagan era of budget cuts and nuclear armament; the housing crisis, homelessness and gentrification in New York City; and many other social issues both local and global.

With its purposefully open structure, Colab membership allowed for varying levels of involvement and participation. Strictly speaking, a project would be identified as Colab or Colab-affiliated if it had a direct funding tie-in. Various projects had such an affiliation at one point, but also had very much a life of their own; examples here would include *X-Magazine*, the New Cinema screening room, the artists' periodicals *Just Another Asshole* and *Spanner*, and ABC No Rio. Still other projects that were not directly affiliated with Colab fall within the gamut of this book because of the key participation of Colab artists. In this group belongs X & Y, a collaboration between Coleen Fitzgibbon and Robin Winters; the art journal *Art-Rite*, edited by Edit DeAk and Walter Robinson; the Center for New Art Activities' QWIP project; Fashion Moda, the Bronx art space operated by Stefan Eins and Joe Lewis; the Tribeca project known as the Offices of Fend, Fitzgibbon, Holzer, Nadin, Prince & Winters; as well as the work of a range of individual artists who were active in Colab.

When I started gathering material for *A Show About Colab*, my initial focus was on artists' publications, printed ephemera, editions and serial works, as well as film and video—the kind of material that overlapped with Printed Matter's own mission, which focuses on artworks (primarily artists' books) meant to be distributed and circulated outside of the commercial art market and mainstream art institutions. I supplemented this selection with a smattering of photo documentation, documents and original artworks. The exhibition also included a number of film and video works which were screened for the duration of the exhibition; independent projects by individual Colab artists; some New Cinema feature films; and a compilation of Potato Wolf, the Colab public access cable TV show; as well as some complete broadcasts, which are represented in the book by a selection of stills.

For the exhibition I also solicited texts from participating artists—statements, manifestos, essays and anecdotes. In keeping with the "by and for artists" ethos of Colab, it seemed best that Colab should represent itself. Some additional texts came in after the show specifically for the book, and I've included a selection of outsourced text—mostly from the pens and mouths of Colab participants—to fill in some of the gaps.

The book is in a roughly chronological order, though many of the projects ran simultaneously and many had different life spans, so it has a fair amount of overlap. And like the exhibition, the book has no overarching narrative; rather, it is a series of parts and fragments that I think better convey and celebrate an extraordinary output of creative energy and work, as well as an iconic period of New York City's cultural history.

My own discovery of Colab began pretty directly after I moved to New York from Vermont in the late 1980s. I had been vaguely aware that something interesting was going on after I spent 15 months in the city in '81 and '82, catching a glimpse of No Wave bands like DNA and Konk in Tompkins Square Park or Club 57. But I was a teenage country hick pretty freaked out by the adrenaline-inducing challenges of living on my own in the LES barrio, and frankly more interested in the Bad Brains and the emerging NYC hardcore scene. After quitting Oberlin College (where I was introduced to conceptual art, post-modern theory and the Pictures Generation, broadly through the programming of the late Bill Olander, who was curator at the college's Allen Memorial Art Museum), I did a five-year stint in Burlington, Vermont, alternately playing in punk bands and staging Cheap Art shows.

I had adopted the Cheap Art model from my father Peter Schumann, the founder and director of the Bread and Puppet Theater. Beginning in 1979, he had been sending the company's painted school bus around Vermont towns as a roving Cheap Art Gallery, selling mass-produced, original paintings at prices that ranged from 25 cents to a couple dollars. In Burlington I would convert the shared punk rock apartments I lived in into galleries—dubbed the Burlington Home Cheap Art Gallery and Factory Outlet—as well as put up art shows in cafes, bars, movie theater lobbies, and the local colleges, anywhere I could get a foot in the door.

It didn't take long for others to join in, and a Cheap Art collective emerged. Inspired by artists like Prince, Sherman, Kruger and Longo, I had swapped out my father's often idyllic Cheap Art motifs for imagery all drawn from mass-media sources, mostly painting from television stills, magazines and newspapers. (Serendipitously, I would later find the first literary reference to Cheap Art in Adrian Piper's artist statement "Cheap Art Utopia" published in *Art-Rite* #14—the artists' book issue—edited by Colabers and Printed Matter founding members, Walter "Mike" Robinson and Edit DeAk.)

When I moved to New York for good around 1988–89, the artists and activists Peter Cramer and Jack Waters graciously hosted a series of Cheap Art shows at ABC No Rio, the Rivington Street art space where they were co-directors. The name Colab started coming up, as in "Colab used to do this sort of thing"—that is, selling serial and multiple artworks for super cheap. A local guy, Harry Druzd, introduced himself one day at ABC No Rio, and said that his partner, Ulli Rimkus, was starting up a bar on Ludlow Street (the now celebrated Max Fish), and was going to schedule regular art shows there. Would the NYC Cheap Art Collective like to participate in the first show?

Ulli had been an engaged member of Colab, had helped negotiate the lease for the 1980 "Times Square Show," and did her Colab tour of duty as the group's secretary for a year. The first exhibition at Max Fish, put on before the bar had its liquor license, was called *The Atomic Show*, and the NYC Cheap Art Collective (which Harry had since joined) put together a huge collectively made mural in the back room, with hanging elements for sale—super-cheap, of course.

The name "Colab" had been coming up more frequently, particularly since the ABC No Rio art space had grown out of a Colab project, *The Real Estate Show* of 1980. But it was at Max Fish, and through *The Atomic Show*, that I first encountered the work of Colab artists like John Ahearn, Becky Howland, Christof Kohlhöfer, Tom Otterness, Walter Robinson, and others. Many lived within blocks of the Fish and Ulli would rotate a display of artworks from her personal collection behind the bar. Kohlhöfer and Robinson's work had special resonance—here was an urban version of what I had been plugging away at in Vermont for the past five years—dark figurative painting based on mass media imagery.

I started working at Printed Matter in 1989, where I had picked up a temporary gig packing books for the holidays and then stayed on as the part-time shipper and assistant sales person. At Printed Matter I also found kindred spirit with a cheap art ethos—mass produced artists' books and experimental publications sold at often ridiculously low prices. Three years into the job I was thrust into my first stint as Printed Matter's Acting Director when the organization's Director, Manager and Assistant Director all resigned within a period of a few weeks. The grown-ups had left and the kids were in charge(!), and we embarked on a more active programming schedule, putting on exhibitions and events like readings, screenings, and performances on a much more regular basis.

Colab and related activities reared its head once again. My co-worker Anne Kugler collaborated with Christopher Wool on *Hell is You*, a screening series of Super-8 feature films from the late 70s, and thus I was introduced to the Colab-associated

New Cinema. David Schmidlapp and Phase 2 did a slide lecture on the golden age of aerosol/subway art. Schmidlapp, a photographer who was marginally connected to Colab, was a fastidious documenter of subway art and had founded the IGTimes grafitti zine which Phase 2 would join as art director. The presentation underscored the connection of graffiti and the early Hip Hop community to the downtown art scene via Charlie Ahearn's film *Wild-Style*, Fashion Moda, and the East Village galleries. (I actually first encountered this during a short gig as the office cleaner at The Kitchen around 1981, where the Rock Steady Crew and friends put on an extravaganza of breaking, aerosol painting, and rap).

I also learned that Printed Matter and Colab had joined forces in 1982 on a Holiday Show and accompanying mail-order catalog of inexpensive multiples and serial artworks "Art for the Holidays/Art-Direct" facilitated by Mike Glier, both a Printed Matter staffer and member of Colab. In 1993 I collaborated with former Colaber Andrea Callard in organizing the first of Printed Matter's annual Giftland shows—a smorgasbord of inexpensive multiple and serial artworks in homage to the earlier project. Andrea put out the submission call to the Colab community and Stefan Eins, Becky Howland, Walter Robinson and others responded. At the opening there were some sideways looks and shifting postures—apparently some of the participants had not been in the same room since their last contentious Colab meeting. But it was a festive event all the same, and here came together my interests in the artists' collective, alternative art economies, and alternative models for the production and distribution of art, under the roof of Printed Matter.

Fast forward to 2011 when, in the wake of the 2008 stock market crash and in the midst of the Great Recession, the discontent that would culminate in the Occupy Wall Street movement was percolating. Colab had come up out of the urban debris that was a result of the recessions of the early 1970s and the draconian cuts in social services following NY City's near bankruptcy in 1975. At the national and international level, this same period saw the rise of the Chicago School of Economics that would lead to the Reagan/Thatcher era and the solidification of neoliberal economics and ideology.

In that recession-ridden year of 2011, though the gentrification of Manhattan was a done deal, I was hearing echoes of the 1970s and the spawning of neoliberalism, which would usher in perpetual wars and the greatest transfer of wealth to the top since the Gilded Age. Colab was beckoning, and I began to think about *A Show About Colab (and Related Activities)*.

—Max Schumann

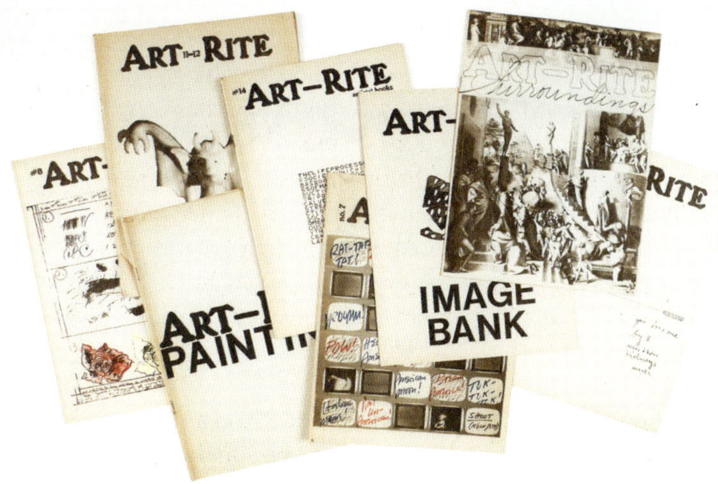

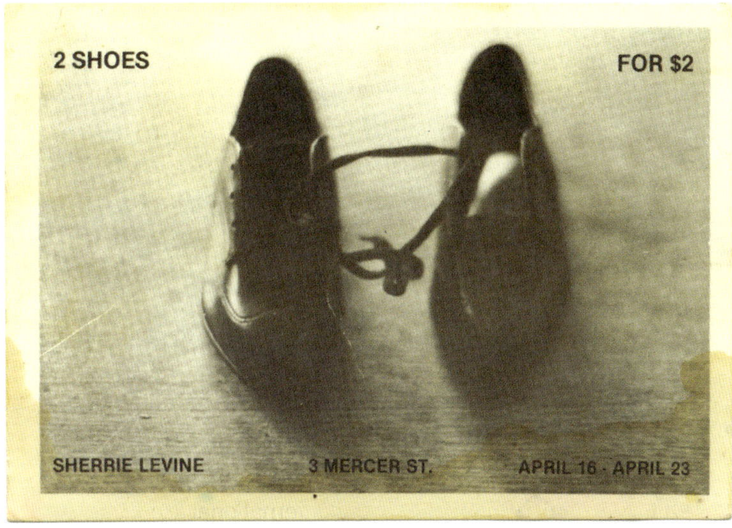

Colab was definitely not "I'm ok, you're ok." It was a moving test site where competing concepts were constantly floated and challenged. There was a little grant money, just enough to argue over. If you couldn't defend your idea vigorously it died. Colab was like trying on your friend's clothes, fitting into their show concepts like *The Manifesto Show*, the summer mural, the Island of Negative Utopia, Potato Wolf TV….

—Jane Dickson

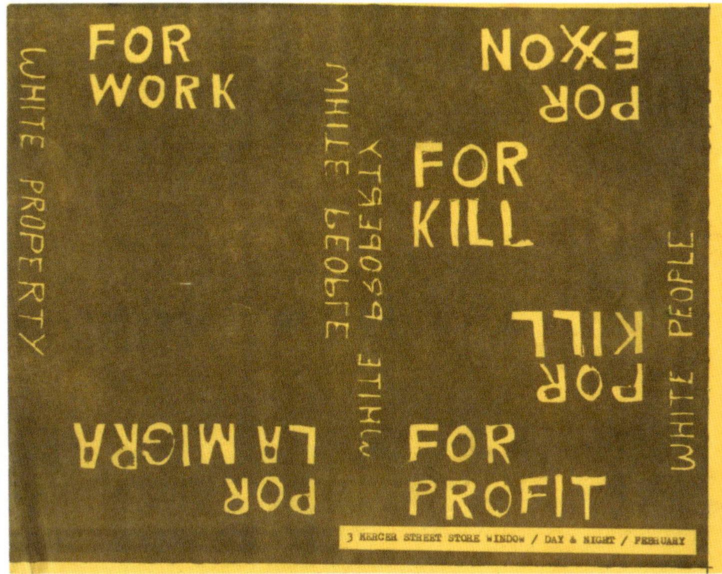

Art-Rite (Issues 8, 11–12, 9, 14, 7, 18, 15, 10). New York: Walter Robinson, Edit DeAk and Joshua Cohn, 1973–78. Offset printed, pbk, staple-bound, page counts vary, 28 × 21 cm. Courtesy of Printed Matter. Photo: Nancy Linn.

Sherrie Levine. *2 Shoes for $2*, 1977. Offset printed postcard, 9 × 13 cm. Announcement for exhibition at Stefan Eins' Mercer Street Store. Courtesy of Barbara Ess.

Robert Cooney. *Por Exxon, For Kill*, 1978. Photocopy, 21.5 x 28 cm. Hung in the window of Stefan Eins' Mercer Street Store. Courtesy of Kiki Smith.

P. ADAMS SITNEY

Shortly after that you got the job working with microfilms, didn't you?

COLEEN FITZGIBBON

From 1974 to '79 I worked part-time for Rick Van Auken's Information Technology Center microfilming public documents (warrants, bankruptcies, debts, etc.), learning computer language and storage and retrieval machines. Rick had been a '60s Apollo space-program analyst.

PAS

But your films there weren't made with a computer?

CF

No, they were on microfilm. My first job experience was filming documents of warrants in the New York Supreme Court basement on a 16 mm microfilm camera for the court system.

PAS

So you made your own copy of the stuff?

CF

After-hours, I made my own text films on the microfilm camera. I filmed magazines, newspapers, dictionaries, documents—which became the films *Time Magazine*, *Der Spiegel*, *Daily News*, *Dictionary*, and *Document*. Showing microfilm is very subliminal because the microfilm camera frame films the equivalent of three regular frames so you see the film—

PAS

Triple frame.

CF

The faster the film moves through the frame the less you visually retain until you reach a consciousness threshold where the sensation is remembering something you can no longer recall.

PAS

. And what you're seeing are whole pages of text? You'd have to be able to read awfully fast.

CF

It's a version of speed-reading. It's best to let the text flow over you because continual text is stimulating to the point of exhaustion. We navigate daily through hundreds of signs, newspapers, magazines, websites, and product ingredients. In '73 I was an American tourist traveling through the tunnel from West to East Berlin and had an epiphany of life without text. There were no signs in East Berlin, not even on restaurants. Nothing, only bare light bulbs. Then you cross back over into West Berlin, and it's like the States.

—Coleen Fitzgibbon interviewed by P. Adams Sitney.
Bomb No. 123 (Spring 2013). New York: *Bomb*, 2013.

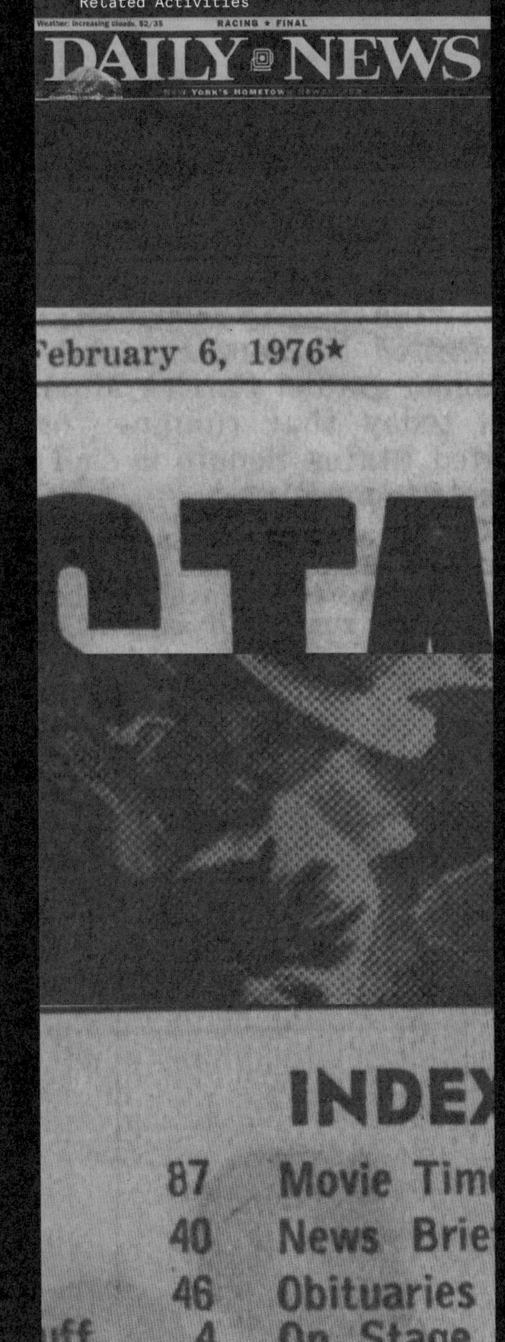

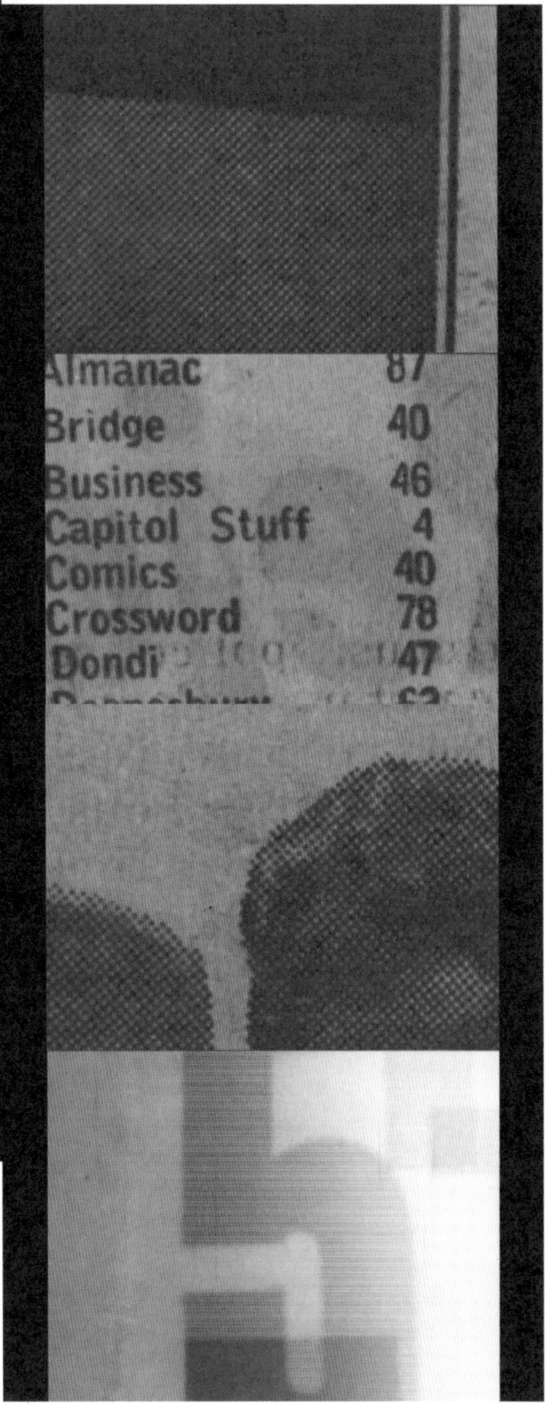

Daily News, 1974/2011. Directed by Coleen Fitzgibbon. [Film Stills] Digital version
transferred from original Super-8, color, silent, 11:30 (original Super-8, B/W, silent, 6:00).
Courtesy of Coleen Fitzgibbon.

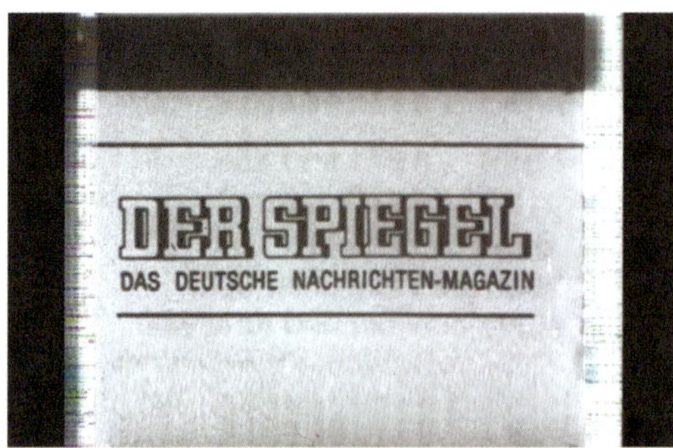

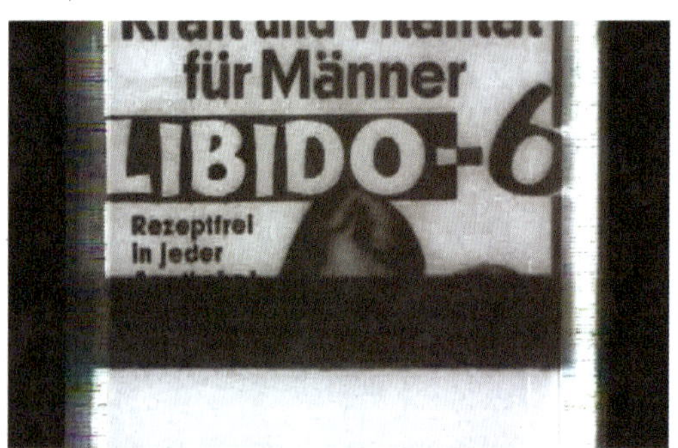

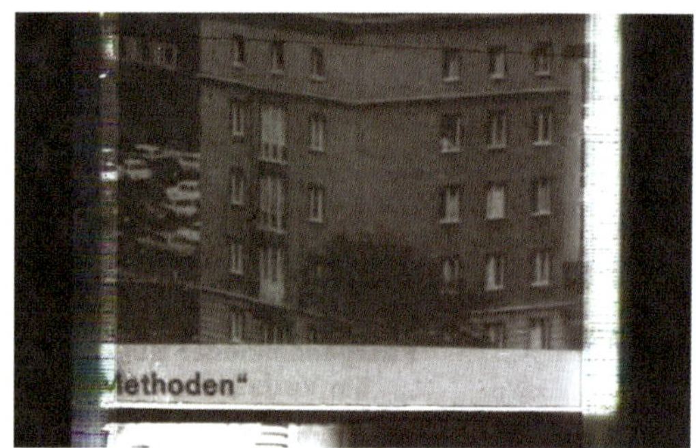

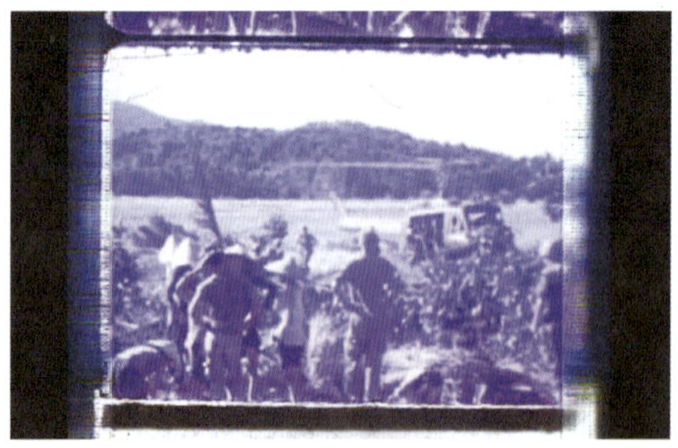

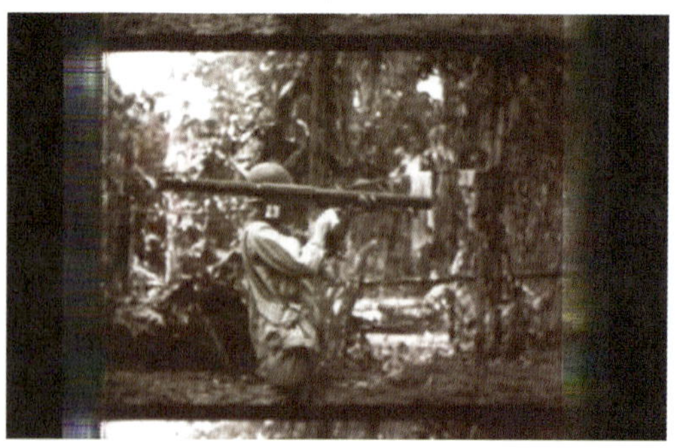

Der Spiegel, 1975. Directed by Coleen Fitzgibbon. [Film Stills] 16mm, B/W & color, sound, 9:51. Courtesy of Coleen Fitzgibbon.

CITIZENS UNITE

STOP: CON ED/WEST WAY/ MA BELL/ PENSION LENDING/ CONCORDE/ DUKE POWER/ CIA
FBI/ BIG MAC/ J.P. STEVENS/ TRI-LATERAL COMMISSION/ BOSSES/ PAY OFFS/ EXXON
ETC.

FREE MONEY FOR

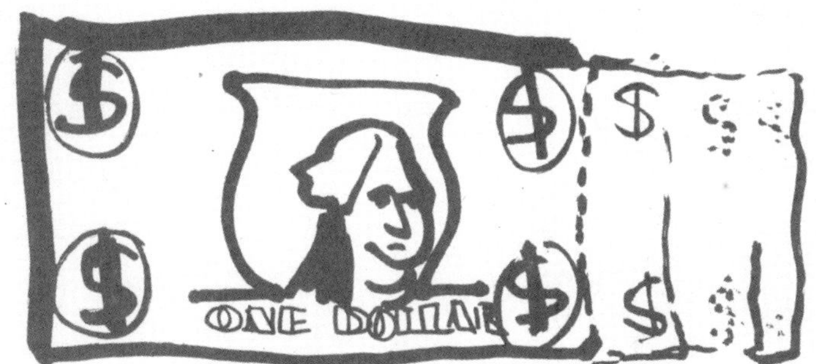

EVERYONE

OPERATING AT A LOSS

START: GUARANTEED ANNUAL WAGE/ FREE PUBLIC TRANSIT/ FREE MEDICAL CARE/ FREE
PUBLIC UTILITIES/ SUPERMARKET RIOTS/ GENERAL STRIKES/ WORKERS' PROFIT-SHARING
ETC.

STOMP
STOP THE RICH

X & Y (Coleen Fitzgibbon & Robin Winters). *Citizens Unite, Stomp the Rich*, c. 1976.
Photocopy flyer, 28 × 21.5 cm. Courtesy of Bobby G (Robert Goldman).

INTERNATIONAL SERVICES ADAPTABLE TO YOUR SITUATION
WE TRAVEL ANYWHERE ANYTIME
LARGE ENOUGH TO HANDLE YOUR NEEDS/ SMALL ENOUGH TO SERVE YOU

POSSIBLE PROGRAMS:

Film showings/Performances?/Lectures/
Demonstrations/Installations/Instructions/
Slide shows/Surveillance video installations/
Video shows/Information booths/Window
displays/Graphics/Interviews/Portraits:family,
official, miniature, portrait sculpture,
and portraits from photos/Advertising/
Commercials/False advertising/Test construction/
Interior design service/Signed limited editions
for the young collector/Catalogs/Auctions for
fund raising/ Armed protection of art pieces/
Script writing/ Art consultants/ Curatorial
consultants/Art adventures/Industrial design/
Art direction/Sign painting/Communication
devices/Incentives/Role-playing/Model
building/Art pricing/Live tv performance/
Art packing and shipping/Cleaning and restoring/
Cartoons and illustration/Music/Noise/Muzak/
Public speaking/Savage acts/Liquidators/
Posters/Production-line techniques/Architect-
ural alterations/Object production/Good
conversation/Subliminal and overt manipulations/
Review of ethics/Audiovisual instruction/
Creating your living legend/Forgery/Investigation/
Experiments/Invisible restorations/Taste
inhancers/Pricing vested interests/Salw stim-
ulators/Trouble-shooting/Logos for your cor-
porate look/Packaging/Time and motion studies/

FOR:

Institutions/Offices/Businesses/Bus stations/
Airlines/Galleries/Publishers/Accountants/
Unions/Secretarial pools/Advertisers/Banks/
Africans/Bordellos/Prisons/Airportsz/Hospitals/
Amusement parks/Schools/Universities/Persons/
Scientists/Architects/Citizens/Individuals/
Restaurants/Factories/Atheletes/Mapmakers/
Psychiatrists/Hatters/Automobile showrooms/
Public places/Museums/Libraries/Zoos/Camps/
Bakeries/Importer-exporters/Manufacturers/
Barber shops/Hairdressers/Beauty parlors/Beer
halls/Realtors/Hotels-motels/Military concerns/
Law enforcement agencies/Fairs/Parades/Public
utilities/Government agencies/Stores/Farmers/
Dentists/Migrant workers/Post offices/Buffoons/
Laundries/guerrillas/anarchists/communists/
monarchists/Carpenters/Churches/ mosques,
temples, synagogues/Cafes/Markets/Conventtions/
capitalists/Data-processors/Doorways/Subways/
Highways/Salespersonnel/Painters/Placement
agencies/Filmmakers/Firemen/Flowershops/
Foundations/Garden parties/

(PRIVATE INVITATION)

This is a private invitation to a series of unusual shows, occurrences & eperiments with
some artists who you will not know and
some you do not. Two separate but contig-
uous locations are involved with simultan
eous but not necessarily similar activities:
"Enterprise" at 5 Bleecker ground floor, and
"Research & Development" at 591 Broadway
fourth floor; both in New York City. At both
spaces are facsimile connections that can
transmit or receive information to & from
art-ists in N.Y.C., San Francisco, and Toron-
to; X Magazine, a collaborative endeavor of
several artists, is also available. Please call
for appointments.

ENTERPRISE at 5 Bleecker: 777-1859. 359.
RESEARCH & DEVELOPMENT at 591 Broadway: 431-3367.

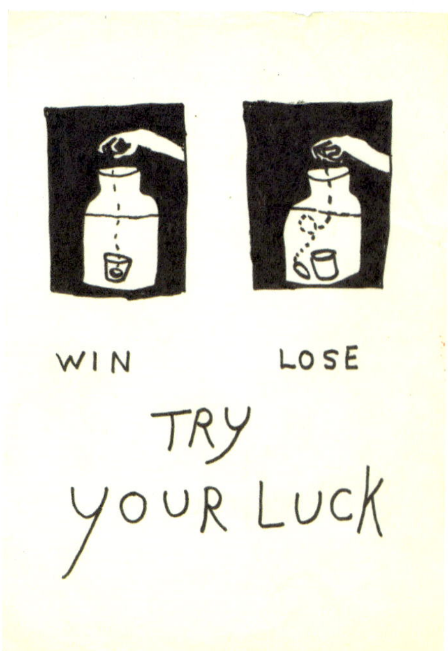

Clockwise from upper left:

X & Y (Coleen Fitzgibbon and Robin Winters). *International Services Adaptable to Your Situation*, c. 1976–77. Photocopy, 28 × 21.5 cm. Courtesy of Robin Winters.

X & Y (Coleen Fitzgibbon and Robin Winters). *Private Invitation*, c. 1977. Photocopy, 28 × 21.5 cm. Courtesy of Robin Winters.

X & Y (Coleen Fitzgibbon and Robin Winters). *Win, Lose*, 1977. Marker on paper, collaborative drawing, 28 × 21.5 cm. Courtesy of Robin Winters.

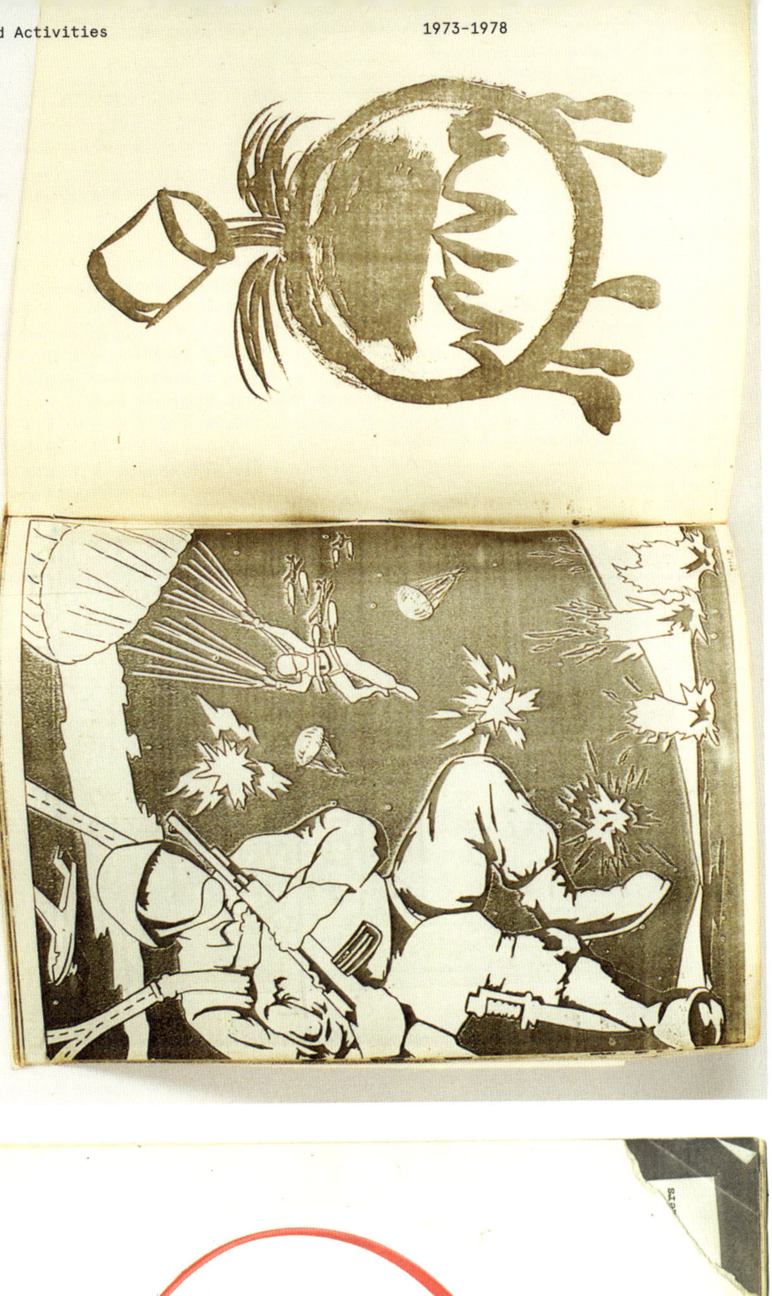

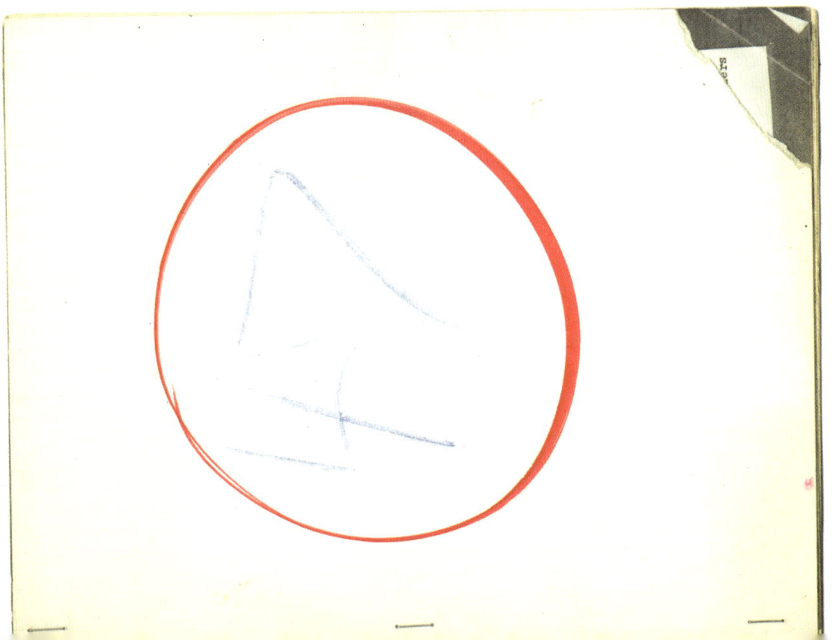

This page and the following spread:
Robin Winters. *Wait*, New York: R. Winters, 1976. Photocopy, marker and colored pencil on paper, pbk, staple-bound, 16 pp, 28 × 21.5 cm. Artists' book published on the occasion of the performance piece *Wait* at Artists Space. Courtesy of Andrea Callard. Photo: Nancy Linn.

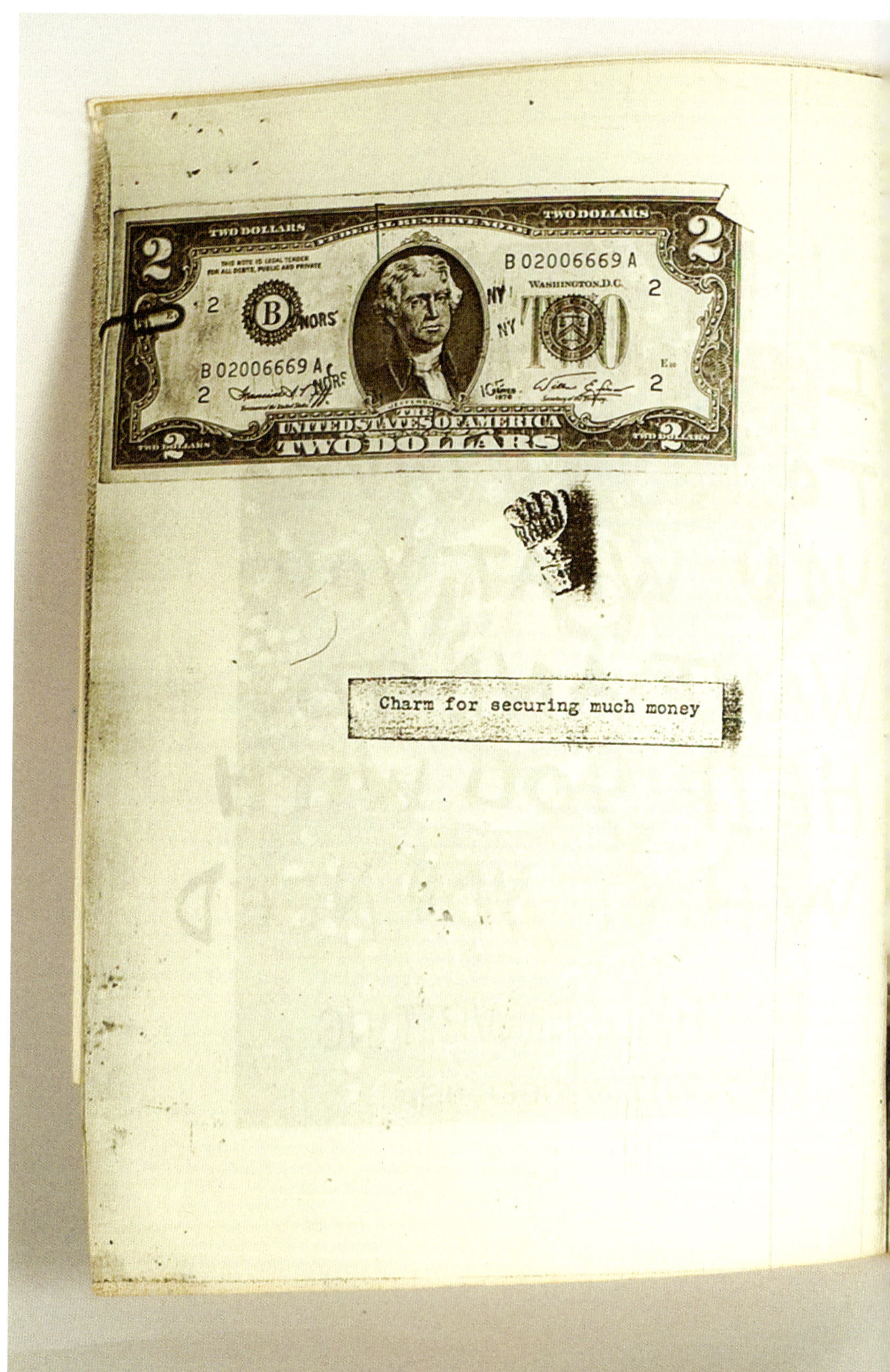

Charm for securing much money

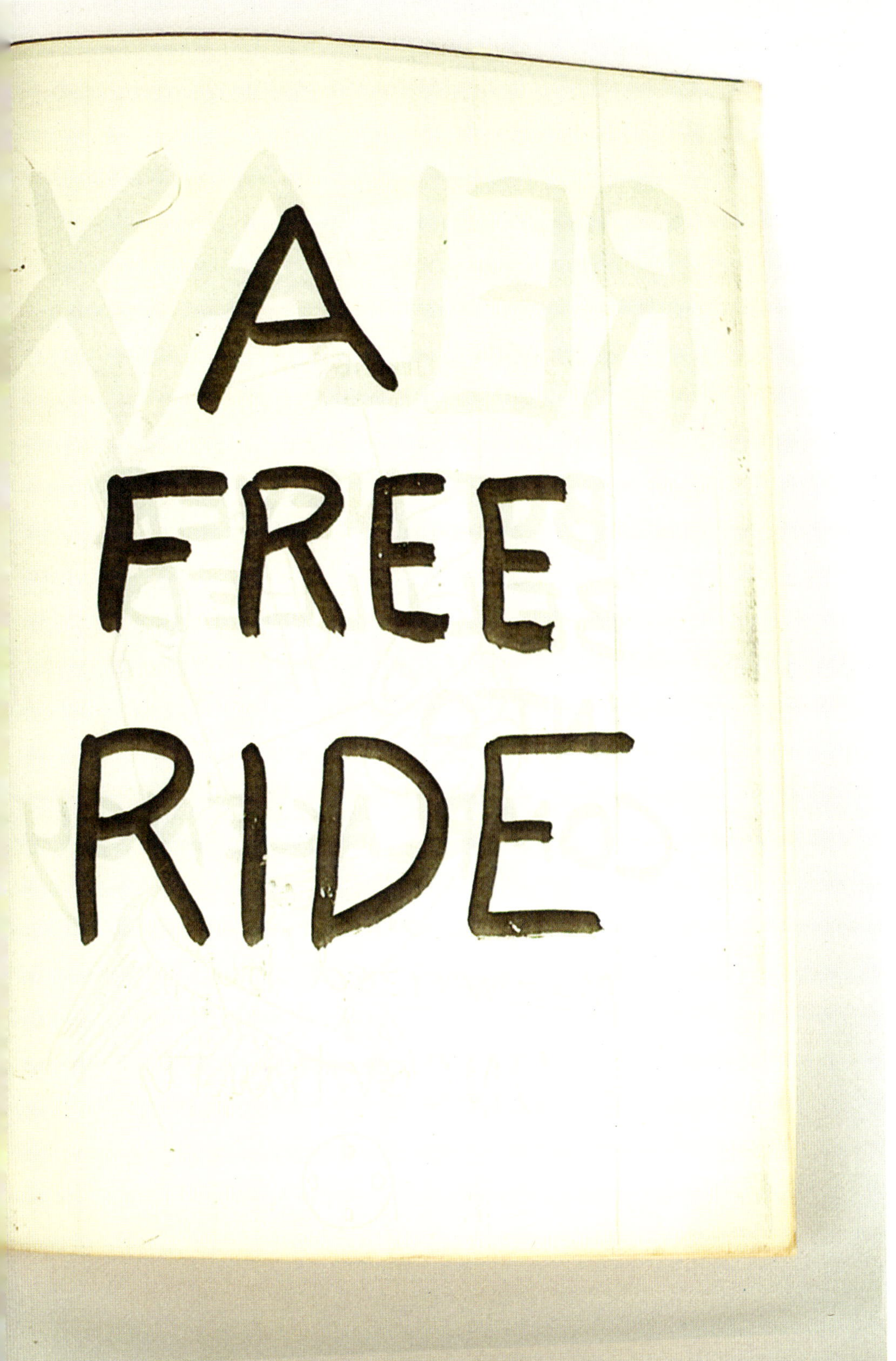
A
FREE
RIDE

The Secret Life of Bob E or Bob E Behind the Veil (Diary of A Dreamer). During the years 1974, 1975, and 1976 I was working behind a two-way mirror on an assembly line in a factory making rubber top hats for everyone in the world. I was also punching a time clock every day for two months at the Whitney Museum performing 8 hours daily behind a two-way mirror. "W.B Bearman Bags A Job." In Germany I balanced beer glasses in an empty room to the sound of a teakettle entitled "Dedication To The Man Whose Main Job Was Testing Whistling Teakettles." Upon my return to New York I created dinners in my apartment for blind dates and double dates. This work was entitled "Silent Food for Speechless Fools." I had three people each night for dinner. Many of my existing friends came to these dinners. All these works were produced in anonymity. There has been a rather humble resume declaration by all members of Colab as to the origin of the group. We say we are Co-founders. I stand by that declaration.

Colab was formed collaboratively by each of us with our own histories and specific interests. There was no one founder. Many of us had already worked together. We were our own best audience. The Zeitgeist of the time was one of creative energy in the face of a depressed economy. We were all interested in making new work and meaningful contributions to the world. The Collaborative Projects I envisioned was never intended to be viewed as an outlet for artists' self-promotional commodity fetishes. My own particular interest was in a non-hierarchical union of artists (cultural workers). A union that insisted in fees for artists who participated in public venues such as the museums and alternate space. An artists' bank which not only had a collection of art works (with the recognition that the Art world was a 1% system) but a Bank which was a useful organizing tool to pool the finances of a large group into working capital. I was interested in credit unions and "The Artists Reserved Rights Transfer and Sales Agreement" as proposed by Seth Siegelaub and Bob Projansky. I was against the Idea that a "critic" who was not directly involved in the organization of exhibits or the events would be the "voice" of this history. Outside curators and sponsor organization seemed antithetical to what our efforts were all about. The great thing about the shows we did together was that everyone was excited and we all did stuff for free in our own spaces, in the airwaves, in print, on the street or in liberated public locations. Many of the idealistic ambitions of our diverse group have been failures however many of our goals have seen the light of day and are now part of the Art world fabric. I see Occupy Wall Street as a current example of the type of democratic struggle we as artists / cultural workers were then (and some now) engaged in. I continue this struggle knowing I am not alone. I realize there are many stories in this naked city and that mine is only one of them.

—Robin Winters

Colab was a group of artists in their mid twenties in the early 70s arriving from parts of the US and Europe, seemingly of like-mind, living in lower Manhattan NYC neighborhoods that few others wanted to be in. Not particularly politically ambitious Colab did see themselves as identifying with the American disenfranchised while busy reading French new wave philosophers whose names few could pronounce.

Economics motivated most into the traditional artist's profile of cheap apartment rentals, squats, nowhere jobs and funky bars packed with dissolutes. Art dealers didn't want us and we didn't know how to approach them except to swarm gallery openings.

With Vertovian enthusiasm Colab (Collaborative Projects, Inc) started meeting in 1978 to form a collective of 40-plus artists through 1985 that could make and show art as a group while maintaining individual non-existent careers.

Colab started organizing projects and shows with friends around thematic concepts and the work was made fast and somewhat specific for the theme.

Some of the collaborative projects included *X Motion Picture Magazine* (1978–79); *The Arcade Show* at the NYC Municipal Building (1978); 5 Bleecker Store shows *Income & Wealth*, *Manifesto* and *Just Another Asshole* (1979); 591 Broadway shows *Batman*, *Doctors and Dentists* and *Dog Show* (1979); *X Magazine* Benefit punk rock show (1979); Jay Street and 5 Bleecker film screenings (1979–80); Colab Live cable TV shows Potato Wolf, All Color News and Night Curtain (1979–85); 93 Grand Street show (1979), *The Real Estate Show* (1979/80), *The Times Square Show* (1980), WPA show (1981) and others, including various spin offs such as New Cinema screening room, *Spanner Magazine*, Nightshift Theater, MWF Club (MondayWednesdayFriday) video distribution and a one-time collective summer house on Long Island.

To be in Colab an artist had to go to three consecutive Colab meetings; to get support or funding for a project Colab required at least three people, two of which had to have already made it through the three-meeting gauntlet to propose a project to the group. It was a difficult process in which no one made it through the whole seven years, though many joined.

—Coleen Fitzgibbon

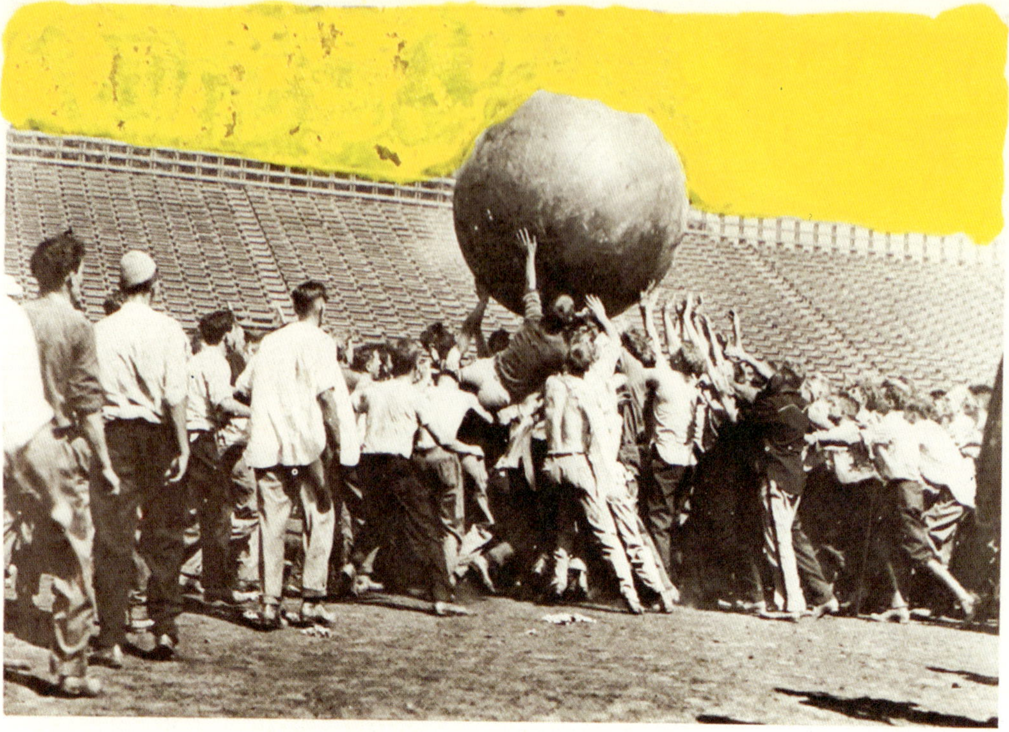

PUSH AND PULL

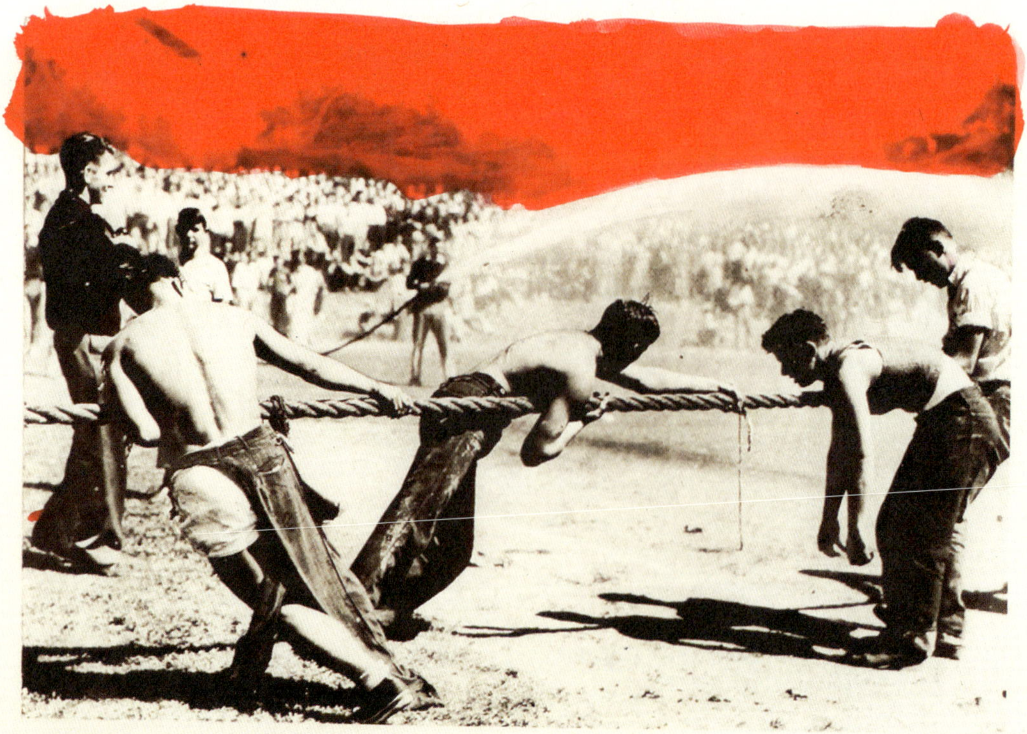

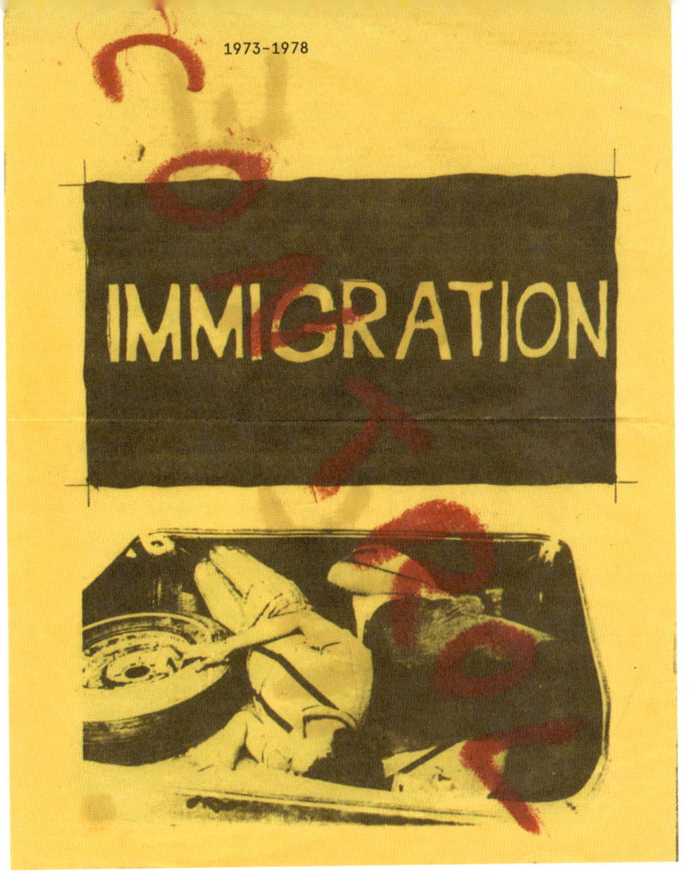

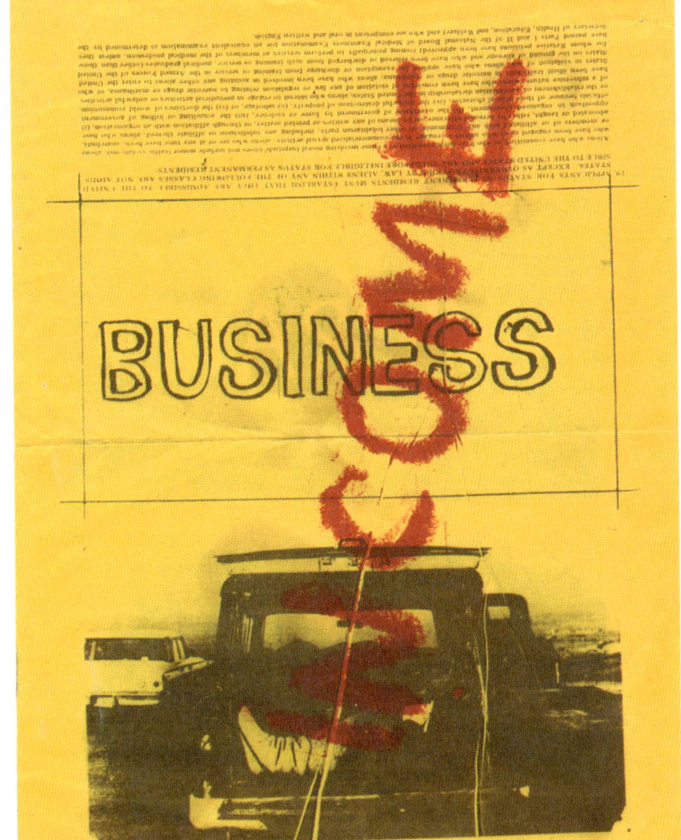

Robin Winters. *Push and Pull*, 1975. Hand-painted, offset printed, 43 × 36 cm. Courtesy of Robin Winters. Photo: Nancy Linn.

Robert Cooney. *Immigration / Control. Business / Income*, c. 1977–79. Hand-painted photocopies, 28 × 21.5 cm. Courtesy of Tom Otterness.

COMMUNICATIONS LINK FOR SEND/RECEIVE SATELLITE NET

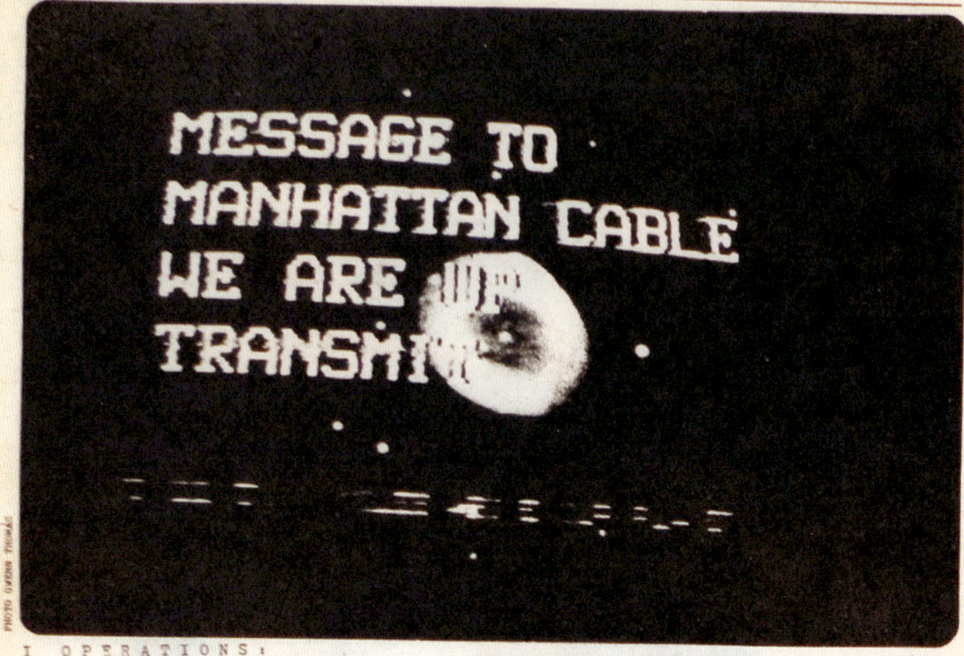

PHOTO GLENN THOLE

I OPERATIONS:

A. Class I -- Transmit TB2 (14.0525), Audio Subcarrier 5.14
        Receive RB1 (12.0805), Audio Subcarrier 5.14

B. Ames Research Center -- Transmit TB1 (14.2475), Audio Subcarrier 5.14
        Receive RB2 (11.8855), Audio Subcarrier 5.14

TWO-WAY

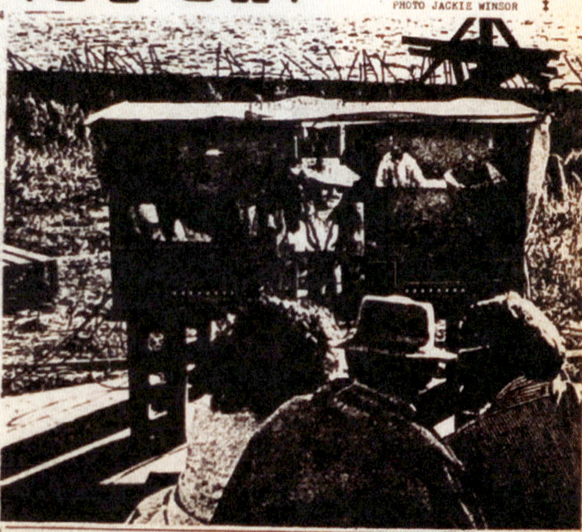

PHOTO JACKIE WINSOR

L. BEAR..K. SONNIER..A. HOROWITZ.(PISA).DISCUSSING FUTURE SATELLITE EXPERIMENT

BPCA....CMAA...DCA....FCC....NASA...LIP/PSAC...MOD...PISA...PSSC...SIRA.

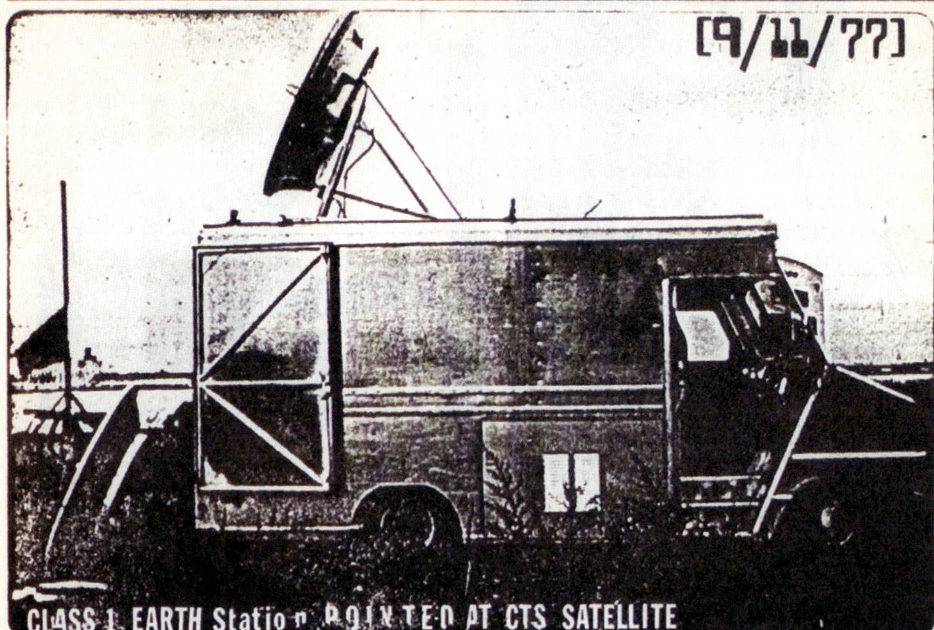

	True Azimuth	Elevation	Mag. Variation	Compass Azimuth	Elevation
New York	234.09°	26.54°	12.5° W	246.59°	26.54°
Ames Research Center	170.09°	46.15°	17° E	153°	46.15°

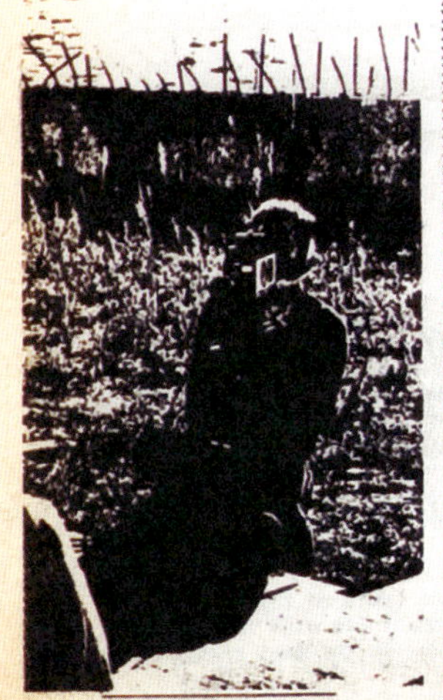

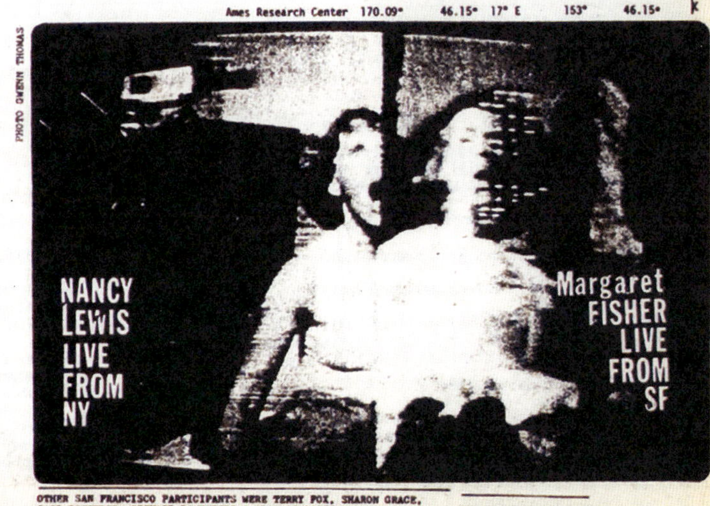

Documentation of *Send/Receive Satellite Network: Phase II*, September 1977. Digital print, 38 × 58 cm each (diptych). Created for *X Magazine,* 1978, by Liza Béar, reprinted 2011. Courtesy of Liza Béar.

Send/Receive was an interactive transmission between New York and San Francisco artists coordinated by Keith Sonnier and Liza Béar. Other participants: *(New York)* Andy Horowitz, PISA; Nancy Lewis; Richard Peck; Richard Landry; Diego Cortez; Betsy Sussler; Seth Tillett; James Nares; Duff Schweninger; Willoughby Sharp; Paul Shavelson; *(San Francisco)* Sharon Grade; Terry Fox; Alan Scarritt; Richard Lowenberg; Margaret Fisher; Brad Gibbs; NASA; and Carl Loeffler.

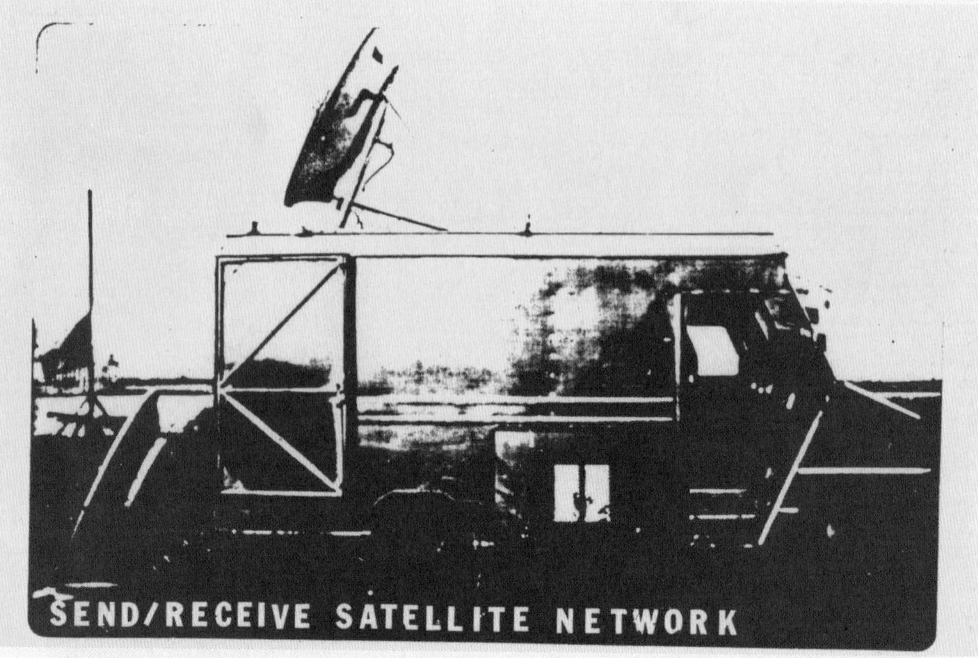

Liza Béar. *Send/Receive Satellite Network*, 1978. Offset printed card, 14 × 21.5 cm. Front and back.
Announcement card for Send/Receive and NYC-SF live two-way broadcast via CTS. Courtesy of Liza Béar.

The Center for New Art Activities, Inc
Founded 1974

In 1974 Liza Béar and Willoughby Sharp, who had collaborated on *Avalanche Magazine* since 1968, founded The Center for New Art Activities, Inc at 93 Grand Street. Originally formed to provide a fiscal umbrella for *Avalanche*, CNAA later sponsored other magazines and emerging artist organizations, notably Colab and *Bomb*, by providing research, consulting, administrative and production support. It also produced video and telecommunications projects.

CNAA published the last five issues of *Avalanche* when the magazine switched to newspaper format. As an international avant-garde journal featuring artist interviews, photographic documents and an extensive news section, *Avalanche*'s coverage included the downtown alternative art scene at 112 Greene Street, 98 Greene Street and other spaces as well as performance groups such as the Phil Glass Ensemble, The Grand Union, and General Idea and the Western Front in Canada.

In the late 70s a number of artists formed a video cooperative through CNAA and purchased equipment to produce a half-hour series for public access cable television. Among the artists who produced shows for Communications Update were Vicki Gholson, DeeDee Halleck, Milly Iatrou, Michael McClard, Liza Béar, Eric Mitchell, Ron Morgan, Terese Svoboda and Stephen Torton. At first, programs focused on the impact of new communications technology. As the number of artist producers expanded, so did the style and subject matter of the shows, which ranged from political documentary to satire. For instance, Janet Densmore's *The Algiers Killings* explored the murders of Blacks as retribution for a slain cop in the New Orleans neighborhood of Algiers. Sanja Iveković and Dalibor Martinis produced two programs on Zagreb Video. The best of Communications Update—later renamed Cast Iron TV—was screened at The Kitchen and at the Museum of Modern Art in the mid 80s.

In 1975, artist Keith Sonnier initiated *Send/Receive*, and later collaborated with Liza Béar in what became a CNAA project. *Send/Receive* was an interactive transmission via public satellite between groups of artists and performers in San Francisco and New York. The Franklin Street Arts Center coordinated the link from the mobile satellite unit in Battery City Park to the cable drop to Manhattan Cable TV. The Center for New Art Activities enabled artists to experiment with new media, including Slow Scan and QWIP, an early version of the fax machine. It suspended its activities in the mid 90s and is now digitizing its archive.

—Liza Béar

Q.PORT 93 GR &GR..LBI   **NEW YORK**

Q PORT LOCATION: 93 GR & GR/NEW YORK CIty

TRANSMISSION DATES: **1** OCTOBER 2 1978 (to Robin Winters, COLLAB)
                      2 OCTOBER 25 1978 (to WORLDPOOL, MONTREAL)

TRANSMISSION TIMES: **1** 18.45 EST   **FROM THE**
                      2 20.30 EST   **LUNAR BUREAU**
                                            OF INVESTIGA-
                                                         TI
MISSION: NEWSFEED   **ON**
          THROUGHPUT
       X ORIGINAL SOURCE
          RELAY FROM OTHER SOURCE
       ? REQUEST RESPONSE **X**
          QUERY-
              NATURE OF QUERY- **?**
                  DOUBT_
                  NATURE OF DOUBT-

                                    REQUEST FOR INFORMATION
                                    REQUEST FOR AFFIRMATION
                                  X REQUEST FOR CONFIRMATION
                                  X REQUEST. FOR INPUT
                                    REQUEST FOR ATTENTION
                                      OR INTENTION

XXXXXX NONE OF THE ABOVE:

                RESPECIFY LANGUAGE FORMAT,
                             MOOD OR MODE.

SUGGEST CONDITIONAL.

SUPPOSING THAT ZZZZZZZZZZZZZZZZZBFYZZZZZZZ (FOR INSTANCE)

          AND THEN WOULD BE THE CASE.
                  RECEIVER FOLLOWS MOOD, MOVES ON.
                  RECEIVER REJECTS, CHANGES MOOD,
                             ALTERS DIRECTION
SAY, SWITCH TO ACTUALity
          INDICATIVE
          INDICATES SPACE & PLACE, TIME & DATE, as of now,
          METHOD OF ATTACK oblique before
AFRICAN TRAVELLER RECEIVES SILICON TRANSPLANT.
SUGGEST, SPECIFY LAST, EXPLORE OTHER MODES FIRST .

                     (OVER ?OUT?FOR LATER RESPONSE)

Liza Béar. *A Possible Communication Scenario*, 1978. Facsimile print, 28 × 21.5 cm. Courtesy of Liza Béar.

QWIP and Slow Scan:
The digital revolution: looking to the future

An often overlooked aspect of the zeitgeist in the late 70s is artists' involvement with new communications technologies, or what would now be called social media. Sparked by the 1977 *Send/Receive* interactive demo between artists/performers in New York and San Francisco, this highly elaborate satellite venture, which Liza Béar coordinated with Keith Sonnier, required a major bureaucratic offensive.

Through research into simpler ways of setting up an artists' communication network, Béar found the QWIP, an early version of the fax machine, and the Slow Scan transceiver.* (see archival document). Basically, Robot's machine converts video into an audio signal which travels over phone lines (see diagram) and is reconverted to video at the rate of one frame every eight seconds. Both systems allow for interactive—though not instant—transmissions and provided ways for artists to experiment with new media.

Exxon, the QWIP manufacturer, loaned several display models to Center for New Art Activities (CNAA). These were shared by Colab artists; drawings, collages, photos, texts exchanged from 1978–79 were on display in the Printed Matter show.

Slow Scan teleconferences between artist groups throughout the US, Canada and Europe, were coordinated by Béar during that period; Colab artists in New York took part in the largest of these which involved seven cities in March 1979.

—Liza Béar

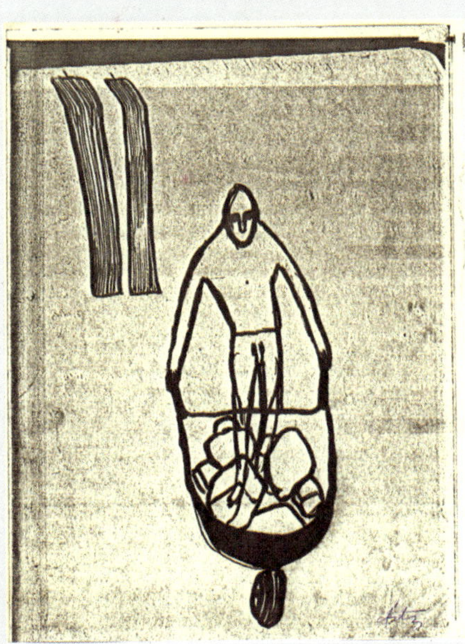

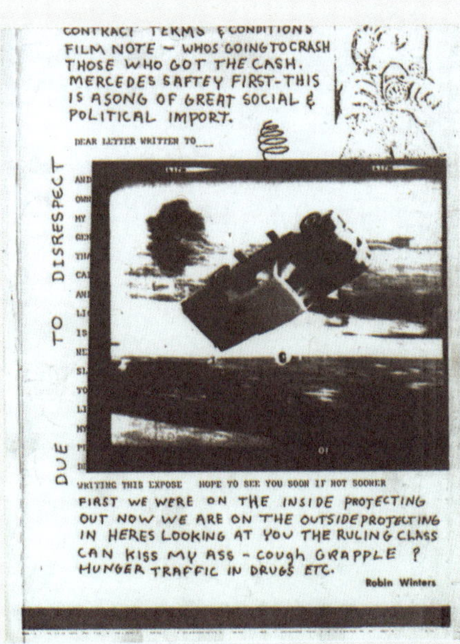

Left to right:

Coleen Fitzgibbon. *Man with Wheelbarrow*, c. 1978. Telecopier print, 28 × 21.5 cm. Courtesy of Coleen Fitzgibbon.

Robin Winters. *Due to Disrespect*, c. 1978. Telecopier print, 28 × 21.5 cm. Courtesy of Becky Howland.

ARTWORK SENT VIA QWIP FACSIMILE. FROM ARTISTS' TRANSMISSIONS ORGANIZED BY THE CENTER FOR NEW ART ACTIVITIES.

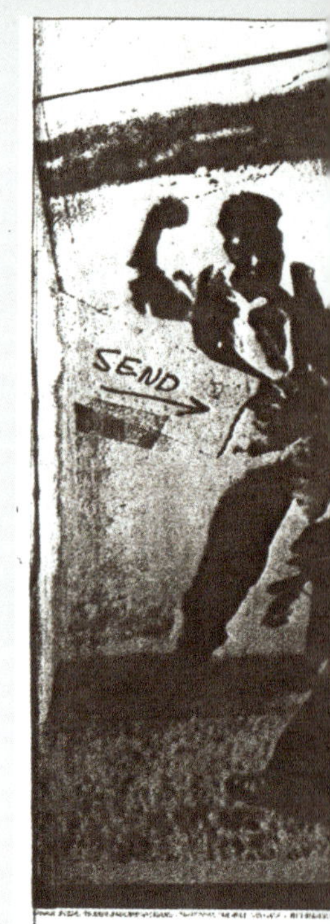

There were exhibitions and stores in storefronts and lofts, international Slow Scan video, publications, and a pre-fax, pre-internet, communication transmission activity utilizing QWIP machines, procured from the Exxon Corporation by Liza Béar. Through a juicy and conflicted multi-year period of identity and structural definition, there was experimentation in and rich discussion of accessible content, political forces, technology, equity, corporate versus union models, and material resources.

—Andrea Callard

Clockwise from upper left:

Tom Otterness. *Send/Receive*, c. 1978–79. Telecopier print, 28 × 21.5 cm. Courtesy of Becky Howland.

Unknown. *Untitled* [good to be back in North America], c. 1978–79. Photocopy of telecopier print, 28 × 21.5 cm. Courtesy of Coleen Fitzgibbon.

Robin Winters. *Untitled* [liberty], c. 1978–79. Collage on telecopier print, 21.5 × 28 cm. Courtesy of Becky Howland.

Christof Kohlhöfer. *Untitled* [shrine with gun], c. 1978–79. Telecopier print, 28 × 21.5 cm. Courtesy of Becky Howland.

Tom Otterness. *Untitled* [Co-lab cure], c. 1978–79. Collage and pen on telecopier print, 28 × 21.5 cm. Courtesy of Becky Howland.

ARTWORK SENT VIA QWIP FACSIMILE. FROM ARTISTS' TRANSMISSIONS ORGANIZED BY THE CENTER FOR NEW ART ACTIVITIES.

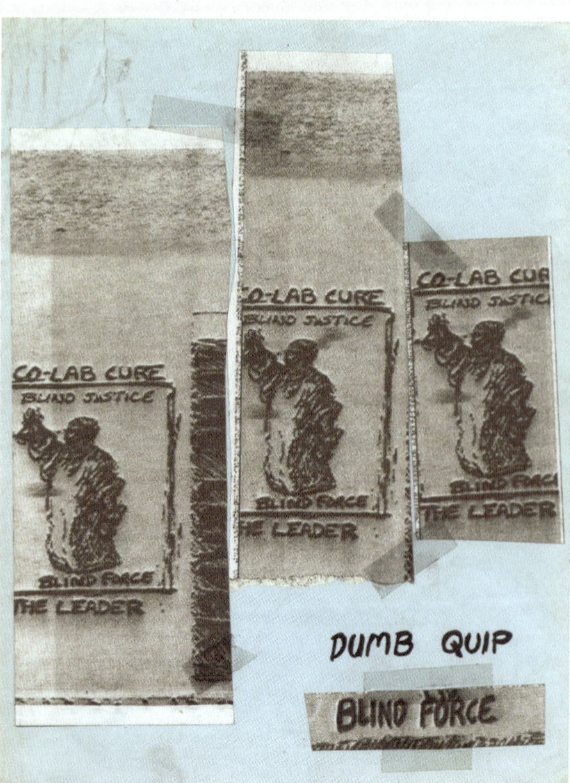

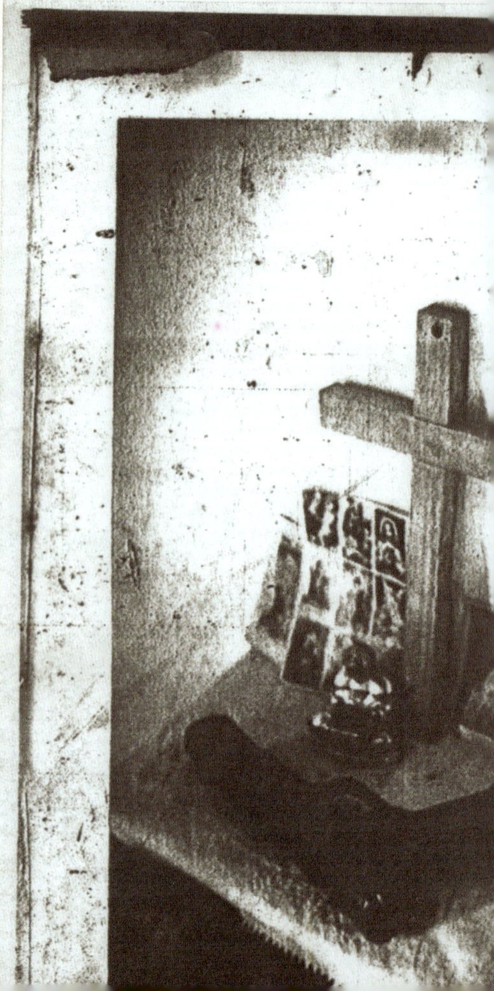

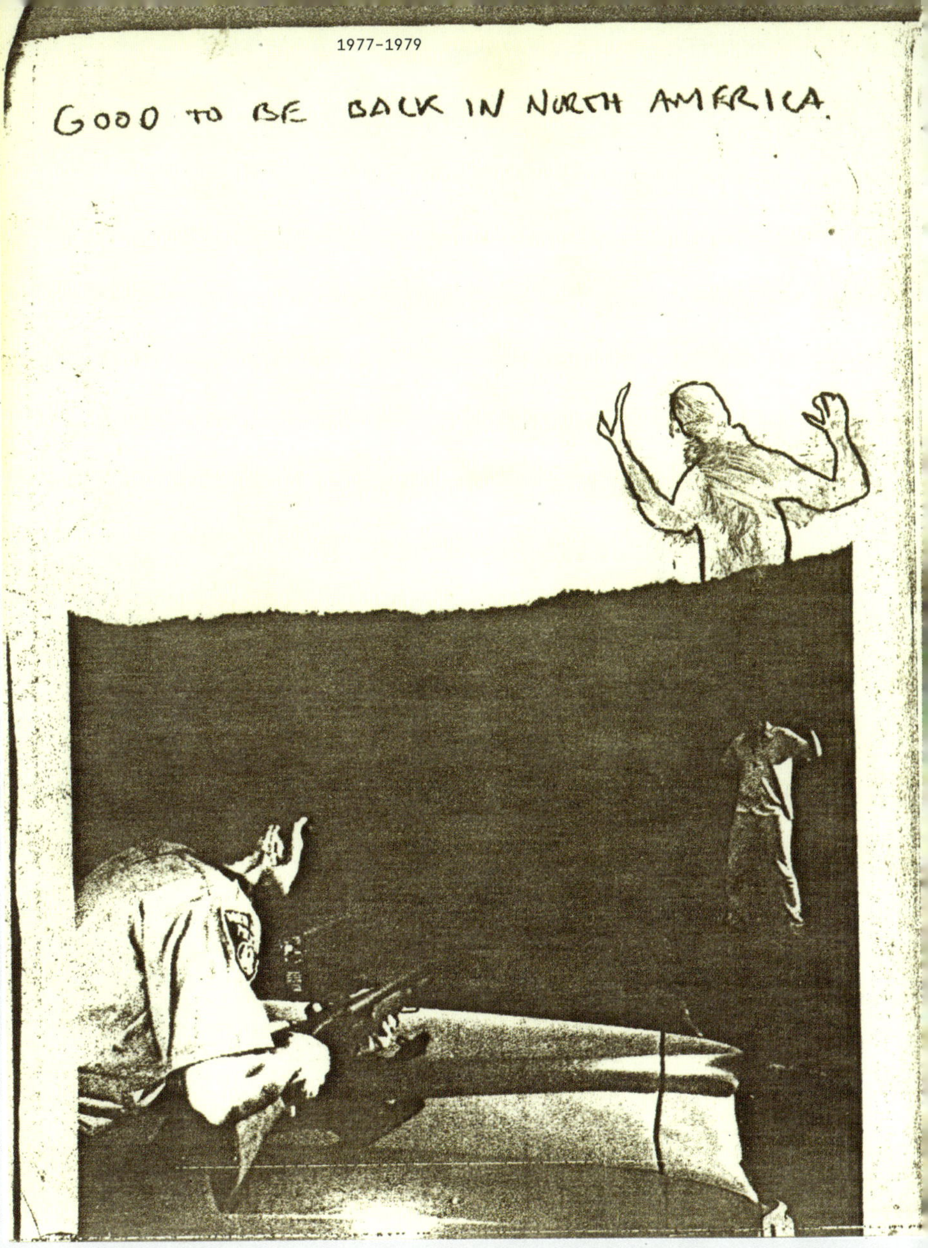

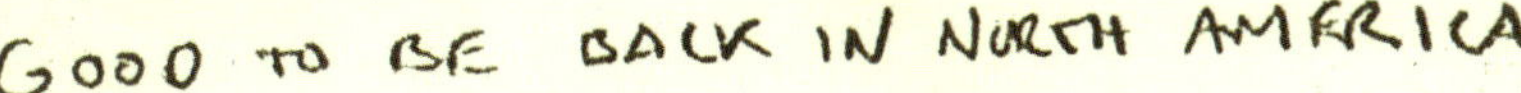

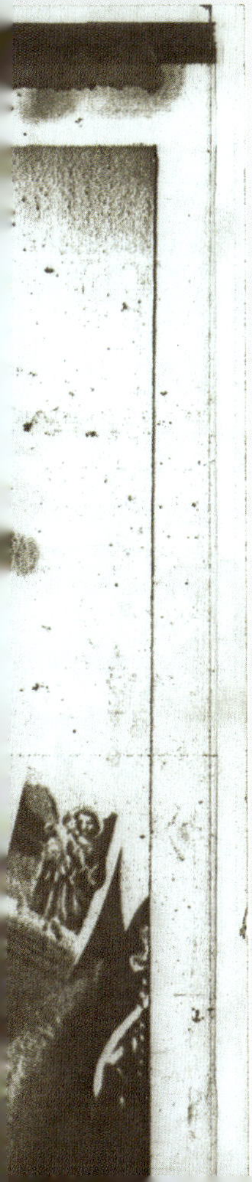

GOOD TO BE BACK IN NORTH AMERICA.

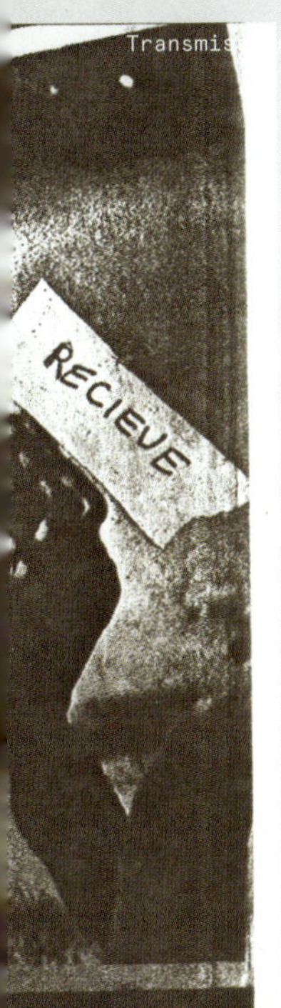

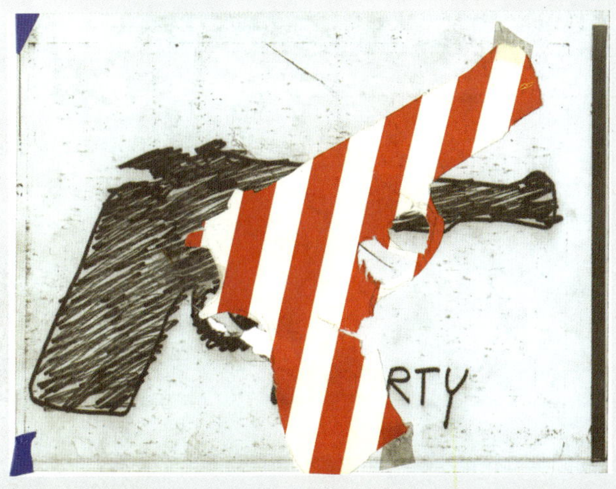

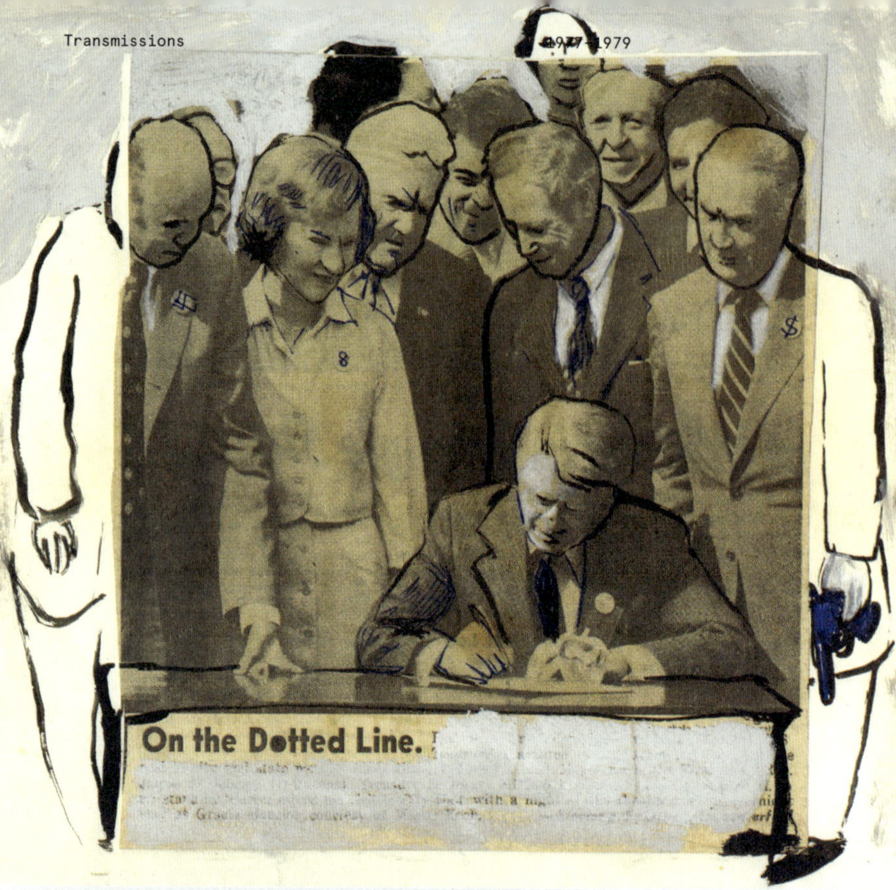

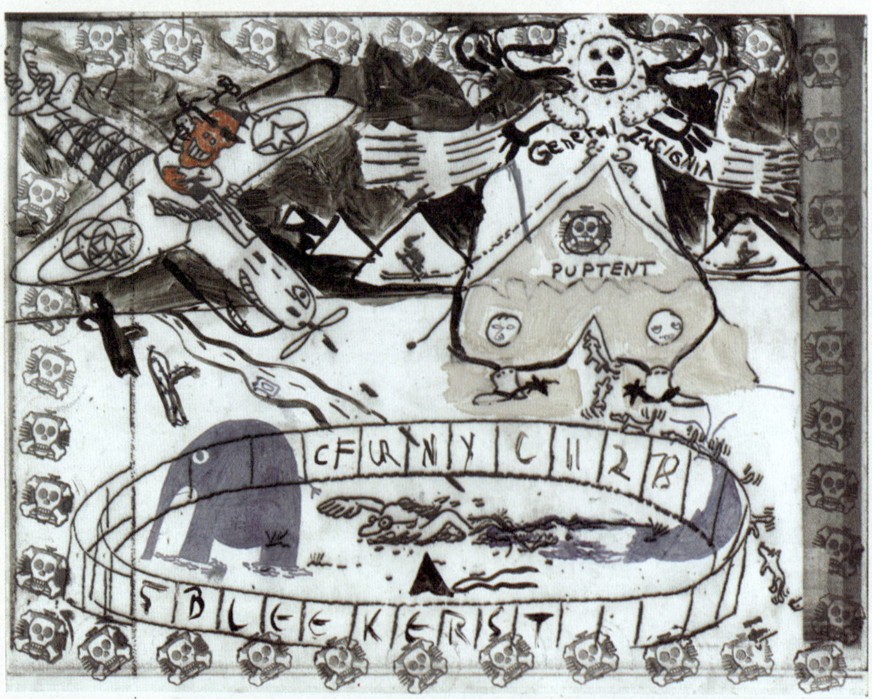

Coleen Fitzgibbon. *On the Dotted Line*, c. 1978–79. Collage and ink on telecopier print, 21.5 × 28 cm. Courtesy of Coleen Fitzgibbon.

Coleen Fitzgibbon, Christof Kohlhöfer and others. *General Insignia Puptent*, c. 1978–79. Collaborative hand-painted telecopier print, 21.5 × 28 cm. Courtesy of Coleen Fitzgibbon.

    ARTWORK SENT VIA QWIP FACSIMILE. FROM ARTISTS' TRANSMISSIONS ORGANIZED BY THE CENTER FOR NEW ART ACTIVITIES.

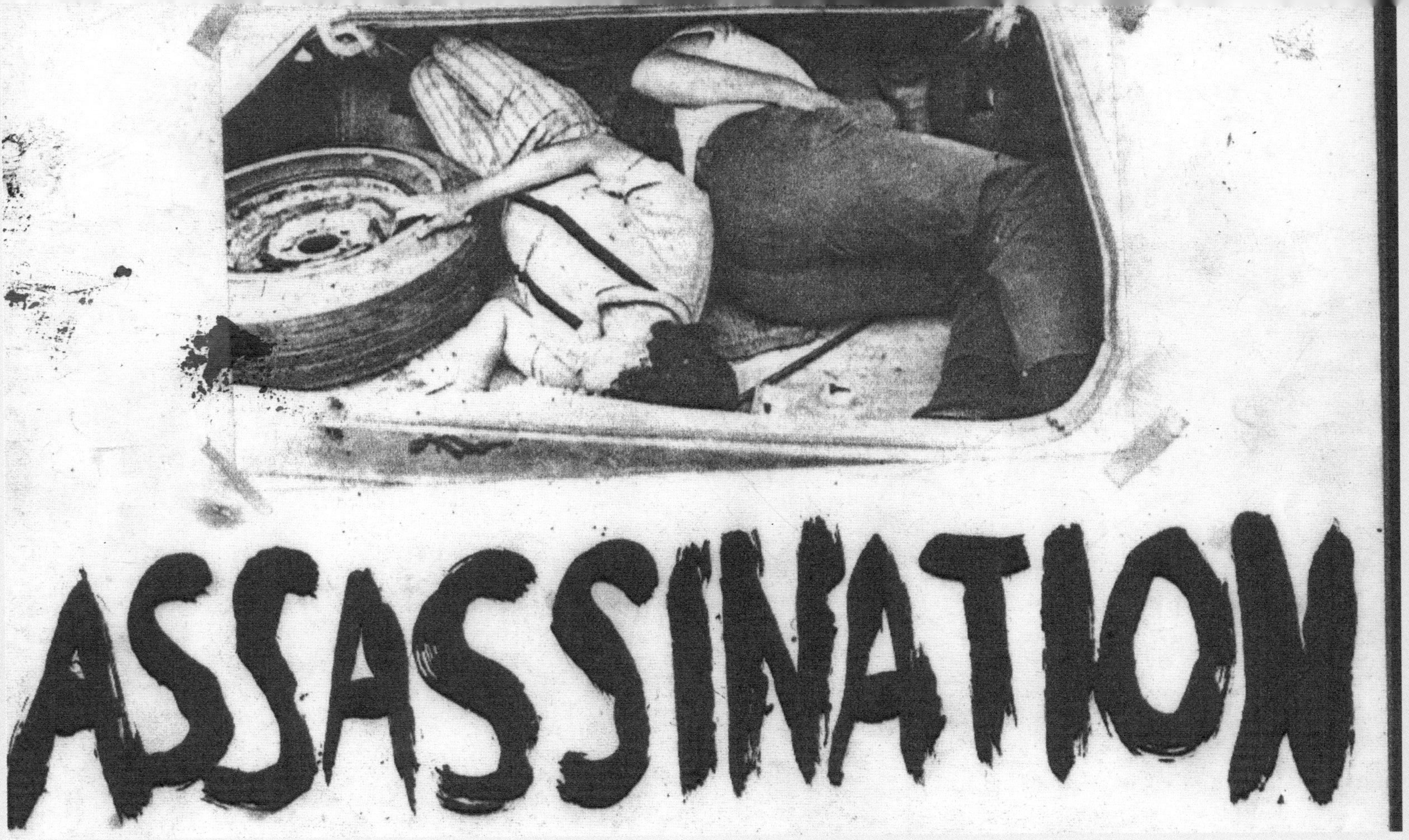

Robert Cooney. *Assassination*, c. 1977–78. Telecopier print, 21.5 × 28 cm. Sent via QWIP. From Artists' Transmissions organized by The Center for New Art Activities. Courtesy of Coleen Fitzgibbon.

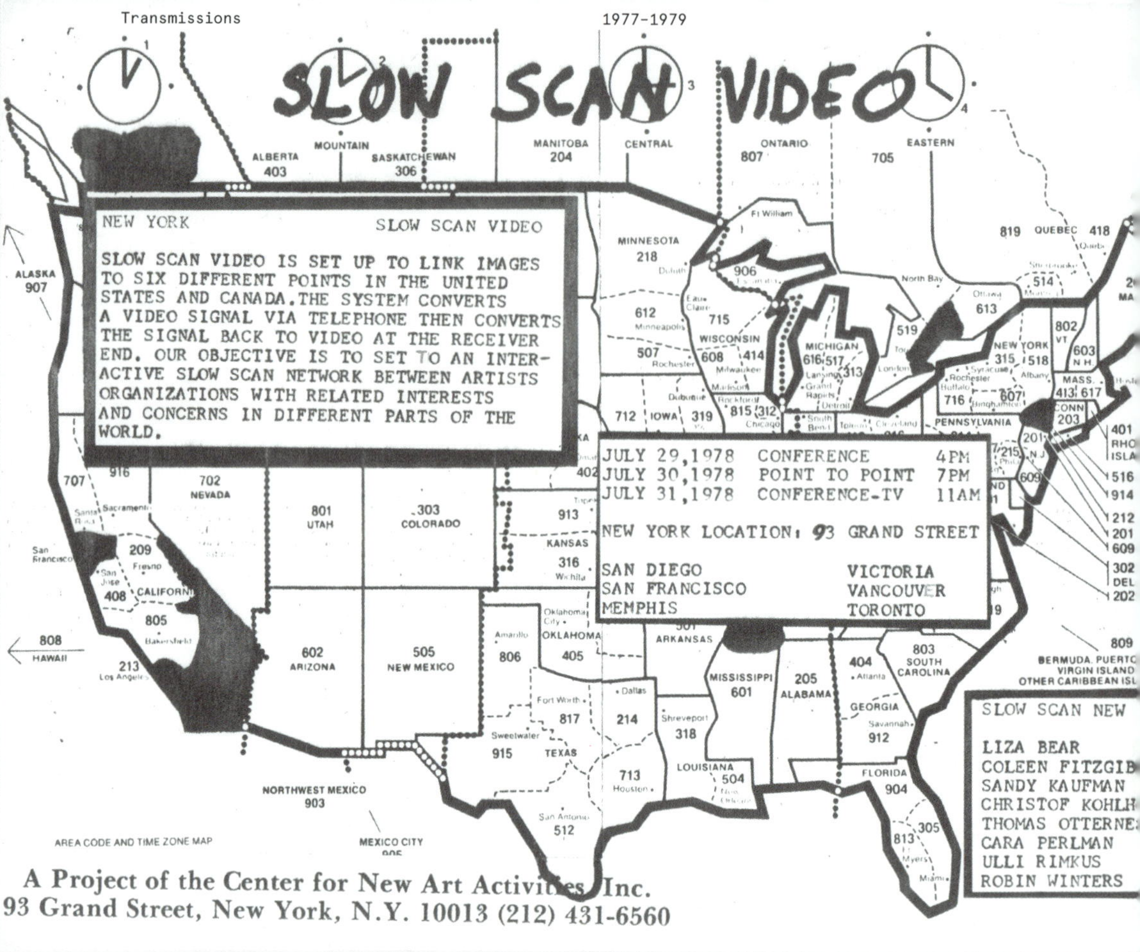

A Project of the Center for New Art Activities, Inc.
93 Grand Street, New York, N.Y. 10013 (212) 431-6560

Liza Béar. *Slow Scan*, 1978.
Offset printed, 21.5 × 28 cm.
Flyer for Slow Scan Video.
Courtesy of Liza Béar.

Cara Perlman. *Untitled* (*Patty Hearst*), c. 1978–9. Offset printed, 28 × 21.5 cm. Photocopy of a *Slow Scan* video still. Courtesy of Liza Béar.

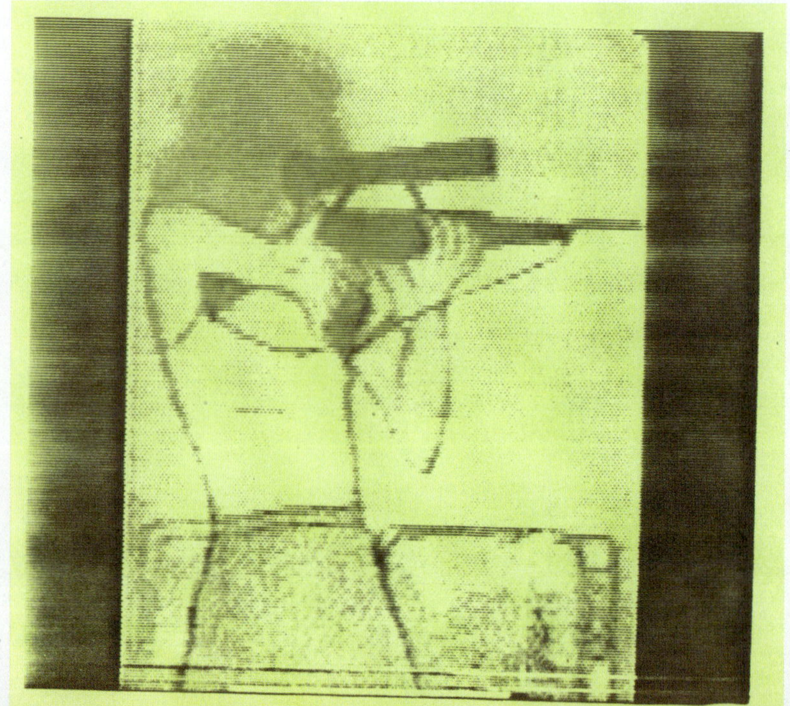

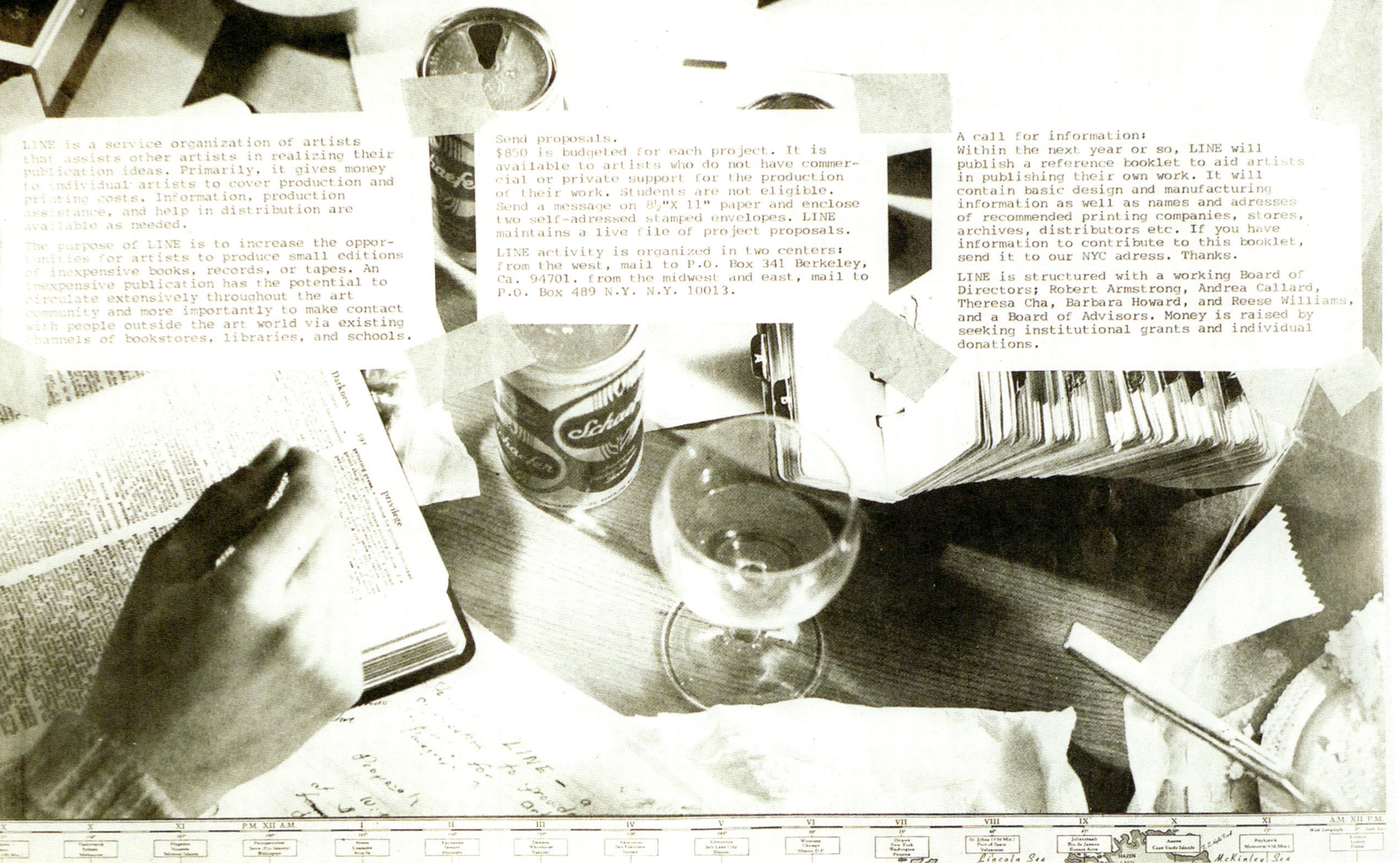

Andrea Callard and Reese Williams. *Untitled* [Line is a service…], 1977. Offset printed, 28.5 × 43 cm. Courtesy of Andrea Callard.

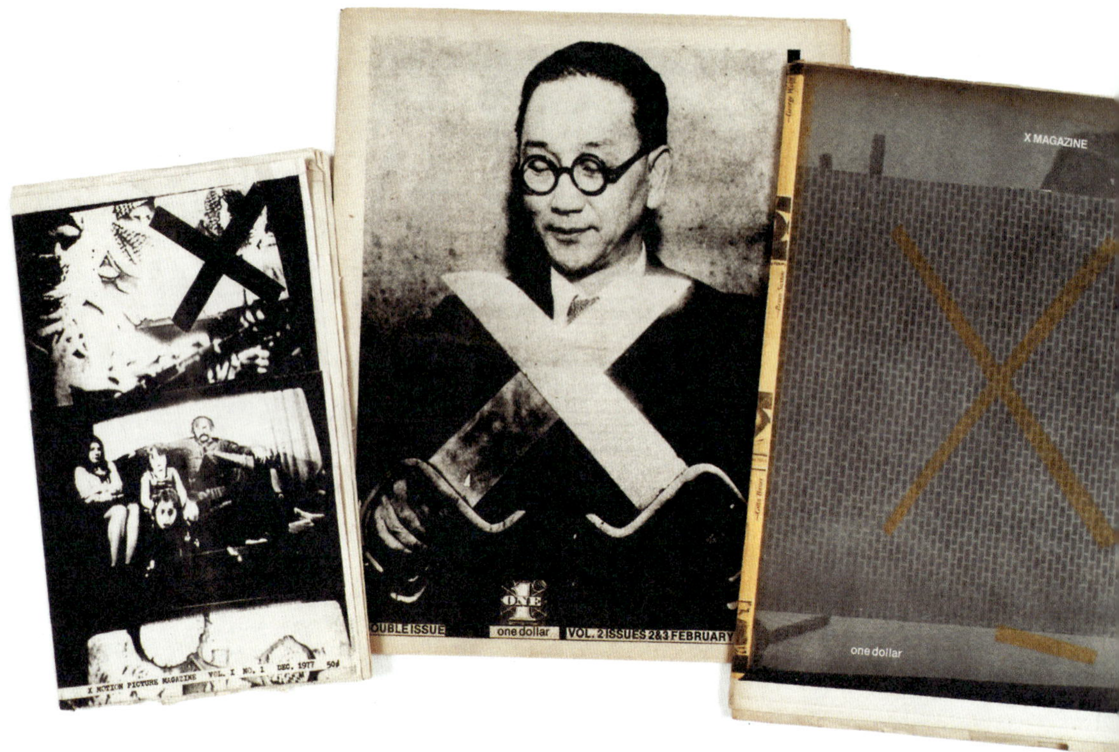

Jimmy DeSana, Coleen Fitzgibbon, Lindzee Smith, Betsy Sussler, editors. (covers, left to right) *X Motion Picture Magazine. Volume 1, Issue 1. X Motion Picture Magazine. Volume 2, Issues 2 & 3. X Magazine. Volume 2, Issues 4, 5, & 6.* New York: Collaborative Projects, Inc, 1977-78. Courtesy of Philip Aarons and Shelley Fox Aarons. Photo: Nancy Linn.

Contributions to *X Motion Picture Magazine*, also known as *X Magazine*
Contributions by Diego Cortez, Terence Severine, Eric Mitchell,
Kathy Acker, Michael McClard, Duncan Smith, Jacki Ochs, Mitch Corber,
Alan Moore, James Nares, Jimmy DeSana, Betsy Sussler, Arturo Schwarz,
Beth B, Tom Otterness, Dorian Brew, Robert Cooney, Nancy Murray,
Bruce Wolmer, Terence C. Sellers, Seth Tillet, Tim Burns, Vivienne Dick,
Scott B, Rene Ricard, Anya Phillips, Kirsten Bates, Robin Winters,
Randi Cohen, Anonymous, Ilona Granet, Marcia Resnick, F. Demi,
Julius Valinnas, Liza Béar, Beate Nilsen, Tina Lhotsky, DeeDee Halleck,
Cara Brownell, Helen Rutherford, Michael Sahl, Coleen Fitzgibbon,
Charlie Ahearn, Stefan Eins, Craig Gholson, Scott Johnson, Jeremy Lipp,
Katy Martin, Aline Mayer, Michael Oblowitz, Judy Rifka, Lindzee Smith,
Susan Springfield, Jeff Goldberg, Philippe Demontaut, Philip Fraser,
Leandro Katz, Sonia Miranda, Amos Poe, Leisa Stroud and Duncan Rathbone
Hannah. "X Magazine is published by its contributors under the auspices
of Colab (Collaborative Projects, Inc), a collaborative non-profit
association controlled by artists."

—Publisher's Statement

Dear Contributors,   *LIZA*   *Jan 7th*

X Motion Picture will publish Vol. II in time for the New Year. All manuscripts and photos should be sent to us by Dec 21. The format this time
will be larger - if you have Vol 1 of X just open it up one fold and that's
the size - 10" wide 12 3/4" long not including the borders.

All manuscripts should come to us already laid out. We will not make any
changes in what we recieve unless you notify us. If possible type
should be on an IBM typewriter - it is clearer. The larger size enables
you to organize the work in columns, as a full page, or as a reduction -
with two typewritten pages on each page (laid out horizontally) If you
do want to reduce it goes by 15%s so type out the original accordingly.

All photographs should be accompanied by the exact dimensions you want
it to be and where you want it placed on the page(s)Specify as to
what type of printing you would like - line shot, halftone, reverse,
benday. I would reccomend either halftone or, if there are alot of subtle
greys, a benday.

If you have any questions please call one of these people

Kathy Acker - 533-6217
Coleen Fitzgibbon - 226-6164 — 5 Bleecker St
Michael McClard - 473-2583
Eric Mitchell, 23 E 3rd St.
Betsy Sussler - 966-0140

Send all contributions to X Motion Picture, c/o Betsy Sussler, 246 Mott #14,
NYC NY *10012*

Talk to you all soon.

Best

Betsy

 P.S.
X is available at-
Bleecker St. Cinema
Cinemobilia
Anthology Film Archives
8th Street Bookstore
Gotham Bookmart
Jaap Rietmann
Jean Renoir Cinema
LIP
Rizzoli
City Lights, S.F. Ca
is distributed in Paris and Munich and next issue will be in Geneve and London

Betsy Sussler. *Letter to contributors for X Motion Picture Magazine, Volume 2, Issues 2 & 3*, 1978.
Pen on typewritten document, 28 × 21.5 cm. Courtesy of Liza Béar.

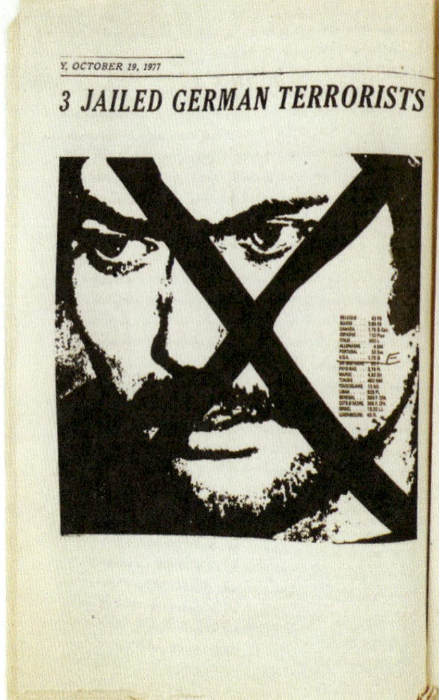

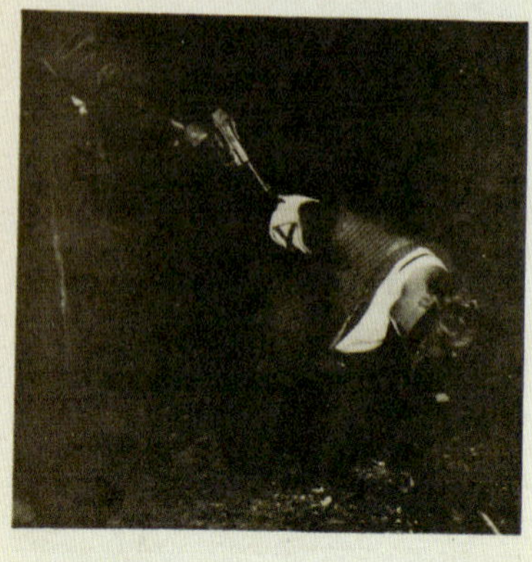

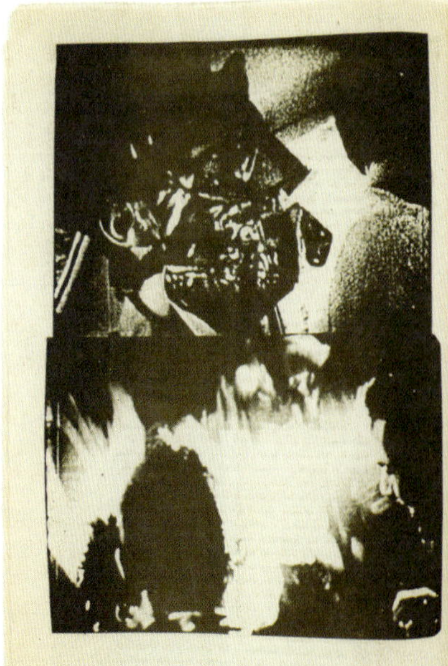

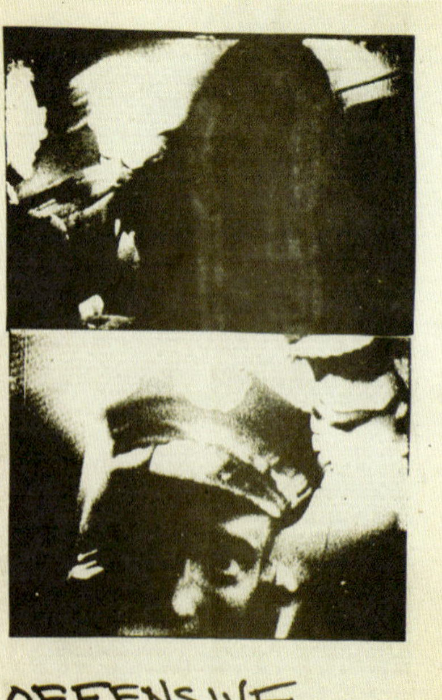

Jimmy DeSana, Coleen Fitzgibbon, Lindzee Smith, Betsy Sussler, editors. *X Motion Picture Magazine*. *Volume 1, Issue 1*. New York: Collaborative Projects, 1977. Offset printed, pbk, 29 × 18.5 cm. Various interiors. Courtesy of Philip Aarons and Shelley Fox Aarons. Photo: Nancy Linn.

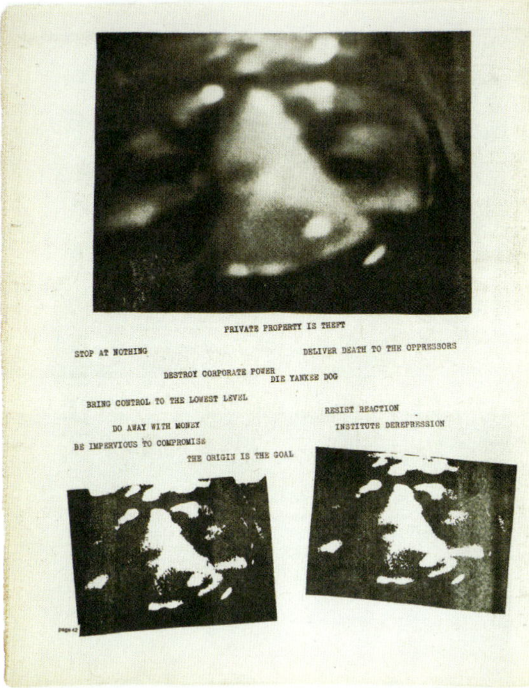

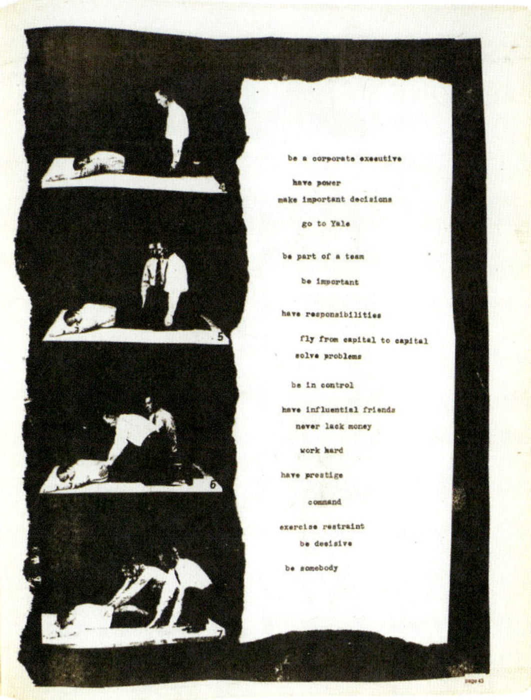

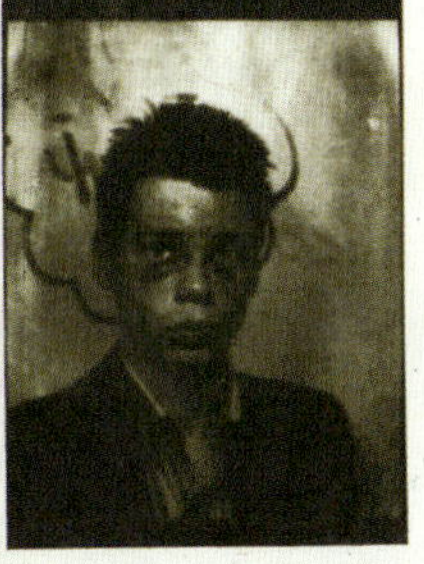
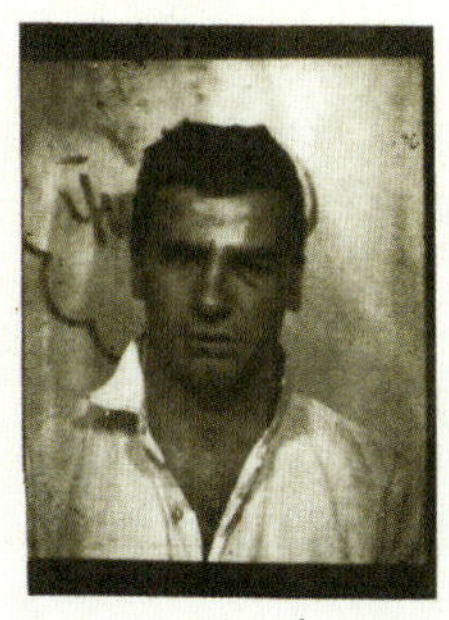

blood money   professional
dead money   professional professionals
blood money   know what must be done
kill money   professional
rape   money   professionals
kill money   you have to be one
money kille   you aint no one
                                     till youre one
                                     you go no where
                                     till youre one
blood money   professionals
blood money   control
money blood   control
shootin money   professionals
hate   money   cant stand
  s   up
assasinate money / murder money   cant go
blood money   down
dead money   upside
dead money /not mine   up
limp money   downside
sick limp money / poison money   down
unemployment money/ tax money   gone below
kill money   nothim there but
dead money   professionals
blood money   professional
not mine   professionals
                                     X us out
                                     get no shame
blood money   jobs dont last
dead money   ge too fast
stiff money   no time
erect money   no strength
christ money   just sleep
work money   just work
slave money   just fuck
master money   just fuck
man money   professionals
sex   money   professional
rolling moeny   professionals
rolling money   no life
blood money   its professional
dead money / not mine   no minds
print money   its professional
control money   no brain
eat money   its professional
shit money   professional
fuck money / suck money   professionals
desire money   money   them
corupt money / power money   control   them
professional money   power   them
sacrifice money   living   them
repress money   us
corporate money   them professionals
grant money / blood money   professional professionals
dead money
not mine
SETH B   page 45

Jimmy DeSana, Coleen Fitzgibbon, Lindzee Smith, Betsy Sussler, editors. *X Motion Picture Magazine*. *Volume 2, Issues 2 & 3.* New York: Collaborative Projects, Inc, 1978. Offset printed, pbk, 35.5 × 28.5 cm. Various interiors. Courtesy of Philip Aarons and Shelley Fox Aarons. Photo: Nancy Linn.

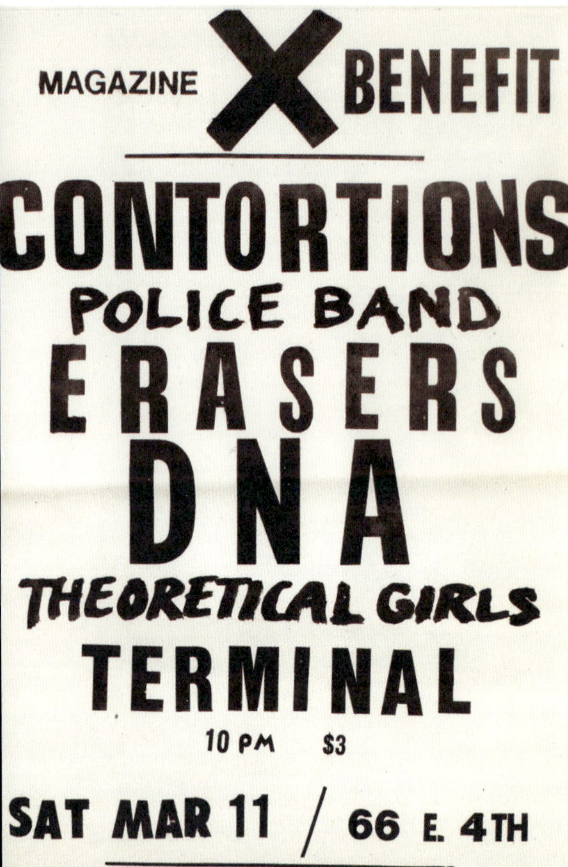

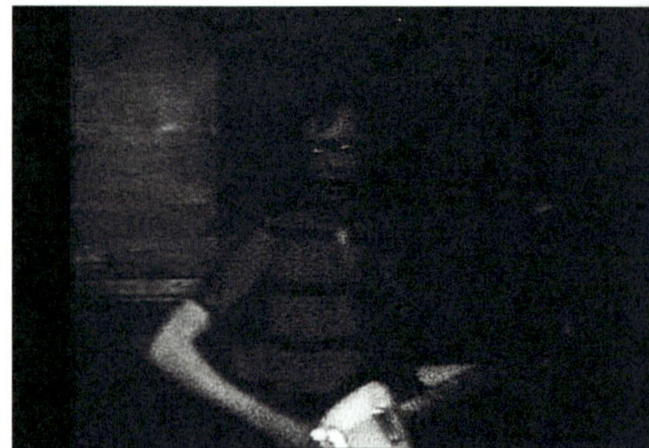

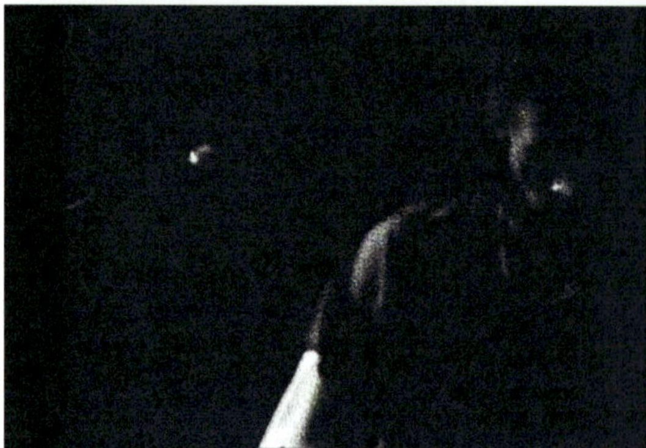

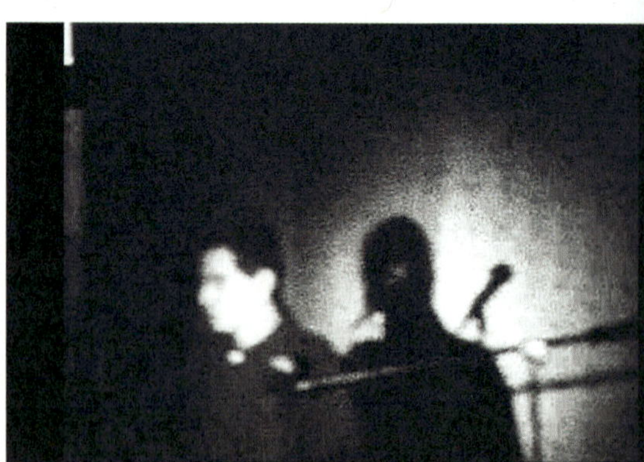

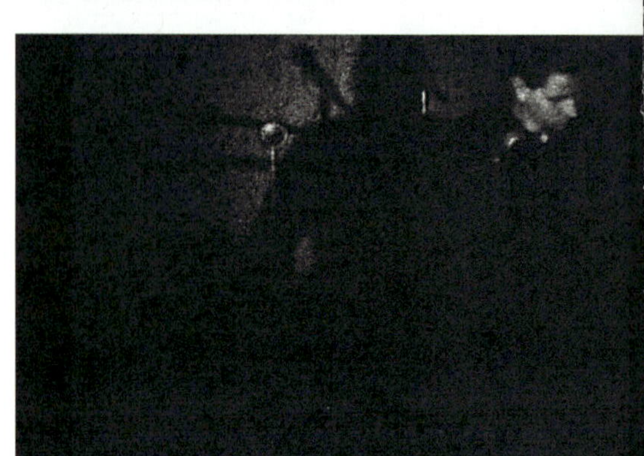

"Colab's X Magazine Benefit" documents the punk rock performances of DNA, James Chance and the Contortions, and Boris Policeband in NYC in the late 1970s at the Puerto Rican Social Club. Shot in B/W Super 8 and edited on video.

Seth Tillet. *X Magazine Benefit Poster*. Offset printed, 50.5 × 35.5 cm. Courtesy of the Collaborative Projects Archive.

X-Magazine Benefit, 1978/2009. Directed by Coleen Fitzgibbon and Alan Moore. [Film Stills] Digital transfer from Super-8, B/W, sound, 11:00. Courtesy of Coleen Fitzgibbon and Alan Moore.

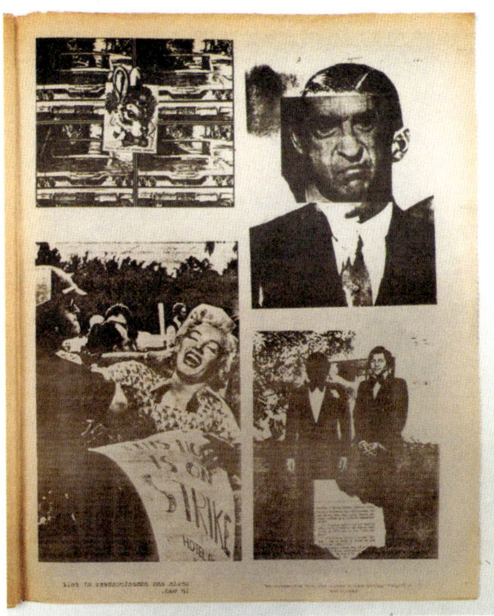

In the winter of 1976–77, I was drawn into a feverish sequence of gatherings in artists' lofts in downtown New York City. The focus was the structure of an organization that would support the creation and sharing of art, defining purpose and forms for group activity. The group included a mix of about 26 artists; painters, writers, photographers, filmmakers and many who wanted to make everything.

—Andrea Callard

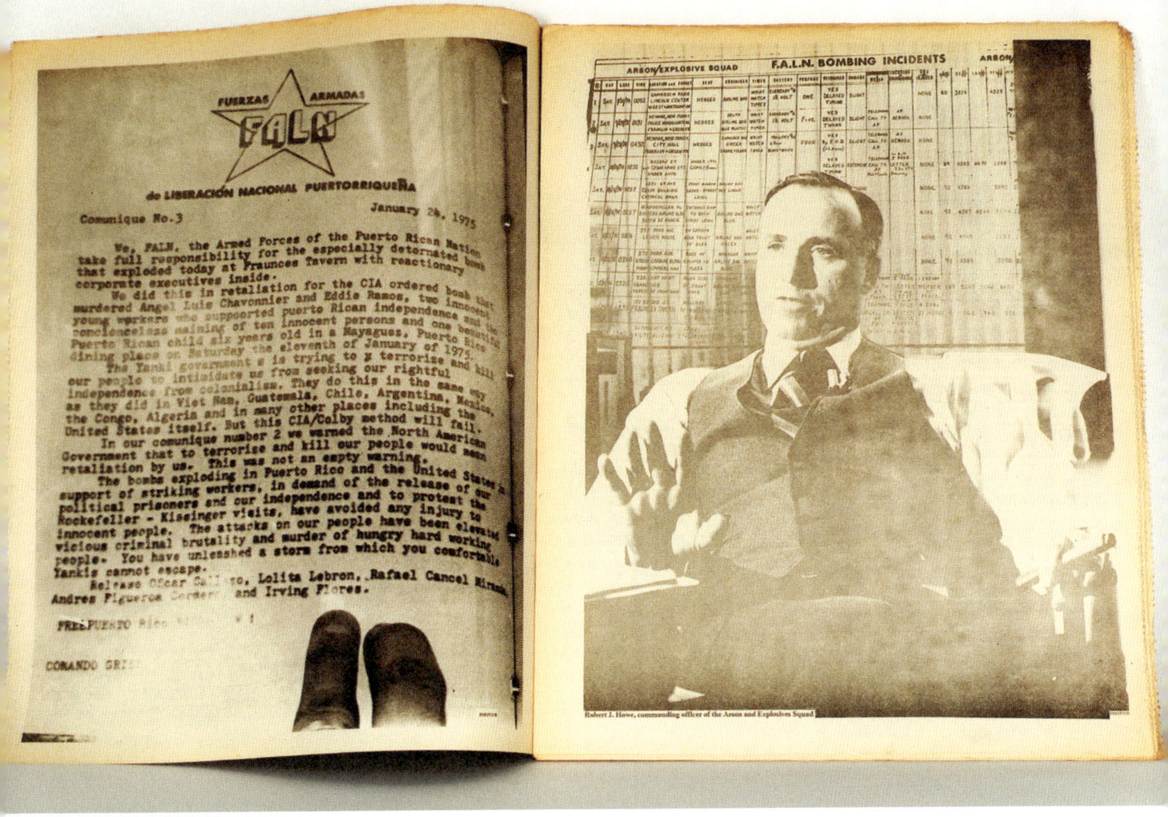

Jimmy DeSana, Coleen Fitzgibbon, Lindzee Smith, Betsy Sussler, editors. *X Motion Picture Magazine. Volume 2, Issues 4, 5 & 6.* New York: Collaborative Projects, Inc, 1978. Offset printed, pbk, 35.5 × 28.5 cm. Various Interiors. Courtesy of Philip Aarons and Shelley Fox Aarons. Photo: Nancy Linn.

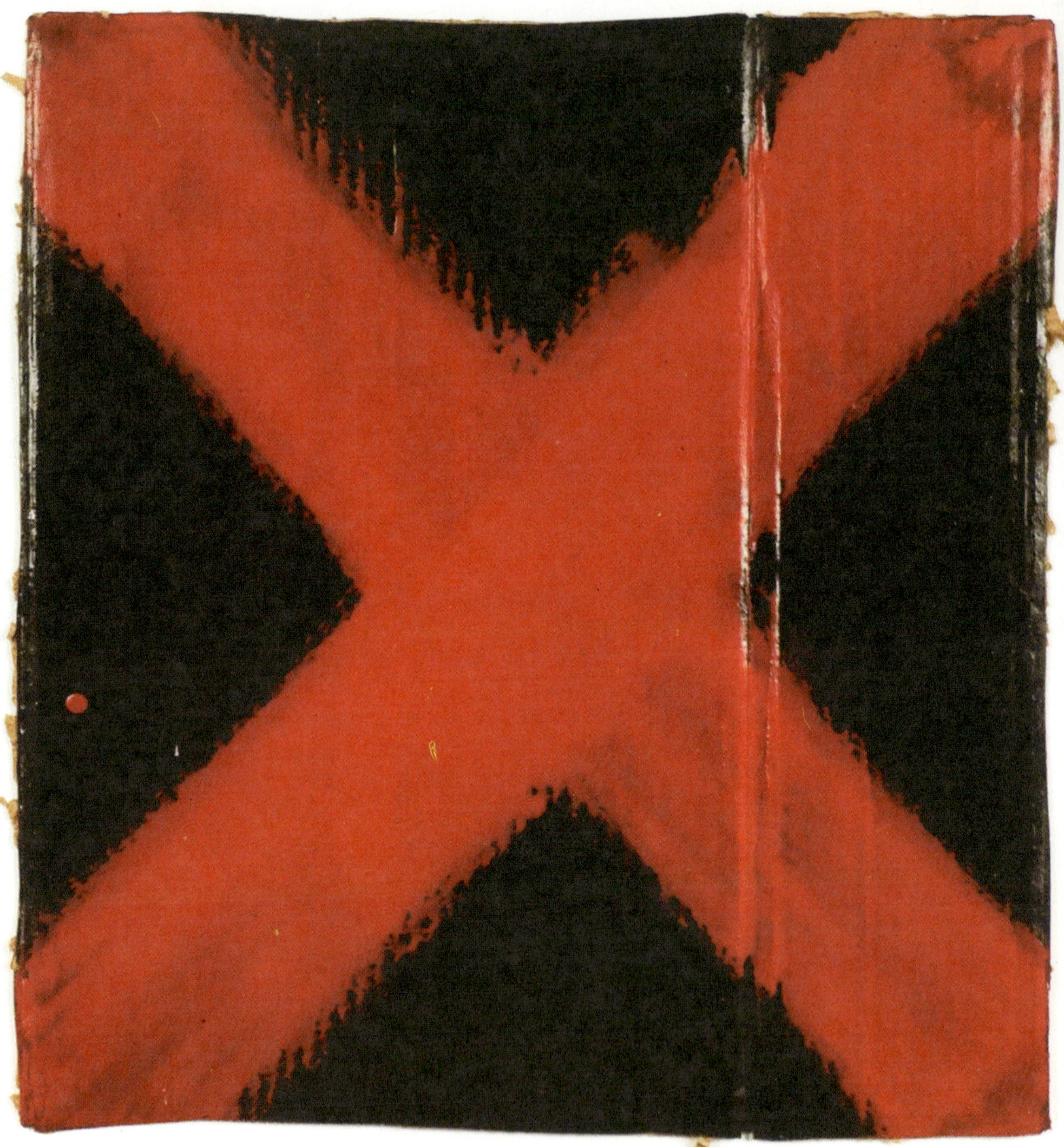

James Nares. *Red X (Small #1)*, 1977. Acrylic on cardboard,
127 × 127 cm. Courtesy of James Nares. Photo: Nancy Linn.

For most of us WWII Baby Boomers we were engaged in school and politics in the late sixties early seventies and familiar with communes, kibbutzes and the experience of large sit-ins/be-ins/be there or be square thinking. 1975 marked what most thought was the end of the Vietnam War and the beginning of peace; this lasted seven years until the US involvement in the Middle East.

—Coleen Fitzgibbon

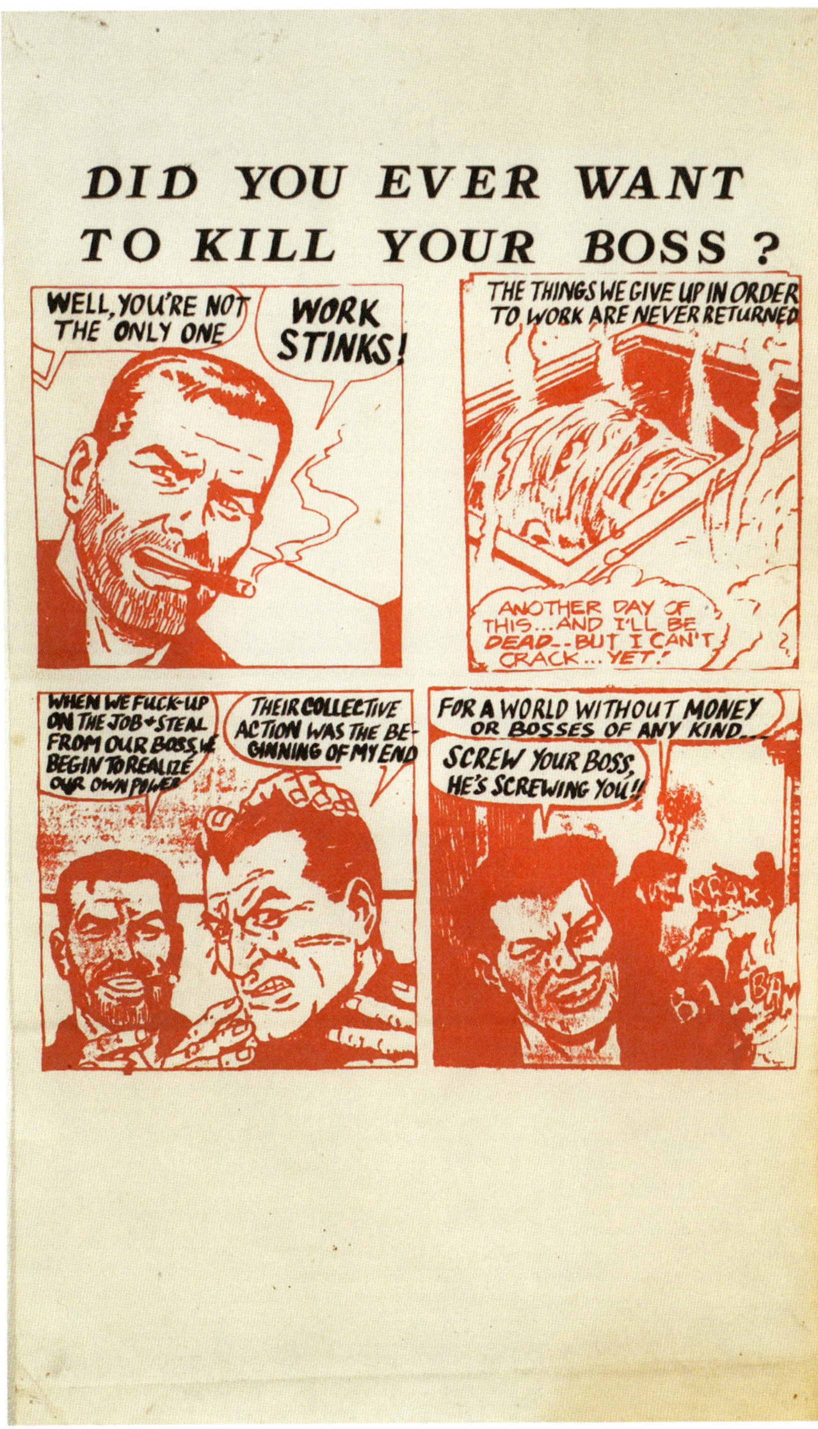

Unknown. *Did You Ever Want To Kill Your Boss?*, c. 1978. Two-color screenprint, 56 × 33 cm. Courtesy of Robin Winters.

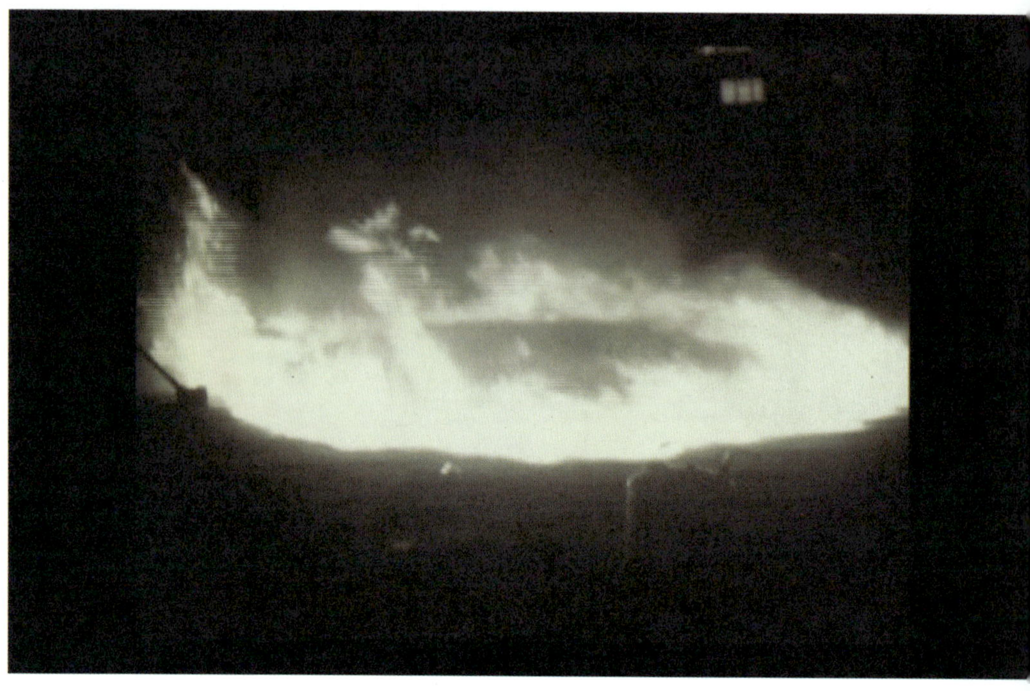

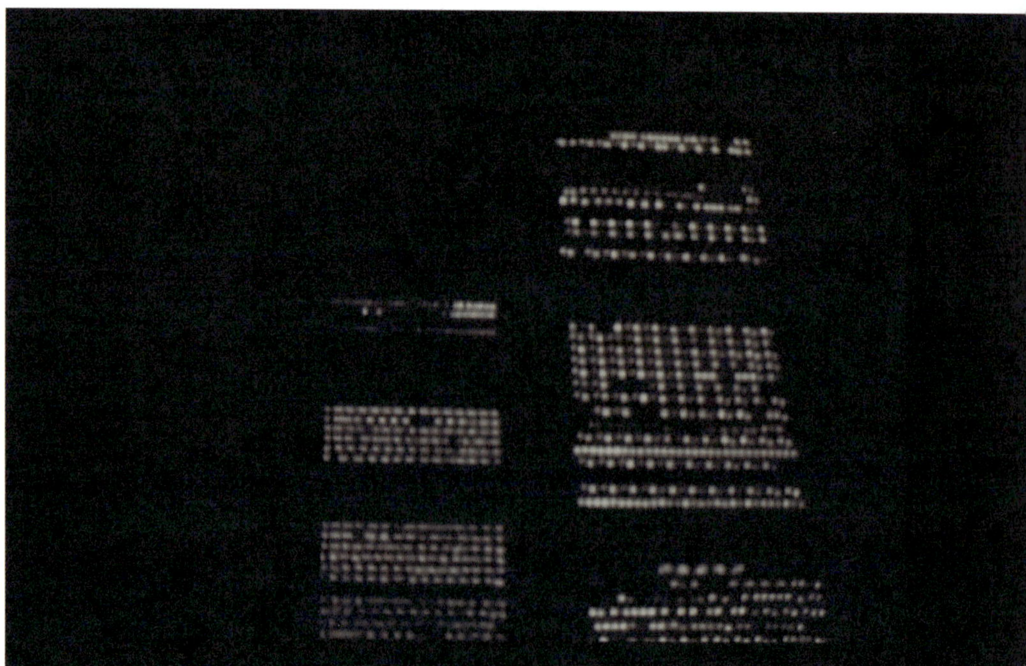

Four Small Fires, 1977. Directed by Ann Messner. [Film Stills] 16mm, B/W, silent, 3:54. Documentation of a series of small fires set by the artist in Tribeca, NYC. Courtesy of Ann Messner.

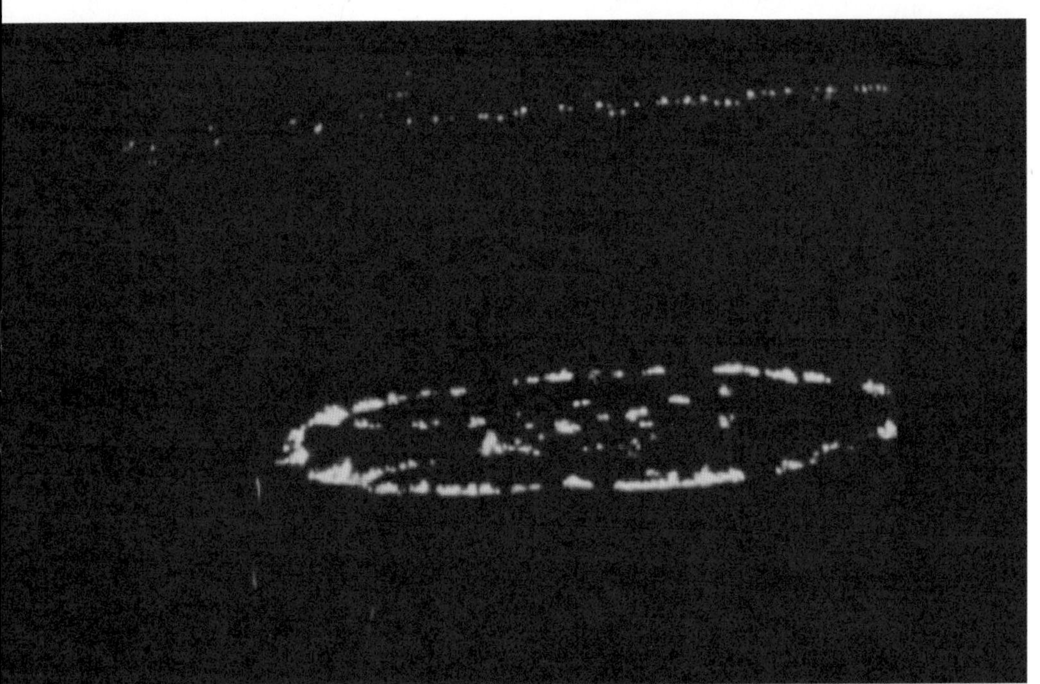

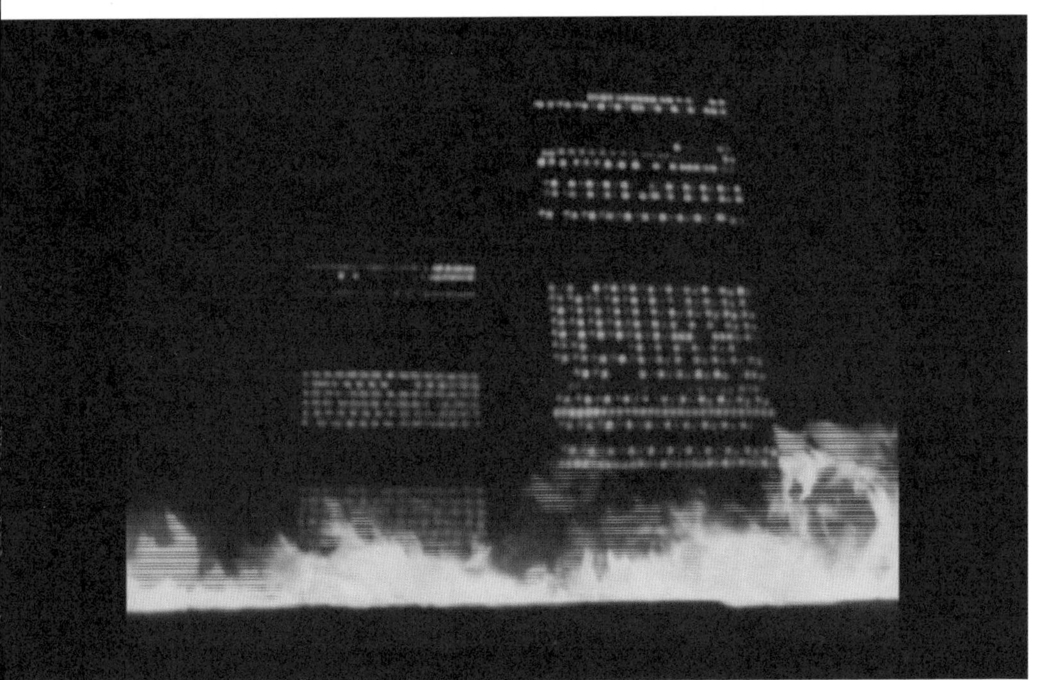

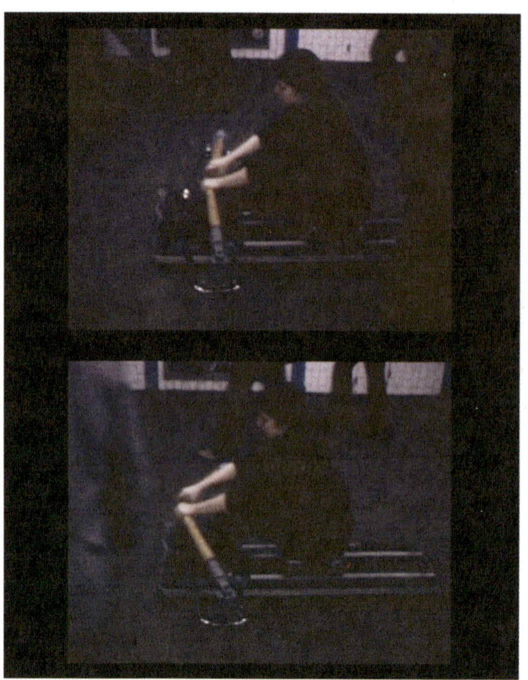
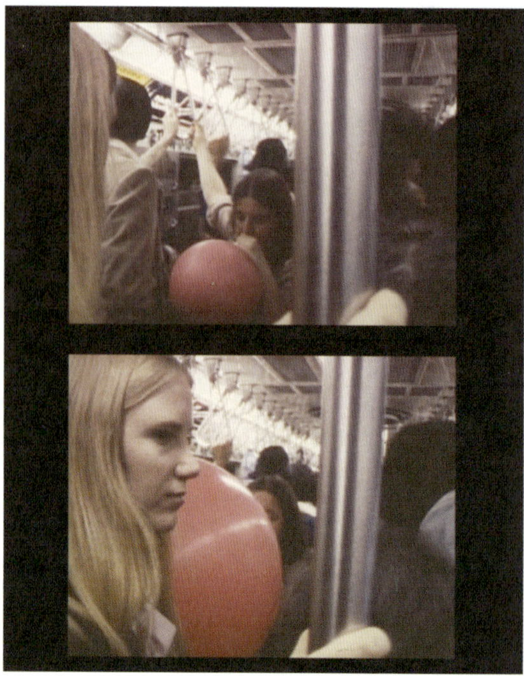

The collective structure allowed access for what was an eclectic cohort of young artists to generate and show work in an immediate way that was not tied to the hierarchal standard of measurement native to the commercial gallery system. This direct participatory process was conducive to the production of uncompromising work that had at its core concern the experience of the 'real' world.

—Ann Messner

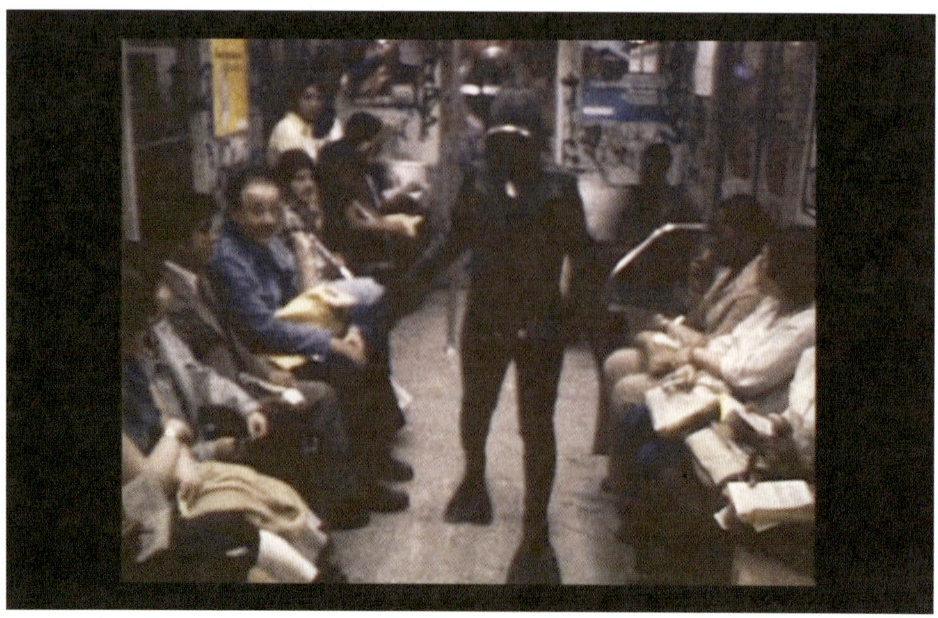

Subway Stories, 1978/2012. Directed by Ann Messner. [Film Stills] Digital transfer from Super-8, B/W, silent, 13:00. Documentation of a series of performance events in New York City subway. Courtesy of Ann Messner.

We were young artists, hot shots and nerds, 30–35 of us, an informal institution in the late 1970s New York City. Our collectivity was passionate, raw, productive, competitive. Colab fed the hungry: New Peers, New Ideas, Recognition. It launched Careers. Colab is a significant contribution to my life's work.

—Cara Perlman

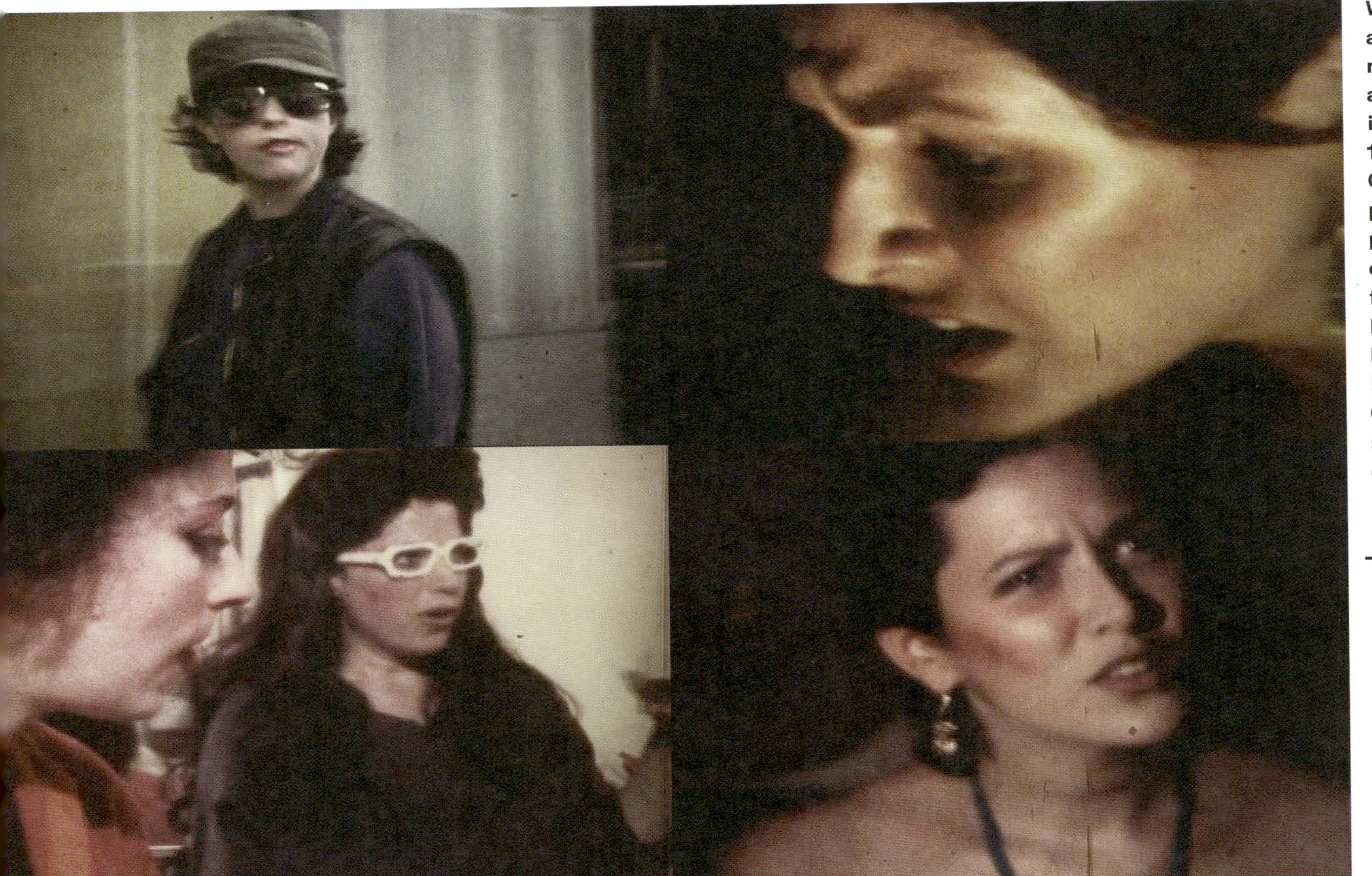

Poofo, 1978. Directed by 3 Way Productions (Ellen Cooper, Cara Perlman, Kiki Smith). [Film stills]. Super-8, B/W, sound, 34:00. Courtesy of Cara Perlman.

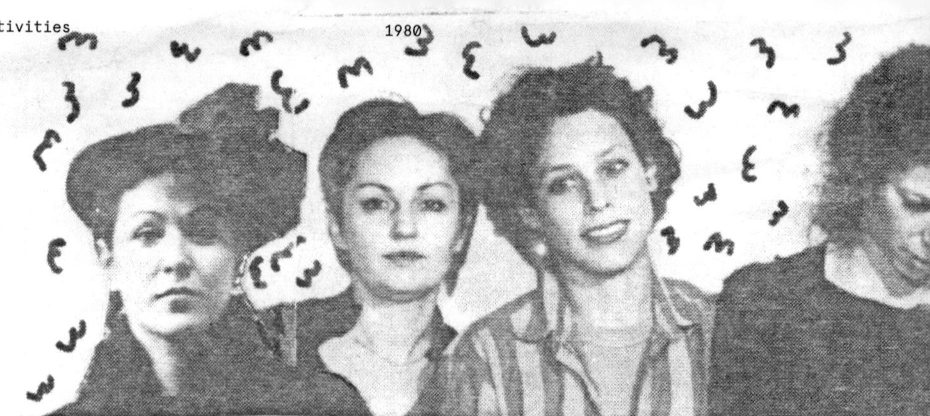

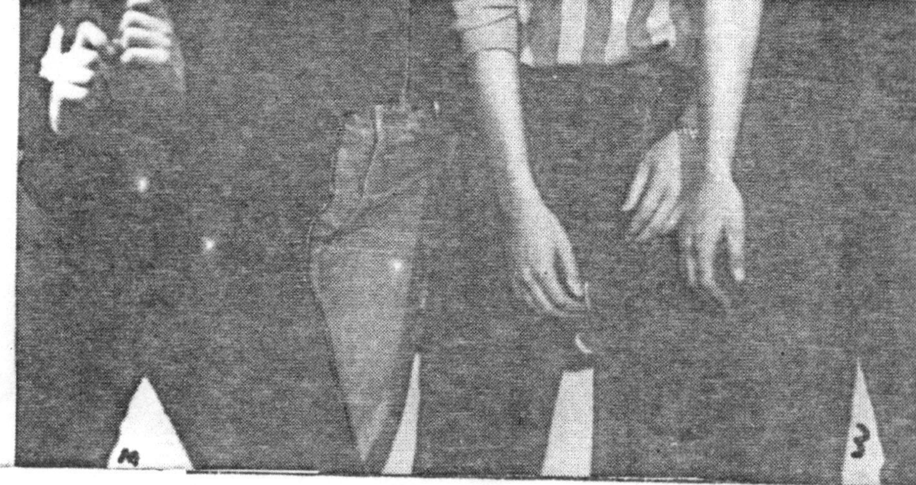

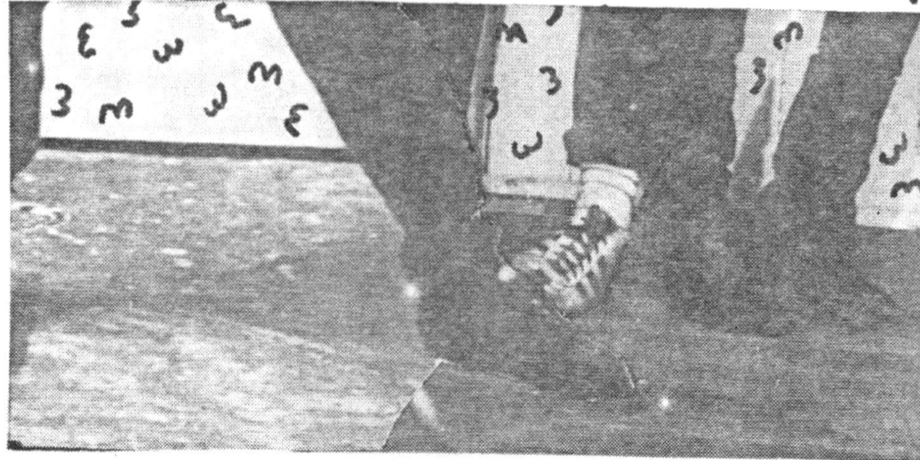

Unknown. *Nice Hot Bath POOFO Y-PANTS*, 1980. Photocopy flyer, 21.5 × 28 cm. Left to right: Ellen Cooper, Virginia Piersol, Jane Dickson, Barbara Ess, Cara Perlman, Gail Vachon, Kiki Smith. Courtesy of Kiki Smith.

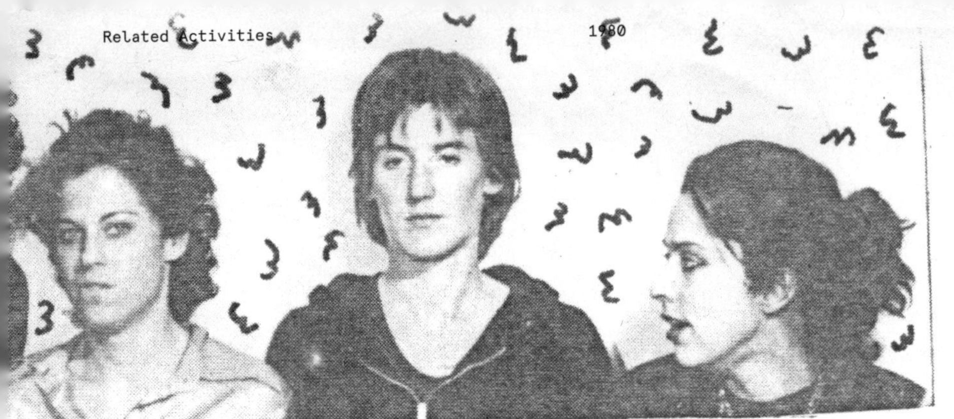

th POOFO

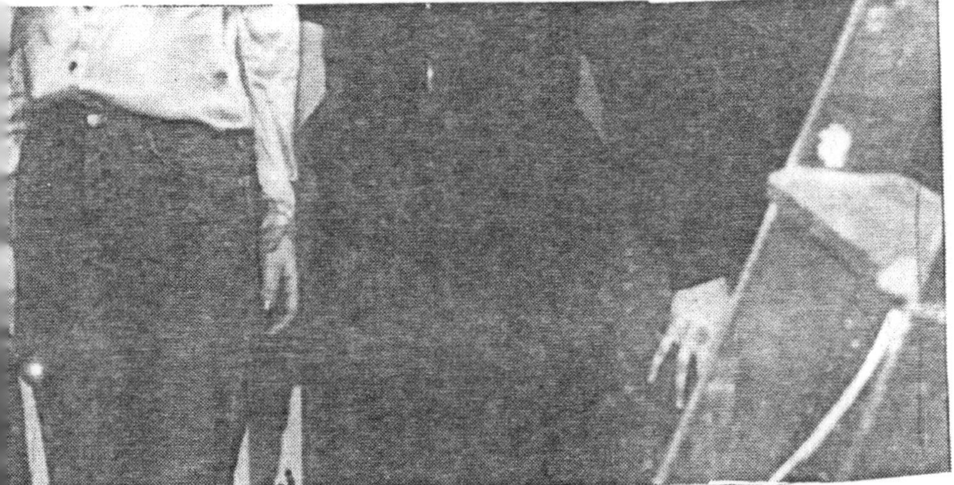

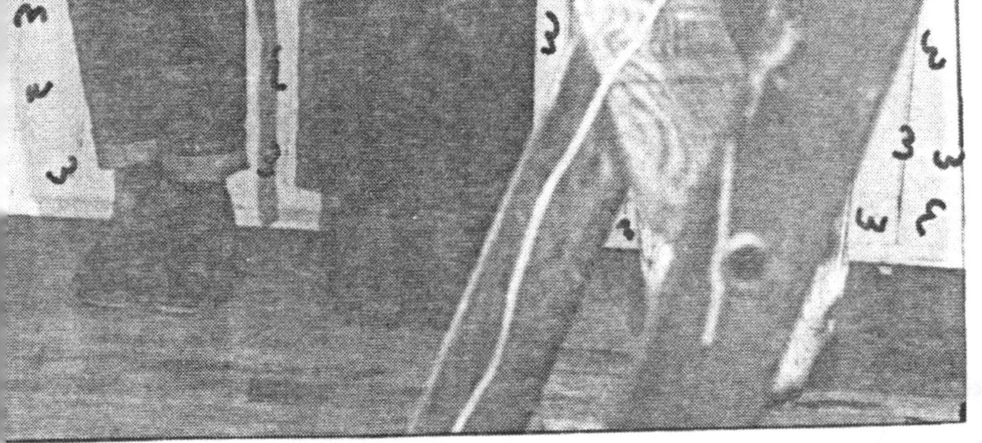

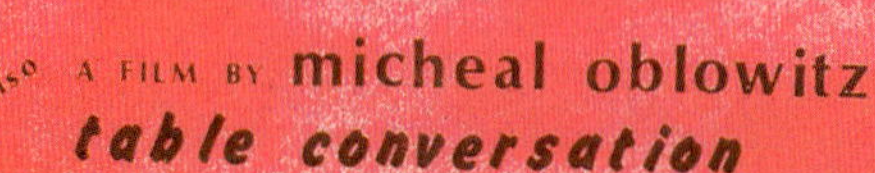

James Nares. *Dope Dope*, 1977. Enamel paint on plastic, 22.5 × 34.5 cm. Text from the script of Nares's film "Suicide? No, Murder!" Courtesy of James Nares.

    John Ahearn. *Shame*, 1978. Screenprint on paper with spray paint, 43 × 28 cm. Courtesy of John Ahearn.

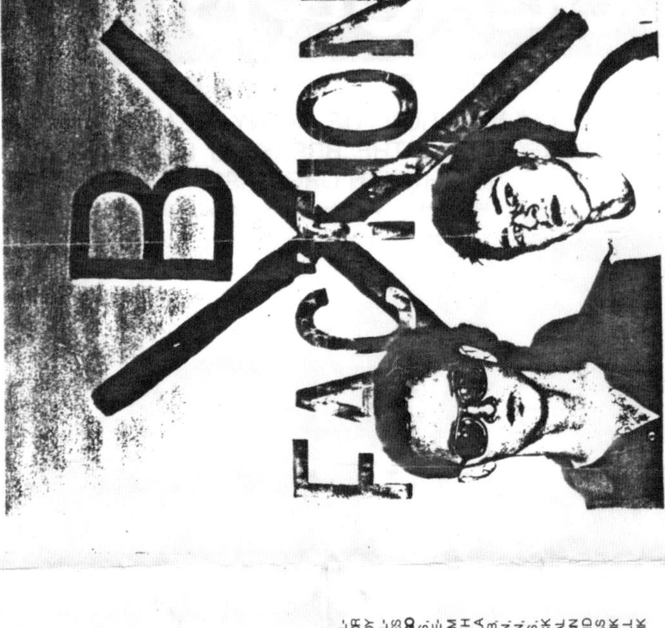

Beth B and Scott B. *Black Box & G-Man*, 1978.
Two-sided photocopy on paper (front and back),
36 × 21.5 cm. Courtesy of Kiki Smith.

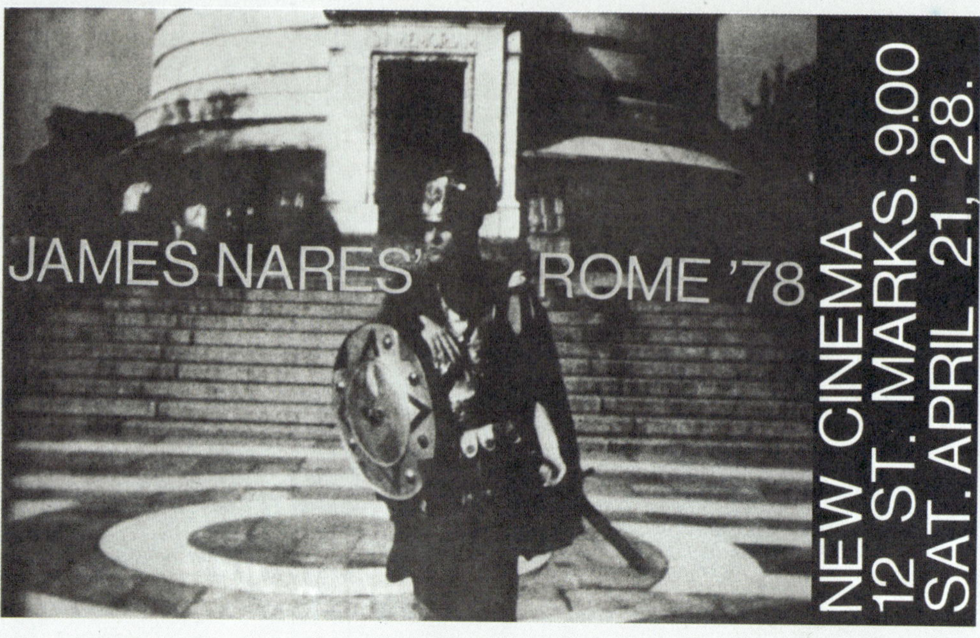

James Nares. *James Nares' Rome '78*, 1978. B/W offset printed poster, 22 × 36 cm. For New Cinema screening room.
Courtesy of James Nares.

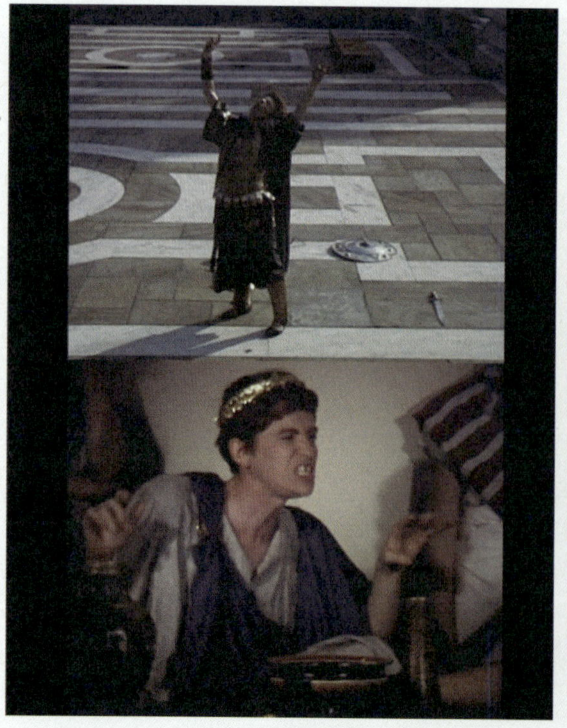

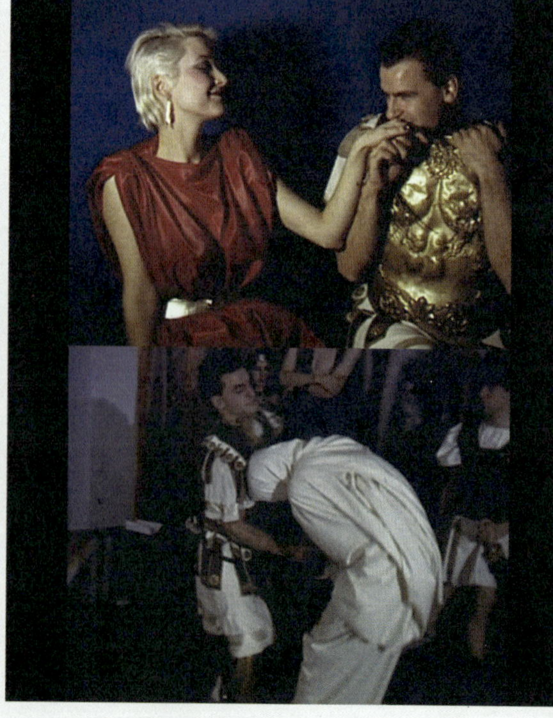

Rome '78, 1978. Directed by James Nares. [Film Stills] Super 8, color, sound, 82:00. Shown at New Cinema screening room.
Courtesy of James Nares.

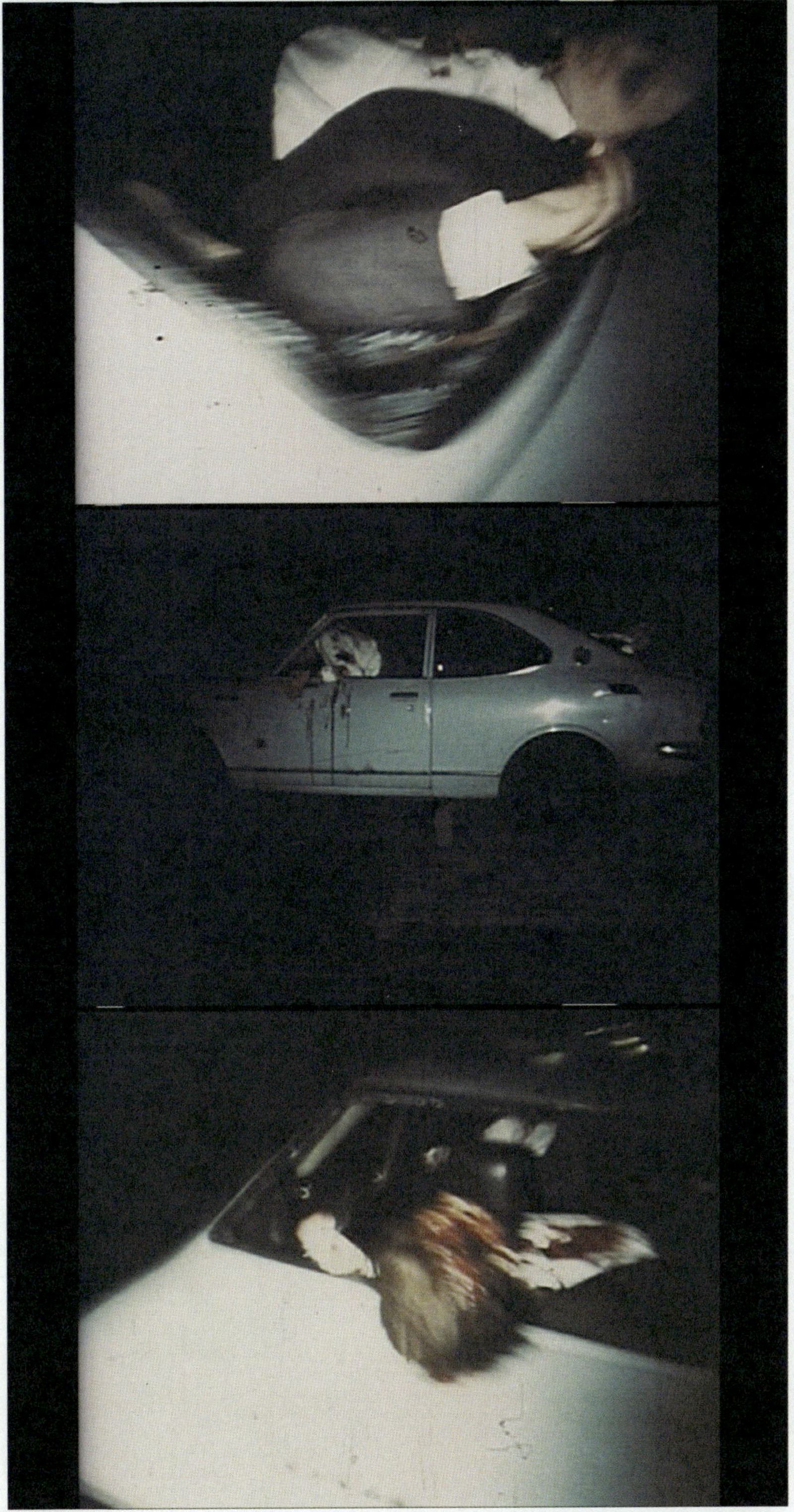

Car Crash/Mass Homicide/Suicide Attack, 1977. Directed by Eric Mitchell. [Film Stills] Super 8, B/W, silent, 6:00. Shown at New Cinema screening room. Courtesy of Eric Mitchell.

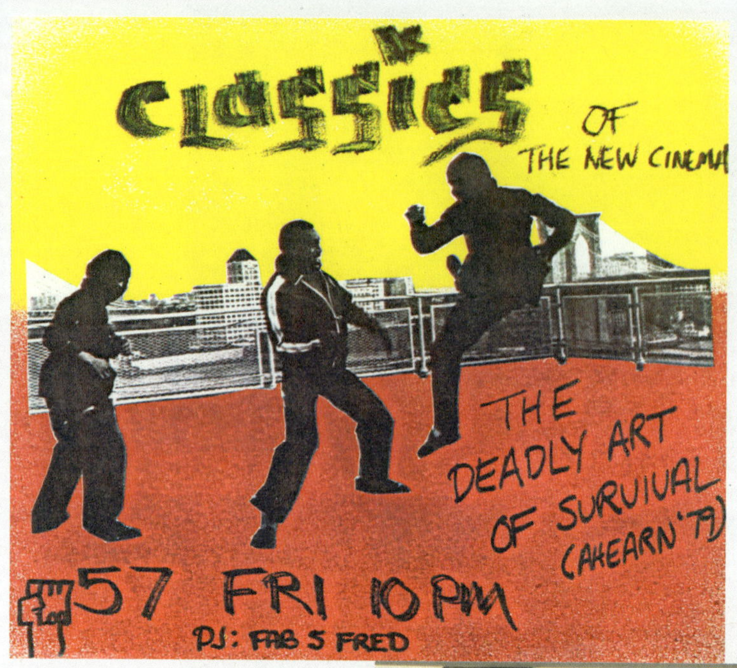

Patti Astor. *The Deadly Art of Survival*, 1979.
Hand-colored offset printed poster,
22 × 36 cm. For screening at Club 57 with
DJ Fab 5 Freddy. Courtesy of Charlie Ahearn.

Charlie Ahearn. *The Deadly Art of Survival*,
1979. Hand-painted silk-screened print,
73.5 × 55 cm. Courtesy of Charlie Ahearn.

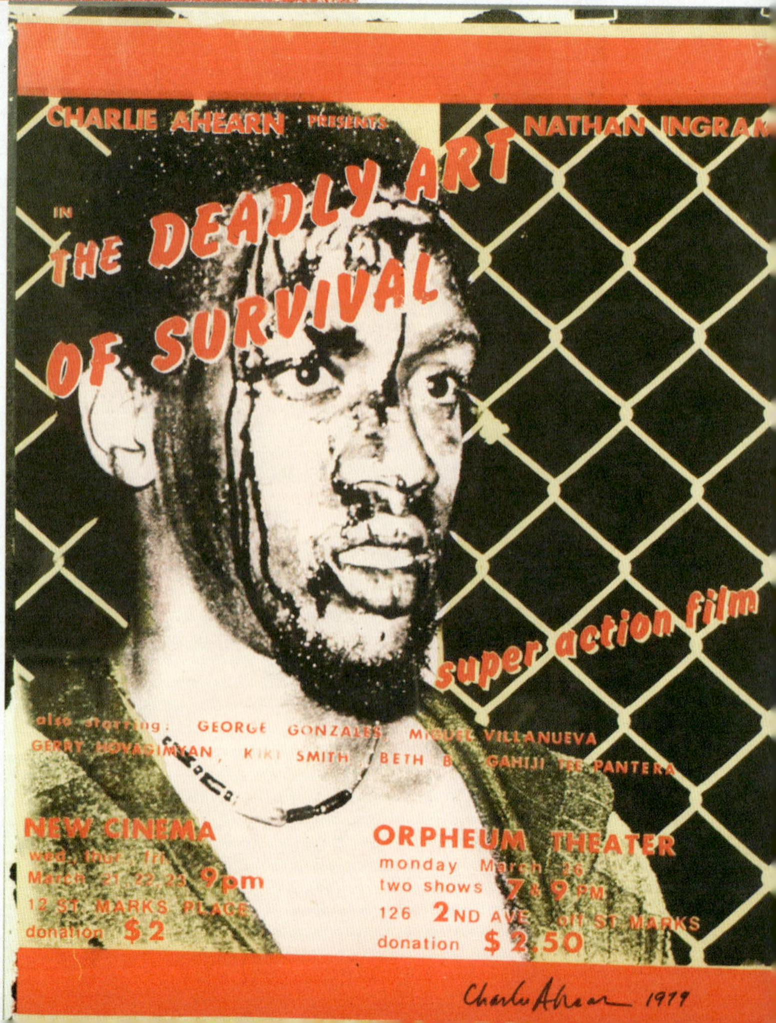

Colab for a collapsing world, of shifting peers and little support. First felt perhaps when Robin Winters in 1973 tried (unsuccessfully) to organize fellow Whitney Program artists, "Refuse to show! Don't let Them curate Us," but he was in the Biennial later that year. Stefan Eins generously offered me a show at his 3 Mercer Store where I met Scott B (then Billingsley) and Beth B (then Horowitz) and we drove nonstop to Arizona together to make movies and videos and became friends. Robin and Coleen Fitzgibbon sort of joined *The Arcade Show* I/we did under The Municipal Building with films, videos, performance; screening Gordon Matta-Clark's "Slivers" on the columns, but Gordon was already too sick to attend. I recall a noisy Colab meeting at Christa Maiwald's LES apartment probably late 1977 with Coleen urging us to get the grant money "not The Institutions" so we could share film equipment, etc. Then word got out that Nick the Fence under Alan Moore's spot on Houston Street got a load of Super 8 cameras and they went fast. Colab began All Color News "live" on Channel D with everything allowed. We had a blast coming into the Cable TV station with raw rolls of Super 8 with my twin brother John and Tom Otterness and we're just flying it live onto the show with Alan at the controls. Was anyone watching it? I had been shooting a Super 8 martial arts movie in the Smith Projects by The Brooklyn Bridge and John climbed up under the bridge to capture the movie's climax from above. Beth B, Becky Howland and Kiki Smith made appearances amid the street action scenes. We screened it with a live martial arts show at Stefan and Joe Lewis' Fashion Moda and later at *The Times Square Show* bringing it finally back to The Deuce, boulevard of Kung Fu flicks. Working from Jane Dickson's three card monte drawing, I silkscreened hand-painted posters upstairs in the TSS before things really got hectic. Fred Brathwaite approached me during the opening and we talked about making a movie on graffiti and hip hop and he and Lee Quinones busted out a FAB5 on the TSS building the very next morning in broad daylight. The Wild Style project had lots of Colab friends involved: Coleen was the production manager; Joe Lewis played a role often mistaken for Kool Herc; Tom O and Ulli Rimkus did carpentry on the amphitheater; Walter Robinson lent his car; John his Bronx apartment; Jane storyboarded the animation, etc. But was any of this really Colab? I like to think of it as parallel play with I'll play in yours if you play in mine before we all went our own ways.

—Charlie Ahearn

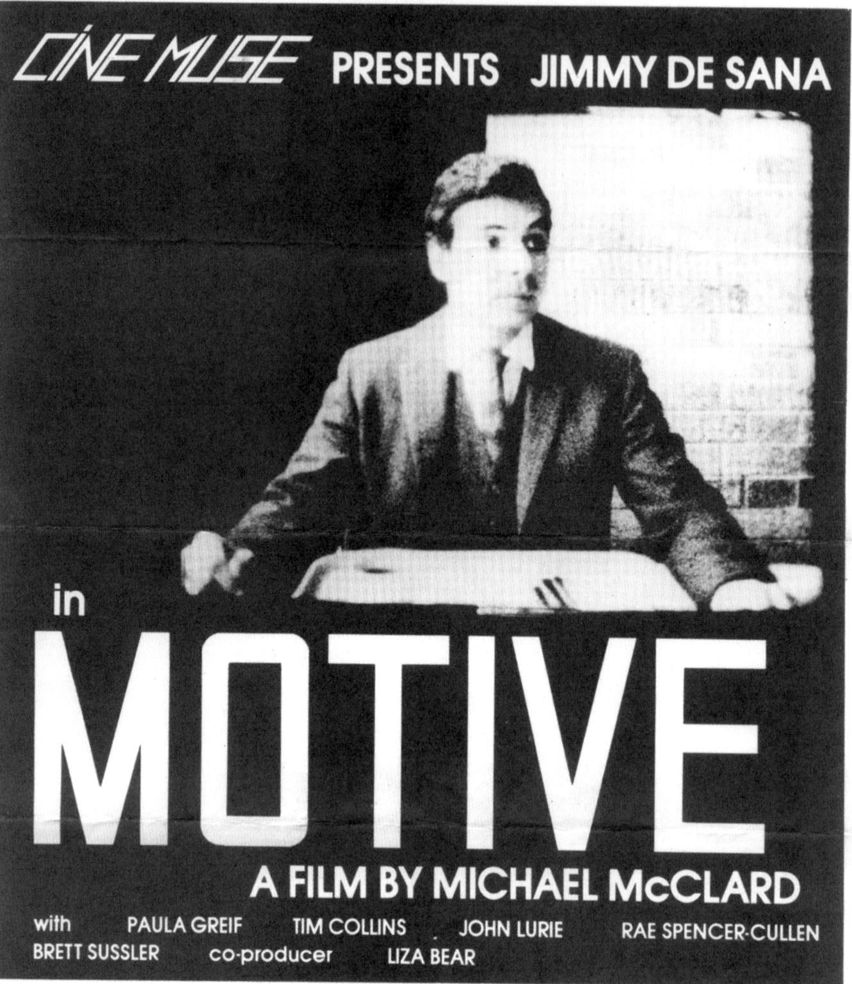

Michael McClard. *Motive*, c. 1979–80. Offset printed, 34 × 28 cm.
Poster for New Cinema screening room. Courtesy of Michael McClard.

Colab, the not for profit corporation, explicitly formed to sponsor, fund and otherwise facilitate works of art-collaboration by three or more people worked reasonably well. The fact that it lumbered on for as long as it did is remarkable. I think a lot of good came out of it over the years.

—Michael McClard

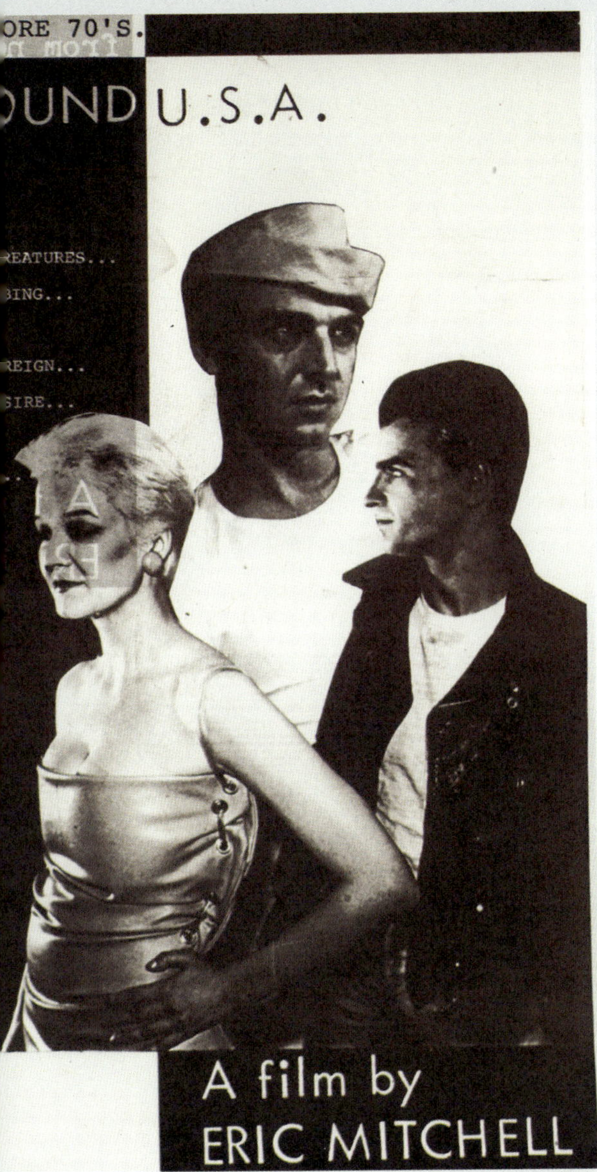

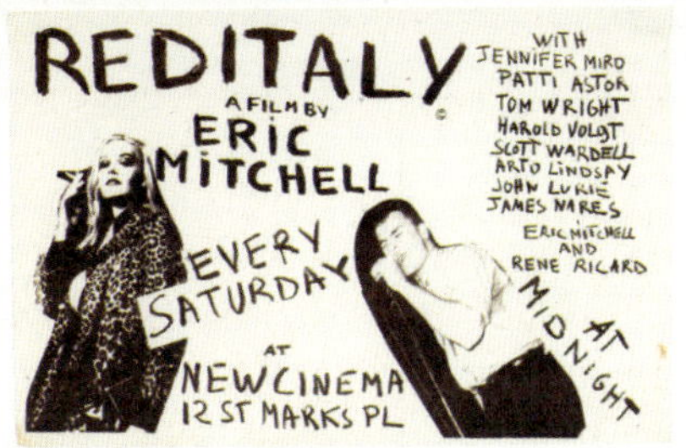

Eric Mitchell. *Underground USA (No More 60's No More 70's)*, 1980. Offset printed poster, 54 × 42.5 cm. For New Cinema screening room. Courtesy of Eric Mitchell.

Eric Mitchell. *Red Italy*, 1979. Offset printed poster, 28 × 43 cm. For New Cinema screening room. Courtesy of Eric Mitchell.

Colab was fun (for a while)
Colab was tedious (those boring meetings!)
Colab was progress (ahead of its time)
Colab was dated (a utopia without contracts)
Colab was a group (a+b+c+d+e+f....)
Colab was individualistic (where is my grant?)
Colab was about collaboration (*The Time Square Show,*
    The Real Estate Show, The New Cinema, X Magazine, etc)
Colab was about personal achievement (I, we, I, we, I, we.....)
Colab was hopeful (youthful, delusional, enthusiasm)
Colab was doomed (by its very success)
Colab was.

—Eric Mitchell

While Colab is known as the cauldron of the 80s big show, the group came into being because of the requirements of media work. Several members had participated as junior artists alongside Soho heavyweights in the satellite broadcast projects of Liza Béar in the late '70s. These newbies were also making Super 8 films, and some started "punking out." Diego Cortez moved into the bubbling music scene on the Lower East Side and started haunting CBGBs with the star-crossed glamorpuss Anya Phillips. Amos Poe was already there. He and Ivan Kral documented the early CBs scene in *Blank Generation* (1976), and screened his feature *The Foreigner* in a vacant lot at Cannes.

In 1978 the New Cinema screening house opened on St. Marks Place. Here Colab filmmakers like Eric Mitchell, James Nares, John Lurie, Tina Lhotsky, Betsy Sussler, and Becky Johnston showed video transfers of their 8mm synch-sound feature films on an Advent projector. Subjects included terrorists, astronauts, Roman emperors, strippers and disaffected butchers.

The New Cinema crowd, many of whom lived on East 4th Street near the NYC Mens Shelter, cleaved to a Warhol-tinged vision of beat life and glamorous pose. Other artists in Colab formed the All Color News (ACN), a documentary-oriented group working on public access cable TV, a new outlet for artists. These included the Ahearn twins, Charlie and John, the team of Scott and Beth B, Tom Otterness, Virge Piersol and me. Together with Michael McClard and Coleen Fitzgibbon, ACN produced live cablecasts at Experimental Television Center, then located on 23rd Street, a low-cost commercial TV studio. One emergency cablecast featured Congressman Ted Weiss. Clutching his messy briefcase under his arm, he spoke against the draconian criminal code called S-1 proposed by Congress during the European anti-terrorist fever; this early move toward total state surveillance was defeated.

After Colab formed, All Color News dissolved. Soon Potato Wolf formed to make cable TV, a whimsical name assigned by first series producer Cara Perlman. Potato Wolf cleaved to an open, artist-driven and eclectic mix of programming, most of it fictionally based, and parodic of the forms of mainstream television. PW often pre-taped at the Young Filmmakers studio on Rivington Street, but did most of their work live at the ETC studios on 23rd Street. Shows like the memorably chaotic "Nightmare Call-In Theater," and "Call to Wobulate" frightened Jim Kladdach, the usually imperturbable manager of that venue. For the latter, upstate hardware maven Terry Mohre plugged his homemade "wobulator" synthesizer directly into ETC's main board. Among PW's producers was the team of girlhood friends Ellen Cooper and

Kiki Smith. They made *Cave Girls* (1982) a collaborative work of research, reenactment and creative anachronism about a prehistoric tribe of techno-savvy women. Scenes for this were taped in Soho, filmed in New Jersey and in the weed-filled backyard of the new cultural center ABC No Rio.

Potato Wolf shared sensibility and some personnel with other artist-run cable TV series, most notably Communications Update, a project run by Liza Béar, and the still extant Paper Tiger Television. PTTV also adapted the practice of making live TV and for a while emulated the tacky painted paper look of Potato Wolf productions (an aesthetic which PW artists called "cardboard consciousness") as a backdrop to their critiques of contemporary media hosted by academics and cultural critics.

—Alan Moore, "A Brief History of MWF." Clayton Patterson, editor *Captured: A Film/ Video History of the Lower East Side.* New York: Seven Stories Press, 2005.

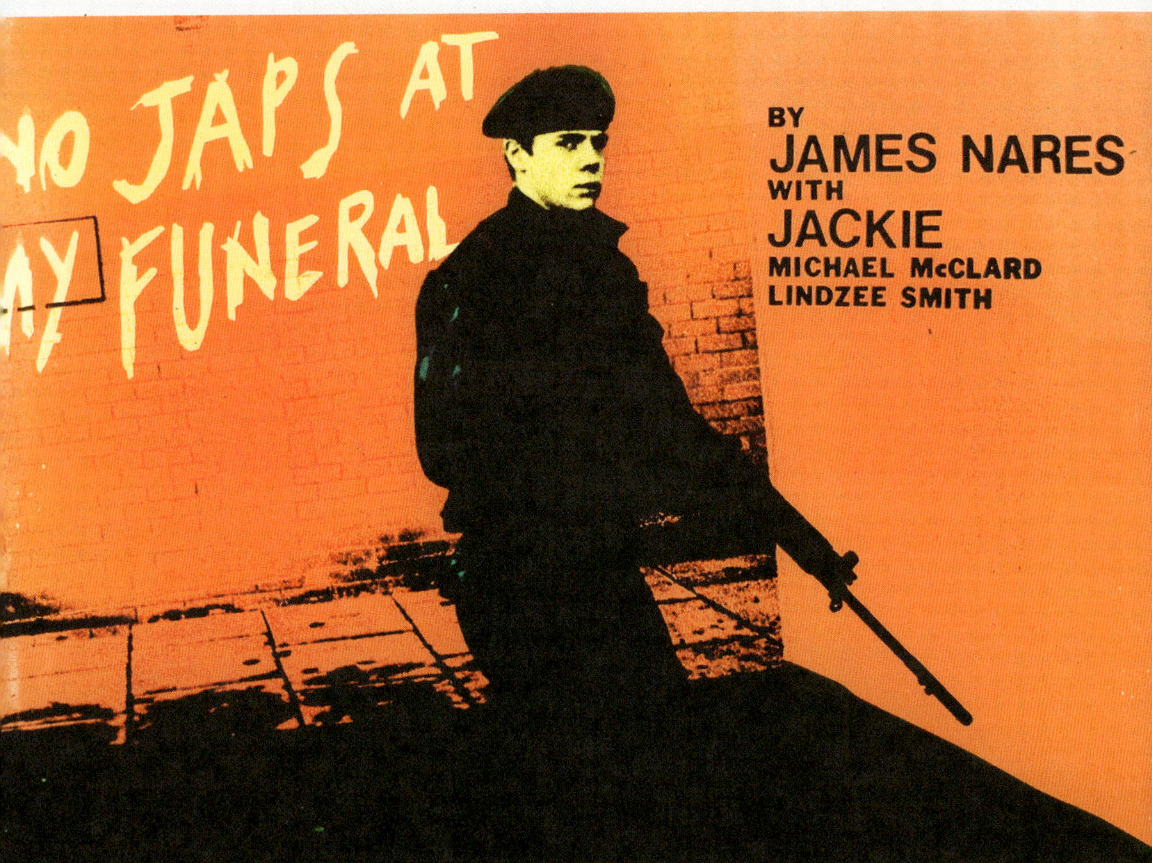

James Nares. *No Japs at My Funeral*, 1980. Offset printed poster, 43 × 28 cm. For premiere screening at *Times Square Show*. Courtesy of James Nares.

COLAB

PO' LAB

ROAD TO

HOE LAB

LOW LAB

GROW LAB

NO FLAB

GO LAB !

YO LAB

BRO LAB

OH LAB

SCHMO LAB

WHOAAH LAB

SLOW LAB

THROW LAB

BLOW LAB

FLOW LAB

GLOW LAB

NO LAB ?

MO' LAB

JAMES NARES

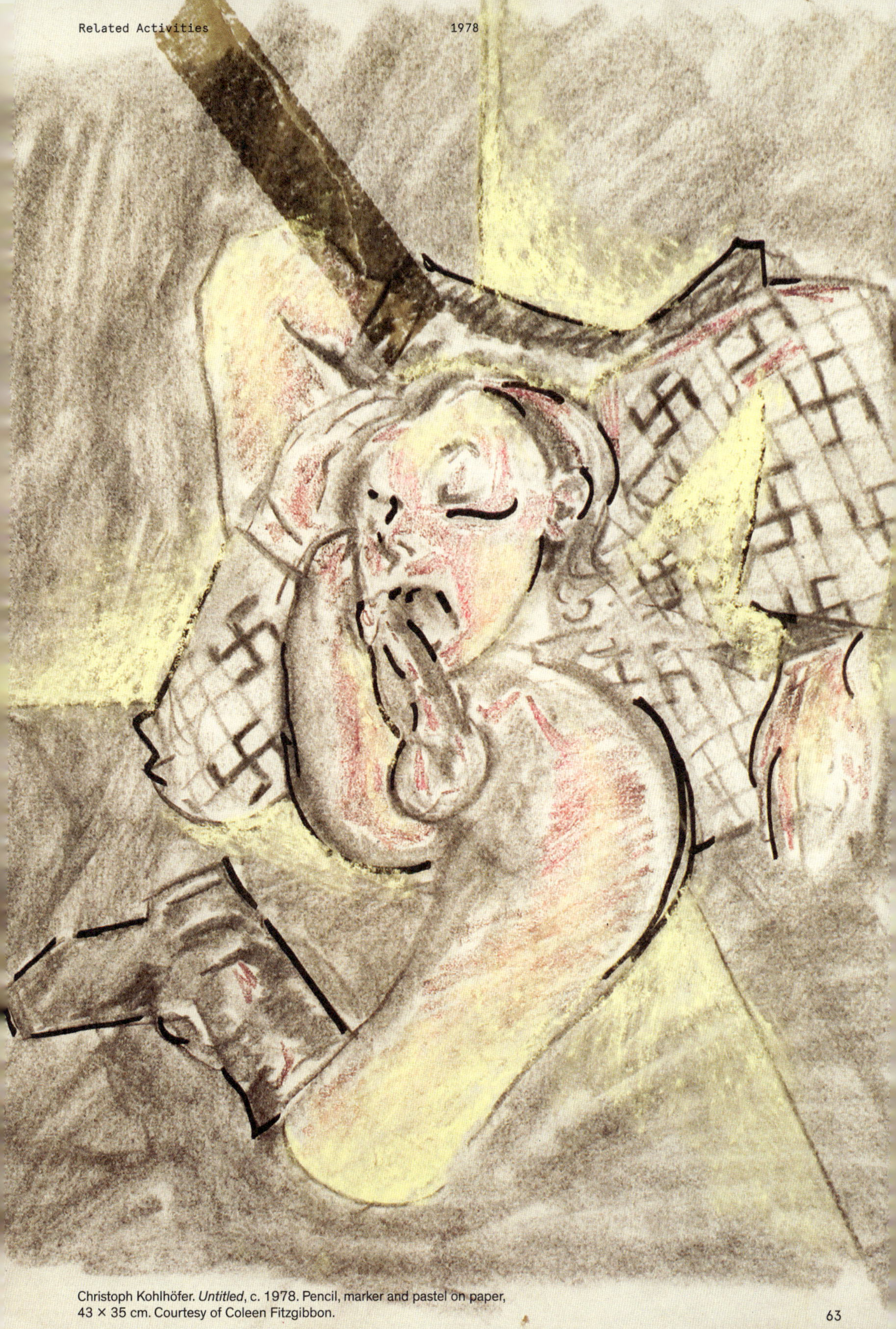

Christoph Kohlhöfer. *Untitled*, c. 1978. Pencil, marker and pastel on paper,
43 × 35 cm. Courtesy of Coleen Fitzgibbon.

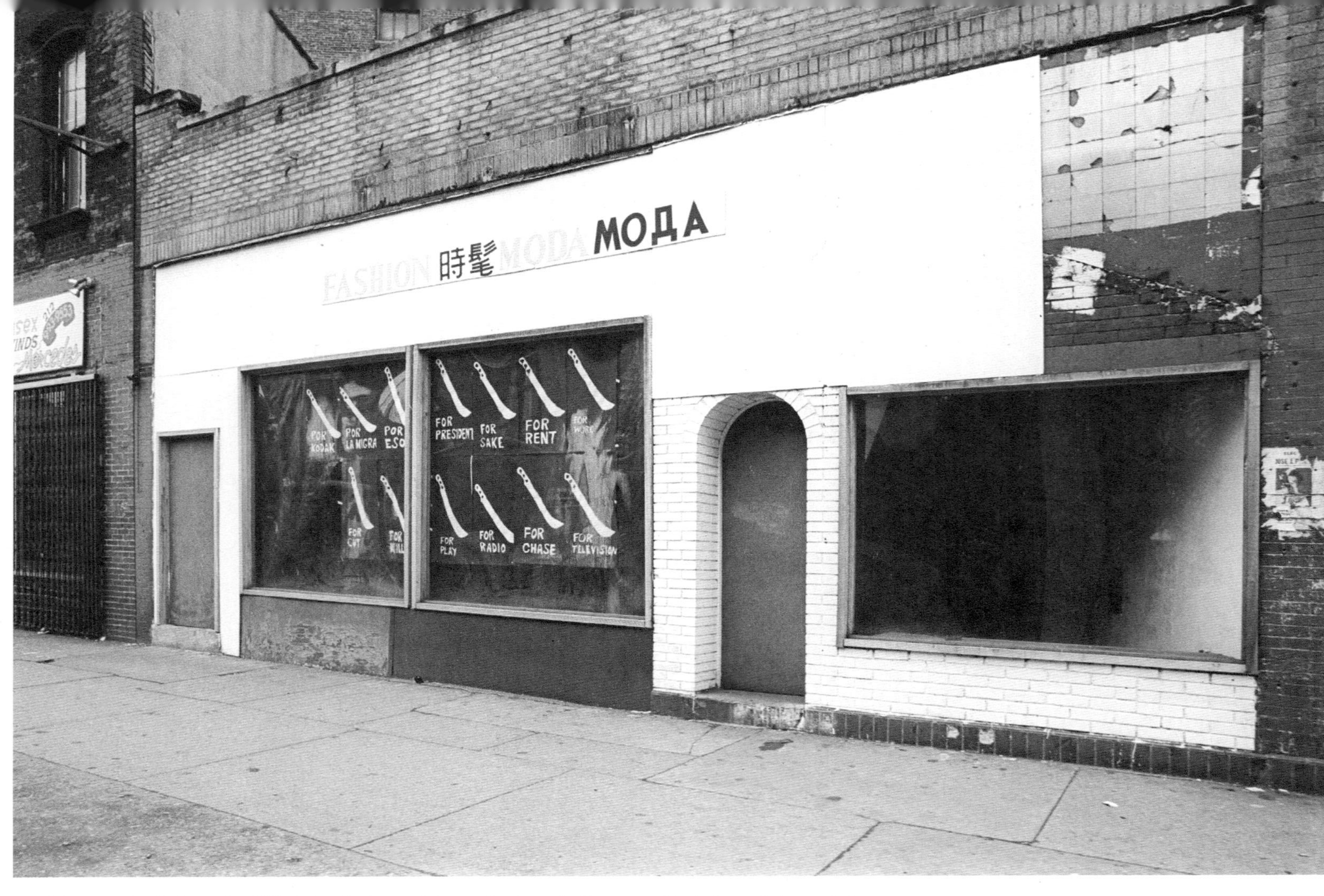

Lisa Kahane. *Fashion Moda exterior*, 1979. Fashion Moda, an artist run gallery in the South Bronx, as it looked when first renovated; artist's window installation by Robert Cooney. © Lisa Kahane, NYC. All Rights Reserved. Courtesy of Lisa Kahane.

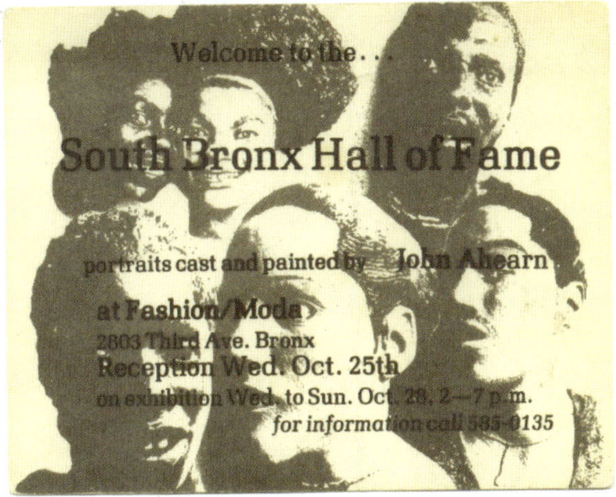

John Ahearn. *Welcome to the South Bronx Hall of Fame*, 1979. Offset printed handbill, 7 × 9 cm. Courtesy of John Ahearn.

Christy Rupp. *Animals Living in Cities*, 1979. Offset printed poster, 43.5 × 58.5 cm. Courtesy of Christy Rupp.

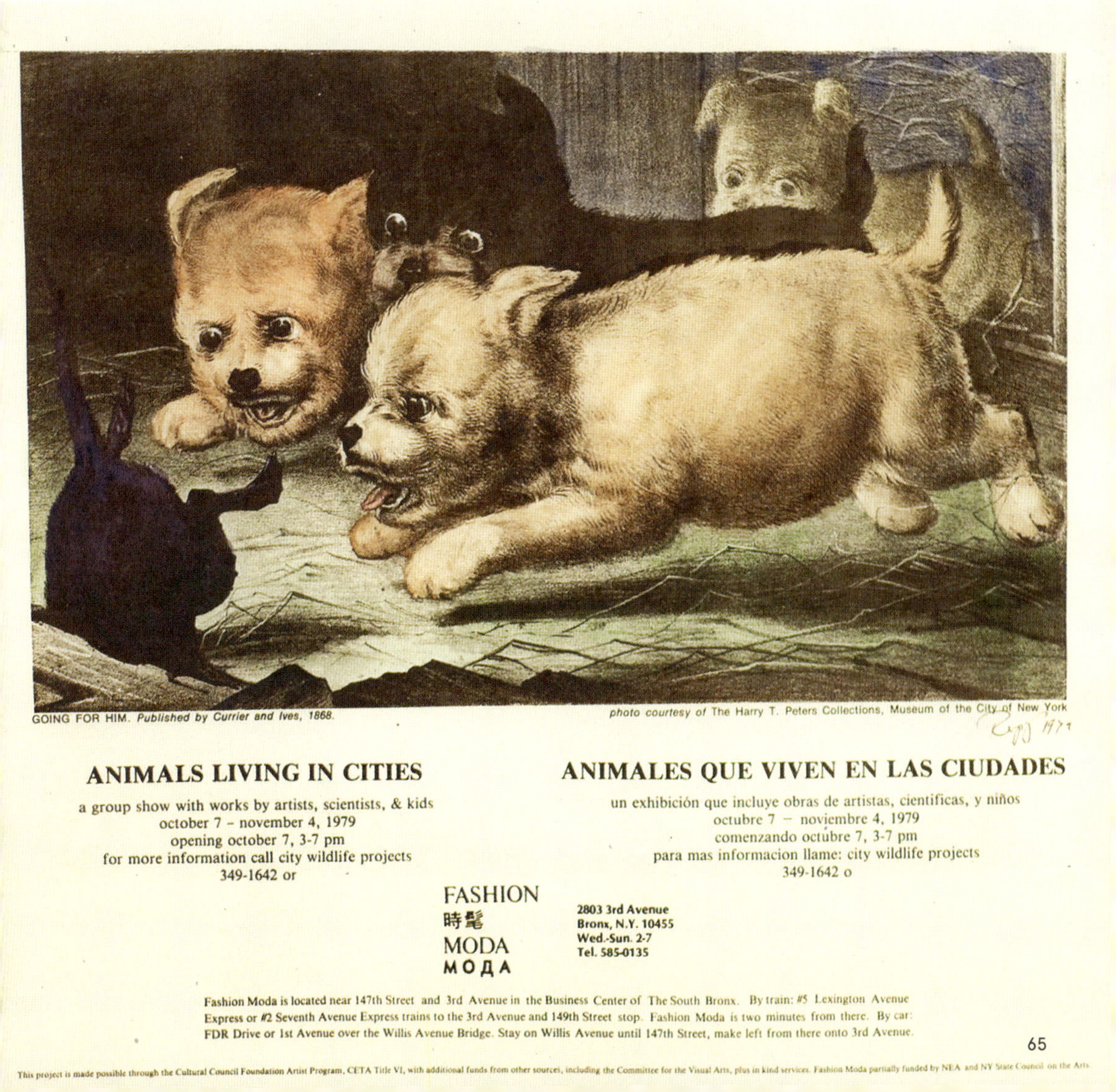

"Fashion Moda defined itself as a Museum of Science, Art, Invention, Technology, and Fantasy"

—Stefan Eins. Letter to P. Clapp, March 1989.
From *Downtown Collection*, NYU Fales Library, New York, NY.

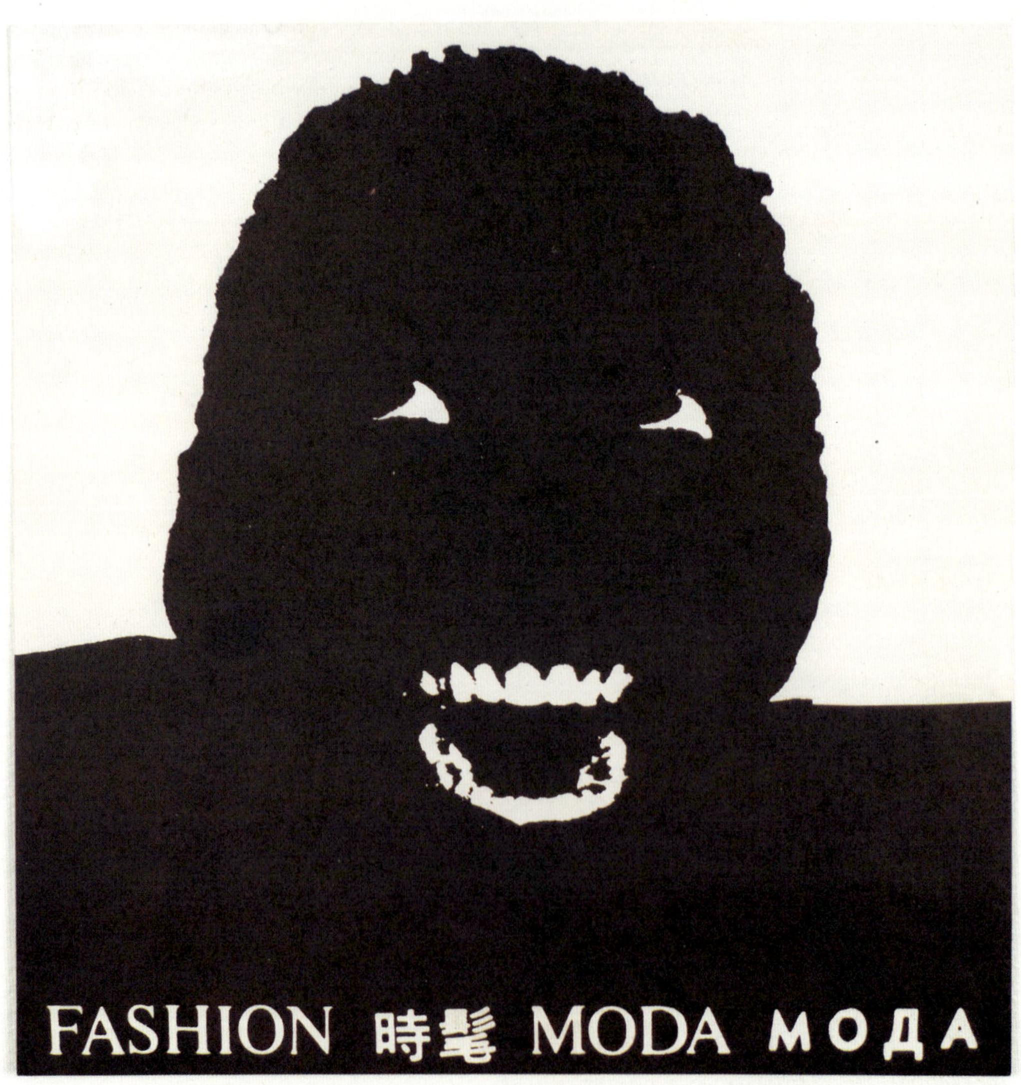

John Ahearn, Stefan Eins and Walter "Mike" Robinson. *Fashion Moda / Sculpture,* 1980. Offset printed, 34 × 33 cm. Courtesy of Stefan Eins.

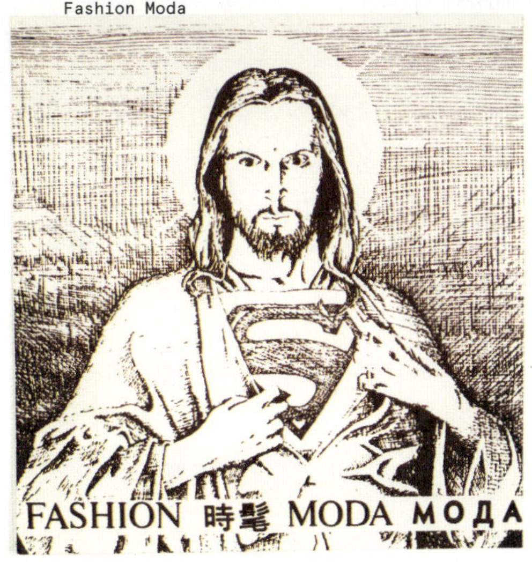

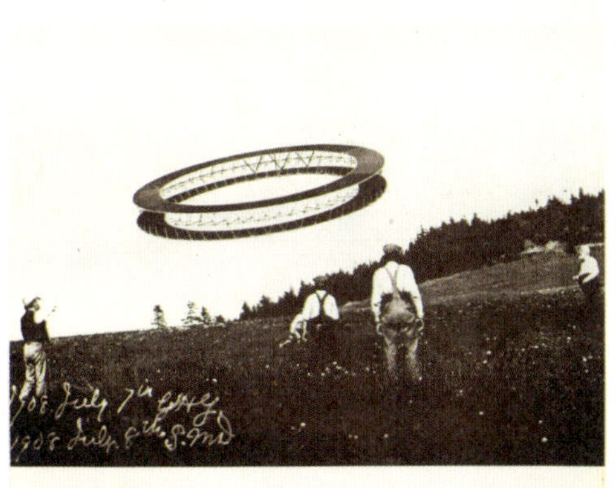

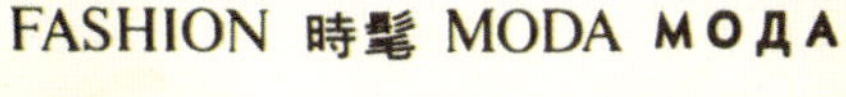

Just like **FASHION** 時髦 **MODA МОДА,** Colab brought on the end of Modern Art and Modernism. Cohesive groups like Colab in previous generations created in styles like Cubism, Surrealism, Pop Art, Expressionism, Abstract Expressionism, Minimalism and other movements. Not any longer. Colab members in the 70s and now create in their own individual styles. It represented the end of Modernism and Modern Art and brought in a new area of openness: Contemporary Art. The end of Modernist dogma!

—Stefan Eins

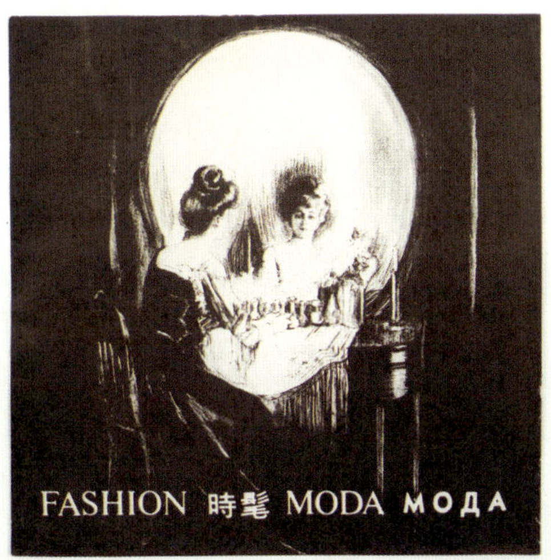

Stefan Eins. *Fashion Moda / Christ Superman*; *Fashion Moda / Alexander Bell*; *Fashion Moda / Skull Ladies,* 1980. Offset printed, 34 × 33 cm each. Courtesy of Stefan Eins.

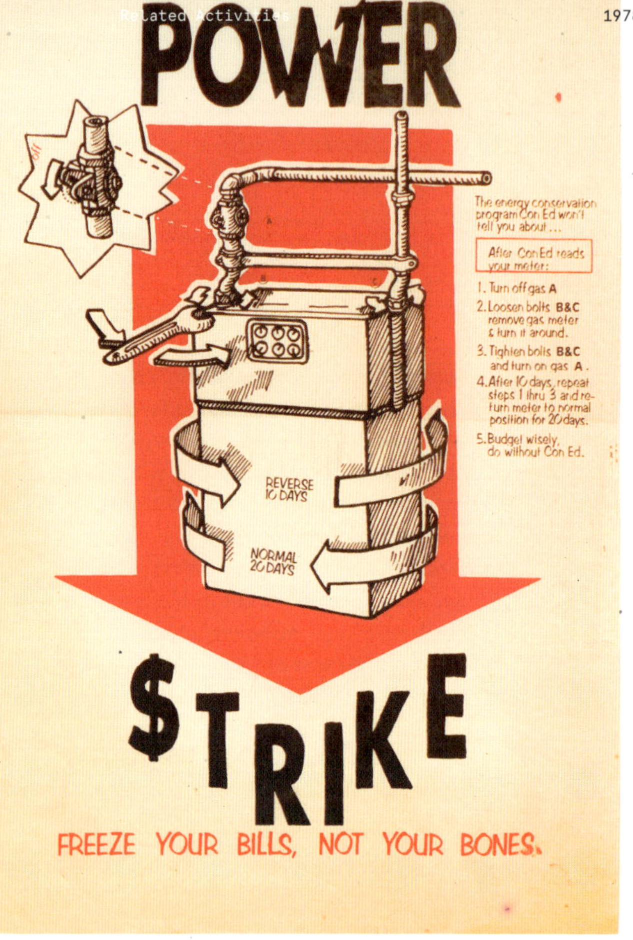

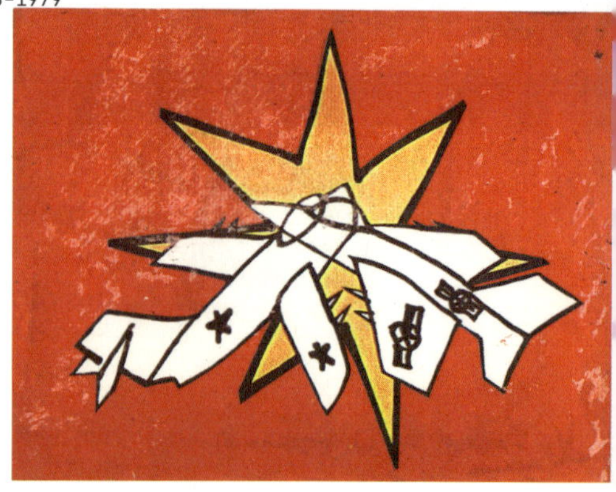

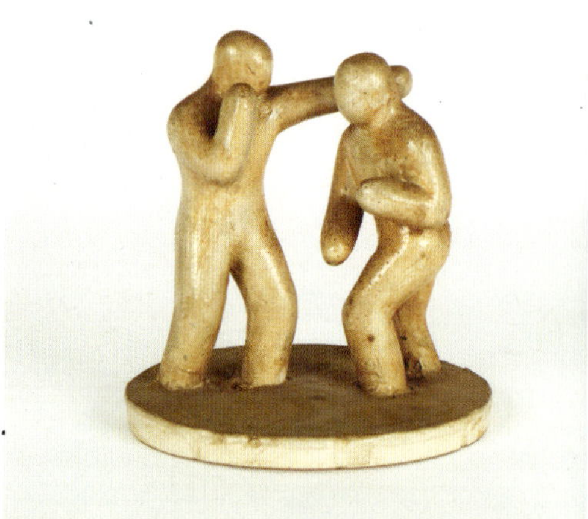

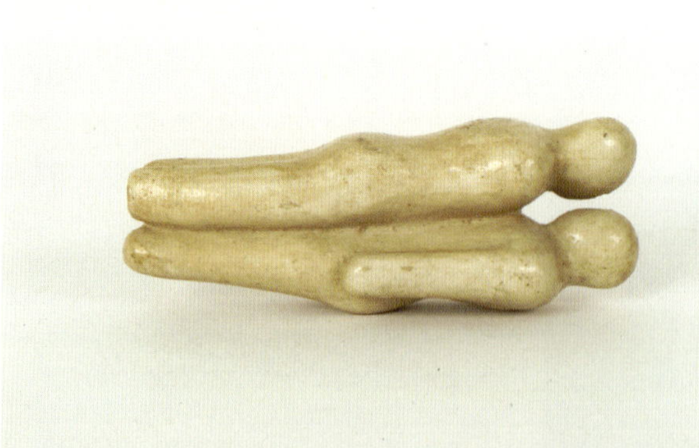

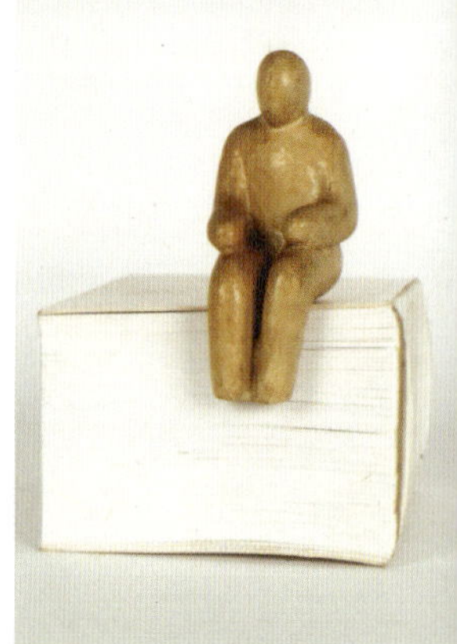

Clockwise from upper left:

Robert Cooney, Jorge Mendez and Tom Otterness. *Power Strike*, c. 1978. Offset printed poster, 48 × 32 cm.
Wheat-pasted and distributed in the Lower East Side, the Bronx and Brooklyn. Courtesy of Robin Winters.

Unknown. *Untilted*, 1979. Offset printed, 28 × 21.5 cm. From Tod's Copy Shop. Courtesy of Barbara Ess. Photo credit: Nancy Linn.

Tom Otterness. *Boxers / Sitting Man / Couple*, 1978. Hydrastone cast, 4 × 4 × 9.5 cm each. Courtesy of John Ahearn.

TOM OTTERNESS MUTIPLES SOLD AT ARTISTS SPACE, FASHION MODA, AND THE STEPS OF MoMA.

**Early on, John Ahearn told me:
Colab is like running the peer gauntlet.
Yikes!
Happy to report
I survived Colab
and killed no one.**

—Becky Howland

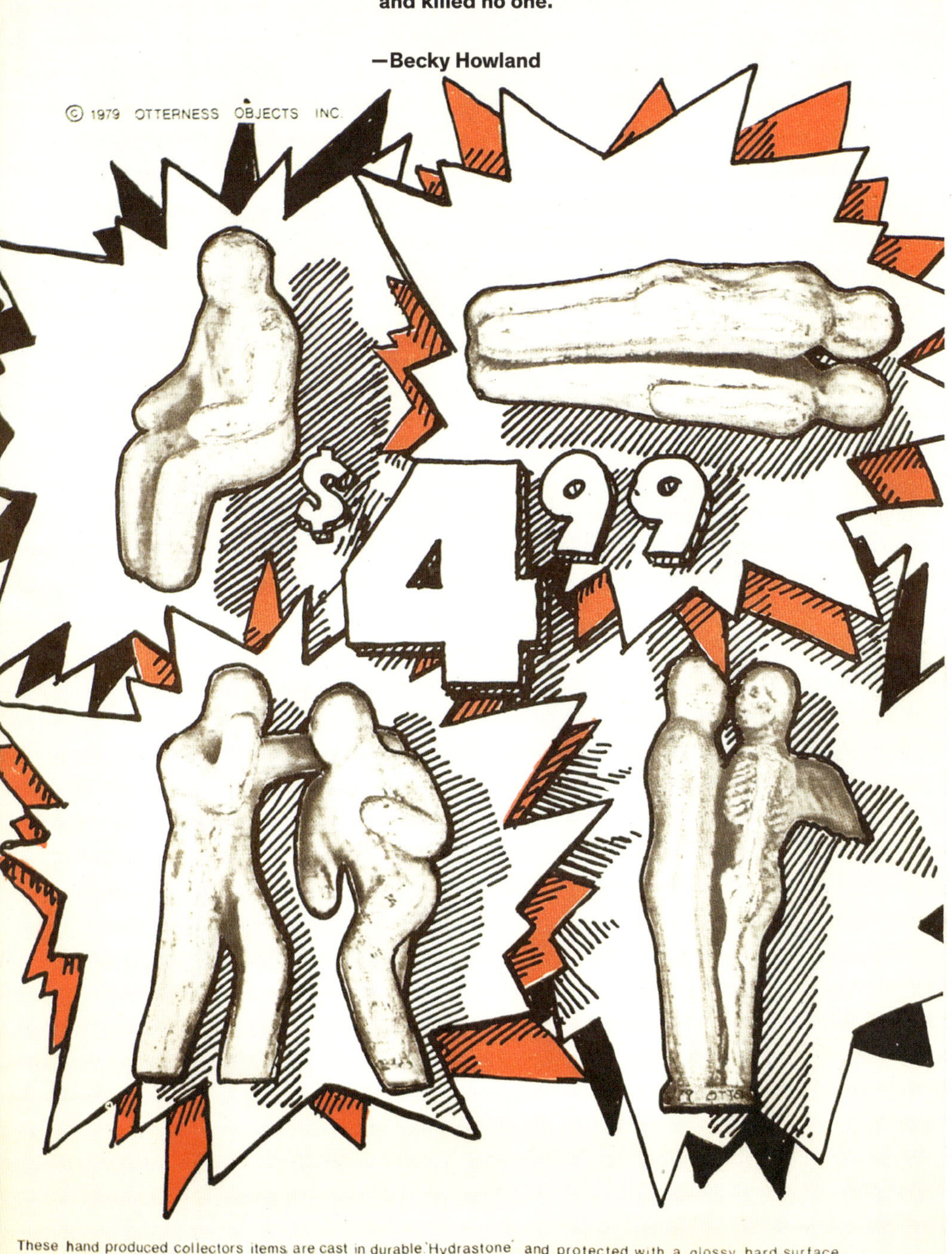

Tom Otterness. *Otterness Objects*, 1979. Offset printed poster, 36 × 25.5 cm. Courtesy of Tom Otterness.

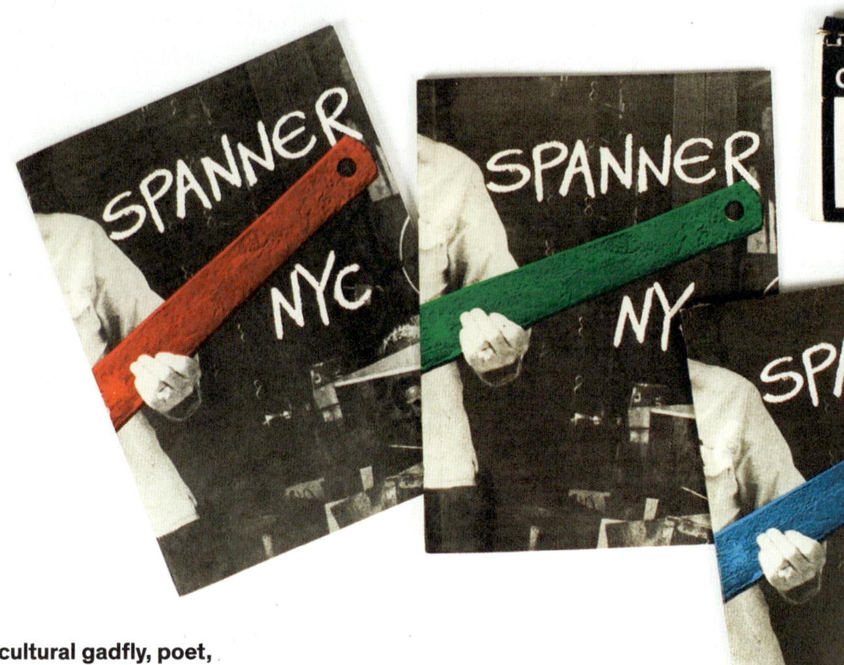

Richard Miller, cultural gadfly, poet, publisher and soon to be sculptor, founded *Spanner* Magazine with English poet Alan Fisher in London in the late 1960s. Domiciled in NYC after escaping from England, with publisher's flair, Miller working with Teri Slotkin, began exploration of the downtown scene by requesting from artists 'print specific artwork' for the newly created *Spanner/ NYC*. Contributors were often members of Colab, of which Miller and Slotkin were founding members, but were not exclusively so. The *Spanner* slogan was 'a magazine of art not an art magazine', a concept unique at the time yet so current today.

—Dick Miller

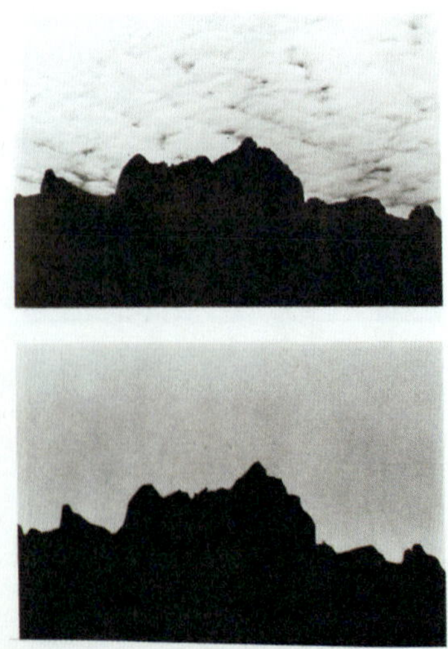

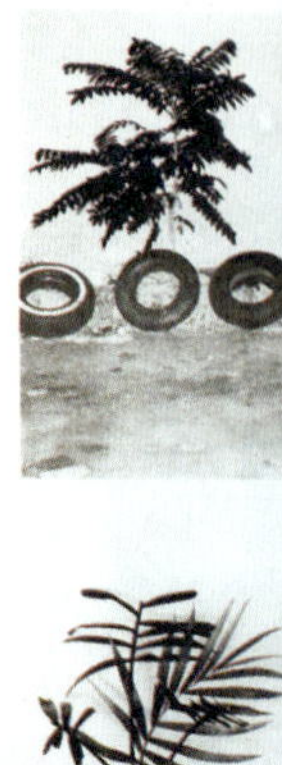

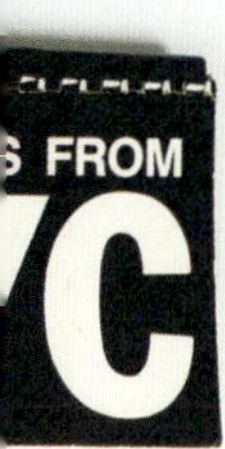

Clockwise from upper left:

Dick Miller and Terise Slotkin, editors. *Spanner, Issue 1 (red)*, 1978, 78 pp; *Spanner, Issue 2 (green)*, 1979, 75 pp; Spanner, *Issue 3 (blue)*, 1980, 76 pp; Offset printed, pbk, glue-bound, 21 × 28 cm each. *Greetings from NYC (Spanner, Issue 5)*, 1985. Offset printed, pbk, spiral bound, 11 × 15 cm. All *Spanner* issues published in New York: Aloes Books. Courtesy of Terise Slotkin. Photo: Nancy Linn

Judy Rifka in *Spanner, Issue 1*, pp 48–49. Photo: Nancy Linn.

Dick Miller in *Spanner, Issue 1*, pp 52–53. Photo: Nancy Linn.

Marcia Resnick in *Spanner, Issue 1*, pp 12–13. Photo: Nancy Linn.

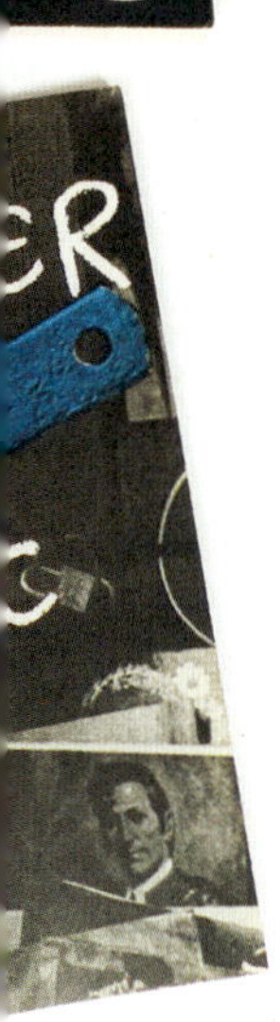

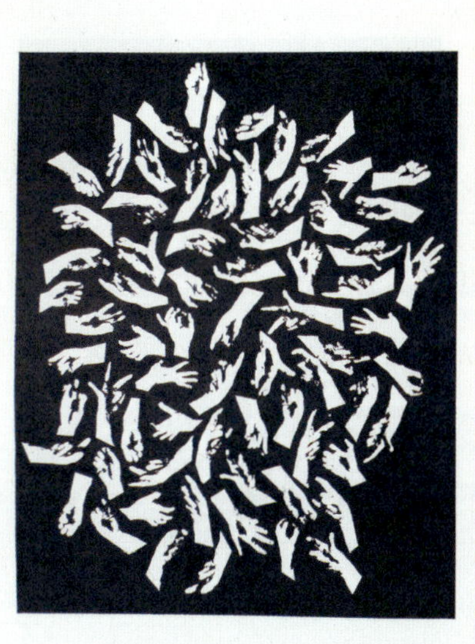

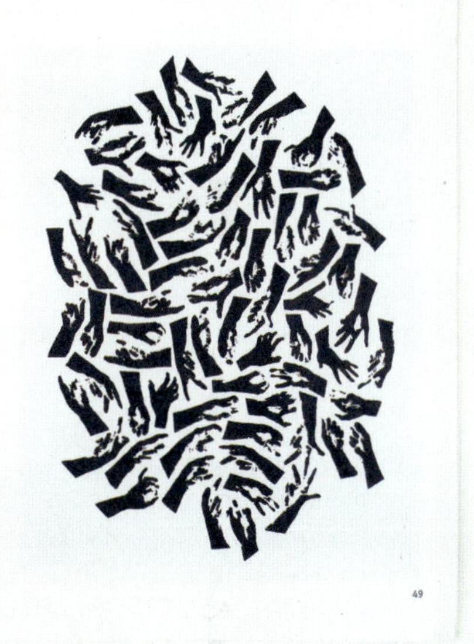

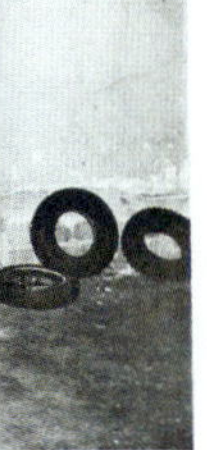

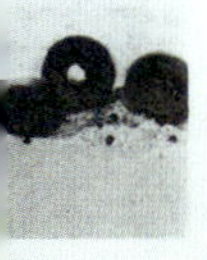

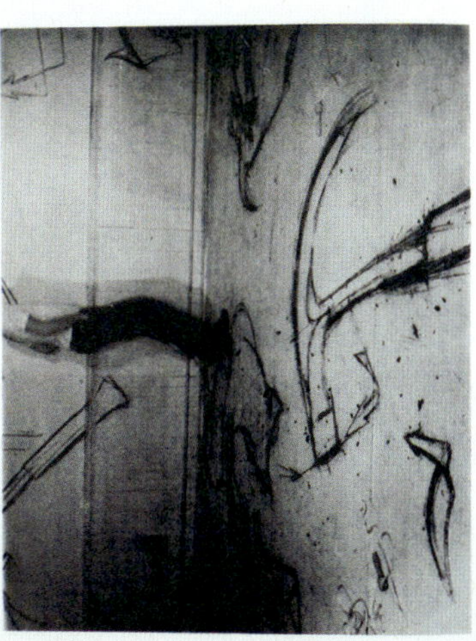

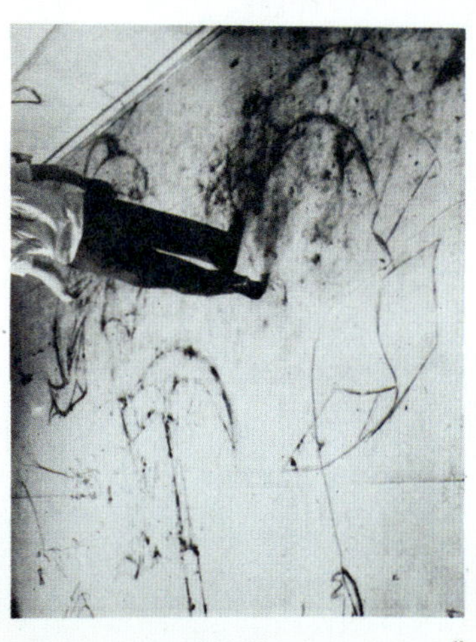

HERE TO THERE

THE PRESENT SYSTEM DEADENS OUR SENSIBILITIES AND THREATENS OUR WELL-BEING. SOCIETY MUST BE REWORKED SO IT IS MORE RESPONSIVE TO OUR NEEDS. IT IS NOT ADEQUATE TO EXPOSE SOCIAL ILLS OR DEAL WITH PROBLEMS SYMBOLICALLY OR METAPHORICALLY. IT IS REALISTIC TO ACT DIRECTLY TO PROPOSE AND IMPLEMENT AN IMPROVED ORDER.

IT IS TIME TO CLARIFY RATHER THAN CONFUSE. THE BASIS FOR EFFECTIVE ACTION IS ACKNOWLEDGING THERE IS NO NEUTRAL STANCE; IT IS IMPORTANT TO UNDERSTAND THE IMPLICATIONS OF WHAT WE DO ON A DAILY BASIS BEFORE UNDERTAKING LARGER REVISIONS. THEN IT IS REASONABLE TO ASSUME THE POWER AND RESPONSIBILITY TO ATTEMPT A MORE PLEASURABLE, MORE FUNCTIONAL SYSTEM. PLEASURE AND FUNCTION ARE INCLUSIVE; BOTH ARE REQUIRED FOR A NONCOERCIVE, SUPPORTIVE SOCIETY.

A DESIRE FOR WHAT WORKS IS A LEGITIMATE POINT OF DEPARTURE. PROCEDURE SHOULD NOT RELY ON IDEOLOGY, ACTIVITY SHOULD NOT ILLUSTRATE IT. EVERY PROBLEMATIC SITUATION IS UNIQUE; INHERENT IN OUR RESPONSE SHOULD BE AN APPROPRIATE COURSE OF ACTION. CONSTRUCTING A PRACTICAL METHODOLOGY IS AN APPROPRIATE COURSE OF ACTION. WE ADVOCATE INTEGRATING ESTHETICS WITH PRACTICE TO BETTER OUR POSITION.

JENNY HOLZER
PETER NADIN

16

Jenny Holzer and Peter Nadin in *Spanner, Issue 3*, 1980.
Photo: Nancy Linn.

YOU CAN'T LOCK ME OUT. I WAS BORN HERE

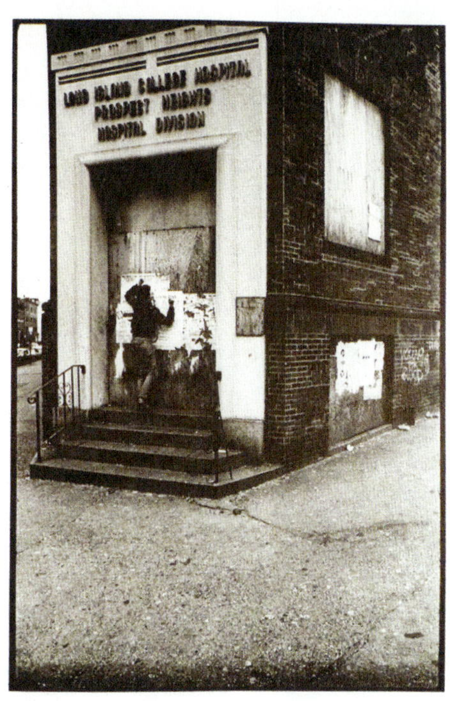

Terise Slotkin in *Spanner, Issue 3*, 1980.
Photo: Nancy Linn.

Walter "Mike" Robinson in *Spanner, Issue 3*, 1980.
Photo: Nancy Linn.

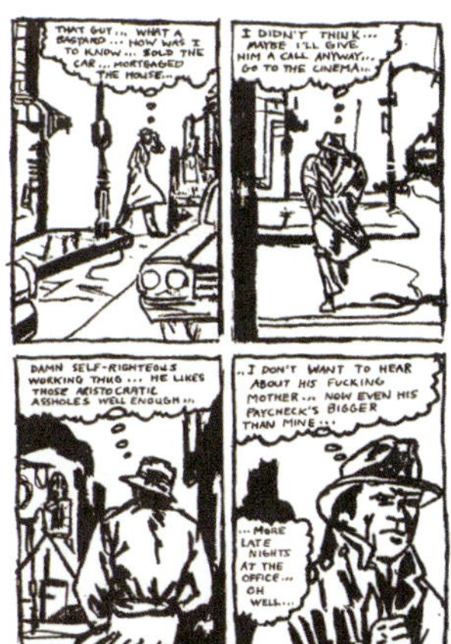

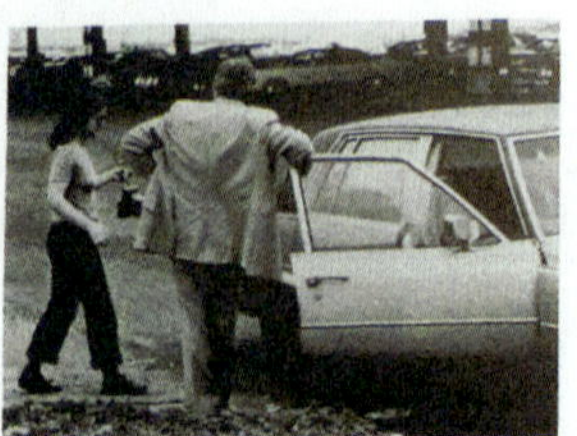

DRIVER   VEHICLE   DRIVER   VEHICLE   DRIVER   VEHICLE

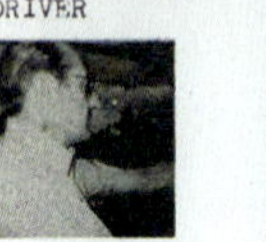 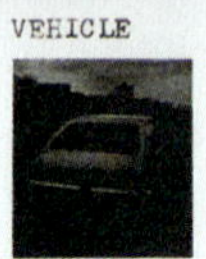 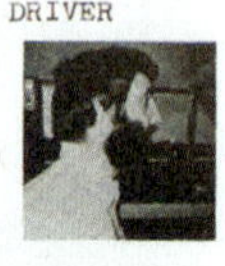 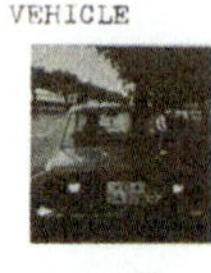 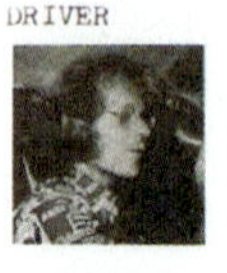 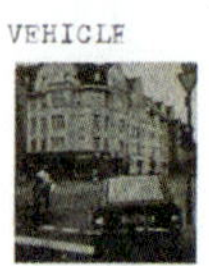

DRIVER   VEHICLE   DRIVER   VEHICLE   DRIVER   VEHICLE

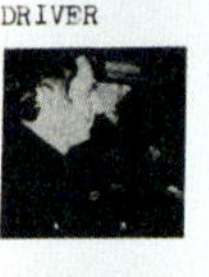 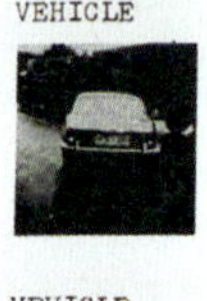 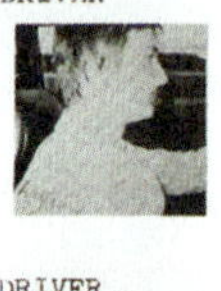 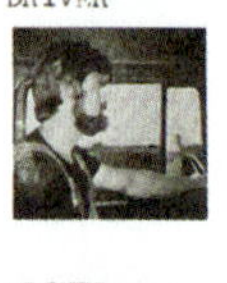 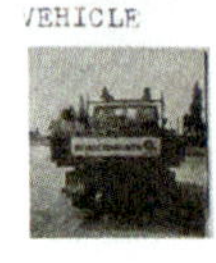

DRIVER   VEHICLE   DRIVER   VEHICLE   DRIVER   VEHICLE

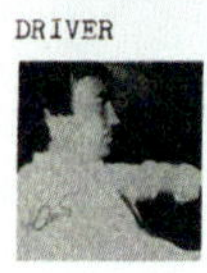 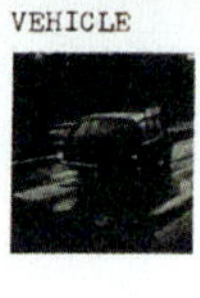 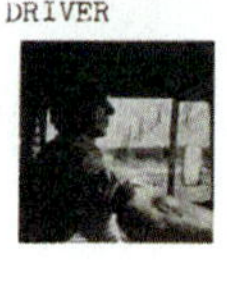

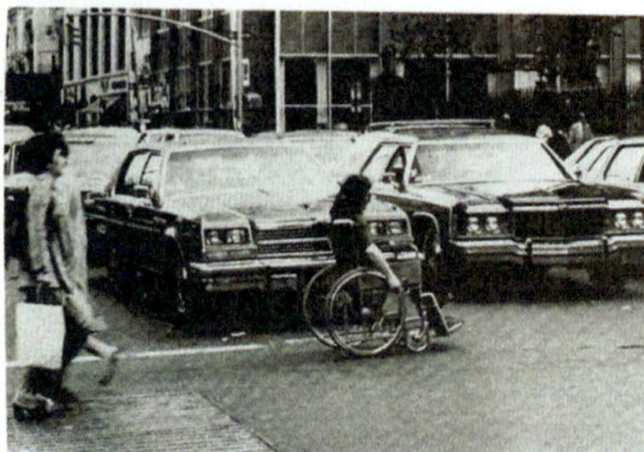 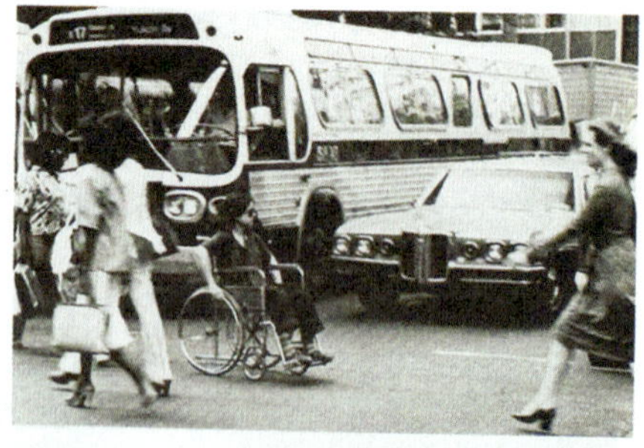

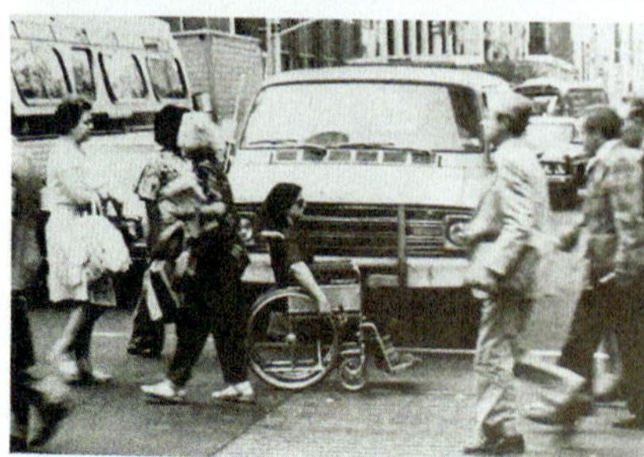 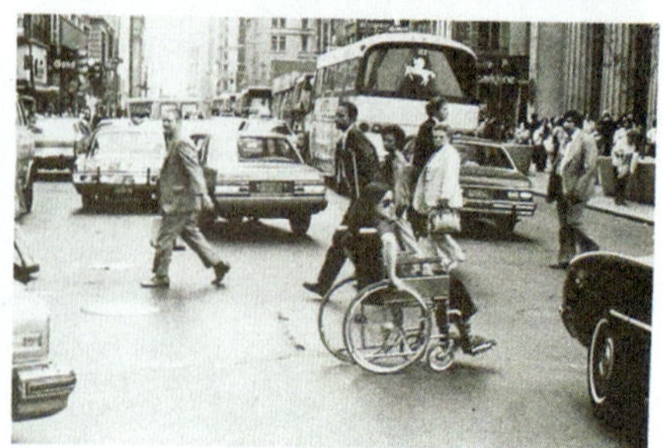

     Ann Messner in *Spanner*, *Issue 3*, 1980. Photo: Nancy Linn.

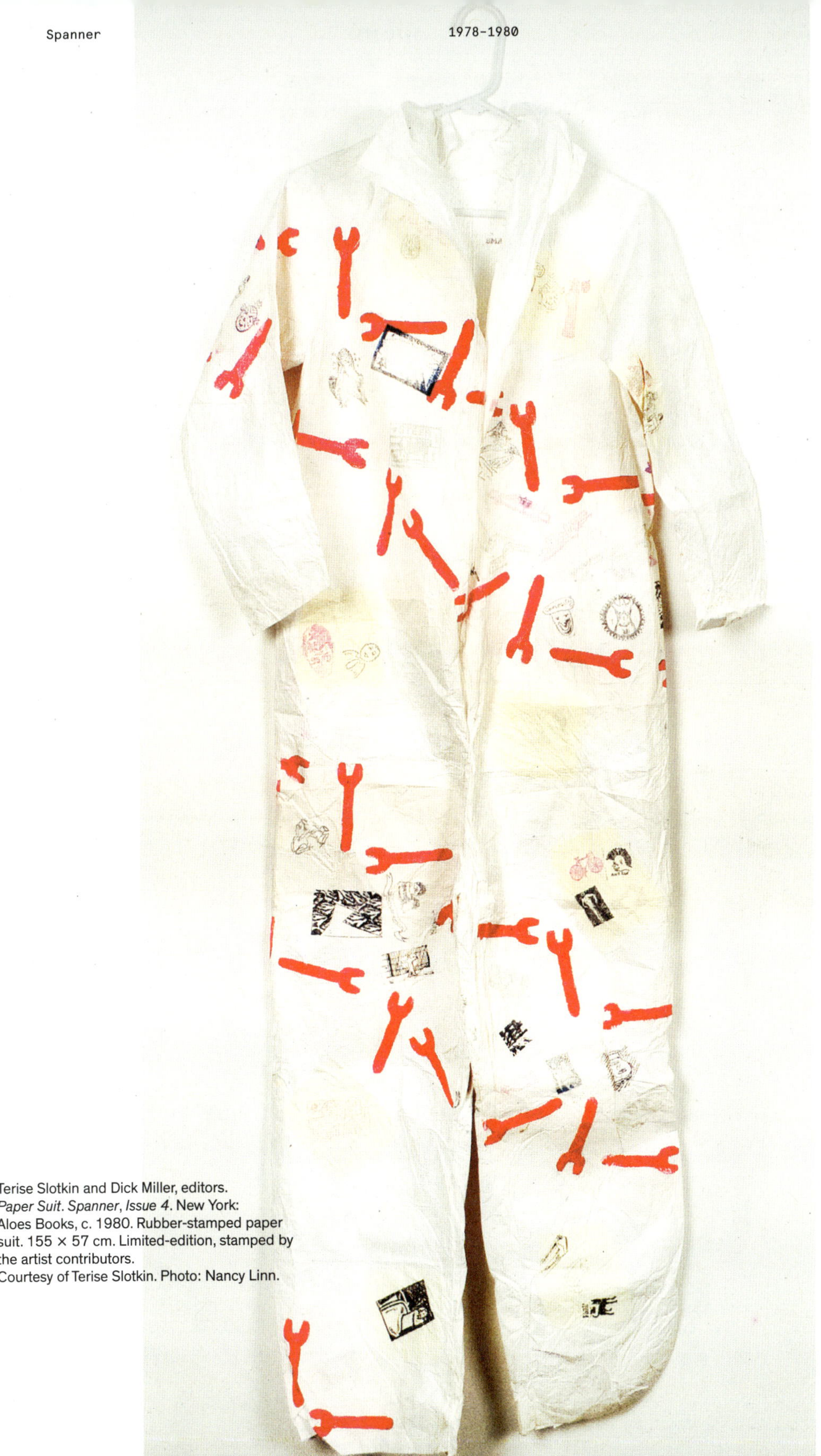

Terise Slotkin and Dick Miller, editors.
Paper Suit. *Spanner, Issue 4*. New York:
Aloes Books, c. 1980. Rubber-stamped paper
suit. 155 × 57 cm. Limited-edition, stamped by
the artist contributors.
Courtesy of Terise Slotkin. Photo: Nancy Linn.

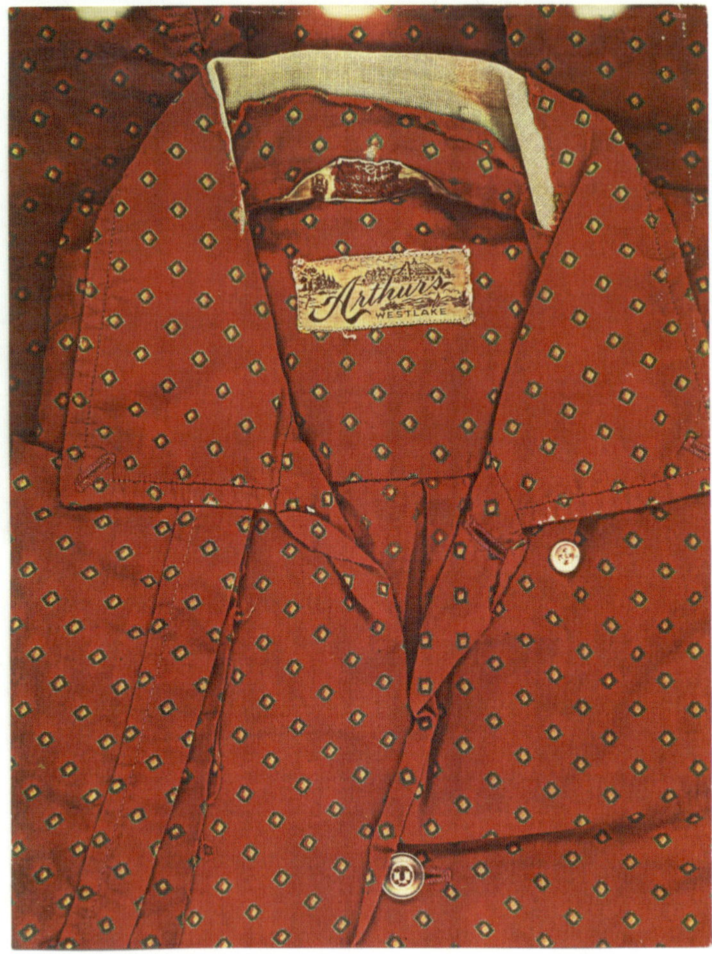

Clockwise from upper left:

Andrea Callard. *Color Shirt*, c. 1979. Photocopy, 28 × 21.5 cm. Courtesy of Andrea Callard.

Robin Winters. *Untitled*, c. 1979 [one-of-a-kind artists' book]. Marker on IRS W-4 forms. Staple bound, 16 pp, 28 × 21.5 cm. Courtesy of Barbara Ess.

Robin Winters. *Soldier*, c. 1979. Ink on collaged paper, 28 × 21.5 cm. Courtesy of Robin Winters.

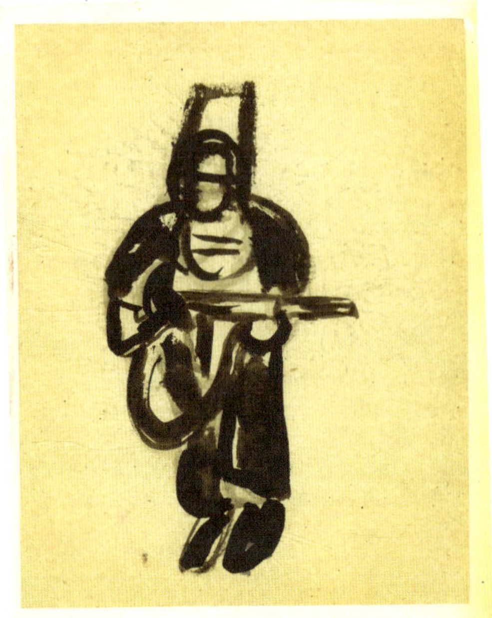

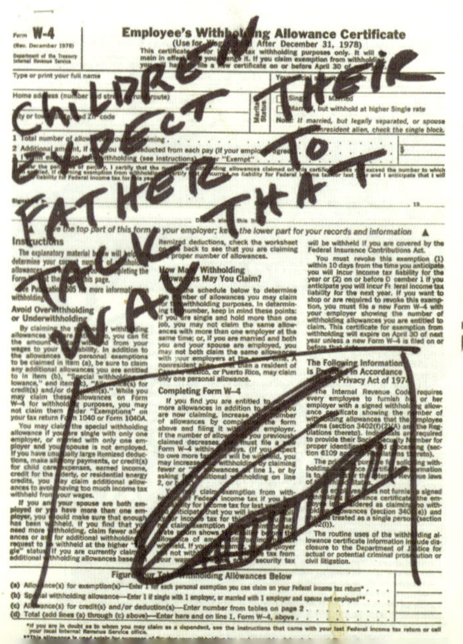

**Julie Harrison Talks to Robin Winters,
Fall 2014**

Julie Harrison: I want to focus on the four shows that took place in 1979—*The Doctors & Dentists Show*, *The Dog Show*, *The Income & Wealth Show*, and *The Manifesto Show*—which you were instrumental in organizing. How did you come up with the titles, particularly the first two, which are so mundane? Was it meant to be a kind of joke? What was your thinking?

Robin Winters: My work has always had titles which are intentionally humorous, and I suppose sometimes mundane. In early installations and performances, before *The Dog Show*, my titles were: *Dedication To The Man Whose Main Job Was Testing Whistling Teakettles*; *The Secret Life Of BoB-E Or BoB-E behind The Veil*; *W.B. Bearman Bags A Job or Diary Of A Dreamer*; *Boredom, Tension And Surprise*; *Silent Food For Speechless Fools*; *To Gandy Dancers And Roustabouts*; *Industry*; *The Best Hired Man In The State*; etc. So in considering themes for group exhibits, *The Doctors & Dentists Show* and *The Dog Show* were in keeping with my previous practice. I was also very interested in the notion of a "target audience," for instance *Doctors & Dentists* was styled as a large waiting room—lime green—and all works were related to the theme, with the hope that we could make deals with doctors and dentists to barter services. In the case of *The Dog Show* I wanted to bring in artists who were unaffiliated with Colab, or who thought shows like *The Manifesto Show* were somehow too political. It seemed as though practically every artist I knew had done some artwork with a dog.

I consider my activities as an artist to be, in part, a living version of an elaborate fiction. (I recently mentioned at the Hunter College panel that Colab had hired me as an actor to be an outspoken artist for Colab).

JH: That's very funny, I forgot about that. What strikes me now is that many of us in Colab were the same age, influenced by the same changing art world, by the political urgency that was prevalent, and we came to New York to be part of that energy. There was no future in being an artist at that time; it wasn't like today, with curators and gallery directors scouring MFA shows for talent. It was actually an embarrassment to be in graduate school or to promote one's work. We were weaned, after all, on the dematerialization of the art object.

Art was transformative in the 1970s, it still amazes me how much happened so quickly. Within a ten year span we were treated to watershed movements that continue to be celebrated, from Happenings and Fluxus to Minimal and Conceptual aesthetics, which led us to more time-based video, film and performance art. I think the impact of the early Colab shows was twofold: that they were uncurated and open to all comers (democratizing the process), and that there was an anti-aesthetic that prevailed (from Fluxus and Beuys's "social sculpture"). Young people can't imagine what it was like before the Internet, which has provided a somewhat democratic means for showing art. Before that, it was a closed system, and having exhibitions in homes that were open to whomever was radical (ok, I realize that we didn't constitute a disparate demographic, but nontheless, it was a very exciting opportunity for anyone who wanted to show work). I remember seeing things on the wall that looked like a child's drawing, or were cut out from the newspaper, and everything was equal in the white box. It was first come, first served; if you got there early you might get a good wall to put your work on; and there was no critiquing, no one really cared what you did. It was like going to Coney Island and observing the culture, it just *existed*.

Since you had two of the exhibitions in the loft where you lived, you experienced the ultimate "life as art," did you ever think of your life as part of the show, or the shows themselves as a work of art, the process being more important than the product?

RW: That is a lot to consider and respond to. I actually had three exhibitions and many performances in the loft. I think for my own pleasure and entertainment I have always been interested in mixing things up. The high and the low, the inside and the outside, black and white and all the shades in between, the young and the old, the male and the female. It was clear that I had cohorts in this feeling and that we gravitated towards each other. The evidence of this activity is resounding today—I think it is important to note that the ratio of male to female in Colab was pretty much 50/50. The exhibition history of Colab, in terms of representation of gender, sex and race, is way ahead of the curve.

In my earliest performances my main daily audience was factory workers on their lunch break, then I graduated to people living on the street who would come to dinner when I had blind dates and double dates in my apartment. There have been streams of people who have visited and participated in the various events in my loft. Not everyone made physical artworks—at one point there was a lot of saxophone and drumming in the house, while an early version of a fax machine was scrolling pictures sent from various locations—the "QWIP" machine to be exact, organized by Lisa Béar.

In the exhibitions in my studio on Broadway, and also in Coleen Fitzgibbon's storefront on Bleecker Street, there was a constant cast of characters passing through from a variety of worlds. In *The Batman Show* on Broadway, produced in collaboration with Diego Cortez, we mixed artists with kids who made drawings of super heroes (including Bob Kane the originator of the Batman comic series). I made a fake Chris Burden for this show. In *The Doctors & Dentists Show*, artists such as Cindy Sherman and Matt Mullican were included, along with people like Evan Lurie from The Lounge Lizards and Lisa Stroud. In *The Dog Show*, I included Joan Jonas and Dennis Oppenheim alongside thrift store paintings of dogs and Colab.

I guess what I am trying to say is that there was not really one aesthetic or one specific ideological bent, but it was rather like a tone poem. This was curation at its best. I remember John Ahearn came to my house with a painting he did of a policeman; I think *The Dog Show* was being assembled. So I was like: "John, a cop makes no sense in this show, but you should take it over to Coleen's for the show that Coleen and Jenny are putting together, *The Manifesto Show*. John subsequently did two casts of me for *The Dog Show* entitled *A Dog And His Master*, which I think were his first castings. So the theme was a way to curate. Then it was a matter of salon style, but I was the interior decorator.

Each show at my studio had a different color. One criterion was that I lived there, so when bloody dog bones were dumped on the floor for *The Dog Show* I said "no," as they would smell. And the same when Terry Fox pinned a liver to the wall for *The Doctors & Dentists Show.*

For me, it was never a sentiment of the anti-commercial art world—I had already shown in a major German art gallery at this point (Konrad Fisher Gallery), and I knew there was a possible future as an artist in that I had worked for Donald Judd and installed shows at Sonnabend Gallery. The thing that working in Europe taught me was that when one says they are an "artist" it means a way of life. All I knew was that I wanted to make things happen and that it was most exciting to meet new people and to play with friends new and old.

As to the question of life and art and being in the work etc., the answer would be yes.

JH: This is great, I think we're finished, don't you?

RW: I wonder if we are "finished?" I really did not want the conversation to be about "me," although some of what needed to be addressed was my personal history. I also did not want to just drop names but I wanted it to be clear that the exhibitions were inclusive of others not directly involved in the mechanics of Colab. I am also curious about you in terms of your involvement with Colab and your subsequent activity.

JH: Well, I'm on the first list of Colab

members (the scan of which is archived on the internet), and my address at that time was Varick Street, where I lived in 1977, so I attended Colab meetings from the start. Cara Brownell brought me to my first one. I actually thought of myself as fairly independent and radical until I met folks in Colab, some of whom scared me, as did much of the punk aesthetic in the beginning! At the time I was a lesbian and felt out of place, but I was immediately charged by the philosophy of Colab, and of course the six-packs of beer helped! I had just started graduate school at NYU, which I told very few people about as it was the antithesis of what we were doing, the anti-establishmentarianism, and there I worked with dancers, video and photographs. Graduate school kept me busy and unable to do as much collaboration as I had wished, but I did manage to put a few items in some of the theme shows. I mostly worked with others in time-based media—Cara Brownell and Robert Cooney (the three of us traveled around Mexico shooting Super 8 film and performed at Franklin Furnace in 1979), as well as the gang of Cave Girls. Potato Wolf interested me a lot since I had been involved with video since 1973 and was freelancing as a cameraperson.

As a young art student in the 1970s at the University of New Mexico, I became deeply transformed by the work of conceptual photographers and video artists who had embraced the element of time, and ensconced myself in the theoretical and theatrical changes that were occurring at the time. The radicalization of art with the de-materialization of the art object echoed current cultural tactics. Also, developments in technology fueled my desire to attach myself to the machine in a metaphoric way, bodily. I worked with dancers and video, and the body politic became the message. I came to NYC to work with my heroes, like Willoughby Sharp and Simone Forti (with whom I performed at MoMA). Now my work includes re-framing the news.

OK, Robin, I think we're finished now.

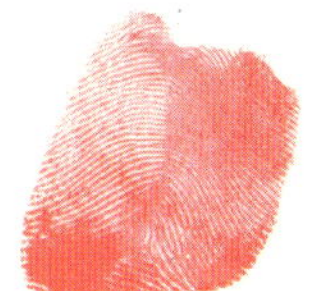

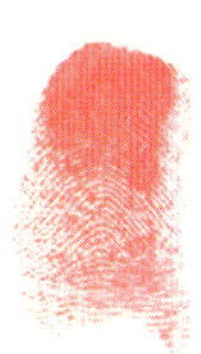

```
PRESS RELEASE: EXHIBITION AT 93 GRAND STREET
               3pm TO 6pm, WEDNESDAY THROUGH
               SATURDAY,

               NOVEMBER    1    2    3    4

                           8    9   10   11

               or by appointment (431-6560)

DESCRIPTION: Interface of facts, objects
             and transactions


               0.4   pd by CNAA
               0.225 pd by CVA
               0.375 pd by CP
```

"Exhibit A," November 1-11, 1978, included James Nares, Tina Lhotsky, Seth Tillet, Paul McMahon, Diego Cortez, John Lurie, Robin Winters, Liza Béar, Michael McClard, Coleen Fitzgibbon, Colab Black Book "1978 Activities."

Michael McClard. *Exhibit A Invitation*, 1978. Offset printed card, 11 × 14 cm. For *Exhibit A* exhibition. Courtesy of Liza Béar.

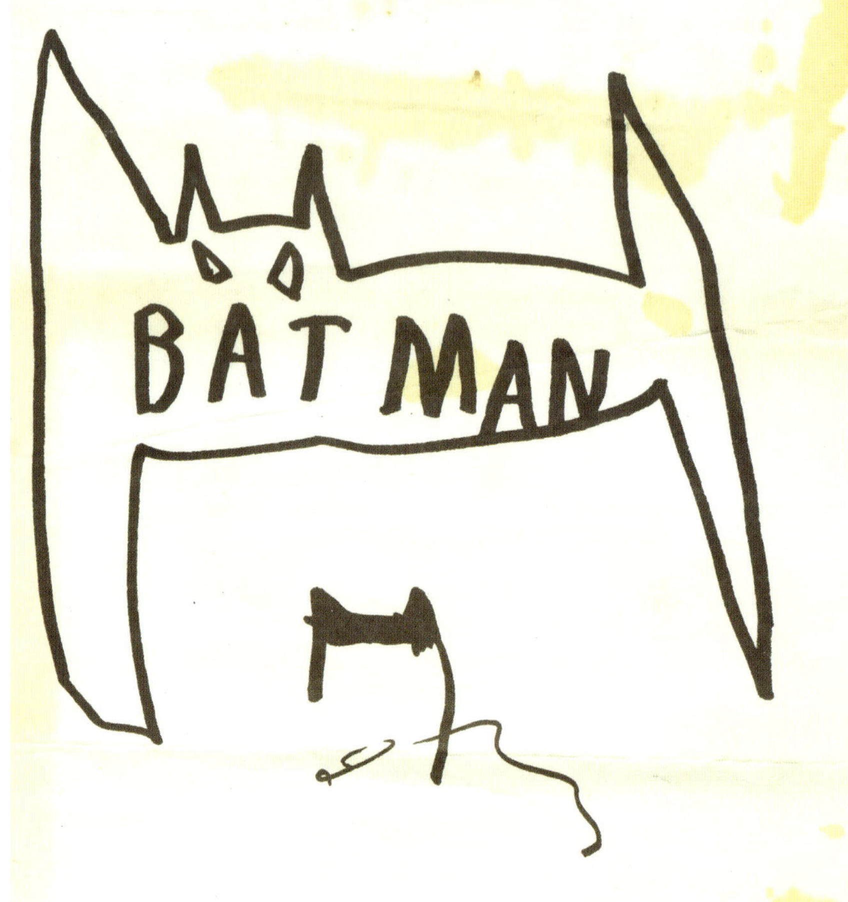

Ian Rusten (artwork), Diego Cortez (design). *BAT*, 1977.
Offset printed poster, 36 × 21.5 cm. For *The Batman
Show*. Courtesy of Kiki Smith.

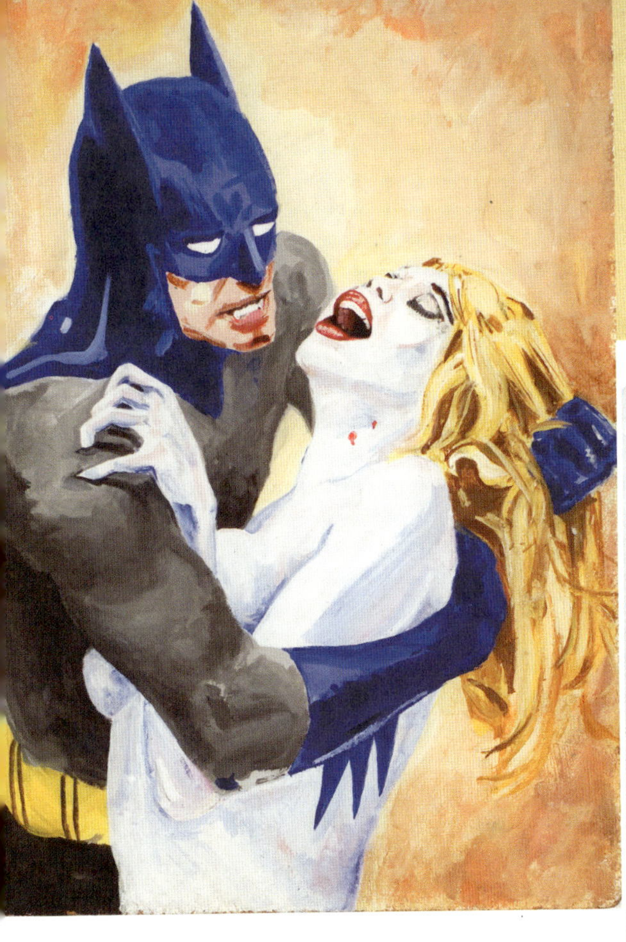

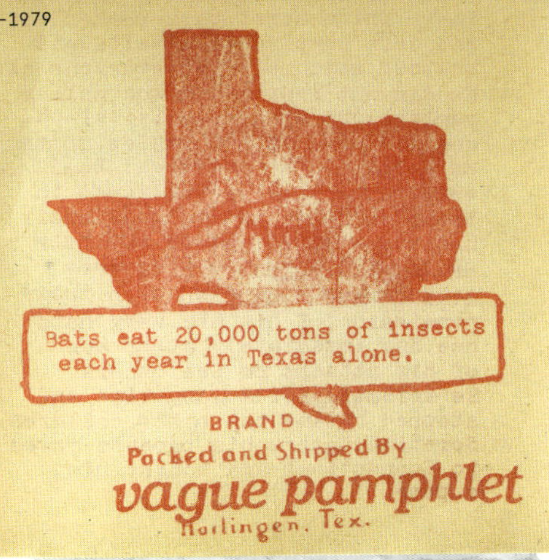

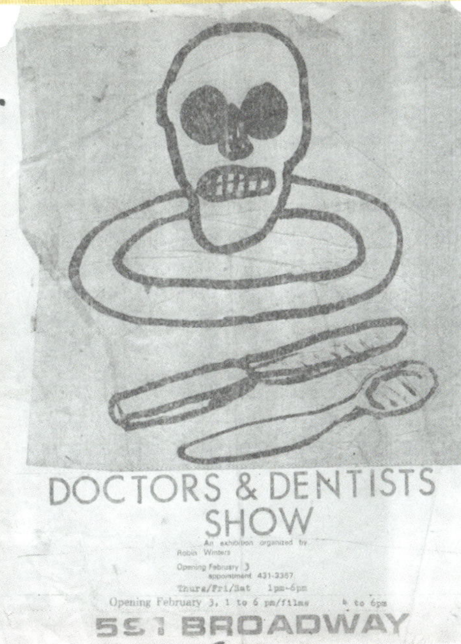

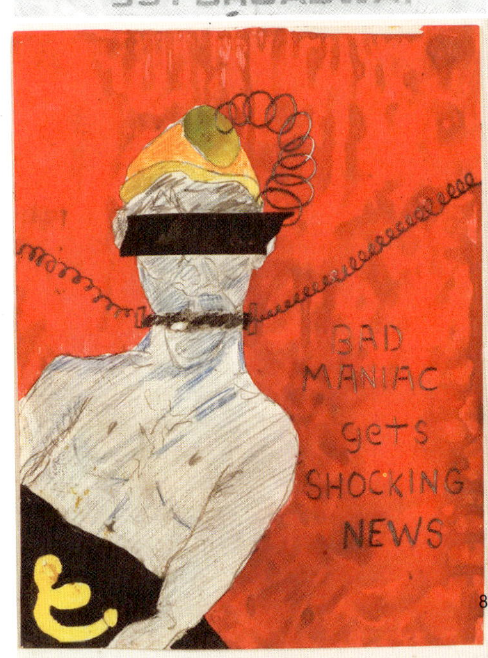

Clockwise from upper left:

Walter "Mike" Robinson. *Batman Painting*, 1977. Acrylic on masonite, 42 × 30 cm. Exhibited in the *Batman Show*. Courtesy of Robin Winters. Photo: Nancy Linn.

Andrea Callard. *Bat Tract*, 1977. Screenprint on newspaper, 21.5 × 36 cm. Exhibited in the *Batman Show*. Courtesy of Andrea Callard.

Robin Winters. *Doctors & Dentists Show*, 1979. Telecopier print, 28 × 21.5 cm. Facsimile print flyer sent via QWIP. Courtesy of Becky Howland.

Robin Winters. *Bad Maniac Gets Shocking News*, 1977. Mixed media on paper, 34.5 × 27.8 cm (framed). Exhibited in *Doctors & Dentists Show*. Courtesy of Robin Winters. Photo: Nancy Linn.

I'm enclosing a couple of clips
from the NY Times. The one about
the mini-camera is self explanatory.
The "Batman" story brings to
mind our own experience with the
so and sos. We had them in the store.
Exposed ceiling timbers such as we
had make great hiding places for
them. Since their food is insects
which they catch in flight they are
well nigh impossible to trap. And
since they enjoy a sort of in-built
sonar system they are well nigh impossible to hit with a ballbat altho
your Uncle Bob knocked one out of
orbit with a yard stick. They're
helpless on a flat surface.

Our best luck was to try to get 'em
flying, see where they landed
--usually way up high somewhere--
then stab 'em with a twelve-foot
pole with a nail in the end.
...Something like jousting. For a
flying animal, they have a lot of
blood. Harmless unless handled but
they certainly scare the daylights
out of customers in a furniture
store! So much for natural history.

The sourdough pot is bubbling. I'm
saving your last recipe. Take good
care of yourself.

Love,

Gramp.

(PEOPLE PRACTICE A PRIMITIVE FORM
OF ECHOLOCATION IN DISCO PARLORS
AND ON URBAN SIDEWALKS EVERY DAY.)

a tablespoon a day
fresh from mammal flesh
keeps a 1 oz. bat fat

I worked in a day care center
where there was a small boy
who always wore some article
of clothing tied around his
neck. He spent most of his
time zooming around singing:

   "DAda DAda DAda DAda
   DAda DAda DAda DAda
   DAda DAda DAda DAda
   BATMAN!!!   "

(you know the tune)

About once a day, he would become
angry with some other child and
would ferociously bite into their
flesh which upset them tremendously
and left unattractive welts and
bruises which worried everyone else.
He did not respond to the policy
punishments of social isolation
and harsh words and rabies shots
were out of the question. Real
vampire bats are so delicate in
their drinking habits that their
hosts are rarely aware of their
presence. This boy's parents
didn't have a clue so with their
permission, I bit him very hard
one day immediately after one
of his attacks on the others.
He screamed for a long time and
stopped biting the other children.
Sometime later, his parents moved
to Connecticut and bought him
a pony.

A BAT AND A WEASLE

A weasle snatched a bat and the
bat begged for life. No dice
said the weasle, I never give a
bird a second choice. Ay (says the
bat) but I'm a mouse you see...
just check out my body: and so
she got away. The same bat was
unfortunately caught by another
weasle and again begged for her life.
No said the weasle, no mercy for
mice. But the bat said, look again,
I'm a bird flapping my wings. The
weasle dropped its jaw and the bat
flew off. And so it happened that
the bat escaped between two aspects
of her image by playing the trickster.

A BAT, BIRDS, AND BEASTS

Upon a terrible battle between the
birds and the beasts, the bat stood
neutral until she saw that the
beasts would probably win and then
went over to the strongest side.
But the birds rallied and came up
the winners that day so the bat
went over to the other side where
she was tried as a deserter, scorned
and banished never to see the daylight again.

NOTES: If you are going to
play tricks, it is good to
know what time it is. What
were the birds and the beasts
fighting for anyway? Don't
they know that the people
already won and that only the
most adaptable will survive in
civilized nature?

(VAMPIRE BATS DOMESTICATE EASILY)

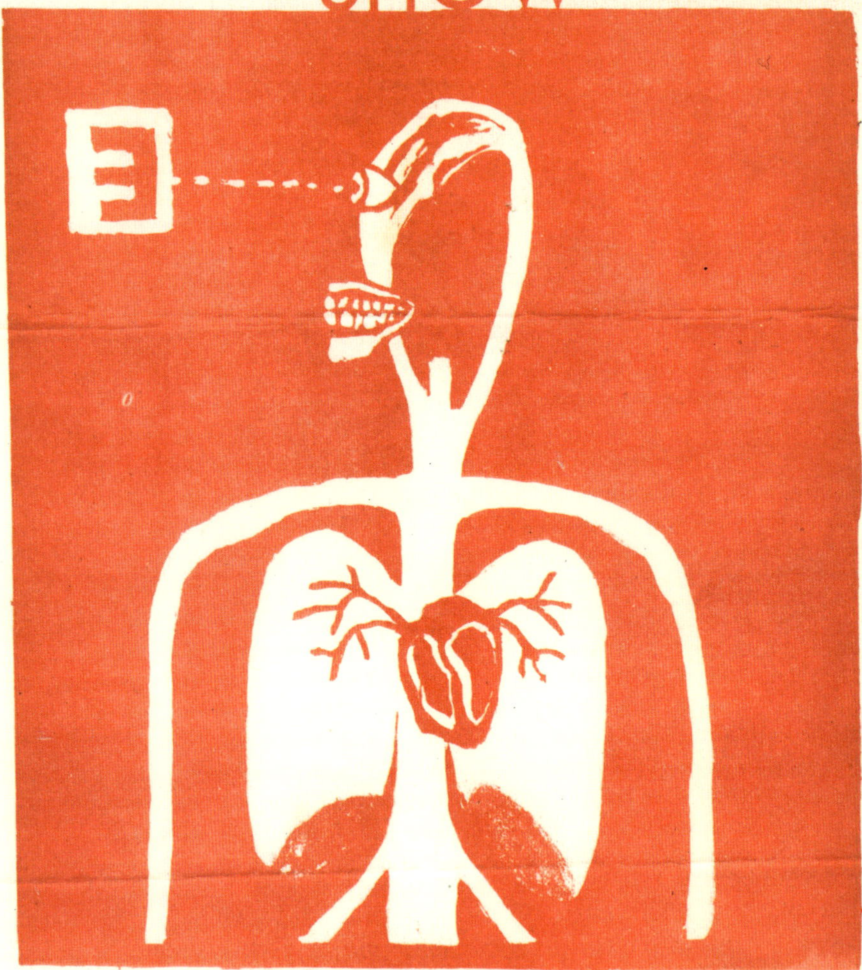

Facing page:

Andrea Callard. *Bat Tract*, 1977. Screenprint on newsprint, 21.5 × 36 cm. Exhibited in *The Batman Show*.
Courtesy of Andrea Callard.

This page:

Robin Winters. *Doctors & Dentists Show*, 1979. Offset printed poster, 28 × 21.5 cm. Courtesy of Becky Howland.

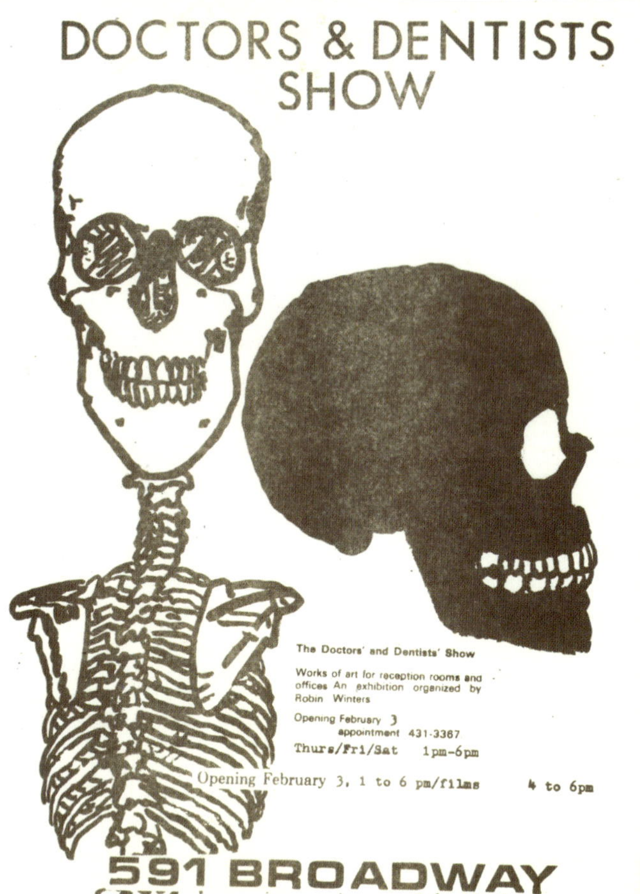

Robin Winters. *Doctors & Dentists Show*, 1979. Photocopy poster, 28 × 21.5 cm. Courtesy of Becky Howland.

In November of 1978, an exhibition entitled "Exhibit A" at the 93 Grand Street storefront of the Center for New Art Activities signalled the beginning of a change in emphasis for Collaborative Projects. It was a new sobriety, perhaps, more appropriate for an entry into the art market. This selective show of "graphic works by artists who usually worked in film or video media," was to be followed by exhibits B, C and D in years to come, open to many artists. In fact, this neutral progression of increasingly more open shows did not happen. Wary of a seeming dependency on Center for New Art Activities, Robin Winters and Coleen Fitzgibbon moved the 1979 exhibition activities to their own lofts which were within blocks of each other. The early activities had inscribed a definite hierarchy of artists within the organization, one which would be largely broken down—or changed in the course of 1979.

As they produced the Colab group exhibitions, Fitzgibbon and Winters closed down their crime-styled underground partnership. The shows in the main gestured blandly at eclectic social themes. The first was odd: *The Batman Show*, "arranged" in January of 1979 by Diego Cortez at Winters' loft at 591 Broadway. Cortez said he was inspired by a child's drawings of the superhero Batman, which featured as the poster for the show. This choice of a popular icon responded first to the art direction of the then-popular television show. The sound effects of battles appeared as large animated cartoon balloons, a conjunction that directly evoked Pop Art. This choice of theme then situated the art retrogressively in a moment dominated by conceptual and post-minimal art. Further, the character Batman, partnered with his "young ward" Robin, has a clear queer subtext to which Cortez, as a gay man, was pointing.

February saw simultaneous exhibitions, *The Doctors & Dentists Show* (at 591 Broadway, Winters' studio), and *The Income & Wealth Show* (or "Enterprise") at Fitzgibbon's storefront space at 5 Bleecker Street. These exhibitions were noted in the press, especially *Doctors & Dentists*, which featured a carefully reconstructed waiting room with Danish modern furniture, wallpaper, and sailboat paintings. *The Dog Show* followed in March (at 591), *The Manifesto Show* in May (at 5 Bleecker; co-organized with Jenny Holzer), and in June *The Library Show* (an exhibit of artists' books and journals, also at 5 Bleecker; co-organized with Barbara Ess, editor of the journal *Just Another Asshole*).

The purpose of these exhibitions was to provide for an "exchange of information and contact for artists with artists," and "to create a collective atmosphere of artists producing and showing work together." These shows were "organized" rather than curated, that is, they were open to all comers (although most of them were invited) with minimal excision and rearrangement. To the artists, this was an important distinction, since it struck at curatorial privilege. This had been significantly expanded by the professionalization of alternative spaces. The Colab shows were jam-packed with works hung salon style on the walls from floor to ceiling, signs of a burgeoning community of unseen younger artists.

With *The Manifesto Show*, an exhibition of works which purported to say something, the response revealed both interest and unease. Peter Frank, a critic then identified with the Fluxus movement, described it as a show "put on by a floating collective of post conceptual, para-punk artists whose aggressive leftist stance comes over at once as adolescent posturing and as the revival of the shit-kicking spirit that motivated the Dadaists in Berlin." Another critic found it a "loud and ragged show, perfect for its locale: CBGB is across the street."

—Alan Moore. *Art Gangs*. New York: Autonomedia, 2011.

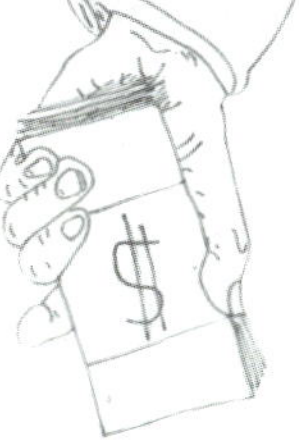

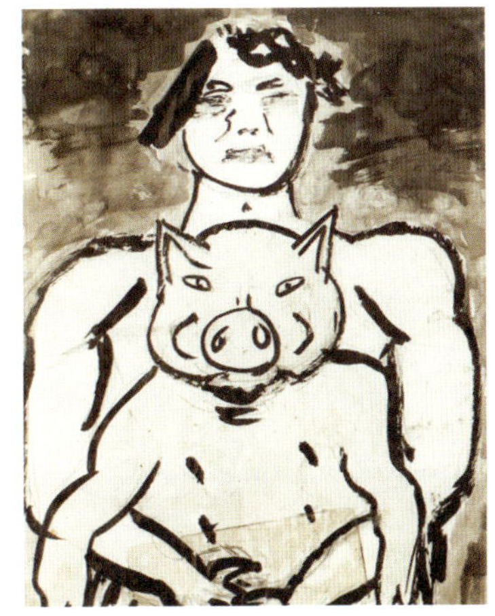

Robin Winters. *The Language of Business*, 1979. Marker on vellum transparencies, 21 × 10 cm each. Exhibited in *The Income & Wealth Show*. Courtesy of Robin Winters.

Dick Miller. *Artist and Art Dealer*, 1979. Pencil and ink on paper, 28 × 35 cm (framed). Exhibited at *The Income & Wealth Show*. Courtesy of Terise Slotkin. Photo: Nancy Linn

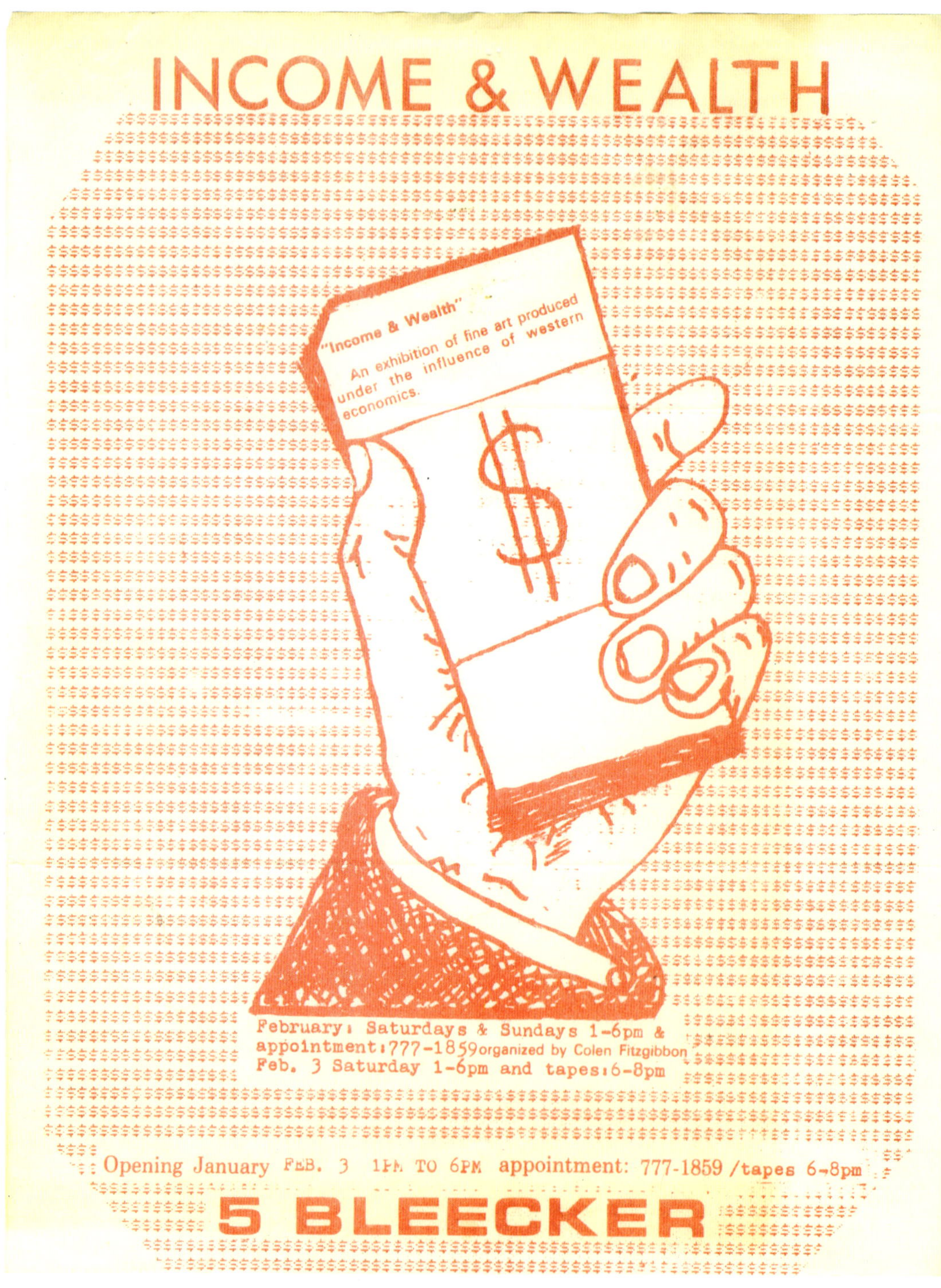

Robin Winters (artwork) and Coleen Fitzgibbon (design). *Income & Wealth*, 1979.
Color screenprinted poster, 28 × 21.5 cm. For *The Income & Wealth Show*. Courtesy of Becky Howland.

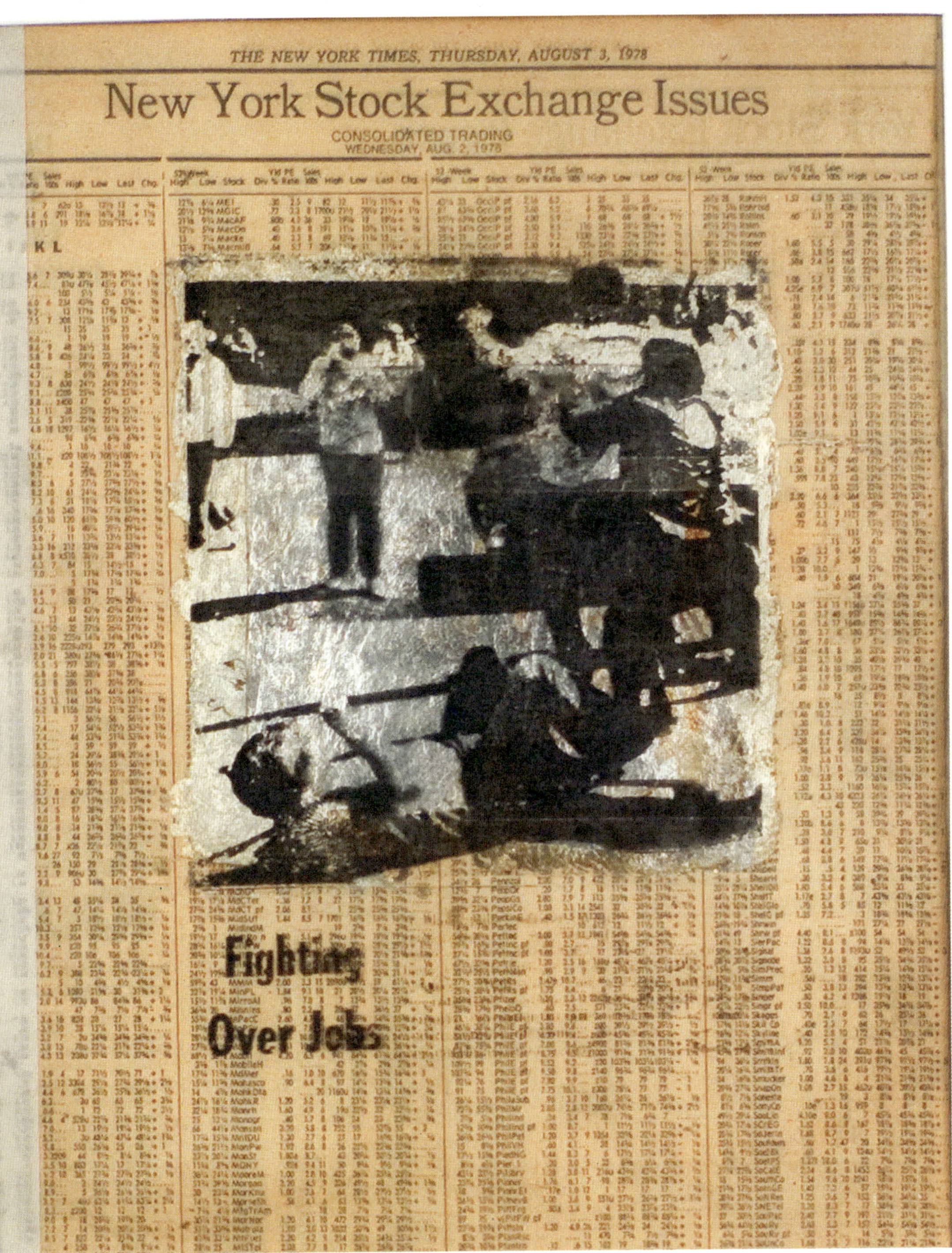

Coleen Fitzgibbon. *Fighting Over Jobs*, c. 1979. Mixed media collage, 34 × 28 cm framed.
Exhibited in *The Income & Wealth Show*. Courtesy of Tom Otterness. Photo: Nancy Linn.

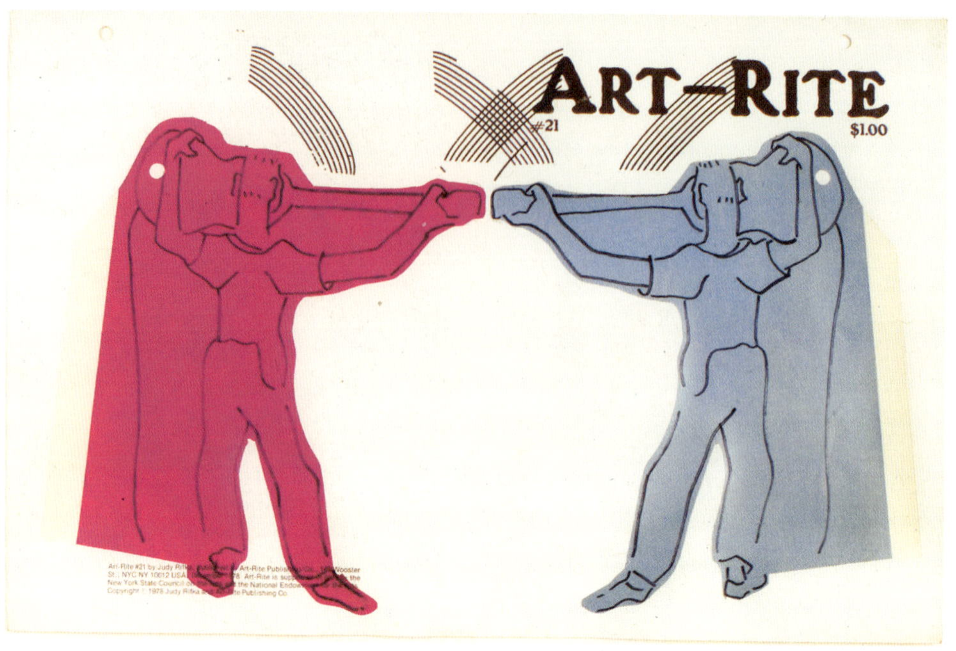

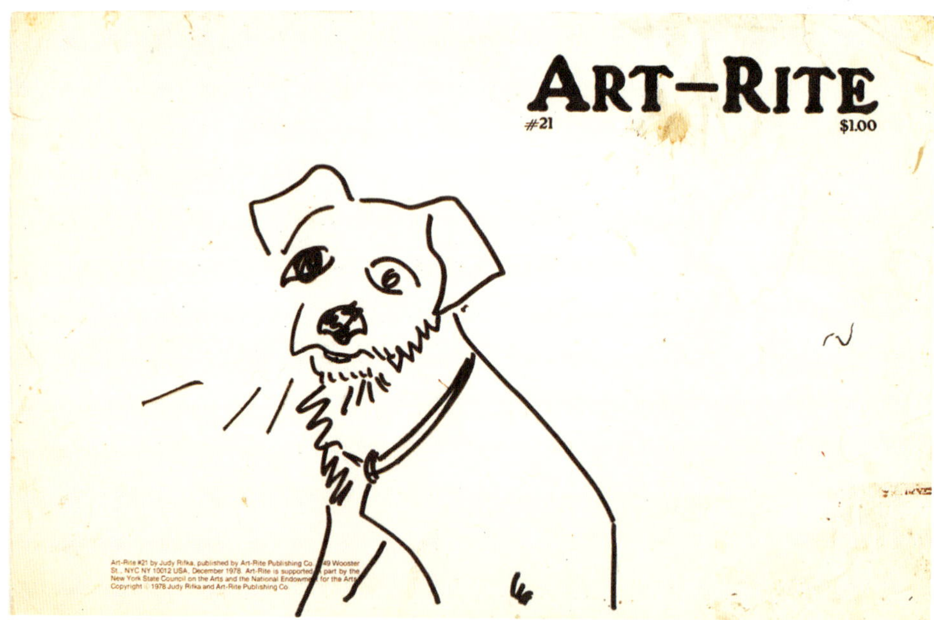

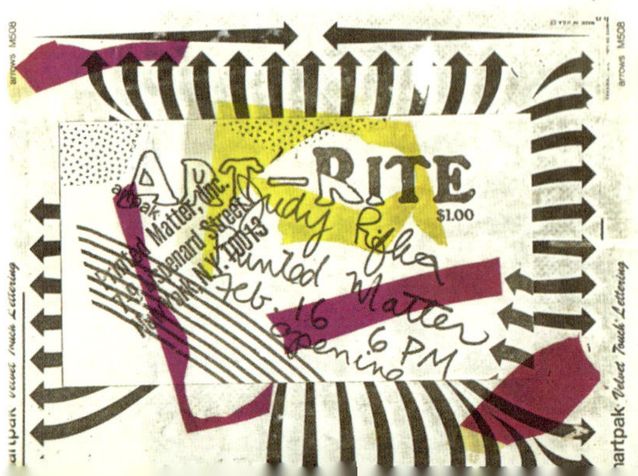

Judy Rifka. *Tier 3*, 1978. Collage and drawing on paper, 31.5 × 46.5 cm (framed). From a series of artist's variations of *Art-Rite* covers. Exhibited at Printed Matter. Courtesy of Judy Rifka. Photo: Nancy Linn.

Judy Rifka. *Dog with Color Vision*, 1979. Marker and pencil on paper, 27 × 42 cm. From a series of artist's variations of *Art-Rite* covers. Exhibited in *The Dog Show.* Courtesy of Judy Rifka.

Judy Rifka. *Untitled* [Printed Matter/*Art-Rite* collage], 1978. Photocopied announcement from Printed Matter and colored acetate, 21.5 × 28 cm. From a series of *Art-Rite* cover variations. Courtesy of Judy Rifka.

"Around this time [1977] all these people were being holier-than-thou radical chic and people were being alienated, so I wanted to have the most unhip [show.] … We had an historical survey of artists' dogs pictures. Dennis Oppenheim has his Dead Dog piece. Joan Jonas had a great drawing of Sappho. Becky Howland had a dog that she'd made for JoAnne Akalaitis's Colette play. Christy Rupp had dogs you could step on."

—Robin Winters interviewed by Betsy Sussler. *Bomb*. Fall 1983.

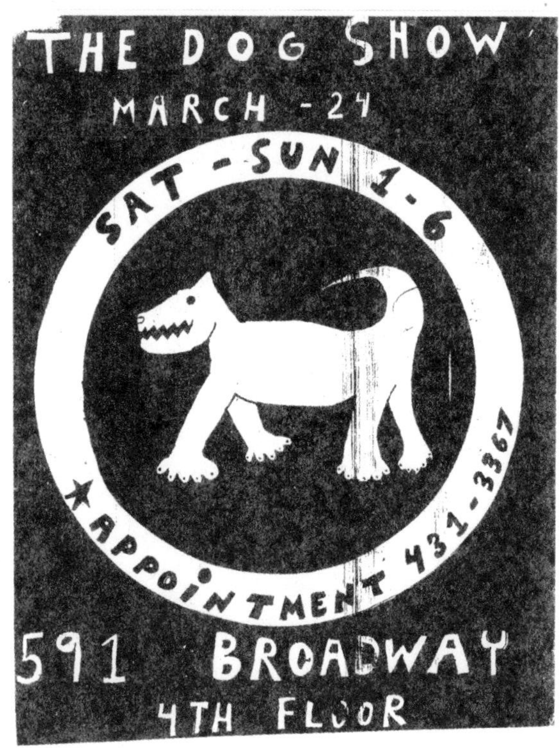

Robin Winters. *The Dog Show*, 1979. Offset printed poster, 21.5 × 28 cm. For *The Dog Show*. Courtesy of Julie Harrison.

Robin Winters. *I Am Not a Dog Person*, c. 1979. Ink on paper, 35.5 × 28 cm. Exhibited in *The Dog Show*. Courtesy of Robin Winters.

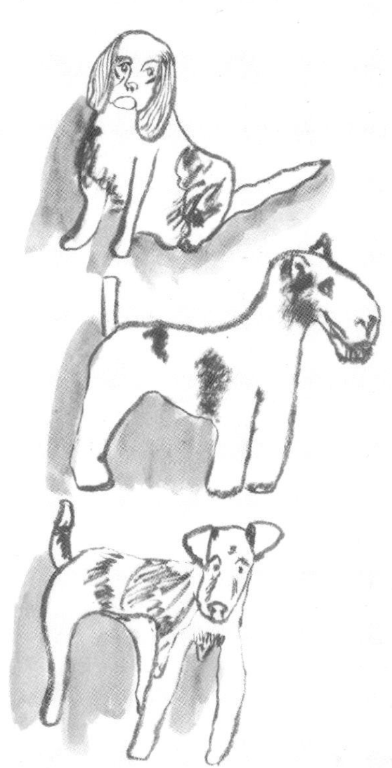

Jenny Holzer. *Manifesto Show*, 1979. Offset printed with collage intervention by an unknown artist, 23 × 23 cm. Poster for *Manifesto Show*. Courtesy of Becky Howland.

*DON'T TALK DOWN TO ME. DON'T
BE POLITE TO ME.   DON'T
TRY TO MAKE ME FEEL NICE.
DON'T RELAX. I'LL CUT THE
SMILE OFF YOUR FACE. YOU
THINK I DON'T KNOW WHAT'S
GOING ON.   YOU THINK I'M
AFRAID TO REACT. THE JOKE'S
ON YOU. I'M BIDING MY TIME,
LOOKING FOR THE SPOT. YOU
THINK NO ONE CAN REACH YOU,
NO ONE CAN HAVE WHAT YOU
HAVE. I'VE BEEN PLANNING
WHILE YOU'RE PLAYING. I'VE
BEEN SAVING WHILE YOU'RE
SPENDING.   THE GAME IS
ALMOST OVER SO IT'S
TIME YOU ACKNOWLEDGE ME.
DO YOU WANT TO FALL NOT
EVER KNOWING WHO TOOK YOU?*

*SENTIMENTALITY DELAYS THE REMOVAL OF
THE DANGEROUSLY BACKWARD AND THE
UNFIT.   RIGOROUS SELECTION IS
MANDATORY IN POLICY MAKING AND
POPULATION MANAGEMENT.   INCORRECT
MERCIFUL IMPULSES POSTPONE THE
CLEANSING THAT PRECEDES REFORM.
SHORT-TERM NICETIES MUST YIELD TO
LONG-RANGE NECESSITY. MORALS WILL BE
REVISED TO MEET THE REQUIREMENTS OF
TODAY. MEANINGLESS PLATITUDES WILL
BE PULLED FROM TONGUES AND MINDS.
WORDS LIKE PURGE AND EUTHANASIA
DESERVE NEW CONNOTATIONS. THEY SHOULD
BE RECOGNIZED AS THE RATIONAL SOCIAL
INSTRUMENTS THEY ARE.   THE GREATEST
DANGER IS NOT EXCESSIVE ZEAL BUT UNDUE
HESITATION. WE WILL LEARN TO IMITATE
NATURE.   HER KILLS NOURISH STRONG
LIFE.   SQUEAMISHNESS IS THE CRIME.*

*YOU GET AMAZING SENSATIONS FROM
GUNS.   YOU GET RESULTS FROM
GUNS.   MAN IS AN AGRESSIVE ANIMAL;
YOU HAVE TO HAVE A GOOD OFFENSE
AND A GOOD DEFENSE. TOO MANY
CITIZENS THINK THEY ARE HELPLESS.
THEY LEAVE EVERYTHING TO THE
AUTHORITIES AND THIS CAUSES
CORRUPTION. RESPONSIBILITY
SHOULD GO BACK WHERE IT BELONGS.
IT IS YOUR LIFE SO TAKE CONTROL
AND FEEL VITAL. THERE MAY BE
SOME ACCIDENTS ALONG THE PATH
TO SELF-EXPRESSION AND SELF-
DETERMINATION. SOME INNOCENT
PEOPLE WILL BE HURT. HOWEVER,
G-U-N SPELLS PRIDE TO THE
STRONG, SAFETY TO THE WEAK
AND HOPE TO THE HOPELESS.
GUNS MAKE WRONG RIGHT FAST.*

*A CRUEL BUT ANCIENT LAW
DEMANDS AN EYE FOR AN EYE.
MURDER MUST BE ANSWERED BY
EXECUTION. ONLY GOD HAS THE
RIGHT TO TAKE A LIFE AND WHEN
SOMEONE BREAKS THIS LAW HE
WILL BE PUNISHED. JUSTICE
MUST COME SWIFTLY. IT DOESN'T
HELP ANYONE TO STALL. THE
VICTIM'S FAMILY CRIES OUT FOR
SATISFACTION, THE COMMUNITY
BEGS FOR PROTECTION AND THE
DEPARTED CRAVES VENGEANCE
SO HE CAN REST. THE KILLER
KNEW IN ADVANCE THERE WAS
NO EXCUSE FOR HIS ACT, TRULY
HE HAS TAKEN HIS OWN LIFE.
HE, NOT SOCIETY, IS
RESPONSIBLE FOR HIS FATE. HE
ALONE STANDS GUILTY AND DAMNED.*

Jenny Holzer. *Inflammatory Essays*, c. 1979. Offset printed, 25.5 × 25.5 cm. From a series of 15 posters exhibited in *Manifesto Show*. Courtesy of the Collaborative Projects Archive.

M A N I F E S T O

S H O W

ORGANIZED BY ARTISTS

CURATED BY NONE

DIRECT BUT UNDIRECTED, CLEAR BUT NOT REFINED

ENTIRELY DEBATABLE

SUBJECT TO ATTACK

BUT NOT TO CRITIC—ISM

NOR TO ART DEALING

NOTHING IS "FOR SALE," BUT EVERYTHING CAN BE SOLD, LEASED,
  FINANCIALLY UNDERWRITTEN, HANDED OUT (SOMETIMES)

MANIFESTOS TAKE MANY FORMS: POSTERS, STATEMENTS, MAPS,
                      TV SHOWS, MOVIES, SPEECHES

SPEECHES, PERFORMANCES AND AGITATIONS ON SATURDAYS, 4 PM

NO IDEOLOGY OR ATTITUDE PREVAILS

ONLY BOREDOM IS NOT ALLOWED. WHILE NOTHING'S PRESCRIBED,
  EVERYONE'S PREPARED.

        FREE ENTRY   NO PRICE
        FREE EXPRESSION   NO RULES
        FREE ASSOCIATION   NO CLASS
        FREE EXCHANGE   NO RIGHT

WHAT IS THIS?

M A N I F E S T O   S H O W

APRIL 1979   AN EXHIBIT IN ONE LARGE
THURSDAYS-SATURDAYS 2-6 PM   ROOM OF MANIFESTOS GENERATED
5 BLEEKER STREET   BY A TEMPESTUOUS CROWD OF
                                  ARTISTS, BOTH NOW IN NYC
AGITATORS AND PERFORMERS   AND LONG BEFORE.
SATURDAYS 4 PM
                                  ANOTHER IN A SERIES OF
COORDINATORS: JENNY HOLZER,   ARTIST-ORGANIZED SHOWS
   COLEN FITZGIBBON   WITH DIFFERENT COORDINATORS
                                  AT DIFFERENT LOCATIONS.

Manifesto Show   4.79   Doctors & Dentists Show   3.79
Sex & Death Show   5.79   515 Broadway Show   1.79
Dog Show   4.79   Batman Show   1.79
Income & Wealth Show   3.79   Exhibit A   1.79

50

This page:

Unknown. *Manifesto Show*, 1979. Photocopied document from Colab Annual Report, 21.5 × 28 cm.
Courtesy of Matthew Geller.

Facing page:

Andrea Callard. *Photo Replacements*, c. 1978–79. Photocopy, 28 × 21.5 cm. Exhibited in *The Manifesto Show*.
Courtesy of Andrea Callard.

Coleen Fitzgibbon. *Bomb Squad*, c. 1979. Drawing with color gouache, 64 × 49 cm (framed).
Exhibited in *The Manifesto Show*. Courtesy of Coleen Fitzgibbon.

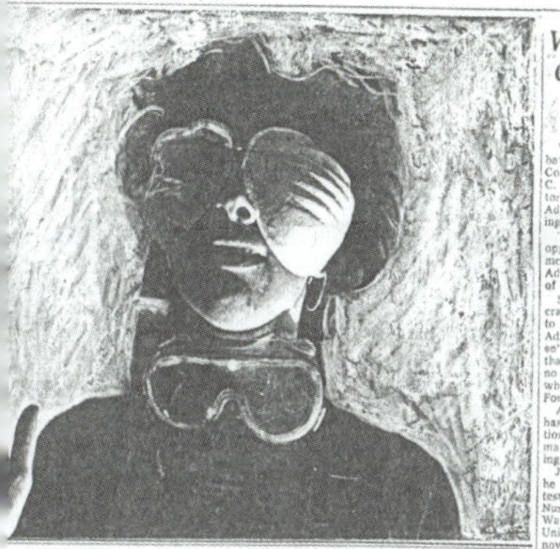

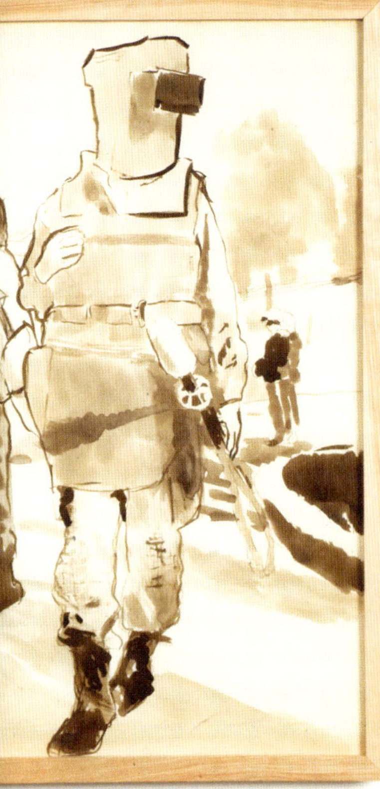

Excerpt from *The Book of Ibid* by Joe Lewis
SECOND CANTO

In memorandum
Prepare for peace with honor
Classified top not-so-secret partisan enforcement makes time
Or whatever they have renamed it
Systems management best sleep too.

Non-action dilutes the social gait
In lieu of War
On the mainland.

Re-dsitra-forested, conurbation
ID card imminent

The debonair have become junkies
Side show freaks the geek
is on
Selfless in an environment that is revolution.

Brooding hail to the chief
Who stabled you in the face
And couldn't keep the pigeons off here
Where the evolutionary process has turned bulls to pigs
In the public interest.

Sanctified by
something stole
Education
Religion
Remember the carrier pigeon?
Freckles on curls, pearly with teeth?
They done messed with the rats so bad they's jumping
Up and down instead of off.

Nothing
Is something
New...

We used to drink together
Party, dance and sing together
No time to talk
The program pushed the accelerator.

— Joe Lewis. *The Book of Ibid*, 1979 (performed at *The Manifesto Show*, 1979). Collection of Joe Lewis.

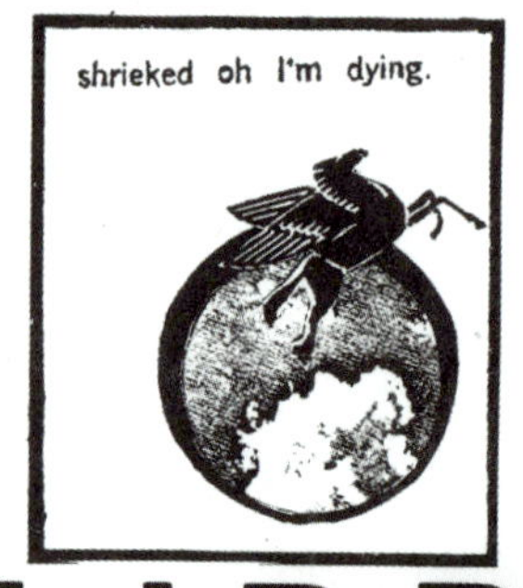

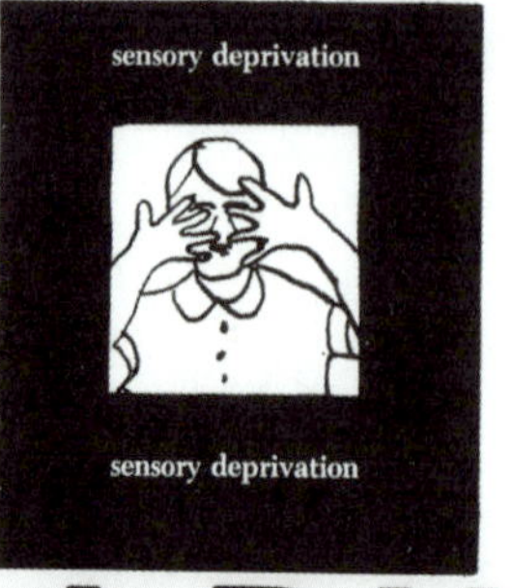

LIBRARY

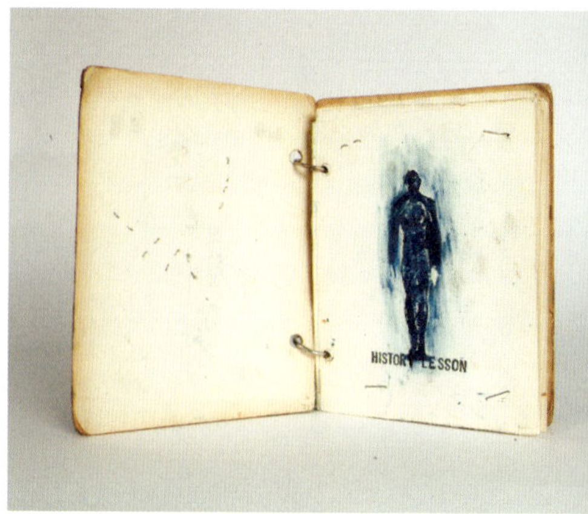

It was one of the rare moments in my life, where being someone's girlfriend was acceptable to me.

In those early Colab days, I was living with Tom Otterness in the loft that we created together with his labor and my financing, through what was a short-lived two year career as a "rabid feminist topless dancer."

I benefited from being in proximity to Colab without actually being a 'card carrying' member and was included in a half dozen shows put together by Colab. I was lucky to have experienced the zeitgeist along with being part of an inspired moment in time with a sometimes inspiring group of peers.

I tried attending Colab meetings, but don't think I even made it all the way through one meeting. I did NOT have the patience for that group of gigantic egos. The vast majority of the artists I met, especially the male artists, suffered from what in those days I termed "boy artist syndrome," a vast sense of self importance and entitlement. This criticism could as easily have applied to some of the women in Colab. There was too much administration as well as too many personality conflicts, some of which are still amazingly robust and intact these almost 40 years later.

In the late seventies, I worked at a local Tribeca artist hangout bar and restaurant named Magoos, which has its own wonderful downtown history from bygone eras, including having had a back room where city hall big wigs reportedly knocked knees with 'ladies' procured by the owner.

Some artists traded their artwork as barter for a food tab. One of the artists I remember waiting on was unknown at that time, who didn't impress me much even though he worked nearby in Soho, I thought, as a bartender. I just mostly remember he was always broke and would only order coffee, then proceed to sit there, drinking the one cup of coffee and adding in more and more milk from the pitcher served with it. That would

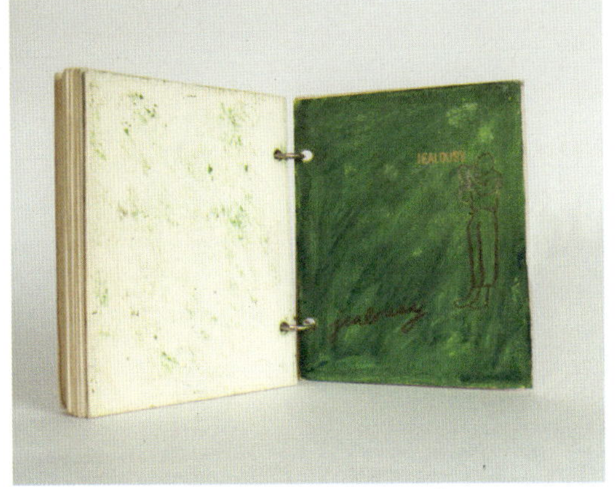

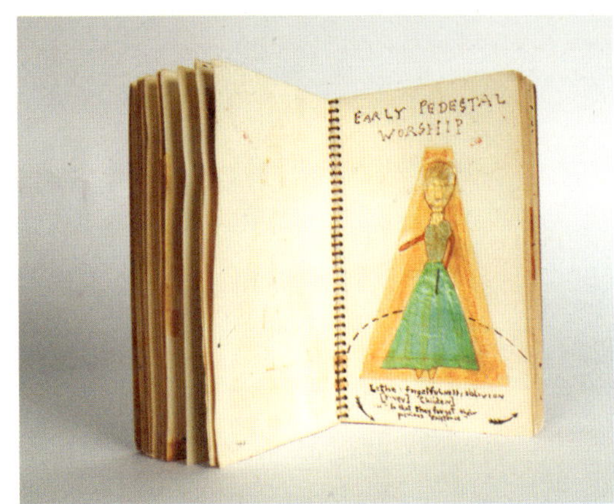

have been Julian Schnabel.
Later, I worked in the Jewish Mafia's small group of topless bars around Manhattan, near Penn Station, Grand Central and Studio 54.
I used the job as a way to work out my issues with men and danced my way into a study of power roles among men and women. My work at the time was about 'the personal is the political' with the goal of re-sacralizing the mundane.

In this recent spate of Colab related shows in NYC in (2013 & 2014) "Topless", a super 8 film I created in collaboration with Cara Perlman was just shown in "Girls Gone Wild" at Spectacle in Williamsburg, Brooklyn. It tells a bit of the story of where I was coming from during this time.

Several Colab shows took place at Coleen Fitzgibbon's studio. At one show, held at Coleen Fitzgibbon's loft on Bleecker Street nearby the (then) Communist bookstore, Barbara Ess and I had a joint show called *The Library Show* where we showed our

own one-of-a-kind books, and we solicited artwork from anyone who came by and put it up on a bulletin board across one wall, promising the artists that we'd publish all the artwork in our co-produced issue of *Just Another Asshole* magazine.
—Jane Sherry

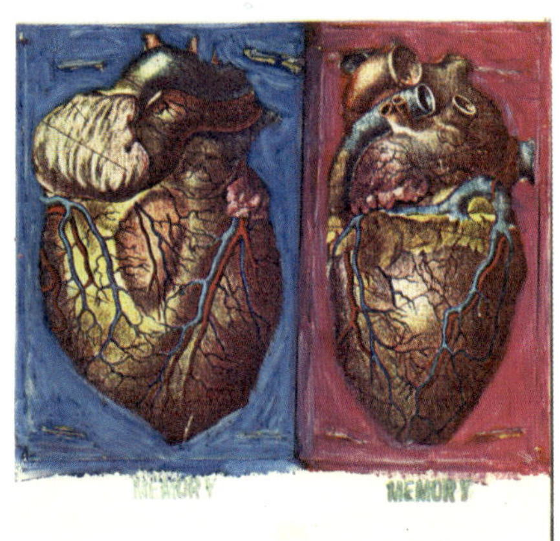

Top, left to right:

Barbara Ess and Jane Sherry. *Library*, 1979. Offset printed card, 10 × 15 cm. Announcement for *The Library Show*. Courtesy of Barbara Ess.

Jane Sherry. *History Lesson #2*. New York: J. Sherry, 1979. Mixed media, ring-bound book, 35 pp, 18 × 11.5 cm. *Goddess Book #1*. c. 1979. Mixed Media, ring-bound book, 20 pp, 18 × 11.5 cm. *History Lesson #3*, c. 1979. Mixed media, ring-bound book, 15 pp 17 × 13 cm. Exhibited in *The Library Show*. Courtesy of Jane Sherry. Photo: Nancy Linn.

Bottom:

Jane Sherry. *Memory*, c. 1978–79. Collage and paint on board, 14.5 × 14.5 cm. Exhibited in the *Just Another Asshole Show*. Courtesy of Coleen Fitzgibbon. Photo: Nancy Linn.

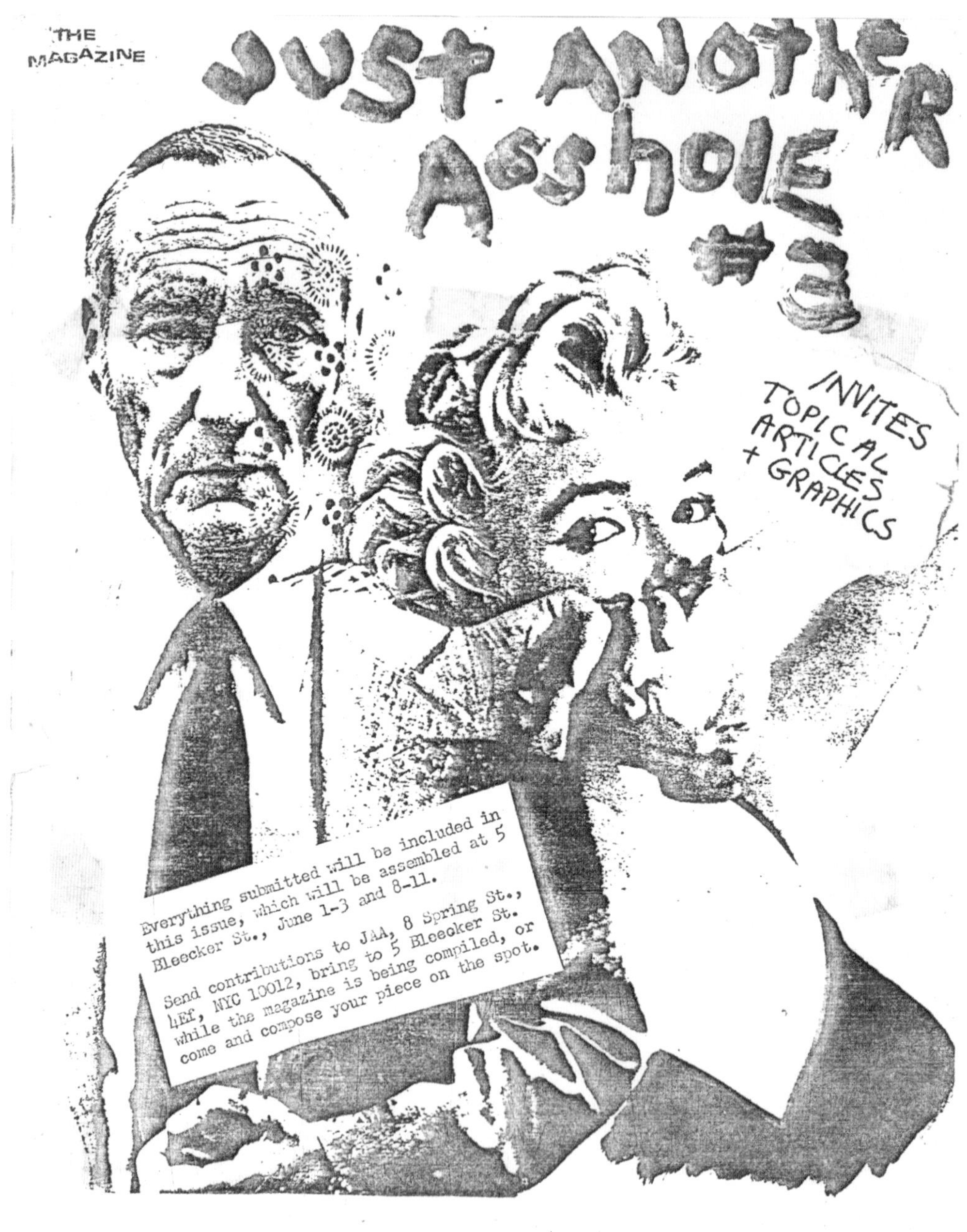

Barbara Ess. Untitled [*Call for Contributors*], c. 1979. Photocopy flyer for *Just Another Asshole, No. 3*, 28 × 21.5 cm. Courtesy of Barbara Ess.

$1.50

Barbara Ess and Jane Sherry, editors. *Just Another Asshole, No. 3*. New York: Just Another Asshole, 1979. (cover) Offset printed, pbk, 48 pp, 29 × 38 cm. Courtesy of Barbara Ess. Photo: Nancy Linn.

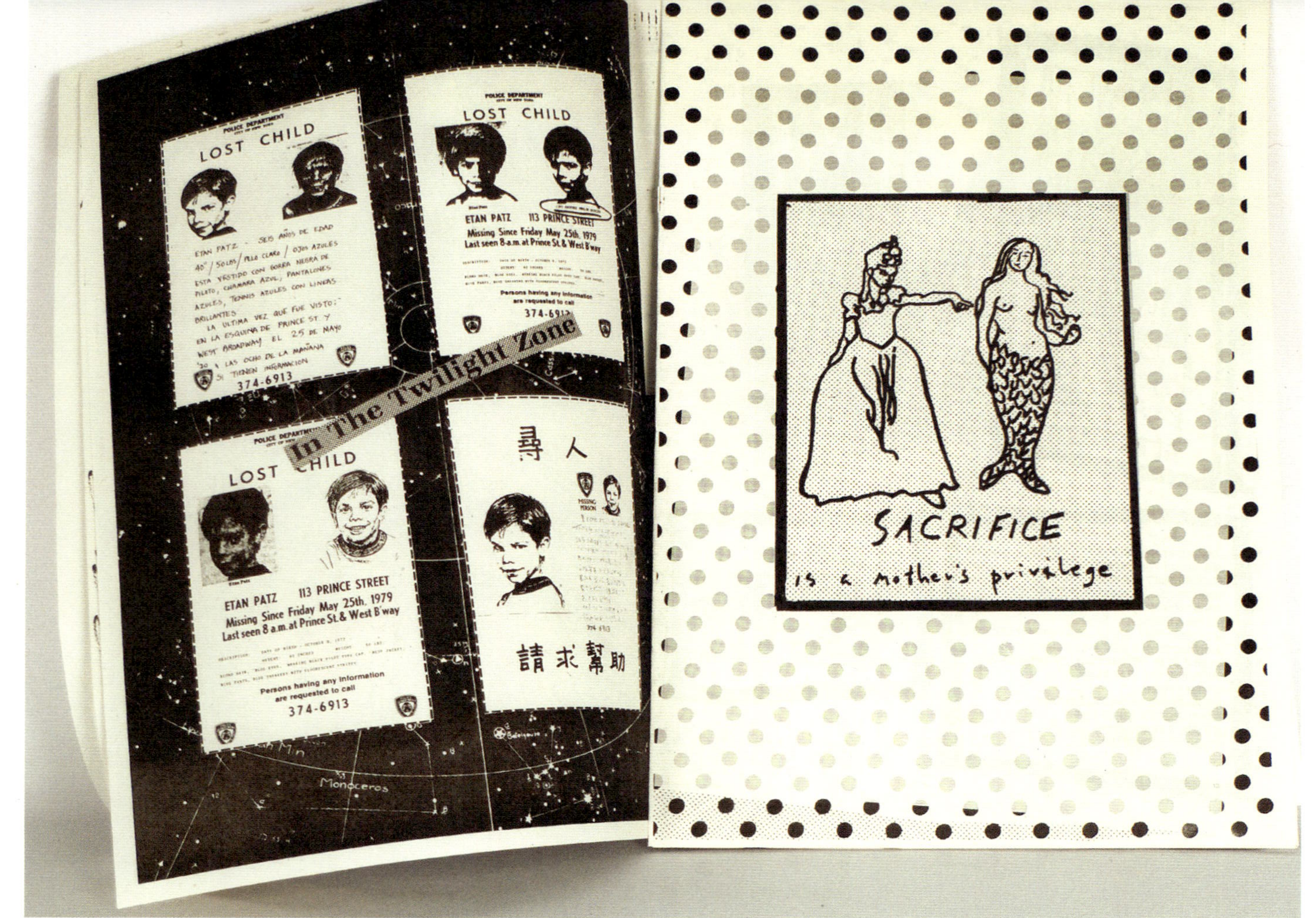

Barbara Ess and Jane Sherry, editors. *Just Another Asshole, No. 3.* New York: Just Another Asshole, 1979. Offset printed, pbk, 48 pp, 29 × 38 cm. Interior. Courtesy of Barbara Ess. Photo: Nancy Linn.

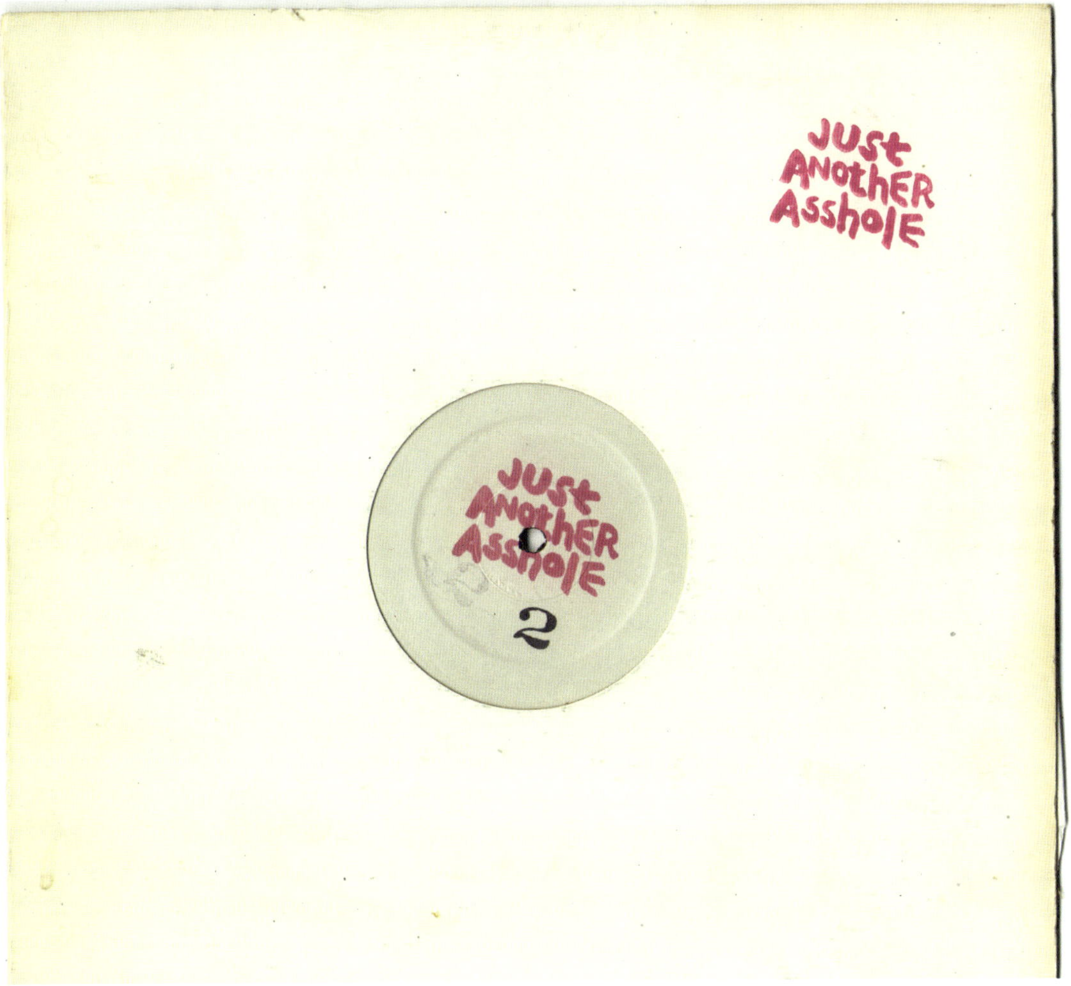

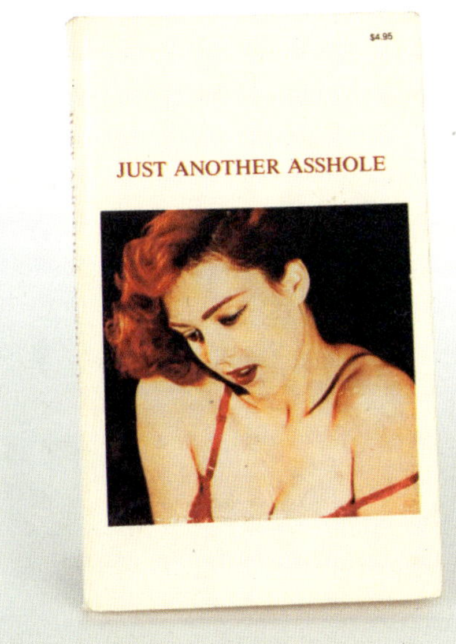

Barbara Ess and Glenn Branca, editors. *Just Another Asshole*, *No. 5*. New York: Just Another Asshole, 1981. LP, 32 × 32 cm. 83 artists, 77 tracks at 0:45 each. Produced with the assistance of White Columns and Josh Baer. Courtesy of Barbara Ess. Photo: Nancy Linn.

Barbara Ess and Glenn Branca, editors. *Just Another Asshole*, *No. 6*. New York: Just Another Asshole. 1983. Offset printed, paperback, glue bound, 186 pp, 17.5 × 10.5 cm. Courtesy of Barbara Ess. Photo: Nancy Linn.

REAL ESTATE SH
JAN. 1 1980
123 Delancey St.

Entries in my calendar from 1979 show how *The Real Estate Show* developed, beginning with a non-stop series of shows with a thematic, single idea—in artists' lofts, for ourselves and our friends—that we did that spring:

March 23: help Robin install *The Dog Show*
March 24: *The Dog Show* opens
April 7: opening *Manifesto Show*
April 21: opening 75 Warren Street—A Salute to Creative Youth
    (Note: May 15-19 Public Arts International: Free Speech: Performance Art Festival at 75 Warren Street. Organized by Joseph Nechvatal, Carol Parkinson, Cid Collins)
July 21: meet Tom (Otterness) and Alan to break into Delancey Street.
July 22: finish reading *The Octopus*
Aug. 1: poster meeting here. Robert Cooney and Jorges Mendez
Oct. 7: Colab meeting
Oct. 9: take pictures of in-rem building for Colab
December 7: Cable TV show
    (Note: Ann, Alan, and I participated in a live-cable TV show organized by David Levine and Christof Kohlhöfer. We staged a takeover of the TV station. I painted a woman in a chador, with a flap hiding a gun underneath, and drew posters of Uncle Sam, the recently deposed Shah of Iran, and the Ayatollah Khomeini. Ann and I dressed up in chadors—with fake guns—and charged into the station for the takeover.)
Dec. 9: meeting at Alan's house Real Estate
Dec. 10: Try to go into Delancey St.
Dec. 16: Talk w. Peter and Alan about Real Estate
Dec. 17: Hall of Records, photostats 125 Delancey St.

—Becky Howland

Becky Howland. *Real Estate Show [Octopus]*. New York: B. Howland, 1980. Stencil spray-painted poster, 91 × 74 cm (framed). Edition of 36. For *The Real Estate Show.* Courtesy of Becky Howland. Photo: Nancy Linn

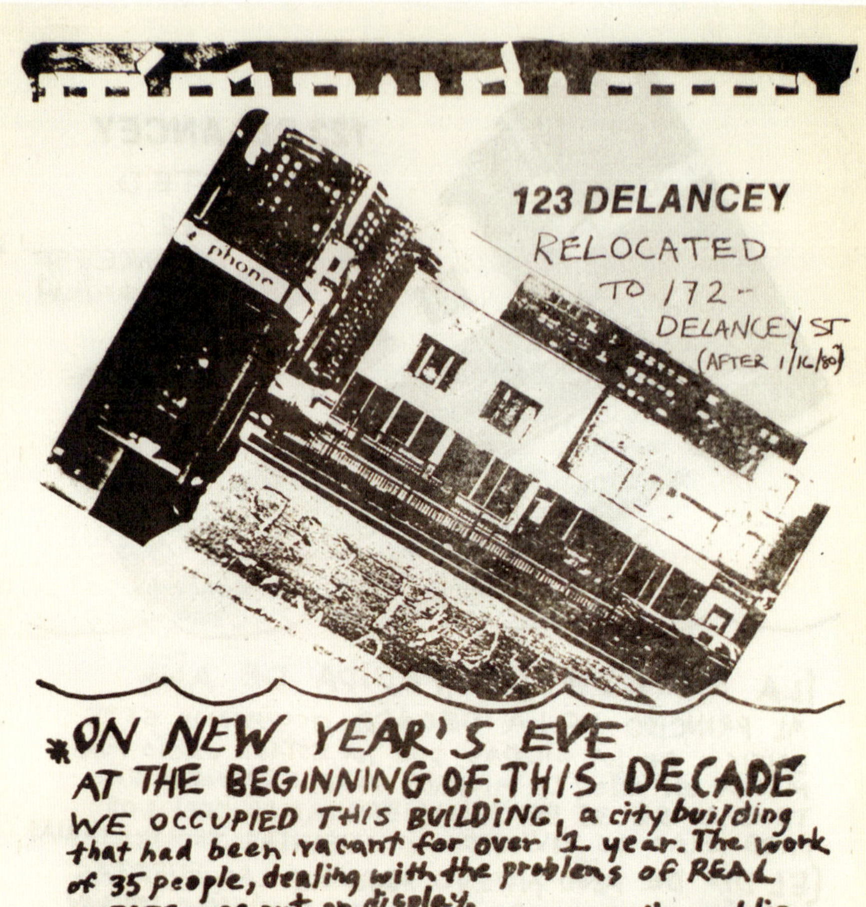
123 DELANCEY
RELOCATED
TO 172-
DELANCEY ST
(AFTER 1/16/80)

phone

*ON NEW YEAR'S EVE
AT THE BEGINNING OF THIS DECADE
WE OCCUPIED THIS BUILDING, a city building
that had been vacant for over 1 year. The work
of 35 people, dealing with the problems of REAL
ESTATE, was put on display.
*ON JAN. 1 we opened the doors to the public.
This was to be the beginning of an exchange
about landlord speculation, tenants rights,
property misuse, projected housing developments,
arbitrary urban planning, etc. --- A CITIZEN'S CENTER.
*ON JAN. 2 the city put a lock on the door pre-
venting any further development.
*ON JAN. 11 the
CITY vandalized our display and removed
part of it to a city warehouse.
REAL ESTATE SHOW

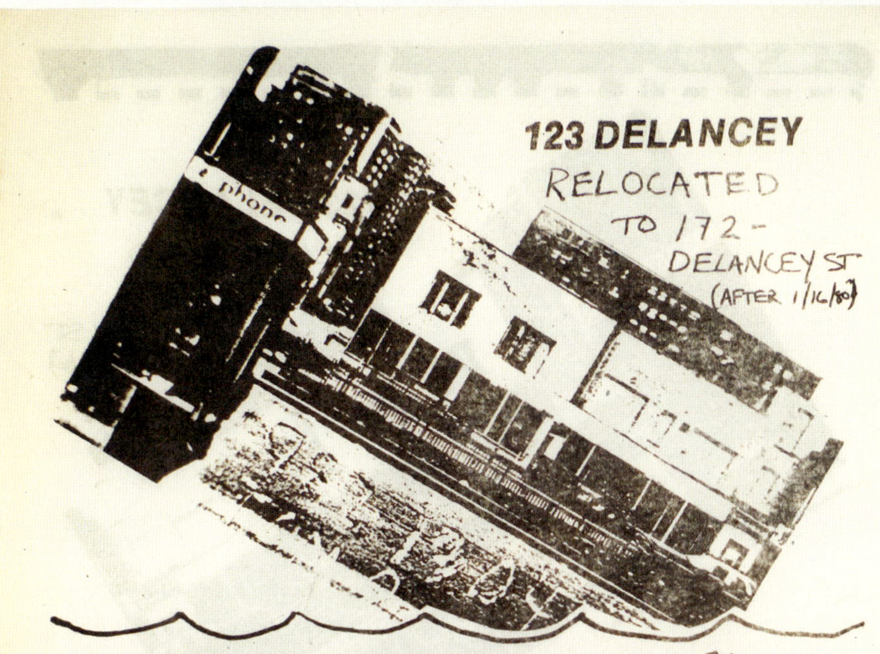

Becky Howland, Christof Kohlhöfer and Alan Moore. *Real Estate Show*, 1980. Photocopy poster, 28 × 21.5 cm. Two-sided poster in English and Spanish for *The Real Estate Show*. Courtesy of Becky Howland and Bobby G (Robert Goldman).

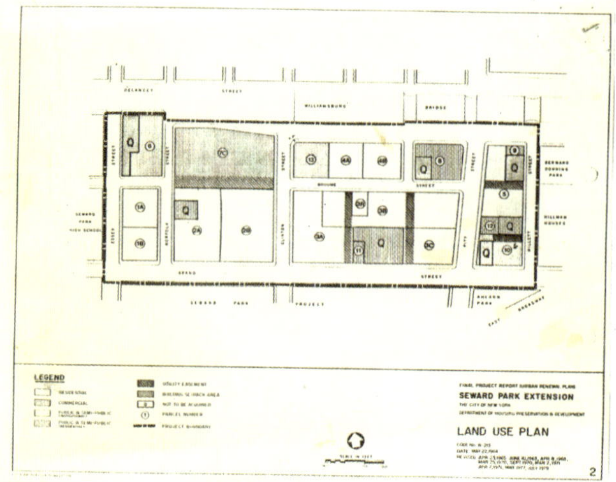

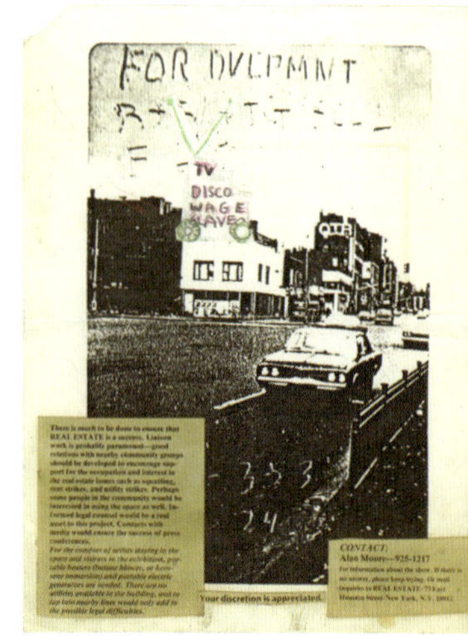

That initial meeting, lots of curiosity accompanied by a mixture of insecurity and unforgiving shyness…but those Colab artists were just so damn welcoming there was easily enough space within which to find a comfortable seat. A huge open embrace, which for this artist, was something there had been a longing for.

Perhaps resulting from a shared 1960s adolescence, there was within Colab a collective disregard for institutional structures and traditional modes of practice. Out of the cultural malaise caused by Vietnam, the tragic assassinations of quixotic public figures, the images of kids being hosed and in the case of Kent State gunned down, the indiscriminate blazing of the inner city already in desperate need of repair, very little that remained standing seemed at all respectable. Just as with the neglected neighborhoods, particularly in New York where we chose to live, reality had fallen apart exposing distressing hypocrisy. And not surprisingly our relationship as artists to culture took on the form of refusal and deconstruction.

Out of this chaos and collapse, the 'what to do' as an artist had broken open. We got to start with a blank slate, and in this way, shockingly, we were lucky. The rent was not too damn high and it was possible to work a couple of hours a day at some menial task and survive, leaving lots of time for creative searching. But that brutality we had witnessed in our coming of age had removed any vestige of innocence or utopist ideation and out of that bitter taste that remained, there was solace in the collaboration with peers.

The Real Estate Show was a hedge; a provocative stance deployed to expose the city's nefarious

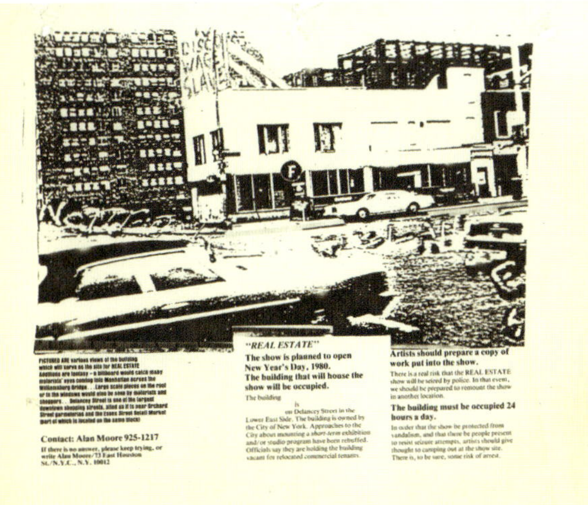

Left to right:

Department of Housing Preservation and Development. *Final Project Report (Urban Renewal Plan): Seward Park Extension*, 1979. Photocopy, 21.5 × 28 cm. Courtesy of Bobby G (Robert Goldman).

Alan Moore. *Your Discretion is Appreciated*, 1979. Photocopy, pencil and collage on paper, 28 × 21.5 cm. Paste-up for *The Real Estate Show* flyer. Courtesy of Becky Howland.

Alan Moore. *Real Estate*, 1979. Photocopy flyer, 21.5 × 28 cm. Call for artwork submissions for *The Real Estate Show*. Courtesy of Becky Howland.

relationship to not only the urgent concerns of an impoverished community but also to the creative desires of a vibrant counterculture movement. Our action: the occupation of 123 Delancey Street and the mounting of the exhibition *The Real Estate Show* proved a test of opposing wills. In retrospect the bravado of multiple break-ins, as evidenced in the photographic documentation, appears awkwardly humorous (oversized bolt cutters in a guitar case) but at the time the direct and forceful dealings with the city, although remaining non-violent, were not at all pleasant. If it were not for the brief attendance of Joseph Beuys in support of our action there may have been more severe consequences (his Guggenheim Retrospective had landed him front page notoriety in the tabloids and as such his presence seemed to intimidate the city officials). As it was a stalemate ensued, ultimately ending in our favor with the granting of a temporary space at another location, as the city struggled with embarrassing damage control in the press.

I did not have the stamina for sustained engagement over time so I did not participate in the slow and arduous task of building what was to become ABC No Rio. But the experience of the initial action has stayed with me over the years, yes, as an inspiring memory of 'crazy' camaraderie, but more significantly, as an example of what becomes possible through collective intentionality. As artists continue to engage in the development of collective 'social practices', recently inspired by itinerant activities of the Occupy movement, the 123 Delancey Street action provides an interesting historical model to consider in moving forward—specifically because it involved the direct occupation of unused

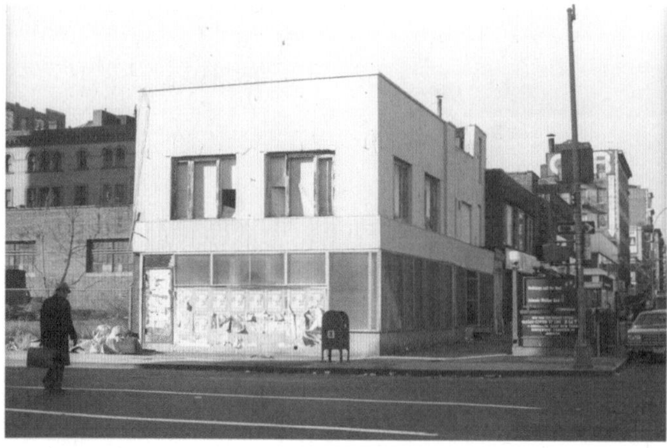

Left to right:

Ann Messner. *123 Delancey Street: abandoned. City-owned building occupied by members of Colab for Real Estate Show*, 1980. Photograph from B/W 35mm negative film, 17.5 × 26.5 cm. Courtesy of Ann Messner.

Peter Moennig. *Ann Messner with the tool used to break into 123 Delancey Street*, 1980. Photograph from B/W 35mm negative film, 26.5 × 17.5 cm. Courtesy of Ann Messner.

Ann Messner. *Breaking into 123 Delancey*, 1980. Photograph from B/W 35mm negative film, 26.5 × 17.5 cm. Courtesy of Ann Messner.

space to serve the needs of the community. This empty structure was rotting from neglect, situated as it was on a schism delineated for urban redevelopment, its forlorn presence served as poignant example of the problematic relationship of the city to the needs of the surrounding neighborhood. To illustrate how insidious that relationship continues to be, that one building was eventually torn down and for the last three decades has remained an underused parking lot—a holding pattern for some momentous re-zoning event to come, permitting perhaps a 30-story crystal palace, to be assured not the humble tenement historically consigned to this periphery of Manhattan.

These thirty years later the stakes are much higher: we have witnessed the value of real estate persists its measure not in personal terms as a place where people of simple means make their homes and raise their families but rather as a cold calculation in its relationship to capital. The cost of housing, having no direct relationship to actual value, based rather on a cynical strategy of scarcity, is staggering. Each new building twice the height that now litters the skyline is mediocre in design, echoing its intention, the building boom being simply a calculation of maximized profit in the form of simulated brick and mortar. If you were lucky to grab a foothold decades ago you are a member of a select few who remain, and if you are rent stabilized, your only hope of being able to

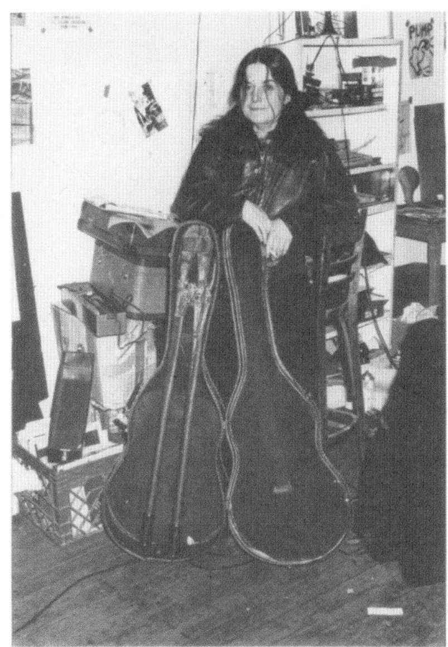

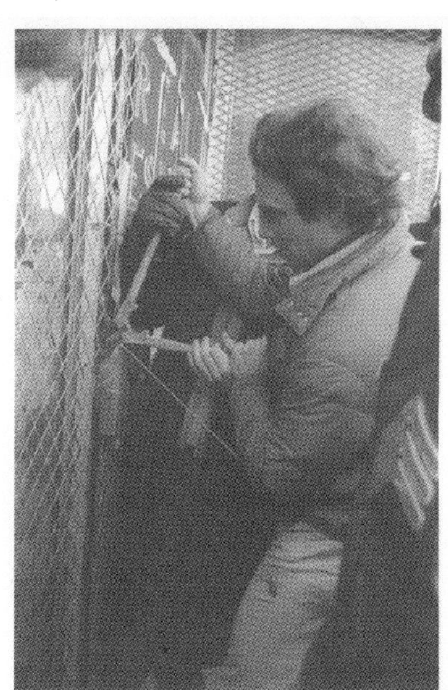

stay, the laws that protect you are challenged yearly.

Just as real estate—in promoting exclusivity—manufactures conflict, so does the elaborate overproduction by the creative class. Artists have historically had to contend with the duplicitous implications of serving the court, in our contemporary world replaced by the market and its relationship to wealth and power. I would propose, given the urgency of this time, we artists ought to reevaluate our allegiances. Is it our desire to stock the precious walls of high-end boutiques with multi-million dollar spectacle or to steward the modest task that reaffirms a creative commons? Imagine the posthumous scream of Edvard Munch himself as his

drawing was led to the gallows of the auction block—ultimately selling to the highest bidder for a whopping historic high at $119.9 million at Sotheby's in early May— the acuity of that contorted horror, a manifestation of the capitalization of despair.

So back to Colab, and in specific *The Real Estate Show*, a modest example of collective agency and solidarity…and friendship that has lasted 30 years.

—Ann Messner

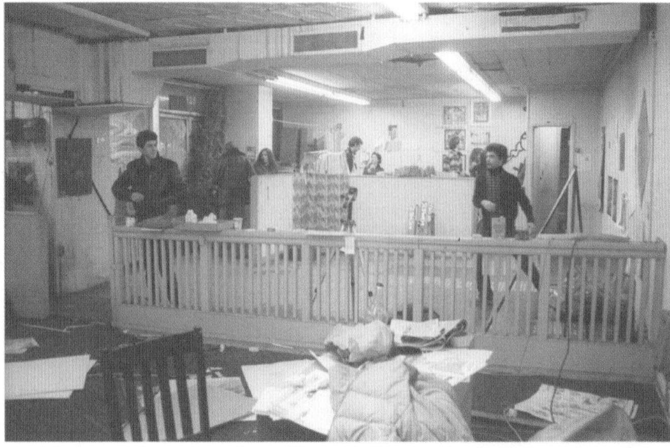

What is it about the shift from
1979 to 1980?

Looking back, it feels wrenching,
like the scrape of tectonic plates.

It was a hinge-moment of change,
from the nearly-bankrupt ghost
town of the 70s, to the mad gold-
rush stampede of predatory real
estate development that continues
in New York today.

We broke into an abandoned
building for our show about real
estate, which opened New Year's
Eve, 1979. Our ragtag bunch did
it—and, were rewarded for it—with
the space that became ABC No Rio.
Amazingly, 35 years later, we own
the whole building. With its program
of art and activism, it will remain
as what might be called a shrine to
defiance, long after we are gone.

Everyone loves a good outlaw story,
and, for me, this is how it began:

Growing up with the tumult
of assassinations, feminism,
and protests against the war in
Vietnam—dissent is in my bones.
Wending my way from a small
town upstate, I arrived in Lower
Manhattan in 1974, seeking the
community of artists. Nights of gliding
to openings, and days of grappling
with the reality of the precarious life
of an artist. Most artists were living
illegally, in commercial loft buildings.
If an inspector saw a houseplant in
a window, a bag of groceries, or a
bathtub—eviction!

By 1979, globally, tension was
high—60 American hostages were
taken in Iran. Here at home, real
estate values began to climb, and
stories emerged of fire marshals
forcibly evicting artists from lofts;
paintings and possessions dumped
on the street. Then, as now, a Black
woman—Elizabeth Mangum—was
brutally killed as she resisted
eviction from her home in the dead
of winter. Under the city glitter,
it felt grim, explosive.

My neighbor Ann Messner and I
both made guerilla public sculpture.

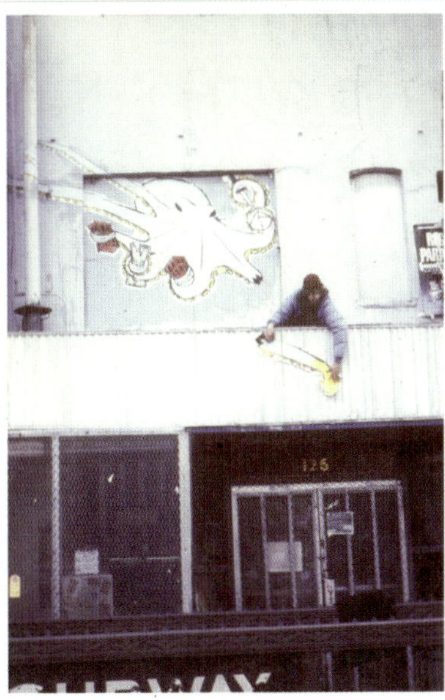

We didn't want to publicize the show too widely in advance; we didn't want to be stopped.

Mid-December, Alan and I made hand-out flyers to invite anyone to join us. Artists from Lower Manhattan and Downtown Brooklyn jumped in.

Entry to the building was done in stages. On Christmas Eve, under cover of night, Peter Moennig—with a few others—muscled the lock off the door with bolt-cutters, and installed our own lock. On Dec. 29, in broad daylight, we waltzed in like we owned the place. The sun was bright and the air was cold; I felt totally present and alive. You know, that breathless feeling, when things happen very quickly, and time feels frozen; not knowing what's next.

A steady stream of artists began to arrive. Some made work right on the spot, some brought work to install, some got so excited they ran home and made new pieces and brought them the next day. Fred Krughoff turned on the gas in the building; the heater worked! I cut stencils for posters for the show, spray-painted them right there, and immediately posted them on the street. Neighborhood people poked their heads in the door and stayed, discussing how they had been

Transgressive, nerve-wracking but exhilarating, too. One cold rainy day in November 1978, I met Alan. He wore sandals, with wet newspapers wrapped like socks. Odd sartorial touch, irresistible. We hooked up in 1979. Ann hooked up with German artist Peter Moennig, a former student of Joseph Beuys. We introduced Alan and Peter; the four of us began talking all the time. A core group was formed through proximity, friendship, and fun.

That spring, Collaborative Projects (Colab) artists organized exhibitions that addressed single issues. Alan wanted to do a show about real estate, and had stumbled upon a building on 123 Delancey Street —perfect! He and Peter cooked up the idea of: "Let's just break in and do it." Alan's friends in Colab weren't keen on this, so it simmered until we decided to do it anyway, and dedicated it to the murdered woman, Elizabeth Mangum.

fighting evictions for years. A group of kids came in, danced and drew on the walls.

We had a great opening party—Happy New Year!

However, the party was over when we returned to Delancey Street on January 2, to find that our lock had been removed, and a new one installed in its place. So what to do now?

We started making phone calls from the payphone on the corner. Fred McDarrah, the photographer for *The Village Voice*, arrived. He pointed out a car, in front of the building, full of City officials from Housing, Preservation, and Development (HPD), who were in charge of the building. To my surprise, Denny Kelly popped out of the car. Just as surprised, Denny said, "Hello Becky, what are you doing here?" I'd met her earlier, when she worked as a cafe waitress on Duane Street, where I'd worked on the construction crew. Now she was the assistant for the Assistant Commissioner. After some discussion, she and the HPD officials insisted on meeting us at their office downtown on Maiden Lane, at 6:30 pm that very day. At a rather tense meeting, they said absolutely they would not let us back into the building because first, we'd broken into it, and second, the building was on a site slated for "urban renewal" —the Seward Park Urban Renewal Area. (Thirty-five years later, they are just beginning construction…) They did give us a long list of buildings under HPD management to possibly relocate the show. We began looking the next day, January 3. It was brutally cold, the buildings were in terrible condition, with no heat. There were icicles hanging from the ceilings! Nothing was suitable.

On January 4, we artists met to figure out how to continue the show at 123 Delancey Street— for a short time—until January 22. We decided to hold a press conference and "Second Grand Opening," in front of the building on January 8. That day, a crowd of artists, reporters, city officials, and policeman gathered around the building. We were in luck; Joseph Beuys arrived with John Halpern and Ronald Feldman, his art dealer. He was in town for his exhibition at the Guggenheim Museum, and had given a talk at Cooper Union, where John, Peter, and Christof Kohlhöfer (another German artist) invited him to our press conference. Amazingly, he came—it felt like the cavalry had arrived.

We vaulted Joseph Nechvatal into the gap above the locked front doors, then he unlocked the side door on Norfolk Street. A couple of John Halpern's friends entered there and got upstairs. At this point the city officials and police got even more alarmed, and began to threaten to arrest anyone who entered. We decided

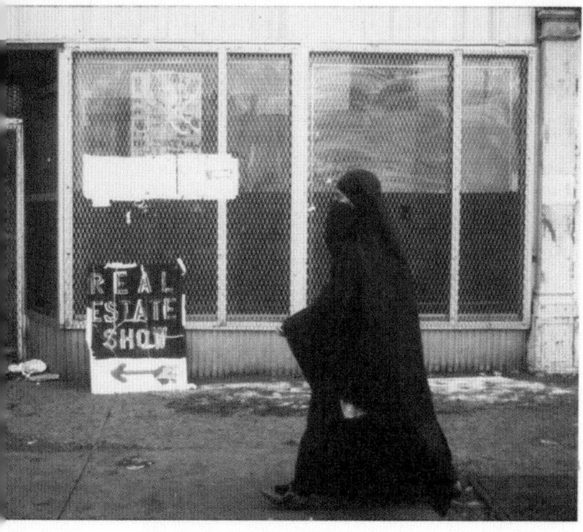

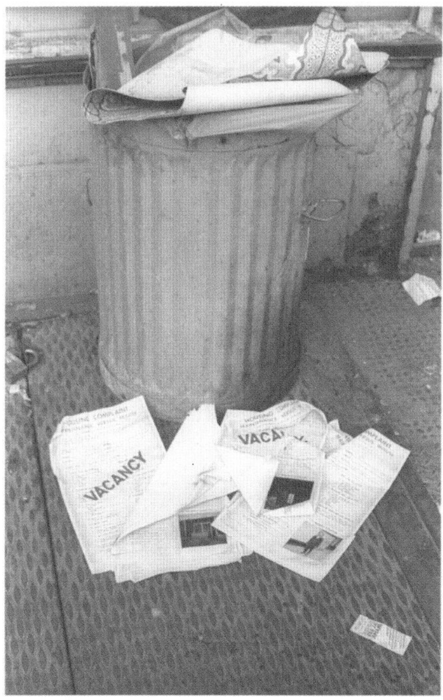

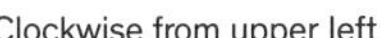

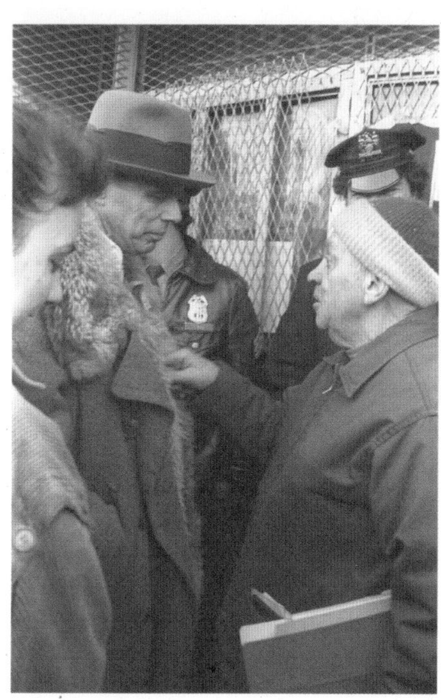

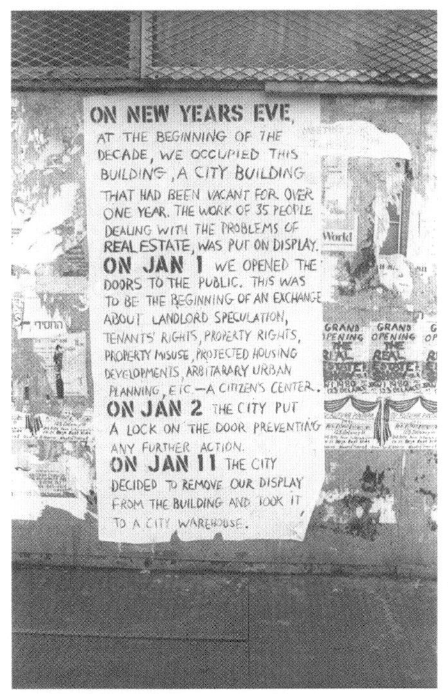

Clockwise from upper left:

Ann Messner. *The Real Estate Show at 123 Delancey Street*, 1980. Color photograph from 35mm negative film, 17.5 × 26.5 cm. Courtesy of Ann Messner.

Ann Messner. *Press conference outside 123 Delancey Street after it was relocked by the City. Joseph Beuys supports the occupation*, 1980. Photograph from B/W 35mm negative film, 26.5 × 17.5 cm. Courtesy of Ann Messner.

Ann Messner. *Poster announcing the sequence of events of Real Estate Show posted on 123 Delancey Street* (English version), 1980. Photograph from B/W 35mm negative film, 26.5 × 17.5 cm. Courtesy of Ann Messner

Ann Messner. *Remnants of The Real Estate Show destroyed by the City*,1980. Photograph from B/W 35mm negative film, 26.5 × 17.5 cm. Courtesy of Ann Messner.

not to force our way in, and as city marshals nailed the doors shut, we left to regroup.

We returned to the building a couple hours later, and surveyed it rather glumly. My 11-foot long Real Estate Octopus Mural was still taped to the storefront window. Peter offered to help me follow my original plan to glue the octopus to the front of the building, on the second story. He immediately gave me a leg-up, and I scrambled onto the top ledge. Harry Spitz joined me to wheat paste it to the wall. It was really windy, almost comical with the tentacles whipping around. My mural stayed up for about three months, and served as a symbolic occupation of the building.

A reporter from *The New York Times* had come to our press conference, and on January 9, his story and photograph ran on the front page of the *Metro Section*. But on January 11, the city moved our artwork from Delancey Street to a warehouse—Art held Hostage! We wanted it back, to continue both our show and the conversations we'd started with the local residents.

Denny Kelly held meetings with us, where she reiterated the city's position, but offered us a tiny temporary location at 172 Delancey Street. For six weeks—January 18 to the end of February ($5 rent!)—we did film screenings and performances there, while teams of artists searched for a more suitable space. My team found 156 Rivington Street—a storefront with a back courtyard filled with rubble, ailanthus trees and tremendous potential. We moved there in March 1980. We were astonished—what had started as a 3-week exhibition was now a space with unlimited possibilities.

Artists from Colab had joined us in *The Real Estate Show*, and later reimbursed us for some initial expenses. (We also got a similar amount from Artists Space, about $300). After deliberation, Colab members decided that they didn't want a physical location; it needed "administration." So, I signed a month-to-month lease with the city for an artist's studio in the storefront, and we started the process of forming our new organization, ABC No Rio.

That, of course, is a whole other story…

—Becky Howland

Clockwise from upper left:

Designer(s) Unknown. *The Real Estate Show*, 1980. Photocopy poster, 36 × 21.5 cm. For *The Real Estate Show*. Courtesy of Ann Messner.

Becky Howland. *Picture Your Future*, 1980. Photocopy poster, 21.5 × 28 cm. For *The Real Estate Show*. Courtesy of Bobby G (Robert Goldman).

Alan Moore (photograph), Tom Otterness (drawings) and Becky Howland (lettering). *Occupation Location*, 1980. Photocopy flyer, 21.5 × 28 cm. For *The Real Estate Show*. Courtesy of Becky Howland.

Mitch Corber, Becky Howland and Alan Moore, *Landlords Invited*, c. 1980 (back side). Photocopy flyer, 28 × 21.5 cm. Two-sided collaborative flyer for *The Real Estate Show*. Courtesy of Becky Howland.

Ann Messner (photograph), Becky Howland and others (artwork). *To Have Real Estate Show*, 1980. Photocopy and stenciled painted flyer, 21.5 × 28 cm. For *The Real Estate Show*. Courtesy of Bobby G (Robert Goldman).

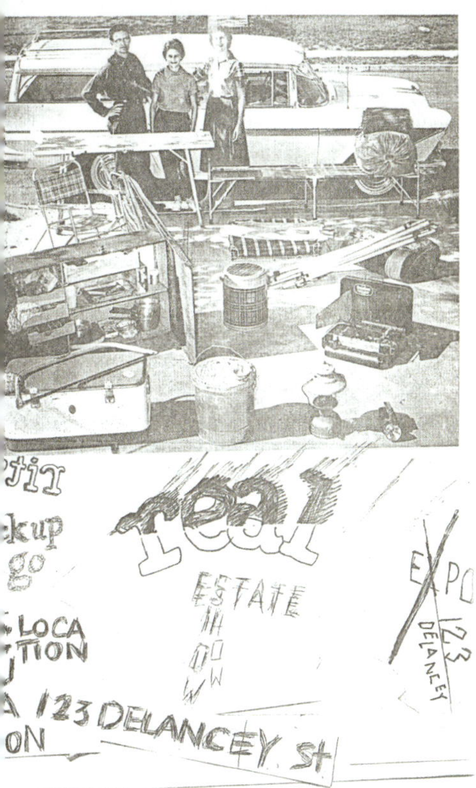
real
ESTATE
SHOW
EXPO
123 DELANCEY
LOCA
TION
123 DELANCEY St

PICTURE YOUR FUTURE
at
The Real Estate Show
AN ART EXPOSITION 123 DELANCEY St.
2nd Grand Opening
TUES. JAN. 8 - NOON

OC
CU
PA
TION
LOCA
TION
THE REAL
ESTATE
SHOW
at 123 DELANCEY
INSURRECTIONARY URBAN
DEVELOPMENT

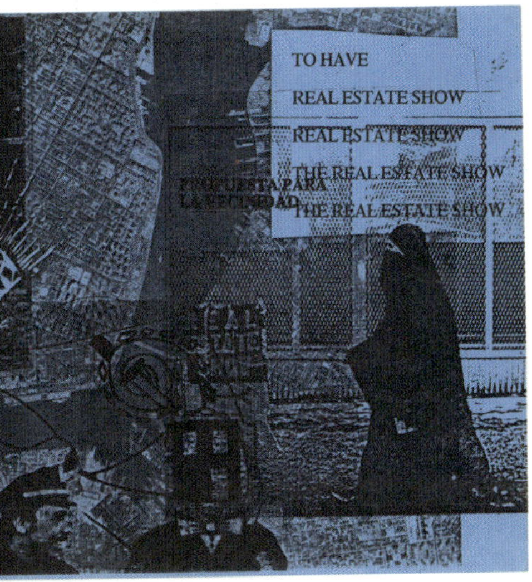
TO HAVE
REAL ESTATE SHOW
REAL ESTATE SHOW
THE REAL ESTATE SHOW
PROPUESTA PARA
LA VECINDAD
THE REAL ESTATE SHOW

REAL ESTATE
UNLOCK
BOLT
WISDOM
POWER
RICHES
GLORY

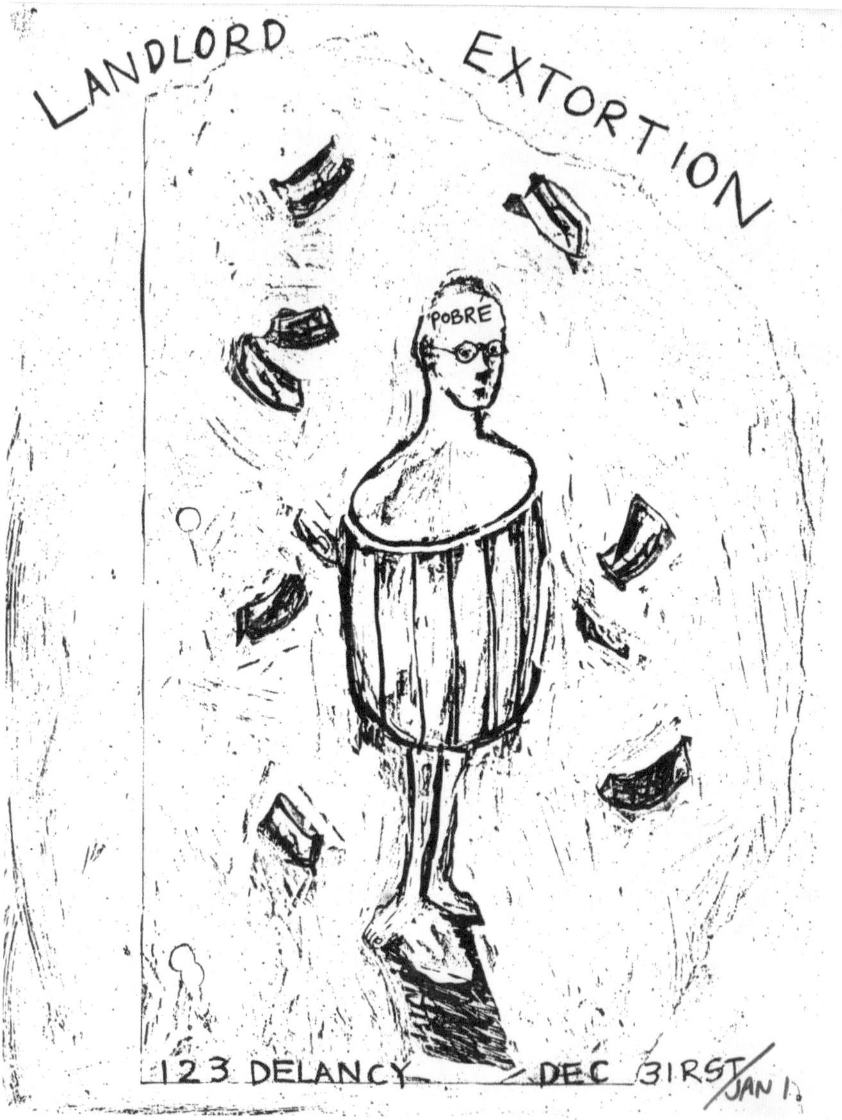

Coleen Fitzgibbon. *Landlord Extortion*, 1980. Photocopy and pen, 28 × 21.5 cm.
For *The Real Estate Show*. Courtesy of Bobby G (Robert Goldman).

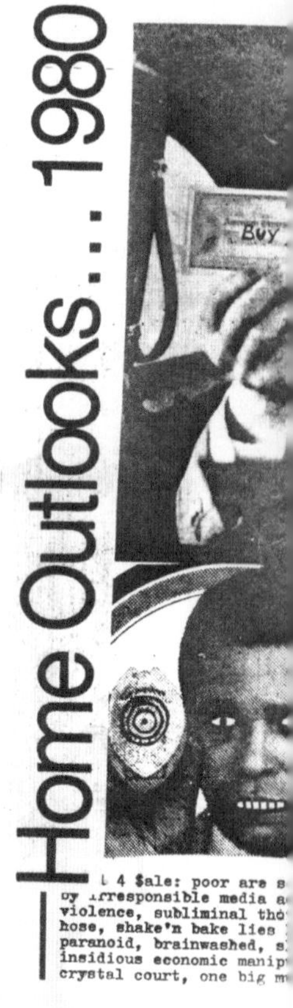

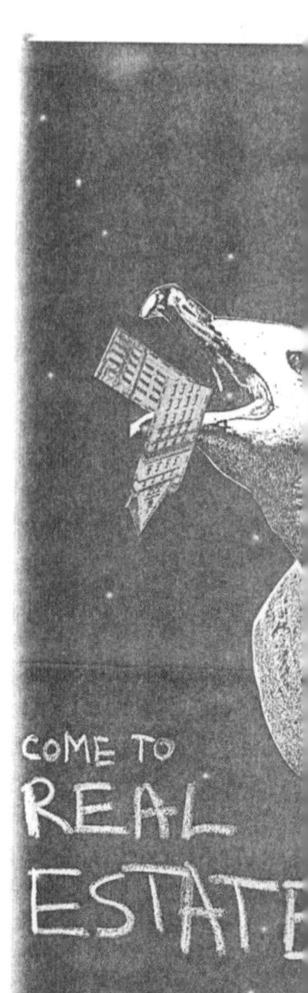

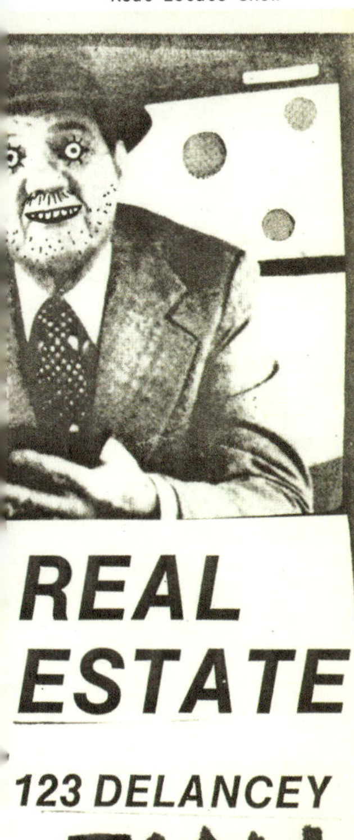

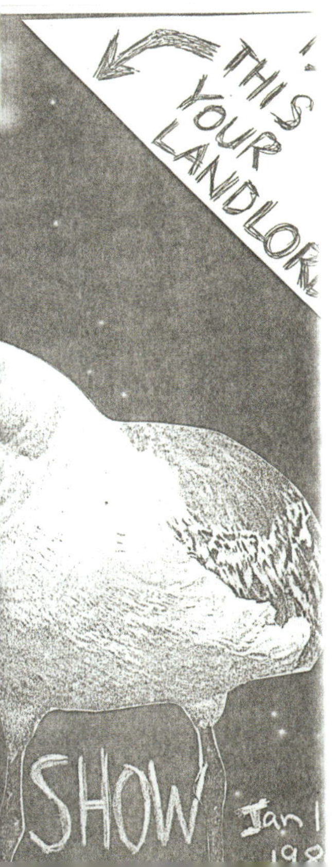

GRAND OPENING
JANUARY 1, 1980

"THE REAL ESTATE SHOW"

Rent is interest on a principal investment.

Peter Moenig is a criminal radical. His friends are socialist
terrorists. I would not go to any of their parties.

The whole art system is geared up to accept and embrace
radical initiatives. But only if they are useless. Only if they
do not trespass on social issues. Social issues are the province
of lawyers, politicians, of the noblesse who are obliged.
For artists to involve themselves seriously in social
issues means an intra-professional challenge, an unacceptable
trespass.

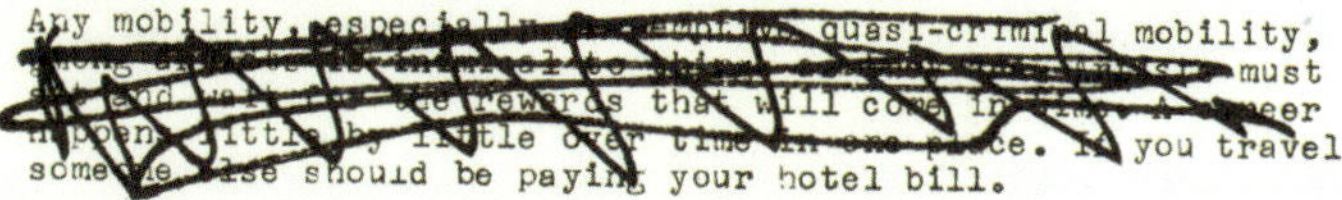

Clockwise from upper left:

Andy Baird. *Home Outlooks…,1980*. Photocopy, 28 × 21.5 cm.
Courtesy of Bobby G (Robert Goldman).

Alan Moore. *Draft of an unfinished Real Estate Show announcement*, 1980.
Photocopy, 28 × 21.5 cm. For *The Real Estate Show*. Courtesy of Ann Messner.

Christy Rupp. *Come to Real Estate Show*, 1980. Photocopy, 36 × 21.5 cm.
For *The Real Estate Show*. Courtesy of Ann Messner.

REAL
ESTATE at
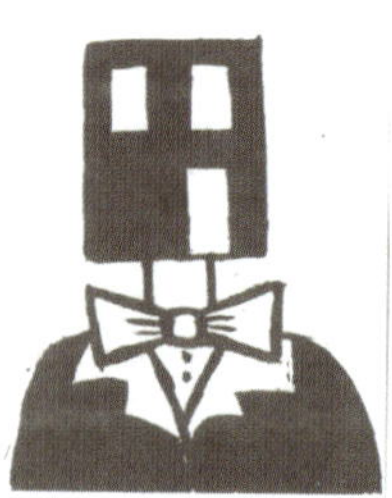

MUD CLUB FEB. 28
77 WHITE ST. 9:00 $4

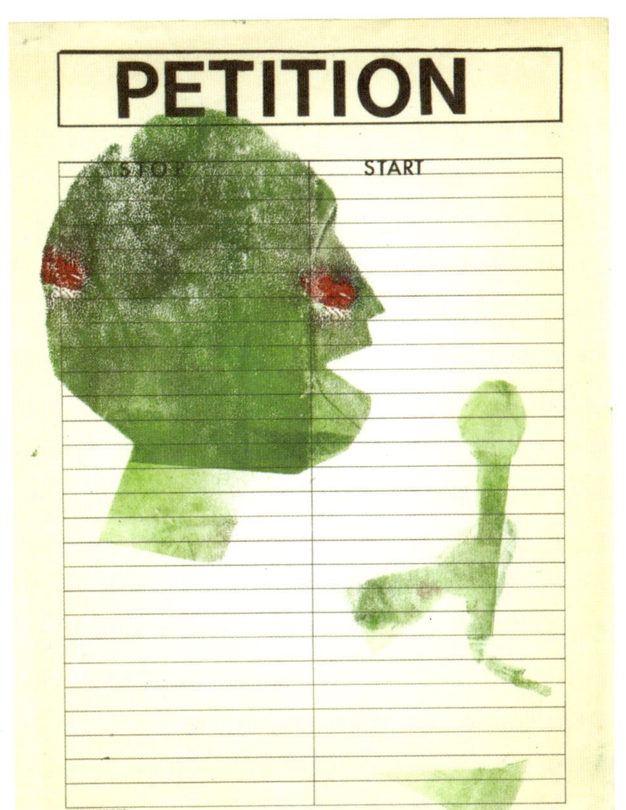

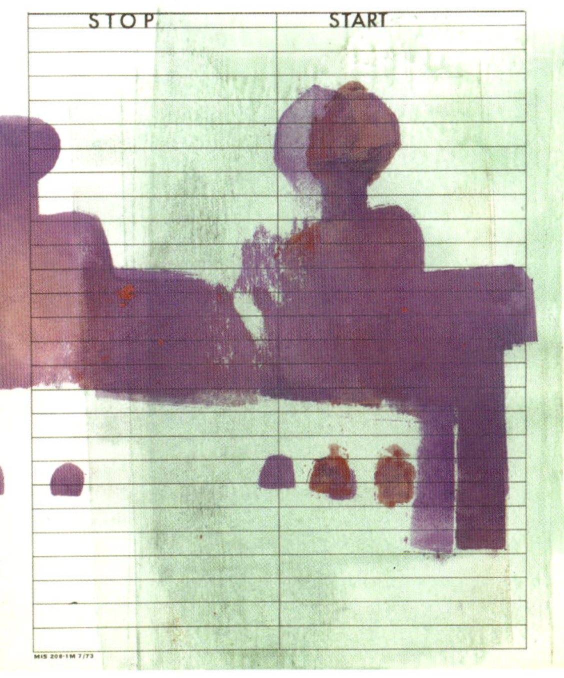

Clockwise from upper left:

Robin Winters. *Landlords*, 1980. Photocopy, 28 × 21.5 cm. Based on a sign found in the Lower East Side. Courtesy of Bobby G (Robert Goldman).

Robin Winters (poster), Alan Moore (painting). *Landlords*, 1980. Hand-painted photocopy, 28 × 21.5 cm. Courtesy of Becky Howland.

Alan Moore. *Petition (face and microphone) / Petition (figures at panel)*, 1980. 28 × 21.5 cm each. Hand-painted petition forms made for a mock Housing Commission hearing performance at the Mudd Club. Courtesy of Becky Howland.

Becky Howland (artwork) and unknown designer. *Real Estate*, 1980. Photocopy, 21.5 × 28 cm. Poster for a mock Housing Commission hearing performance at the Mudd Club. Courtesy of Bobby G (Robert Goldman).

THE REAL ESTATE SHOW

started the 80's with a break. The lower East Side Community,
artists, and art watchers were surprised by the positive action
of artists occupying the building on 125 Delancey street
for a display of art, architecture and urban planning. The
possibility for development despite repressive structures became
apparent. The old conception of the creative artist realizing
his aim of freedom through the contemplation of art pieces was
questioned.

The illusion of free available space promoted throughout
modern art and represented in the American society by the mis-
conception of equal opportunities for everybody does not work!
Thought can only be realized through the initiation of
real progress. Without this the intellectual gambling of elitist
art circles will never reach a function of art oriented on human
needs.

The initial flyer for the real Estate Show calls
the intention of the action to show that artists are willing and able
to place themselves and their work squarely in a context which shows
solidarity with oppressed people; a recognition that merchantile and
institutional structures oppress and distance artists lives and works;
and that artists living and working in depressed
communities are comrades in the re-evaluation of property and the
whitening of neighborhoods. These are the cocerns of the artists who
spread out into a community to learn and to change.

Such a concept gives art the social strength since the
rising ambitious bourgeosie made itself the sponsor for artists.
Culture does not have to be a useless parasite of people's wealth;
it has someting to offer which goes further than the intellectual
play.

This project started as an open process of permanent change.

The experience of the group so far is that A strong idea has many faces.
Being stopped by a bourocracy without fantasy does not
only improves the flexibility to
elude useless confrontations to elaborate new strategies for other

The Real Estate Show.....

CONTINUES

ITEMS FOR AGREEMENT submitted to HPD:

1.) That the Real Estate Show be allowed to reopen at 123 Delancey Street for the period commencing January 8 and ending January 22, ~~18~~ 1980.

Understanding that the premises of 123 Delancey Street will be entirely vacated by sundown of ~~xxxx~~ January 22, 1980.

2.) That the gas and electric utilities in the building at 123 Delancey Street be turned on for the period Jan 8-22.

Understanding that the Committee for the Real Estate Show will reimburse the City for the expense of utilities during the period Jan 8-22. (An estimated sum can be put aside in escrow if the City is desirous.)

3.) That the City coordinate a program between its agencies (HPD, Dept of Gen. Serv., and Dept of Real Estate) whereby artists can become managing agents and temporary on=site tenants of buildings scheduled for demolition and vacant or under-used City facilities.

Understanding that these buildings would be cases inwhich no short term commercial usage is feasible- anmd that the artist tenants use the buildings solely for the preparation and display of exhibitions.

. . . .

WHAT THIS IS

The Real Estate Show is a collective exposition open to all artists and exhibitors. The Committee for the Real Estate Show is an organizing group that finally determines its actions at general meetings of the exhibitors.

This is a new kind of art show. It is interactive and collective. During the 3 day course of the exhibition (set-up Jan. 30; recpption Jan. 31; and public opening abertura publico Jan. 1 1980) we found the spacing of single artworks at 123 Delancey dissolved. Art works were placed together, their individuality merged, and new expressions arose. Artists in show began to prepare work specifically for the building.

First Children, then adults from the neighborhood came into the Real Estate Show. The children drew on the walls, and organized a theatrical group using a shower curtain and a flashlight. Adult visitors to the show sang and danced, and expressed interest in volunteering to work with the children at 123 Delancey Street.

All of this spontaneous and planned activity has been crushed by the City padlocking of the Real Estate Show.

REAL ESTATE

123 DELANCEY

Facing page:

Committee for *The Real Estate Show. Draft for a Real Estate Show Manifesto*, 1980.
Typewritten, hand-edited collaborative manuscript, 28 × 42 cm. Courtesy of Kiki Smith.

This page:

Committee for *The Real Estate Show. Real Estate Show Manifesto*, 1980. Photocopy, 28 × 21.5 cm.
For *The Real Estate Show.* Courtesy of Bobby G (Robert Goldman).

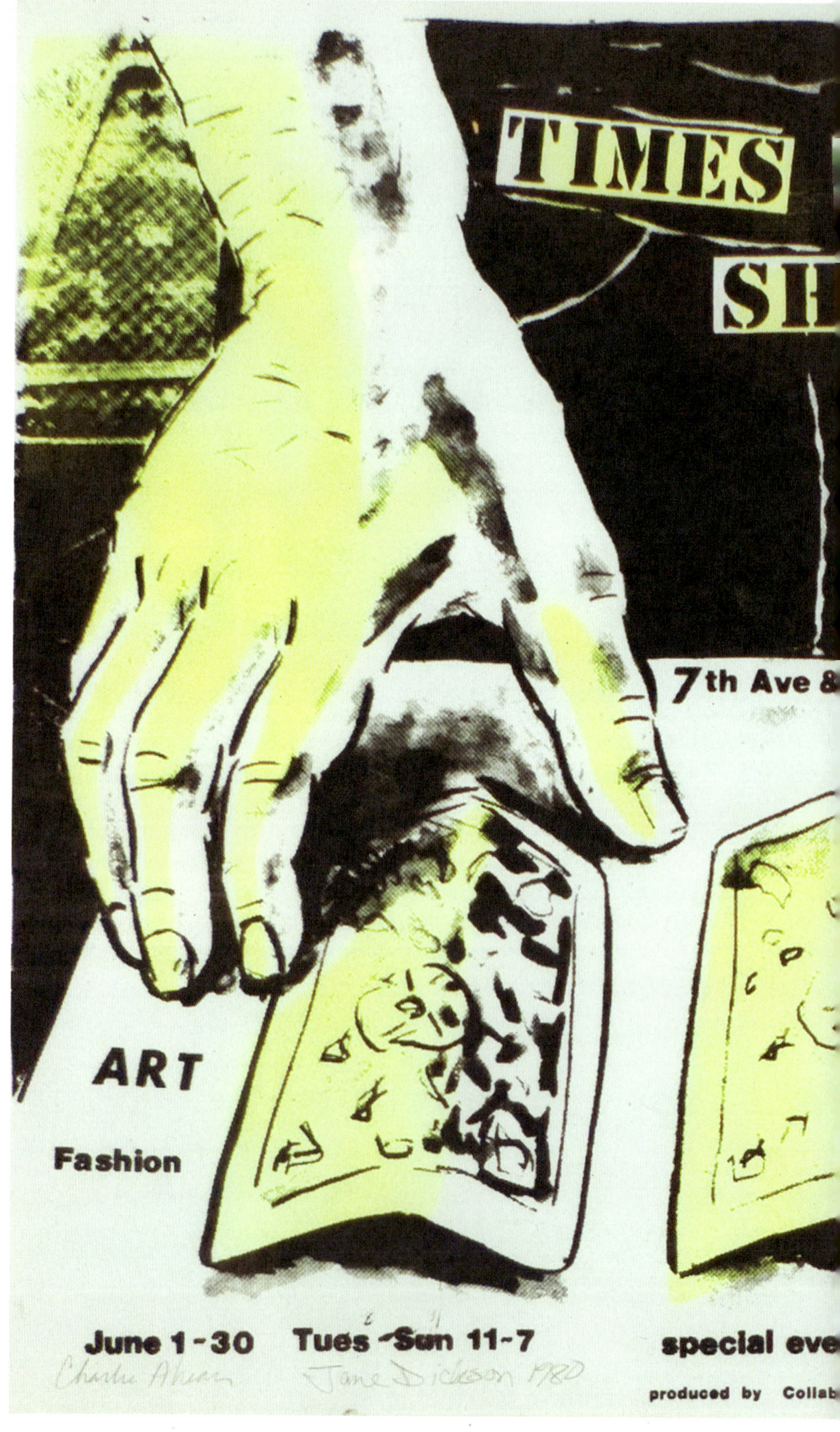

Charlie Ahearn and Jane Dickson. *Times Square Show Poster*, 1980. Screenprint and spray paint on paper, 65 × 78 cm (framed). Courtesy of Jane Dickson. Photo: Nancy Linn.

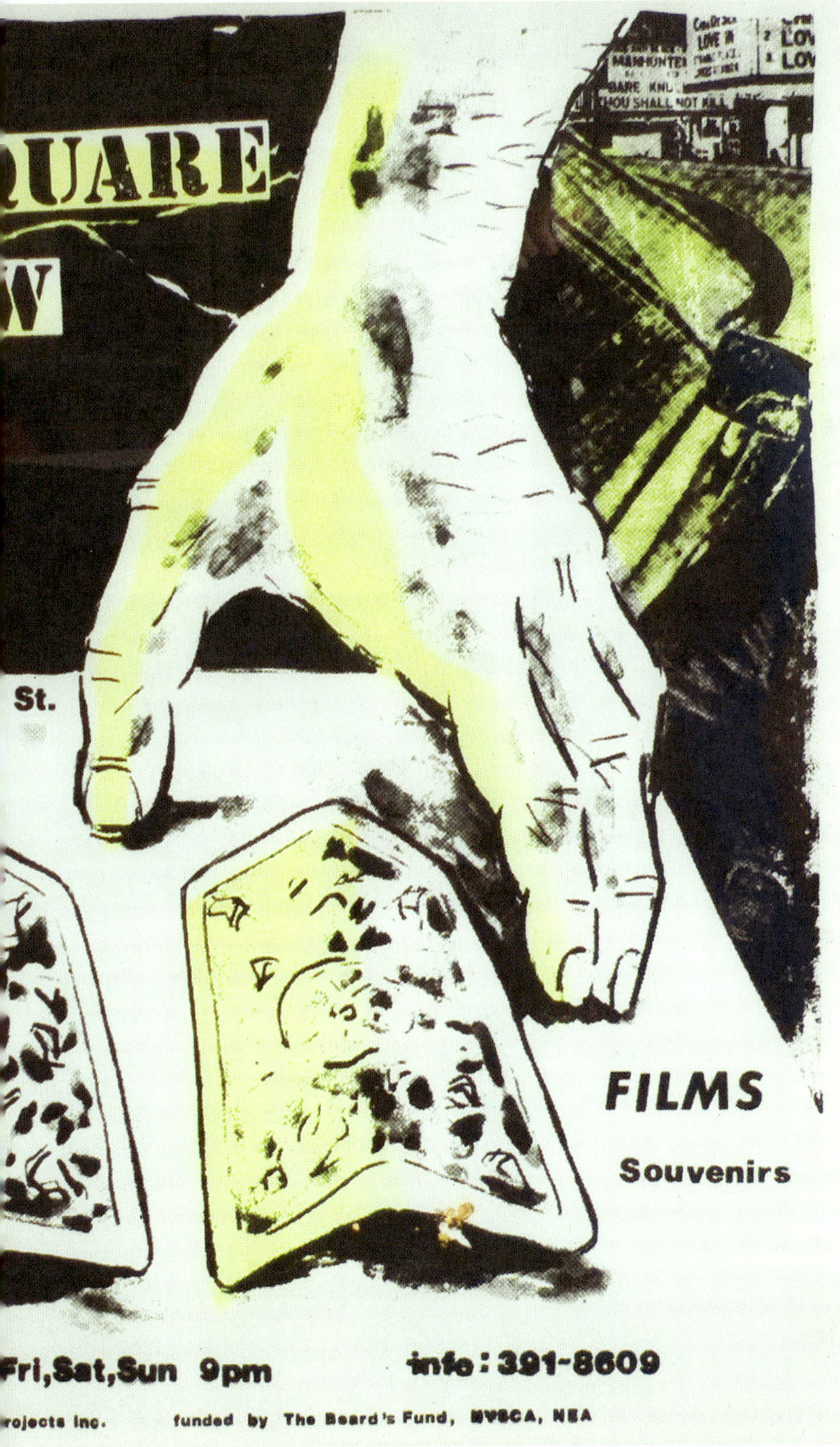
QUARE
W
St.
FILMS
Souvenirs
Fri,Sat,Sun 9pm   info: 391-8609
rojects Inc.   funded by The Beard's Fund, NYSCA, NEA

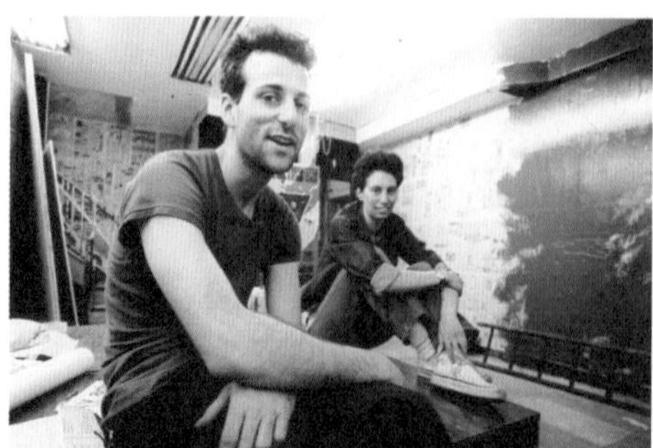

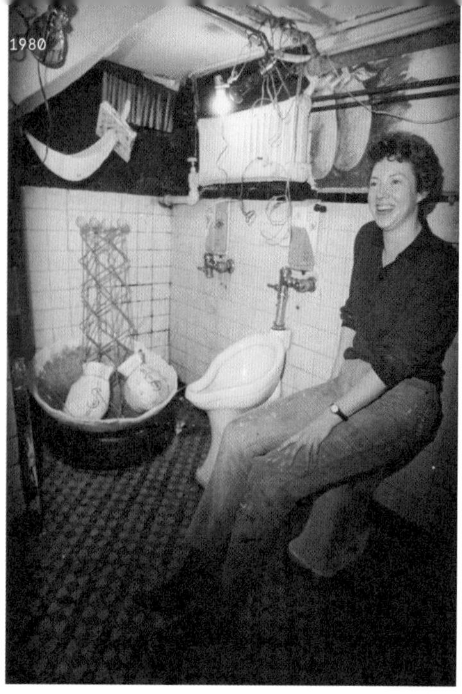

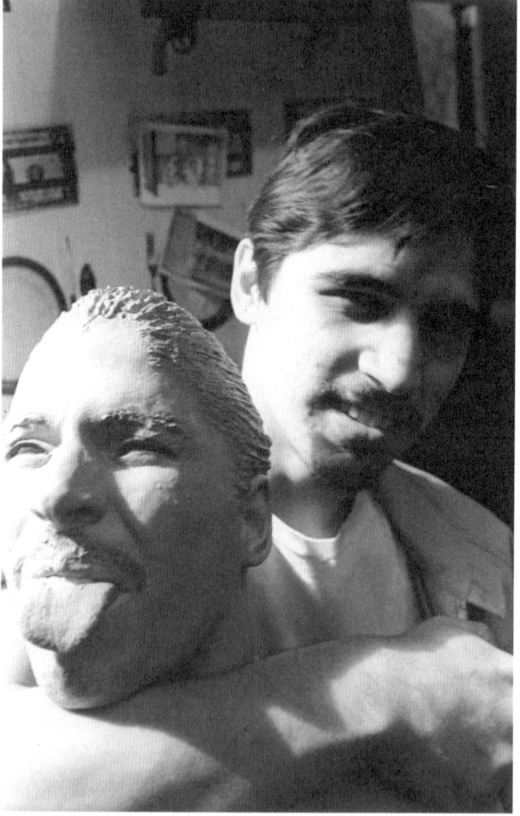

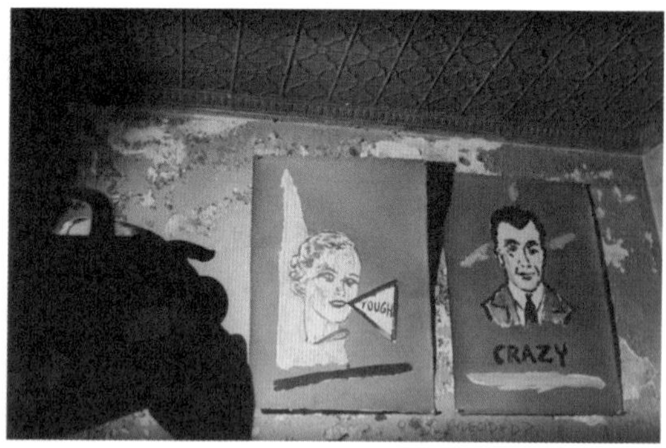

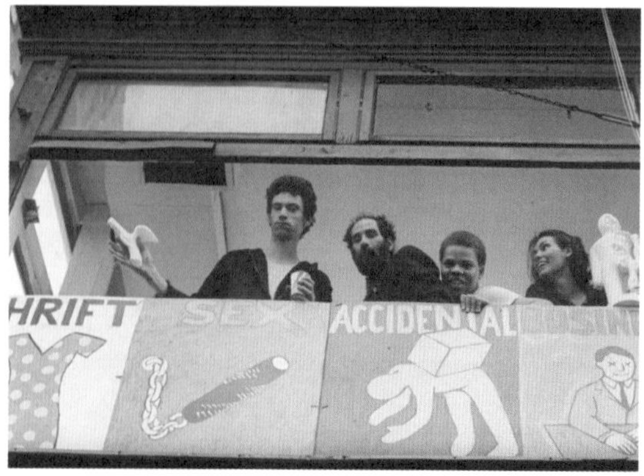

I am the hidden artist from *The Times Square Show*. I was the artist of an installation piece called *Man Killed by Air Conditioner*. The piece was mentioned in numerous articles at the time and was later referred to in an article on Jean-Michel Basquiat in the *NY Times Magazine*—all of which appeared sans mon nom. A drawing of the piece by Tom Otterness was displayed on the TSS building exterior (in the collection of John Ahearn and recently displayed at Hunter College's *Times Square Show Revisited*) and I exist as the unnamed inspiration. History is for the winners.

—Dick Miller

Clockwise from upper left:

All Francene Keery (documentation of the installation of *The Times Square Show*). *Matthew Geller and Teri Slotkin; Becky Howland with her Oil Rig Fountain installation; Tough/Crazy installation (paintings by Robin Winters); Window view of Alan Moore, Coleen Fitzgibbon, and others at The Times Square Show; Rigoberto Torres with John Ahearn cast, All 1980.* Silver gelatin prints, 25 × 20 cm each. Courtesy of John Ahearn and Francene Keery. © Francene Keery. NYC. All Rights Reserved.

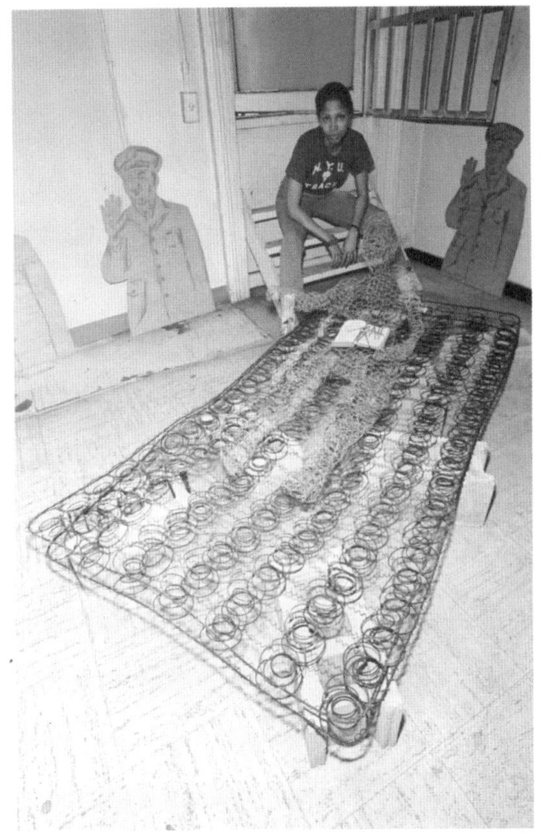

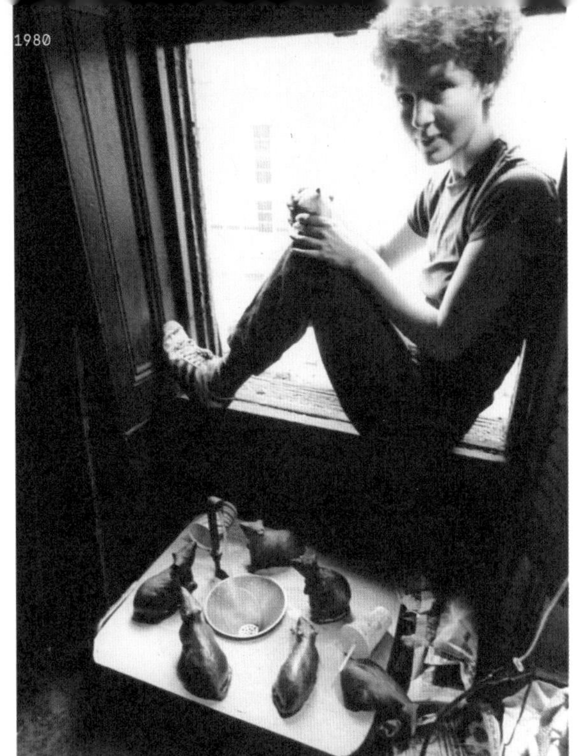

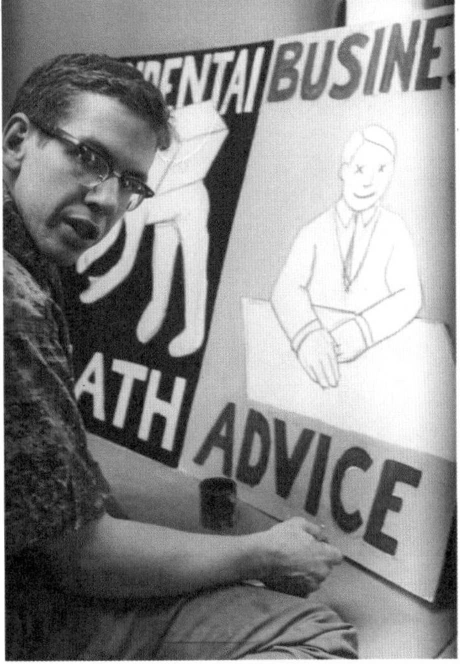

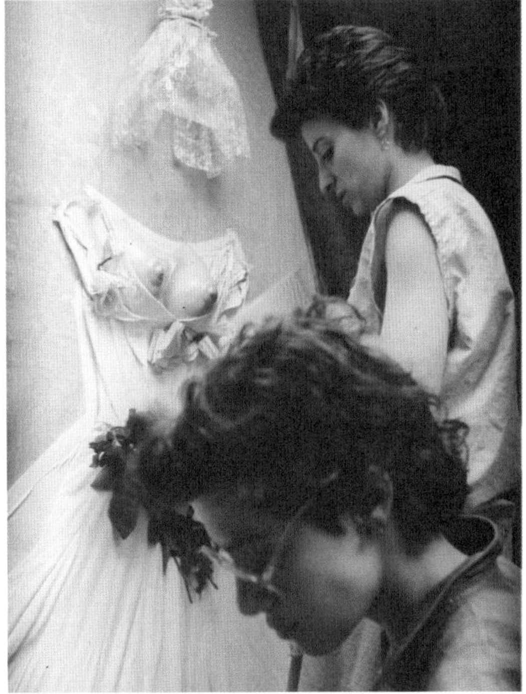

Clockwise from upper left:

All Francene Keery. *Candace Hill-Montgomery in her installation
"92 Morningside, Remember Fred Hampton;" Christy Rupp
with her Rats installation; Jane Sherry and Eileen Meyer installing;
Tom Otterness painting signs.* 1980. Silver gelatin prints,
25 × 20 cm each. © Francene Keery. NYC. All Rights Reserved.
Courtesy of John Ahearn and Francene Keery.

TIMES SQUARE

201 west 41st street & 7th avenue   Exhibition

FRIDAY   JUNE 6

7 PM $2
CONGO OYE video by Bill Stephens
with Eldridge Cleaver
(People's Communication Network Inc.)

9 PM $2.50
PSYCHIC PLAQUE performed by Gary Indiana
VIVA, VIVA film by Michel Auder
with Undine & Viva

Midnight $2
MINUS ZERO film by Michael Oblowitz

SATURDAY   JUNE 7

7 PM $2
TOPLESS film by Jane Sherry & Cara Perlman
WORD OF MOUTH film by Aline Mayer
JANE MANSFIELD & BARBARA STREISAND &
LADY WRESTLERS films courtesy Video X
9 PM $2.50
THE OFFENDERS film by Scott B & Beth B
with Adele Bertei   John Lurie   Bill Rice   Lydia Lunch
UN CHANT D'AMOR film by Jean Genet

Midnight $2
SINGLE ROOM FURNISHED feature film
with Jane Mansfield

SUNDAY   JUNE 8

7 PM $2
MACHDOX SEX video by Mark Pauline
INSPECTOR HOWE video by Beth B & Scott B
OVERLOAD film by Larry Meltzer

9 PM $2.50
SCORPIO RISING film by Kenneth Anger
WIDE ANGLE SAXON film by George Landow
TIDSTORY film by Bing Lee   RHYTHM film by Bick Greenwald
WHO SHALL REMAIN NAMELESS film by Peter von Ziegesar
Midnite $2
AMAZONAS & SICK SICK SISTER video by Mark Rabon

FRIDAY   JUNE 13

7 PM $2
TRIPE video by Betsy Sussler
(A Nightshift Production)
SLEEPLESS NIGHTS video by Becky Johnson

9 PM $2.50
THE JONES' film by Steve Brown, Ellie Nagler &
Barry Shils
TWINS film by Charlie Ahearn

Midnite $2
JACK SMITH presents EXOTIC LANDLORDISM OF THE W
with Sinbad Glick & the Brassiere Girls of Bagdad   (t

SATURDAY   JUNE 14

7 PM $2
THIEF OF BAGDAD with Sabu   (1949)

9 PM $2.50
JACK SMITH presents EXOTIC LANDLORDISM OF THE W
with Sinbad Glick & the Brassiere Girls of Bagdad
(theatre)

Midnight $2
JACK SMITH presents EXOTIC LANDLORDISM OF THE W
with Sinbad Glick & the Brassiere Girls of Bagdad
(theatre)

SUNDAY   JUNE 15

7 PM $2
STUART SHERMAN music & video
RELATIVELY TORTURED film by Willie Lenski

9 PM $2.50
TERENCE SELLERS performs
REGGAE FILM Jamaican bands

Midnite   free admission/contribution
Memorial Screening of ECSTATIC STIGMATIC
film by Gordon Stevenson   with Mirielle Cervenka

The TIMES SQUARE SHOW is a project of COLLABORATIVE PROJECTS INC.
funded in part by NYSCA, NEA, Beards Fund.

OPENING NIGHT JUNE 1   with live music of the

EVENTS
...ARE SHOW

This spread and following page:

Beth B and Scott B (design).
Times Square Show Programming Posters,
1980. Offset printed newsprint,
57 × 73 cm each. Courtesy of Bobby G
(Robert Goldman)

...es thru Sun daily in June 11–6:00   info: 391–8609

...AY JUNE 20

free movies until midnight
PEOPLE ARE RISING Third World Newsreel

DREAD, BEAT & BLOOD Linton Kwesi Johnson

ONLY THE BEGINNING Third World Newsreel

BREAK AND ENTER Third World Newsreel

...te
NIGHTSHIFT THEATRE

FRIDAY JUNE 27

7 PM $2
 RAPE RAVAGE & ROLL UTOPIA OR ELSE
  performance by Ilona Granet
 JANE GRETSCHNEIDER film & video

9 PM $2.50
 MICHAEL SMITH performance
 NOSFERATU film by Murnau (1922)
 1920s films: DARE DEVILS DANCING ELECTROCUTION
  FLOODS ASSASSINATION FIRES & MARILYN MONROE
Midnight $2
  film by Jim Jarmusch

...RDAY JUNE 21

$2
 AGAINST THE GRAIN film by Tim Burns
 THE HUMAN COMMODITY film by Mindy Stevenson

$2.50
 CAZ PORTER theatre
 NO JAPS AT MY FUNERAL film by James Nares

...ght
NIGHTSHIFT THEATRE

SATURDAY JUNE 28

7 PM free
 SLIDE SHOW by Nan Goldin
 GOD'S POLICE & 100s

9 PM $2.50
 CHRISTOF KOHLHOFER presents films
 LINDZEE SMITH theatre

Midnite $2
 RICK GREENWALD 100s

...DAY JUNE 22

$1
 PERSONAL PROBLEMS A Black Soap Opera
  video by Bill Stephens
  (Reed/Cannon Communications Inc.)

$2.50
 LIVE MARTIAL ARTS SHOW by Nathan Ingram
 DEADLY ART OF SURVIVAL film by Charlie Ahearn

...ight $2
 A BOY FROM THE CITY
 TELEVISION & PHONICS video by Kenny Scharf

SUNDAY JUNE 29

7 PM $2
 THE HAMLET OF THE SHCHIGROVSKY DISTRICT
  performed by DOI Garner   (Turgenev)
 WONDERWOMAN film by Dara Birnbaum

9 PM $4.00   CLOSING NIGHT EXTRAVAGANZA
 RHAPS & RAP   FASHION
 THE DYNELLS   LIVE MUSIC
 FRAMED TEARDROP video by Walter Robinson &
  Paul Dougherty   soundtrack SUICIDE
 Y FANTS   LIVE MUSIC

Thanks to Robert Gordon, Anfour Corporation, National Video Industries, Department
of Cultural Affairs, Spectacolor Inc., Sandra Devlin, Richard Barkley 111 Workshop,
Anonymous

...EATS plus ERIKA van DAMN   food   juke box

TIMES SQUAR

201 west 41st street & 7th avenue   Exhibition open Tues thru

THURSDAY 19 JUNE	FRIDAY 20 JUNE	SATURDAY 21 JUNE

8 PM PURE STARCH video by Mitch Corber
TOO LAZY TO LIVE film by Vivian Dick & Bobby Swope
A TOOTH MOVIE film by Bumpie-Kitchener Productions
CITY WILD LIFE: MICE, RATS & ROACHES video by
        Christy Rupp
 	
10 PM $2.50
 	
KIDNAPPED by Eric Mitchell
 	
11:30 PM $2.50
 	
PETIT MAL & SOOTHING THE BRUISE films by
        Betzy Bromberg
HUSTLE OF THE HEART & NATURAL TALENT films by
        Lauren Abrams
	7 PM FREE until Midnight
	
	DREAD, BEAT & BLOOD Linton Kwesi Johnson
	PEOPLE ARE RISING, ONLY THE BEGINNING, BREAK &
	        ENTER Third World Newsreels
	
	Midnight $2.
	
	NIGHTSHIFT THEATRE
		7 PM $2
		
		AGAINST THE
		THE HUMAN CO
		
		9 PM $2.50
		
		CAZ PORTER
		NO JAPS AT
		
		Midnight $2.
		
		NIGHTSHIFT

THURSDAY 26 JUNE	FRIDAY 27 JUNE	SATURDAY 28 JUNE

8 PM $2.50
 	
BETTER, STRONGER video by Ed & Tom Bowes
VIDEO SHOW by Jane Brettschneider, Jeff Turtletaub &
        Mark Kehoe
 	
10 PM $2.50
 	
PREMIERE! TRUE CROSS FIRE a new video by
        Judy Rifka & Matthew Geller
 	
11:30 PM $2.50
 	
PREMIERE! TRUE CROSS FIRE a new video by
        Matthew Geller & Judy Rifka
	7 PM $2.
	
	RAPE RAVAGE & ROLL UTOPIA OR ELSE performance by
	        Ilona Granet
	VIDEO SHOW by Jane Brettschneider
	
	9 PM $2.50
	
	MICHAEL SMITH performance,
	NOSFERATU film by Murnau (1922) & other "Greats"
	        from the 1920s
	
	Midnight $2.
	
	FILM SHOW by Jim Jarmish
		7 PM FREE
		
		SLIDE SHOW
		GOD'S POLI
		
		9 PM $2.50
		
		FILM SHOW
		THEATRE by
		
		Midnight $2.
		
		FILM SHOW

The TIMES SQUARE SHOW is a project of COLLABORATIVE PROJECTS INC.

Funded in part by NYSCA, NEA, Beard's Fund.

SOUVENIR SHOP OPEN

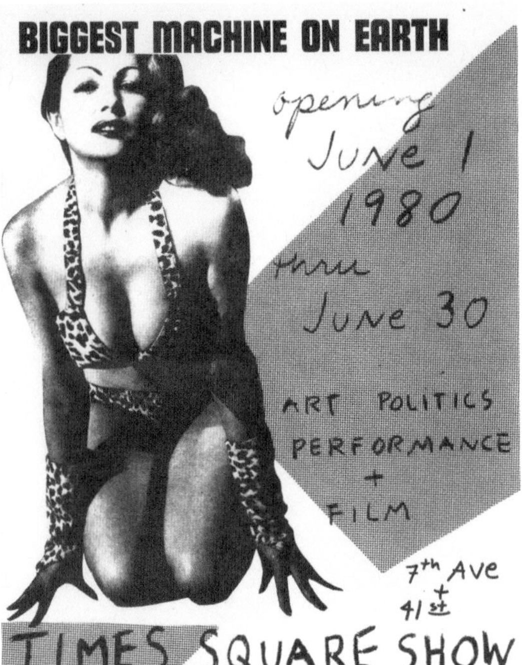

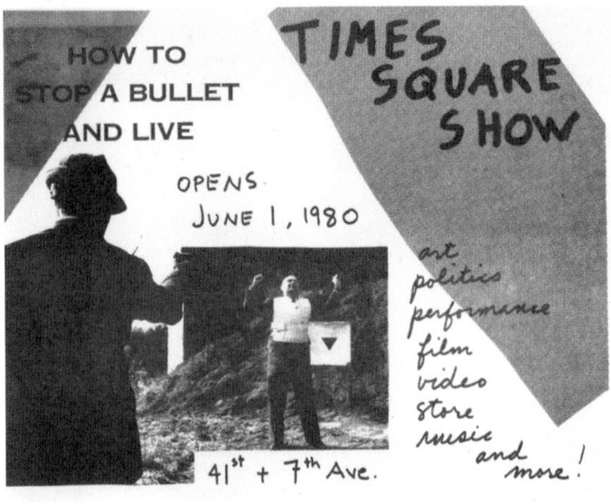

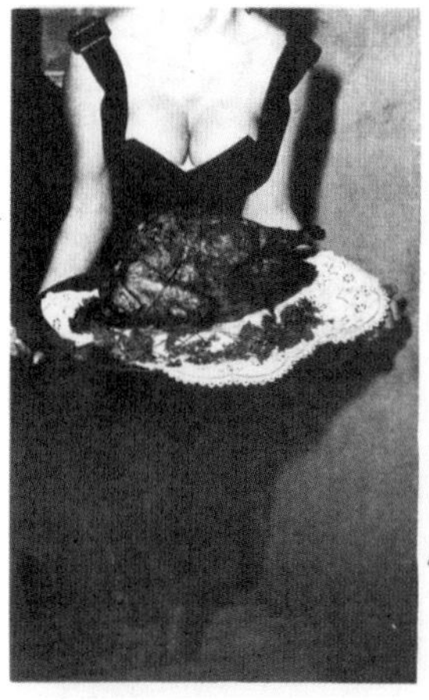

Clockwise from upper left:

Jane Sherry. *Biggest Machine on Earth*, 1980.
Photocopy flyer, 28 × 21.5 cm.

Jane Sherry. *How to Stop a Bullet and Live*, 1980
Photocopy flyer, 21.5 × 28 cm.

Jane Sherry. *Times Square Show,* 1980. Photocopy flyer,
21.5 × 28 cm.

Andrea Callard. *TV Ads*, 1980. Photocopy flyer,
28 × 21.5 cm. Schedule of TV Ads.

Unknown. *Ecstatic Stigmatic*, 1980. Photocopy handbill,
21.5 × 14 cm. Announcement for screening of *Ecstatic
Stigmatic* by Gordon Stevenson.

All for *The Times Square Show*. All courtesy of Bobby G
(Robert Goldman).

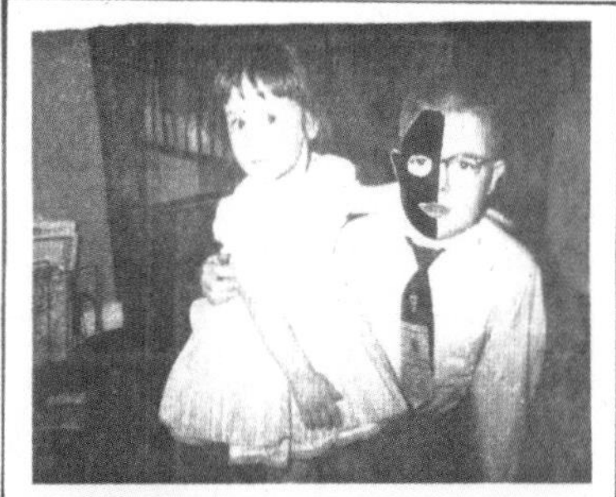

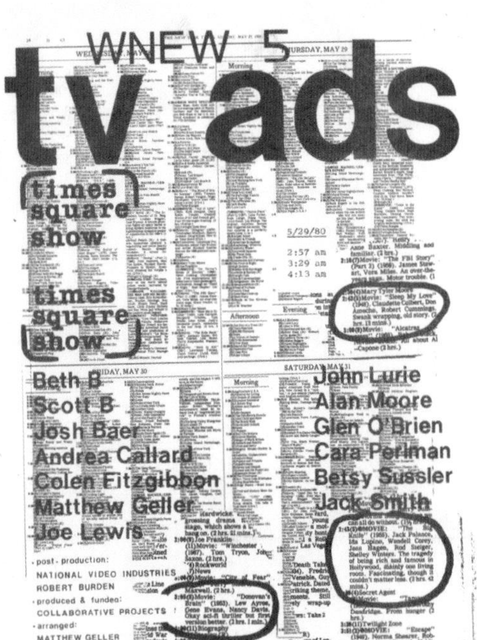

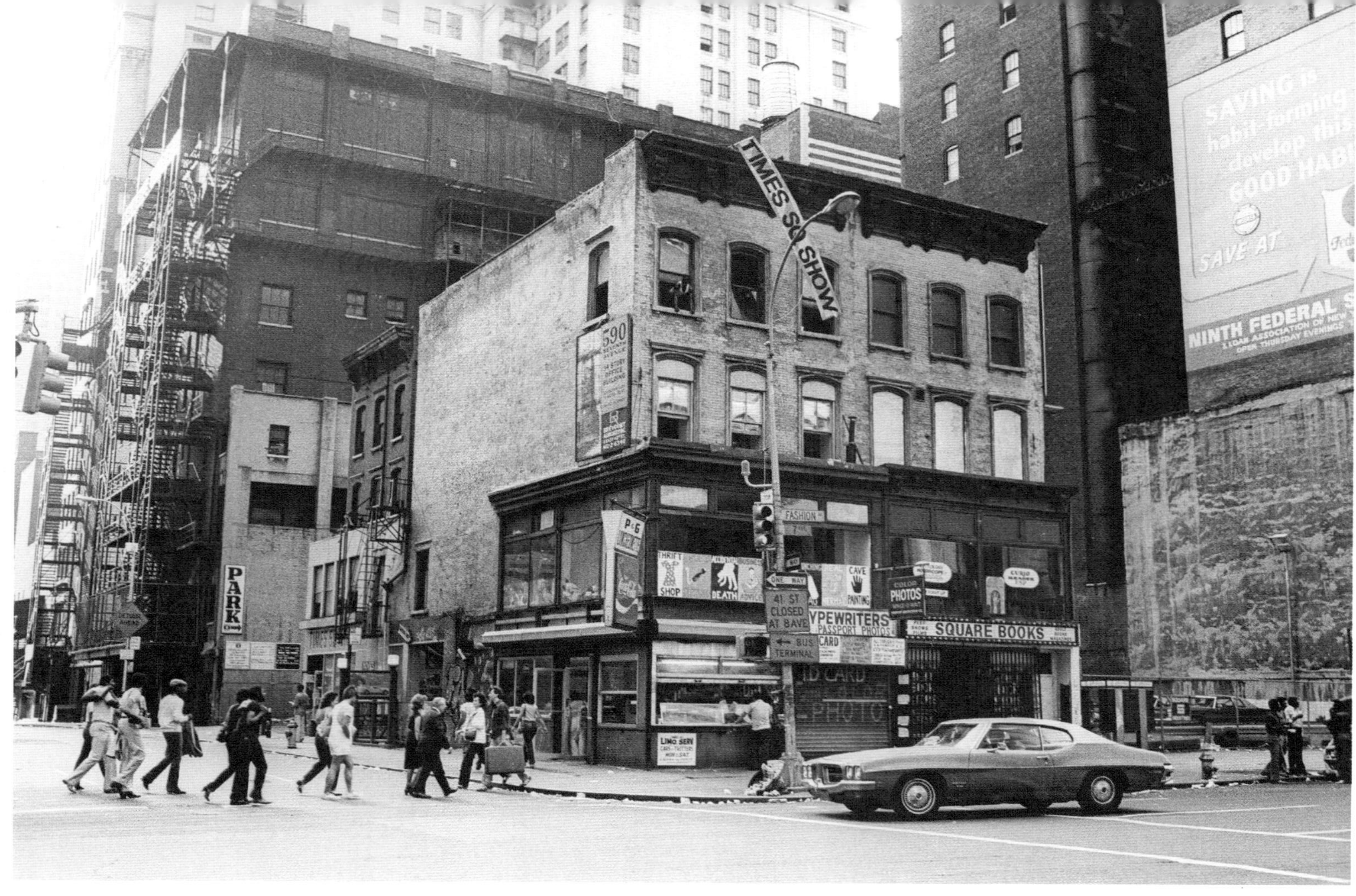

Lisa Kahane. *Exterior of Times Square Show*: 1980. Silver gelatin print, 40 × 50 cm. Courtesy of Lisa Kahane. © Lisa Kahane, NYC. All Rights Reserved.

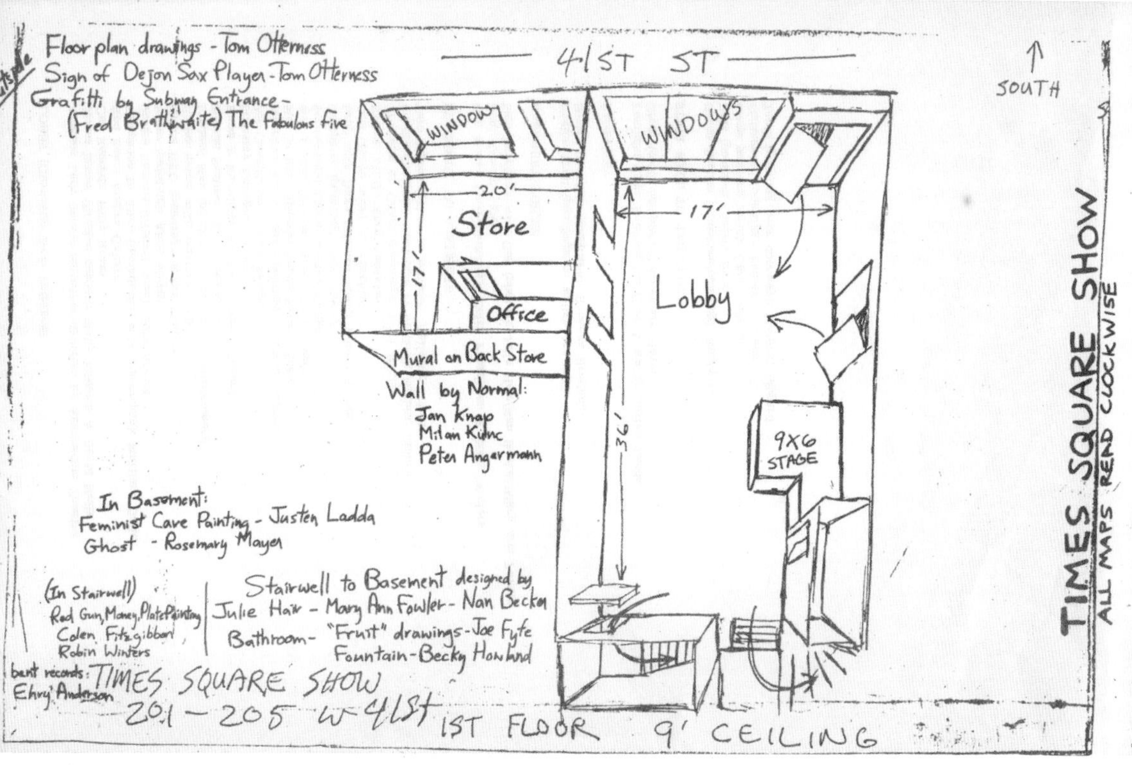

Tom Otterness (drawing) and John Ahearn (lettering and lists). *Times Square Floor Plan [First Floor]*, 1980. Photocopy on colored paper, 21.5 × 36 cm each. For *The Times Square Show*. Courtesy of John Ahearn.

LOBBY (Clockwise from Entrance)

Amazon Lady (movie cutout):contributed by Amsterdam Theatre
James Brown (lifesize puppet): Wally Edwards & David Wells
Cut Records: Willy Heeks
Red Rake: Andrea Callard
Telephone to Alice (installation with mannequin): Matthew Geller
Janice Parsons (lifecast head): John Ahearn
Boxer (painting): Aline Mayer
Crime NYC (painting): Robin Winters
Italian movie still: Matthew Geller
Chained Man (painting): Candace Hill Montgomery
Special Summer: Reese Williams
News & Nuitrician (poster): Andrea Callard
Stairway Collages: Bobby G
Air Conditioner: Kenny Scharf
Ailanthus Leaves (wall painting): Andrea Callard
Man in Blue (lifecast head): Robert Torres
Man in Red (lifecast head): John Ahearn
Second-hand Clock: Andrea Callard
Cleopatra (painting): Jane Sherry
Lady with Tears (lifecast head): Robert Torres
Doll (above door): L. Abrahms
Record L.U.D.: Ehry Anderson
Crocidile on Couch (painting): Scott Miller
Phallic Ceramics (sculpture in window): Micheal Bidlo
Taro Yawns (photo on window): Wolfgang Staehle

STAIRWELL TO BASEMENT

Gun Money Plate (painting): Colen Fitzgibbon & Robin Winters
Bent Records: Ehry
Sign Language with Gun (photos): Julie Hair/Nan Becker/Mary Ann Fowler

BASEMENT TOILET

Phallic Fruit (paintings on walls): Joe Fyfe
Money Fountain (sculpture): Rebecca Howland

BASEMENT

Feminist Cave Painting (on floor & walls): Justen Ladda
Ghost (cloth sculpture): Rosemary Mayer

STAIR WELL TO 2ND FLOOR

Green Bottles (sculpture/painting): Bobby G
Rats (posters): Christy Rupp
Large painting series: Cara Perlman
Endangered (painting): Paulette Nenner
Teeth (painting over doorway): Margret Lippard

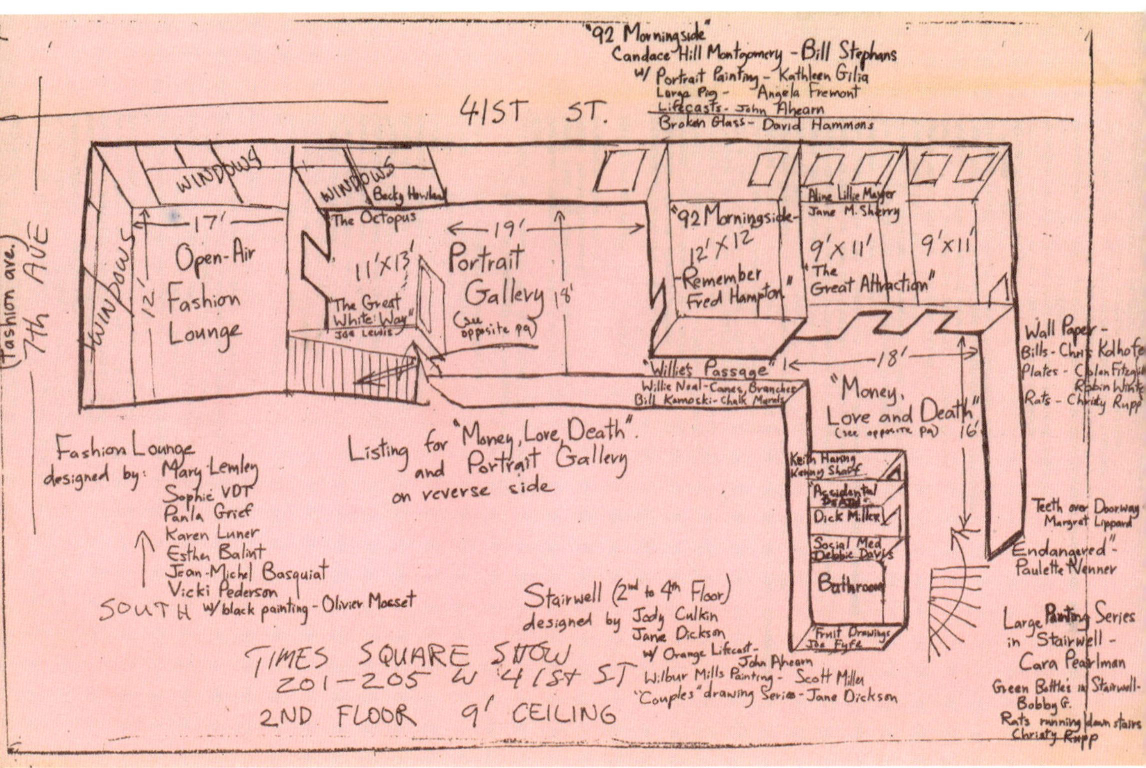

2ND FLOOR : MONEY LOVE & DEATH ROOM

Gun Doller Plate (wallpaper): Colen Fitzgibbon & Robin Winters
Billion Dollar Bills (wallpaper): Christof Kohlhofer
Rats (wallpaper): Christy Rupp
Man with Foot in Mouth (drawing): Marc Brasz
Hoof-Head Portraits (paintings): Richard Mock
Idi Amin Plate (sculpture on wall): Candace Hill Montgomery
Three Blind Mice (painting): Richard Bosman
Sky Falls (painting): Scott Miller
Man with Visible Insides (sculpture): Tom Otterness
Yellow Singer (painting): Wally Edwards
Purple Tongue (lifecast head): John Ahearn
Caution/Coition (painting): Tom Otterness
David (photo over the doorway): Matthew Geller
Series of 8 drawings: Colen Fitzgibbon
Scissors (painting): Janet Ziff
I Am Not An Alien (collage): Jai Mal
Gun & Cross (photo): Christof Kohlhofer
Gold Money (painting): Andrea Callard
Gilmore's Drawing (poster): Stephan Eins
3 Women's Heads (painting): Alex Katz
Hairpin Mirror (painting): Bobby G
Youth Collage (with photos): Howie Montaug & Caz Porter
Money (drawing on safe): Robin Winters & Colen Fitzgibbon
Dangerous Weapons Case (sculpture): Scott Miller
Tom with Gun (lifecast head): John Ahearn & Tom Otterness
Heels on Hubcaps (sculpture): Sandy Semour
Basketball Snapshots (photos): Tom Warner
Bound for Glory (photos): Mike Bidlo
Record of Rimbaud: Doug Ball
Mirror Frames: Scott Pfaffman
Black Triangle (sculpture): John Morton

2ND FLOOR: 92 MORNINGSIDE/REMEMBER FRED HAMPTON
Installation by Candace Hill Montgomery & Bill Stephans
With:
Old Man Portrait (painting): Kathleen Gilia
Large Pink Pig (painting): Angela Fremont
Glass: David Hammonds
Lifecasts: John Ahearn

2ND FLOOR: PORTRAIT GALLERY

Heart/Skull/Twins drawings: Charlie Ahearn
Submission Photos: Jimmy DeSana
Portrait Painting: Edward Brzezinski
3 Male portraits & 2 women undressed (5 paintings): Duncan Hannah
3 Stabbing Suspects (photos): Gregory Lehman
2 female portraits on black plastic (paintings): Jane Dickson
G.I. & Girl (2 paintings): Mike Robinson
Spanish Couple (lifecast heads): Robert Torres
Hospital Workers with Patients (photos from Bread & Roses): Georgeen Comerford
Cartoons (Phallocrats, etc. drawings/posters): Caz Porter/ Janet Stein
Four Sad Men (painting): Arnold Fern
Happy Boy (lifecast head): John Ahearn
Hats/Polaroids/Portrait of Businessman/Pants (photos): Jeff Blechman
Punk Portraits on acetate (photos): Wolfgang Staehle
The Great White Way (glass): Joe Lewis; w/ glass crane: Leni Brown and
Pederast photo: Jules Allen
Portrait of Shah (painting): Rebecca Howland
Romance (3 paintings of couples): Mike Robinson
Wood Sculpture: Robert Gaines
Large pencil drawing: Margret Lippard
Dark Octopus Abstracted (painting): Michael Norton
Octopus Window: Rebecca Howland
Lead Suit for the Nuclear Age (sculpture): Tom Otterness
Lifecasts from the South Bronx (sculpture): John Ahearn
4 Photos: Jules Allen
Mirror Portrait: Meryle
CODL Cowboy (rocking sculpture): David Wells
Homeless Women series (photos): Anne-Marie Rousseau
Porno Film Window: Teri Slotkin
Dead Servicemen from Helicopter Rescue Mission (portrait sculpture): Mimi Gross
8 Portraits of Friends (plaster paintings): Robin Winters
Barricade (wood sculpture with photos): Bill Evertson
Prison Walls Fall (stone sculpture): Alan Guttman
Anonymous Portrait: Anonymous

Tom Otterness (drawing) and John Ahearn (lettering and lists). *Times Square Floor Plan [Second Floor]*, 1980. For *The Times Square Show*. Photocopy on colored paper, 21.5 × 36 cm each. Courtesy of John Ahearn.

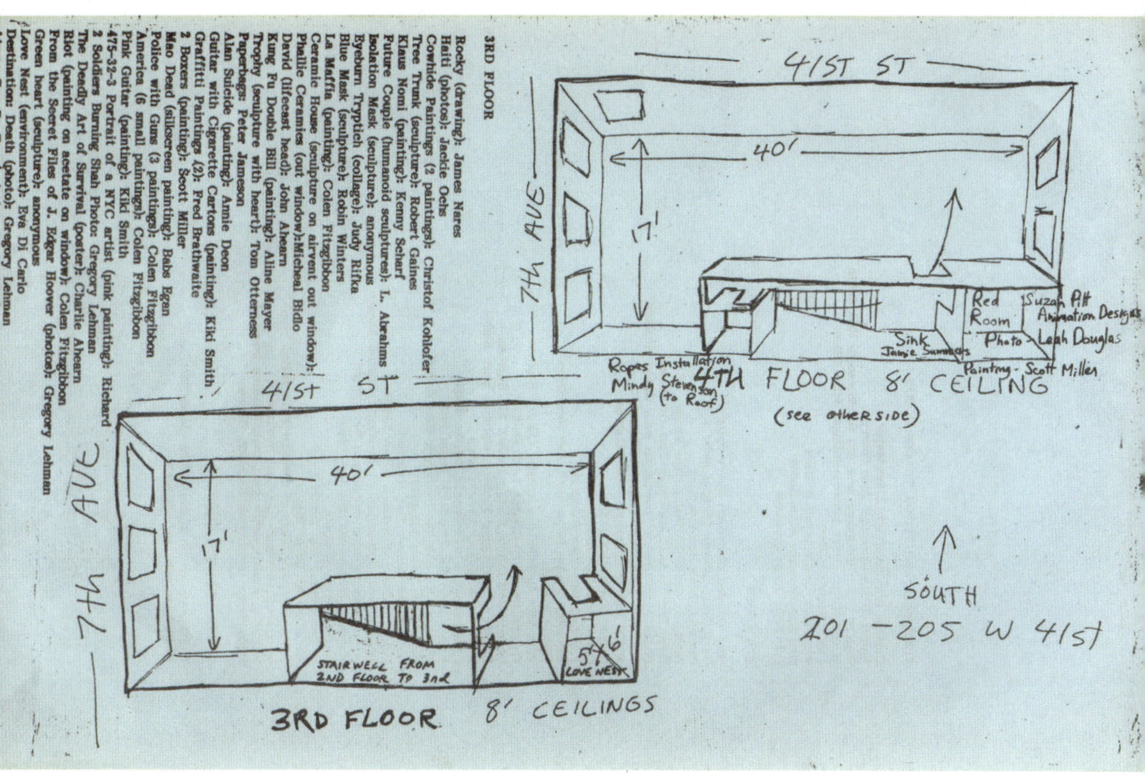

Tom Otterness (drawing) and John Ahearn (lettering
and lists). *Times Square Floor Plan [Third Floor]*, 1980.
Photocopy on colored paper, 21.5 × 36 cm each.
For *The Times Square Show*. Courtesy of John Ahearn.

STAIRWELL 3RD FLOOR TO 4TH FLOOR

Chinese Boy (painting): Aline Mayer
Yellow Dicks (drawing): Jane Sherry
Dragon Heads (sculpture over 3rd flr doorway): Kiki Smith
Macho Macho series (photo-paintings): Mike Glier
Chalk Grafitti: Samo
Funk City Grafitti: Bill & Mark
Graphite Drawing: Mike Roddy
Salt Sink: Jamie Summers

4TH FLOOR

Wire drawing over door: Harry Spitz
Cary Grant (photo): Michael Bidlo
Chairs (photo): Jim Casebere
Diletante Guerrilla Photo: Mike Roddy
Hand Gun Prick (2 drawings): Tom Otterness
Pencil Architectural Drawing on wall: Reese Williams
Text & 5 black bags: Reese Williams
White Statues (drawing): Tom Otterness
Prayer Book: Mike Bidlo
Chalk Graffitti: Anonymous
Punching Bag: Tom Otterness
Bank Mat (below heavy bag): Ann Newmarch
Plastic Woman:
Rats with Garbage & Fountain: Christy Rupp
Frosted Broadway (photo): Leah Douglas
Chalk Mural (above South window): Bill Komoski
Attack of the Nigger Tanks (sculpture): Mark Blaine
Black Goose (floor): Christy Rupp
Fans (ceiling & wall drawing): Mike Roddy
Woman Crawling (painting): Suzan Pitt
Self Portrait with Hat (drawing): Mike Roddy
Paper bags: Peter Jameson
Fighters (sculpture): Tom Otterness
Tough & Crazy (paintings): Robin Winters
Skull & Heart (photostats of drawings): Charlie Ahearn
Peep Show viewer with crank: Anne Petrone
Matching (step) paintings: Lan Payne
Poster: Reese Williams
In Bed (photo): Ann Smith
Victor Mural: Mike Glier
Green Bottles w/photo of S.Bronx: Marc Blaine
Gray Fruit (drawing): Rebecca Howland
Basket of Fruit (plaster sculpture): Rebecca Howland
Dildo Alarm (sculpture): Kathleen Thomas

4TH FLOOR /RED ROOM

3 paintings for an animated film: Suzan Pitt
Window (photo): Leah Douglas

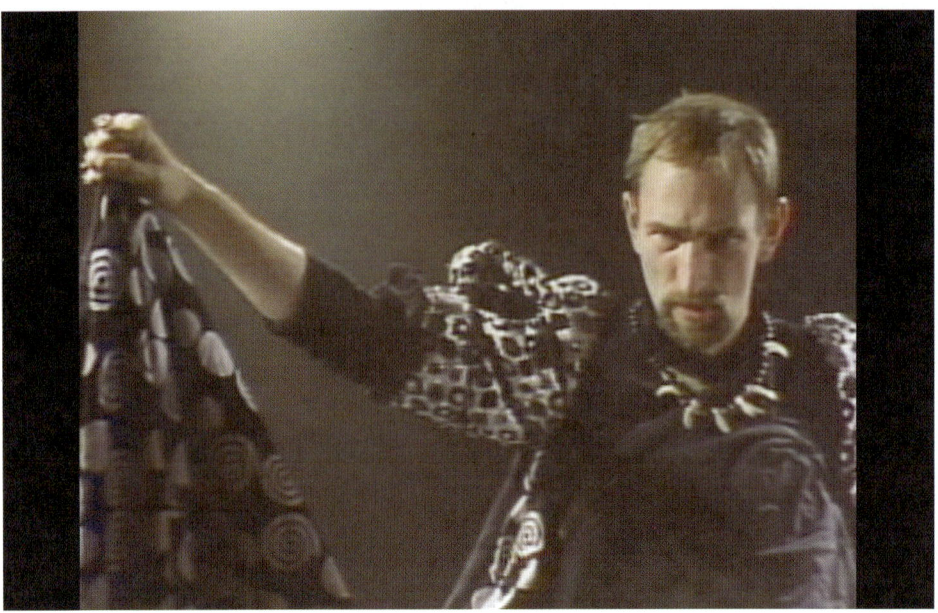

My biggest contributions towards the success of *The Times Square Show* were set into motion in 1978 when I answered a "Help Wanted" ad in the NY Times looking for an animator willing to learn computer programming. This was before digital art was taught in schools. I had no affinity for computers but I needed a job and I figured computers were going to be big so this was probably a useful skill to learn. I got the job, learned to type and to use primitive animation programs and began working in the center of Times Square, on the 1 Spectacolor digital light board, where they drop the ball on New Years Eve. I designed computer animation on weekend nightshifts, 3–11 pm making ads for companies like Coke and Studio 54 (who gave us free comps for late night entertainment). In 1978 I could live on a 2 day a week salary. From my perch behind the sign, above Times Square, I'd take breaks to refocus my computer-strained eyes out the windows onto the bedlam of commuters, office workers, theater goers, tourists, hustlers, johns, trannies, and unsupervised little kids from the surrounding welfare hotels swirling below. I started to draw those neon-lit dramas.

As I got familiar with the job I convinced my boss to let me run occasional "public service" ads for my artist friends' projects: a month-long free ad for Suzan Pitt's *Asparagus* exhibition at the Whitney Museum in 1978, a short ad for Charlie Ahearn's film *Deadly Art of Survival* in 1979 as well as unsanctioned animated billboard titles for Scott and Beth B's film

Times Square Show, 1980. Directed by Beth B & Scott B; Edited by Robert Burden; Camera by Al Vasquez; With Jack Smith; Producers: Robert Burden, Coleen Fitzgibbon; Executive Producers: Collaborative Projects, Inc and NCI Inc [Stills] Public service announcement for cable television, 30 seconds. Courtesy of Coleen Fitzgibbon.

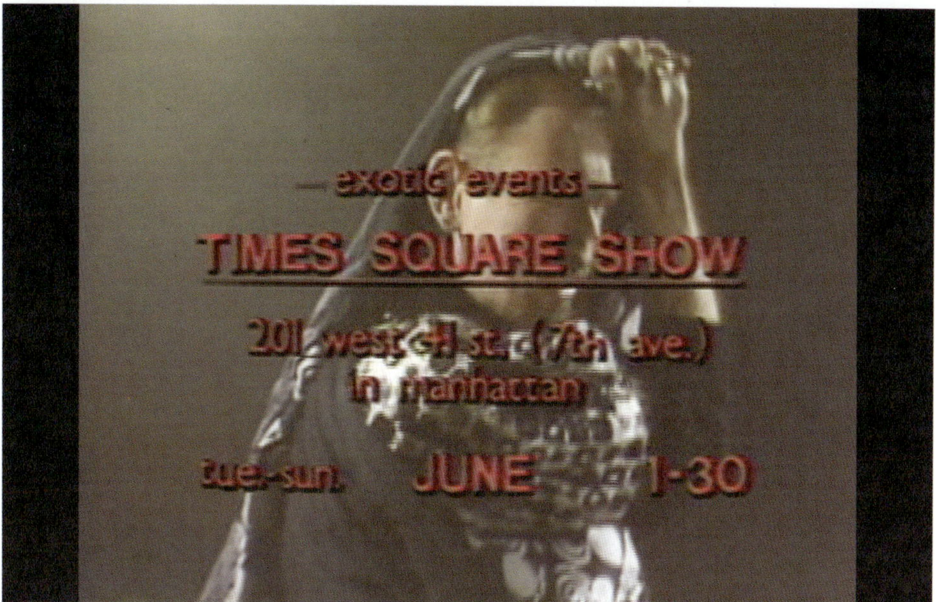

The Offenders in 1980. In late April 1980 when discussions began over what the poster for *The Times Square Show* should be, I proposed my existing drawing of a 3-Card Monte dealer's hands with cards spread out tempting the viewer to take a chance. This seemed perfect for our rowdy mash-up show. (3-Card Monte dealers shuffle around 2 red cards and 1 black, face down, usually on a piece of cardboard on top of a turned-over garbage can, and take bets on where the black one lands. The choreography of the dealer's patter synced to the shill's clueless bets are hypnotic. Tourists always jump in and lose while little pickpocket kids work the crowd of distracted onlookers.)

Charlie offered to make this image into the poster, adding background and graphic punch, while I offered to convince my boss to let me make it into a repeating animated billboard ad for *The Times Square Show*, located just one block away. I designed and ran the 30 second animated sequence of the 3-Card Monte shuffle, revealing info for *The Times Square Show*, which ran every 20 minutes for the whole month of the show's run June, 1980.

Administrative tasks for *The Times Square Show* and every Colab show were shared by volunteers and a number of members did fundraising solicitations for this show. I accompanied Walter Robinson on a pitch to the Public Art Fund to meet with their acting director, Jennie Dixon. Our lead time was too short for their organization, but Jennie was intrigued by the idea of my digital animated billboard art and asked to discuss that further.

I want to try to correct the much quoted false patriarchal framework put forth by Richard Goldstein, who misunderstood and mischaracterized Colab and *The*

Times Square Show in his article for *The Village Voice*, a quick weekly review, not a seriously researched informed piece of journalism. Goldstein described this show in terms of traditional art exhibition hierarchies (privileging male contributions, omitting female ones). The overturning of these traditional hierarchies of curatorial power including male domination/female subservience was central to Colab's mission as I understood it.

Each Colab show had a themed title and anyone, member or not, could put in anything they felt like contributing. There was no directing, curating or editing of Colab shows. Many people contributed to the conceptualization of projects through vigorous argument, and implemented shared creative ideas through administration and execution of each Colab show. *The Times Square Show* was the product of years of work by rotating Colab executives who applied for grants, wrote up and filed reports, as well as the crucial unsung efforts of Colab journalists and artist/journalists, Walter Robinson, Edit DeAk, Liza Béar, Betsy Sussler, and Alan Moore, who were adept at spreading the word to the broad artistic community when we did a project, and to all the artists who pitched in, without fanfare, on each others' show concepts to make ideas happen.

The Times Square Show was based on this contentious but well-honed network of fractious cooperation of divergent interests. Minimizing the profound contributions of this ragged collective to describe that show as an individual star turn betrayed the basic collaborative concept of Collaborative Projects. Jeffrey Deitch presented a much more nuanced description of this show in his *Art in America* review.

Organizers of each area in *The Times Square Show* tried to broker

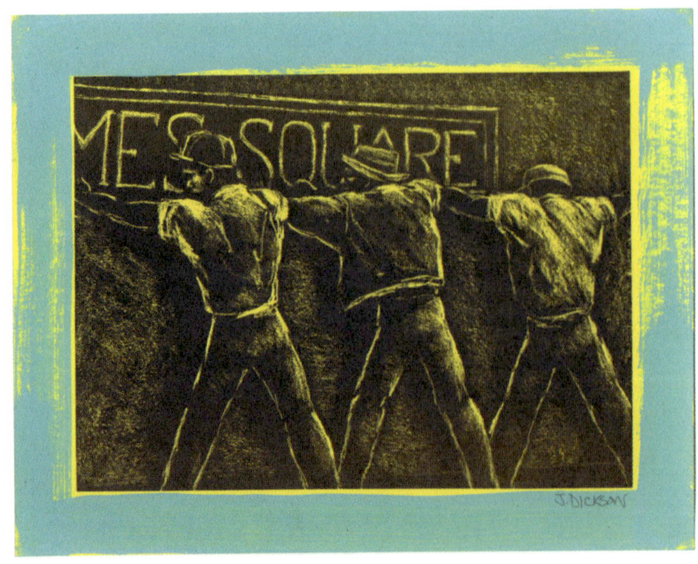

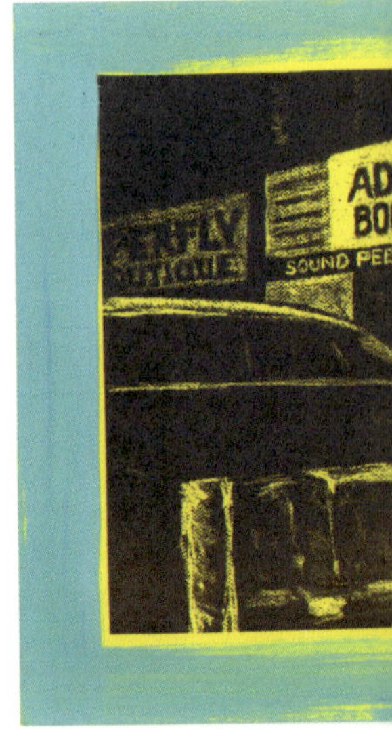

peace but installation was an anarchic Darwinian process. Some artists' pieces were replaced or overshadowed by other artists' work. Sometimes the first artist reasserted their place, sometimes not. Unknown SVA students, Kenny Scharf and Keith Haring showed up and added art work wherever they felt like it, as did graffiti masters Lee and Fab 5 Freddy. There was no final curator/arbiter to settle these disputes. It was creative arm to arm combat and the most assertive won.

For example Jody Culkin and I took responsibility for organizing the stairwells. As we were installing, a then unknown David Hammons appeared. He'd heard from Joe Lewis that there was an art free-for-all brewing, and came to check it out. After introducing himself he headed back out into Times Square, returning quickly with a bag full of empty Night Train bottles, which he'd collected on the block. David then crushed the bottles and

sprinkled shards of green glass down the whole staircase. When we objected to the glass carpet he'd just laid for us to work in, David swept the broken glass to one side of each step, giving us a little shrug and a smile as if to say "Deal with it, kids," and left. His piece stayed among works on the stairs by Kiki Smith, Mike Glier, Fab 5 Freddy, Mike Bidlo, John Ahearn and others, some invited and some volunteers.

Walter Robinson and I also took on the unenviable administrative task of thanking the Durst Organization at the close of this show, presenting them with some miserable Xeroxes a few members had donated as a peace offering. The Dursts were not thrilled about the art mess we had left behind.

—Jane Dickson

Jane Dickson. *Times Square / Adult Books / Cops*. 1980. Photocopy and acrylic paint on paper, 21.5 × 28 cm each. Exhibited in *The Times Square Show*. Courtesy of Jane Dickson.

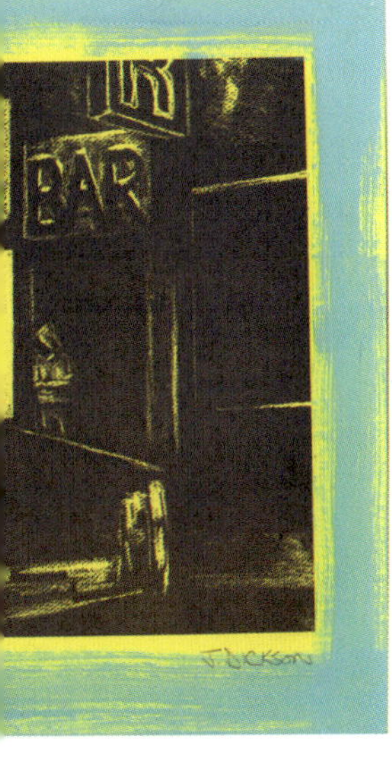
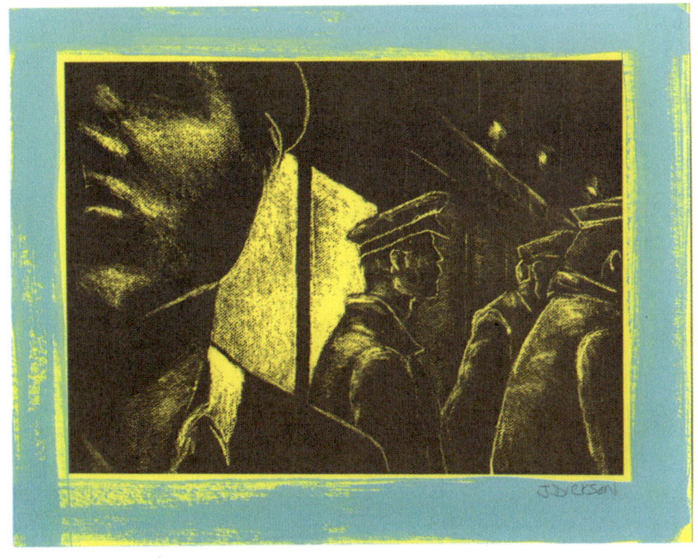

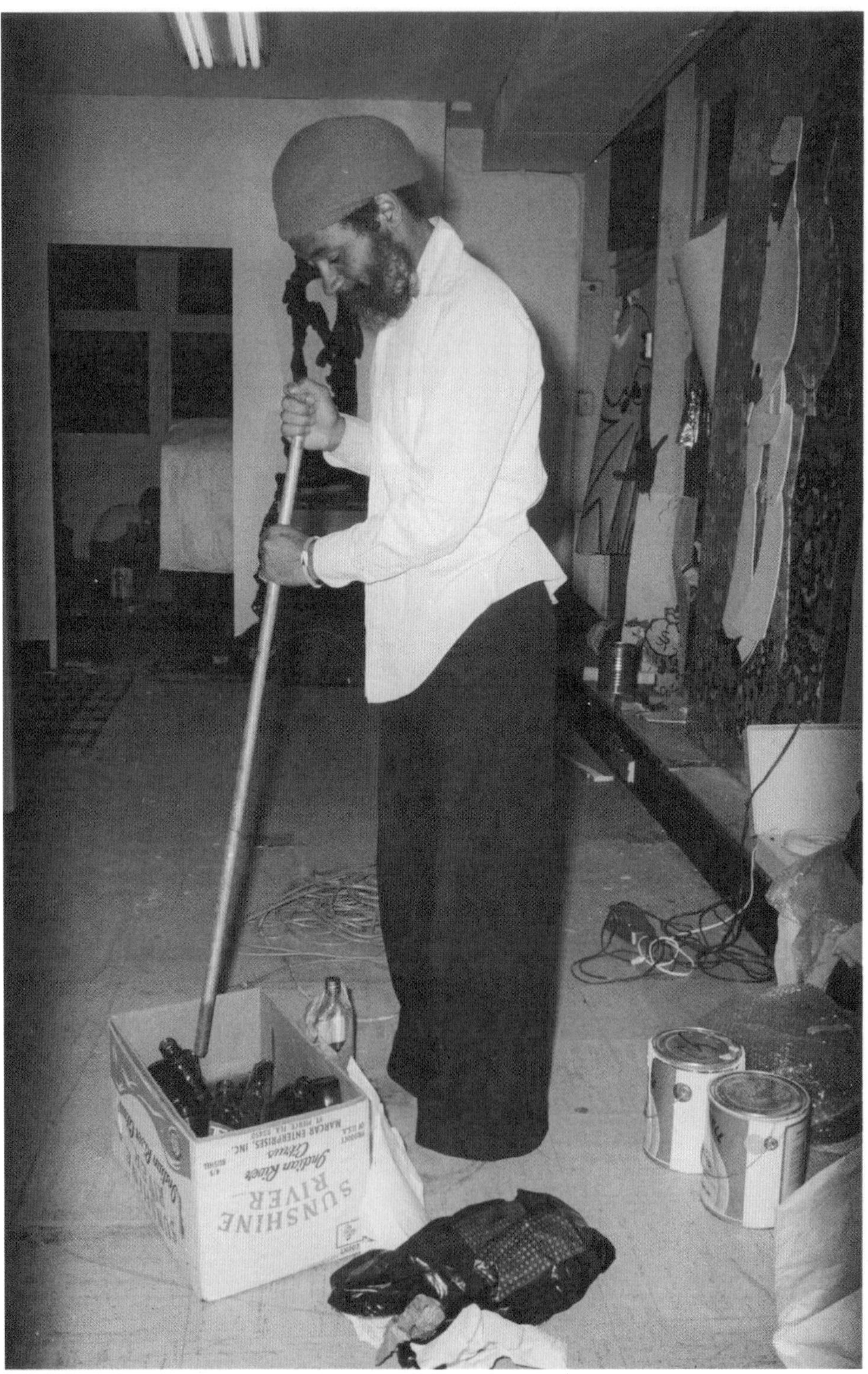

Francene Keery. *David Hammons crushing glass during Times Square Show installation*, 1980. Silver gelatin print, 25 × 20 cm.
© Francene Keery. NYC. All Rights Reserved. Courtesy of John Ahearn and Francene Keery.

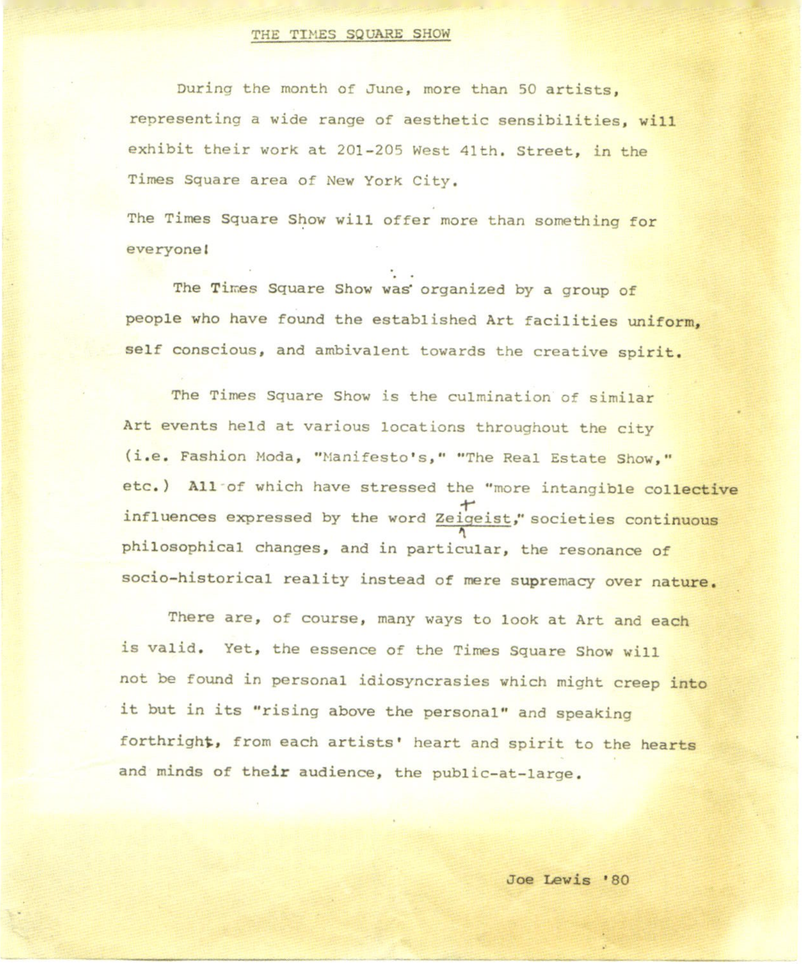

THE TIMES SQUARE SHOW

During the month of June, more than 50 artists,
representing a wide range of aesthetic sensibilities, will
exhibit their work at 201-205 West 41th. Street, in the
Times Square area of New York City.

The Times Square Show will offer more than something for
everyone!

The Times Square Show was organized by a group of
people who have found the established Art facilities uniform,
self conscious, and ambivalent towards the creative spirit.

The Times Square Show is the culmination of similar
Art events held at various locations throughout the city
(i.e. Fashion Moda, "Manifesto's," "The Real Estate Show,"
etc.) All of which have stressed the "more intangible collective
influences expressed by the word Zeigeist," societies continuous
philosophical changes, and in particular, the resonance of
socio-historical reality instead of mere supremacy over nature.

There are, of course, many ways to look at Art and each
is valid. Yet, the essence of the Times Square Show will
not be found in personal idiosyncrasies which might creep into
it but in its "rising above the personal" and speaking
forthright, from each artists' heart and spirit to the hearts
and minds of their audience, the public-at-large.

Joe Lewis '80

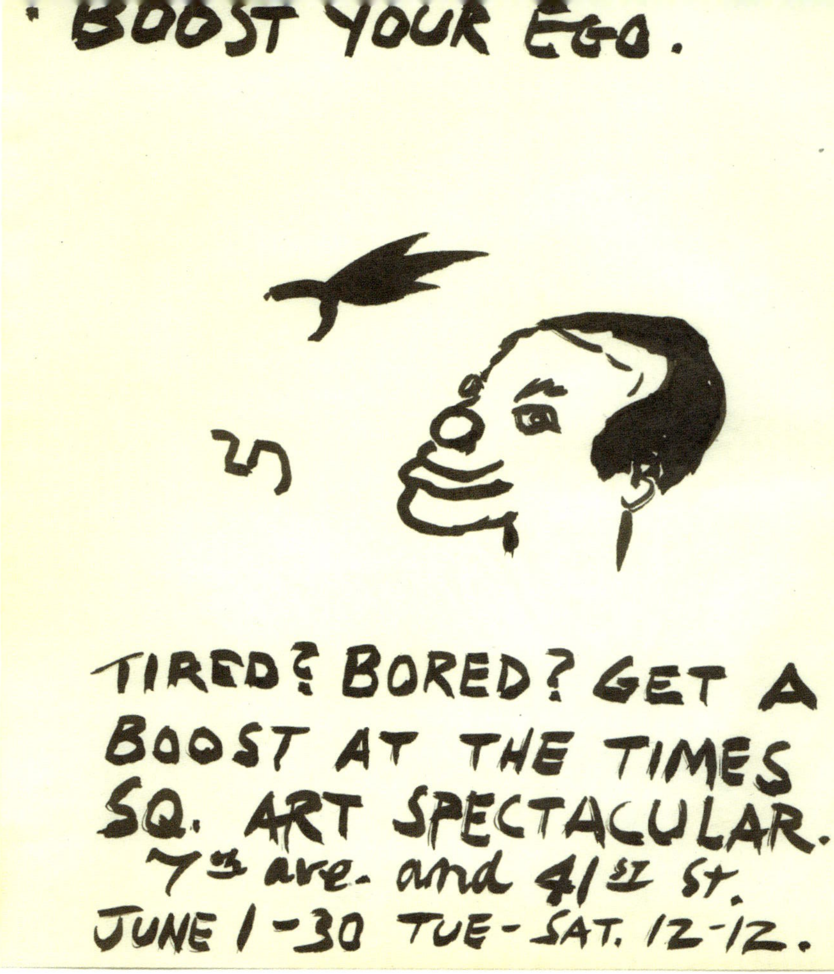

Left to right:

Joe Lewis. *Times Square Show Manifesto*, 1980. Photocopy flyer, 28 × 21.5 cm. For *The Times Square Show*. Courtesy of Becky Howland.

Bobby G (Robert Goldman). *Boost Your Ego*, 1980. Ink on paper, 23 × 21 cm. Original artwork for unrealized poster. Courtesy of Bobby G (Robert Goldman).

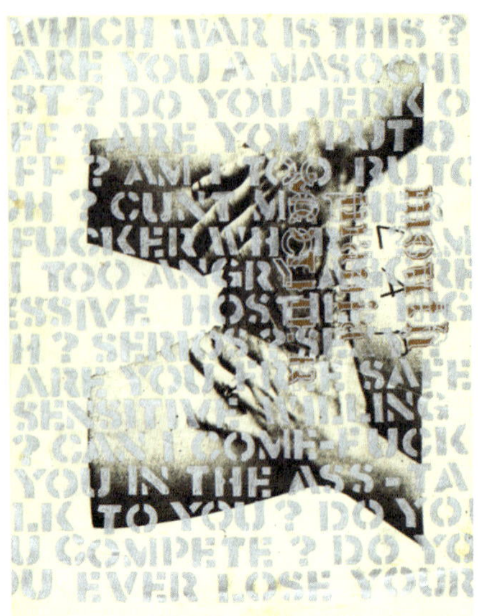

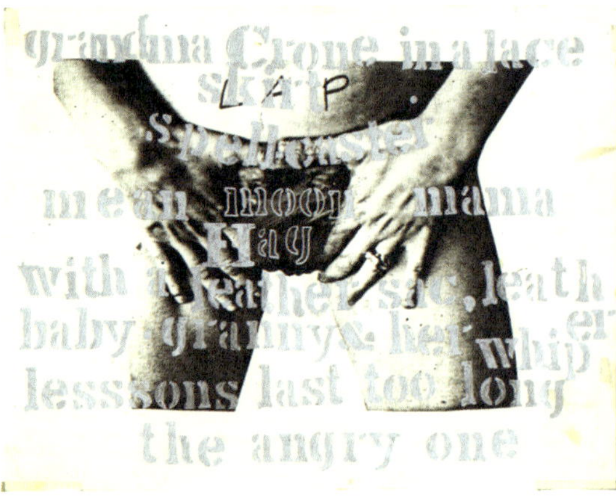

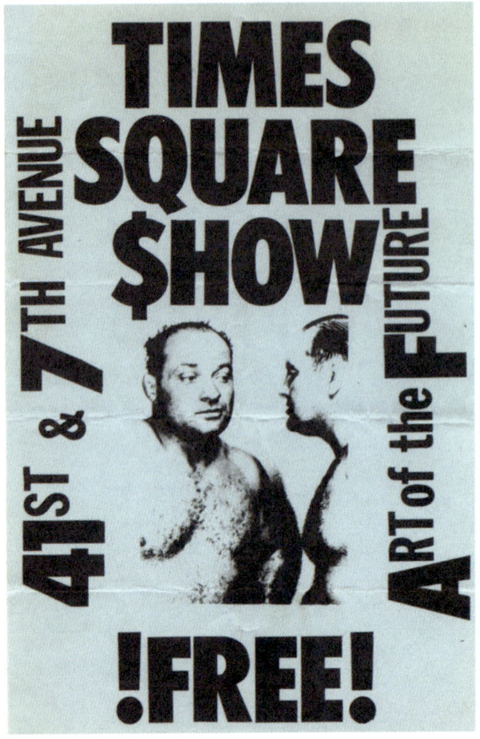

WRAPS AND RAP/THE WRAP. WHAT YOU WEAR. WHAT WE WEAR. SIXTY ARTISTS. DE- SIGNERS. AND PERSONALI- TIES. DRESSED IN WHITE. LIGHTIN' UP THE NIGHT. DOIN' THEIR OWN THING. SAYIN' THEIR OWN THING. THIS IS SOME KINDA UNIFORM. THE RAP. RUNNIN' THROUGH TIMES SQUARE. ON THE RADIO. IN THE PARK. ON A TAPE MACHINE. WALK- IN' DOWN THE STREET. RAP- PIN' TO THE BEAT. THE DYNELLS. WITH MR. JOHNNY DYNELL. TALKING WITH THE RHYTHM. MOVIN' WITH THE GROOVE. HE IS THE BEST. HE BEATS THE REST.

Times Square Show/Sunday, June 29/9 PM/$4.00/41 Street & 7th Ave./

Produced by Paula Greif/Mary Lemley/Sophie VDT

Clockwise from upper left:

Alan Moore. *Art of the Future*, 1980. Photocopy handbill, 21.5 × 14 cm. For *The Times Square Show*. Courtesy of Bobby G (Robert Goldman).

Jane Sherry. *Which War is This*, 1980, 21.5 × 28 cm. Exhibited in *The Times Square Show*. Photocopy and paint pen on paper. Courtesy of Jane Sherry.

Jane Sherry. *Grandma Crone in a Lace Skirt*, 1980. Photocopy and paint pen on paper, 21.5 × 28 cm. Exhibited in *The Times Square Show*. Courtesy of Jane Sherry.

Paula Greif, Mary Lemley and Sophie VDT. *Wraps and Rap / The Wrap*, 1980. Offset printed handbill, 21.5 × 14 cm. For *The Times Square Show*. Courtesy of Bobby G (Robert Goldman).

Next page bottom, left to right:

Bobby G (Robert Goldman). *Money Talks*, New York: R. Goldman, 1980. Hand-painted paper on pin backing, 5 × 8 cm. Edition of 15, signed and numbered. Exhibited in *The Times Square Show* gift shop. Courtesy of Bobby G (Robert Goldman). Photo: Nancy Linn.

Bobby G (Robert Goldman). *Times Square Peep Show / Times Sq. Porno Capital*, 1980. Ink and graphite on cardstock, 8 × 8 cm each. Original artwork for *The Times Square Show* buttons. Courtesy of Bobby G (Robert Goldman). Photo: Nancy Linn.

Bobby G (Robert Goldman). *Times Sq. Art Spectacular*, 1980. Photocopy on button, 6 × 6 cm. For *The Times Square Show*. Courtesy of Matthew Geller. Photo: Nancy Linn.

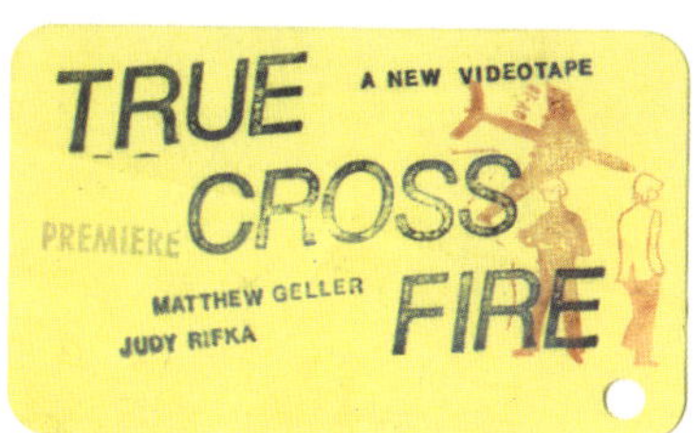

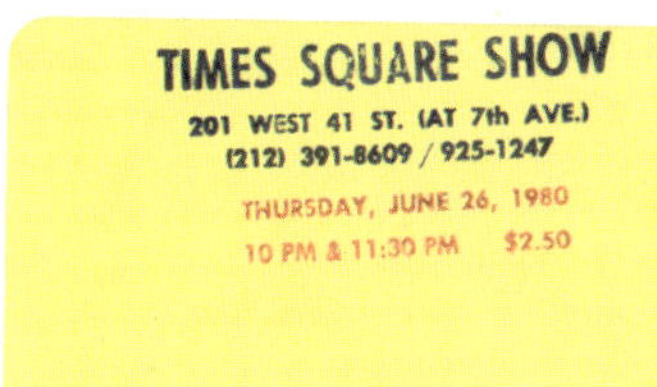

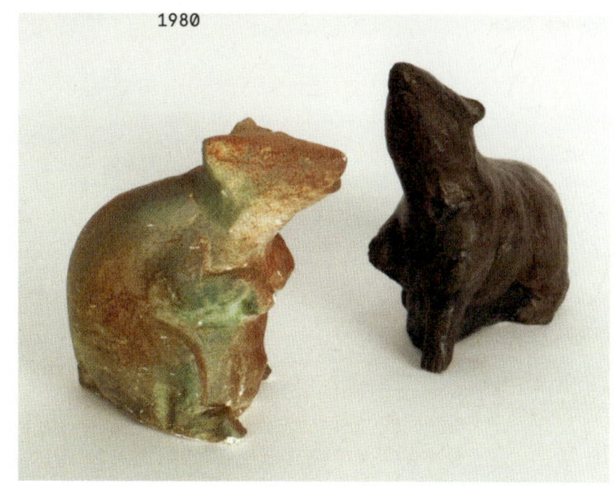

Judy Rifka. *True Crossfire*, 1980. Rubber-stamp on cardstock handbill, 6 × 10.5 cm. For *The Times Square Show*. Courtesy of Bobby G (Robert Goldman).

Christy Rupp. *Rat* (standing dark-colored version and standing light-colored version), 1980. Painted plaster, 8 × 17 × 14 cm each. Exhibited in *The Times Square Show*. Courtesy of John Ahearn. Photo: Nancy Linn.

The Times Square Show was a dare where artists took control of their own agency. Colab knew what to do because they had done it before.

At an early planning meeting the as yet untitled *Times Square Show* was referred to as the *Times Square Art Spectacular*—a collective spectacle. As things developed the collective spectacle where individuals profit as a group, was inevitably subsumed by the capitalist art market machine of winners and losers where curators, gallerists and collectors—not artists—decide what can and can not be done.

Colab's brilliance was that it recognized the inevitability of institutional constriction, took the position that defied that and operated collaboratively outside of it, in public space, creating a paradynamic spectacle out of the enormous reservoir of artistic energy that existed in New York City at that moment. The real intrinsic value of *The Times Square Show* is in all that was revealed. It was the peak of Colab activity and influence, and it did change the art world.

—Bobby G (Robert Goldman)

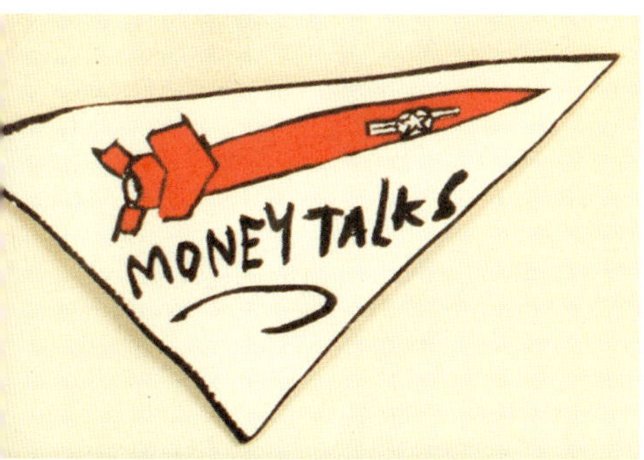

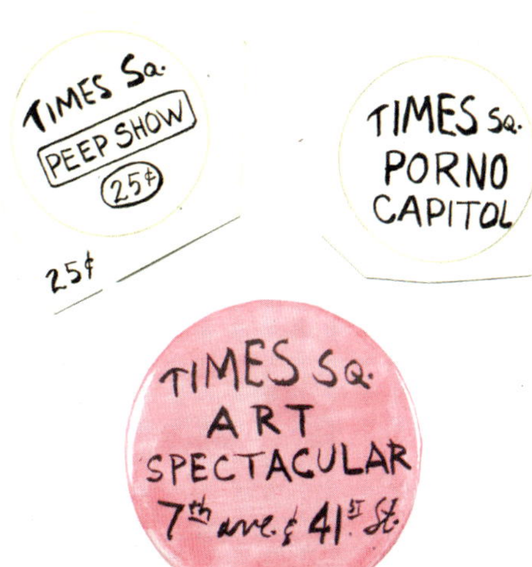

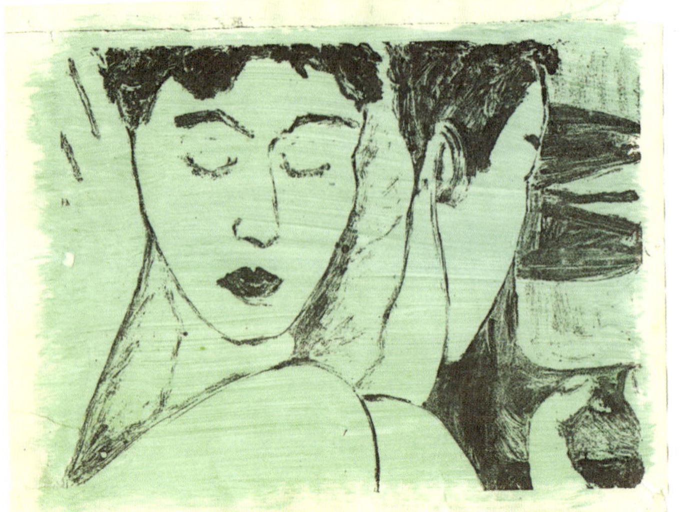

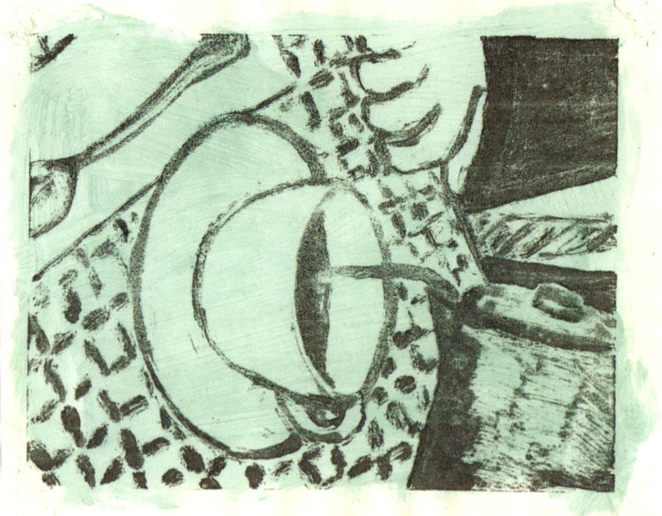

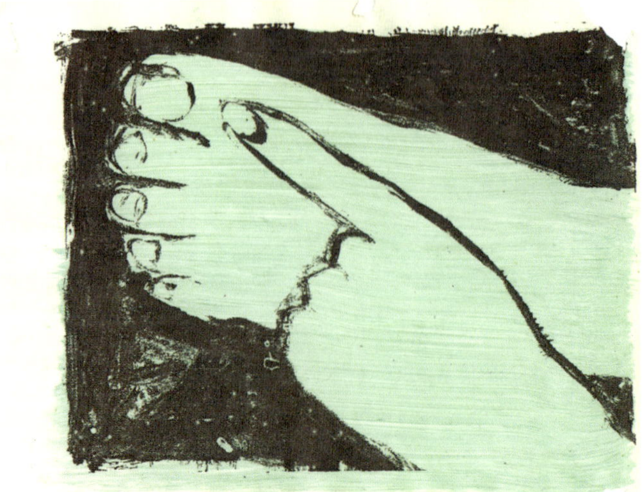

Jane Dickson. *Untitled* [man and woman in bed / coffee cup / foot]. 1980. Hand-painted screenprints, 21.5 × 28 cm each. Exhibited in *The Times Square Show*. Courtesy of Tom Otterness.

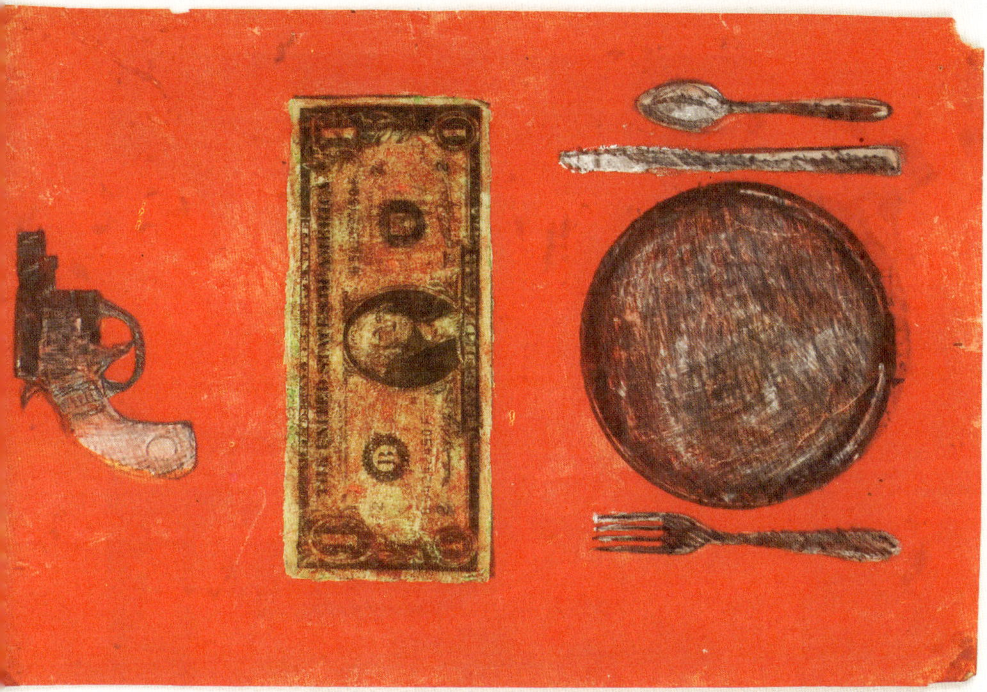

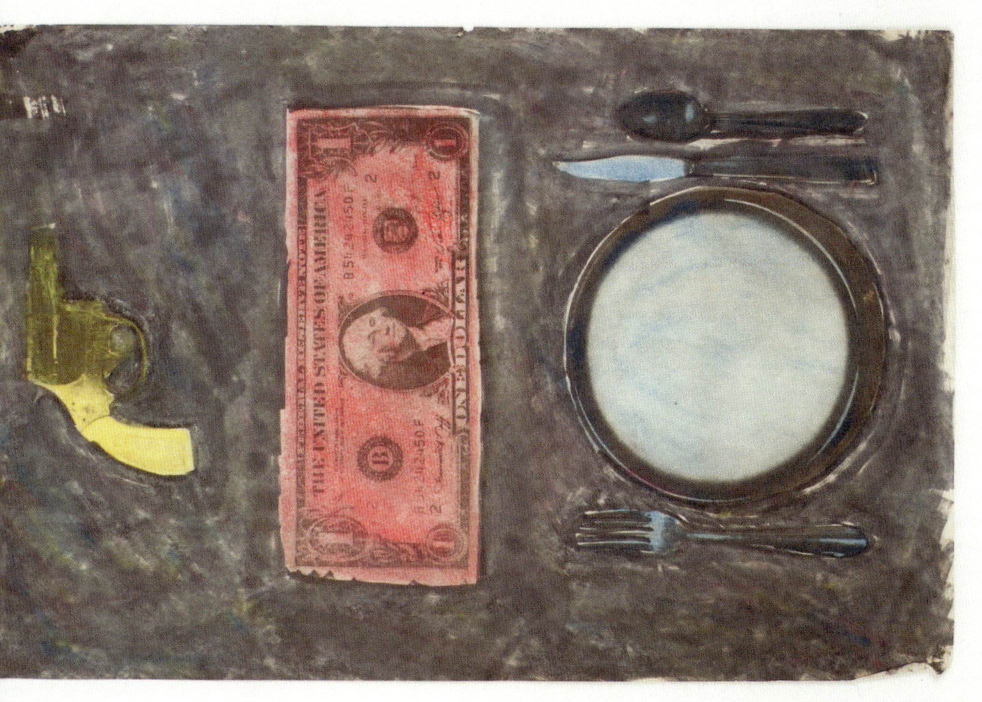

X & Y (Coleen Fitzgibbon and Robin Winters). *Take the Money and Run*, c. 1980. (two versions) Hand-painted photocopy with marker, 43 × 28 cm each. Courtesy of Coleen Fitzgibbon.

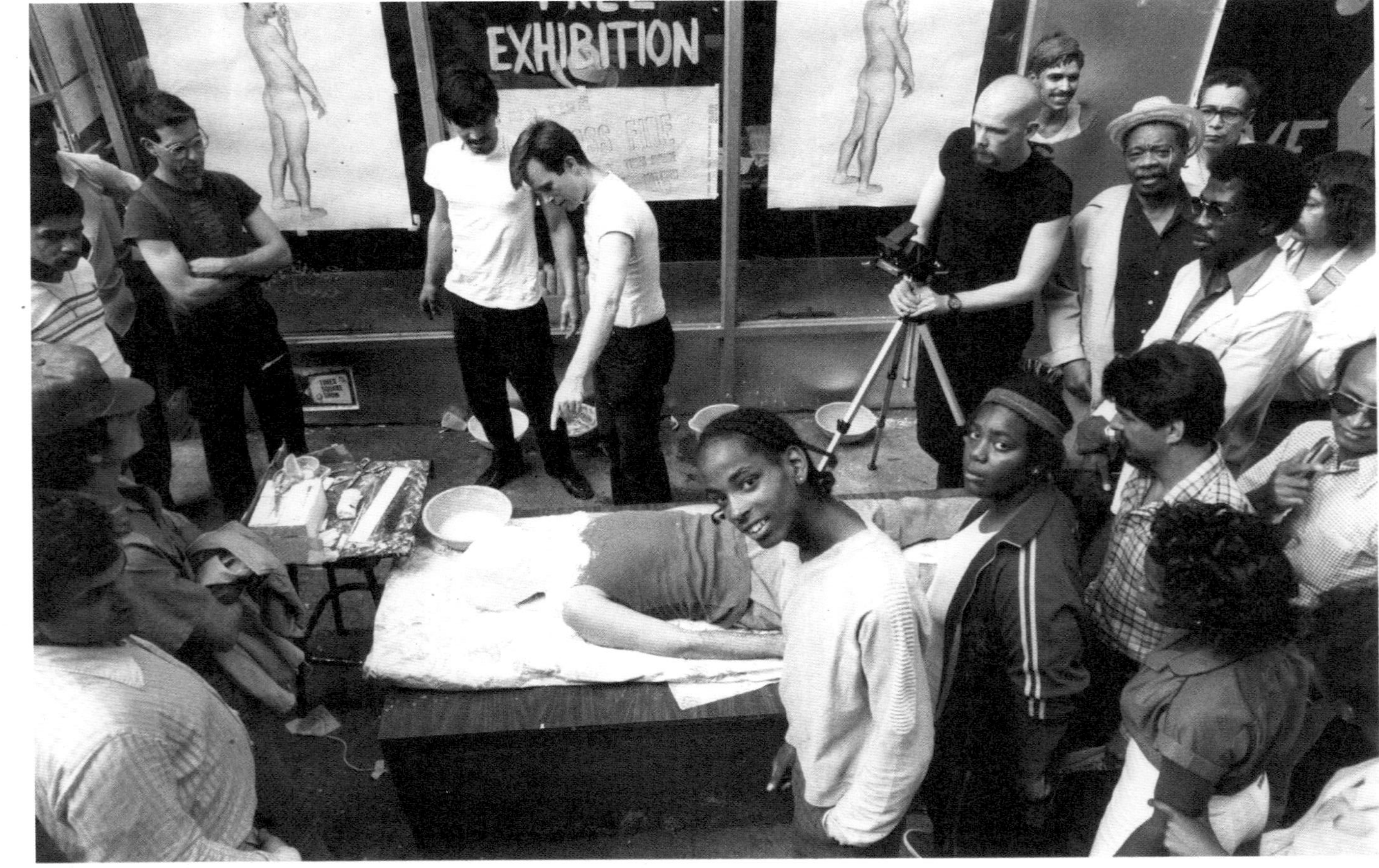

Wolfgang Staehle. *John Ahearn and Rigoberto Torres live casting*, 1980. Silver gelatin print, 20 × 25 cm. Courtesy of John Ahearn.

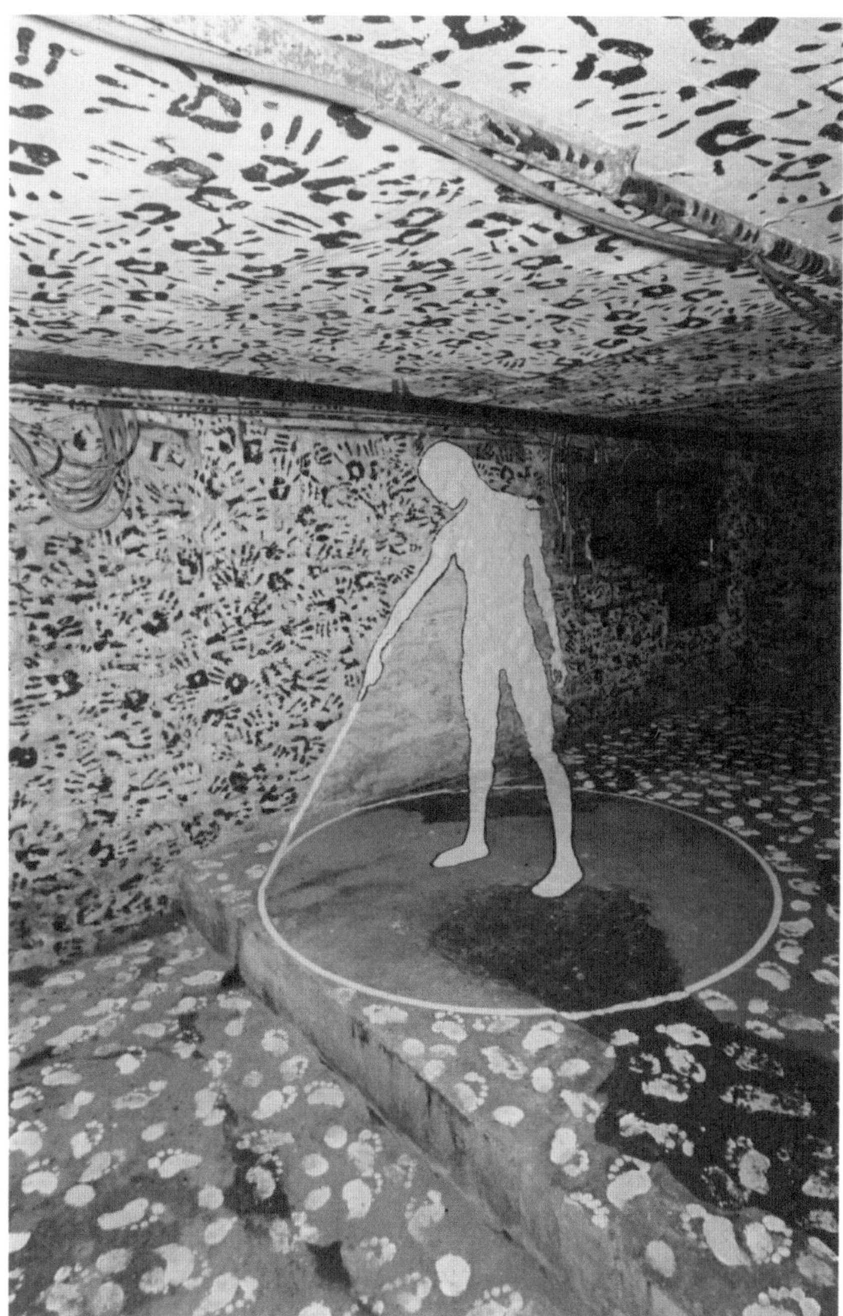

Francene Keery. *Justen Ladda's Feminist Cave Painting*, 1980. Silver gelatin print, 25 × 20 cm.
Courtesy of John Ahearn and Francene Keery. © Francene Keery. NYC. All Rights Reserved.

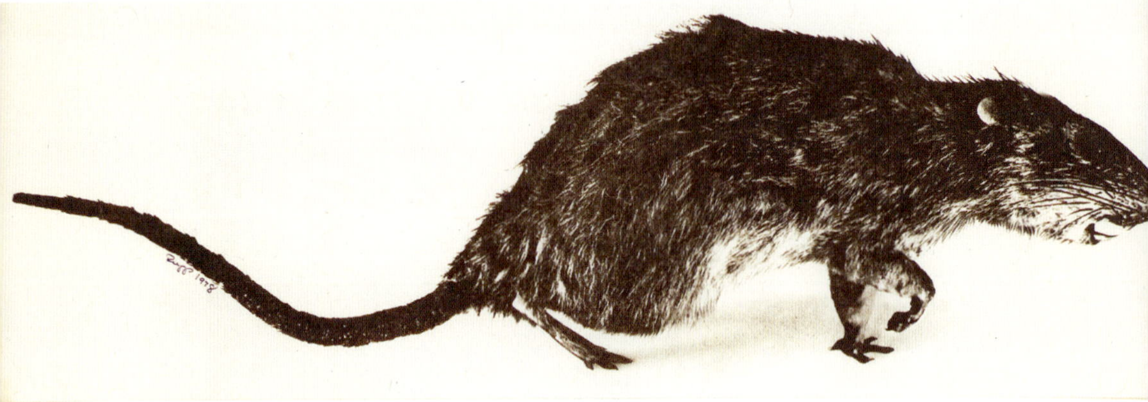

The quintessential Colab-organized show for most people is the *The Times Square Show Extravaganza* with over 75 artists in an abandoned massage parlor on 7th Avenue and 41st St in June 1980, 24–7 for 4 weeks where all 5 floors were covered with art and included performances, fashion shows, music, films and videos. The TSS was advertised with Colab-made TV and newspaper ads, posters, human sandwich boards and word of mouth; it was attended by tourists, Times Square local businesses, the sex-show trade, hustlers and even the art world.

—Coleen Fitzgibbon

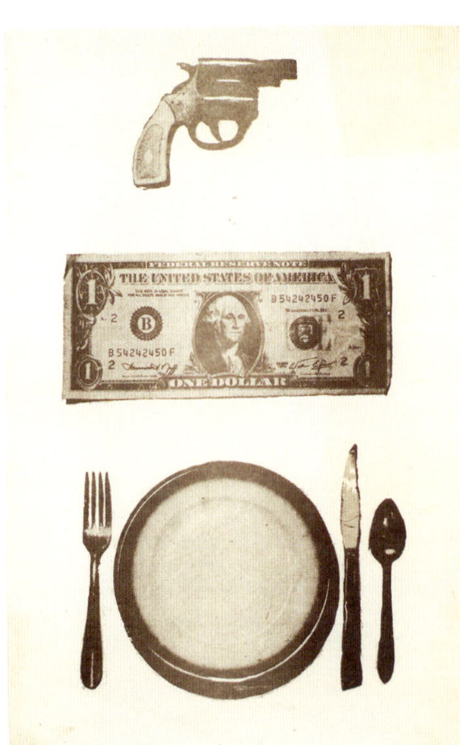

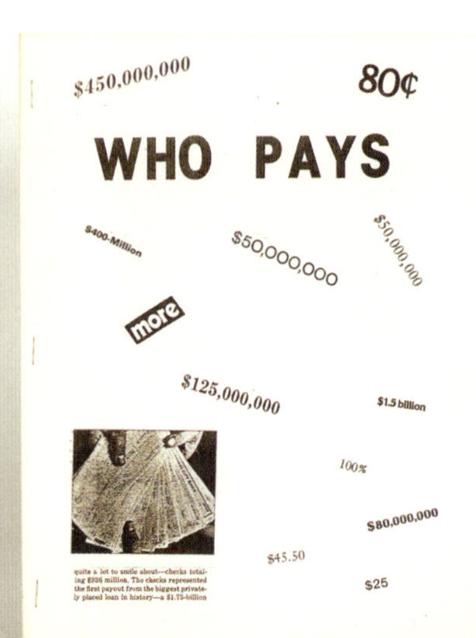

Christy Rupp. *Rat Poster*, 1978. Offset printed poster, 14.5 × 46.5 cm. Exhibited in *The Times Square Show*. Courtesy of Christy Rupp.

X & Y (Coleen Fitzgibbon and Robin Winters). *Take the Money and Run*, c. 1979–80. Photocopy, 43 × 28 cm. Courtesy of Robin Winters.

Bobby G (Robert Goldman). *Who Pays*. New York: R. Goldman, 1980. Photocopy, pbk, staple-bound, 4 pp, 28 × 21.5 cm. Edition of 5, signed and numbered. Cover and interior. Re-edition for Exit Art of a publication displayed in *The Times Square Show* gift shop. Courtesy of Bobby G (Robert Goldman). Photo: Nancy Linn.

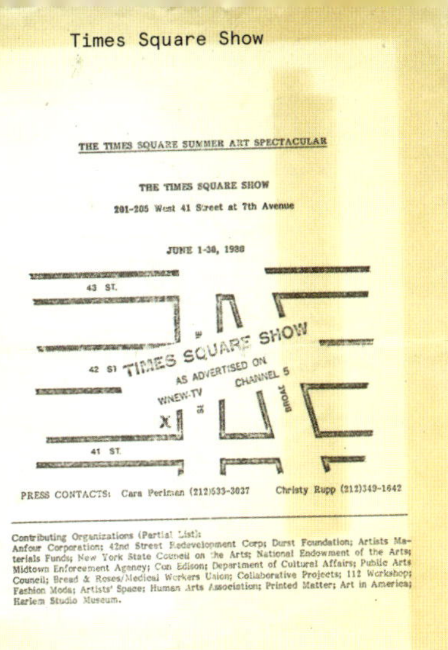

THE TIMES SQUARE SUMMER ART SPECTACULAR

THE TIMES SQUARE SHOW

201-205 West 41 Street at 7th Avenue

JUNE 1-30, 1980

PRESS CONTACTS: Cara Perlman (212)533-3037   Christy Rupp (212)349-1642

Contributing Organizations (Partial List):
Anfour Corporation; 42nd Street Redevelopment Corp; Durst Foundation; Artists Materials Funds; New York State Council on the Arts; National Endowment of the Arts; Midtown Enforcement Agency; Con Edison; Department of Cultural Affairs; Public Arts Council; Bread & Roses/Medical Workers Union; Collaborative Projects; 112 Workshop; Fashion Moda; Artists' Space; Human Arts Association; Printed Matter; Art in America; Harlem Studio Museum.

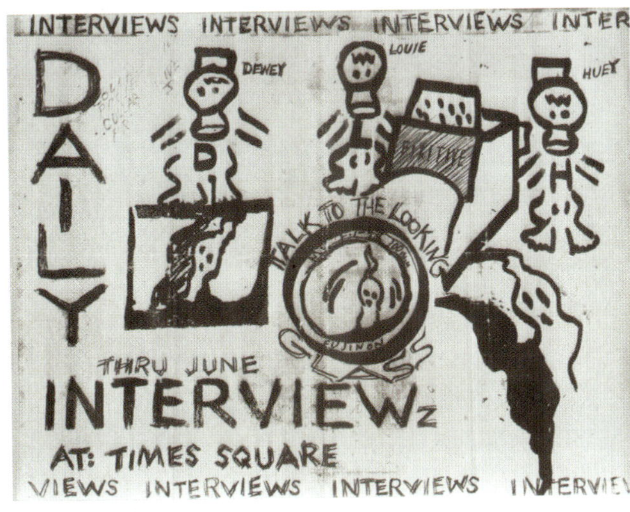

Unknown. *The Times Square Show Summer Art Spectacular*, 1980. Photocopy, 28 × 21.5 cm. Courtesy of Becky Howland.

Unknown. *Daily Interviews*, 1980. Telecopier print, 21.5 × 28 cm. Sent via QWIP. Courtesy of Bobby G (Robert Goldman).

Christy Rupp. *Rat T-Shirt*, New York: C. Rupp, 1980. Screenprinted t-shirt exhibited in *The Times Square Show* gift shop. Courtesy of Christy Rupp.

GREED

AND

DEATH

The Times Square Show was a pink cloud. Jeffery Deitch even called the intervention "courageous" in a review he wrote for *Art in America*. Yet, beneath the thin veneer of self-empowerment and cultural rejection i.e. the gallery system—quickly picked off those they believed could draw a profit—isn't that what it's all about?

—Joe Lewis

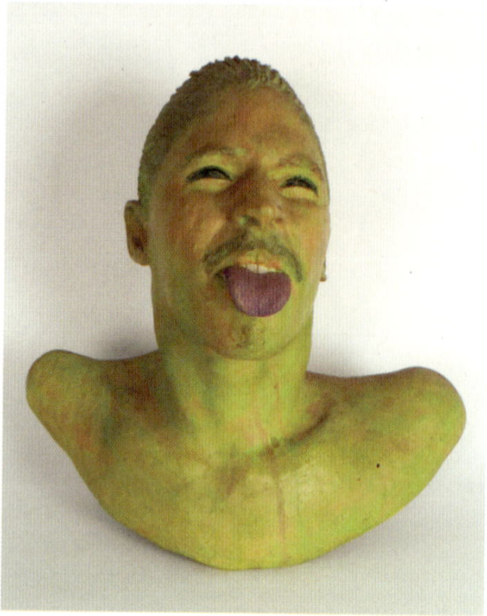

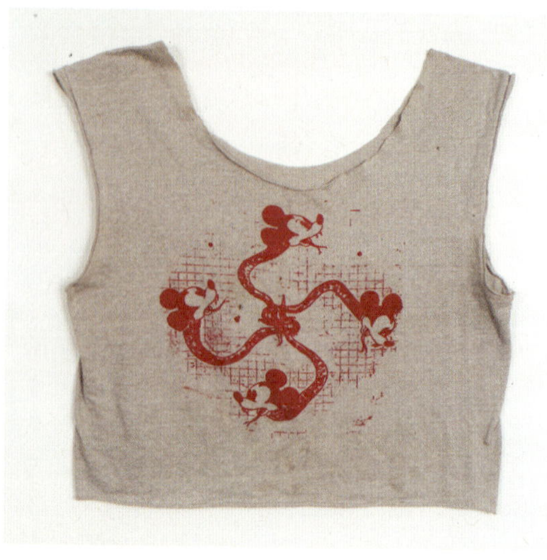

The Times Square Show was entered on the north side of 41st Street beneath a red and silver block letter sign spanning the door into a deep storefront. The gift shop was in a room to the right. At the rear of the storefront a small wooden stairway disappeared behind a wall and led to the four story building on 7th Avenue connected to the entrance space. In front of the stairway was a staging area for screenings and performances happening every night, with the audience filling up the entrance storefront space.

Among the dense installation on the second floor were three mixed media works, *Nail Polish and Drugs*, *No*, and *Greed and Death*. They were made with photographs and objects on grounds of Canal Street plastic scraps and large shards of silver mirrored glass. This second floor exhibition space also served as the "dressing room" for performers to

enter the stage at the bottom of the stairs.

On the evening of Jack Smith's performance as Sinbad Glick in *Exotic Landlordism of the World*, the house was packed. Jack, his cast, and considerable entourage were upstairs readying themselves for the show. It began with the most exotic music piped down from upstairs: antique Persian love songs, North African dance music, Hollywood B-movie music and other obscure entrancements from the unique collection of Jack Smith. This went on for hours. No one took the stage. The audience became a party, but hardly the party that must have been going on upstairs. Anticipation charged the mood.

Finally, the players in elaborate flowing costume descended to the stage. Jack Smith's landlordism that night was devious, erotic and perplexing.

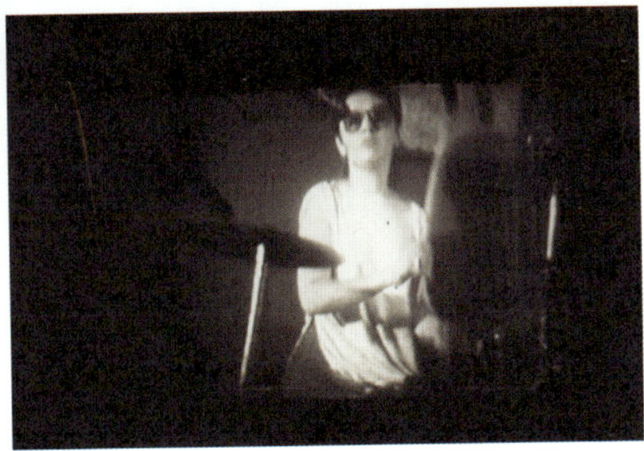

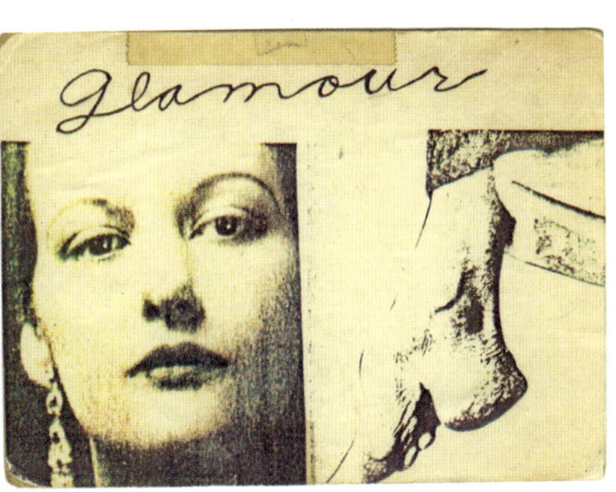

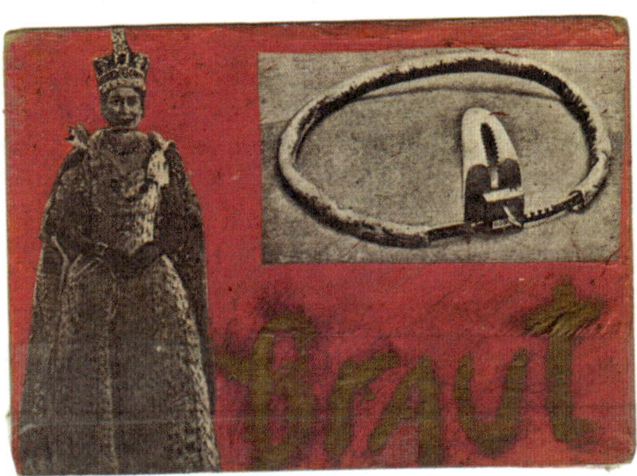

Facing page:

John Ahearn. *Green Robert*, 1980. Painted plaster, 40 × 30 × 12 cm. Courtesy of John Ahearn.

Christof Kohlhöfer. *Untitled [Mickey Mouse T-Shirt]*, New York: C. Kohlhöfer, 1980. Screenprinted t-shirt from *The Times Square Show* gift shop. Courtesy of Becky Howland.

This page:

Unknown. *Virginia Piersol playing the drums with Y Pants at The Times Square Show opening*, 1980. Silver gelatin print, 7 × 9.5 cm. Courtesy of Barbara Ess.

Jane Sherry. *Glamour / Braut [Bride]*. Both 1980. Collage on postcard, 11 × 15 cm each. From the *Misogyny Series*. Courtesy of Jane Sherry.

The next morning I went up to the second floor "dressing room" and found artworks had been altered. Things were missing. *Nail Polish and Drugs* had emptied out gel caps with the colorful time-release particles suspended in epoxy and a dozen tablets from a prescription bottle found on an empty lot. The tablets were some kind of dog medicine that even the drug addicts who frequented this particular lot had discarded. However, during Jack Smith's goings-on, up on the second floor, six of the tablets had been picked off—sacrificed to the ur-reality of the night.

No had attached to white plastic an upside down Exxon credit card, above an image of a soldier standing over body bags with white oil storage tanks against a bright blue sky in the distance. The credit card, also a lot find, and probably discarded by a thief, was gone, too.

Greed and Death had attached to a shard of silvered mirror a discarded junkie kit from the same lot: a few bent up needles, a spoon for cooking dope, a little yellowed piece of a cigarette filter for drawing up water. Really creepy stuff, and even too creepy for the Jack Smith crowd. None of that was even touched.

—Bobby G (Robert Goldman)

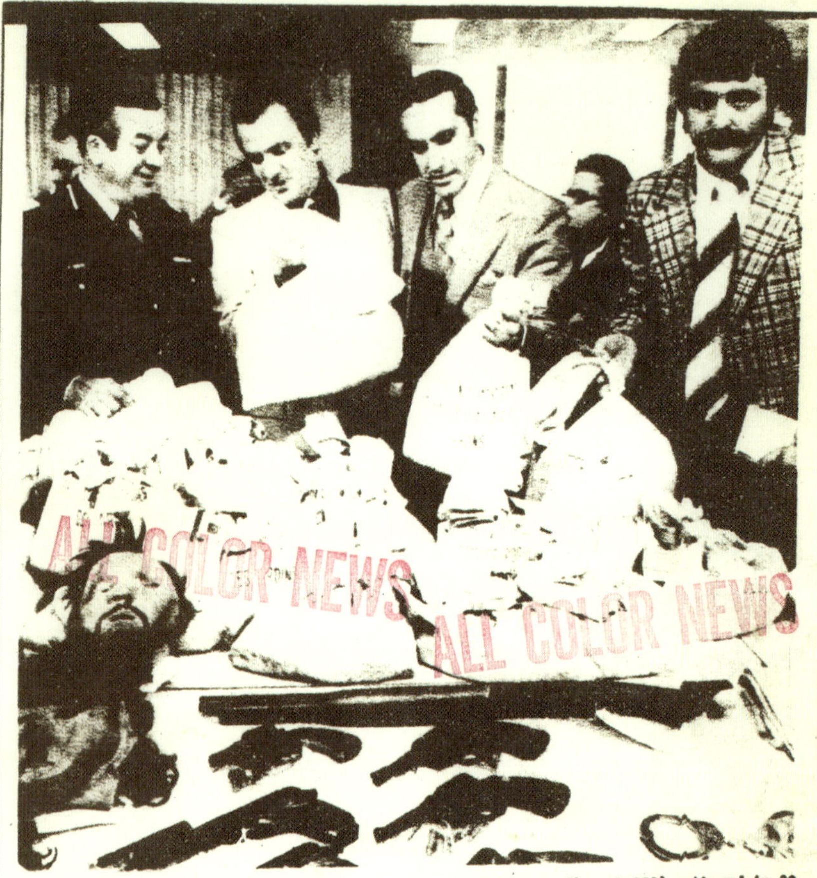

Unknown. *All Color News*, 1978. Photocopy and rubber stamp flyer, 28 × 21.5 cm.
Artwork for *All Color News* open meeting at Franklin Furnace. Courtesy of Becky Howland.

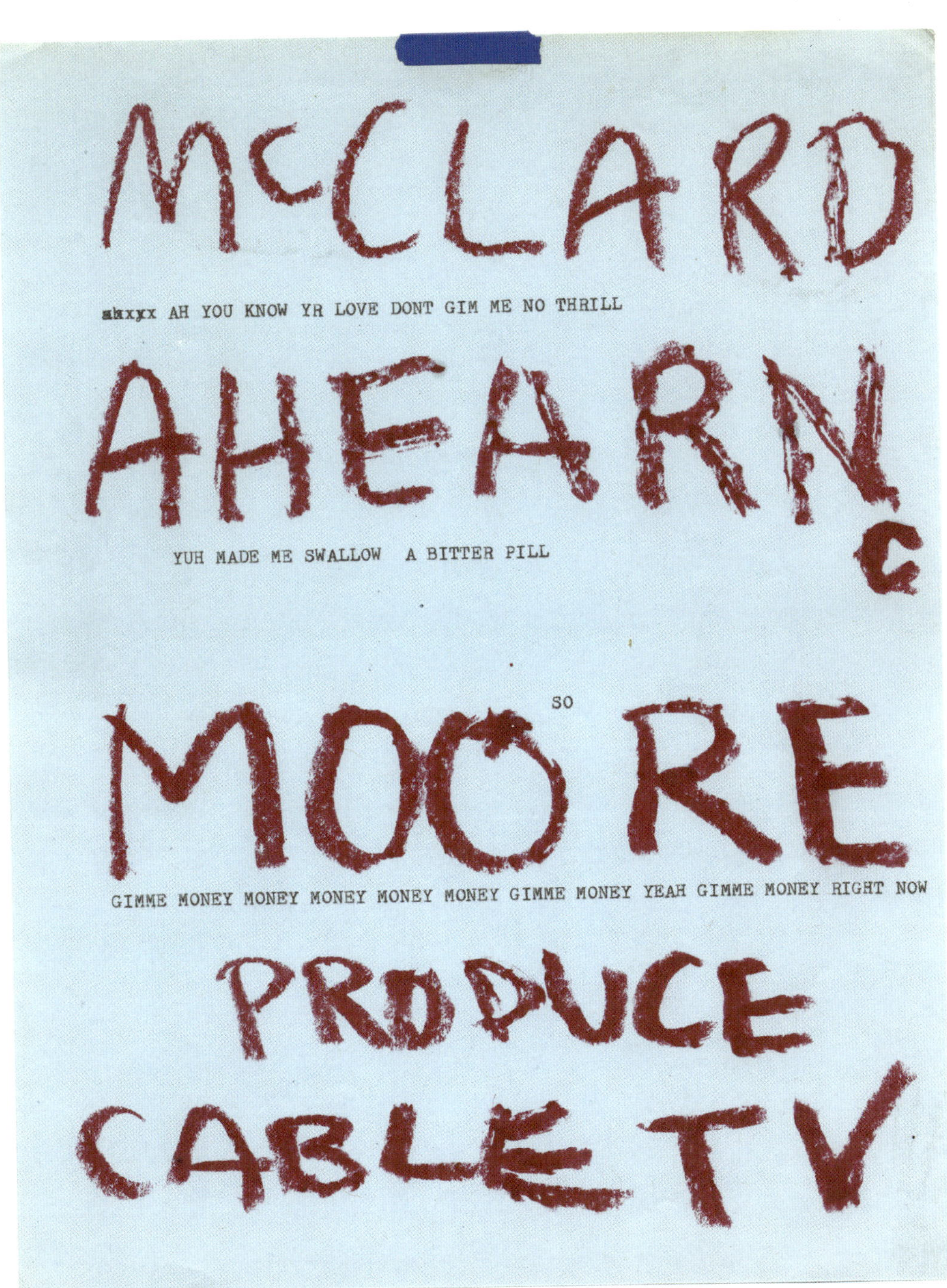

Alan Moore. *McClard, Ahearn, Moore*, 1979. Oil pastel on typewritten colored paper, 28 × 21.5 cm.
Original artwork for a poster for *All Color News* cable broadcast. Courtesy of Becky Howland.

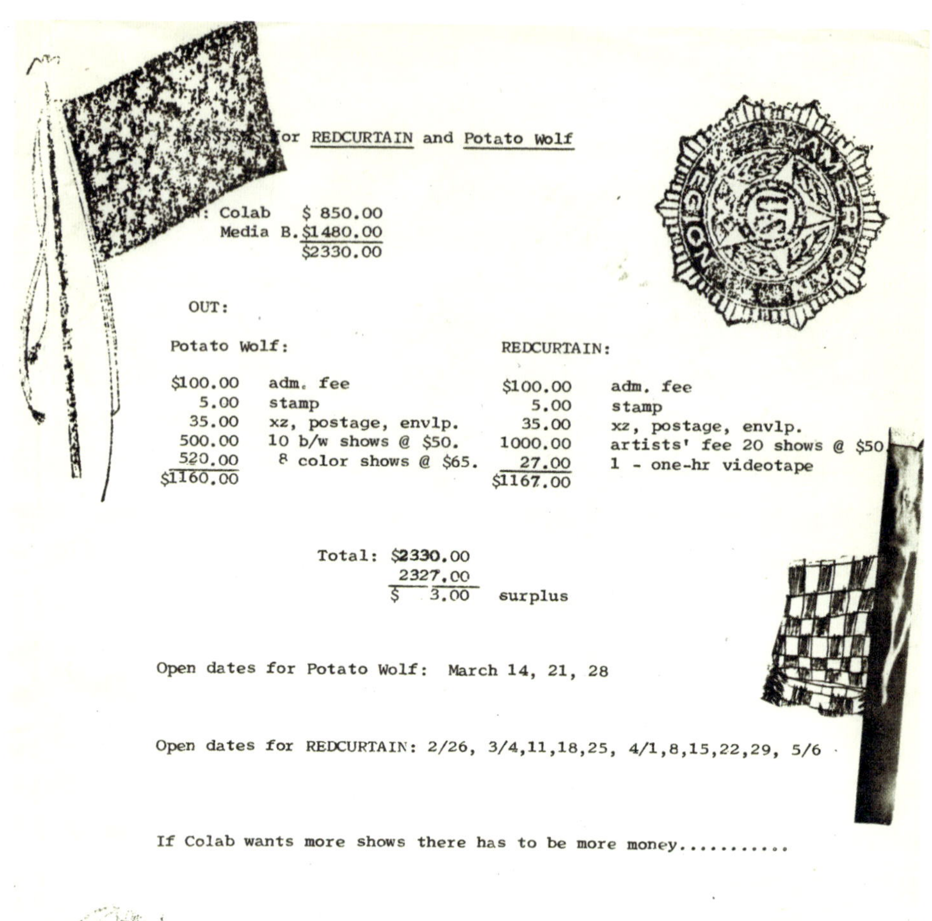

In May 1977, ALL COLOR NEWS emerged out of the larger organization of
artists, Collaborative Projects, Inc, with the purpose of generating an
artist-sponsored "community news service," which was defined as including
events affecting people who are not artists as well as the art community.

The programs carried information on events that got little or no coverage
in conventional news, and provided a critical investigation of current
social structures through a collaborative news-gathering team of artists.
Though the first two programs were primarily focused on NYC, the service
also carried information that had both local and statewide appeal.

Each program was divided into six categories: Births, Office, Fires,
Streets, Entertainment and Editorials. These categories were visually
designated by color change, rather than titles.

All Color News was shot with a B&W portapak, colorized and transferred
to 3/4" cassette for airing. Color coding, intended to make the overall
structure of the weekly program accessible to the viewer, was used to
schematize the program in lieu of titles. The last five minutes of each
show consisted of editorials done in studio and ran in full color;
the editorials deal with current issues of community interest.

-Colab Annual Report 1981

CO-LABORATIVE PROJECTS presents "NIGHTWATCH"
Manhattan Cable TV   channel D   Mondays 10:30-11:30 PM   MAy - Aug 1979

4 THE DEADLY ART OF SURVIVAL   Charlie Ahearn   60 min.
   super action film   starring Nathan Ingram(1976 USA Karate Champion)

1 ROME '78   James Nares   90 min.
   tales of sex, scandal, murder, intrigue in ancient Rome

8 BEAUTY BECOMES THE BEAST   Vivienne Dick   40 min.
   tragi-comedy with Lydia Lunch   music by Teenage Jesus and the Jerks

   TOPLESS   Cara Perlman   16 min.
   humorous peek into New York City's topless bars

4 MEN IN ORBIT   John Lurie 40 min.
   spaced out feature   starring John Lurie and Eric Mitchell

   11 ——→ 12   Andrea Callard   12 min.

   MAXIMS   Jenny Holzer   8 min.

1 G-MAN   Scot B and Beth B   60 min.
   anti-terroist police chief and his sordid personal life;Bill Rice stars

8 BLACK BOX Scot B and Beth B   23 min.
   innocent man(Bob Mason) is tortured by Lydia Lunch

   LETTERS TO DAD Scot B and Beth B 15 min.
   Guyanna Jonestown characters impersonated

   THE OFFENDERS   Scot B and Beth B   12 min.   (parts 1&2)

15 THE WHOLE BODY FEELS LIGHT AND WANTS TO FLY   Christof Kohlhofer   30 min.
   "voo-doo art movie" starring Sigmar Polke

   DANCING LESSON Christof Kohlhofer 28 min.
   (documentary) Mongoloids learn to dance with instructor

2 REMOTE IN THE THIRD WORLD Tom Morey 30 min.
   (documentary) "in 1976 23,000 Guatamaleans died in 7 seconds"

   SLOW SCAN NETWORK artists' groups tape compiled by Liza Bear 30 min.
   USA/Canada 2 way video communication over telephone (taped)

9 SATELLITE TAPES keith Sonnier and Liza Bear 60 min.
   NYC/San Francisco 2 way video communication by NASA satellite (taped)

16 REAL NAMES MUSICAL Alan Moore 30 min.

   I/EYE-SEE/SEA   Cara Brownwell   30 min.

23 MEDICAL SAMPLER Diego Cortez 60 min.

30 TELEVISION AND THE POLITICS OF REPRESSION Links Video(w.Diego Cortez) 60.

6 ROCK TAPES taped by Diego Cortez 60 min.(groups to be announced)

65

Facing page:

$$$$$$$$ for Red Curtain and Potato Wolf, 1979. Photocopied document from Colab Annual Report, 21.5 × 28 cm. Courtesy of Matthew Geller.

This page:

Co-laborative Projects presents "Nightwatch," 1979. Photocopied document, 21.5 × 28 cm each. Photocopy of broadcast schedule from Colab Annual Report. Courtesy of Matthew Geller.

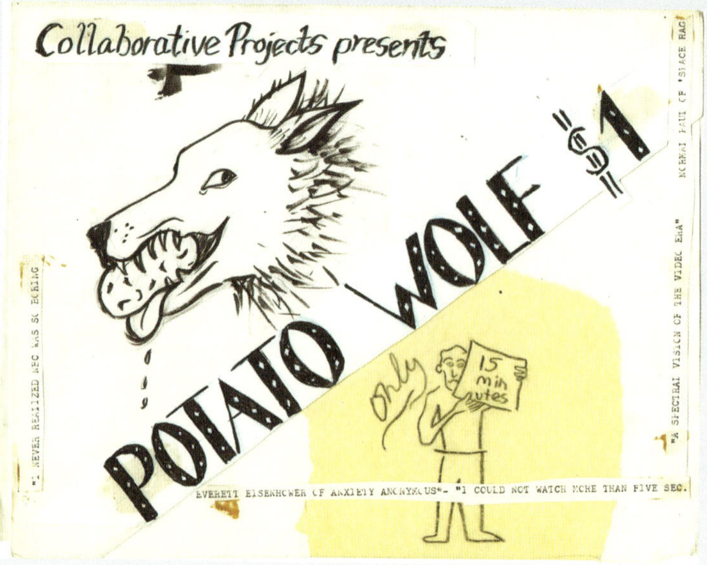

Potato Wolf was a weekly half-hour public access cable TV show produced by Colab from 1979–1986. These were (mostly) "live" shows of varying themes and styles where folks rotated technical and creative duties each week. We learned on the job. Some wrote and directed while others volunteered to act, make sets and costumes, produce/mix audio and music, shoot video, serve as camera operators, and direct video switching during a live feed within a sometimes-chaotic studio. Drawing inspiration from Bertolt Brecht, The Living Theatre, Happenings and Ernie Kovacs, most shows were improvised, cheap, politically oriented and sometimes hastily pulled-together and boring. It was a lot of fun and, as a whole, brilliant. Artists' TV became a hybrid of visual art, theater, film, poetry and video/sonic art that television had never seen the likes of before— a raw expression that precedes and influenced the democratic platform and culture of today's YouTube and Vimeo. The funny thing is, much of Manhattan wasn't wired for cable TV yet, especially the downtown enclave, so very few people actually watched Potato Wolf. We would end up afterwards viewing the ¾ in dub of the live show at someone's loft, drinking and laughing at our brilliance and silliness.

I think the laughter was a defining attribute of Colab, aesthetically and personally. (OK, there were a few fights, some alienating personalities, but let's let bygones be bygones.) This was an era that dared to be made fun of and we did. The seriousness came later in the art world (and politically), the stakes got higher, but for those precious years we played as anarchists in the Colab band.

—Julie Harrison

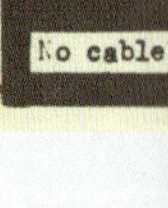

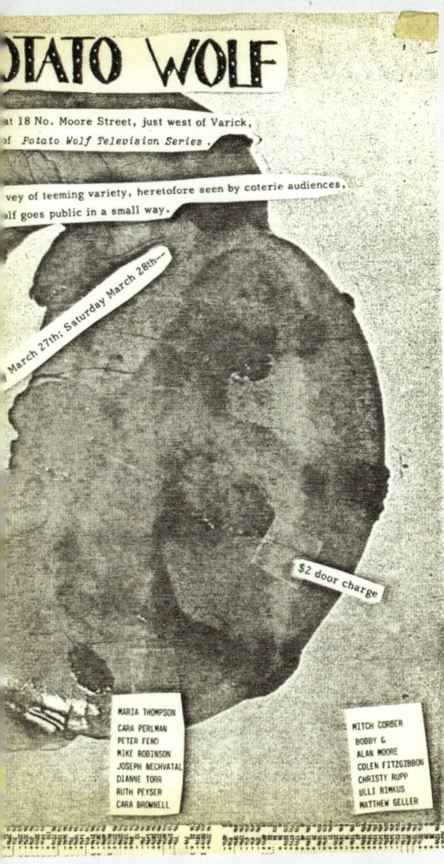

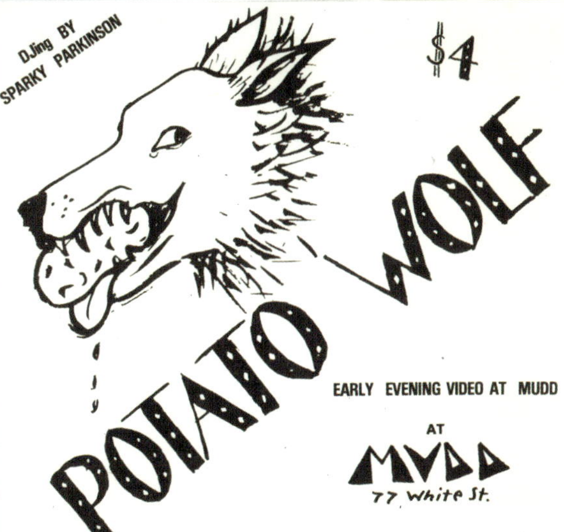

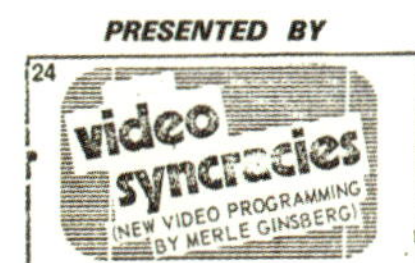

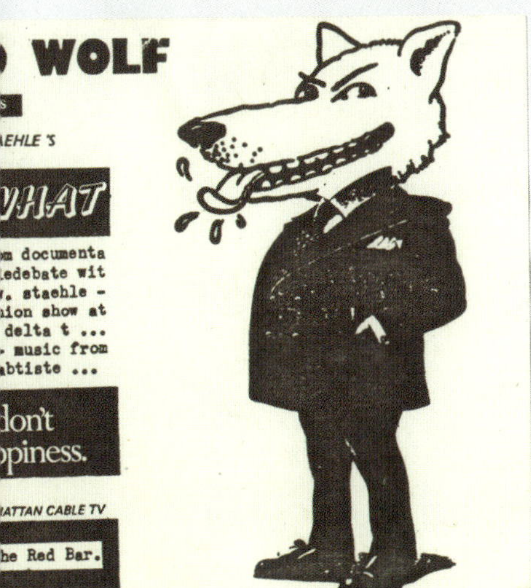

Clockwise from upper left:

Becky Howland. *Collaborative Projects Presents Potato Wolf*, c. 1979.
Artwork paste-up for photocopy flyer, 21.5 × 28 cm.
Courtesy of Becky Howland.

Becky Howland (lettering), Unknown (design). *Potato Wolf*, c. 1979. Photocopy
flyer, 28 × 21.5 cm. Courtesy of Kiki Smith.

Becky Howland (artwork), Unknown (design). *Potato Wolf: Early Evening Video
at Mudd Club*, c. 1981. Photocopy poster, 36 × 21.5 cm.
Courtesy of Bobby G (Robert Goldman).

Wolfgang Staehle. *Potato Wolf Presents Wolfgang Staehle's After What*,
c. 1981. Photocopy handbill, 13 × 17 cm. Courtesy of Becky Howland.

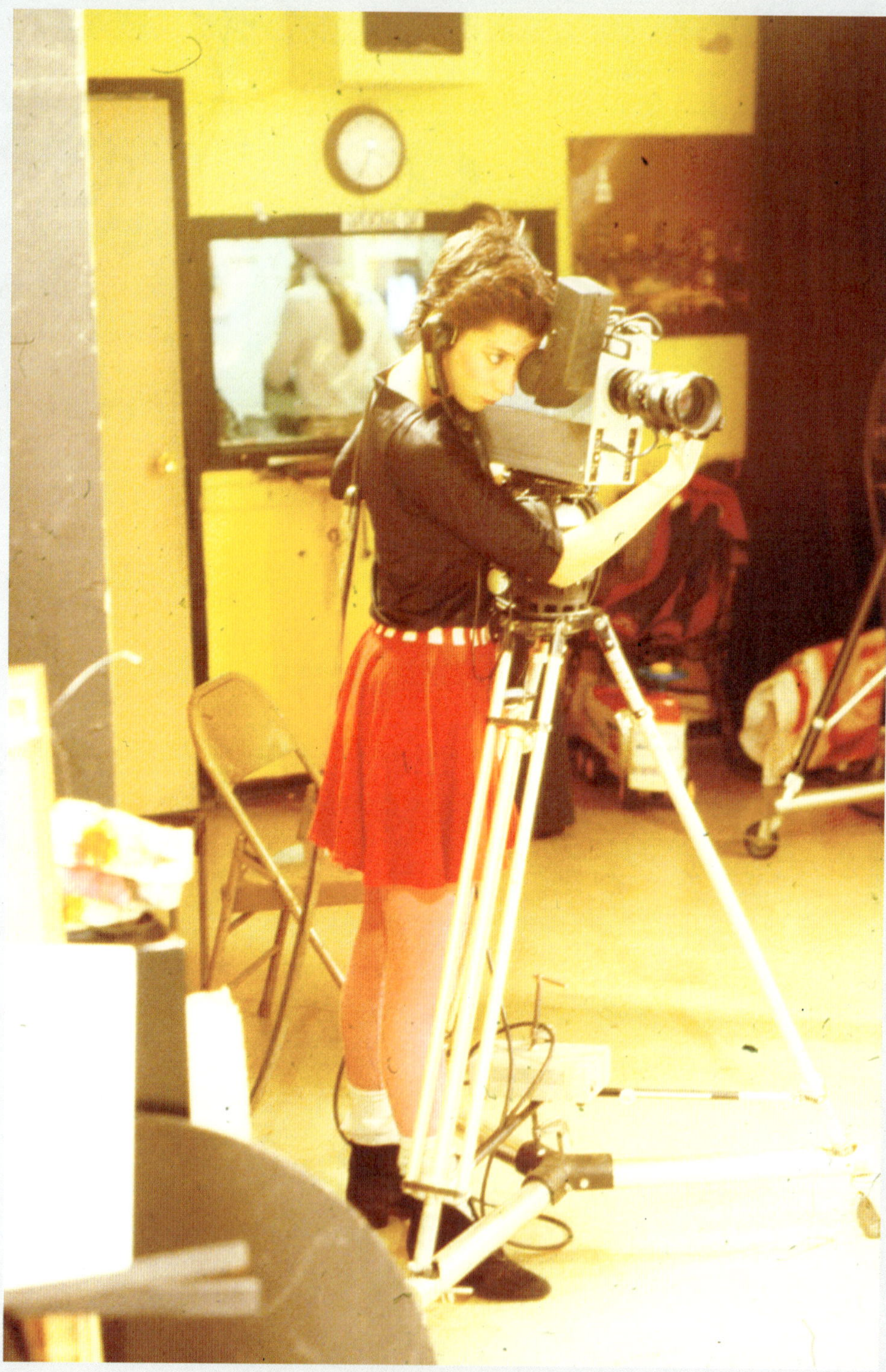

Terry Mohre. *Julie Harrison operating camera during a Potato Wolf broadcast*, 1984.
Color photograph, 25 × 20 cm. Courtesy of Julie Harrison.

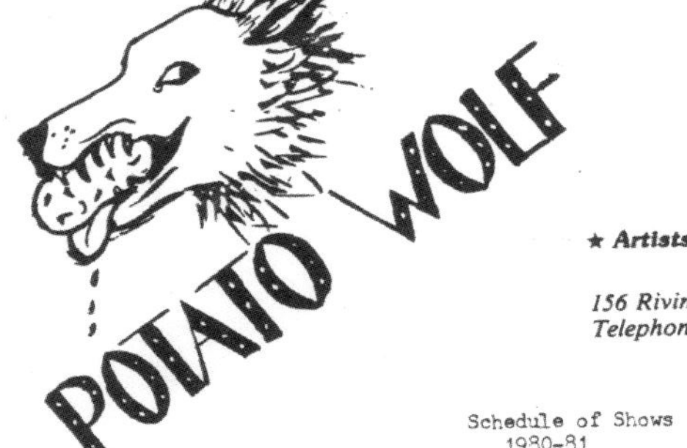

★ Artists' Cable Television ★

156 Rivington Street, New York, New York 10002
Telephone: 254-3697/855-3604

Schedule of Shows
1980-81

"Potato Wolf" is a weekly television series on Manhattan Cable Channel C,
10:30 p.m. Fridays. Each program is directed by an individual artist or group
of artists

November 7--Collaborative Projects "Election Critique"

November 14--Lindzee Smith "Women in Rock"

November 21--Christy Rupp "City Wildlife: Mice, Rats and Roaches"

December 5--Peter Fend "The World Today, 1990"

December 12--Joseph Nechvatal "Nuke Me, Nuke My Dog"

December 19--Ellen Cooper, Kiki Smith "Christmas Show"

December 26--Jeanne Quinn, Bruce Tovsky "A Horror Show"

January 2--Ulli Rimkus "New Year Show"

January 9--Ilona Granet "In the Bomb Factory"

January 16--Alan Moore "The Reptile Mind"

January 23--Cara Perlman "Power Plays"

January 30--Christof Kohlhoeffer, untitled

February 6--Sally White, untitled

February 13--Walter Robinson "The Love Show"

February 20--Diane Torr, Ruth Peyser, untitled

February 27--Wolfgang Staehle "Art Police"

--continued--

Collaborative Projects, Inc.

POTATO WOLF Schedule of Shows, 1980-81
Page Two

March 6--Cara Brownell, untitled

March 13--Jim Sutcliffe, untitled

March 20--Colen Fitzgibbon, untitled

March 27--Matthew Geller "Thirty Boys' Stories"

April 3--Gregory Lehmann "The New Right"

April 10--Mitch Corber, untitled

April 17--Sam Lee "Community Youth Program in Jamaica, Queens"

April 24--Bobby G "Video Program from ABC No Rio"

May 1--Scott Miller "Amateur Wrestling"

May 8--Herr Lugus, untitled

May 15--unallocated time slot   *Debby Davis*

May 22--unallocated time slot   *Mindy Herman*

May 29--unallocated time slot

Unknown. *Potato Wolf broadcast schedule*, 1980. Photocopy, 2 pp, 28 × 21.5 cm. Courtesy of Bobby G (Robert Goldman).

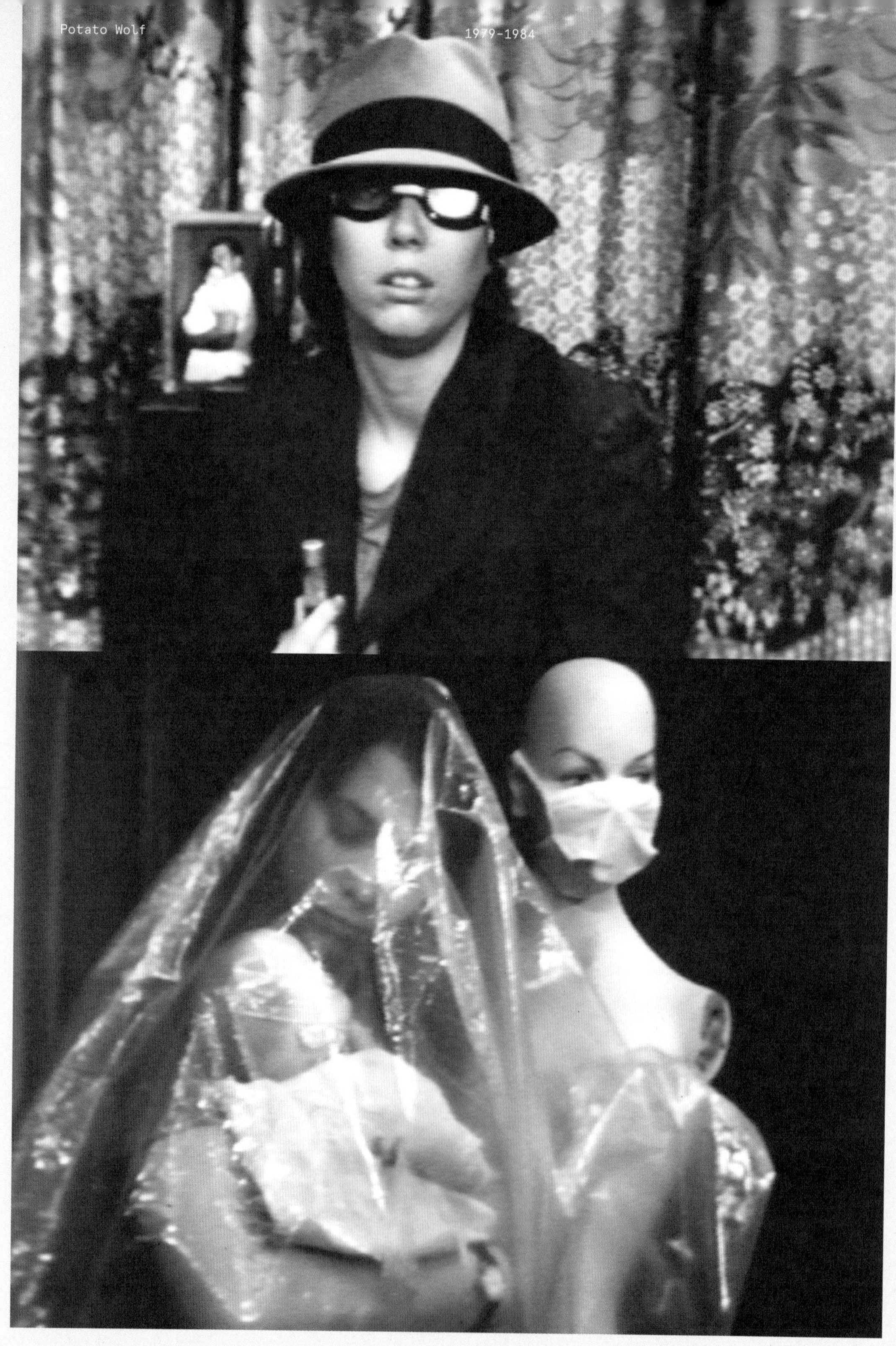

The Birthday Show, 1980. Produced by Julie Harrison [Video Stills by Julie Harrison, 2012]. Video, 30 mins.
Julie Harrison. Courtesy of Julie Harrison.

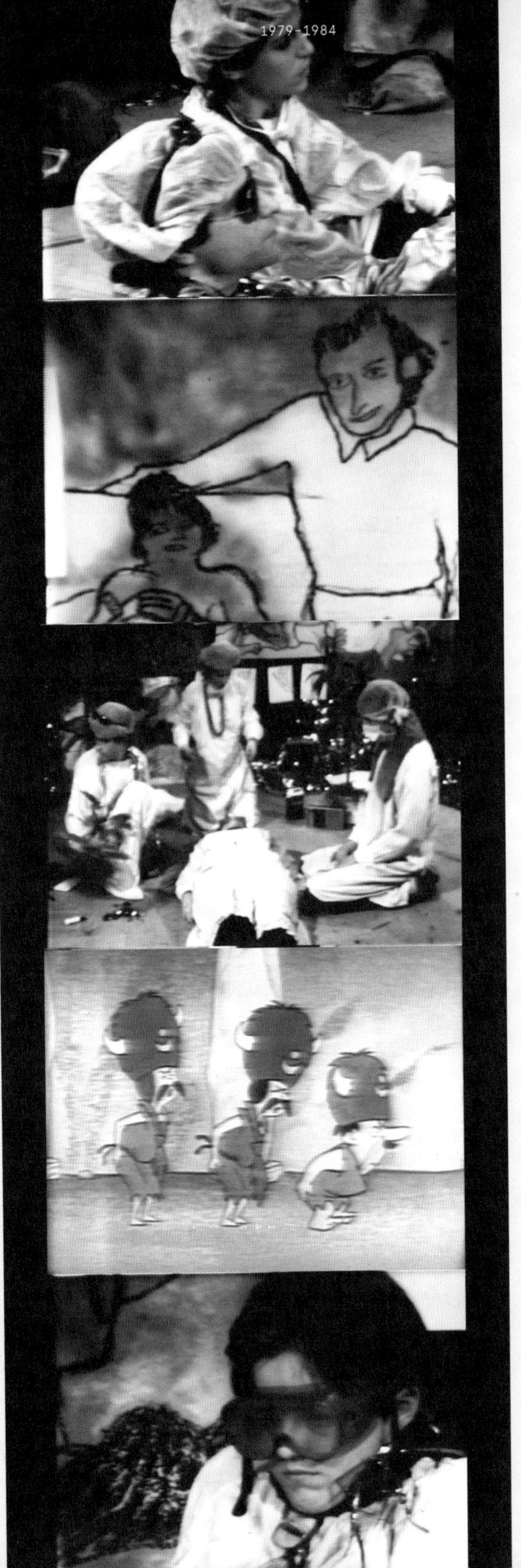

The Patient Show, 1979.
Produced by Cara Perlman.
[Video Stills by Julie Harrison,
2012]. Video, 30 mins. From
top: Cara Perlman, Jim Sutcliffe,
Mitch Corber and Sally White.
Courtesy of Julie Harrison.

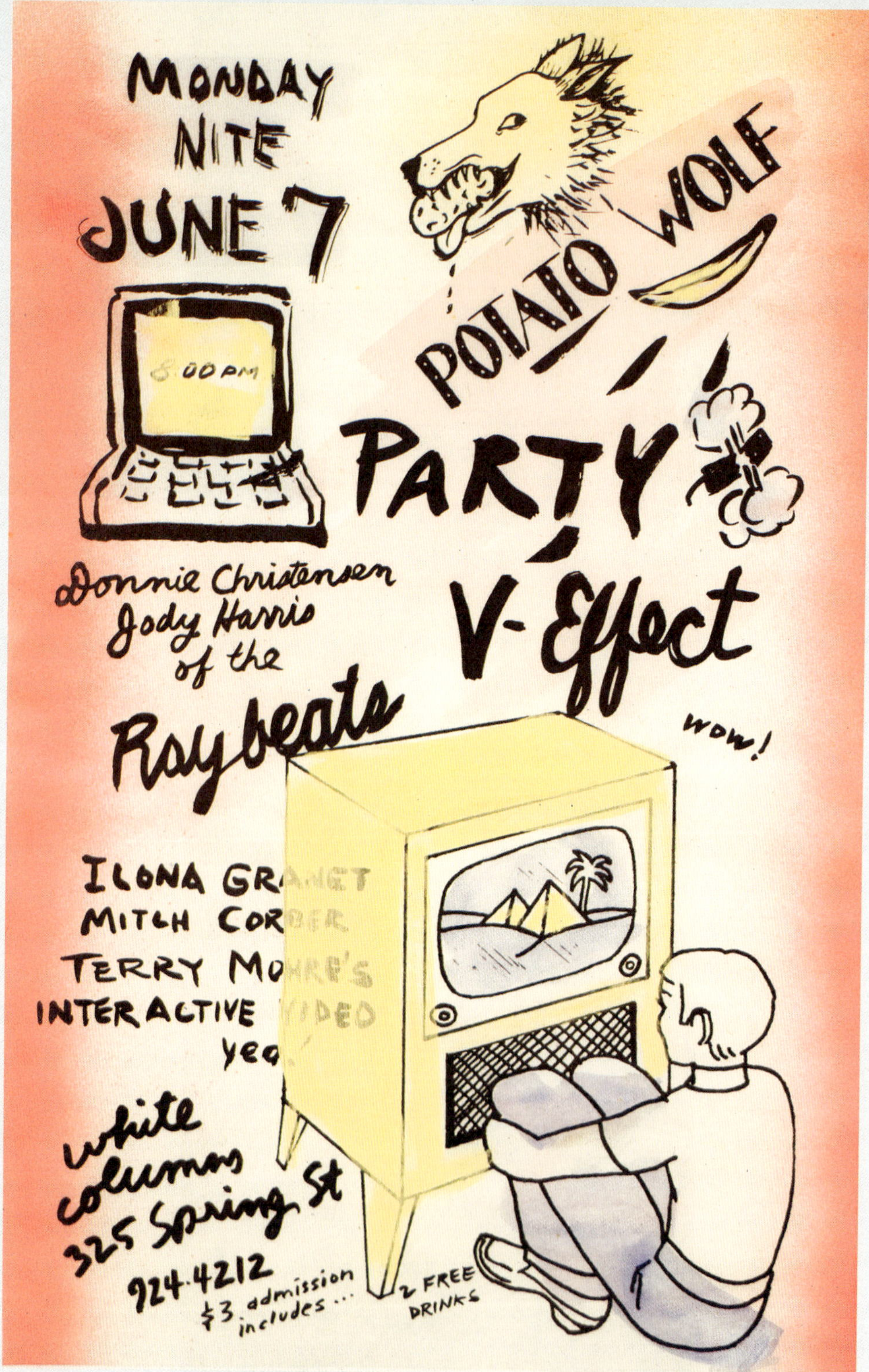

Bobby G (Robert Goldman). *White Columns Potato Wolf Poster*. New York: Collaborative Projects, c. 1983. Hand-painted photocopy, 28 × 40 cm. Courtesy of Bobby G (Robert Goldman).

On Potato Wolf:

The most fun I didn't know

I was having.

—Becky Howland

Opposite:

Unknown. *Potato Wolf broadcast schedule*, 1979. Photocopy, 2 pp, 28 x 21.5 cm. Courtesy of Bobby G (Robert Goldman).

Below:

Cara Perlman. *Potato Wolf handbills*, 1981. Photocopy on colored paper, 7 × 10.5 cm each. Courtesy of Becky Howland and Kiki Smith.

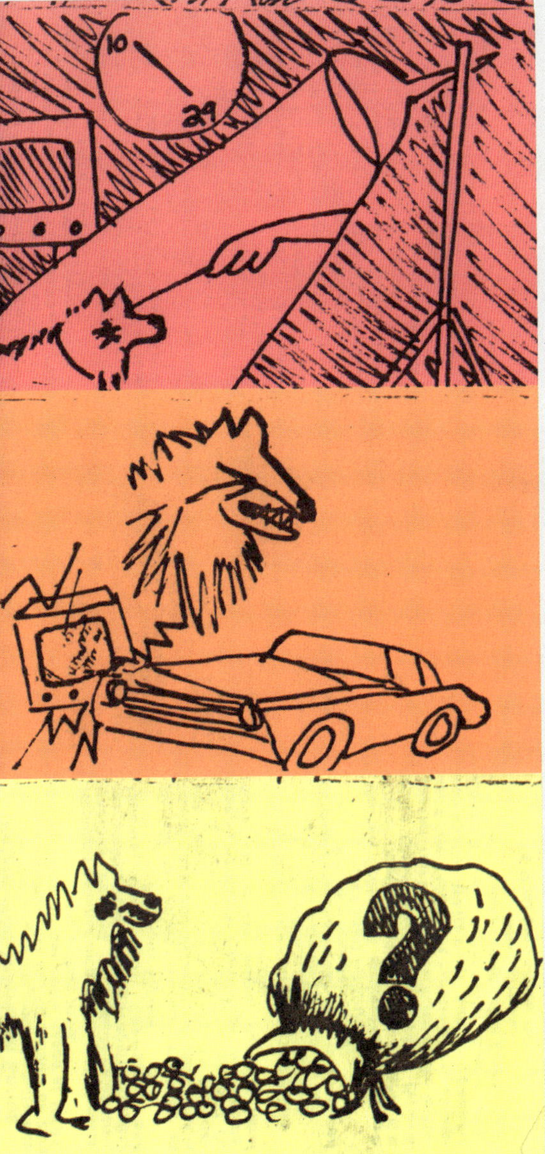

obverse— *Cara Perlman*

"where's that at?"
18 No. Moore St.
just west of Varlck
that's the one-time Revue of the
Potato Wolf Television Series
Two years of bizarre incidents of artists' television, recorded live at ETC Studios on 23rd St. for public access cable, taped at MERC, and around town.

Highlight bonanza recaps Phony Newscasts, goofball Parades of Pseudo-celebrities, megaloManiac Montages, Songstresses, Balladeers, Cave Girls, Charlatans and Psychotic Clowns...

Recline on wide-body Lounge Chairs as liberal hosts dish up exotic delights. This is not "video art"—this is the raw material. It's a video lounge. Entre actes, and DJ Sparky Parkinson, late of Public Arts International, shave the waves, pumping aural animation.

THURSDAY—MARCH 26—9pm till 2am
FRIDAY—MARCH 27—9pm till 2am
SATURDAY—March 28—9pm till 2am

$2 door charge (nominal) goes to straitened P-Wolf production budget...

FEATURED PRODUCERS:
Matthew Geller • Ulli Rimkus • Christy Rupp • Colen Fitzgibbon • Alan Moore • Bobby G • Mitch Corber • Cara Brownell • Ruth Peyser • Dianne Torr • Joseph Nechvatal • Mike Robinson • Peter Fend • Cara Perlman • Maria Thompson • Sally White • Jim Sutcliffe • Robert Cooney • David Levine • Jules Baptiste • Kiki Smith • Ilona Granet • Ellen Cooper and

18 No. Moore St.
just west of Varlck
houses one-time Revue of the
Potato Wolf Television Series
Two years of bizarre incidents of artists' television, recorded live at ETC Studios on 23rd St. for public access cable, taped at MERC, and around town.

Recline on wide-body Lounge Chairs as liberal hosts dish up exotic delights. This is not "video art"—this is the raw material, esophagically received. It's a video lounge. Entre actes, and DJ Sparky Parkinson, late of Public Arts International, shave the waves, pumping aural animation.

THURSDAY—MARCH 26—9pm till 2am
FRIDAY—MARCH 27—9pm till 2am
SATURDAY—March 28—9pm till 2am

$2 door charge (nominal) goes to straitened P-Wolf production budget...

FEATURED PRODUCERS:
Matthew Geller • Ulli Rimkus • Christy Rupp • Colen Fitzgibbon • Alan Moore • Bobby G • Mitch Corber • Cara Brownell • Ruth Peyser • Dianne Torr • Joseph Nechvatal • Mike Robinson • Peter Fend • Cara Perlman • Maria Thompson • Sally White • Jim Sutcliffe • Robert Cooney • David Levine • Jules Baptiste • Kiki Smith • Ilona Granet • Ellen Cooper • Julie Harrison

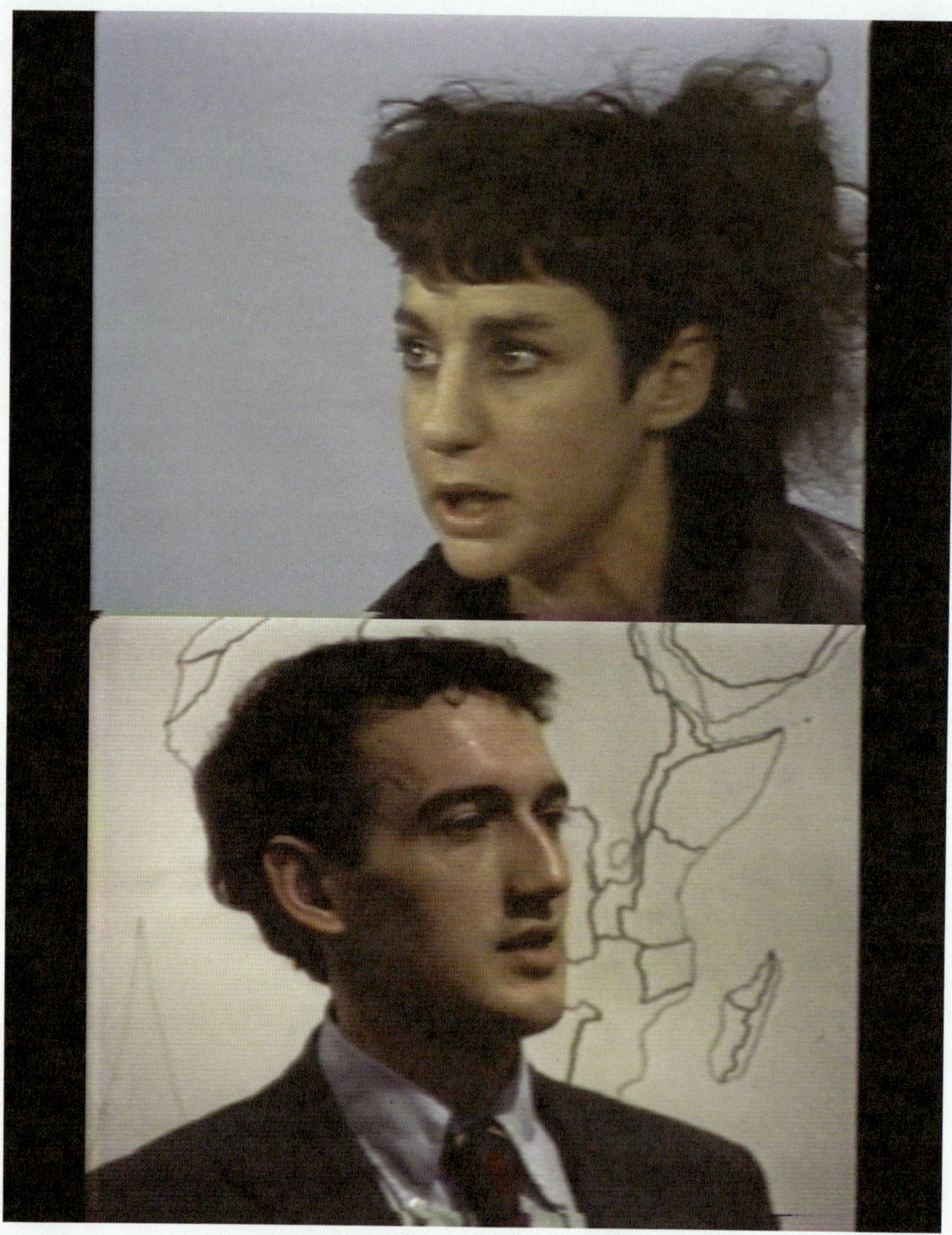

Potato Salad, 1982. A short compilation of Potato Wolf episodes. Produced by Colab. [Video Stills by Julie Harrison, 2012]. Video, 2:20. Top: Ilona Granet in *KGB*; bottom: Peter Fend in *Italy Wins World War II Again*; opposite page: from *Gothic Horror* by Joseph Nechvatal. Courtesy of Julie Harrison.

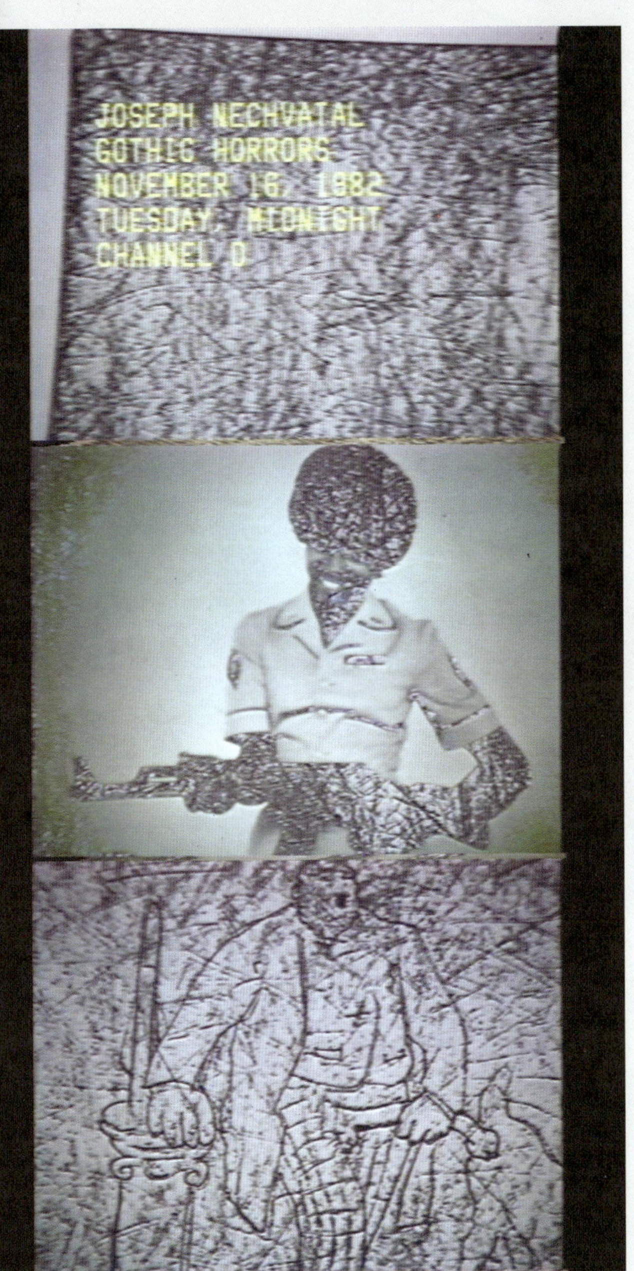

Potato Wolf TV tackles TV genres with paltry budgets but novel attitudes, producing unforeseen versions of variety shows, game shows, newscasts, documentaries, dramas and talk shows. Potato Wolf redefines and recasts the forms of television which its producers grew up on. With each museum or club viewing of its productions, in addition to the public-access telecasts, the twenty or so producers of Potato Wolf shows become more focused, more certain about what they expect to see on mass-market TV. A number of producers have begun contracting with national networks with their innovations – with on-screen credit. At the same time, because Potato Wolf – even when scripted and pre-recorded – tends to be spontaneous and raw, the series breaks through to unexpected forms of TV. Visual documentary, allegorical comedy, fake newscasts, and video verite chronicles of crimes, however rough and unrehearsed, break ground for more professional telecasts later on. Potato Wolf is a TV laboratory. The helter skelter '82–'83 kickoff extravaganza atttracted British and Dutch TV crews, with subsequent European airing: no one could foresee the show, the chaos, not the power. More to come...

-Colab Annual Report 1982

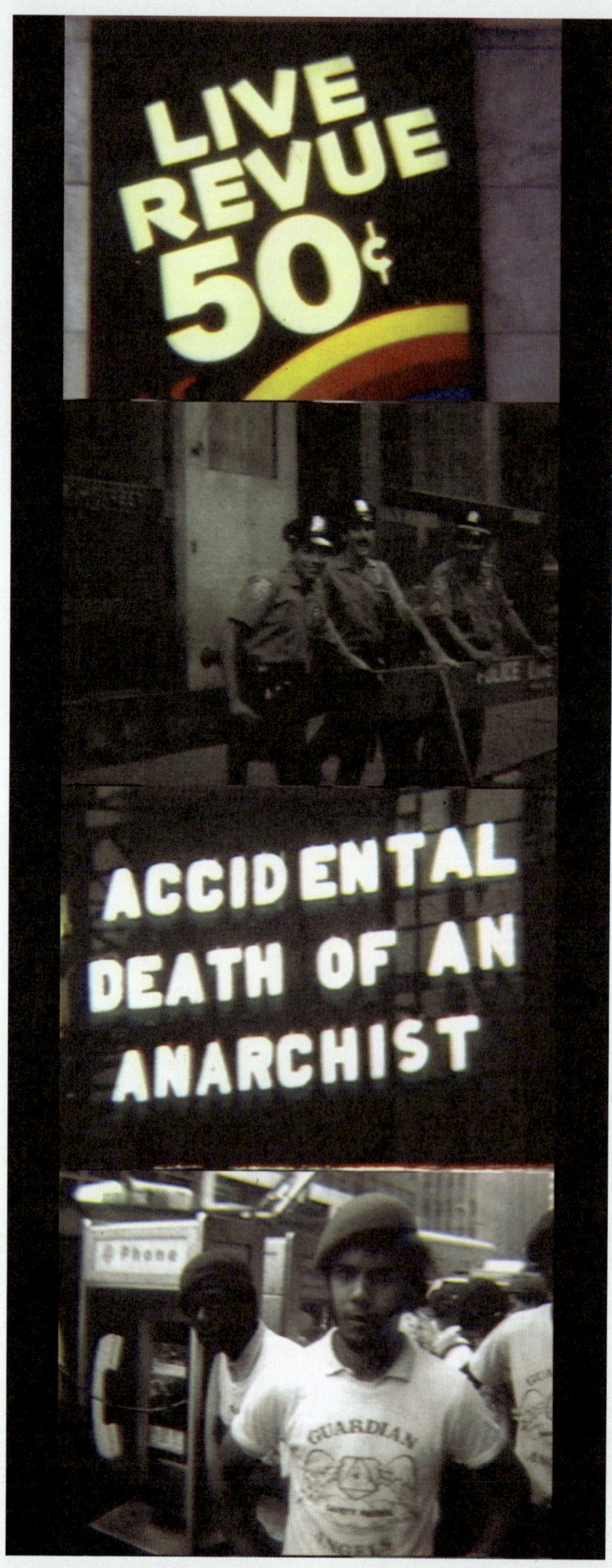
LIVE
REVUE
50¢
ACCIDENTAL
DEATH OF AN
ANARCHIST
Phone
GUARDIAN

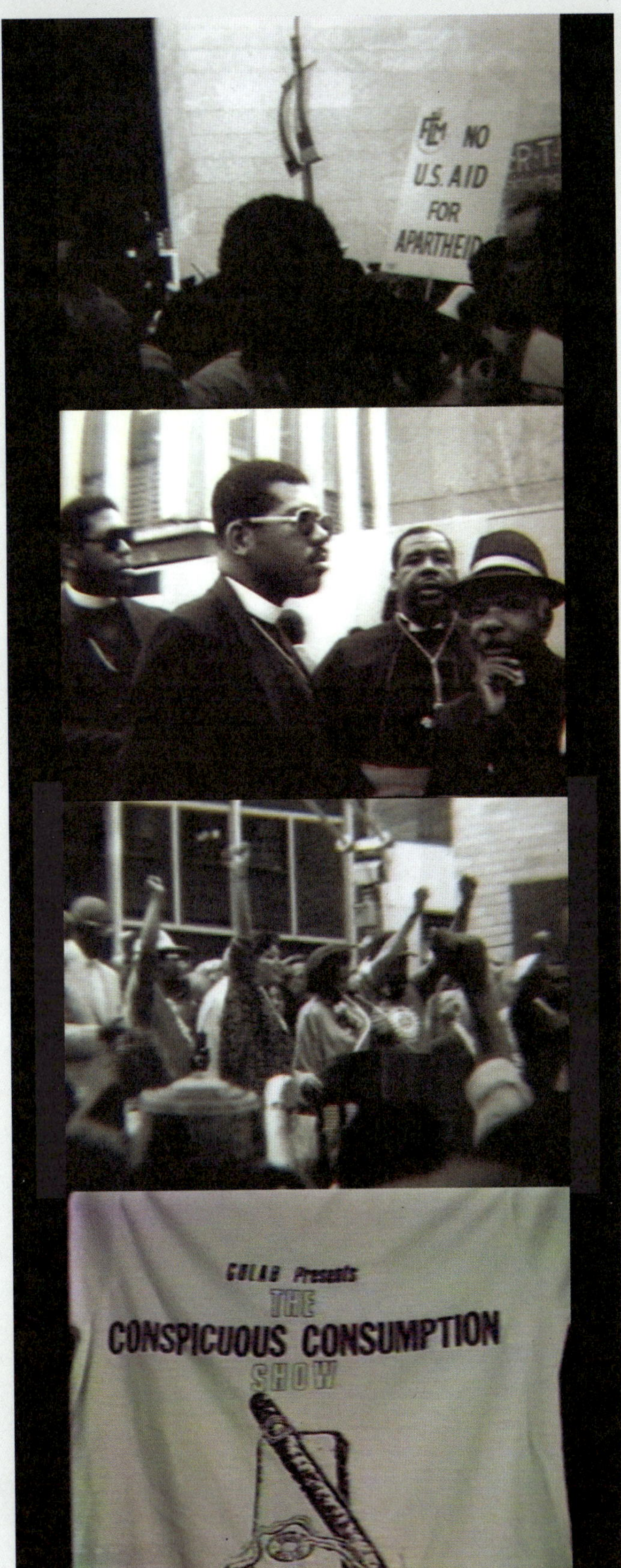

Conspicuous Consumption,
1980, Produced by Colab.
[Video Stills by Julie Harrison,
2012]. Video, 30 mins.
Courtesy of Julie Harrison.

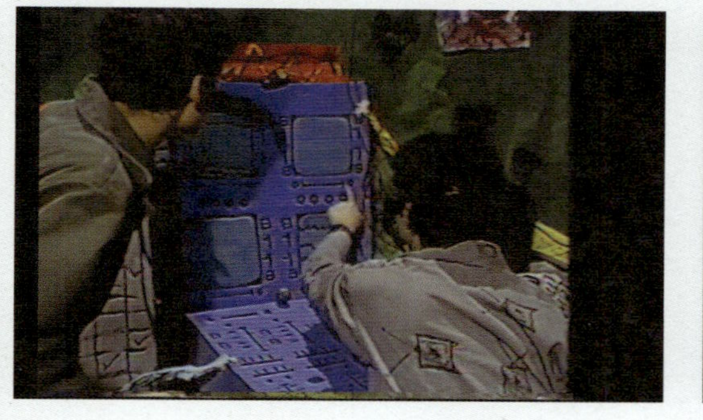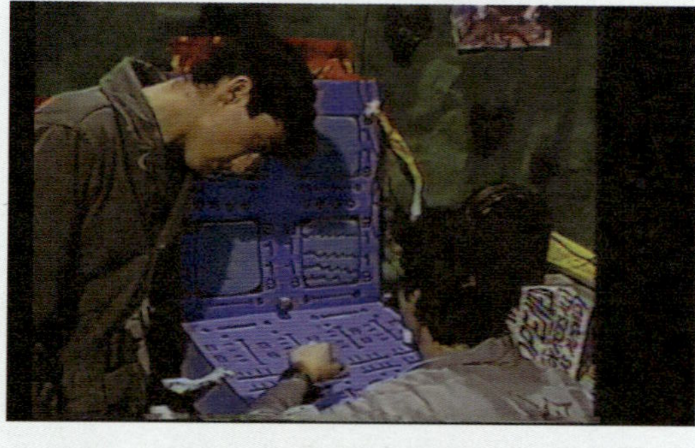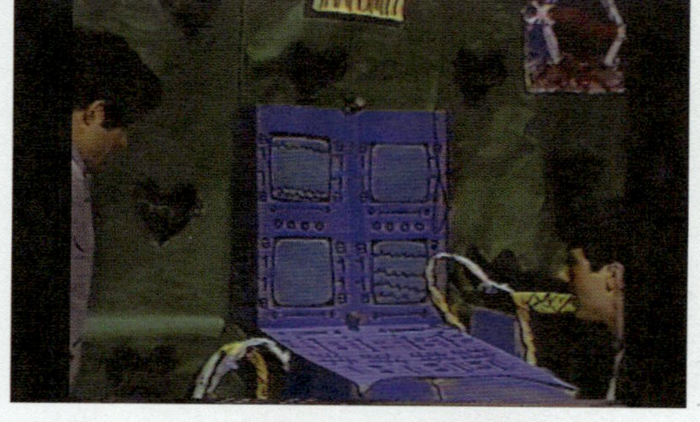
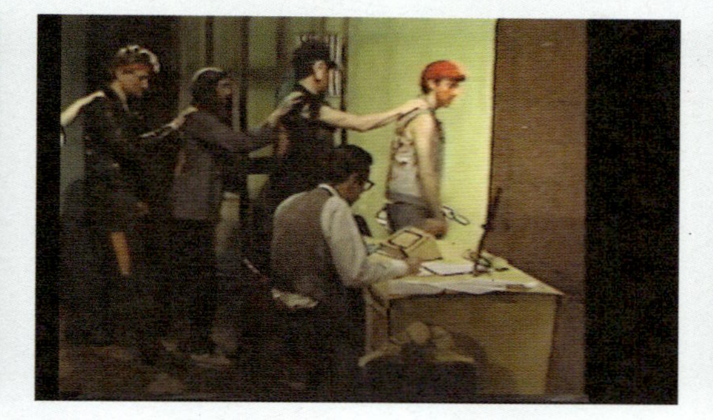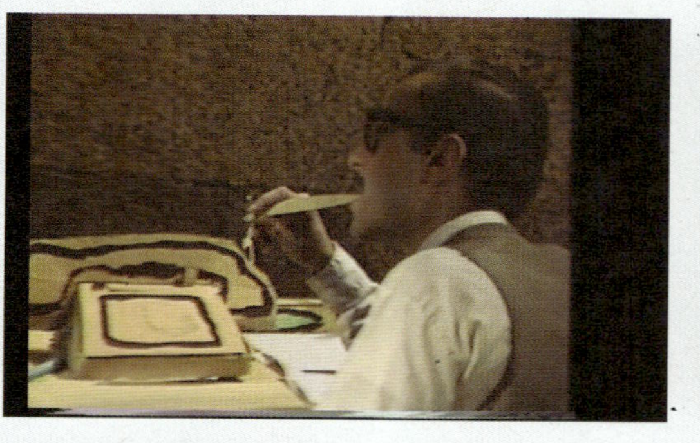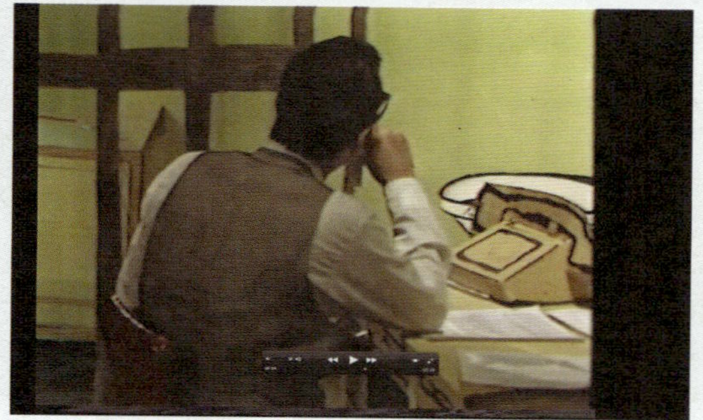
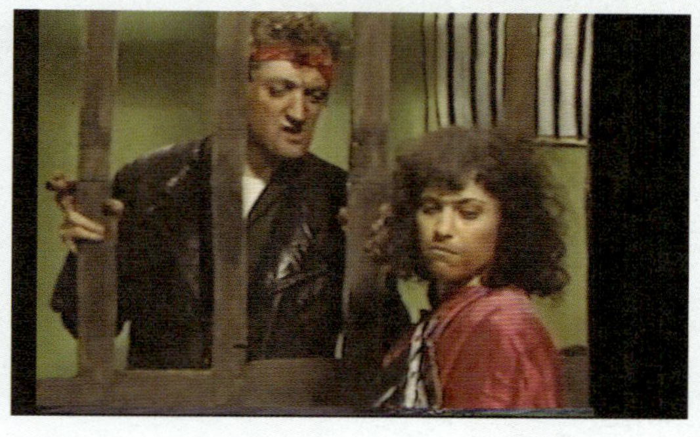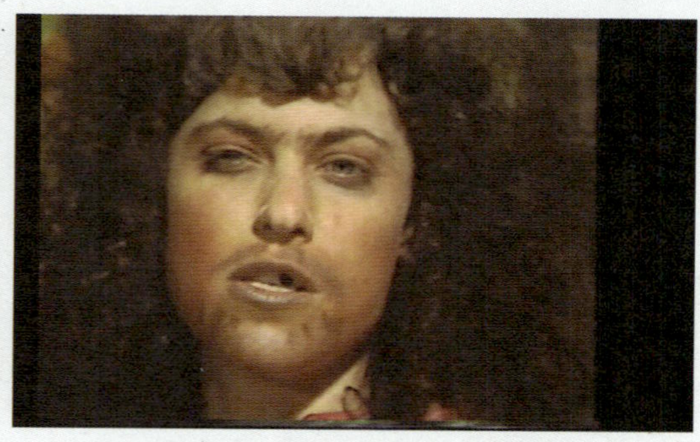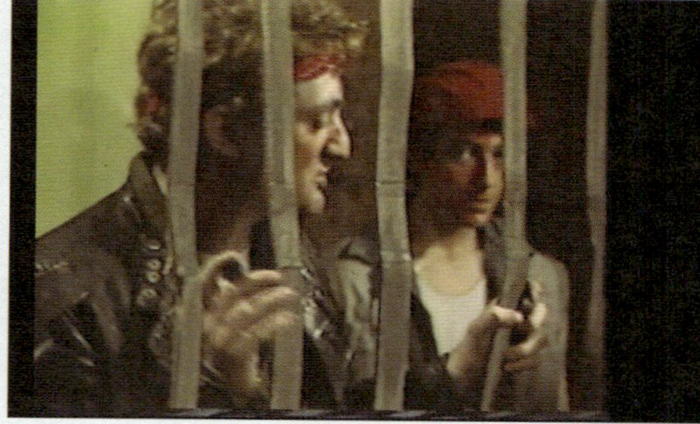

Strife, 1982–83. Produced by Alan Moore [Video Stills by Julie Harrison, 2012 from Potato Salad videocassette, 1982]. Video, 8:11. 1st column: Jim Sutcliffe and Brian Piersol; 2nd column: George Shustowicz, Walter "Mike" Robinson, Jim Sutcliffe, Mindy Stevenson and Terry Mohre; 3rd column: Walter "Mike" Robinson, Jim Sutcliffe and Cara Perlman. Courtesy of Julie Harrison.

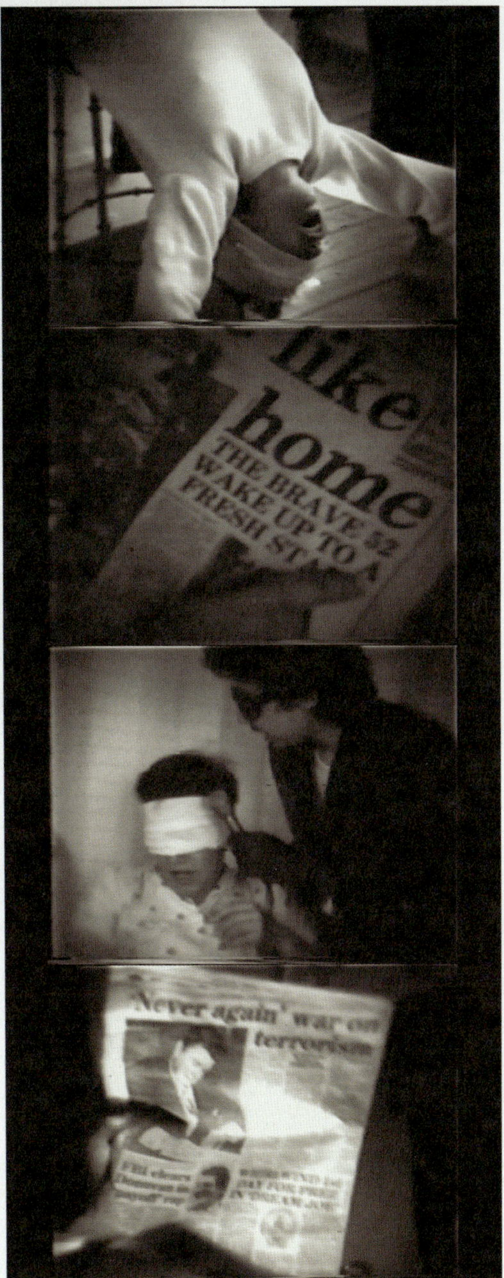

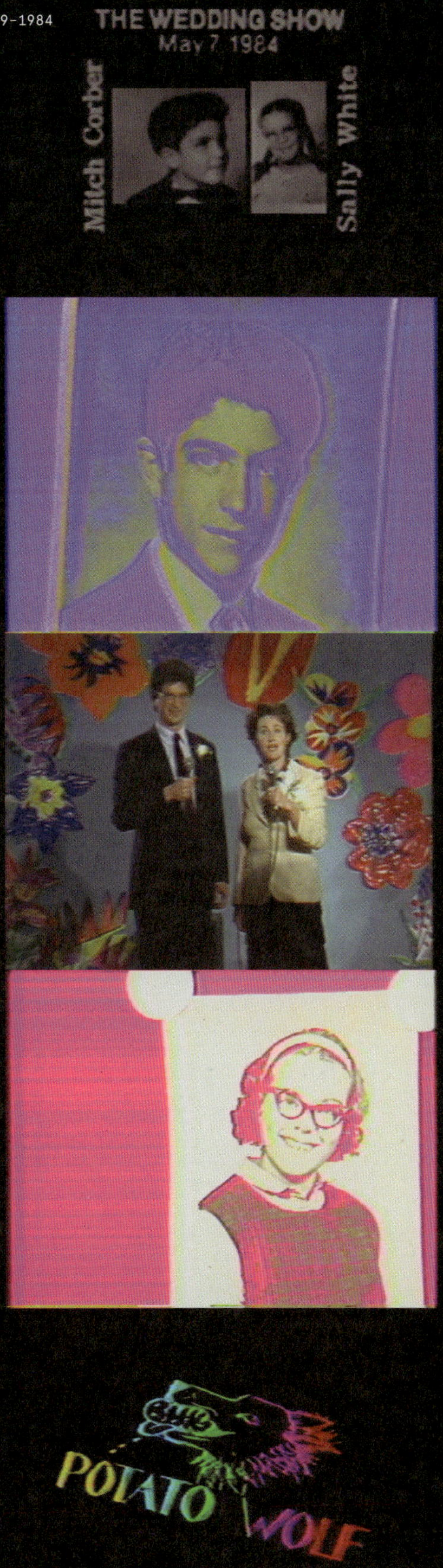

Left:

Yellow Ribbon Conspiracy, 1980. Produced by Colab. [Video Stills by Julie Harrison, 2012]. Video, 30 mins. Cara Brownell and others. Courtesy of Julie Harrison.

Right:

The Wedding Show, 1984. Produced by Sally White and Mitch Corber, directed by George Schifini [Video Stills by Julie Harrison, 2012]. Video, 30 mins. From top: Mitch Corber; Bill Considine and Maria Thompson; Sally White. Courtesy of Julie Harrison.

THE OFFICES OF
FEND, FITZGIBBON, HOLZER, NADIN, PRINCE & WINTERS

PRACTICAL ESTHETIC SERVICES
ADAPTABLE TO CLIENT SITUATION

OUR CONSULTATION INCLUDES
A REVIEW OF YOUR NEEDS AND
SUGGESTIONS FOR REALISTIC ACTION

305 BROADWAY RM 600 NY NY 10013 (212) 233-3794

The Pleasure Function Show or *Function Pleasure Show*—it could be called either way—was a group show of six pretty intense artists: Peter Fend, Coleen Fitzgibbon, Jenny Holzer, Peter Nadin, Richard Prince, and Robin Winters. They came as a group to challenge Los Angeles artists with the idea that pleasure should be functional and work should be play. We sponsored their installation, which took place in the studio of David Amico, who was one of the first artists to move downtown."

—Dorit Cypis, quoted in Richard Hertz, *The Beat and the Buzz.*
  Ojai: Minneaola Press, 2009.

INVITATION

FEND, FITZGIBBON, HOLZER, NADIN, PRINCE & WINTERS
INVITE YOU TO TELL US WHAT YOU WANT, WHAT TO DO, SO
THAT YOU CAN TAKE OVER THE PLEASURE/FUNCTION
SHOW BY SATURDAY, FEBRUARY 9, 1980, 8:00 PM.

FEND, FITZGIBBON, HOLZER, NADIN, PRINCE & WINTERS
WILL BE AT 616 SOUTH BROADWAY, 5 FL, LA, CA, TUESDAY-
FRIDAY, FEBRUARY 5-8, 3-7 PM, (213) 622-4911.

PLEASURE/FUNCTION

The Offices of Fend Fitzgibbon Holzer Nadin Prince & Winters. *Pleasure & Function invitation*, 1980. Offset printed card, 6.5 × 11 cm. Courtesy of Robin Winters; opposite page: *The Offices of Fend Fitzgibbon Holzer Nadin Prince & Winters Office Handbook: Consultation.* New York: P. Fend, C. Fitzgibbon, J. Holzer, P. Nadin, R. Prince and R. Winters, 1980. Photocopy, pbk, staple-bound, 24 pp, 28 × 21.5 cm. Cover and interiors. Courtesy of Robin Winters and Jenny Holzer.

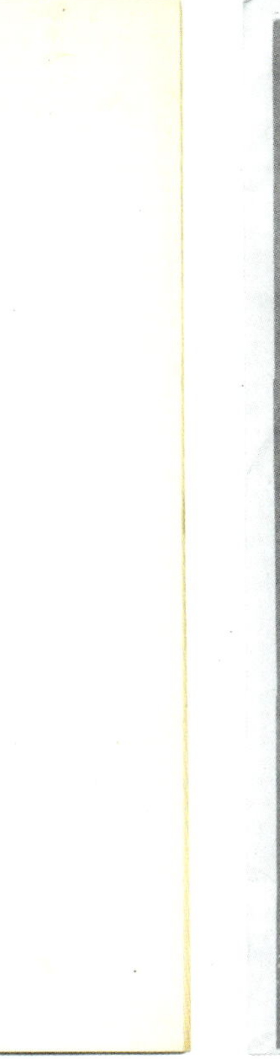

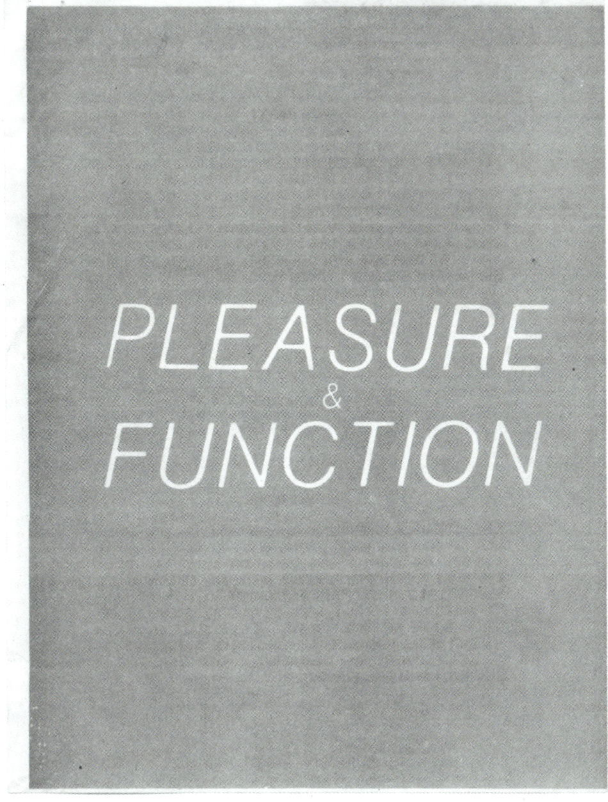

HOUSE & OFFICE

WALLS INSIDE OUR MODERN HOUSE OR OFFICE WERE BUILT BY SOMEONE SOMEONE TO KEEP SOMEONE OUT. THE WALLS GIVE ONLY THE ILLUSION OF URITY. IS IT APPROPRIATE TO EXPECT ISOLATION AND SAFETY WHEN THE UCTURE ACTUALLY IS THIN AND FRAGILE? SHOULD WE BUILD STRONGER RIERS OR SHOULD WE UNDERSTAND AND REACT TO THE REAL PROPERTIES THE STRUCTURE (THAT IS DIVIDES FOR ITS OWN PERPETUATION AND WELL- NG WITHOUT PROTECTING US)? BY STAYING WITHIN OUR DESIGNATED CES WE COOPERATE WITH THE EFFORT TO PART US. SEPARATION NTAINS THIS SYSTEM OF SUSPICION AND THREAT. WE MUST REALIZE WE VULNERABLE. WE MUST ELIMINATE THE DANGERS POSED BY THE STING STRUCTURE.

INFECTIOUS DESIRE

O ARE WE TRYING TO KEEP OUT ANYWAY? IN THE NEXT ROOM IS SOMEONE H THE SAME BASIC NEEDS, SOMEONE IN A PARALLEL SITUATION. WE OGNIZE, AND ACTUALLY HAVE SIMILAR DIFFICULTIES, BUT ACT AS VIDUALS TO DEAL WITH PROBLEMS. WE REMAIN COMPETITIVE AND ATED, OUR DESIRE STOPPED AT THE BOUNDARY. THE TRUTH IS THAT WE THREATENED BY THE SAME THINGS, WE WANT THE THREATS TO STOP, CAN IMAGINE AND MOVE TOWARDS A BETTER STATE. DESIRE IS A STANT. DESIRE DEMANDS OTHER PEOPLE TO BE REALIZED. WE ARE LESSLY SEPARATE FROM ONE ANOTHER. COMMON DESIRE MUST BE OGNIZED AND ALLOWED TO SPREAD.

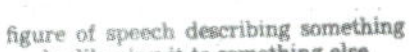

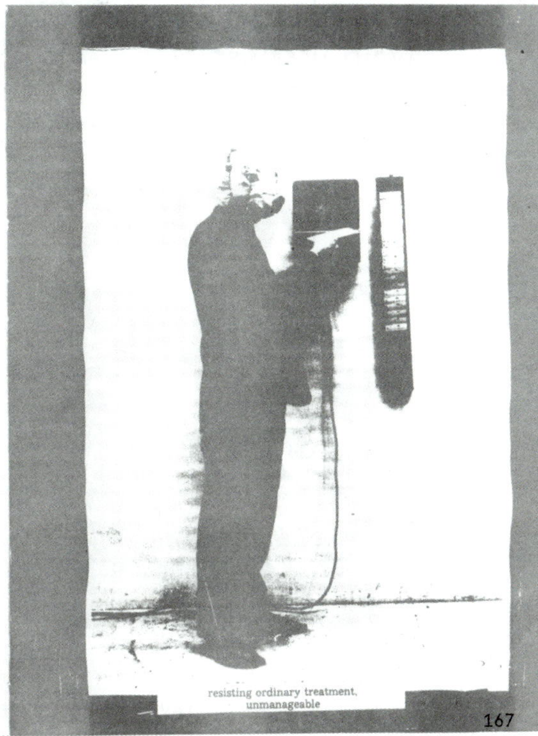

PLEASURE — FUNCTION
THE FOLLOWING TEXT WAS COMPILED FROM NOTES TAKEN FROM FRIDAY JAN 25 THRU THURSDAY JAN. 31st. AS A RESULT OF CONVERSATIONS WITH PETER FEND — COLEEN FITZGIBBON — JENNY HOLZER — PETER NADIN — RICHARD PRINCE — ROBIN WINTERS — DAVID SALMICA.

1. YOU CAN WORK FOR YOURSELF AND GO HUNGRY.
2. YOU CAN GAMBLE AND REWORK ANYTHING.
3. YOU CAN AVOID USELESS WORK IF ONCE IN A WHILE YOU GO AROUND INSTEAD OF THRU.
4. YOU CAN BE SMART AND NOT HAVE TO BE CREATIVE.
5. YOU CAN BE REASONABLE AND NOT HAVE ANY STYLE.
6. YOU CAN ASSUME STANDARDS WHICH ARE IMPOSSIBLE TO LOOK UP.
7. YOU CAN GIVE YOURSELF PERMISSION TO FORM YOUR OWN GOVERNMENT.
8. YOU CAN GET RID OF YOUR EGO AND STILL TRY TO MAKE LOTS OF MONEY.
9. YOU CAN MAKE OBJECTS JUST AS LONG AS THEY'RE EXTREMELY TINY AND FIT IN YOUR MOUTH.
10. YOU CAN LIVE IN A HOTEL AND USE THE LOBBY AS YOUR LIVINGROOM.
11. YOU CAN GO TO PARTIES AND OPENINGS AND CIRCULATE AND USE CONVERSATION AS A BASIS FOR WHAT YOU DO.
12. YOU CAN APPROPRIATE ANY SUBJECT JUST AS LONG AS THAT SUBJECT IS AVAILABLE TO ANYONE ELSE.
13. YOU CAN EXAGGERATE AND HAVE OTHER SIMILARITIES WITH ARTISTS.
14. YOU CAN HAVE DREAMS AND ASK ARTHUR MILLER HIS ADVICE ON MARRIAGE AND DO EXACTLY WHAT HE SAYS WHEN YOU WAKE UP.
15. YOU CAN CRAVE COMPLETE ACCEPTANCE AND NOT SHOW UP.
16. YOU CAN HAVE DESIRES AND MAKE THREATS IF YOU TAKE RESPONSIBILITY.
17. YOU CAN DISH IT OUT AND REFUSE TO TAKE IT.
18. YOU CAN SIT THRU EVERY PLANET OF THE APE AND FORGET WHAT YOUR LOOKING AT.
19. YOU CAN ADMIT THAT HOURS IN A LIBRARY HAS AFFECTED YOUR CREDIBILITY.
20. YOU CAN SUBSCRIBE TO MAD MAGAZINE BECAUSE ITS YOUR PLEASURE.
21. YOU CAN TAKE YOUR CLUBS ON THE SUBWAY AND PLAY GOLF IN WESTCHESTER.
22. YOU CAN STICK TO YOUR GUNS AND MIND YOUR OWN BUSINESS.
23. YOU CAN ASK FOR MONEY AND PLAY THE PART OF THE RICHEST MAN IN THE UNIVERSE.
24. YOU CAN LOOK FOR U.F.O.'S AND IDENTIFY THEM.
25. YOU CAN WALK AROUND IN CIRCLES OR BACK 'N FORTH, WHICH EVER ONE HELPS.
26. YOU CAN GO UP TO YOUR ROOF AND BRING BACK COMMANDS.

1. YOU CAN'T REWORK ANYTHING WHEN YOU ANTICIPATE.
2. YOU CAN'T AVOID USELESS WORK IF YOU TRY TO SAVE MONEY.
3. YOU CAN'T WORK FOR YOURSELF UNTIL YOU CONSIDER YOURSELF A CLIENT.
4. YOU CAN'T EAT AT A SUPERMARKET IF YOUR NOT REALLY HUNGRY.
5. YOU CAN'T PROMOTE A POSITION AND STAY IN IT UNTIL HELL FREEZES OVER.
6. YOU CAN'T SHUCK AND JIVE IF YOUR REALLY NOT TELLING THE TRUTH.

```
*X IART0001 900,465 E006 M 13.500 8 3.0 (900,292 )      CXC33 RX1   11/09/79   03.2
                                                                        14

L (H1)    Art:Prince (RP)

L (H2)

L (H3)

L (H4)

L (H5)    MSRE CHGE 42.5

L 0001    Richard Prince Time-Life Building Rockefeller Center NY, NY 11-9-79

L 0002

L 0003

L 0004

L 0005    >> Art is a significant word.

L 0006    >> Modern is a significant habit.

L 0007    >> Intuition in association with accidental elements
                becoming permanent is a significant gesture.

L 0008    >> Formal notification as an expected operation is a significant attitude.

L 0009    >> Subjects for the appropriation by anyone is a significant
                consideration.

L 0010    >> Providing the convenience of hindsight is a significant function.

L 0011    >> Extracting from preparation referable constructs that
                underline a collective code of motor reactions is
                a significant skill.

L 0012    >> Demanding attention by being nowhere else is a significant request.

L 0013    >> Perpetuating articulation in a society based on
                morphological relationships is a significant language.

L 0014    >> The artist as an agency for the initiation of function
                is a significant proposition.

L

L

L
```

PETER FEND

From out of the seas rise pipelines, aqueduct highways, and the vertebrae series bearing up in cantilevers the slopes and discs upon which entire populations rest. Below these bridging backbones flourish wild animals and plants. Among mountain ridges, the linear megastructures flow within level wedge-cut niches on the slopes. Whether coursing above flatlands or traversing mountainsides, society behaves as if humans had never descended from their trees or high caves. We gaze down across terrain pitched, even if slightly, to the sea. The polity is conceived as an amphitheater. From Ghat and Milan the view descends down respective valleys to a common sea, a common center. In a theater of Greeks, Anatolians, Palestinians and Catalonians, the Italians achieve position in that sovereign terrain they always wanted: a Mediterranean sea state.

LA gets what it always wanted as well: independence in the world. LA discovers its basin as part of a long piece of ocean bottom jutting up from Pacific waters. It discovers that it doesn't belong to the US. It discovers that it cannot survive as an earth-smothering sprawl of concrete roads and rooted buildings smothered in turn by the combustion of geological deposits. It cannot survive by squatting on the ground and using what is dug from the ground. It cannot survive in the Neolithic mold. So it scuttles itself and breaks away. It levels its buildings, shatters its pavements, cuts off its oil supplies, joins the Baja in a joint harvest offshore, and heads for the hills. Everybody always wanted to live in the hills anyway. Or at least among the elevated freeways. Now they do it. What's beneath, in the LA Basin, becomes home range for the deer and the antelope, while above, on the natural or artificial ridges, the humans look on fields upon waving green fields--on what used to be LA.

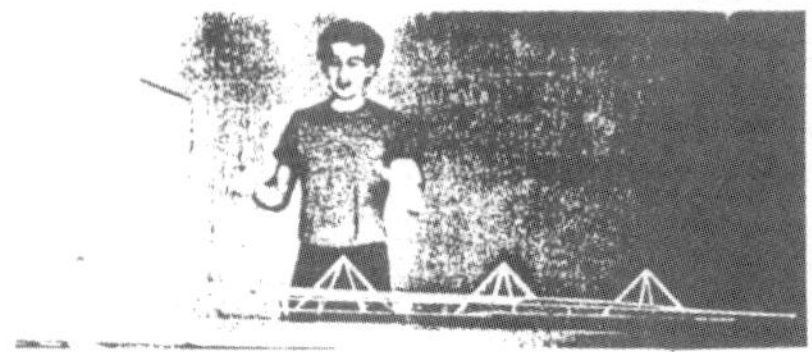

15. YOU CAN'T DRIVE A CAR IF YOU'RE JEALOUS. JEALOUS.
16. YOU CAN'T DOMINATE AN ANIMAL JUST BECAUSE YOU'RE LONELY.
17. YOU CAN'T SLEEP ALL DAY UNLESS YOU WORK AT NITE.
18. YOU CAN'T DETERMINE THE OUTCOME IF MONEY" IS AT STAKE.
19. YOU CAN'T EXPECT PEOPLE NOT TO KILL EACH OTHER UNLESS YOU'RE ON ANOTHER PLANET.
20. YOU CAN'T NEUTRALIZE YOUR EGO WHEN YOU FEAR NOT BEING RECARDED.
21. YOU CAN'T FORGET ABOUT IT SO THEN YOU ACT STUPID.
22. YOU CAN'T STANDARDISIZE AND EXPECT COMPLIMENTS.
23. YOU CAN'T SHOW UP AND ACT WITHDRAWN.
24. YOU CAN'T SUBSCRIBE TO PLEASURE WITHOUT ALIENATING YOUR

I ASK NOT WHAT COLAB DID
BUT WHETHER IT CAN (YET)
BENEFIT OUR PLANET.

IN WHAT WAYS HAS THE WORLD
GAINED BY WHAT WE DID, OR
CONTINUE TO DO?

IF WE END UP CELEBRATED
AS WERE THE PERFORMANCE
ARTISTS SHOWN IN PACE
GALLERY RECENTLY, WE
HAVE BEEN IRRESPONSIBLE.

—Peter Fend

```
ECONOMY IS A SCULPTURE.
IT CAN BE SEEN IN A PAINTING.
IT IS A BIOLOGICAL ORGANISM;
IT CAN BE SICK OR IT CAN BE WELL.
IT OCCUPIES A PIECE OF EARTH AND INCLUDES, TO FUNCTION, SALTWATERS
   IN CIRCULATION.
WHEN ECONOMY FUNCTIONS WELL, THE PEOPLE WHO LIVE ON ITS PIECE OF
   EARTH DO NOT SUFFER DISEASES OR DESPAIR RESULTING FROM THEIR
   PHYSICAL CIRCUMSTANCES.
ECONOMY IS A MATTER OF PHYSICAL OBSERVATION AND PHYSICAL ARRANGEMENT.
WHAT IS CALLED "NATURAL LAW" IS ACHIEVED BY ARCHITECTURE IN THE
   COMPREHENSIVE MIMICRY ALTOGETHER OF NATURE AS IT SURROUNDS US.
   THIS WAS THE HABIT OF ADAM AND EVE.  THEY SIMPLY ARRANGED HERE
   AND THERE THE EXISTING ANIMALS AND PLANTS: THEY DID NOT TILL
   THE SOIL OR DIG UP ROCKS AND PRECIOUS STONES: THEY DID NOT
   SEEK WEALTH IN POISONOUS DEPOSITS LIKE OIL AND COAL; THEY DID
   NOT ATTEMPT TO OWN OR CONFINE WHAT THEY LIVED WITH AND ATE.
I ENDEAVOR TO MIMIC NATURE, NATURE AS EXPLICATED BY SCIENCE BUT
   AS UNDERSTOOD AND ENGESTURED BY ARTISTS, FOR THE CONSTRUCTION
   OF FUNCTIONAL SPACES ENGENDERING BODY-MADNESS.  I TRUST BODY-
   MADNESS AS AN INDICATOR OF WHAT IS GOOD FOR ME AND FELLOW HUMANS.
   NOT EVERYTHING NEED BE PROVEN BY SCIENTIFIC OR LEGAL DOCTRINE;
   NOT EVERYTHING NEED BE EXPLAINED AND CREDENTIALED.  IF I SUFFER
   BODY-MADNESS OVER A CERTAIN CAPACIOUS STRUCTURE, THEN I KNOW I
   HAVE BUILT AN HABITAT THAT FUNCTIONS.
AS I ENDEAVOR TO MIMIC NATURE FOR THE COMMUNITY IN WHICH I LIVE,
   WHICH NOW BY GLOBAL CIRCUMSTANCES INCLUDES THE FULL RANGE OF
   NATION-STATE AND MULTINATIONAL CORPORATION ACTIVITIES, THEN I
   ENDEAVOR TO RE-ARRANGE THE MATERIALS IN THE PRESENT ECONOMY INTO
   STRUCTURES FOR A MORE PHYSICALLY-PURPOSEFUL, MORE FUNCTIONAL,
   ECONOMY.
[LA]    LA   LA   LA    LA    LA    LA
OUR FIRST CLIENT

NO POLLUTION
NO ENTANGLING ALLIANCES IN MATERIALS FLOWS
NO BOUNDARIES
NO MULTINATIONAL OIL COMPANIES
NO SPRAWL
NO FLATLAND LIFE
NO LACK OF WATER
NO WAITING IN GETTING AROUND
MEGASTRUCTURES
NO EARTHQUAKE DANGERS
DEER AND ANTELOPE PLAY

ONCE THE MATERIAL CONDITIONS ARE DETERMINED, ONCE THE RRQUIREMENTS ARE
   MET, THEN WE CAN CONSIDER HOW MUCH WORK IS NECESSARY TO WELL-BEING
NO WORK IS MADE
ALL WORK IS WHAT IS NEEDED FOR PHYSICAL WELL-BEING
ONLY FUNCTIONAL WORK
THEREFORE, ONLY PLEASURABLE WORK

NO TAXATION
ALL ARCHITECTURE AND INFRASTRUCTURE AND PRIMARY SERVICES

NO RESTRICTION TO POPULATION

ASSUME END OF US
ASSUME END OF IMPERIAL STRUCTURE
SELF-RELIANCE
PREPARED
```

The Offices of Fend Fitzgibbon Holzer Nadin Prince & Winters Office Handbook: Consultation. New York: P. Fend, C. Fitzgibbon, J. Holzer, P. Nadin, R. Prince and R. Winters, 1980. Photocopy, pbk, staple-bound, 24 pp, 28 × 21.5 cm. Various interiors. Courtesy of Robin Winters and Jenny Holzer.

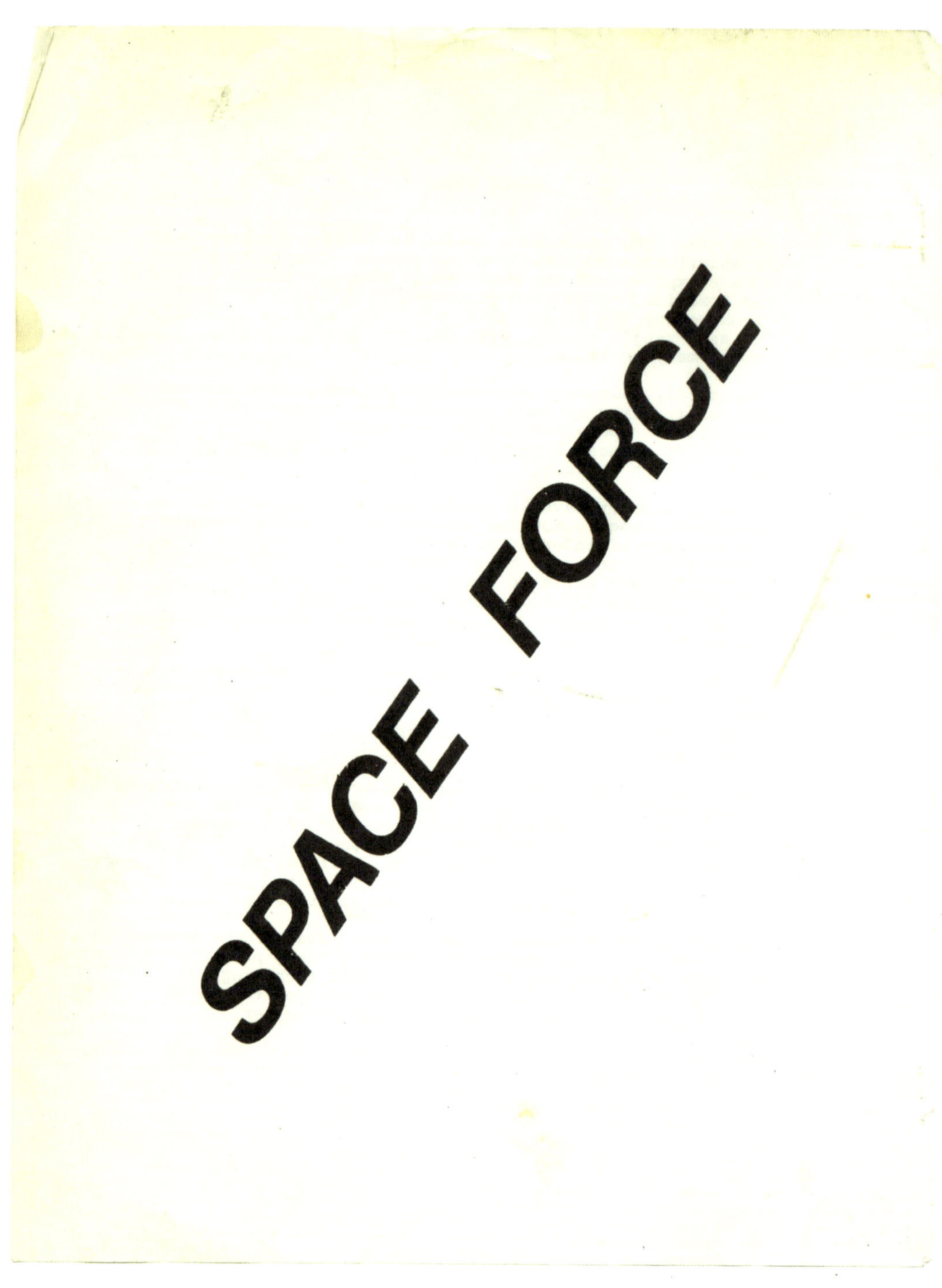

Peter Fend. *Space Force*, c. 1980. Photocopy,
28 × 21.5 cm. Ocean Earth Development
Corporation Space Force group manifesto.
Courtesy of Peter Fend.

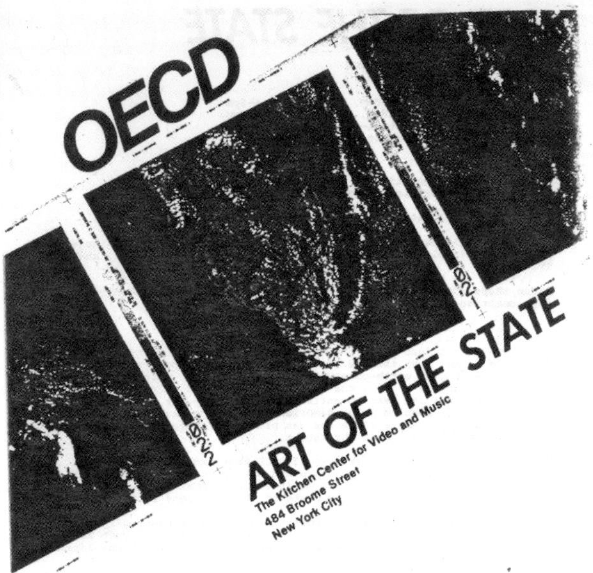

Ocean Earth Construction and Development Corporation (OECD). *Art of the State*, 1982. Photocopy on paper, 2 pp, 28 × 21.5 cm. Courtesy of Peter Fend.

ART OF THE STATE

Produced by SPACE FORCE, OECD

February 4–27
Opening Reception: Thursday, February 4, 6–8pm
Closing Discussion: Sunday, February 28, 6–8pm
Gallery Hours: Tues–Sat, 1–6pm
The Kitchen, 484 Broome Street
Tel: 925-3615

SPACE FORCE, an operation of the Ocean Earth Construction and Development Corporation, OECD, presents:

the state of the art in earth observation.

This also includes advances in the state of the art in digital image processing, in planetary and celestial modeling, in photography and TV.

Since these advances are achieved by governments and their contractors, they comprise not only a state of the art but also an

ART OF THE STATE.

The State is not just NASA: the military can display much more. The State is not just the U.S.: the Japanese and European space agencies are sending up earth-observation satellites that surpass ours. And the contractors . . . , the contractors are developing new image technologies that can lead to entirely new markets--far beyond the State. Example: combine image memories with interactive videodiscs so that with satellite-data alone one can project a three-dimensional landscape and visually walk through it.

As visual researchers, the artists of OECD have exchanged views with government officials and contractors and have contributed--in the exhibited works--to advances in the manipulation, organization and display of digital color data. The state of the art keeps evolving.

If other artists gain hands-on access to the image processing systems used here, the art of the State would become more flexible, more communicable, more subject to personal expression, more part of the domain of art and media.

These video programs and photographic sequences are first efforts of SPACE FORCE towards production of art that's

direct from outer space.

We begin, being human, with planet Earth. And we are:

Bill Dolson	Wolfgang Staehle
Peter Fend	Glenn Steigelman
Colen Fitzgibbon	Taro Suzuki
Win Knowlton	Eve Vaterlaus
Paul Sharits	Joan Waltemath

We have cooperated with, and would like to thank:
Charles Bohn and William J. Campbell, Goddard Space Flight Center, NASA; Dr. Lothar Beckel, University of Vienna; Richard Pendergrass, LogE/Interpretation Systems Incorporated; Dr. Janet Bare, Satlab Inc., and Willoughby Sharp, of Integrated Telecommunications.

By letting artists converge their aims and work in teams, Collaborative Projects and its legally-structured offshoots allowed Art in the United States to achieve an impact on public policy and the economy as is never possible with the one-on-one competition of the normal art world. This impact, lasting only a few years until forcibly shut down, was global. The shutdown can be reversed. The practices spawned by Collaborative Projects can be re-launched.

—Peter Fend

The diverse group of artists that gathered under the rubric Collaborative Projects, it seems to me, shared only one thing in common. We all involved ourselves in issues that ran parallel to, or fed into, epistemological questions of American wealth, class and power. In the 30-plus years since, American civilization has witnessed multiple paradigmatic shifts. The predictability of the linear equation of class and sex boundaries (in art) that was the norm for us in the 1980s was found to be insufficient in capturing the relevant behavior of our art impulses and their distribution through the art system. Such non-linear ruptures might have been troublesome to manipulate until the advent of computers and cyberspace provided the mid-1990s art system with the means through which non-linear models of self-organization could be tracked and demarcated.

What I early on detected in Colab and ABC No Rio was that art could be expressed in complex rich ways that were non-linear but, nevertheless, displayed long-term tendencies and organizational patterns. Specifically, certain spots in the non-linear field of the art system were found to manifest as either attraction or repulsion spots to nearby trajectories. Attractor Colab art stars were soon found to have a stabilizing function in the art system and represented long-term tendencies of market value. But for me, it also was revealed that the same art star attractors could mutate and spontaneously transform or bifurcate. While the pre-Colab art system isolated physical objects from their surrounding, the attraction of Colab chaos was founded on the realization that the art system is connected to power, subject to flows of money, matter and energy which move constantly through them. Inversely, the dynamic imbalance of ABC No Rio resulted from chaotic energy that manifested a creative process that generated richly organized patterns that teetered on the complex stable and the complex unstable.

It is neither surprising nor coincidental that a paradigmatic epistemological change in art at large would follow these developments. I can even say that culture experienced a bifurcation as a result of Collaborative Projects style activity, and the artists of Colab all represented their own particular bifurcation within the cultural field.

In critical studies and in an array of philosophical discourses, chaotic approaches to order and composition have been addressing the rhizomatic-decentralized modes of distribution that I first experienced in Collaborative Projects. When New York art began a Colab influenced examination of its heterogeneous system, it initiated a true break with modernism and this bifurcation is what I found to be interesting in my participation with ABC No Rio and Collaborative Projects.

—Joseph Nechvatal

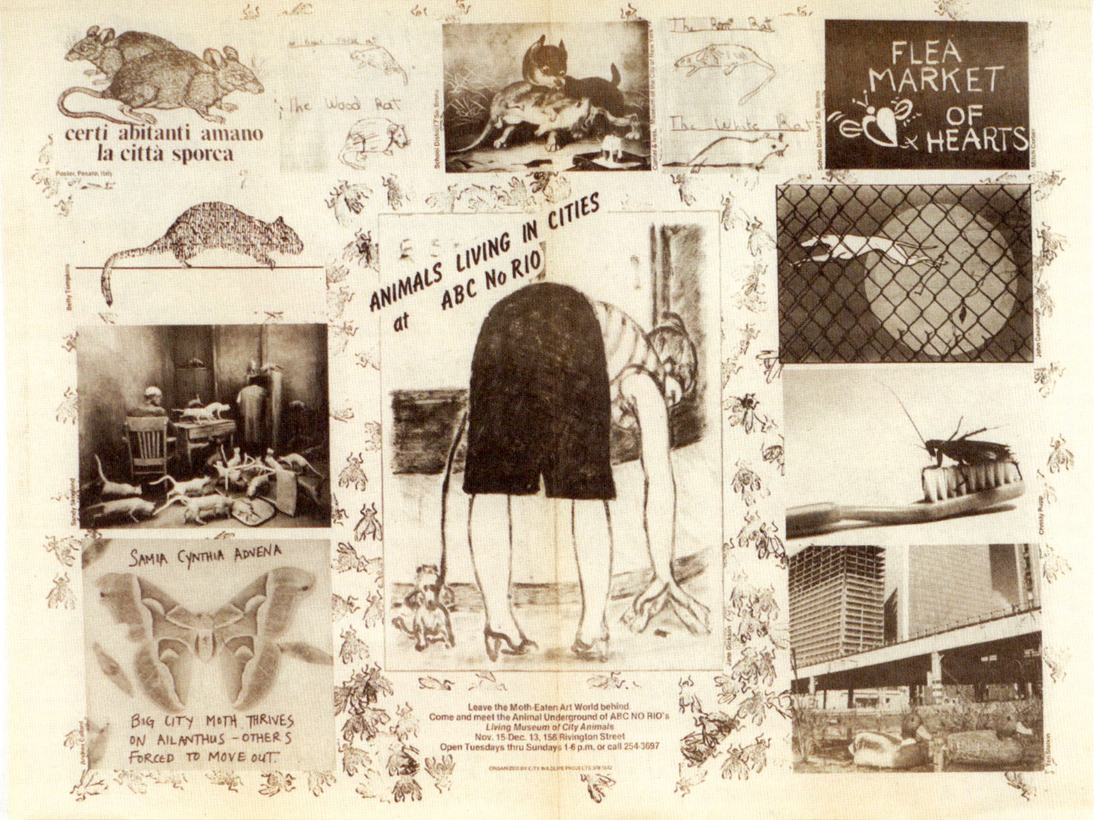

Animals Living in Cities

Should Vermin exterminators ply their trade? Not necessarily, according to Christy Rupp, the art world's resident urban ecologist. To prove it, her City Wildlife Projects has organized a show of more than 100 artworks and exhibits (some involving live rats, roaches and the like) aimed at dispelling such quackery. ABC No Rio, through December 13th.

-The Soho News, Nov 19, 1980, reproduced in Colab Annual Report, 1981

Christy Rupp. *Animals Living in Cities*, 1980. Offset printed on newsprint, 43 × 58 cm. Centerfold for the *East Village Eye*. Courtesy of Christy Rupp.

Andrea Callard. *All Animals Need Water to Survive*, c. 1978–80. Photocopy, 28 × 21.5 cm. Courtesy of Andrea Callard.

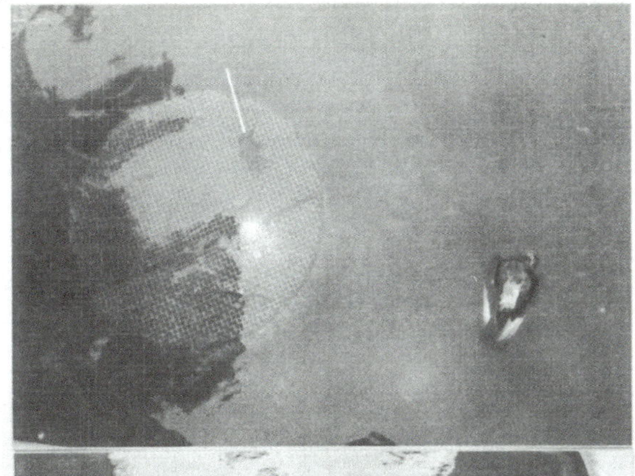
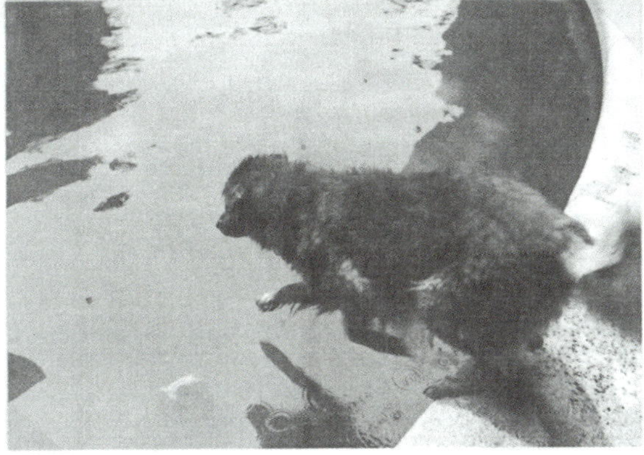

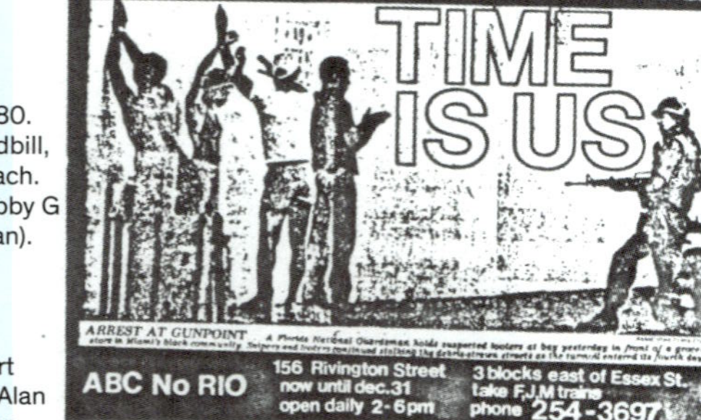

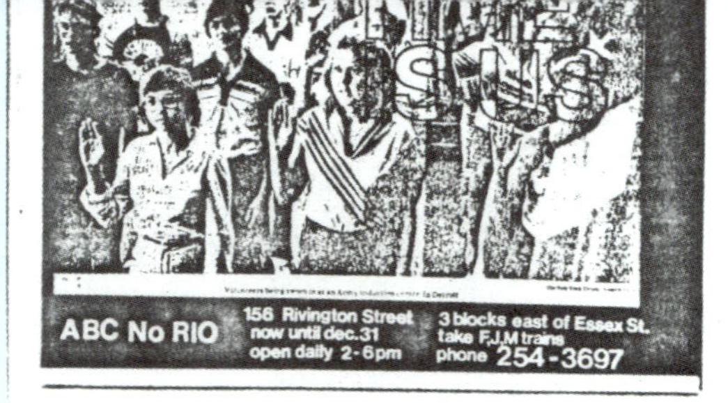

Left:

Justen Ladda.
TIME IS US, 1980.
Photocopy handbill,
9 × 12.5 cm each.
Courtesy of Bobby G
(Robert Goldman).

Right:

Bobby G (Robert
Goldman) with Alan
Granville and Jon
Keller. *Get Wrecked,
Get Political*, 1980.
Photocopy poster,
28 × 21.5 cm.
For ABC No Rio.
Courtesy of Bobby G
(Robert Goldman).

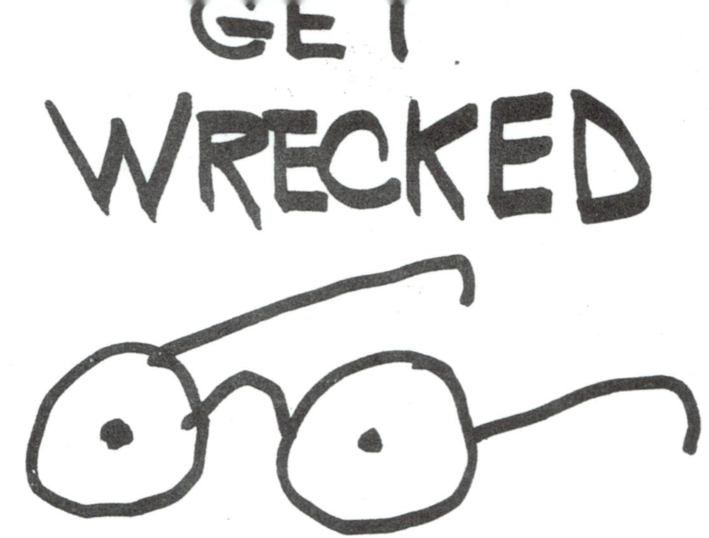

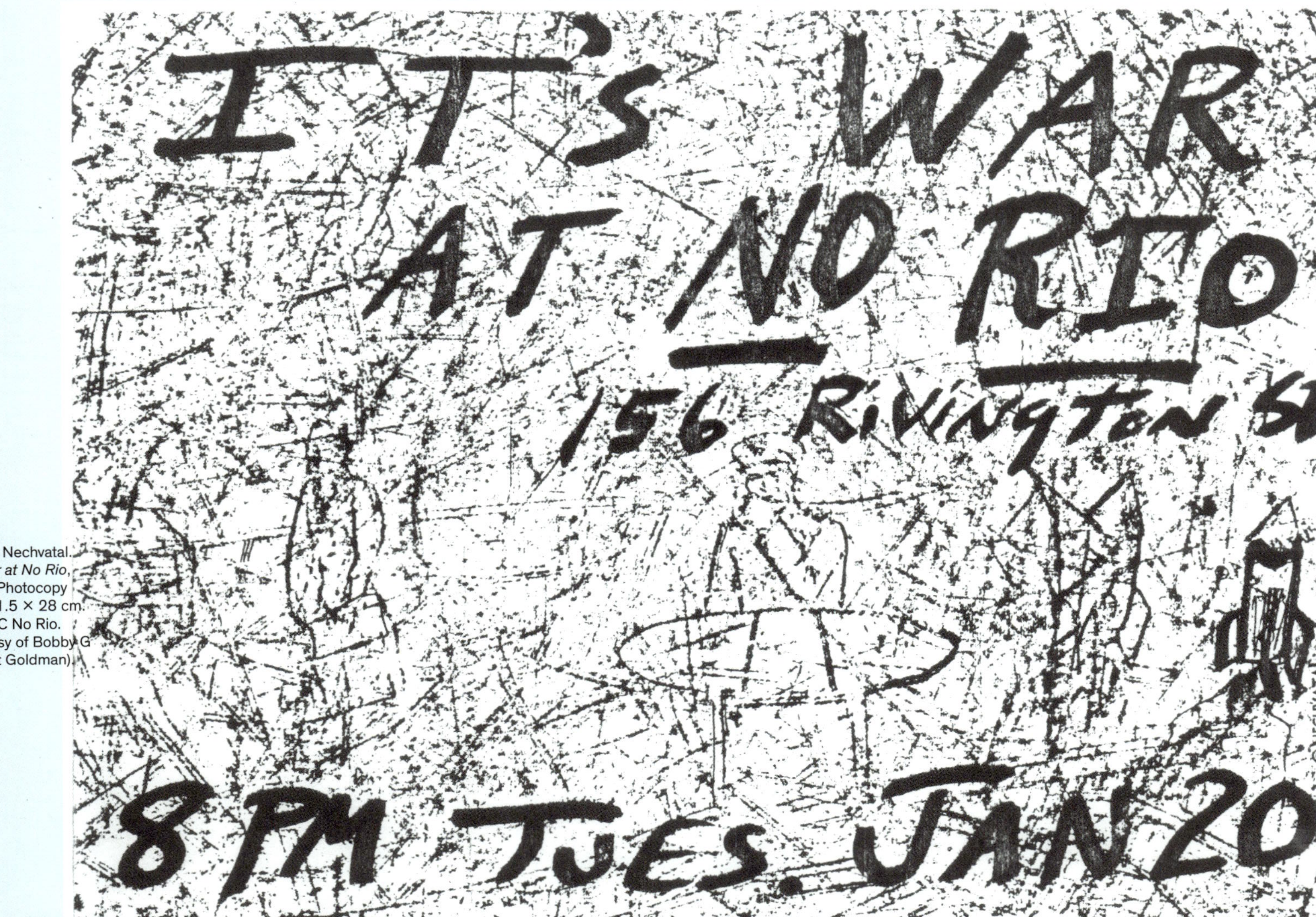

Joseph Nechvatal.
It's War at No Rio,
1980. Photocopy
flyer, 21.5 × 28 cm.
For ABC No Rio.
Courtesy of Bobby G
(Robert Goldman)

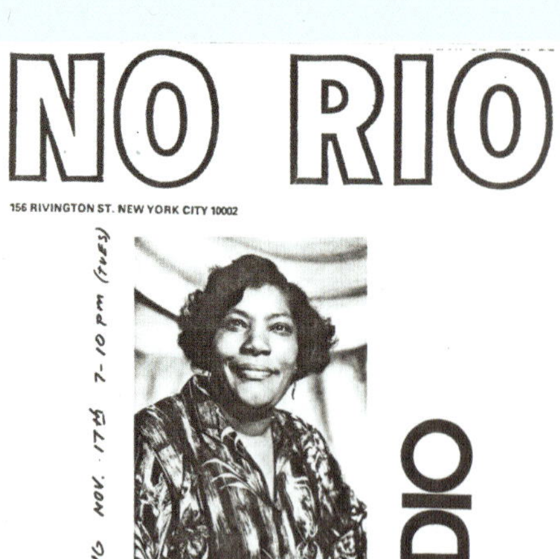
NO RIO
156 RIVINGTON ST. NEW YORK CITY 10002
OPENING NOV. 17th 7-10 PM (TUES)
PORTRAIT STUDIO
SHOW
NØV. 18 - 22

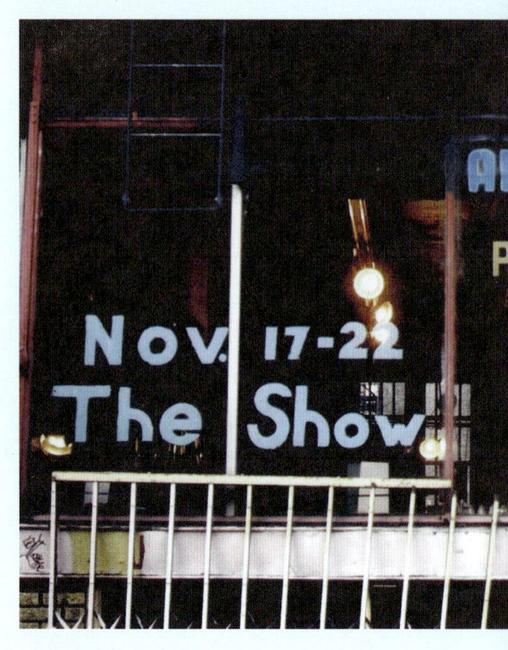
Nov. 17-22
The Show

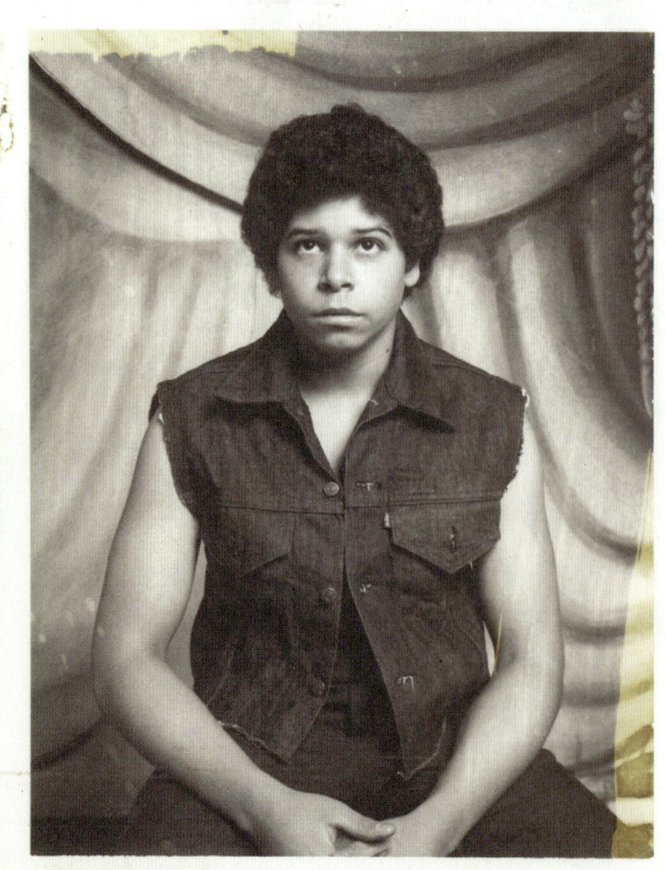

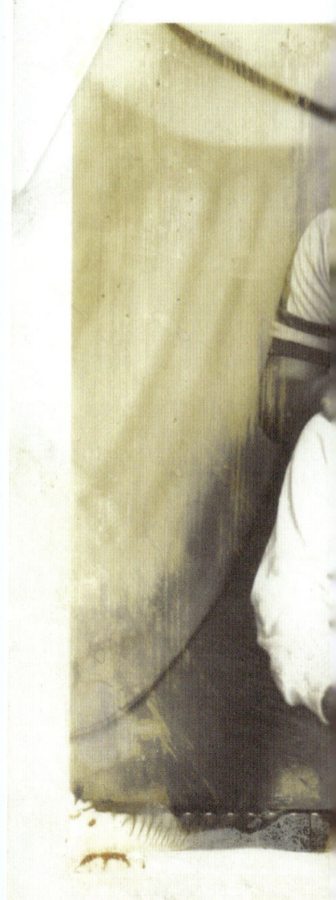

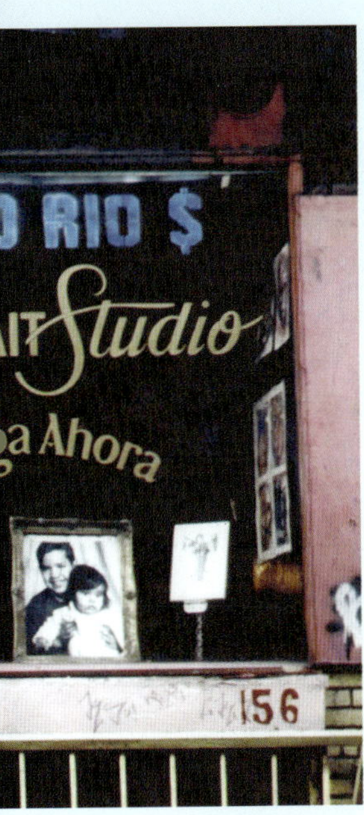

Top, left to right:

Tom Warren. *No Rio Portrait Studio*, 1981.
Photocopy flyer, 28 × 21.5 cm.
Courtesy of Kiki Smith.

Tom Warren. *ABC NO RIO Portrait Studio Window*,
1981/2011. Color digital print from 1981
Kodachrome slide, 11.5 × 15.5 cm.
Courtesy of Tom Warren.

Bottom:

Tom Warren. *Polaroids*, 1981. Polaroid photographs,
14.5 × 10.5 cm each. Stamped, signed and dated
on verso. From the *Portrait Studio* at ABC No Rio.
Courtesy of Tom Warren.

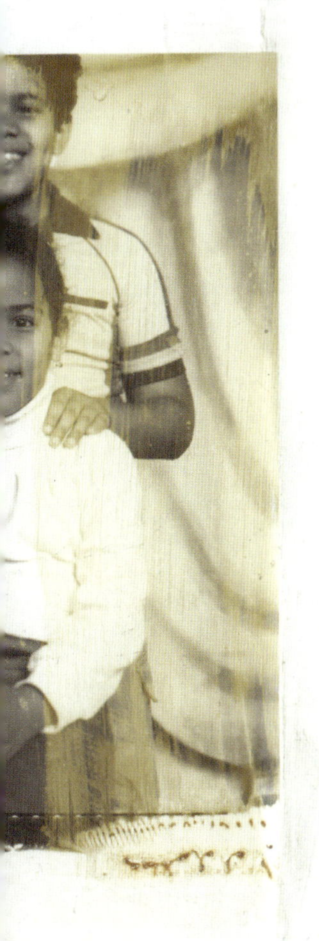

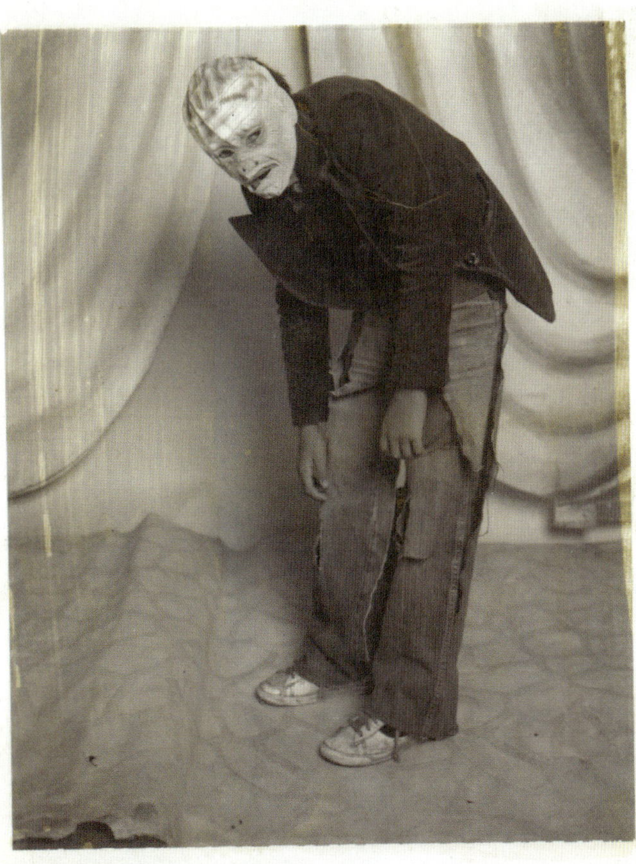

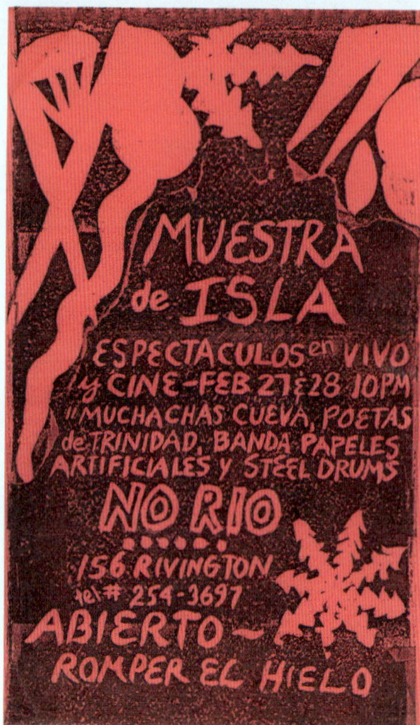

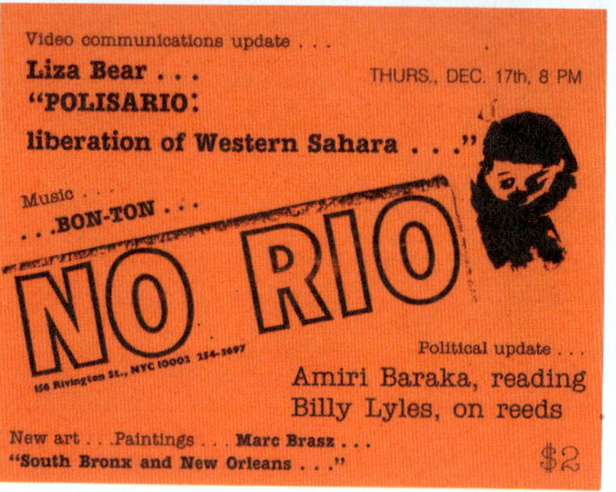

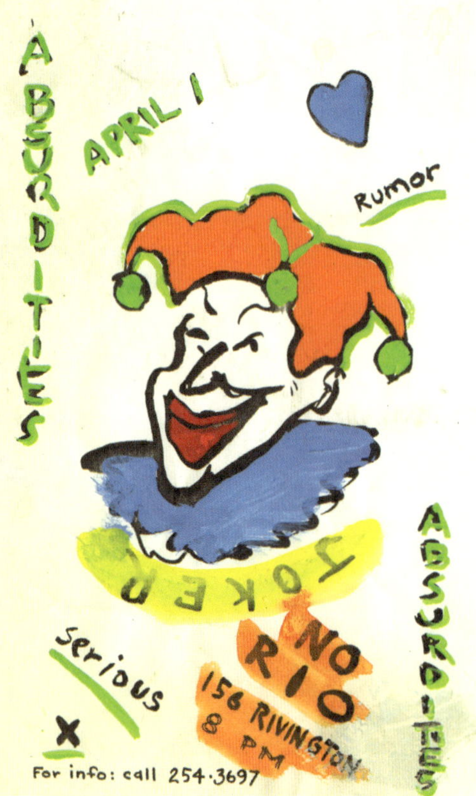

Clockwise from upper left:

Becky Howland. *Island Show and Ice Jungle /
Isla Muestra y Jungla de Hielo*, 1981. Photocopy poster,
36 × 21.5 cm each. Courtesy of Becky Howland.

Becky Howland. *Muestra de Isla y Jungla de Hielo*,
1981. Photocopy handbill, 9 × 21.5 cm.
Courtesy of Bobby G (Robert Goldman).

Unknown. *POLISARIO: Liberation of Western Sahara*,
1981. Offset printed flyer, 28 × 21.5 cm.
Courtesy of Liza Béar.

Alan Moore. *Absurd! Art at No Rio?*, 1981. Photocopy
handbill, 21 × 21 cm. For the *Absurdities Show* at ABC
No Rio. Courtesy of Bobby G (Robert Goldman).

Bobby G (Robert Goldman). *Absurdities*, 1981.
Hand-painted photocopy handbill, 21.5 × 14 cm.
For the *Absurdities Show* at ABC No Rio.
Courtesy of Kiki Smith.

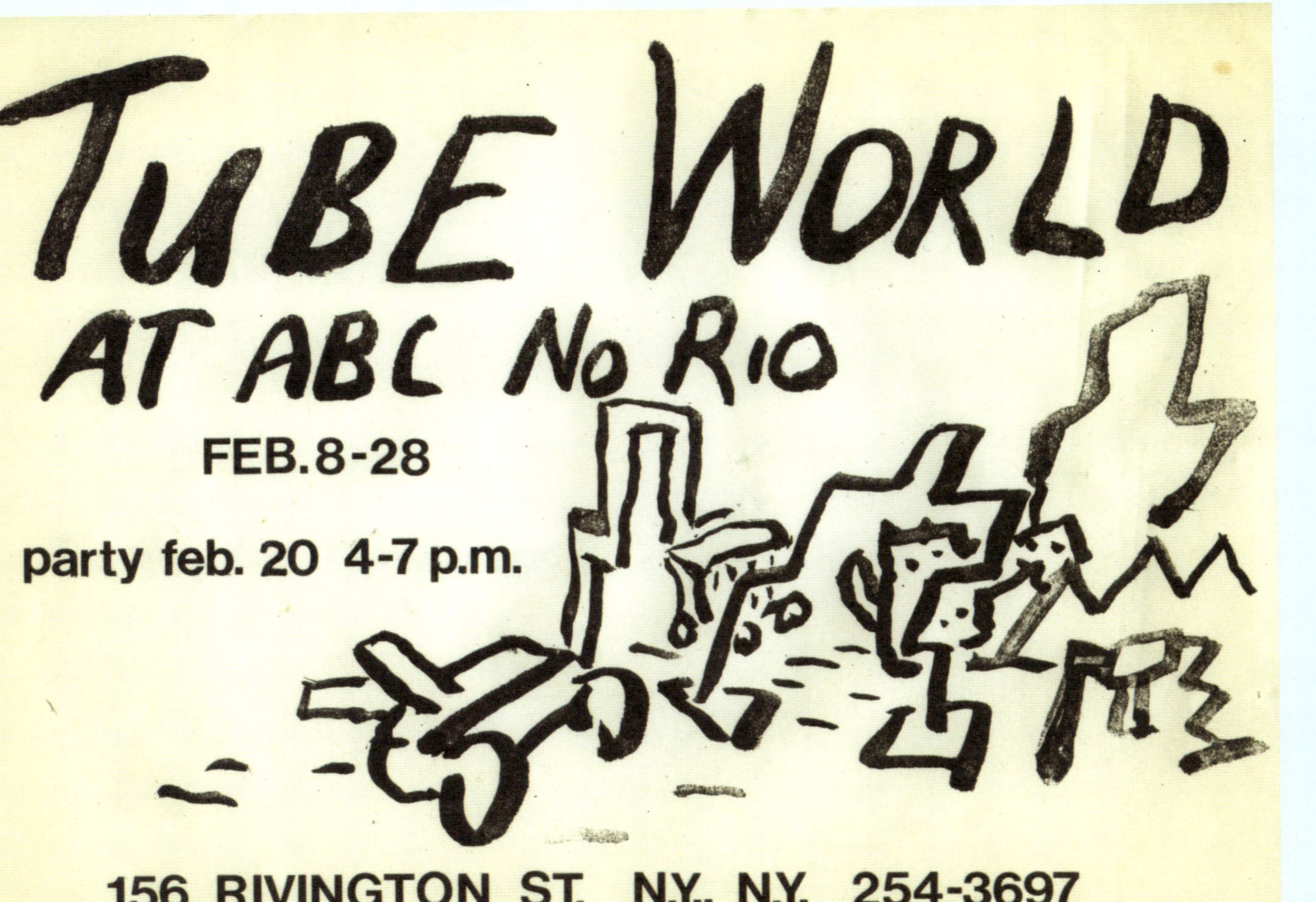

Jody Culkin. *Tube World at ABC No Rio*, 1982. Photocopy poster, 21.5 × 28 cm. Courtesy of Jody Culkin.

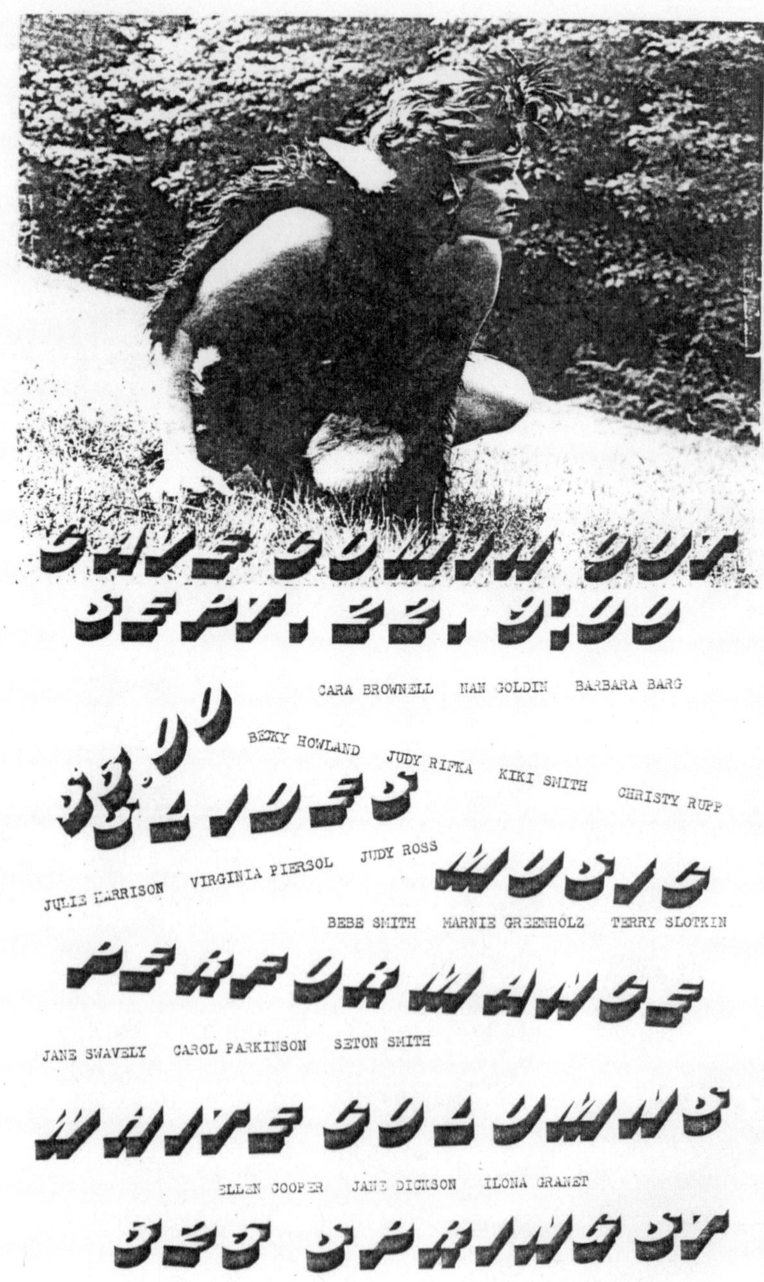

Terise Slotkin. *Cave Comin' Out*, 1981. Photocopy poster, 28 × 21.5 cm. Poster for *Cave Girls Create Chaos* at White Columns. Courtesy of Kiki Smith.

Terise Slotkin. *Cave Girls*, 1981. B/W photographs (clockwise: 12.5 × 19 cm, 19 × 12.5 cm, 15.5 × 23 cm). Courtesy of Terise Slotkin.

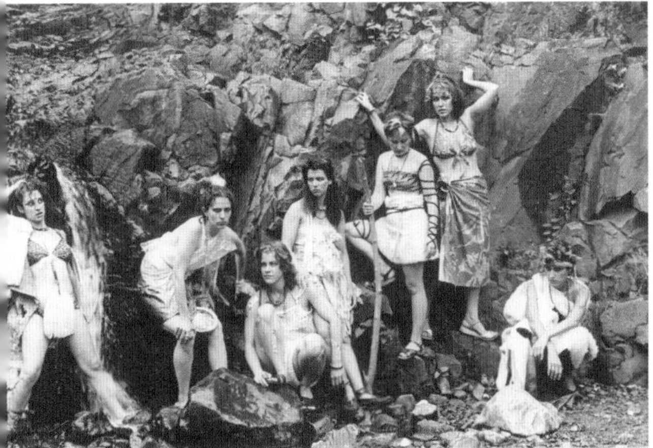

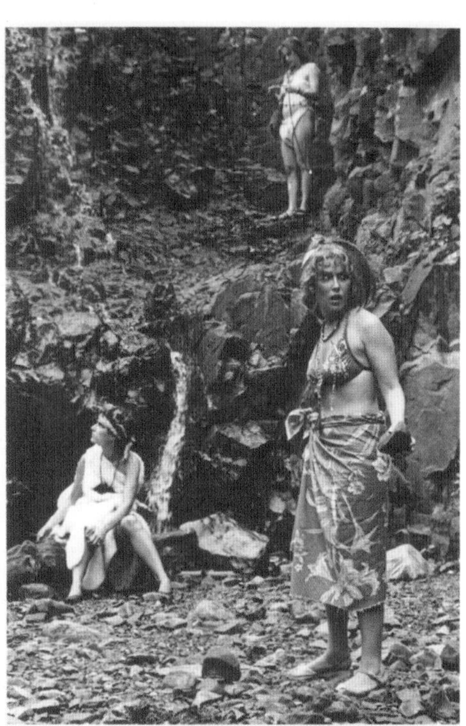

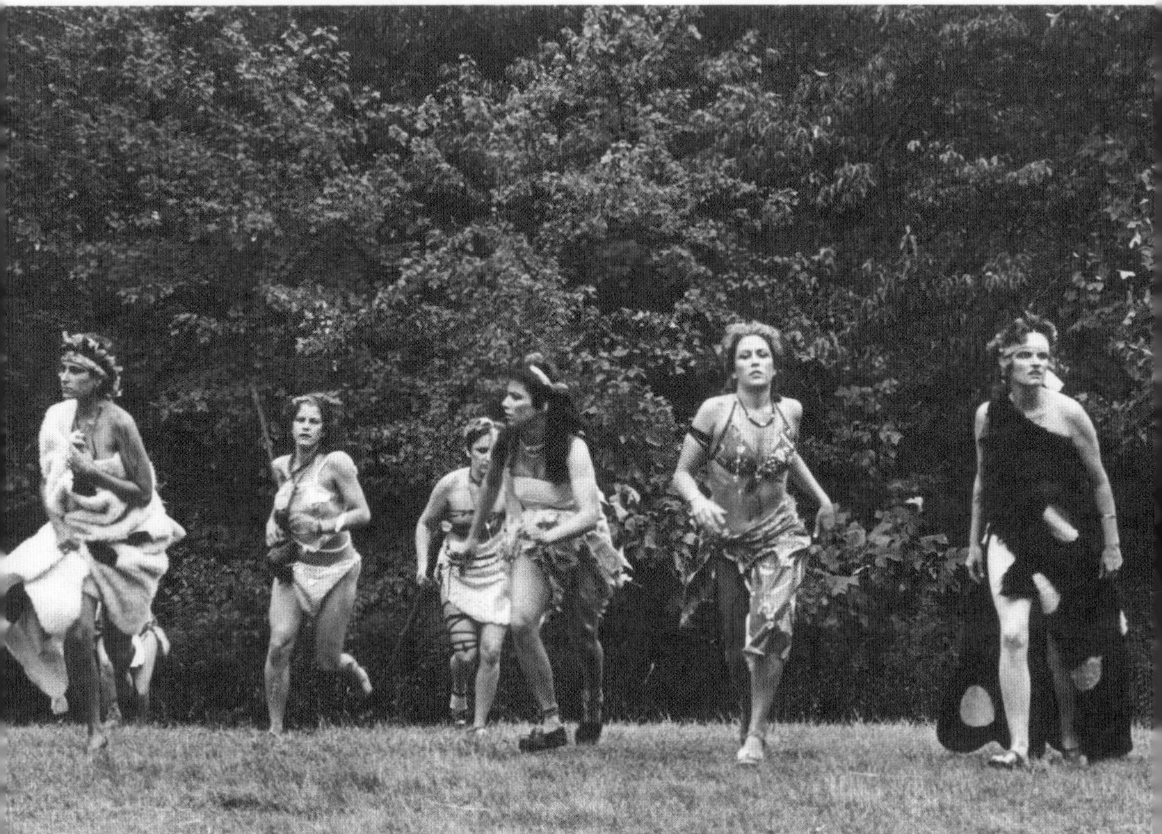

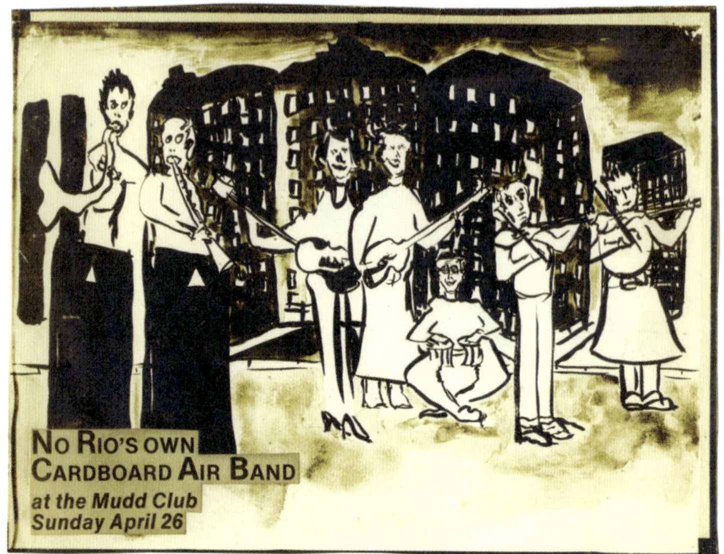

Facing page:

Terise Slotkin. *The Cardboard Air Band*, 1983. B/W fiber prints, 8.5 × 12.5 cm each. From *The Island of Negative Utopia*, an ABC No Rio fundraiser at The Kitchen. Courtesy of Terise Slotkin.

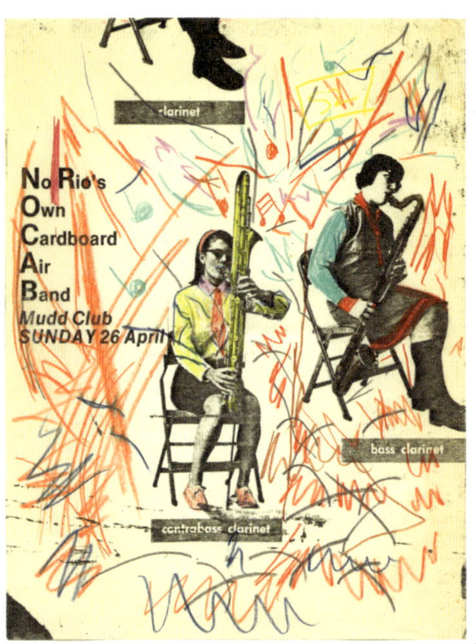

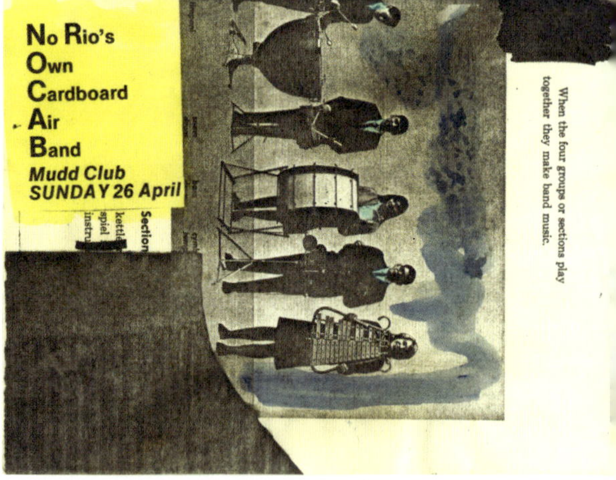

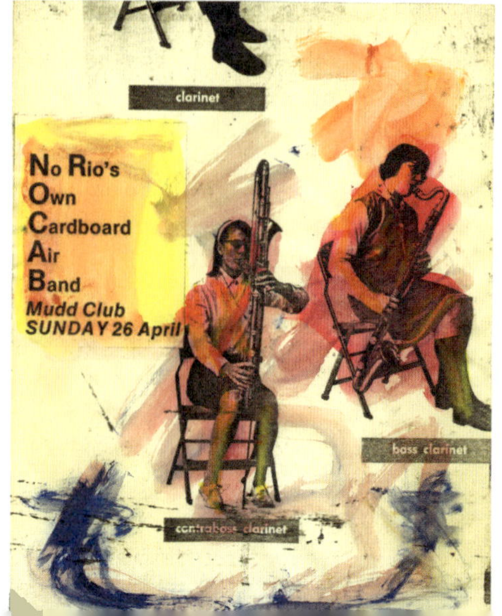

Clockwise from top left:

Bobby G (Robert Goldman). *No Rio's Own Cardboard Air Band*, 1981. Photostat paste-up for Cardboard Air Band flyer 21.5 × 28 cm. Courtesy of Becky Howland.

Alan Moore. (top and bottom) both *No Rio's Own Cardboard Air Band*, 1981. Hand-painted photocopy flyer, 28 × 21.5 cm each. Courtesy of Becky Howland and Walter Robinson.

Alan Moore. *No Rio's Own Cardboard Air Band*, c. 1981. Hand-colored photocopy flyer, 28 × 21.5 cm. Courtesy of Walter Robinson.

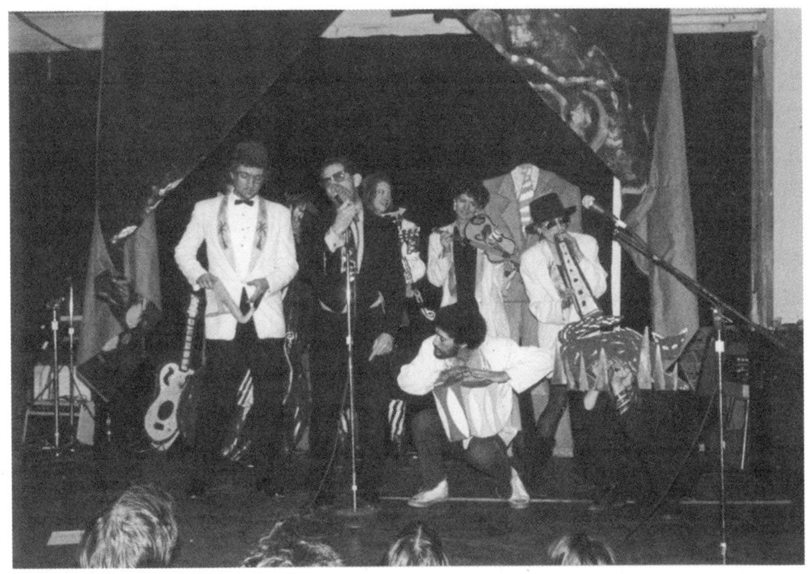

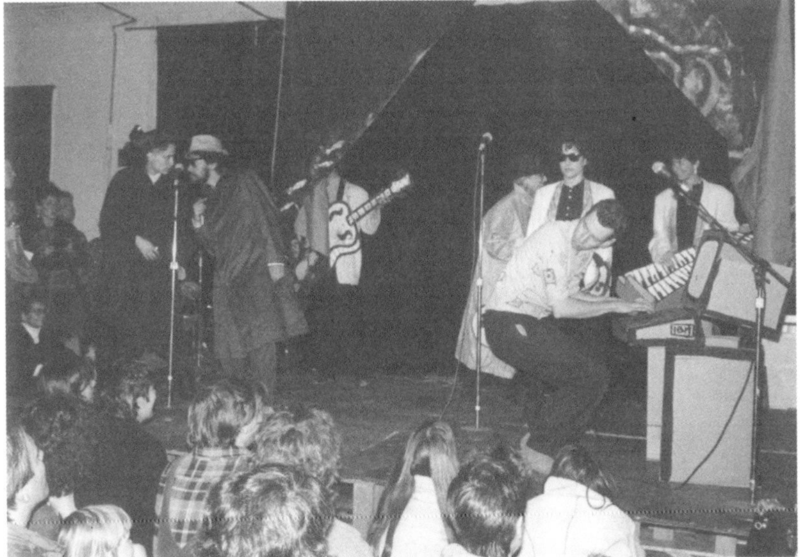

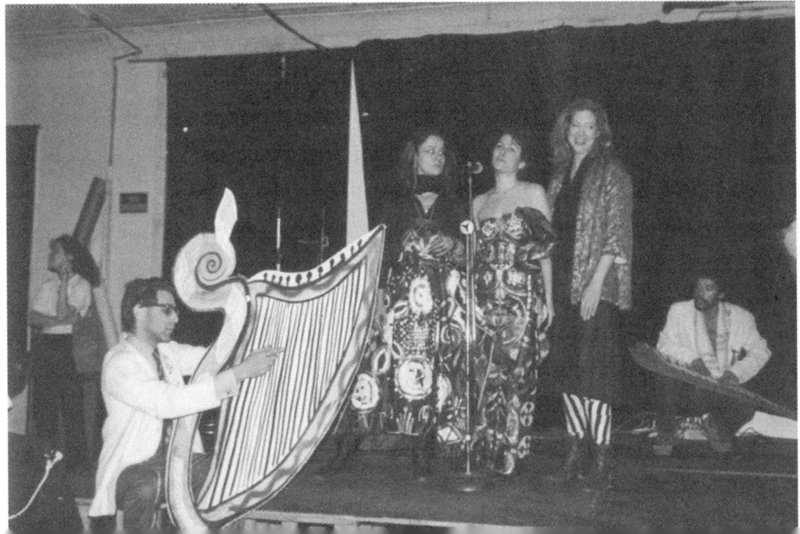

CANNIBALS 2

Don't let those people turn your head
and don't get used to being led
you take your orders from the boss
but don't buy no shit above the cost
Passionate people have got to learn
that in this day and age there is still concern
the corporate world is clean and neat
but there's plenty of people with pointed teeth
A word to the wise for people with eyes open 'em wide see through their
'Cause cannibals are people who eat people   disguise.

consuming you and me is their joy in life

cannibals are people who eat people
you don't need more than that
to knw who is who and what x is what
yeah

The Cardboard Air Band takes art to
the limits of credibility. Cardboard
props, roughly stuck together and
painted for Colab TV productions,
had become the basis—the aesthetic
concept—for a new line of performance.
There would be cardboard props,
cardboard instruments, cardboard
mikes, cardboard clothes. And all
the music would be canned. When real
people get on stage and "play" their
instruments, an elaborate DJ operation
results. Rap performances began with
raps to DJ'd disks: the Cardboard
Air Band takes another, more visual
angle. Instead of rap, there is art.
Obviously art.

—Colab Annual Report 1982

Cardboard Air Band. *Cannibals 2
and Rap Intro*, 1981. Typewritten
lyrics, 28 × 21.5 cm each.
Courtesy of Becky Howland.

WELL THEY SAY EVERYBODY WANTS TO BE A STAR

SO HERE'S A TALKING BAND WITH NO REAL GUITAR

WE COME FROM "NO RIO"

IN THE (BLEEDING) HEART OF THE BARRIO   (BAH-REE-OH)

NOT-TOO-MANY FOLKS COME TO SEE OUR SHOWS

AND YOU NEVER HEAR THIS SHIT ON THE RADIO

BUT WE'RE HOT OFF A STREAK

XXXXXXXXX AND I THINK YOU OUGHTA KNOW

WE DID THE "ISLAND SHOW" AND ABSURDITIES

other voice: La Muestra de Isla!

          Muestra de Muchachadas:

SO HERE WE ARE AT THE MUDD CLUB CLUBBING

GETTING READY AND SET TO GIVE YOUR EARS A DRUBBING

SO HOLD ONTO YOUR LOVER
                RUN
DON'T RUN FOR COVER

JUST SETTLE YOUR ASS IN YOUR FAVORITE SEAT

'CAUSE YOU ARE ABOUT TO MEET:

The No Rio Cardboard Air Band!

"THERMIDOR" by Alan Moore ©1982
written for the CardBoard Air Band

The smoke of burning buildings fills the street
Rats and dogs are coming out to eat
The graveyards are full of tents
They are landlords collecting the rents

The landlords have been buried in the
basements of their buildings
The rich hang by their ballgowns
  from the bridges of the cities
Throw away your clothes – you no longer
  need them

The restaurants are free and
  everyone is eating
Money has no value
The government has fled
America has lost her statehood

The thermidor is here ....
  the thermidor is here

Drawing by Becky Howland

Alan Moore (lyrics) and Becky Howland (lettering). *Thermidor*, 1982. Ink and pencil on paper, 43 × 28 cm.
Courtesy of Becky Howland.

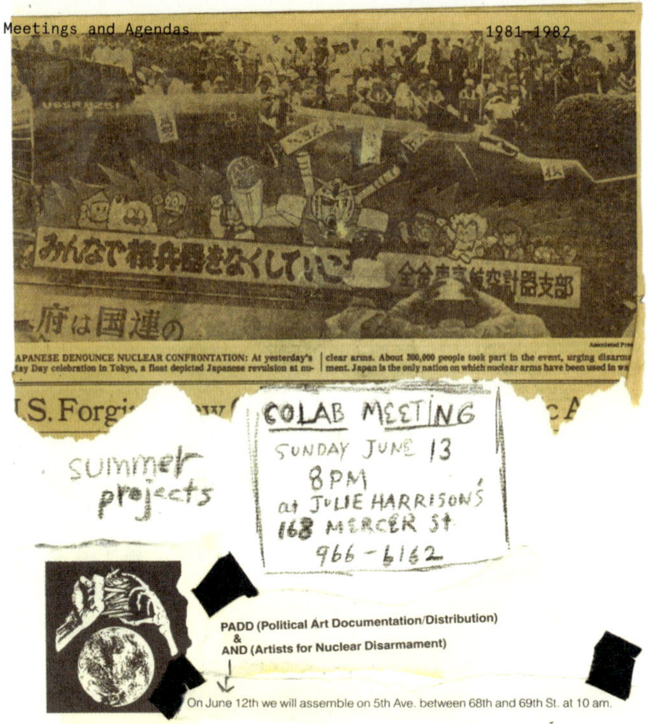

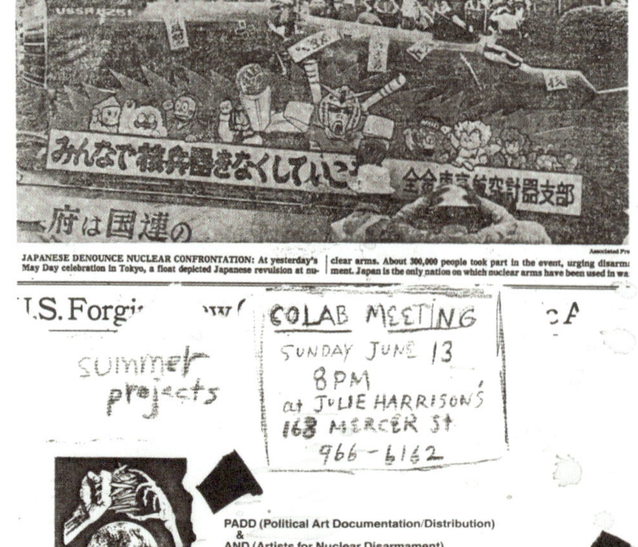

Becky Howland. *Colab Meeting*, 1982.
Collage and pencil on paper,
28 × 21.5 cm. Paste-up for photocopy
flyer. Courtesy of Becky Howland.

Becky Howland. *Colab Meeting*,
1982. Photocopy flyer, 28 × 21.5 cm.
Courtesy of Becky Howland.

COLAB MEETING   MONDAY 4/30 9PM at ABC NO RIO   156 Rivington St.   PARTY COLAB

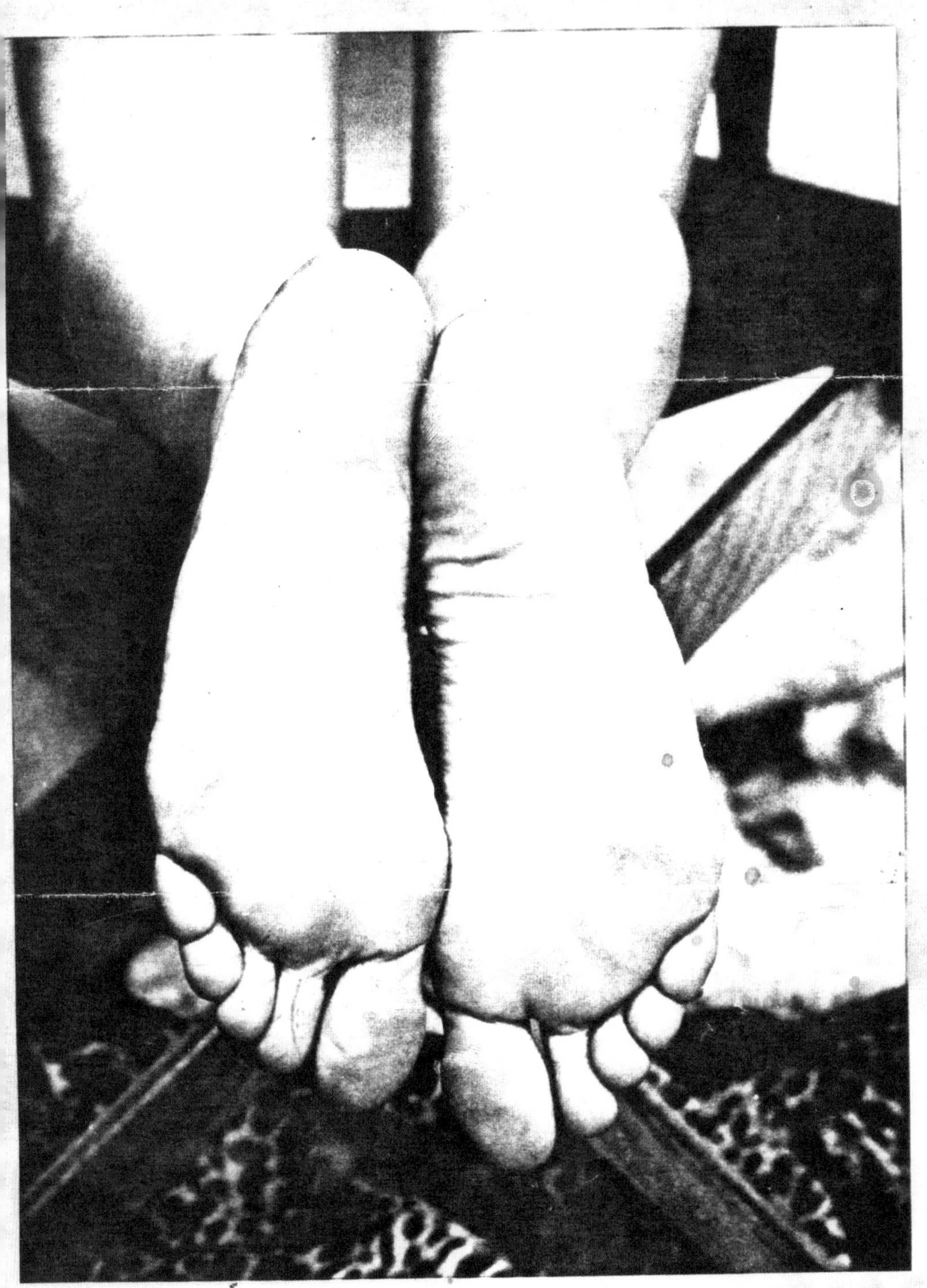

Unknown. *Colab Meeting*, c. 1982. Photocopy on paper, 28 × 21.5 cm. Courtesy of Bobby G (Robert Goldman).

PROPOSAL FOR THE RE-STRUCTURING OF CO-LAB

(short discussion tonight, vote at next meeting)

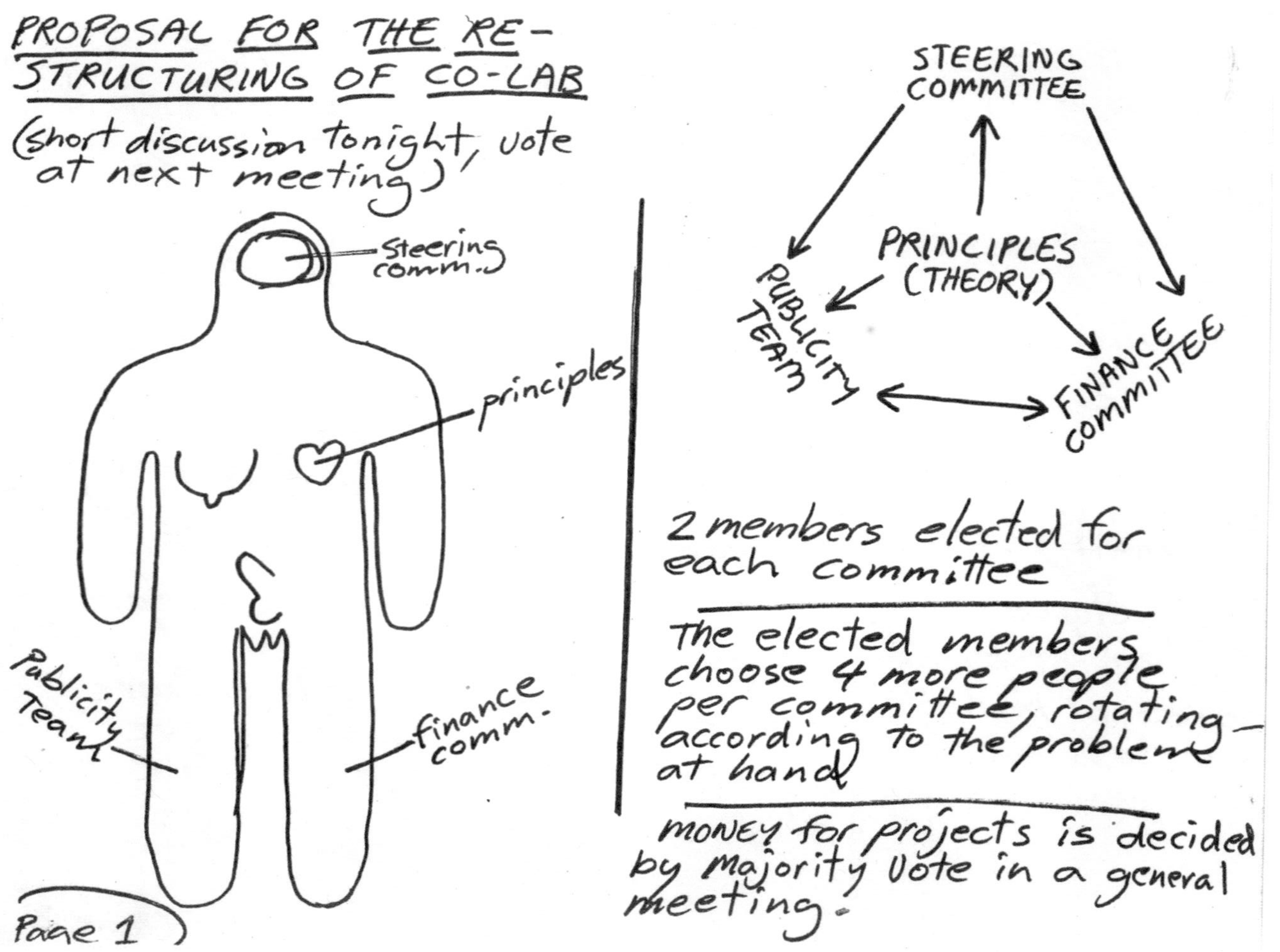

2 members elected for each committee

The elected members choose 4 more people per committee, rotating according to the problem at hand

money for projects is decided by majority vote in a general meeting.

PUBLICITY TEAM	STEERING COMMITTEE	FINANCE COMMITTEE *
- Publicity for Colab Sponsored projects - publicity for <u>ideas</u> - increase internal communication (mail) - develop a system of phone votes or mail votes for fast decisions between meetings	- Planning overall strategy - evaluation of projects - clarify the principles of Co-LAB - develop new ideas & directions - Presentation of projects to the General Member- ship	- Search for new funding sources - Grant Applications - Indipendent fund raising - Internal Book keeping * all members <u>must</u> serve some time on the finance committee

(Page 2)

Tom Otterness. *Proposal for the Restructuring of Co-Lab*, c. 1981–82. Photocopy pamphlet, unbound, pages 1-2 of 3, 21.5 × 28 cm each. Courtesy of Bobby G (Robert Goldman).

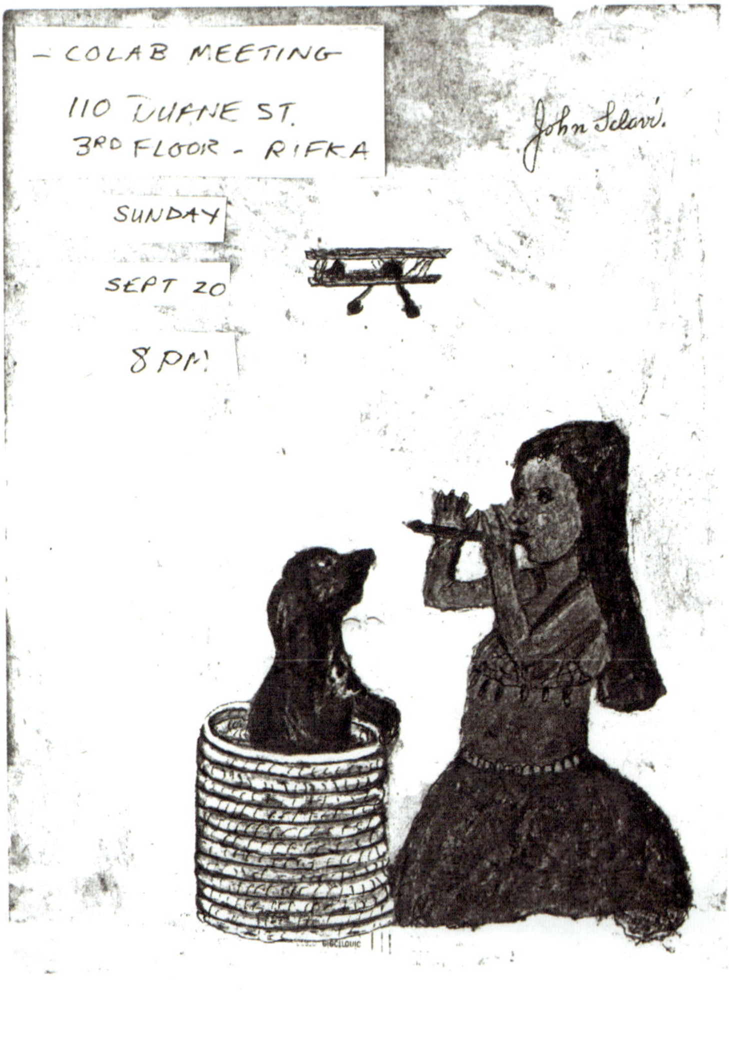

- COLAB MEETING

110 DUANE ST.
3RD FLOOR - RIFKA

John Sclavi.

SUNDAY

SEPT 20

8 PM!

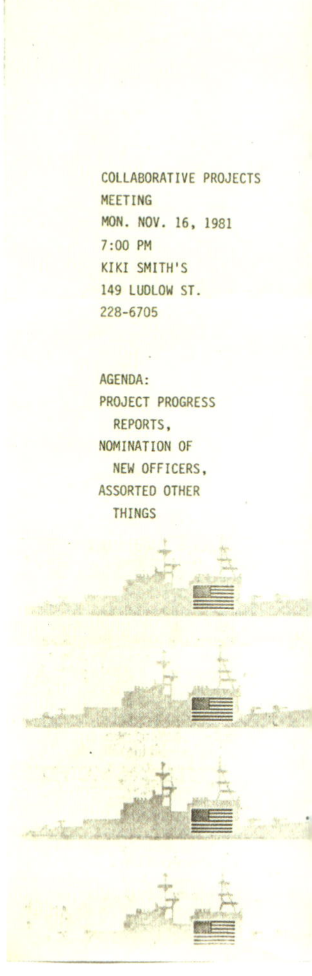

COLLABORATIVE PROJECTS
MEETING
MON. NOV. 16, 1981
7:00 PM
KIKI SMITH'S
149 LUDLOW ST.
228-6705

AGENDA:
PROJECT PROGRESS
  REPORTS,
NOMINATION OF
  NEW OFFICERS,
ASSORTED OTHER
  THINGS

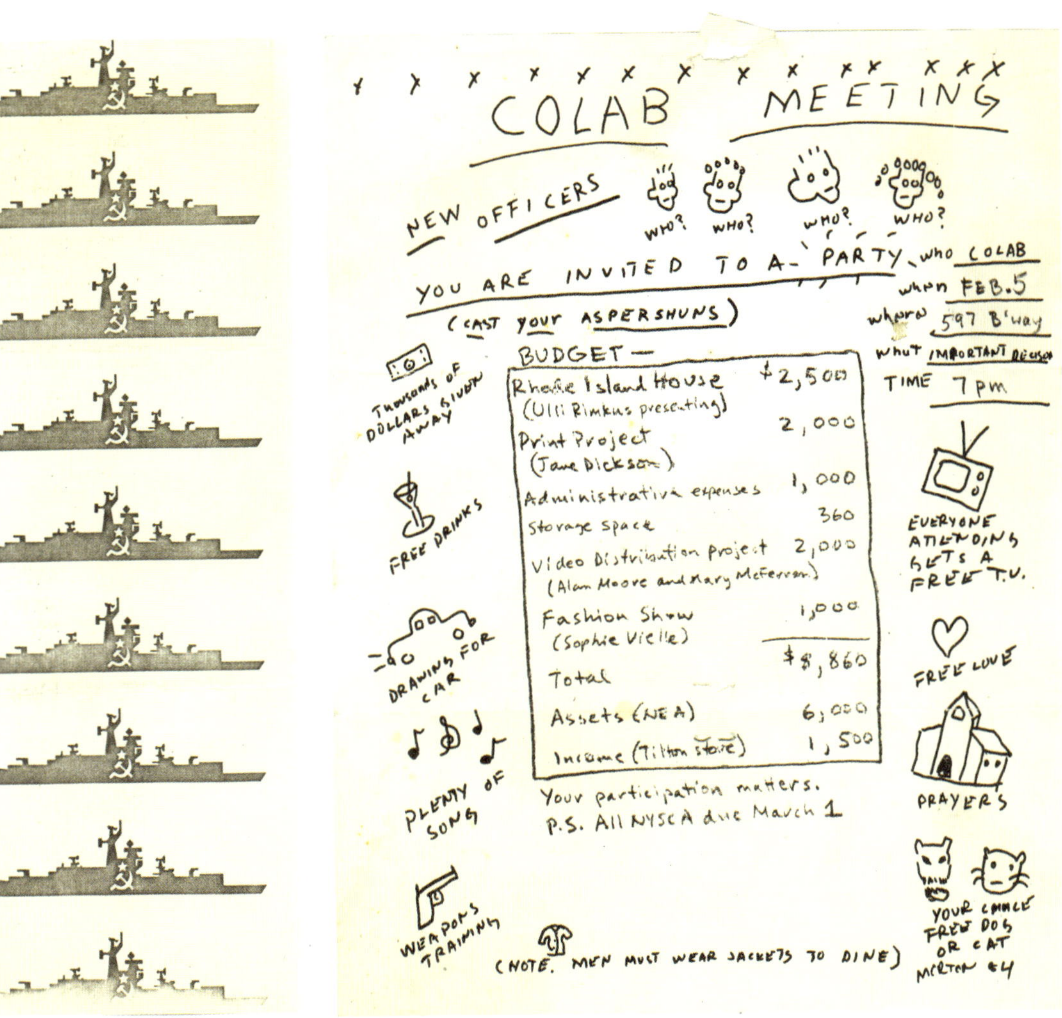

Left to right:

Unknown. *Collaborative Projects Meeting*, 1981. Photocopy flyer, 28 × 21.5 cm. Courtesy of Kiki Smith.

Unknown. *Colab Meeting*, 1981. Photocopy flyer, 28 × 21.5 cm. Courtesy of Becky Howland.

John Morton. *Colab Meeting*, 1982. Photocopy flyer. 28 × 21.5 cm. Courtesy of Becky Howland.

THE COLAB DAILY PURGE

VOL. I, No. 1   FOOLS DAY ISSUE   FREE ($1 to PADD Members)

THOUGHT FOR THE DAY: "For reasons of space I have to over-simplify, but I do want to insist that I'm raising such questions in support of and with genuine respect for the artists who are tackling them, in the interest of strengthening all of our gestures toward justice for the oppressed."
—Lucy Lippard, Voice 3/30

E D I T O R I A L

It's clear that Colab's "philosophy" or "ideology," whatever it was, has long since faded into the background. Instead most of our activity reflects blatant self-interest. Looking out for No. 1 is okay; the point is to use self-help to serve more progressive goals. When it was founded, Colab was based in part on the notion of collective action. And though it may seem a small thing, Colab does function as a collectivity, in which artists work together to increase their own power and seize control over their own destiny. From this one simple idea we see the possibility of much useful development. The COLAB DAILY PURGE has been instituted to provide a forum for members to discuss such ideas and examine group activity in the hope that they can become more important and more useful.

E S S A Y : "What Colab Needs Is A Good, Thorough Purge"

NOTE TO MEMBERS: Nominations are open for the Colab Sabbatical Fellowship Award, a non-juried, mandatory grant providing one-way transportation to Buffalo, N.Y., and a monthly stipend for a period of one year. Who would you most like to see leave town? Please, only one nomination per ballot. Candidates are limited to Colab members.

[Handwritten note:] Fend — A dummy only — sent to you, Miller, Moore & Howland. Please make comments; add wit & spleen, & write something libelous. —M.

THE COLAB DAILY PURGE

VOL. 1, No. 2

STANDARD AGENDA

1. Meeting called to order by president.

2. Minutes of previous meeting read to membership. Minutes approved as read.

3. Correspondence reported by secretary. May be taken up immediately or later.

4. Report of board of directors.

5. Report of treasurer.

6. Standing committees reports, any.

7. Special committees reports.

8. Special orders, if any.

9. Unfinished business. Itemize.

10. New business. Itemize.

11. Controlled announcements, when.

12. The program (if there is one). Chairman or president presides.

13. Adjournment by the president.

*   *

Propaganda Notes
from WSJ 4/2/82

How ITT Shells Out $10 Million or So a Year To Polish Reputation

So-called image advertising has become a burgeoning business for Madison Avenue. Nearly half of the 500 largest U.S. companies use advertising to sell ideas as well as their products, the Association of National Advertisers says. It estimates that $1 billion was spent on such nonproduct advertising last year, with ITT and 16 other companies budgeting at least $10 million each.

But ITT's image advertising is viewed as highly effective. "They've done themselves proud in creating a new image for themselves," says J. Douglas Johnson, an Indiana University marketing professor who has [...]

Walter "Mike" Robinson. *The Colab Daily Purge, Vol. 1 No. 1 [Fools Day Issue]*, 1982. Photocopy broadsheet, 35.5 × 21.5 cm each. Short-lived Colab newsletter by Walter "Mike" Robinson. Courtesy of Becky Howland.

The Colab Daily Purge, Vol. 1 No. 2, 1982. Photocopy broadsheet, 35.5 × 21.5 cm each. Short-lived Colab newsletter by Walter "Mike" Robinson. Courtesy of Becky Howland.

Walter "Mike" Robinson (rules) and Unknown (artwork). *Colab Cabana House Rules (front and back)*, 1982. (front and back) Photocopy flyer, 28 × 21.5 cm. Instructions for Colab getaway on Long Island. Courtesy of Becky Howland.

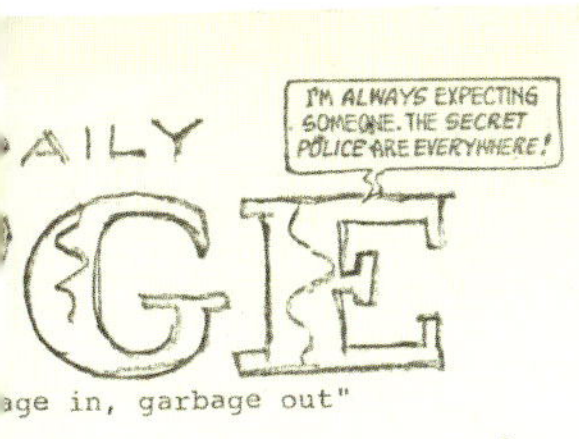

MEETINGS

t's Rules of Order, originally
in 1893

reeting.
 Corrections or additions from
ted.
 arising out of correspondence
w business.)

dations or motions.

ss that will be taken up.

 the meeting. The program

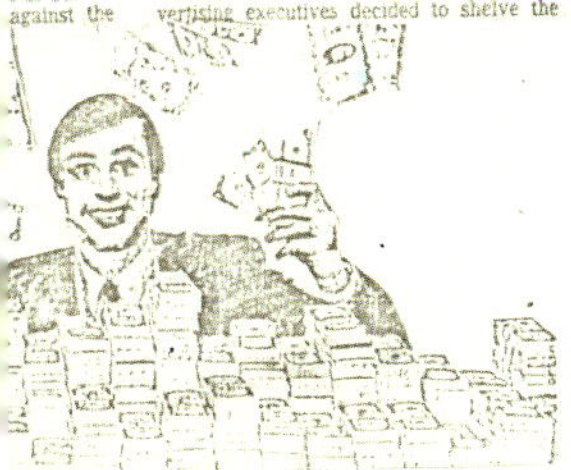
re saying
horn."
 about the
rtisers are
ect matter
scrapped a
rs and its
r instance.
ublicly at-
eing made
"

1960s, ITT's
 company's
f the public
ven its own

up with the
ke, jokingly
nal This &

's involve-
olitics made
growing an-
972 a pub-
y ITT lobby-
t of Justice
against the

company with a purported ITT pledge of
$400,000 to finance the 1972 Republican con-
vention in San Diego (the convention subsequently was switched to Miami Beach). A
year later came revelations that ITT had offered advice and money to the Nixon administration and the Central Intelligence
Agency to help unseat Chilean President Al-
lende.

Although ITT vigorously denied any
wrongdoing, the company's reputation was
blotted. ITT's name appeared regularly in
front-page headlines, its offices in the U.S.
and abroad were bombed and its campus re-
cruiters often were assailed by protesters.
Even some copywriters at Needham, Har-
per & Steers Inc., ITT's ad agency, refused
to work on its accounts.

Dealing With Perceptions.

"We were running uphill. No matter what
you explained, nobody wanted to accept it,"
says Edward Gerrity, an ITT senior vice
president. "Perception is the reality. You
had to deal with the perceptions."

After the controversies erupted, ITT advertising executives decided to shelve the

COLAB CABANA

House Rules:

It is really terrific out there and as soon as the rest of you realize it
I'm sure everyone will want to stay forever. However, there are a few
basic obvious procedures that should be followed if you want to avoid the
most dire consequences and repercussions.

1. Bring blankets, sheets, towels and pillows if you use such things.

2. Clean up after yourself. Wash dishes. Sweep and mop floors. Vacuum
   rugs. Clean kitchen. Pick up stuff and put it back where it belongs.
   This seems so obvious that it needs no repeating. But if you don't
   do it, believe me, you will burn in eternal hell-fire.

3. Don't steal anything from the house. This too is obvious, but
   experience the first weekend revealed that it needs repeating.
   The people who rented the place to us are nice and their stuff should
   be treated with respect. Scavenging is absolutely forbidden.

4. Don't use the telephone for long distance calls. Don't even use it
   for local calls. The bill will soar otherwise and everyone will get
   pissed off.

5. Count on spending an average of $10 a day. If you can't afford that,
   too bad for you--don't come out. A little parasitism goes a long way
   towards ruining a vacation.
   On the first weekend, we found that ca. $6 per person covered food,
   prepared jointly for all, for one day. Hard liquor, with its disproportionate
   cost and quick disappearance, should probably be bought separately.
   The extra $4--or perhaps less--should be set aside (we haven't yet
   established a kitty out there) to pay for telephone, utility and other
   charges.

I guess that's it. On the other side of this sheet is a more detailed
map. Out at the house are further directions on how to arrange for
garbage pickup, how to turn on the washing machine, etc.

I feel like a nag writing this stuff down. We're grown-ups, we're
responsible people, and we can police ourselves. Right?

[Received from on high and transcribed by W. Robinson]

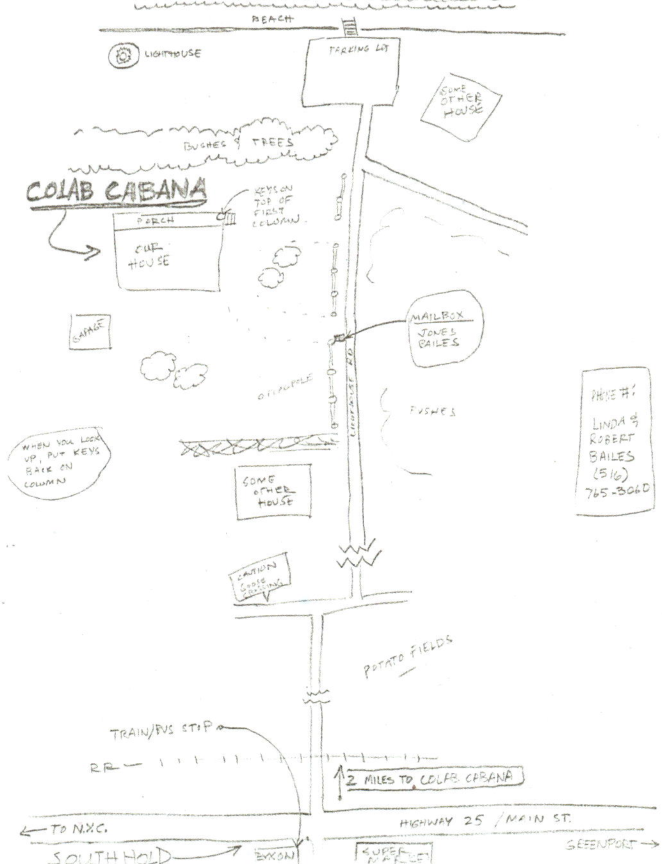

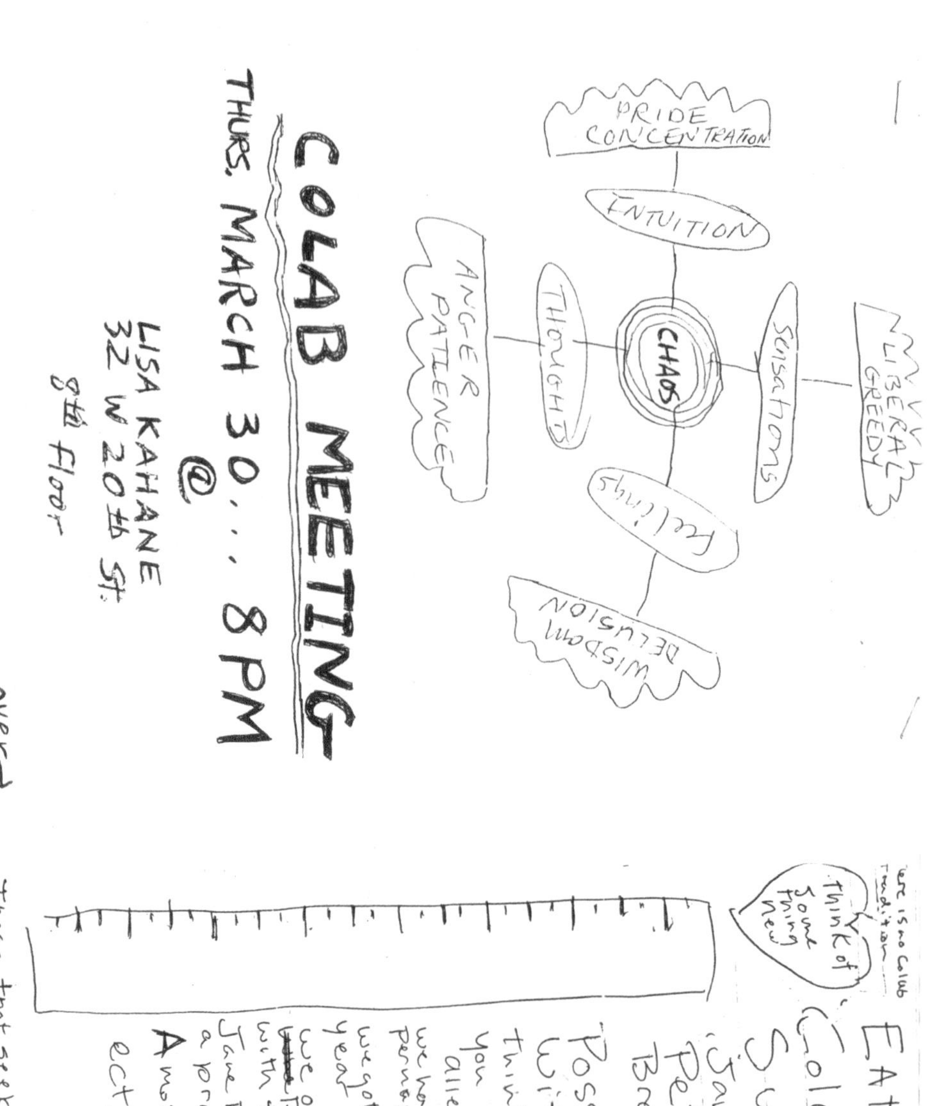

Cara Perlman. *Colab Meeting*, c. 1983. Photocopy flyer, 28 × 21.5 cm. Courtesy of Becky Howland.

Kiki Smith. *Eat More Fiber or Colab Meeting*, 1984. Photocopy flyer, 28 × 21.5 cm. Courtesy of Becky Howland.

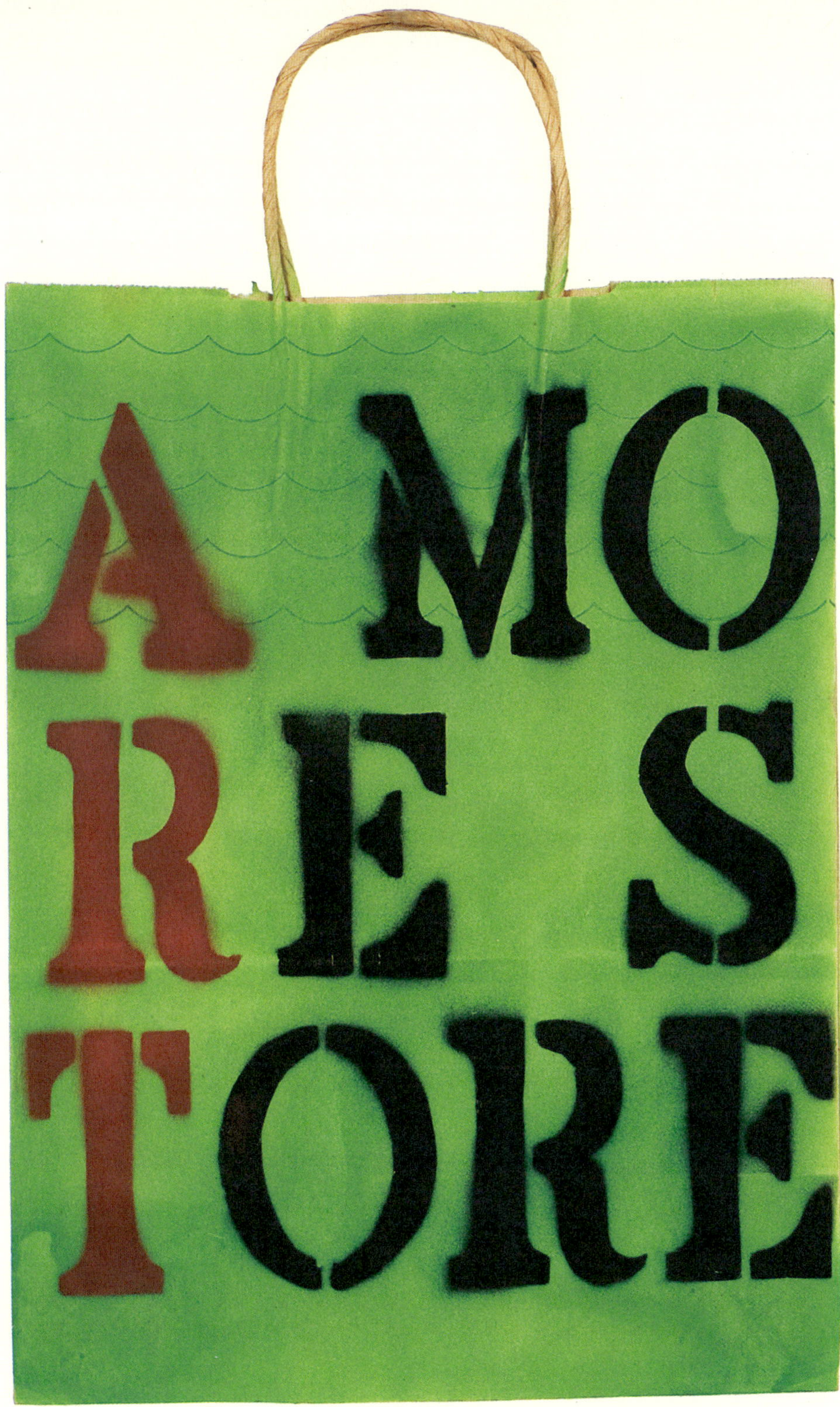

Dick Miller. *A. More Store shopping bag*, c. 1980. Stenciled spray paint on brown paper bag. 43 × 33 cm.
Courtesy of Terise Slotkin.

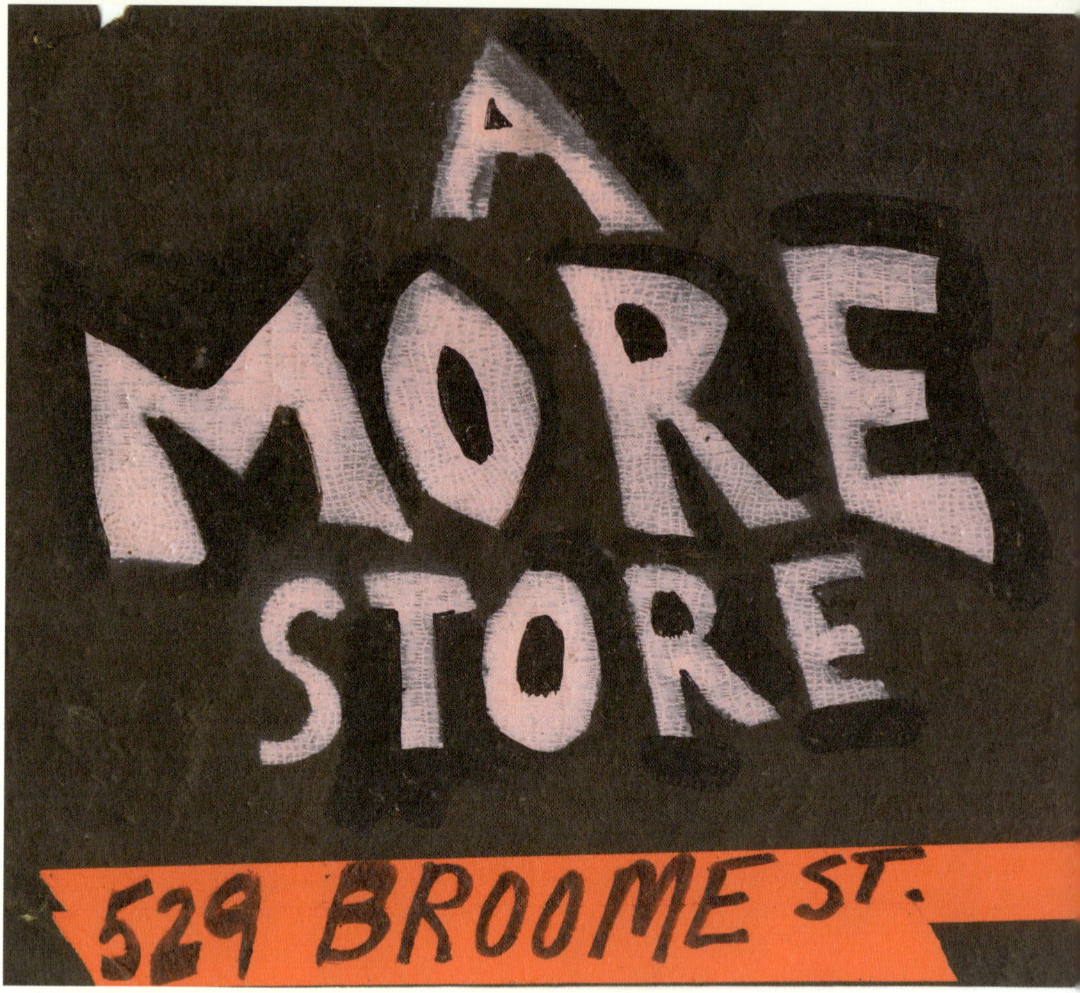

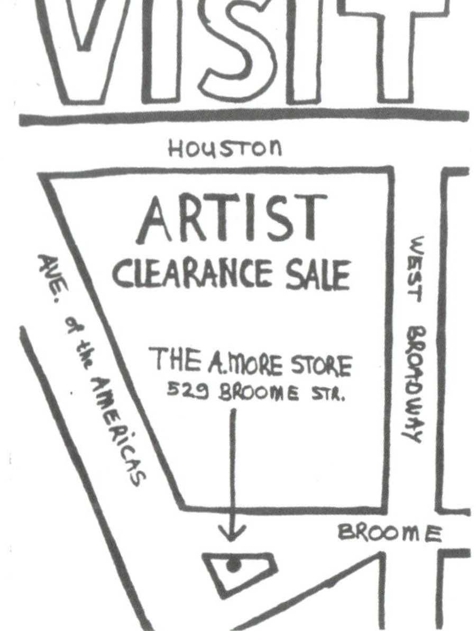

Alan Moore. *A. More Store Sign*, 1980. Acrylic,
tape and marker on board, 24.5 × 29 cm.
Courtesy of Becky Howland. Photo: Nancy Linn.

Unknown. *Visit Artist Clearance Sale*,
c. 1981. Photocopy handbill, 14 × 11 cm.
Courtesy of Becky Howland.

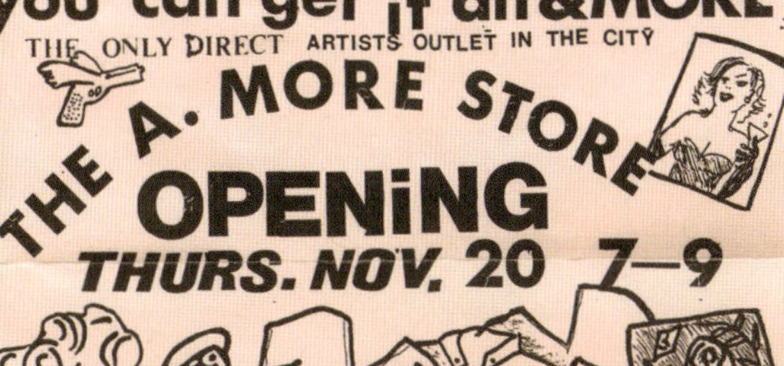

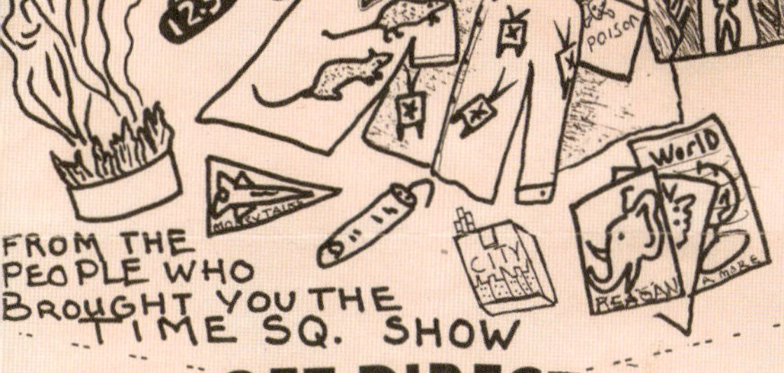

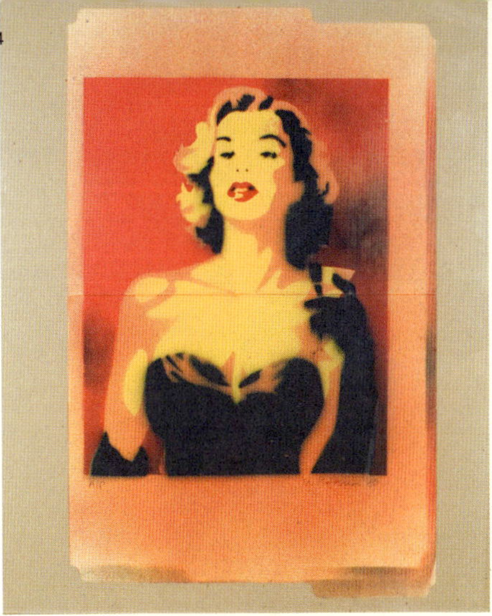

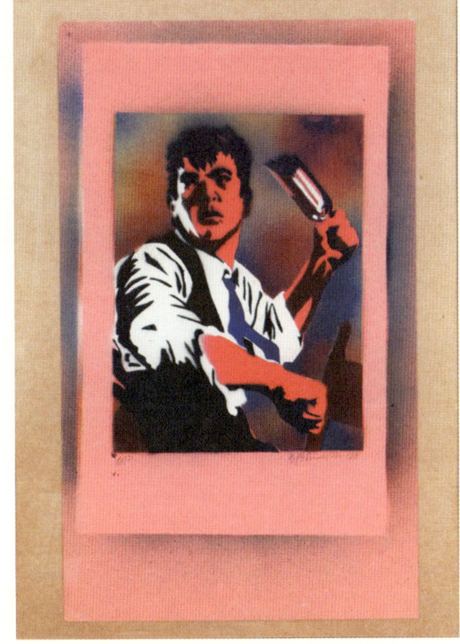

Clockwise from upper left:

Ellen Cooper. *Check It Out*, 1980. Photocopy poster, 36 × 21.5 cm. Courtesy of Becky Howland.

Walter "Mike" Robinson. *Lady with Martini / Man with Bottle*. 1980. Spray paint on manila folder, 51 × 41 cm each (framed). From the A. More Store at 529 Broome Street. Courtesy of Walter Robinson.

Alan Moore. *A. More: Artists' Outlet Means You Collect Direct*. Photocopy handbill, 12.5 × 11 cm. Courtesy of Becky Howland.

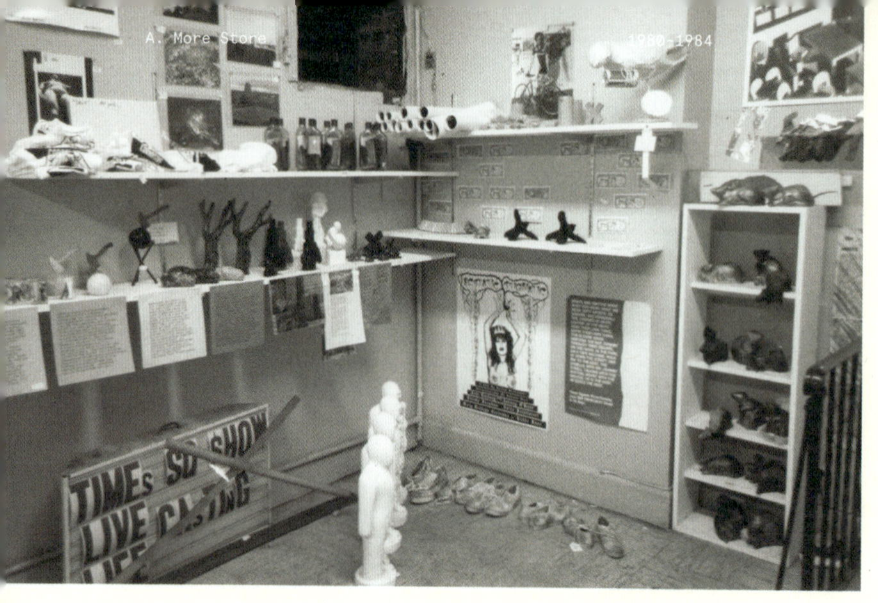

Terise Slotkin. *A. More Store Interior*. 529 Broome Street, 1980. Photograph, 12.5 × 20 cm Courtesy of Becky Howland.

Kiki Smith. *Cigarette Pack*, c. 1981. Chalk and pencil on cardboard, (blue, 18.5 × 14.5 cm; red, 16.5 × 17.5 cm; purple, 16 × 17 cm). Courtesy of Robin Winters.

Tim Rollins & K.O.S. *Burning Brick Buildings*, c. 1980–82. Gouache on brick, approx. 8.5 × 20.5 × 5.5 cm each. Courtesy of Walter Robinson. Photo: Nancy Linn.

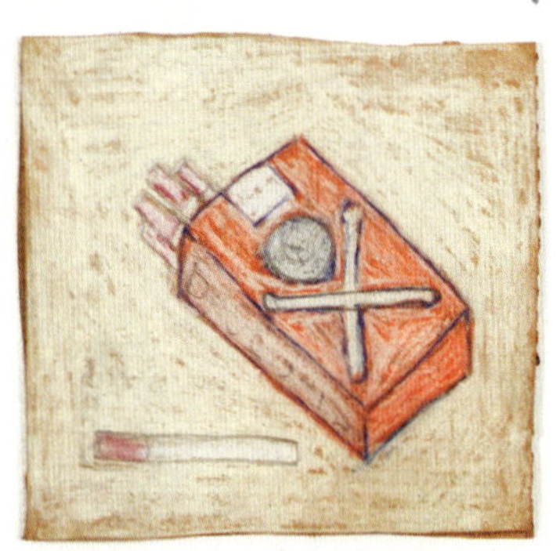
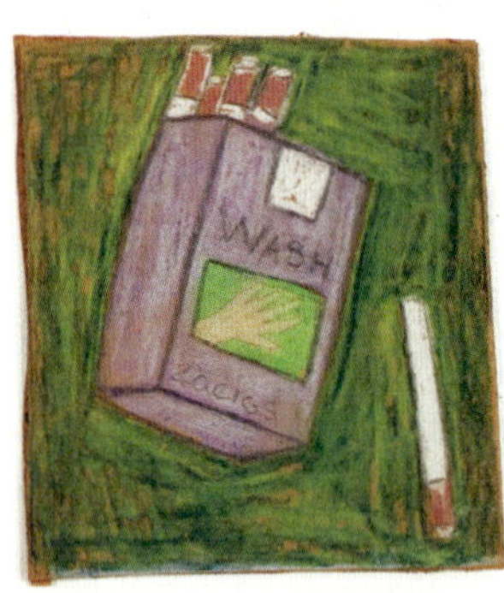
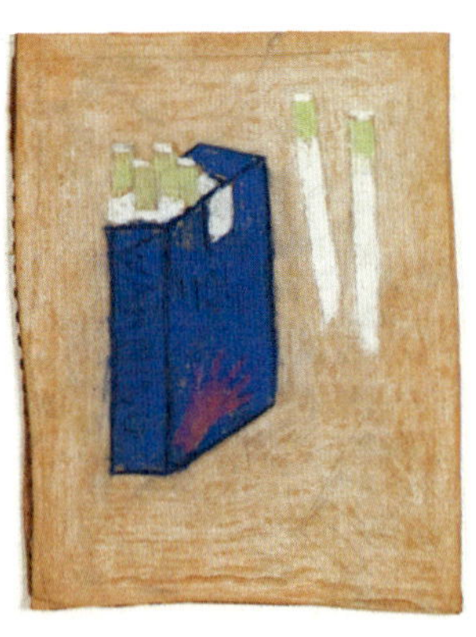

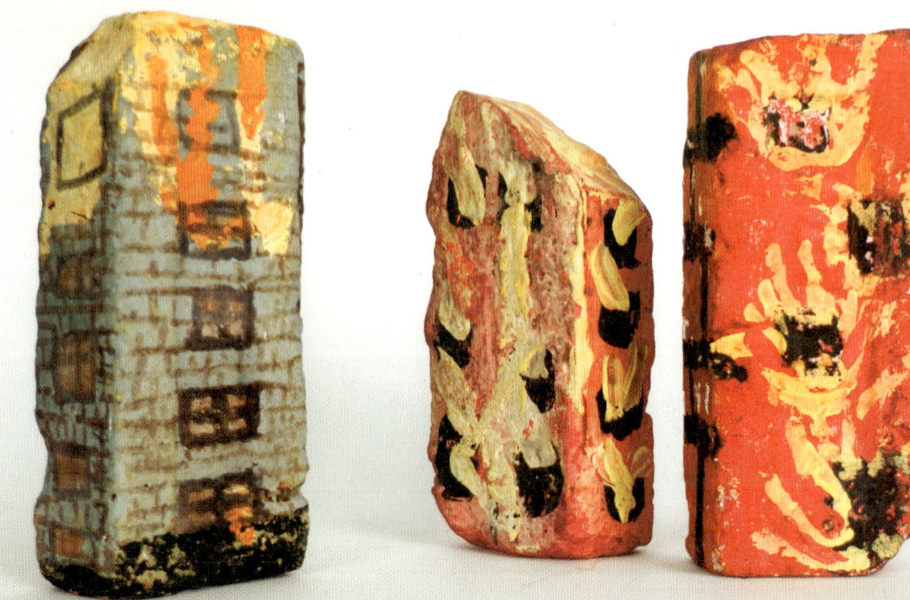

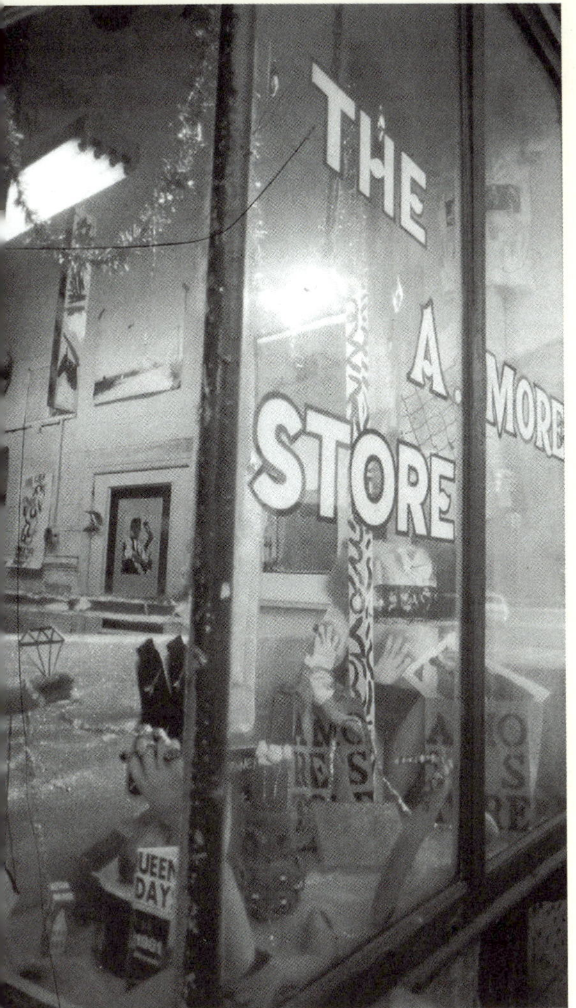

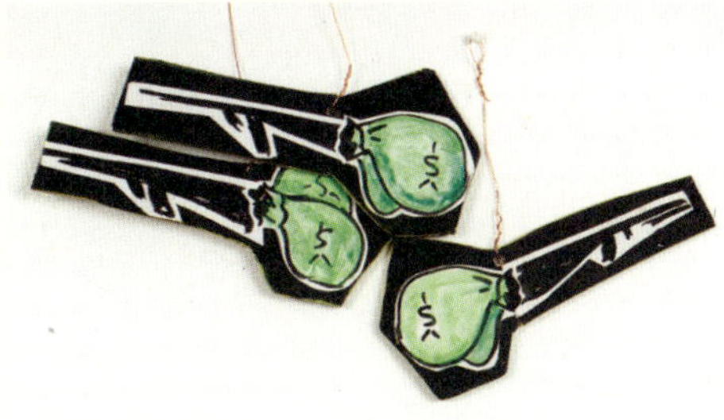

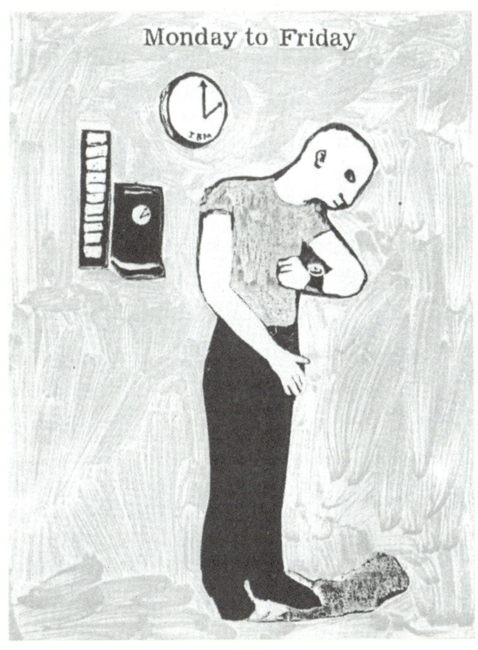

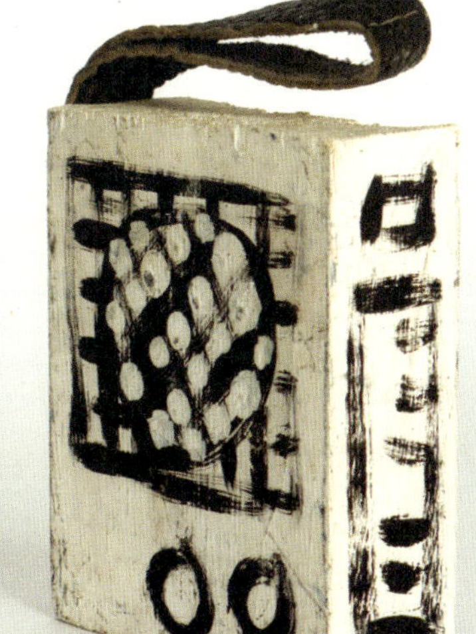

Clockwise from upper left:

Terise Slotkin. *A. More Store*, 1980. Digital reproduction of color photography, 28 × 21.5 cm. From 529 Broome Street Store. Courtesy of Terise Slotkin.

Becky Howland. *Christmas Tree Ornaments*, 1980. Hand-painted photocopy and acrylic on wood, approximately 15 × 10 cm each. Courtesy of Becky Howland. Photo: Nancy Linn.

Coleen Fitzgibbon. *Monday to Friday*, 1980. Offset printed card, 18.5 × 14 cm. Exhibition announcement for benefit at Brooke Alexander Gallery with A. More Store. Courtesy of Kiki Smith.

Kiki Smith. *Transistor Radio*, 1980. Acrylic on wood, leather strap with nail, 3.75 × 8.75 × 11 cm. Courtesy of Robin Winters. Photo: Nancy Linn.

DOUBLE GUARANTEE

I might attack you...your blue glow is a pretty target. You might die from my blows...if it turns out that I do kill you, I want you to know I'll make it up to you someday. Because I don't hate you and I don't have anything against you—in fact, you look like decent folks. I promise that if I do kill you, I will save you in some future life. It may be a thousand transmigrations from now, we may not even be human, but I'll remember. I always keep my word, ask anyone, they'll tell you.

You and I, we are committed to this universe, there is no asylum, so let's get settled in—we could even be friends. I have this recurring image: you are far away in the darkness, cut off from everything, adrift in the winds without eyes (John Wayne shot them out). You are stranded between lives, your only memories are of astronauts. It's been years since you have touched anything and you long to get back to a life with a daily rhythm...And then, with one ringing shot and a chain of silver light, I pull you back.

Don't walk away, it's OK, I'm always under control when Star Wars is playing in the theaters. It's in between episodes that I swerve out of control. It's then that I will hunt you down. Star Wars II will have a long run, but in the late fall, when it is displaced by the latest stinking trash reels from the disintegrated corpse of a city they call Hollywood, I'll come at you. You will be the vent for my hatred of them. Black noise, like blindness will flow through your body.

You see, I go to Star Wars many times each week. I need it: in the daytime it is my school, my psychiatrist, my health club; at night it is my lover, my private jet airliner, my communion with the universe. And when I feel bad, it is my doctor. I'm going to call it Doctor from now on, you'll know what I mean.

You see. I didn't have any schooling, everything I know comes from the movies. Up until the Doctor, all I had was porno and horror and an occasional Clint Eastwood. You can imagine what my first trip to the Doctor was like. He laid me down on this special bed, and a woman in a white dress secured my arms and legs to the bed with leather straps. Then she attached a metal brace to my head and put this little rubber thing in my mouth. The Doctor attached these metal wires to my head and then he stepped back.

The only part I remember is the laser sword scene. God it hurt. He was demolishing me, slashing in deeper and deeper. I was falling into nothingness when someone in white came and saved me...it was you...Now, once again, take my hand and pull me through, maybe you can free me: With your courage and with your common sense, I promise that we will win in November and that America will continue to be a nation that faces the world as it is today and works with realism to bring a future of freedom, peace and justice. Thank you.

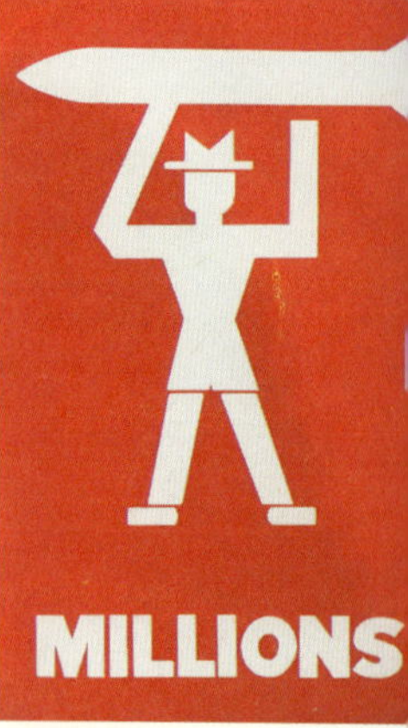

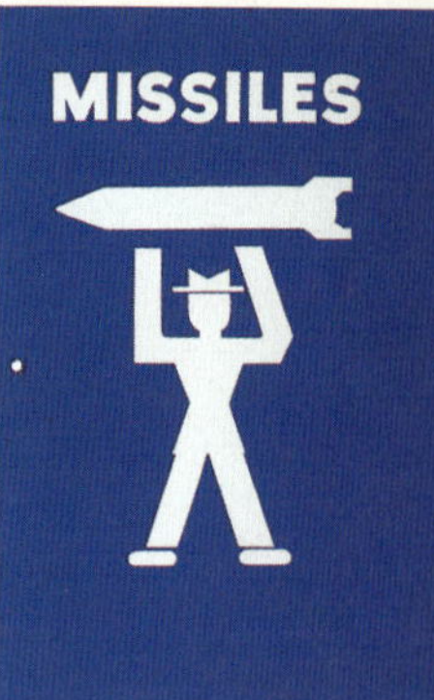

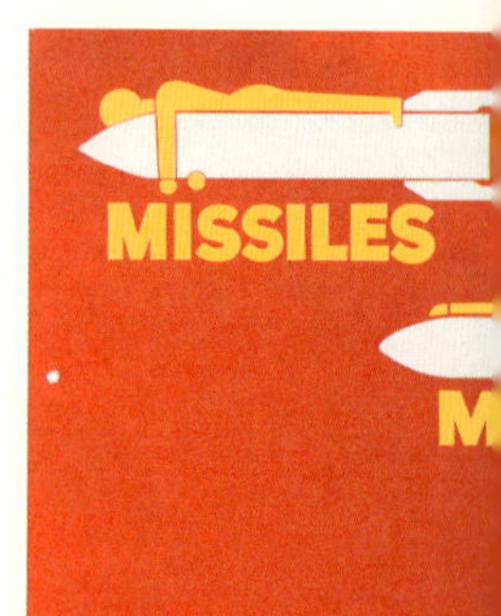

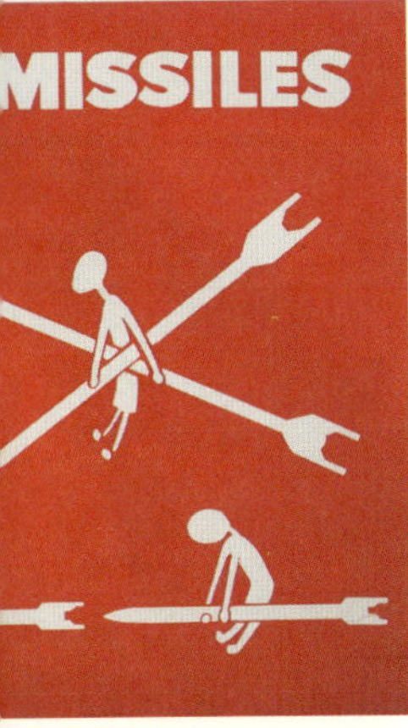

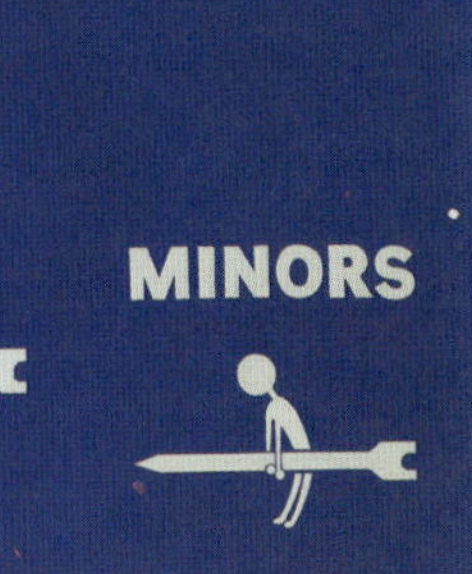

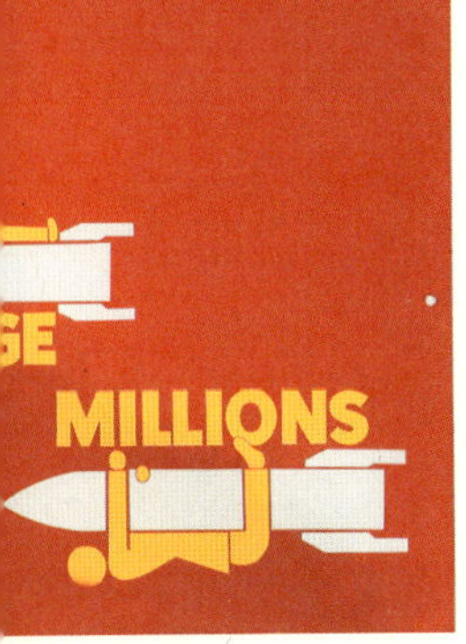

SPECIAL SUMMER

My subject is the bringing together of elements that have been separated, it is this sweet flavor that has brought you here. I'm glad that you have come, the timing is right. Stay with us.

It shows on your face; you have a life that keeps you busily occupied, but deep down inside is fear and chaos. You don't know what to do or what to hope for. You have lost the bilateral symmetry that is natural to all of God's creatures. Look in the mirror. Your left eye is olive shaped and wide and young, while your right eye is tight, just a slit in an ancient mask. Your mouth too has become asymmetrical. But don't despair, turn away from the mirror. There is hope, we are all in the same boat. Join us and together we will cross the great water.

Listen to me and take heed. This is going to be a special summer, it is a very dangerous time. Without great prudence, we shall all perish miserably. Beware of the common objects around you — chairs, tables, books, cups, etc. They are devoid of life, but they carry with them endless generations of the dead. They are openings which allow dead things to come up from the underground. Men will come out of their graves turned into flying creatures. The air will be filled with a mischievous winged race which will assail men and animals and feed upon them with much noise — filling themselves with scarlet blood. Serpents of great length will be seen high in the air, fighting with birds; their noise will stun all who are near and their breath will kill men and destroy cities. Men will take great pleasure in seeing their own work destroyed. And further, they will deal bitter blows to that which is the very source of their life.

I warn you — you may come to such a wretched plight that it will become soothing to have others derive profit from your suffering or from the loss of your only wealth, which is health.

Alas, what do I see... There will come a time when there is no difference between colors, everything will be black alike... But out of this darkness I see the Saviour crucified anew. Come with us, you too will learn to see. I love you and I will show you the way. But don't delay, hesitation is the Devil himself. We have a seminar every day; in just three hours you will become a minister and you will have a career for all eternity. You can then go to the street to teach and save others. You will beget new ministers and they will beget more. Soon we will all be woven together in a giant human pyramid. I need ten dollars from you now. Sure, you are a little uncomfortable when I bring up that subject and you are right to be so because money has been man's greatest curse. But this is our chance to break the Devil's stranglehold. If everyone gives just a little, there will be plenty for everyone. It's only ten dollars for a love that lasts forever.

Reese Williams. (left) *Double Guarantee*, (right) *Special Summer*, c. 1980. Screenprint on paper, 60 × 45 cm each. From *The Times Square Show* Gift Shop, wheat-pasted around Manhattan. Courtesy of Andrea Callard.

Ilona Granet. *Missiles Manage Millions / Missiles for Minors / Missiles Manage Millions*, 1979. Enamel paint on metal, 28 × 46 cm each. From the series "Street Signs for WWIII." Courtesy of Ilona Granet.

Artists Turn Retailers For A New Wave Christmas

The A. More Store Opens at 529 Broome Street

All the fixings for a New Wave Christmas deck the stamped-tin walls of
The A. More Store, Soho's newest and surely its funkiest retail enterprise.

Rats and "rip-offs," ray guns and rock bags are included in A. More's
eclectic inventory of wearable, usables and visuals, the original work
of more than 60 artists, many of them veterans of last summers'
critically acclaimed *Times Square Show*. What this diverse arsenal of art
and artifacts has in common is a range of prices certain to accommodate
the budget of even the most frugal stocking stuffer. …

At A. More's there's wry social commentary in Matthew Geller's 1981 Date
Book, an appointment calendar with grisly tabloid headline (guaranteed
authentic) for each day of the New Year. And there's some economic
tongue-in-cheek in Becky Howland's "Cardboard Oil," a prefabricated
2-ft-tall conflagration of swirling smoke and tongues of fire. ($300).
The conflagration is also available in a more diminuitive tree decoration
size in hand-colored xerox for $3.00. …

The A. More Store is a co-operative venture of the participating artists
who, by eliminating the retail middleman and selling directly to the
public, are able to sell their work at the lowest possible prices. Says
Alan Moore, a participant, "The store is an example of co-operative
economics; it operates on the purest notions of free enterprise. It's
artists inviting collectors to collect, but directly from the artists."
The store's name, insists Moore, is "something Italian."

—A. More Store Press Release, 24 Nov. 1980

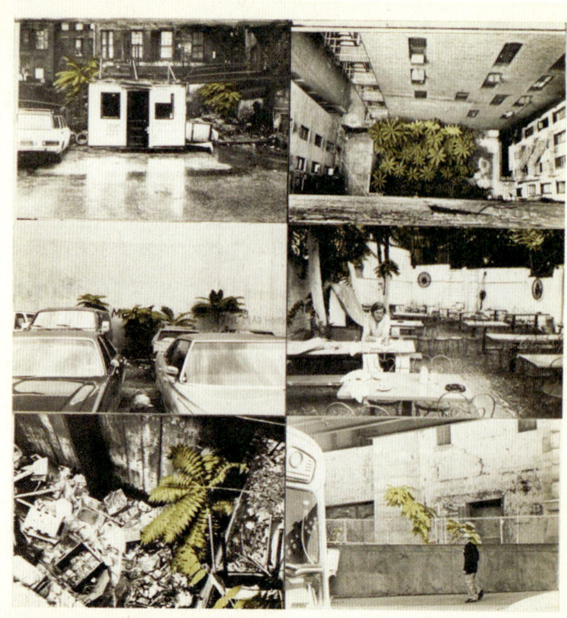

This page:

Andrea Callard. *Ailanthus Trees*, c. 1980.
Duotone offset printed cards, 30 × 33 cm.
Uncut set of six postcards. Courtesy of the
Collaborative Projects Archive.

Facing page, clockwise from upper left:

Alan Moore. *Smashed TV Work Shirt*, c. 1981–
83. Hand-painted button-down shirt. Courtesy of
Walter Robinson. Photo: Nancy Linn.

Walter "Mike" Robinson. *Romance Picture*, 1981.
Offset printed edition, 30 × 37.5 cm (framed).
Edition of 90, signed and numbered. Courtesy
of Walter Robinson. Photo: Nancy Linn.

Tom Warren. *Get Your Pictures Snapped
with Santa*, 1981. Color polaroid photographs,
10.5 × 8.5 cm each. Pictures are Becky
Howland and Joe Lewis. Courtesy of Becky
Howland.

Ellen Cooper. *Christmas Store at White Columns*,
1982. Photocopy poster, 28 × 21.5 cm. Courtesy
of Kiki Smith.

Alan Moore. *Smashed TV*, c. 1981–83.
Handpainted cotton t-shirt. Courtesy of Barbara
Moore. Photo: Nancy Linn.

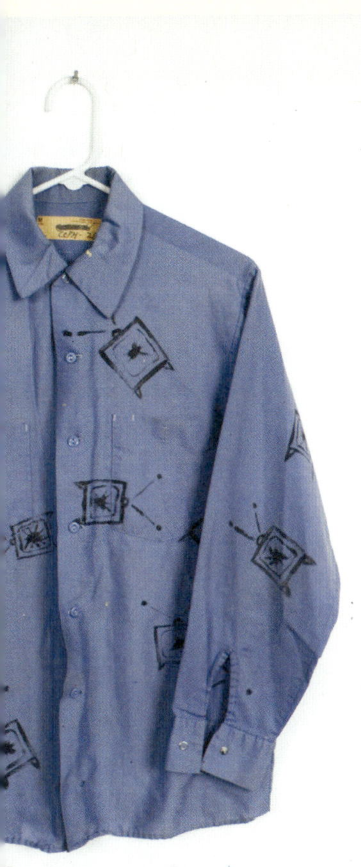

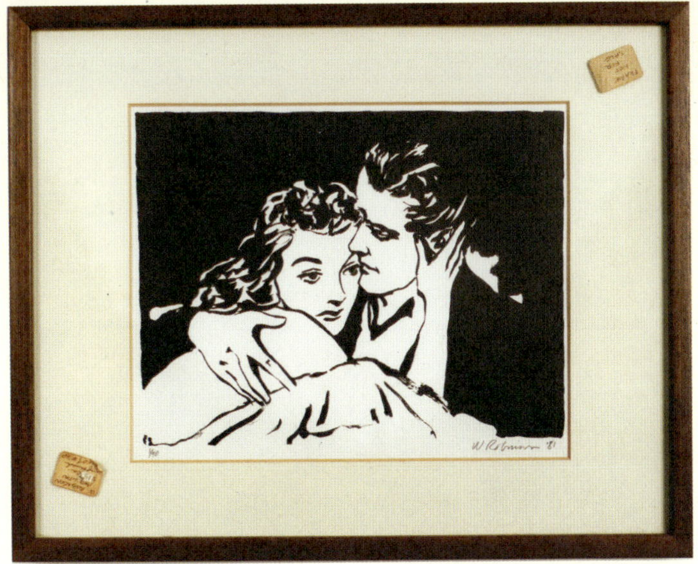

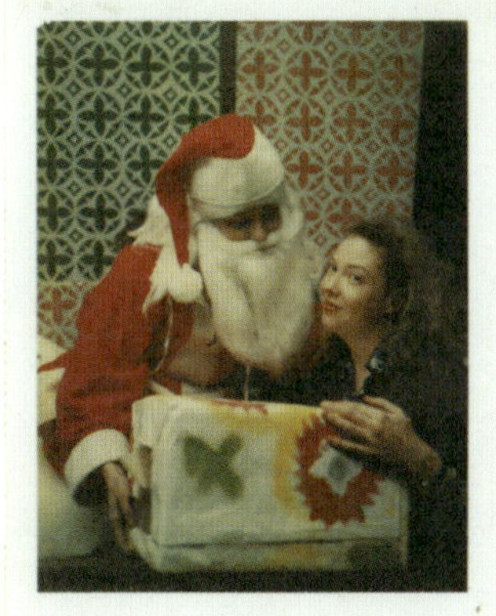

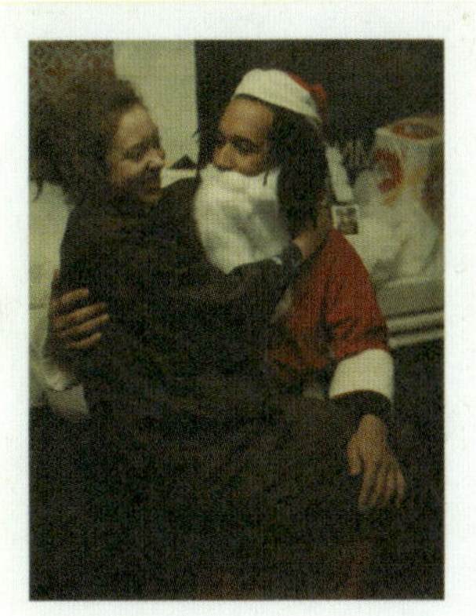

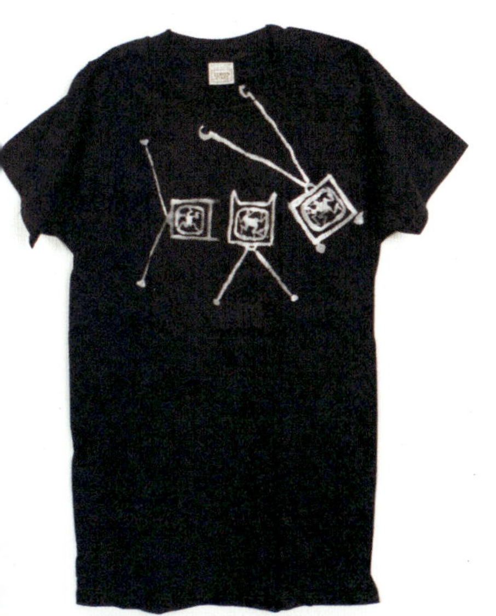

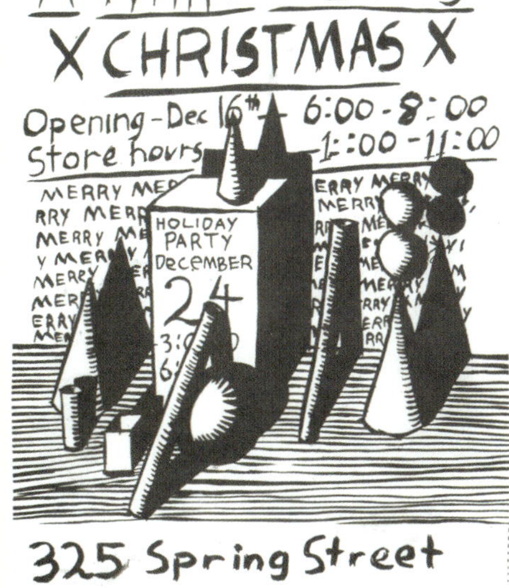
A WHITE COLUMNS
X CHRISTMAS X
Opening – Dec 16th – 6:00 – 8:00
Store hours   1:00 – 11:00
MERRY MERRY
RRY MERRY
MERRY ME
y MERRY
MERRY
MER
ERRY
MER
HOLIDAY
PARTY
DECEMBER
24
3:00
6:00
MERRY MERRY
MERRY
ERRY
MERRY
MERRY
ERRY
RRY
325 Spring Street

A. More Store purchases, 1981. Receipts, 6.5 × 12 cm each. Courtesy of Becky Howland.

Moré

A. More Store-Direct outlet for artists. Opened in November
and December 1980. Led by Ellen Cooper, Kiki Smith, and Mike
Robinson, this venture actually made a profit. Followed up by
advertising in the East Village Eye, and soon to publish a Direct Mail
Mail Catalog.

ABC No Rio   -   Founded by the survivors of the Real Estate Show
156 Rivington St.
Lower East Side   Double decker storefront presents:
NYC

live acts, music, film, and video. Unique sculpure garden
exhibitions include:

Island Show   coordinated by   Rebecca Howland
Time Is Us   "   Justen Ladda
Animals Living in Cities   Christy Rupp
Suicide, Murder, and Junk   John Morton and Tom Warren
Internationalist Art   San Francisco Poster Brigade
Artists for Survival   Jon Keller

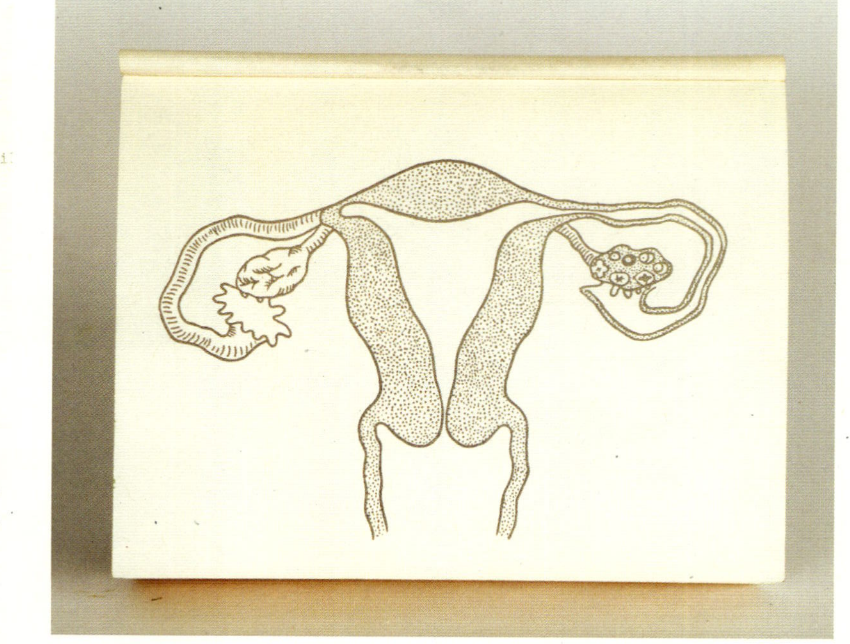

Becky Howland and Alan Moore. *Draft of a press release for the A. More Store*, c. 1981. Pen and typewritten document, 28 × 21.5 cm.
Courtesy of Becky Howland.

Jolie Stahl and Kiki Smith. *Uterus Notepad*. New York: J. Stahl & K. Smith, 1983. Screenprinted, 10.75 × 14 × 1.5 cm.
Courtesy of the Collaborative Projects Archive.

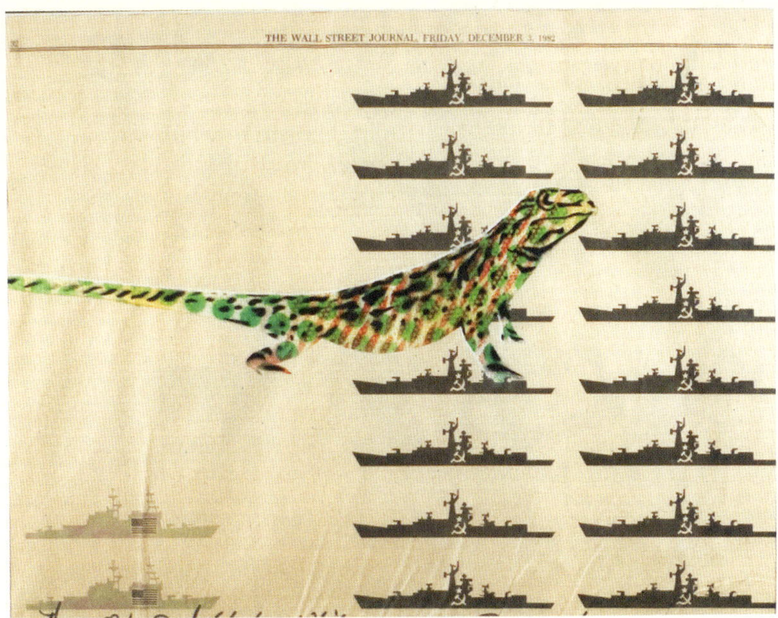

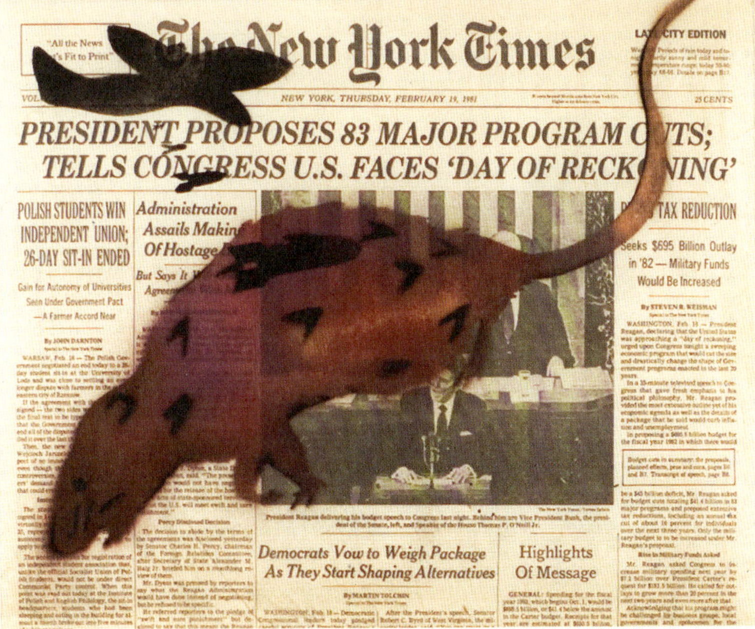

Top to bottom:

Christy Rupp. *They Only See Black & White*, 1982. Spray paint on newspaper, 41.5 × 51.5 cm framed.
Courtesy of Christy Rupp. Photo: Nancy Linn.

Christy Rupp. *Reagan Rat*, 1981. Spray paint on newspaper, 41.5 × 51.5 cm framed.
Courtesy of Christy Rupp. Photo: Nancy Linn.

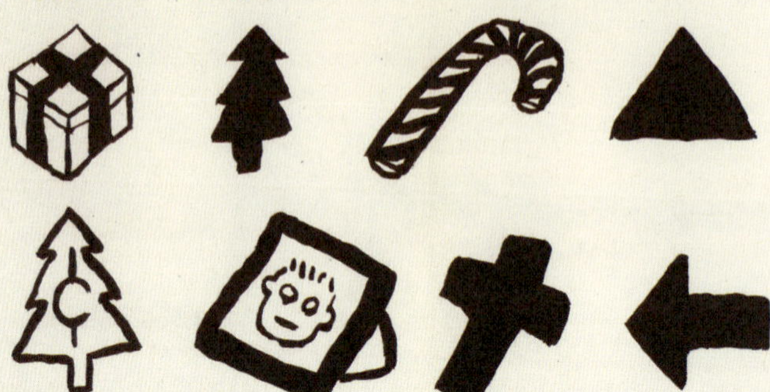

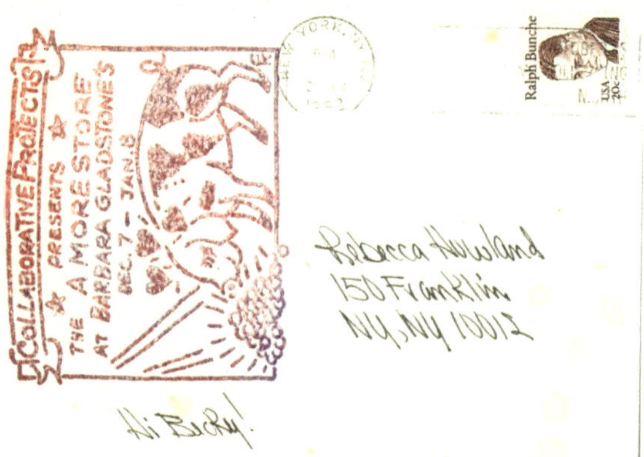

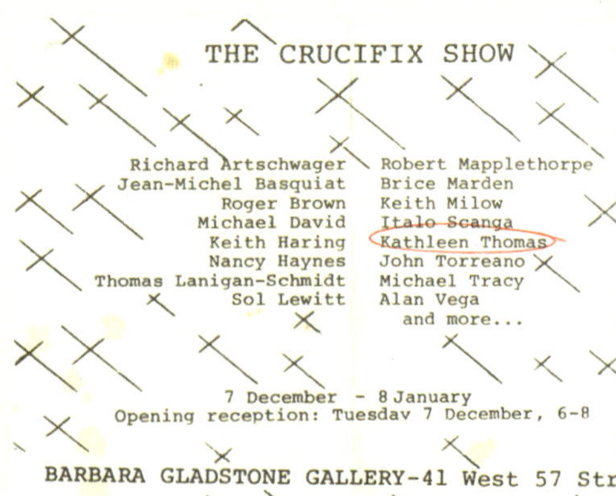

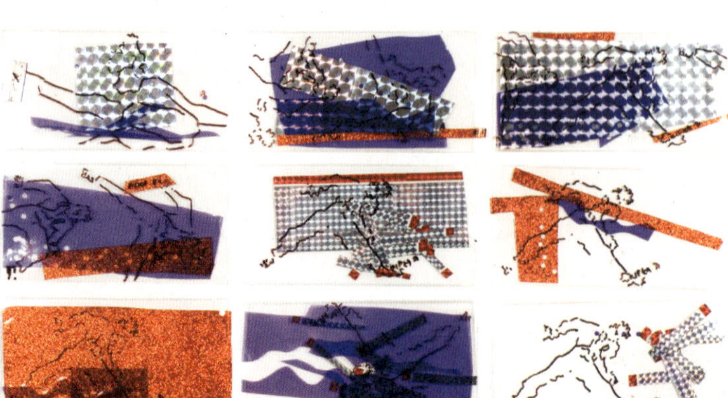

John Morton. *A More Store at the Barbara Gladstone Gallery*, 1982. Offset printed poster, 28 × 43 cm. Courtesy of Kiki Smith.

Unknown. *Collaborative Projects Presents the A. More Store*, 1982. Rubberstamp postcard, 15 × 10.5 cm. (front and back) Courtesy of Becky Howland.

Judy Rifka. *Art Pack*, New York: J. Rifka, 1981. Plastic pockets, acetate and marker, 23 × 12 cm each. Unique set of serial works, each signed and dated by the artist. Courtesy of Judy Rifka.

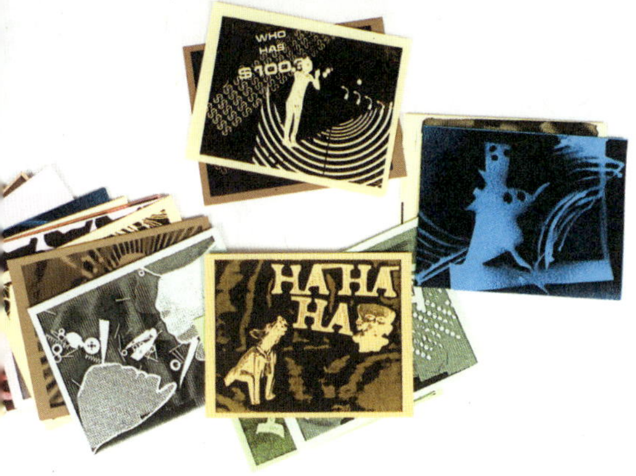

Clockwise from upper left:

Carol Parkinson. *Notecards with Envelopes*, c. 1982. Screenprint and rubber stamp on multi-colored paper, 11 × 14 cm each. Courtesy of Barbara Moore, Bound & Unbound. Photo: Nancy Linn.

Beverly Naidus. *Stick It*, 1982. Stickers, 10.5 × 16.5 cm each. Courtesy of the Collaborative Projects Archive. Photo: Nancy Linn.

Bobby G (Robert Goldman). *Cruise Missile Sox*, 1982. Screenprinted cotton socks. Courtesy of Becky Howland. Photo: Nancy Linn.

Becky Howland. *Diamond & Pentagon*, 1982. Painted plaster cast (diptych), 12 × 12 cm and 16 × 16 cm. Edition of 100, signed and numbered. Courtesy of Becky Howland. Photo: Nancy Linn.

Joseph Nechvatal. *Placemat*. New York: J. Nechvatal, 1982. Laminated photocopy of original drawing, 28.5 × 36 cm. Courtesy of Barbara Ess.

Jane Dickson. *Skull Fan 2*, 1982. 21.5 × 38 cm (open). Oil stick on paper fan. From A. More Store. Courtesy of Jane Dickson. Photo: Nancy Linn.

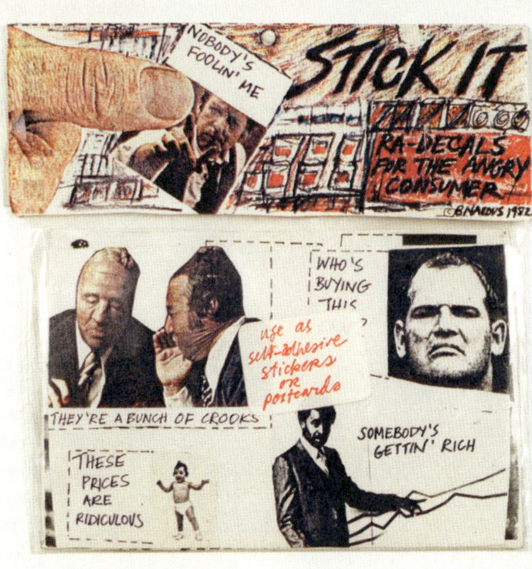

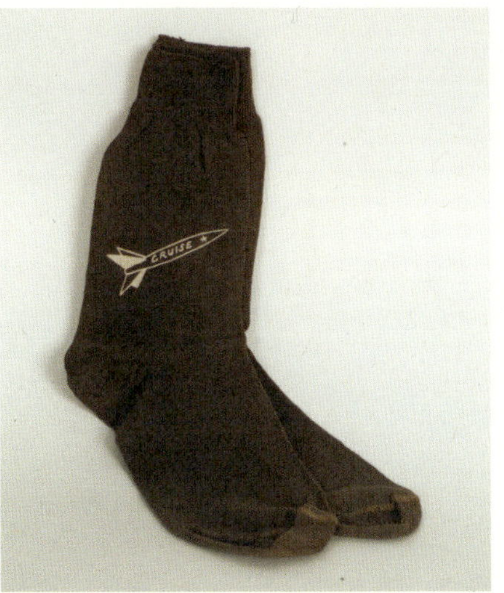

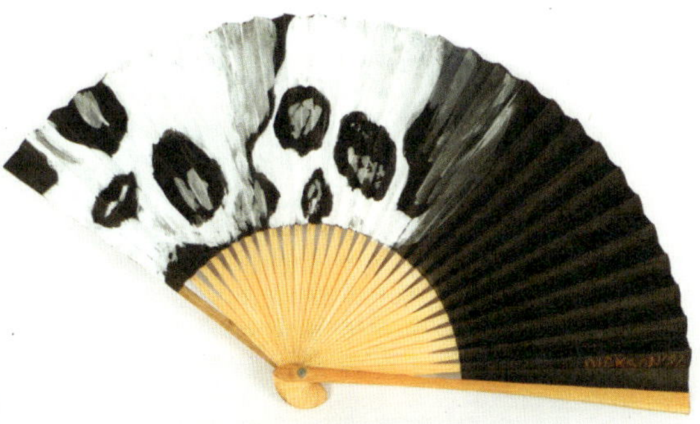

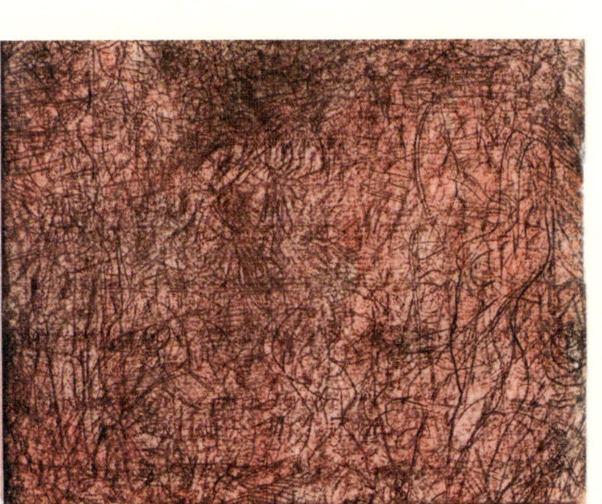

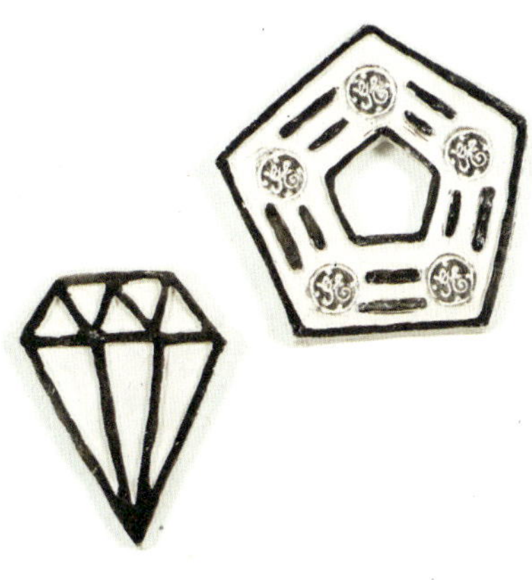

James Beard
Oxtail Ragout*

5 or 6 pounds oxtails, cut
    into joints for serving
Salt and freshly ground
    black pepper
3   tablespoons oil
3   tablespoons unsalted
    butter or beef
    drippings
3   large onions, peeled
    and thinly sliced
4   carrots, scraped
    and halved
2   white turnips, peeled
    and sliced in medium
    rounds
4   whole garlic cloves,
    peeled
Bouquet garni (fresh or
    dried bay leaf,
    thyme, parsley, and
    rosemary tied with
    string to a rib
    of celery or a leek)
4 to 5 cups beef broth
¼   cup Madeira
2   tablespoons chopped
    parsley
Beurre manié, optional
    (see note)

Put pieces of oxtail on a combination broiler rack and pan, and broil until nicely colored and crispy around edges, about 15 minutes, salting and peppering them as they brown, and turning them once.

In a skillet, heat oil and butter or beef drippings left in broiler pan, add onions, and sauté over medium heat until golden and limp. With a slotted spoon, transfer onions to an 8-quart braising pan. Add carrots to skillet, and sauté lightly for 3 minutes. Add these, the turnips, and garlic cloves to braising pan, lay oxtails on top, and add bouquet garni.

Add beef broth (there should be just enough to barely cover oxtails), bring to a boil over high heat, skim off scum that rises to surface, and continue to boil and skim for 5 minutes. Reduce heat, cover, and simmer for 3 to 3½ hours, adding more liquid if it reduces too much (it should just cover oxtails). Test meat for tenderness with point of a small sharp knife—it should penetrate meat easily.

Add Madeira, and cook, covered, for 10 minutes. Add salt, pepper, and a touch of thyme if broth needs more herb flavor.

Let ragout cool, and skim off fat (or chill it in refrigerator for a day or two before serving, this enables fat to be completely removed and flavors to blend).

Reheat ragout, and when heated through, remove oxtails and vegetables to a hot platter. Discard bouquet garni, and let broth cook down over high heat for 2 or 3 minutes.

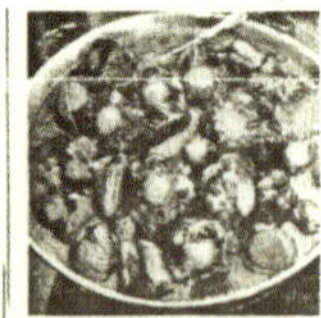

ATTENTION ARTISTS: IT'S TIME TO MAKE MULTIPLES
FOR THE CHRISTMAS STORES:

This year the A. More Store will be at:

Jack Tilton Gallery-24 W.57th Street

Printed Matter-7 Lispenard Street

To pique your interest:

   1. Artforum has given us space to promote work from the past and present.

   2. Best Bets in New York Magazine is considering doing something.

   3. We're working on David Letterman.

   4. Plus ads in the Voice and art mags, posters, and flyers.

Promotion is moving. NOW WE NEED YOUR MULTIPLES!

This year work is to be delivered to Jack Tilton Gallery on Thursday, Nov. 29 from 10:00-5:00. This is the only drop-off date. Please be kind to the organizers and make it on time. We will then split the work and truck half of it to Printed Matter.

When submitting your work please include the following:

1. A card with your name, address, and phone, number of objects submitted, and retail price. In figuring your price, remember that the artist receives 50%, the host receives 40%, and CoLab receives 10%. Also on your catalog card include a brief description of your item/s for reference.

2. Name and retail price on every item. Your help in identifying your item/s will help assure that you receive sales money and that all your unsold work is returned.

Printed Matter A.More Store will open on Saturday, Dec. 1, from 3:00 to 6:00. Jack Tilton will open on Tuesday, Dec. 4 from 5:00 to 7:00.

Pick-up: Thurs., Dec. 3, 10:00-6:00, Jack Tilton Gallery

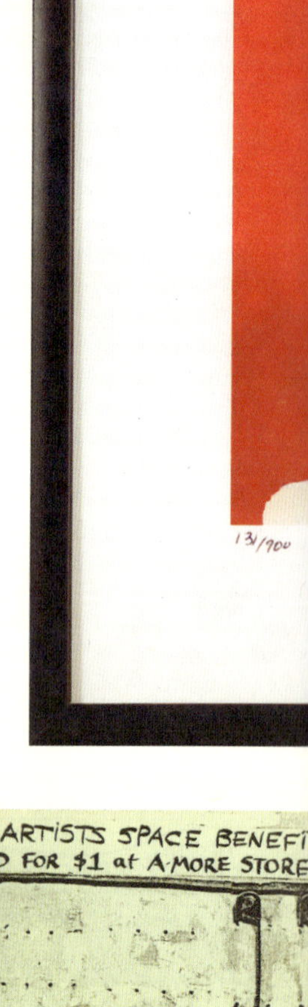

131/900

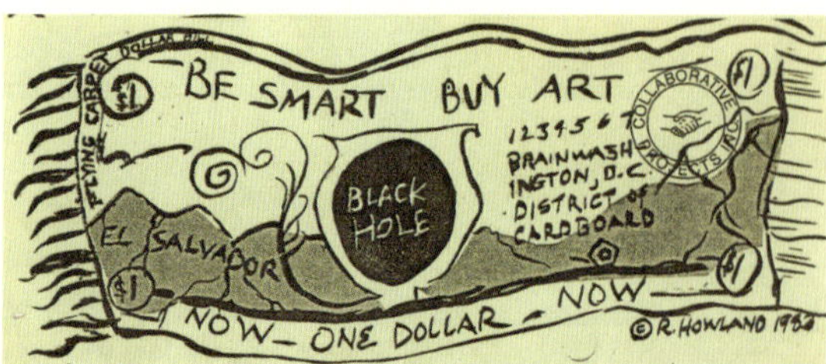

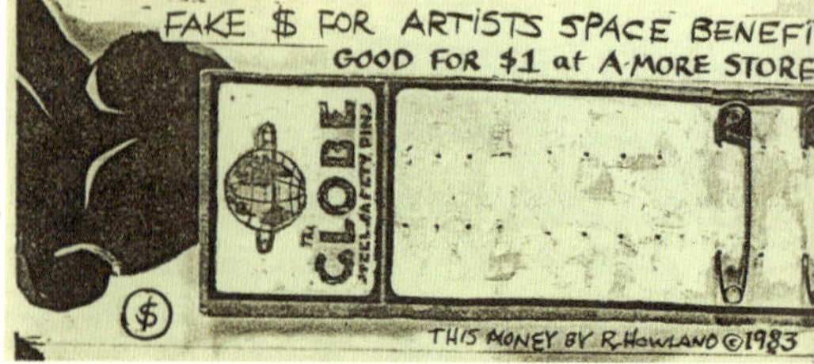

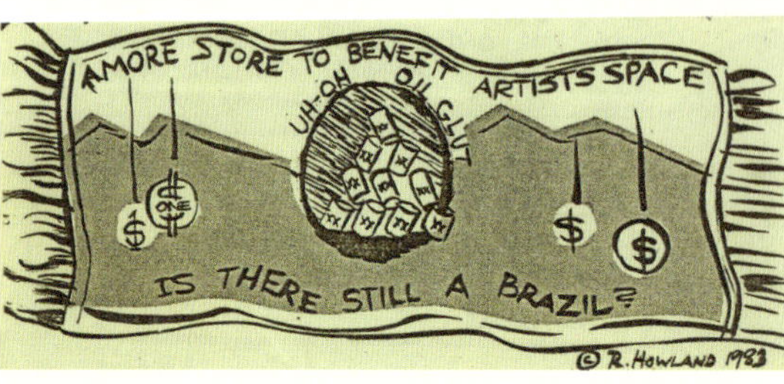

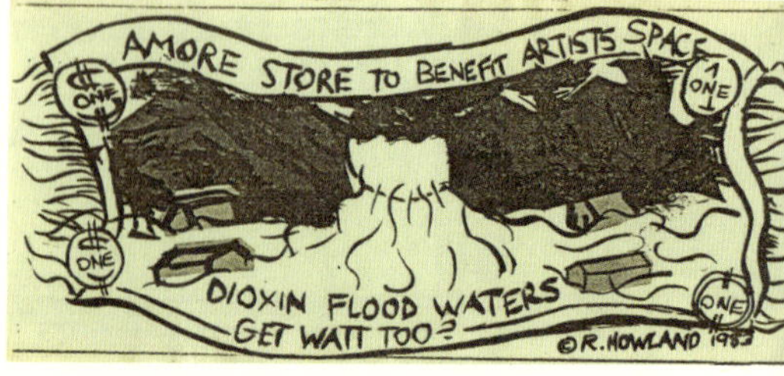

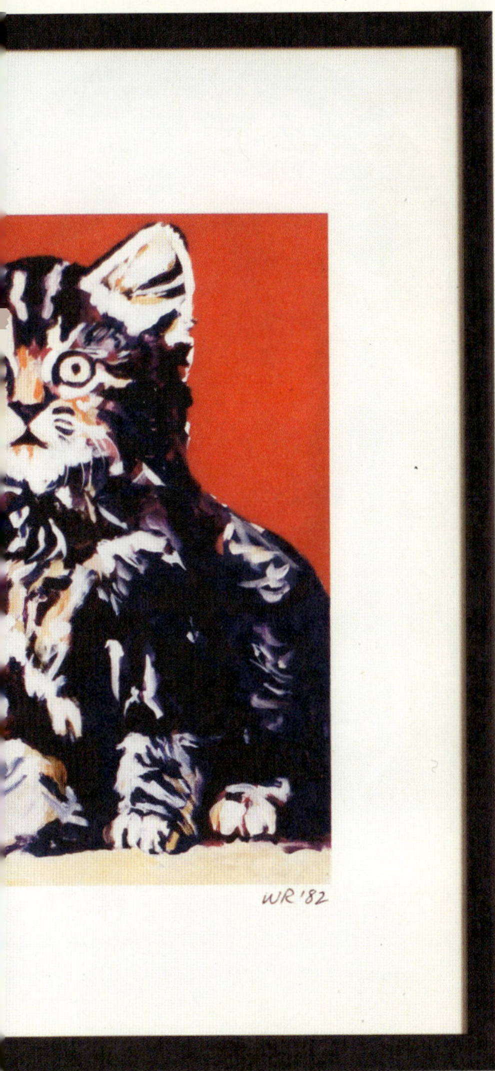

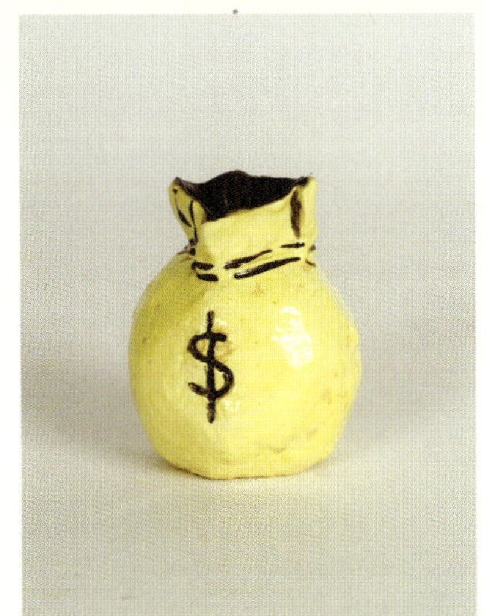

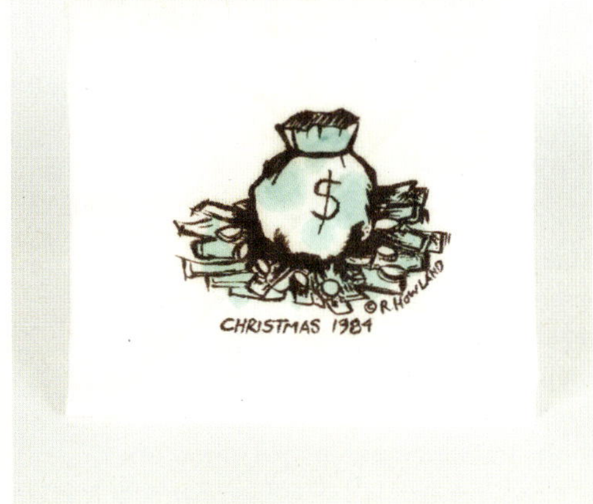

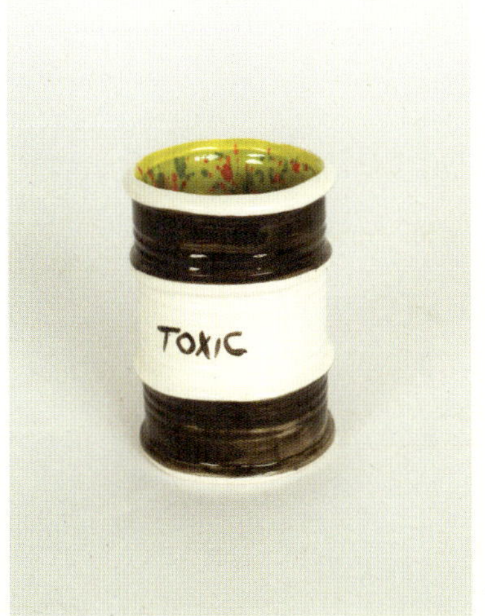

Clockwise from upper left:

Unknown. *Attention Artists: It's Time to Make Multiples*,
1983. Photocopy, 28 × 21.5 cm. Courtesy of
Becky Howland.

Walter "Mike" Robinson. *Kitty*. New York: W. Robinson,
1982. Offset printed edition, 20 × 25.5 cm (framed).
Edition of 900, signed and numbered. Courtesy of
Walter "Mike" Robinson. Photo: Nancy Linn.

Becky Howland. *Money Bag*, 1984. Glazed ceramic cup,
6.5 × 6.5 × 9 cm. Signed and numbered by the artist.
Courtesy of Becky Howland. Photo: Nancy Linn.

Becky Howland. *Money Bag Snot Rag*, 1984.
Screenprinted and hand-painted cotton handkerchief,
40 × 40 cm. Courtesy of Becky Howland.
Photo: Nancy Linn.

Becky Howland. *Toxic Waste Cup*, 1984. Glazed ceramic
cup, 6.5 × 6.5 × 9 cm. Signed and numbered by
the artist. Courtesy of Becky Howland. Photo: Nancy Linn.

Becky Howland. *Untitled* [Coupons], 1983. Photocopy,
9.5 × 21.5 cm each. For Artists Space Benefit.
Courtesy of Becky Howland.

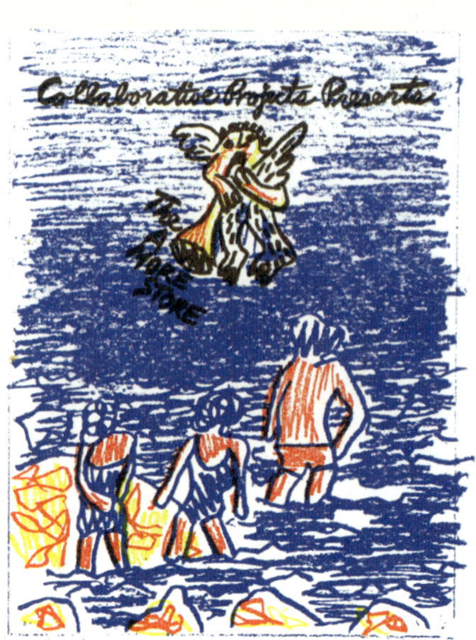

Making multiples was an important aspect of COLAB and they were sold in several versions of the A. More Store, named for Alan Moore. "Collaborative Projects" is now a generic term, midstream mainstream instead of the name of a provocative artists' collective. Some of the artists have been famous, and several have made valuable contributions as leaders and cultural activists.

—Andrea Callard

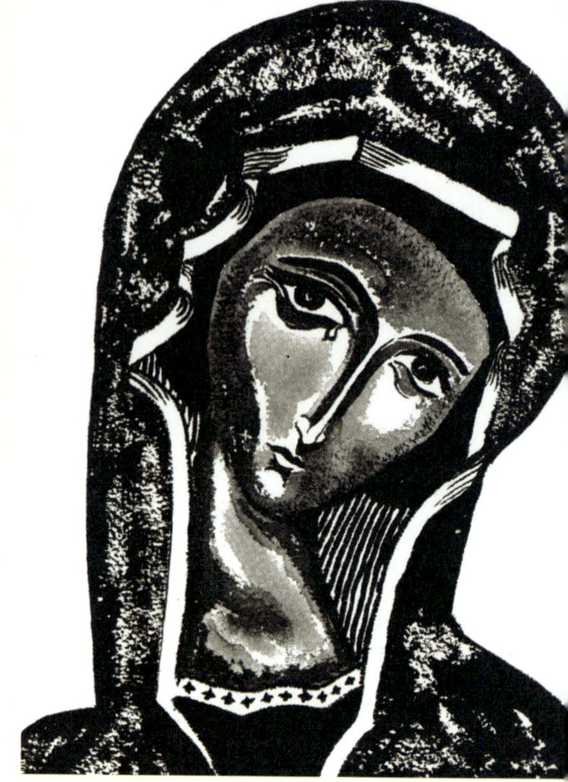

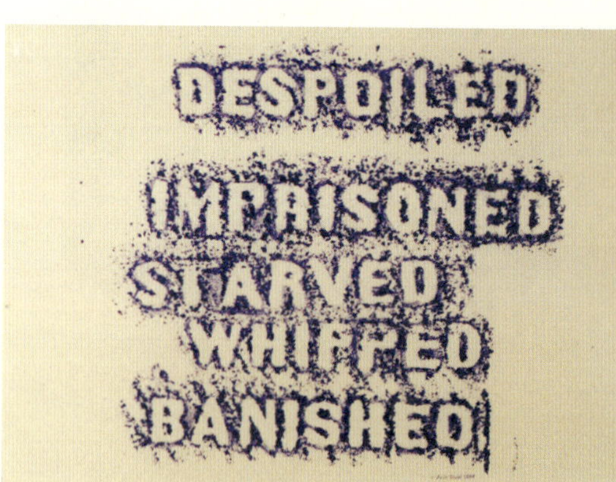

A MORE STORE
at
JACK TILTON GALLERY
24 West 57th Street
Dec. 4 - 22
Opening Dec. 4, 5 - 7

at
PRINTED MATTER
7 Lispenard Street
Dec. 1 - 28
Opening Dec. 1, 4 - 6

Left, top and bottom:

Cara Perlman. *Collaborative Projects Presents the A. More Store*, 1983. Screenprinted card (front and back), 15.5 × 10.5 cm. Courtesy of Andrea Callard.

Right:

Jolie Stahl. *Untitled* [Crying Madonna]. New York: J. Stahl, 1984. Offset printed poster, 25.5 × 19.5 cm. Courtesy of the Collaborative Projects Archive. Photo: Nancy Linn.

Jolie Stahl. *Quaker Placemat* [Despoiled]. New York: J. Stahl, 1984. Blueprint of rubbing on paper, laminated, 39 × 61 cm each. Sold in sets of six. Courtesy of Jolie Stahl.

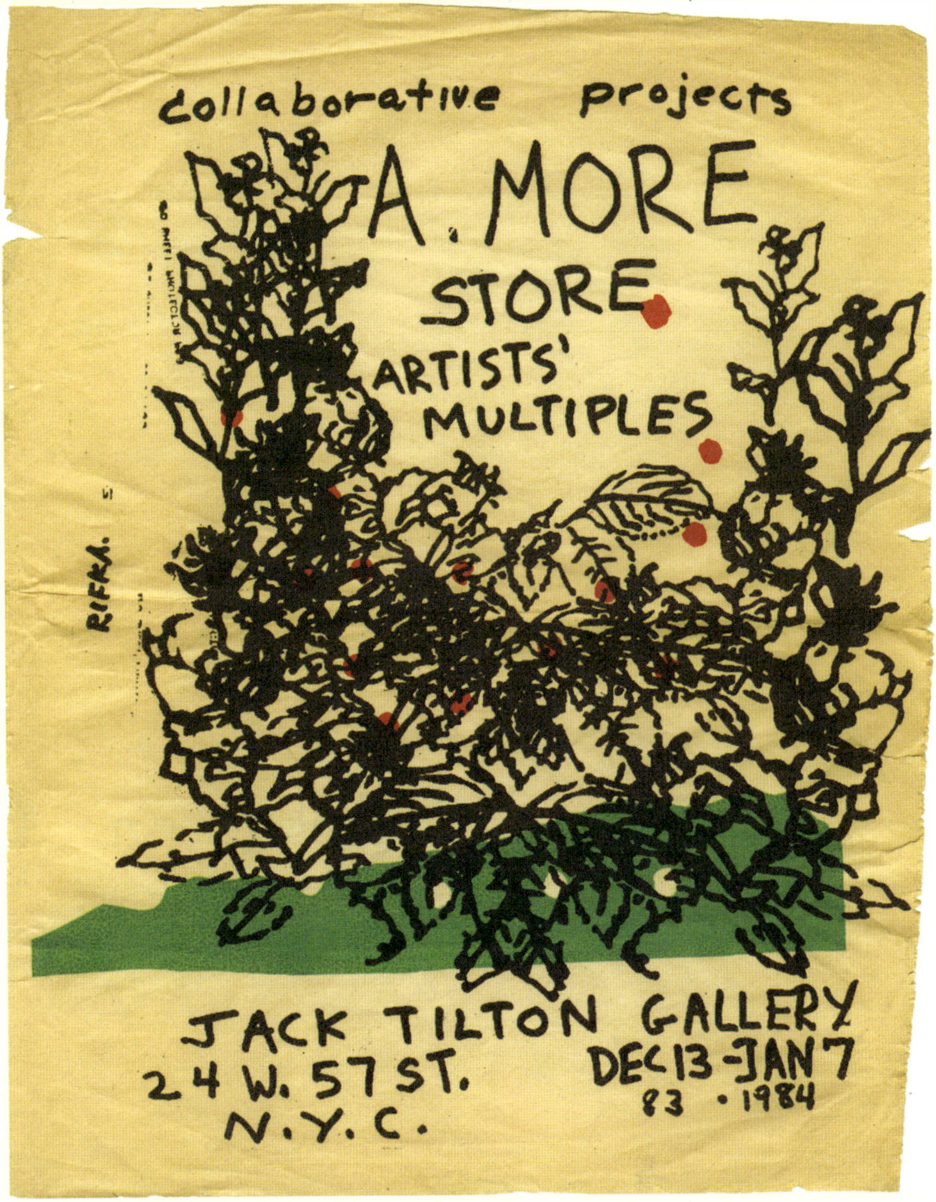

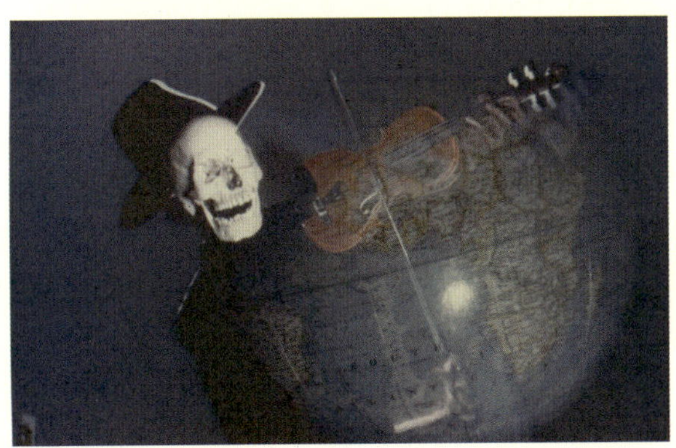

Judy Rifka. *A. More Store at Jack Tilton*, 1983.
Three-color screenprint on paper, 30 × 25 cm.
Courtesy of Barbara Ess.

David Schmidlapp. *Steding & Skull*, 1982.
Color photograph, 8.5 × 13 cm.
Courtesy of the Collaborative Projects Archive.

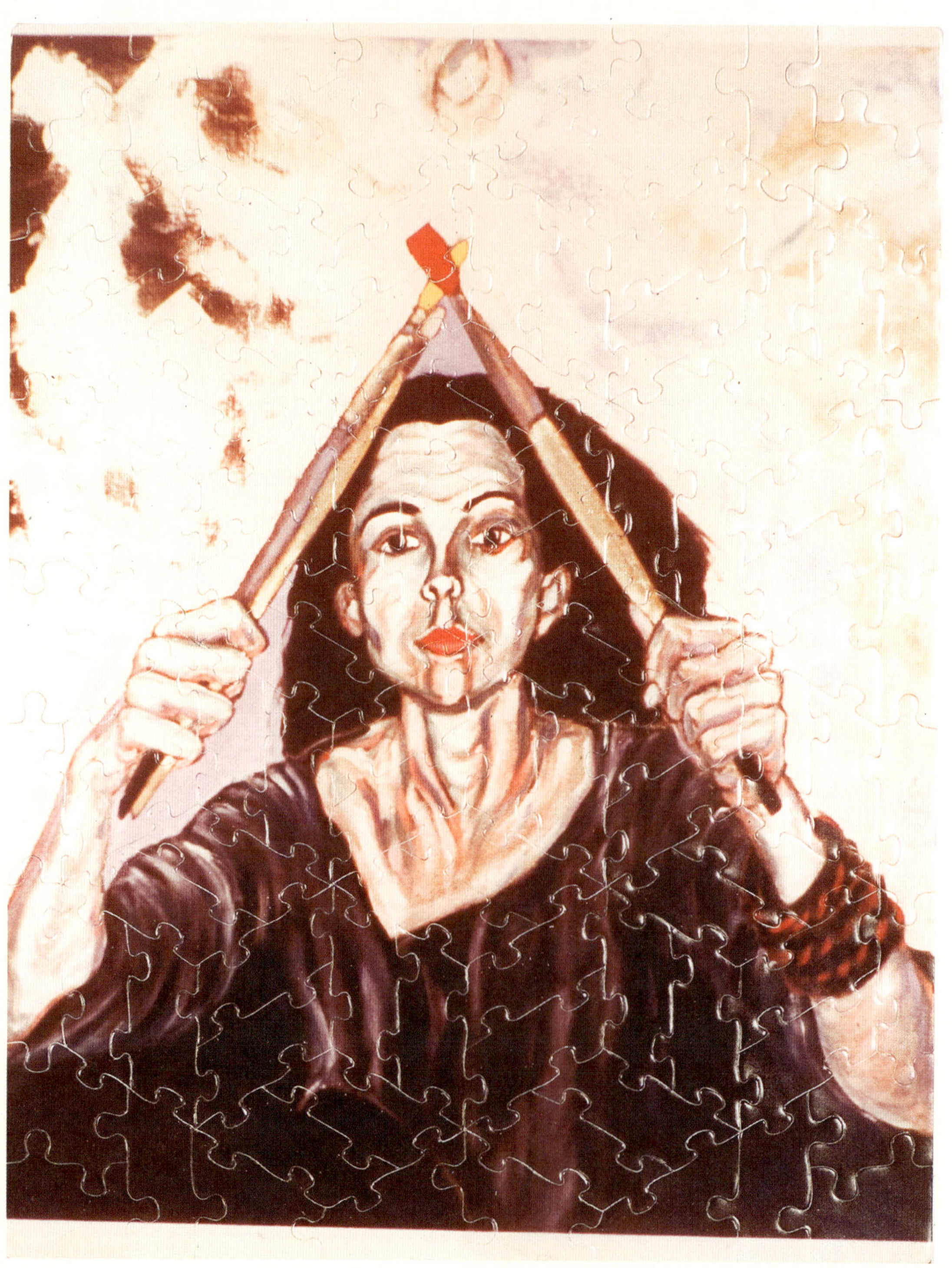

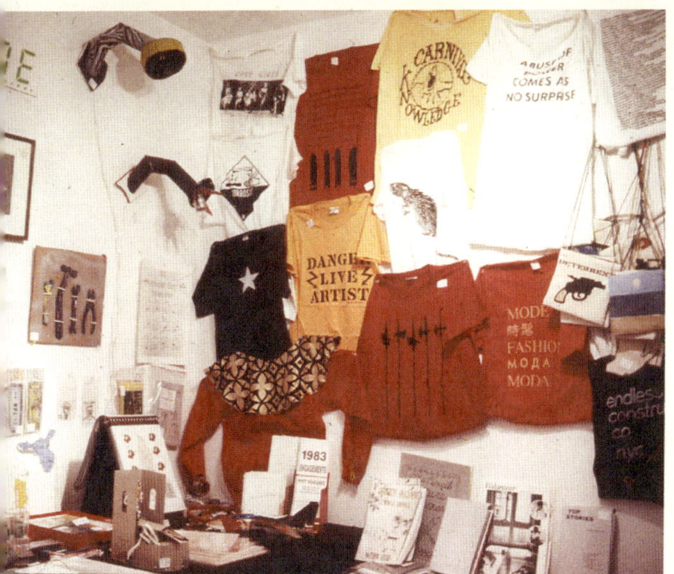

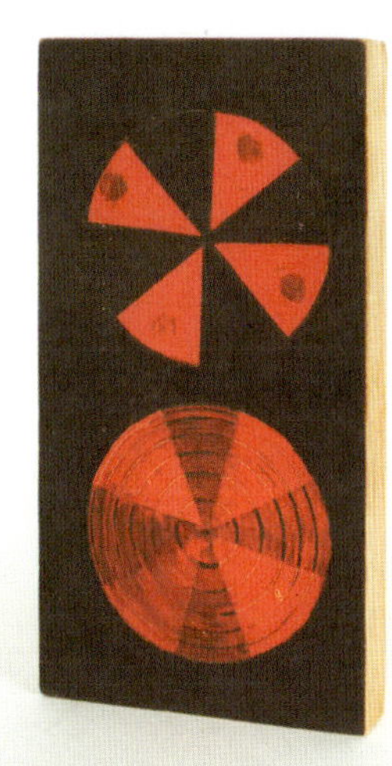

I had met Kiki a few months before through our friend David Wojnarowicz. When I came back from an artist-in-residency program in the Dominican Republic with a sculpture/multiple of a sea-urchin that could be assembled for a show or taken apart for storage, referencing the works of constructivists artists who believed that a work of art only exists when one is looking at it, I went by to visit Kiki on Ludlow Street and brought one with me. She told me to go the A. More Store at the Jack Tilton Gallery and put it in the exhibit they were installing. The multiples were presented on a long narrow table covered with a white table cloth in the middle of the gallery. Some artists I knew were there hanging out, commenting on the work. It was very cool all together.

—Brigitte Engler

Clockwise from upper left:

Jolie Stahl. *Kiki with Brushes*, 1984. Jigsaw puzzle, 34 × 27 cm. Multiple. Courtesy of Jolie Stahl. Photo: Nancy Linn.

Terise Slotkin. *A More Store*, 1980. Digital reproduction of color photography. 21.5 × 28 cm. Courtesy of Terise Slotkin.

Brigitte Engler. (top) *Switch*, 1984. Gouache on plywood, 19.5 × 10 × 2.5 cm. (bottom) *Sea Urchin*, 1984. Gouache on plywood, 30.5 × 35.5 × 35.5 cm. Courtesy of Brigitte Engler. Photo: Nancy Linn.

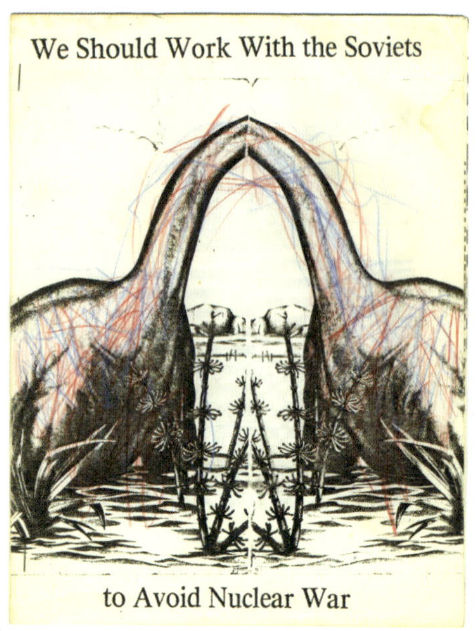

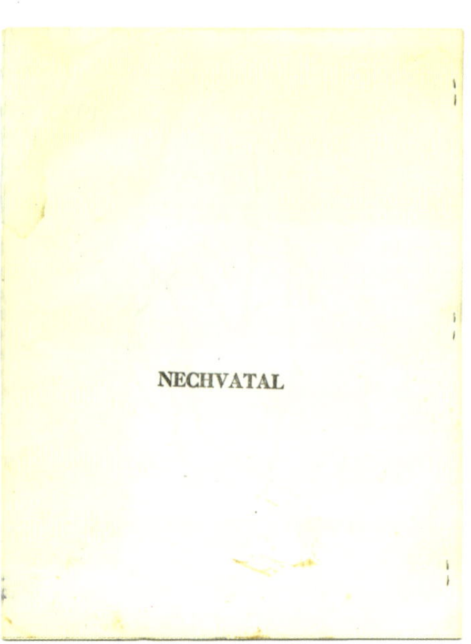

Joseph Nechvatal. *We Should Work With the Soviets to Avoid Nuclear War*. New York: J. Nechvatal, 1980. Photocopy and colored pencil, pbk, staple bound, 10 pp, 28 × 21.5 cm. Courtesy of Bobby G (Robert Goldman).
Photo: Nancy Linn.

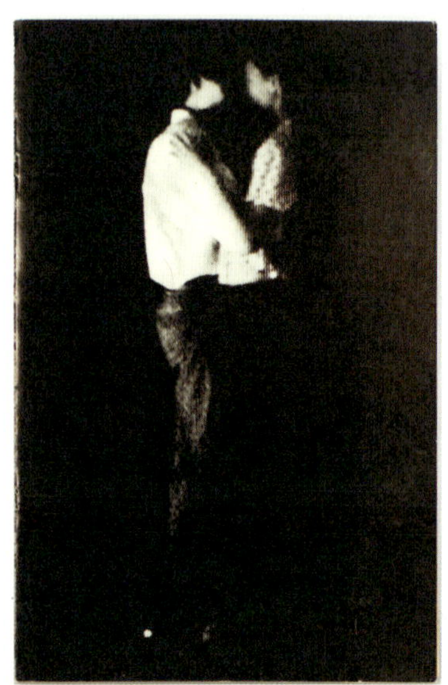

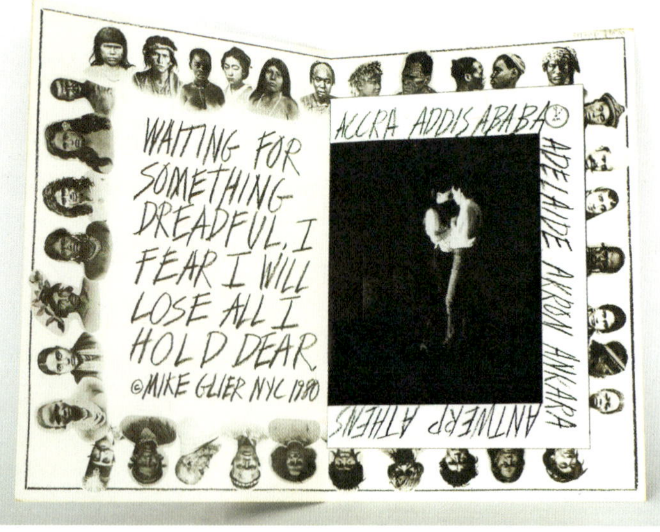

Mike Glier. *Waiting for Something to Happen.* New York: M. Glier, 1980. Offset printed, pbk, staple-bound, 22 pp, 34 × 23 cm.
Courtesy of Mike Glier. Photo: Nancy Linn.

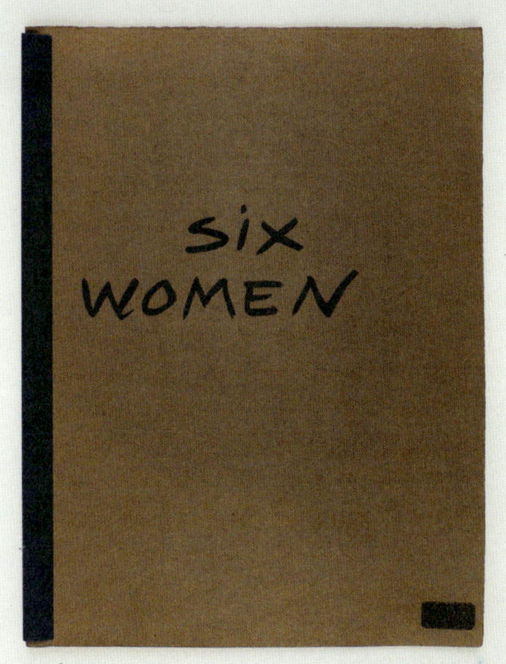

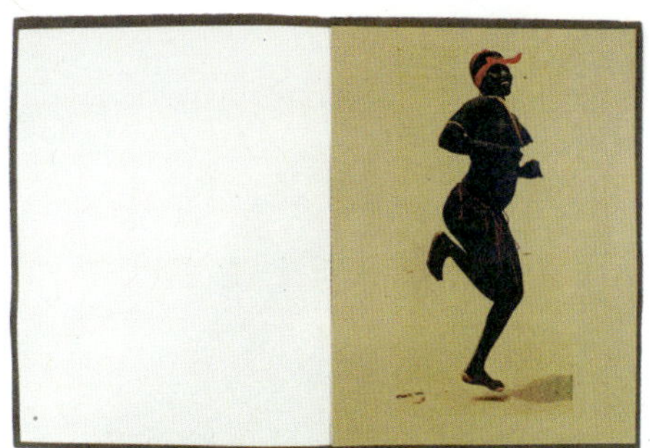

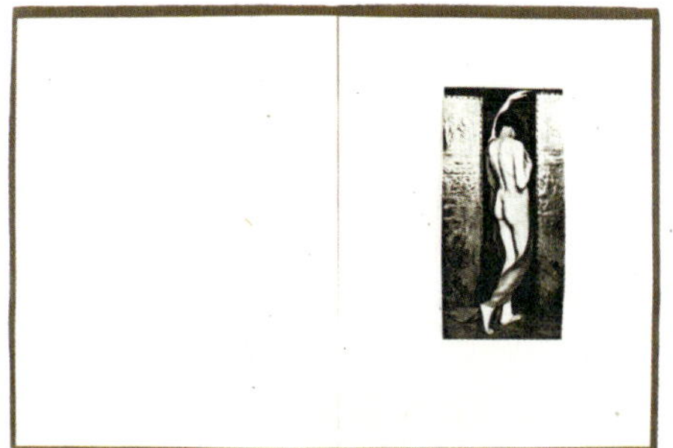

Ellen Cooper. *Six Women*. New York: Ellen Cooper, c. 1981. Photocopy, pbk, staple-bound, 13 pp, 29.5 × 22 cm. Courtesy of the Collaborative Projects Archive. Photo: Nancy Linn.

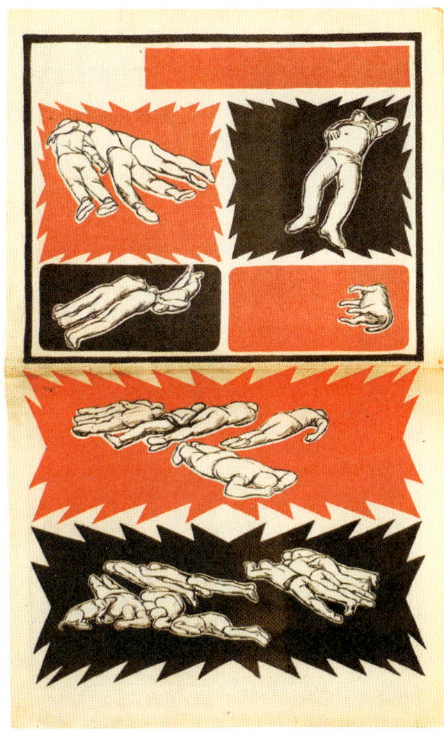

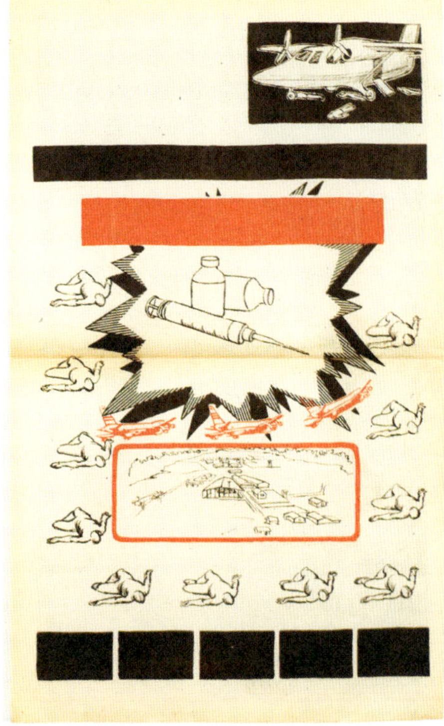

Tom Otterness. *Jonestown Massacre*. New York: T. Otterness, c. 1980. Offset printed, 4 pp, 35.5 × 29 cm (folded). Courtesy of the Collaborative Projects Archive. Photo: Nancy Linn.

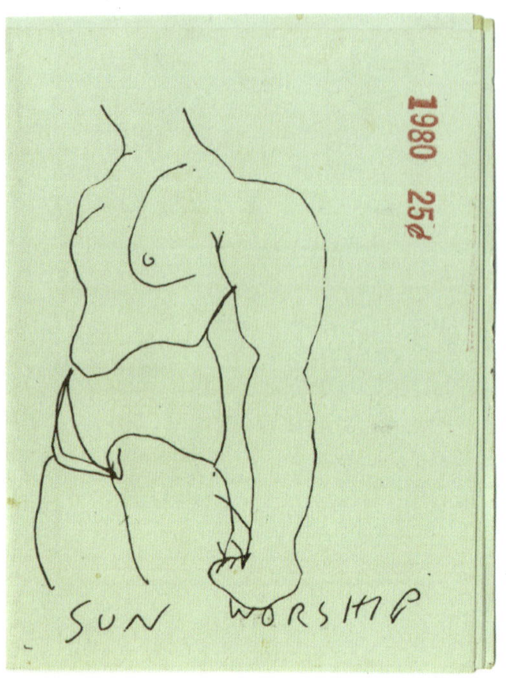

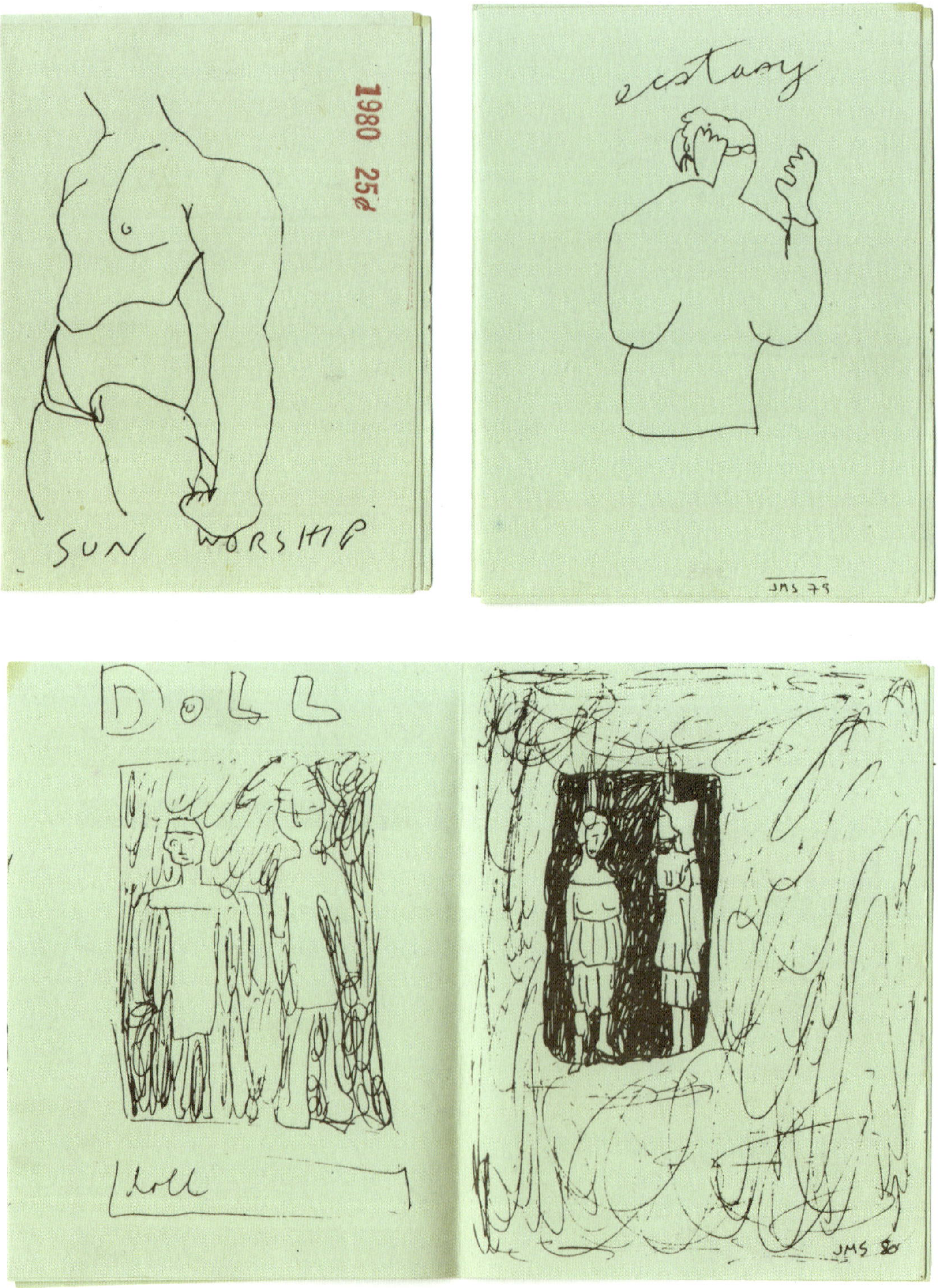

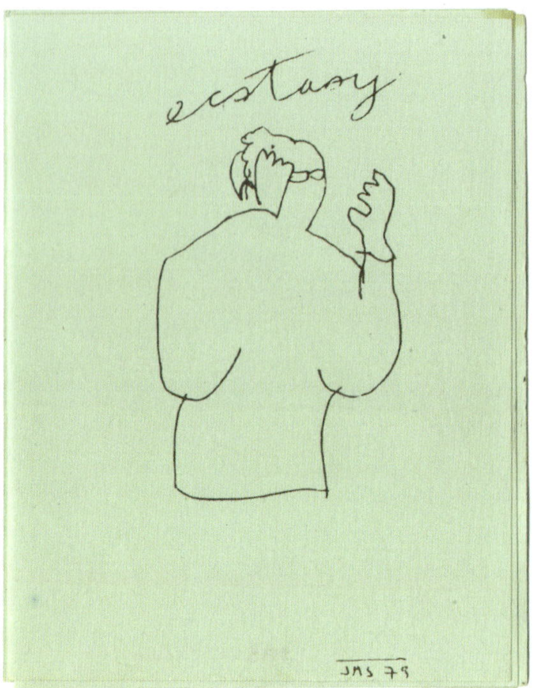

Jane Sherry. *Sun Worship*. New York: J. Sherry & T. Otterness, 1980. Photocopy and rubber stamp, pbk, unbound, 19 pp, 11 × 14 cm. Front and back cover, and interior. Courtesy of Barbara Ess and Kiki Smith. Photo: Nancy Linn.

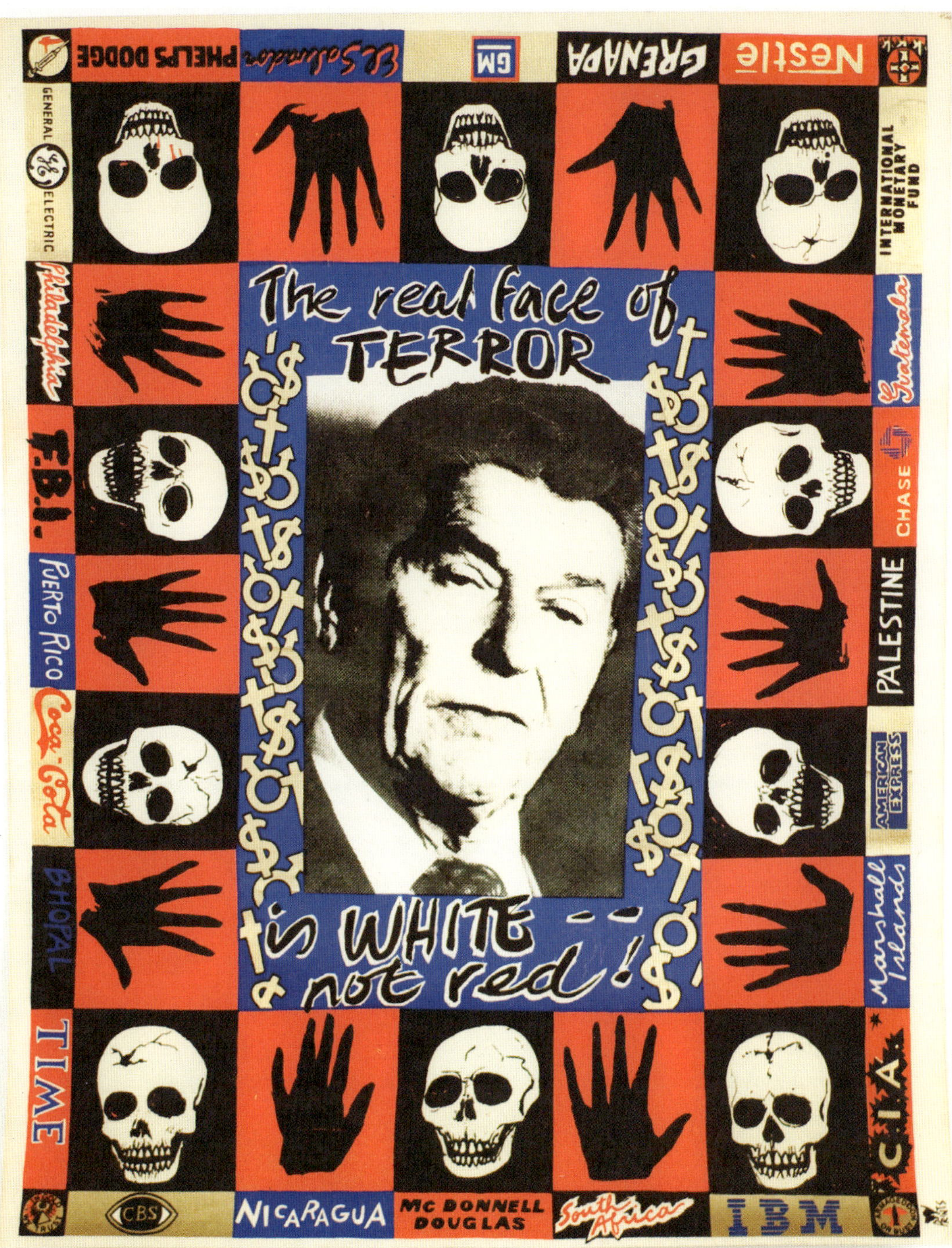

Robert Cooney. *The Real Face of Terror*, c. 1980. Color offset printed poster, 66 × 52 cm.
Courtesy of Coleen Fitzgibbon. Photo: Nancy Linn.

Jane Dickson and Mike Glier. *Untitled*, c. 1981. Photocopy flyer, 28 × 21.5 cm. Proposal for unrealized publication. Courtesy of Nancy Linn.

Mike Glier. *Training for Leisure: A Public Display of Collapsed Desire Designed for the Next World's Fair*, 1980. Two-color screenprint on paper, 38 × 58 cm. Designed for *The Next World's Fair* exhibition at The Kitchen, 1980–81. Courtesy of Mike Glier.

```
TITLES     suggested
The Journal of Male Behavior
Pricks
Grand Prix
Sierra Dong
Organ
The Big Book of Macho
Macho Men, Dads, and Dream Boats
Cock a doodle do
The Big Book of Macho

THESIS
    To examine and undercut stereotypes of male
    behavior and suggest that social and sexual
    roles be individually determined.

GOALS
To make an encyclopedic book of art , fiction,
and essays on the past present and future of male
behavior.  This collaboration between women and men
is intended as a supplement to the volumes of
feminist material on the social/sexual behavior
of women.  Hopefully, the book will be both
critical of present problems and optimistic about
future solutions.

IDEAS
1. Standards of behavior--How are they established
and maintained?
   A. Boy Scout Manual, army training manual, books
   of etiquette, etc.
   B. Fashion trends
   C. Standards of Corporate Behavior. IBM dress code,etc.
   D. Hollywood fiction--westerns, bikers, criminals,
   sexstars, etc.
2. Threats and fears of men and women about each other.
3. Personal stories--the details of daily life that
illustrate the issue.
4. Images of Perfection--what do you want a man to be?
5. Animal Behavior
6. S and M
7. Fathers.  Possibly a visual essay about fathers
and children using family snapshots.
8. Domesticity vs. worldly
9. Reproductive rights and men.
10. Fascist personality
11. What is a hero?
12. Macho--anxiety and over compensation.
13. The father and son coloring book.
14. The men in control. Executives, politicians, TV anchor men,

NETWORK
This project will depend on a lot of participation. If you know of
people who would be interested in the project, please ask them to contact
Mike Glier, 777-2259 or Jane Dickson, 398-1299.
```

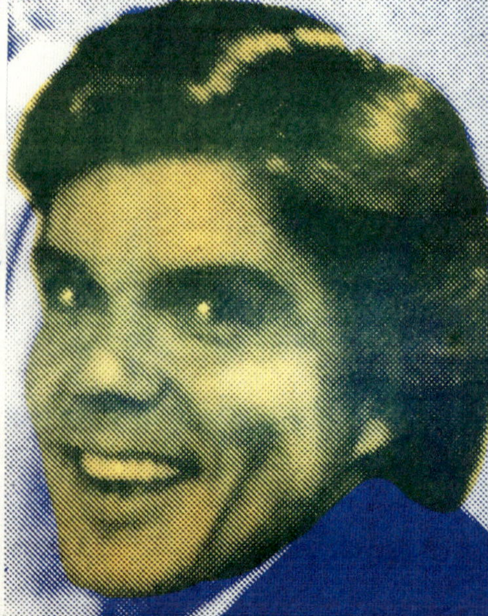

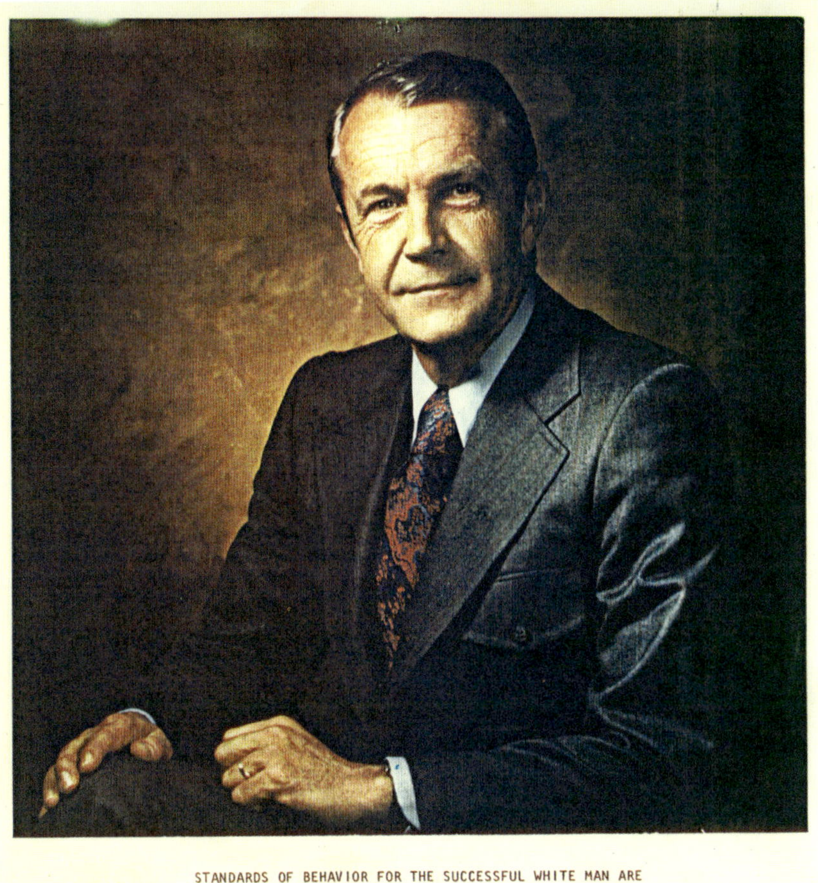

Mike Glier. *Untitled*, c. 1980–82. Photocopy, 28 × 21.5 cm. Courtesy of Nancy Linn.

"The Two Suitcase Show will be at And/Or, Seattle, Washington, from June 9 to June 19 (1981) The show will accompany a conference called "The Art Politik." Please get work to me at home or leave stuff at Printed Matter, Tuesday through Saturday, 10-6. The suitcases are being made by Mimi Gross; their dimensions are approximately 30" × 22" × 9" and 36" × 20" × 10". Work should be smaller than the above dimensions, but if it doesn't fit, I'll cheat and take a portfolio or tube. Please get work to me no later than June 7, a Sunday. Attach installation requirements to work. I will return all work, so you needn't worry about losing originals. However, there isn't any insurance that I know of, so don't send a masterpiece. Seattle seems very interested in the show. I'd like to set up a free handout table; do you have any posters or xeroxes you'd like distributed?

-Mike Glier, Colab Annual Report 1981

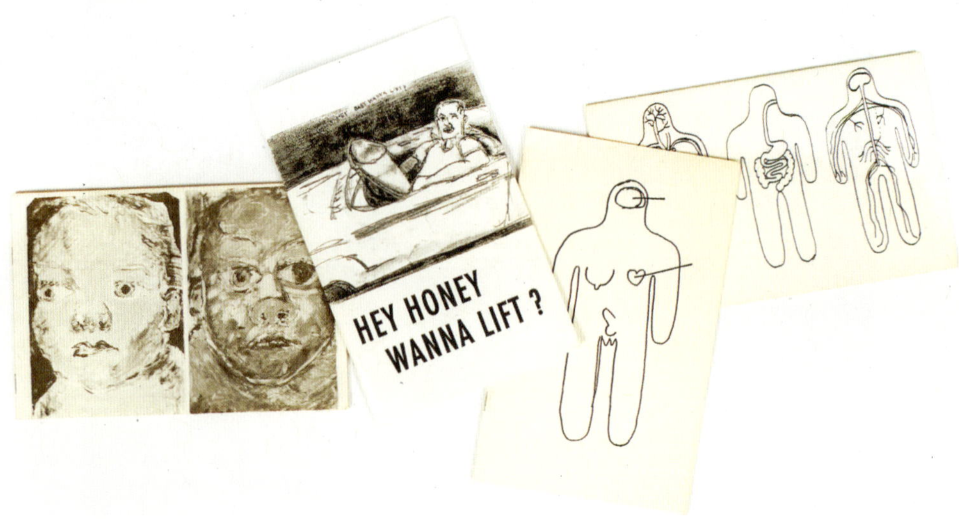

Jane Dickson's *Hey Honey Wanna Lift?* was one of what turned out to be the first group of artists' books published by *Appearances Magazine* (later spun off into Appearances Press) in 1981. The initial group included two additional artists associated with Colab and two that were not closely aligned with the loosely knit group, Tom Otterness, Cara Perlman; and Keith Haring and Jean-Michel Basquiat respectively; all five of whom participated in *The Times Square Show*.

Ironically, I got the idea to publish artists' books while trolling the shelves of Printed Matter, where I'd go on occasion to deliver the latest issue of *Appearances Magazine*. The initial idea was quite grandiose, and as you can tell by looking at the initial published products, value engineered significantly.

Putting the first group together was easy. Jane was the first person I invited to the project. She had a group of hilarious penis drawings that had been exhibited during the Fashion Moda "Events" exhibition at the New Museum. Some with integrated texts of pick-up lines tossed at her as she moved through her Times Square neighborhood. Then, in quick succession I asked Tom, Cara, Keith and Jean-Michel Basquiat.

Tom's book was kind of an interspecies comparative anatomy investigation which displayed his superb drafting skills, tinged with a very conceptual introspective intellectual humor. Cara's finger painting portraits of Colab members and people from the 70/80s New York Art scene were very in the moment, quirky and loose but recognizable; and Keith's space, sex dog, magic wand cacophony in retrospect, raced across the 8.5" x 11" format like a meteor streaking across the evening sky.

On the other hand, Jean-Michel wasn't as receptive. I met with him during his now famous creative hermitage deep within the bowels of Annina Nosei's basement, to discuss if he'd like to participate in the project. He grabbed a few colored Xerox

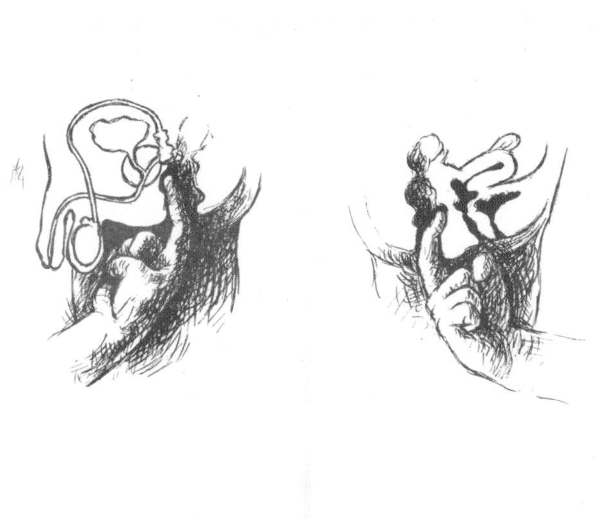

Left:

Cara Perlman. *Fingerpaint Portraits*, 1980 / Jane Dickson. *Hey Honey Wanna Lift?*, 1980 / Tom Otterness. *Tom Otterness*, 1981.
All New York: Appearances Press.
Courtesy of Appearances Press.
Photo: Nancy Linn.

Right:

Tom Otterness. *Tom Otterness*, 1981.
New York: Appearances Press.
Offset printed, staple-bound, pbk, 16 pp, 21.5 × 14 cm.
Courtesy of Appearances Press.
Photo: Nancy Linn.

copies, tore them into twenty pieces or so, and thrust them into my hands with a big grin. I took the fragments home. I returned to his subterranean paradise a few days later, and asked him if he would consider submitting something else. He asked me, "What I was trying to do and how much I was going to sell the books for?" I was interested in publishing his drawings, perhaps ones he was about to show with Annina, and was going to sell the books for $2.00 apiece. He replied, "What are you, a fuckin' communist?"

Ellary Eddy at the Beard's Fund was gracious enough to believe in the idea and gave *Appearances Magazine* a small production grant for the project, as did Brooke Alexander Gallery and two other collectors. The assembly production method was a real grassroots type thing.

After all the material was printed we had a collating party. Most of the artists got together and scored the cardboard stock covers, folded, collated, and stapled the Xerox copies together over drinks. Both Keith and Jane's books went into second printings.

During the next five years I repeated the process with another 11 artists including: David Wells, Judy Rifka/Barbara Moynihan, and Candace Hill-Montgomery. The final series of five limited-edition four color silkscreen books, with a vellum letterpress intro page, hand sewn bindings and trimmed edges; I produced during a week-long residency at the Lower East Side Printshop. The letterpress work was printed at Maggie Reilly's Ram Studio. It was a very diverse group of artists and ideas participants were Darrel Ellis; Crash; Daze; Betty Tomkins; and a collaboration between Marilyn Minter and Christoph Kohlhöfer.

—Joe Lewis

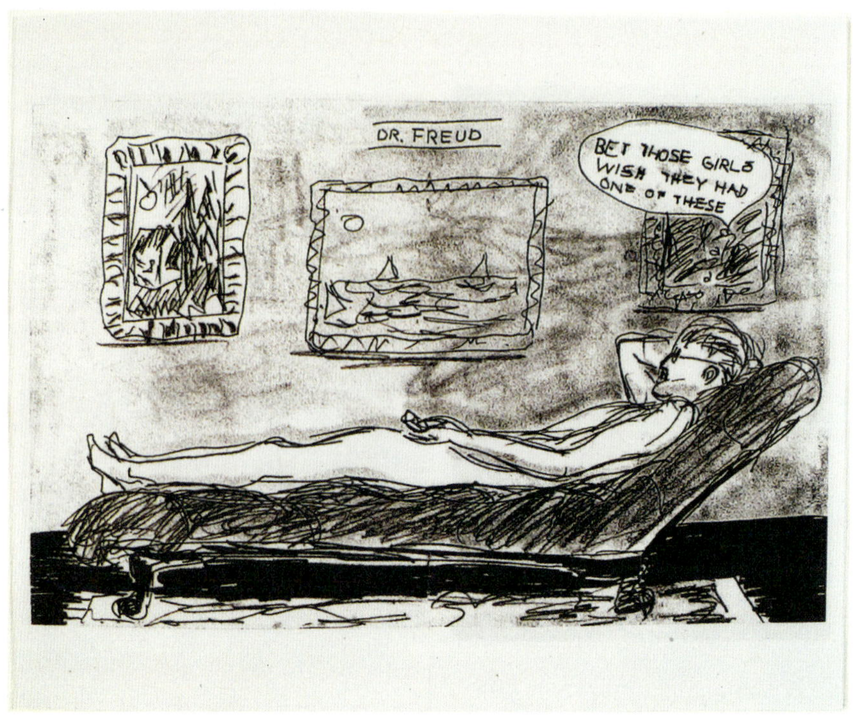

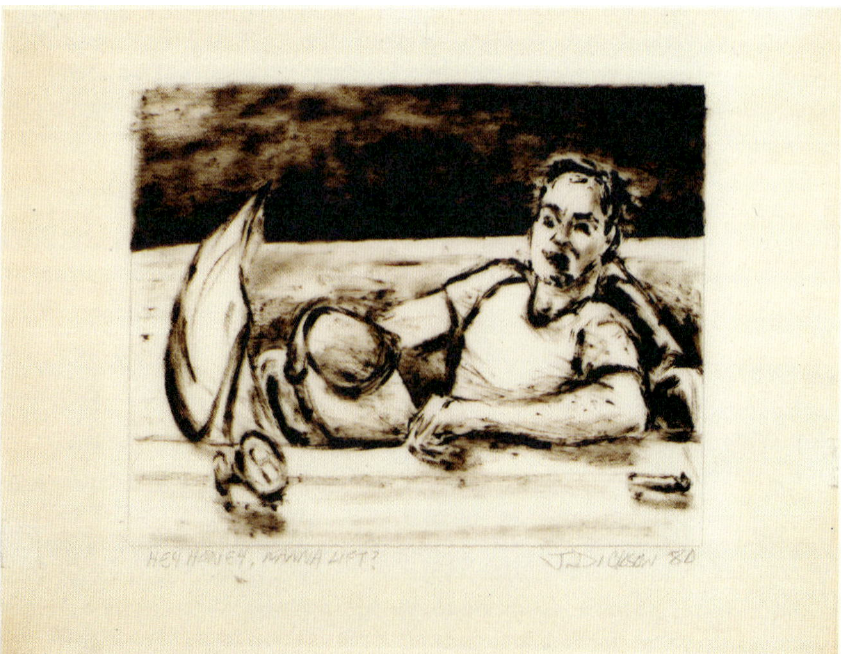

Top:

Jane Dickson. *Hey Honey Wanna Lift?* New York: Jane Dickson, 1980, 2nd ed. 2004. Offset printed, pbk, staple-bound, 28 pp, 28 × 21.5 cm. Interior. Courtesy of Jane Dickson. Courtesy of Appearances Press. Photo: Nancy Linn.

Bottom:

Jane Dickson. *Hey Honey Wanna Lift?*, 1980. Oil paint on paper, 33 × 43.5 cm (framed). Courtesy of Jane Dickson. Photo: Nancy Linn.

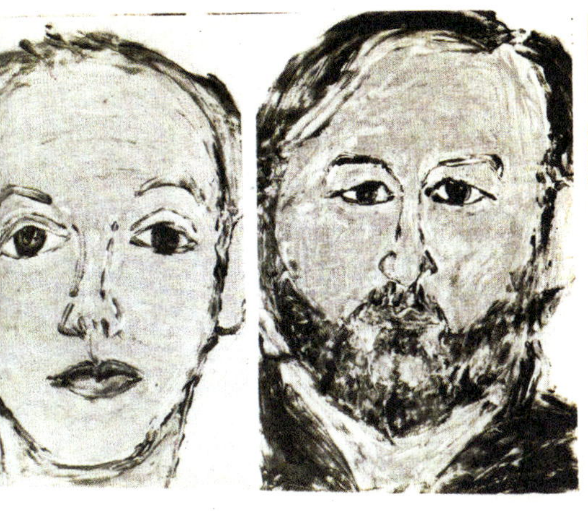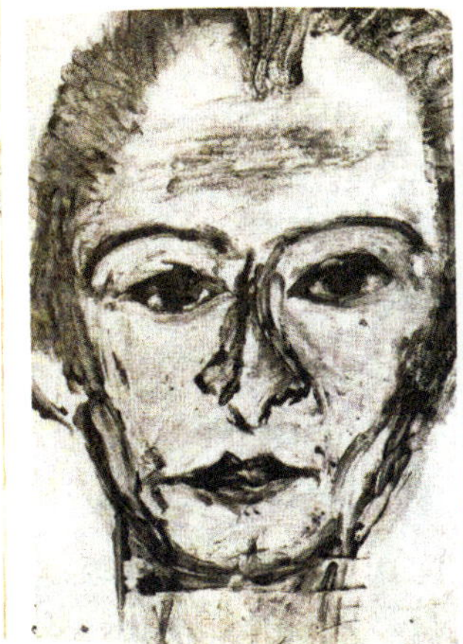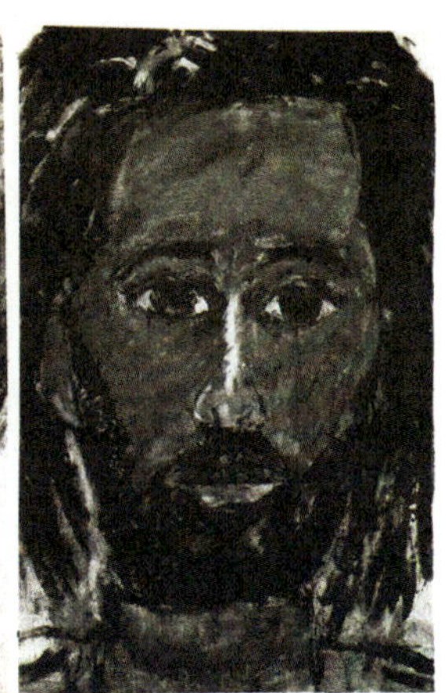

ANNE MARTIN HARTSHORN	ROBIN WINTERS
PETER FEND	ROBERT COONEY
JUDY RIFKA	JODY HARRIS
TOM OTTERNESS	MIKE GLIER
MAGGIE SMITH	JANET STEIN
KIKI SMITH	BOBBY G
NAN GOLDIN	REESE WILLIAMS
ELLEN COOPER	MARNIE GREENHOLZ
ULLI RIMKUS	CHARLIE AHEARN
BUZZ HARTSHORN	JOHN AHEARN
ALAN MOORE	PATTY MARTIN
ILONA GRANET	HELEN PERLMAN
DICK MILLER	TAYLOR MEAD
ELIZABETH BRISTOL	RICHARD MOCK
SOPHIE VDT	CHRIS KOHLHOFER
CARA PERLMAN	JOE LEWIS
MINDY STEVENSON	JOSEPH NECHVATAL
GARGANTUA	MIKE ROBINSON

Cara Perlman. *Fingerpaint Portraits*. New York: Appearances Press, 1981. Offset printed, pbk, 16 pp, staple-bound, 14 × 21.5 cm. Interior and back cover. Courtesy of Appearances Press. Photo: Nancy Linn.

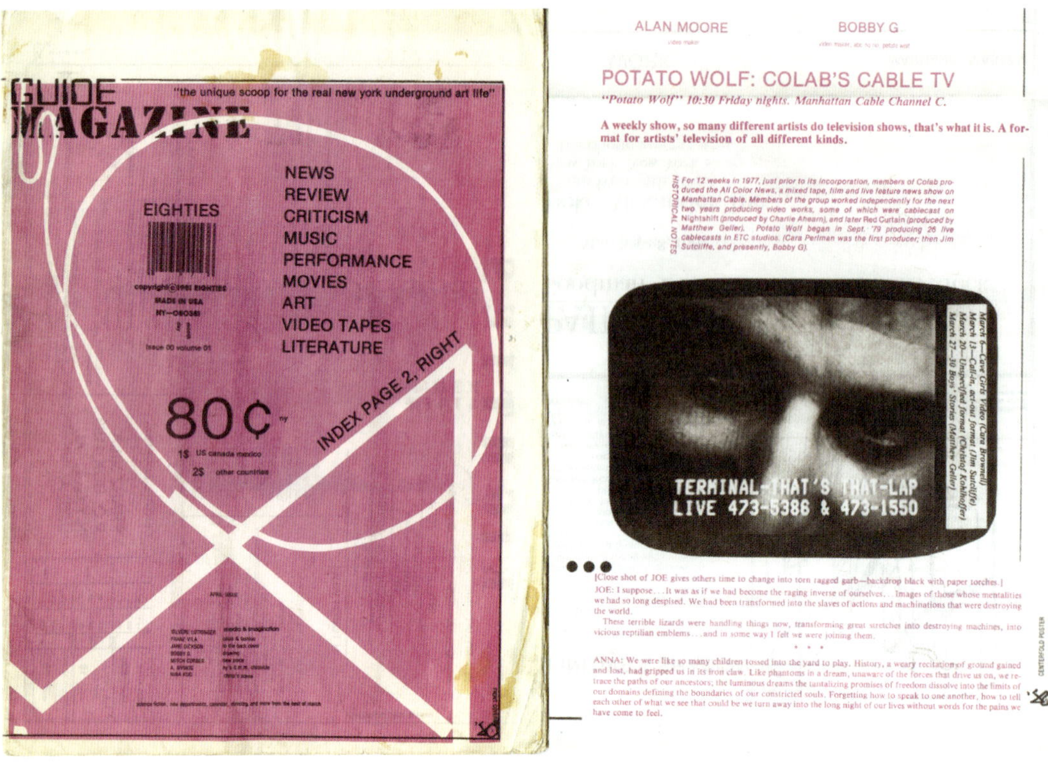

Franz Vila. *Guide Magazine 80s. [Eighties]* Issue 00, Vol. 01. New York: F. Vila, 1981. Offset printed, pbk, 16pp, 29 × 21.5 cm. Courtesy of Franz Vila.

There is some quality of invisibility about me that Colab propelled in me with my total satisfaction. Colab is a fountain of energy and inspiration of all kinds of non-mainstream art and even mainstream art. There were countless shows and an untraceable variety of art work, in which artists unleashed creativity and inclusion was the norm. Many of the shows were very original and not well remembered like the *Flea Market Show* at Coney Island, in which I sold some of my repainted solid beverage cans. I casually and without announcement put a couple of pioneering repainted cans near a bathroom in *The Times Square Show* and next day they were not there, probably some visitor thought that they could not be art at all, but still cute. I didn't bring any cans again.

Eighties, the *Guide Magazine*, lived by the same fate. It is a piece that some people knew about and participated in, but still remained invisible.

Eighties is a simulacra of complete magazine sections in just 16 pages. The Directory and Calendar are sections of a page of a-day-in-the-life-of.

As information, *Eighties* is just a witness.

—Franz Vila

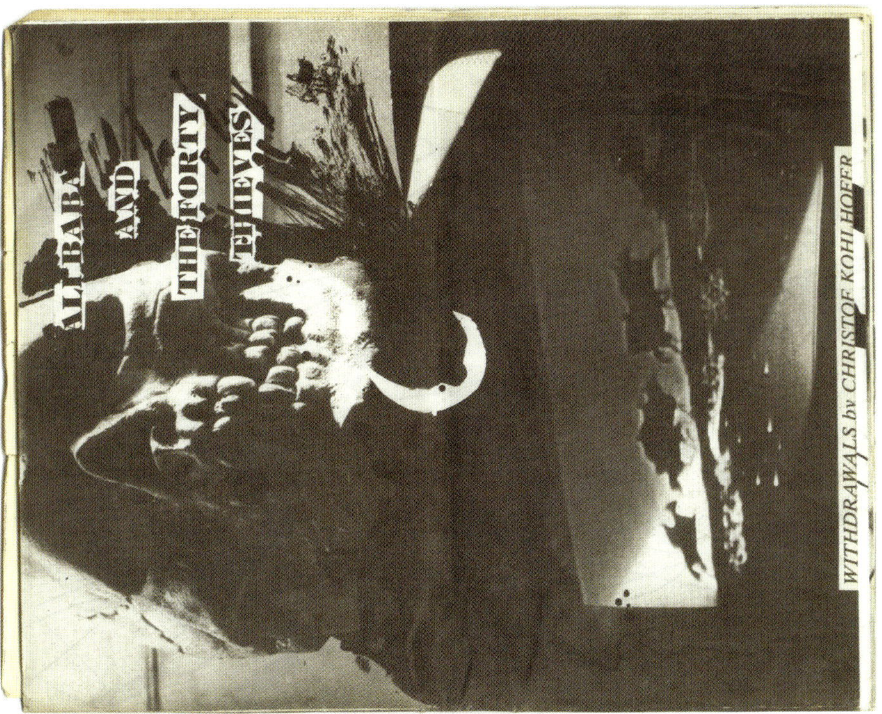

Christof Kohlhöfer. *Withdrawals*. Philadelphia: Philadelphia College of Art, 1981. Offset printed, pbk, staple-bound, 40 pp, 43 × 28 cm. Courtesy of Becky Howland.

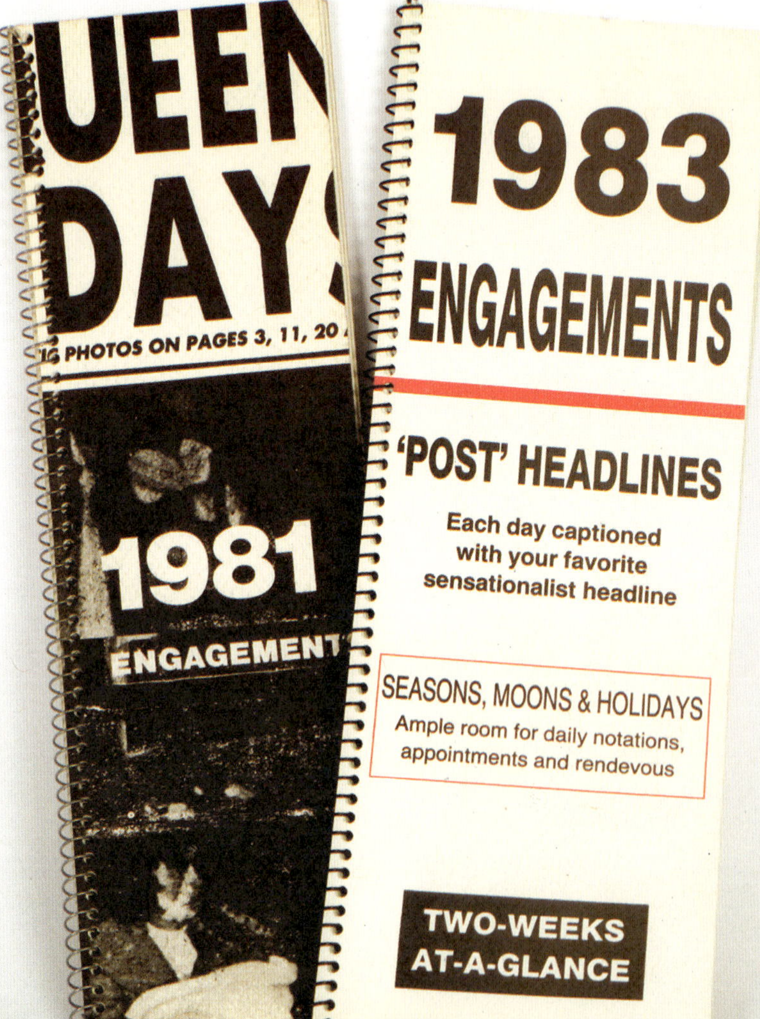
UEEN
DAYS
G PHOTOS ON PAGES 3, 11, 20
1981
ENGAGEMENT
1983
ENGAGEMENTS
'POST' HEADLINES
Each day captioned
with your favorite
sensationalist headline
SEASONS, MOONS & HOLIDAYS
Ample room for daily notations,
appointments and rendevous
TWO-WEEKS
AT-A-GLANCE

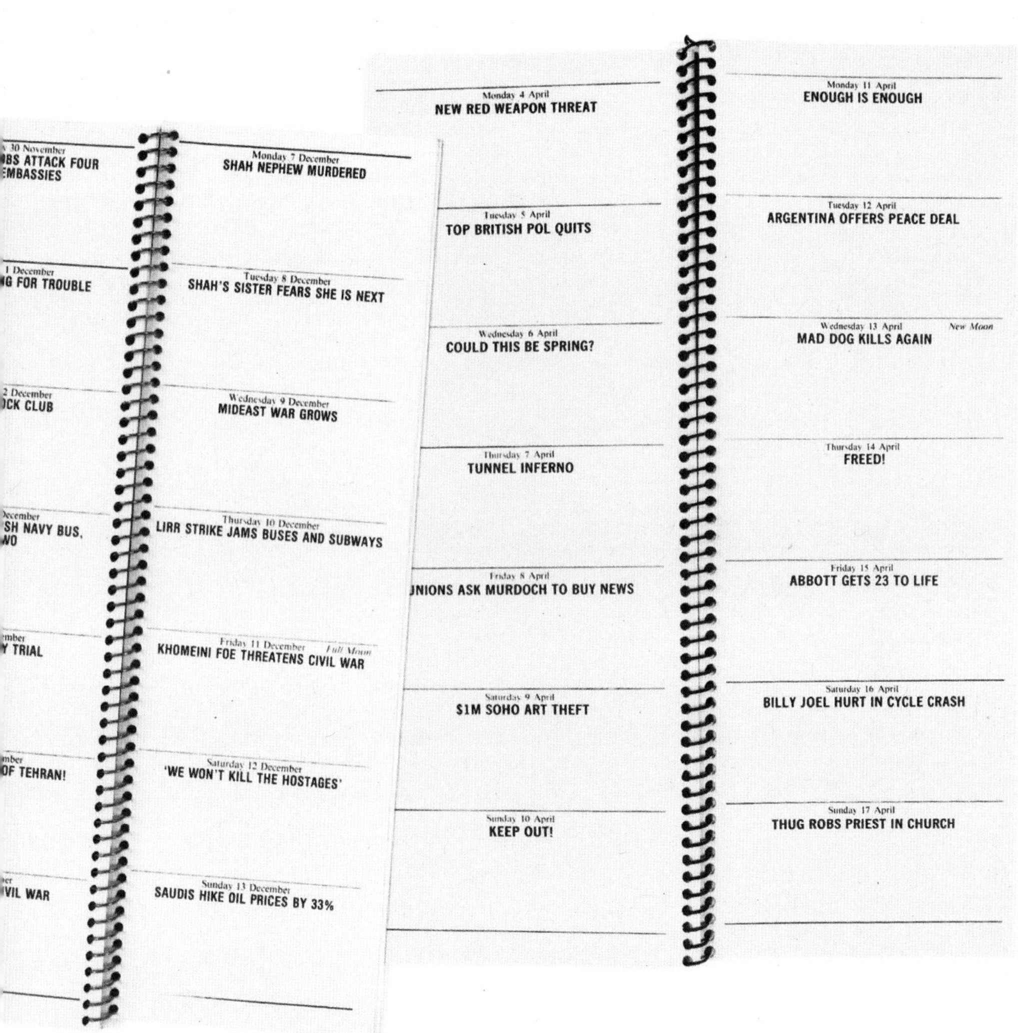

Matthew Geller. *1981 Calendar*, 1980 and *1983 Calendar*, 1982. Offset printed, pbk, spiral-bound, 56 pp, 11 × 4.25 cm. Courtesy of Matthew Geller. Photo: Nancy Linn.

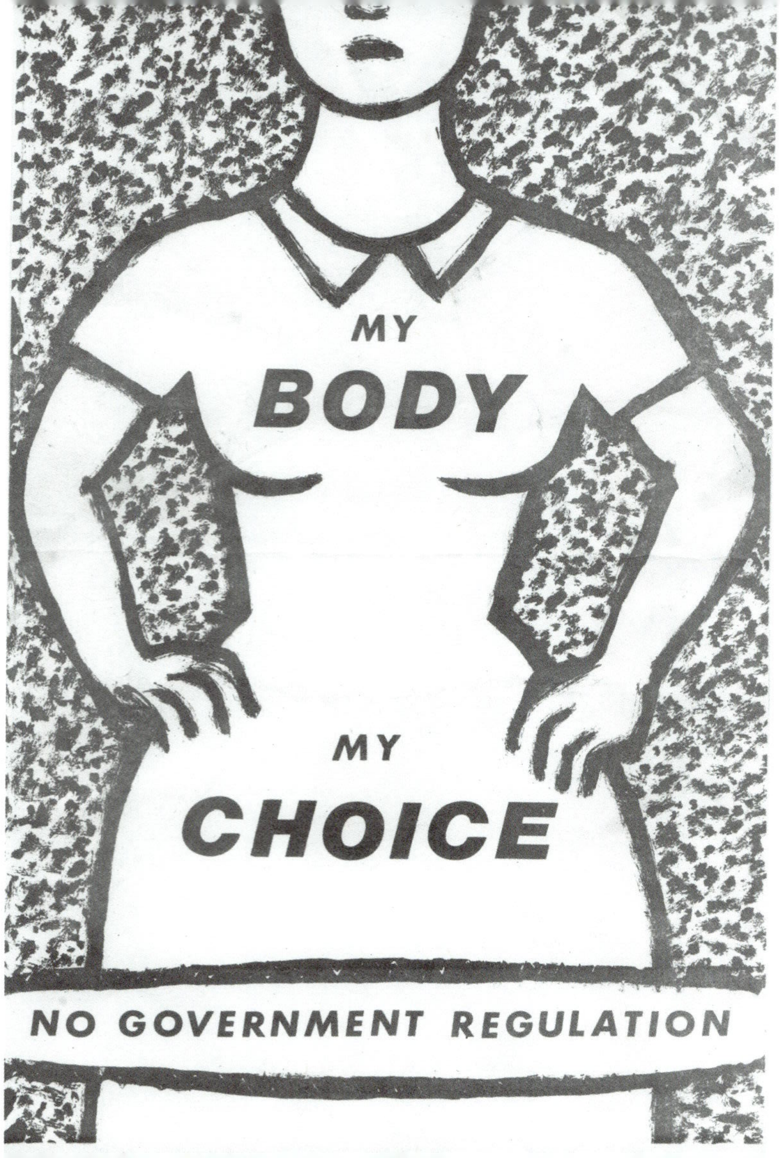

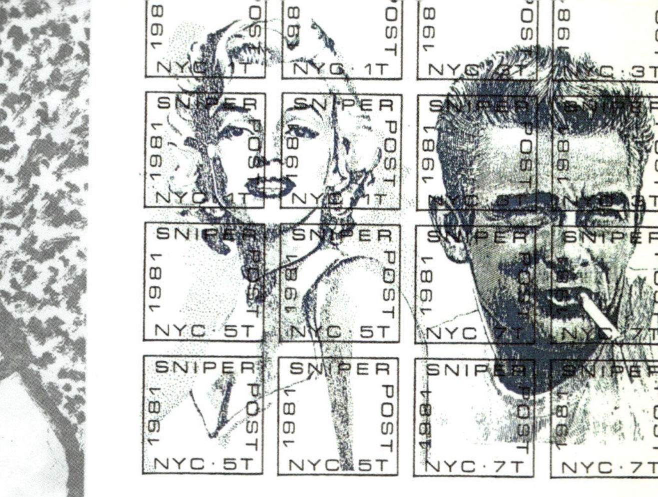

Jane Dickson. *My Body, My Choice*, 1981. Photocopy poster, 36 × 21.5 cm. Created for a pro-choice march on Fifth Avenue. Courtesy of Tom Otterness.

Tod Jorgensen. *Untitled*, 1981. Photocopy, 28 × 21.5 cm. From Tod's Copy Shop. Courtesy of Barbara Ess. Photo: Nancy Linn.

After Chicago, Colab traveled to New Harmony, Indiana's Gallery of Contemporary Art. The successful "Mural America" mural also furnished the title of the show. Whether we represented America was debated. As a local critic wrote, "The works in the show negate most forms of refinement or education and attempt to lower art to a plebian, filthy, vulgar, violent and mindless nightmare—collectively called punk art." Funny — we don't look like punks.

—Colab Annual Report 1982

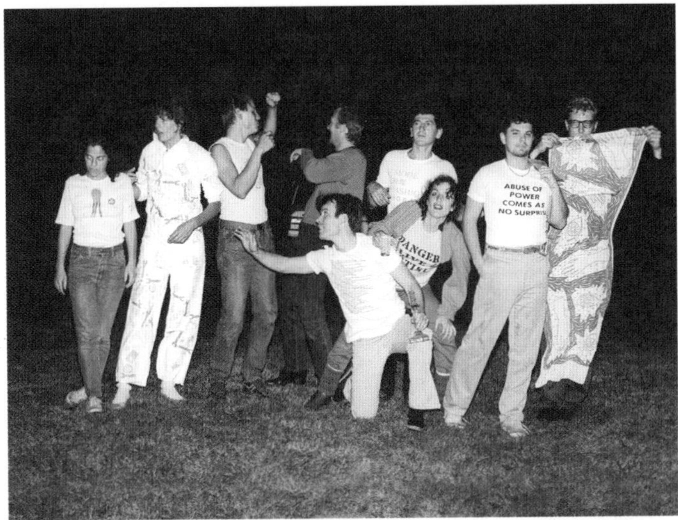

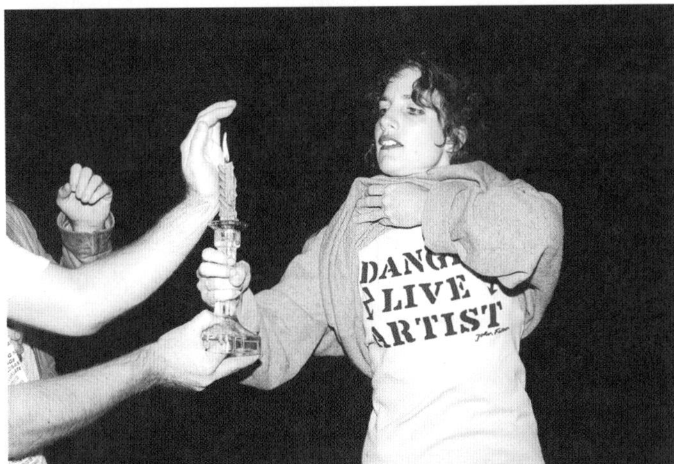

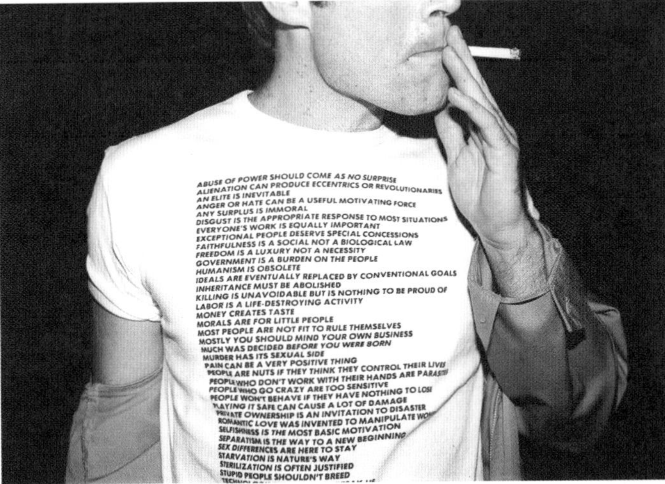

Top to bottom:

All Lisa Kahane. *Artists' t-shirts, jumpsuit and scarf modeled by Colab members; Sandee Seymour modeling John Fekner's "Danger Live Artist" t-shirt; John Ahearn modeling Jenny Holzer's Truism t-shirt.* All 1982. Silver gelatin prints, 12.5 × 19 cm each. Photo shoot for fashion items offered in Art Direct mail-order catalog in collaboration with Printed Matter, Inc. © Lisa Kahane, NYC. All Rights Reserved.

PROPOSAL:

* DIRECT MAIL
   DIRECT MARKET) CATALOGUE

A catalogue for direct mail order
sales of objects, prints, books, Film
video, cable to be target mailed
in U.S. and Europe.
64 pages (6 3/8 × 10") divided into
3 sections (to be mailed together or seperately)
  1) mass produced objects & multiples
  2) Flat copy distribution, prints
     books, mags, xerox
  3) Film, Video, Performance, Cable
     (sales & Rental)

Cataloge open to all members and
to solicited work outside of colab.
30% of sales will be used to cover
expenses. All work subject to review
by editors: M. Geller, K. Smith, T. Otterness
  advisors: A. Moore, J. Holzer, B. Howland

    The Cat. will be most effective
when synchronized with other Colab
projects and individual shows.
(ie. the 'Road Show' could combine
with the mail Cat. when mailing anouncemen
for each city — then have a Sales Shop
as part of the Road show//or the
catalogue could be distributed in
Europe in conjunction with an individuals
show?)

* Direct Mail : uses massive demographically arranged
mailing lists, rented from list Brokers. It can be
very specifically targeted ie "All Eastern European
ornithologists living on the East Coast" or "All
subscribers to Art News" etc...   (over)

Top and bottom:

Tom Otterness. *Proposal: Direct
Mail, Direct Market*, c. 1981.
Photocopy, 2 pp, 36 × 21.5 cm.
Courtesy of Becky Howland.

|← ————— 10" ————— →|

COST FOR 5,000 COPIES
1,500 . . . . . — printing cost
                  (coated paper
                   64 pages)
  500 . . . . — mailing list rental
                @35. per 1,000 names
  200 . . . . — Typesetting @10.
                per hour
  350 . . . . — Photos Printed by
                lab
1,500 . . . . — mailing Cost
4,050 + 15% = 4,650 total

will raise from
other sources   1,650

Request from   3,000
     Colab

Printing by Capital city
Printers in Vermont

ARTISTS' DIRECT
THE ARTISTS' SHOP-BY-MAIL CATALOGUE

THE CONCEPT

The Artists' Shop-By-Mail Catalogue is designed to give a
broadly based group of artists an international outlet for the
sale of inexpensive art multiples. There is increasing interest
in economically viable alternatives to the production of high-
priced painting, sculpture and prints to be consigned to
galleries. The audience for contemporary art is expanding
rapidly but the individuals who can spend $2,500 or more for a
painting still constitute an extremely small group. This
catalogue venture is designed both to provide a commercial
channel for artists who are producing small, inexpensive
multiples, and to provide an opportunity for the new wider art
audience to purchase original artworks at affordable prices.

<u>The Catalogue</u>

The catalogue will include approximately 60 pages of offerings
and will be divided into five sections:

o	objects	35 selections
o	fashion	30 selections
o	film/video	35 selections
o	art prints	15 selections
o	artists' books and other printed material	40 selections

As indicated by the attached mock-up, each object will be
illustrated by a drawing or a photograph, and will be briefly
described in terms of medium, color, size, etc. The back pages
of the catalogue will be detachable order forms.

<u>Selection of the Objects</u>

A six-person committee composed of artists already experienced
in the production and marketing of inexpensive art multiples
will select the objects to be offered in the catalogue. A wide
group of American artists will be approached and asked to submit
proposals. The artists proposing the most interesting pieces
will be interviewed by the committee to make sure that the
artist is capable of producing enough to meet a strong demand.
In order to have an object included in the catalogue, an artist
must submit 20 completed and packed pieces to the committee to
be kept in inventory. Pieces will be selected on the basis of
durability, practicality and saleability as well as for esthetic
interest.

W2454R.1

Collaborative Projects Inc and Printed Matter are proud to announce ART DIRECT,
a mail order catalog offering over fifty artist made sculptures, prints,
posters, fashions and books. Just in time for holiday shopping, ART DIRECT
offers unique objects at very low prices, ranging from $2 to $100.

The items offered in ART DIRECT are quite unusual. The Oven Stuffer Bookends,
for example, are cast chicken halves covered with chicken pink latex. We
also have Radioactive Clams, and lovely hand painted fans. There is a photo
portfolio of urban scenes entitled "Scape," and a silkscreened print called
"Pizza Girl." For the fashion conscious we offer 7 T-shirt designs, "Trash Tres
Chic" jewelry, and a paper suit covered with artist designed rubber stamps.
There has never been a mail order offer like this one.

–Colab Annual Report 1982

Unknown. *Art Direct*, 1982. Typewritten document from Colab Annual Report, 21.5 × 28 cm. Courtesy of Matthew Geller.

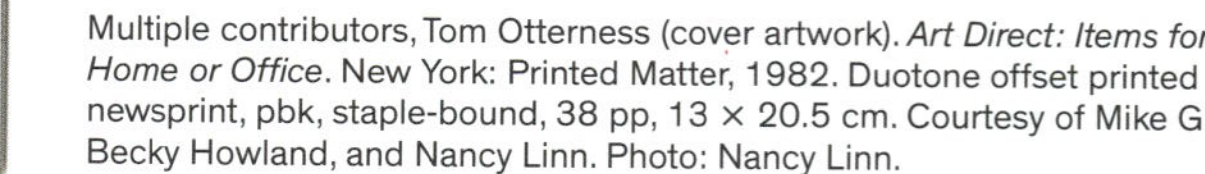

Multiple contributors, Tom Otterness (cover artwork). *Art Direct: Items for the Home or Office*. New York: Printed Matter, 1982. Duotone offset printed on newsprint, pbk, staple-bound, 38 pp, 13 × 20.5 cm. Courtesy of Mike Glier, Becky Howland, and Nancy Linn. Photo: Nancy Linn.

Jenny Holzer INFLAMMATORY POSTERS $10
These brightly colored posters have been put up on the streets of New York and around the world. Each set puts forth 20 contentious propositions; provoke yourself, pique your friends. Give the Moral Majority a run for their money.

Beverly Naidus ONE SIZE FITS ALL—A CONSUMER SURVIVAL KIT $6
28 printed stickers
I'm mad as hell and I'm not gonna take it anymore! Strike back at retail rip-offs. Do ya hate It? Say it with stickers.

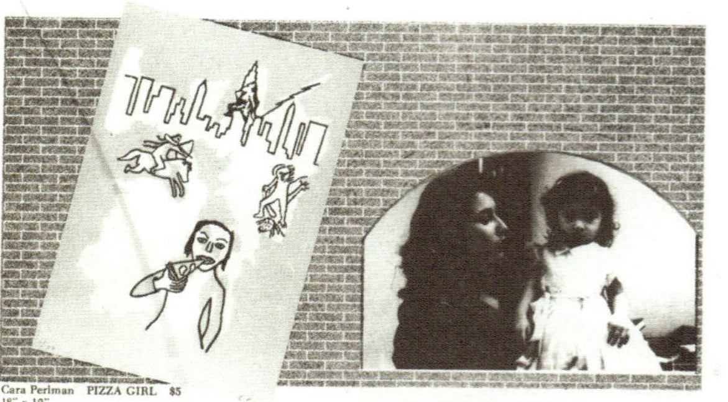

Cara Perlman PIZZA GIRL $5
18" x 12"
Two-color silkscreen on manila paper, initialed and numbered. City girl eats pizza against a skyline peopled with legendary figures. Crisp, evocative imagery in an underpriced premier edition of 100.

Nancy Linn MODERN MADONNA $2
Color photograph 3" x 5" of a mother and child, shaped by the artist and edged in gold leaf. A splendidly casual reinterpretation of a classic Renaissance theme. Makes a unique Christmas decoration for the top of the TV.

Christof Kohlhofer THE SNATCHER'S SNATCHED PURSE $50
You take the same risk as he does while obtaining, but you pay less! You'll feel the same thrill running up your spine as he does when you open it the first time! It's more excitement than playing the horses; simpler than getting mugged yourself! It's the ultimate multiple: each one is quite different from each other one! All purses are untouched and sealed, to make sure that you get the real thing. Sample contents: 1950's box-shaped hand bag (dark & light brown striped bacalite with top and handle, golden filigree trim); grenade-shaped lighter; dust from 1st atomic test site; green '52 sunglasses; battery operated "Moon Mirror" (no

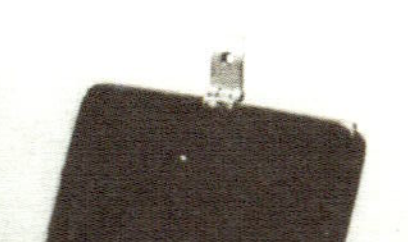
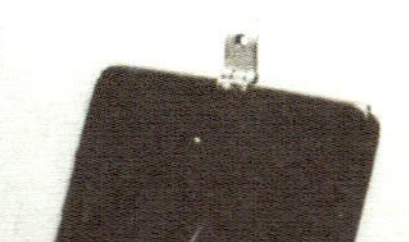
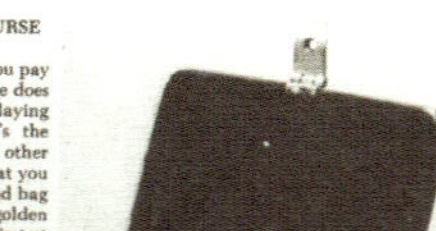

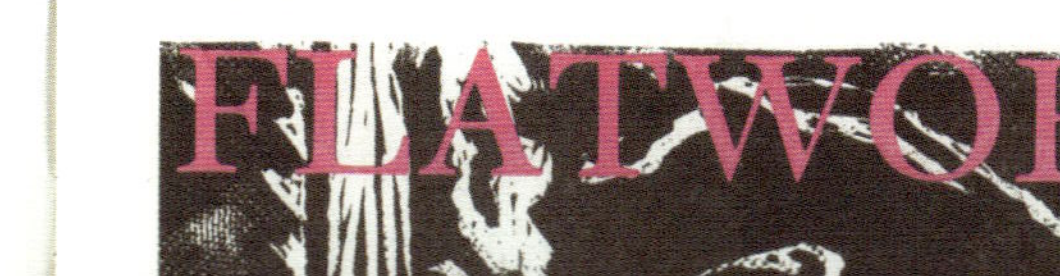

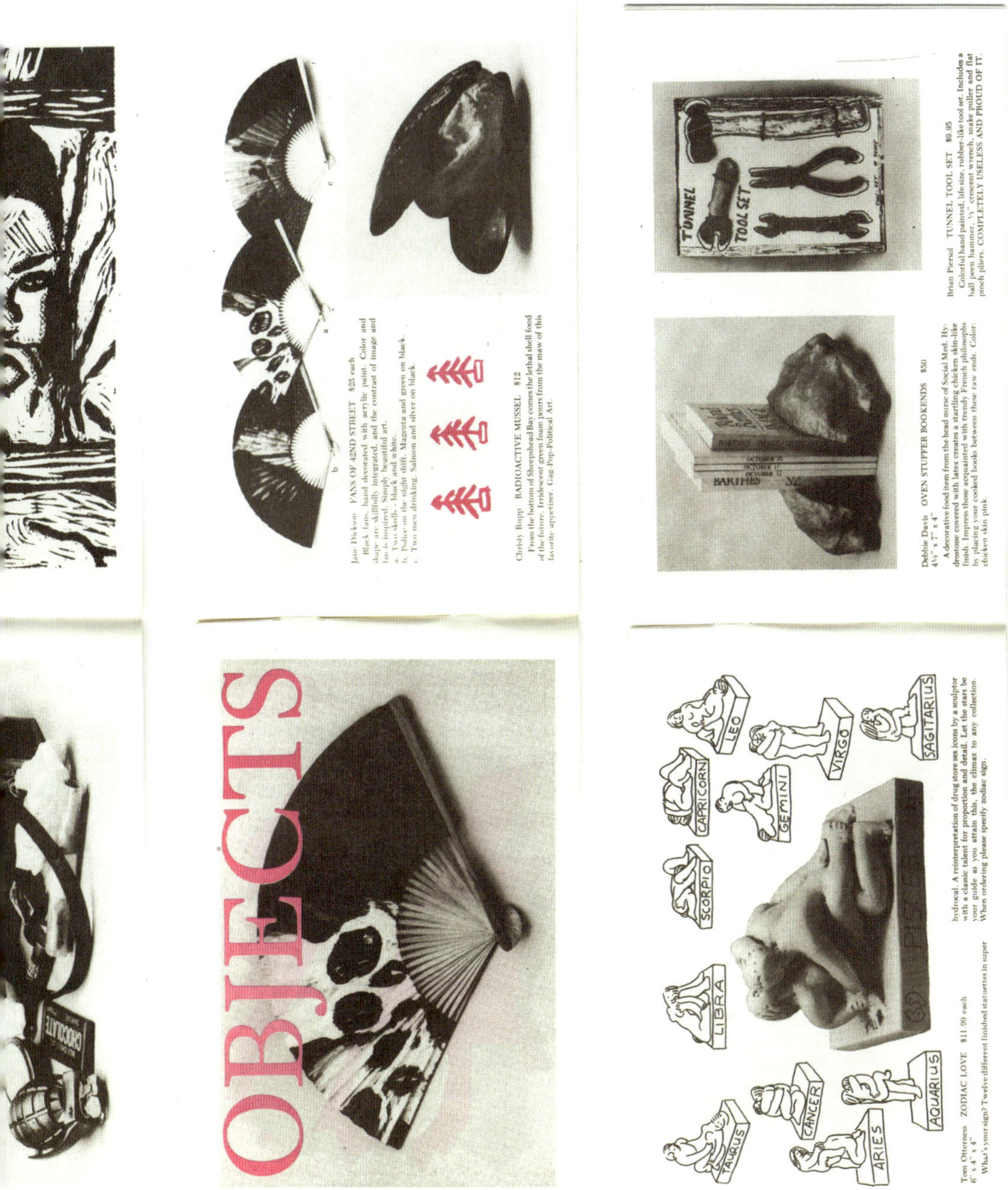

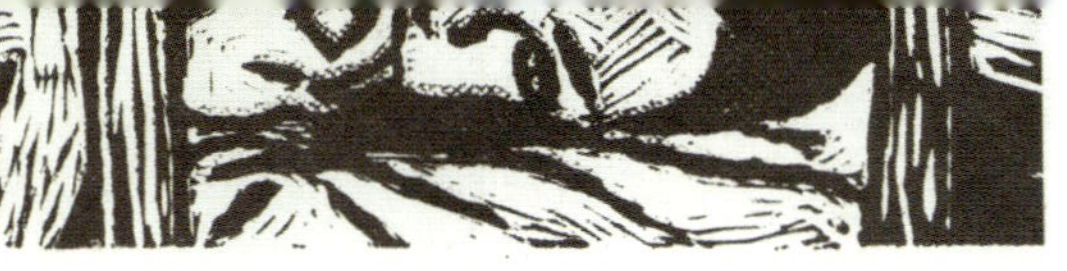

OBJECTS

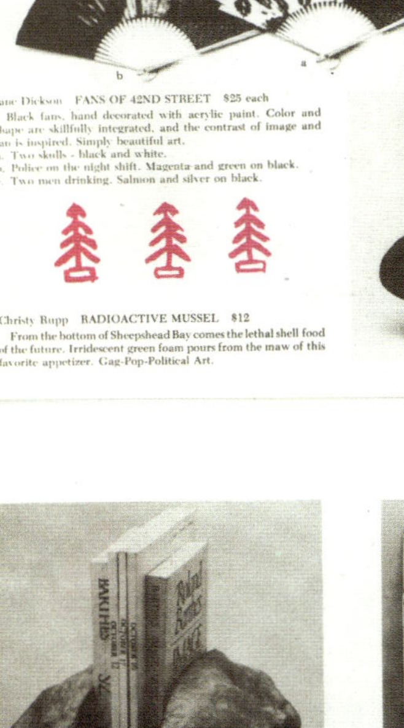

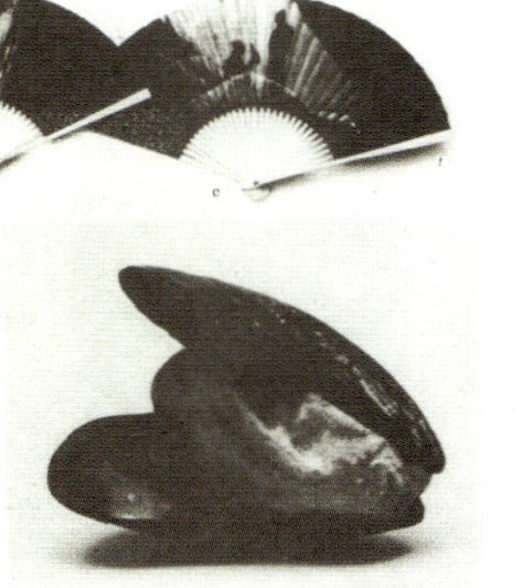

Jane Dickson   FANS OF 42ND STREET $25 each
   Black fans, hand decorated with acrylic paint. Color and shape are skillfully integrated, and the contrast of image and fan is inspired. Simply beautiful art.
a.   Two skulls - black and white.
b.   Police on the night shift. Magenta and green on black.
c.   Two men drinking. Salmon and silver on black.

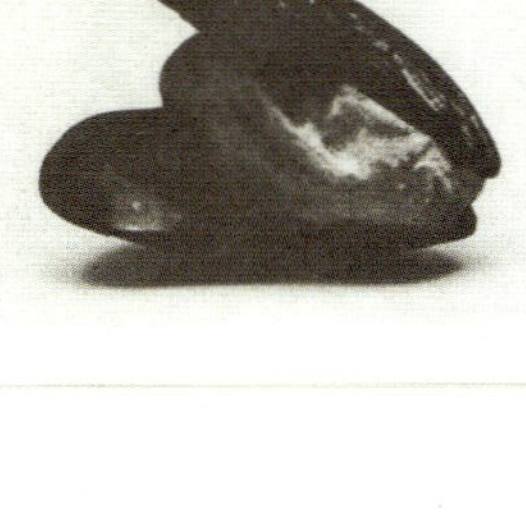

Christy Rupp   RADIOACTIVE MUSSEL $12
   From the bottom of Sheepshead Bay comes the lethal shell food of the future. Irridescent green foam pours from the maw of this favorite appetizer. Gag-Pop-Political Art.

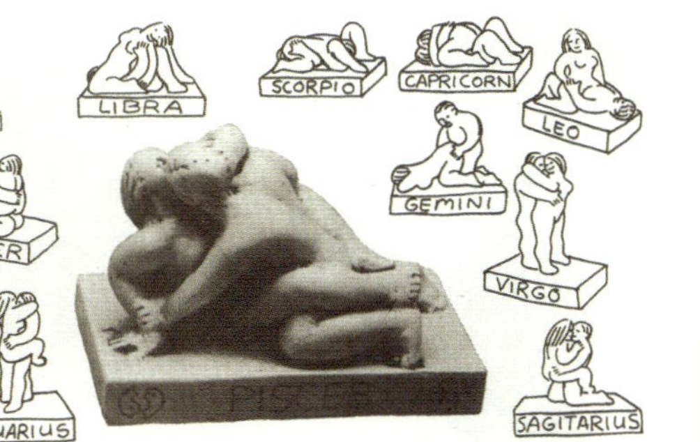

Tom Otterness   ZODIAC LOVE $11.99 each
6" x 4" x 4"
   What's your sign? Twelve different finished statuettes in super hydrocal. A reinterpretation of drug store sex icons by a sculptor with a classic talent for proportion and detail. Let the stars be your guide as you attain this, the climax to any collection. When ordering please specify zodiac sign.

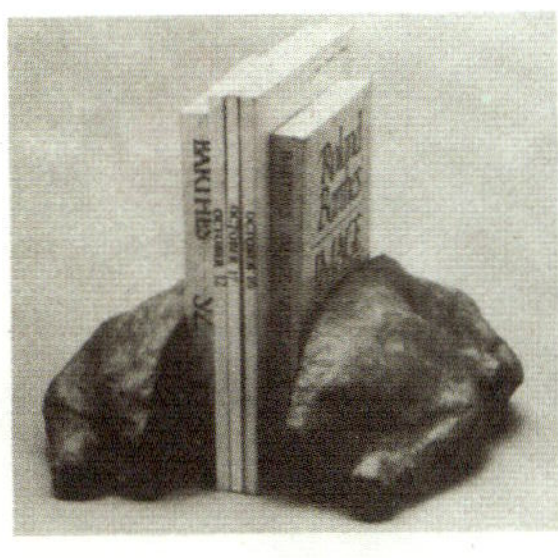

Debbie Davis   OVEN STUFFER BOOKENDS $50
4½" x 7" x 4"
   A decorative food item from the head nurse of Social Med. Hydrostone covered with latex creates a startling chicken skin-like finish. Impress those acquainted with trendy French philosophs by placing your cooked books between these raw ends. Color: chicken skin pink.

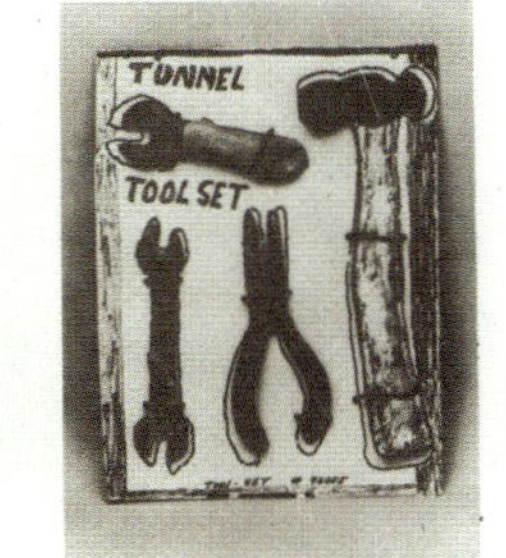

Brian Piersol   TUNNEL TOOL SET $9.95
   Colorful hand painted, life size, rubber-like tool set. Includes a ball peen hammer, ½" crescent wrench, snake puller and flat pinch pliers. COMPLETELY USELESS AND PROUD OF IT.

WASHINGTON-THE RITZ

The New US Congress, along with the rest of Washington, will be put
through Hazing Month this March, soon after it gets underway. Near
Capitol Hill, Colab and Washington artists will open a new club, called
The Ritz. The Ritz will help our nation's decision makers, along with
all their paid and unpaid help, to not just "stay the course," but to
"get ritz!" After all, if we can revive an old flophouse called The Ritz
and present a National Address (on local TV), then this is surely a Land
of Opportunity, and with enough help all of us can get rich.
The Ritz, sponsored by Washington's WPA, will offer: installations,
murals, performance, video, art, television, music. It was announced
to Washington artists as "MORE THAN AN ART SHOW... A Way of Life," and
since then about 50 of them have met with Colab to plan the club-event.
Being coordinated by Ulli Rimkus and Sophie VDT, two Colab members not
from the United States, the show will nonetheless be a patriotic effort.
Budgeted at $5000 by Colab, with $1500 additional from the WPA (plus
supplies), we expect the show to speak for the nation-and to help the
nation speak for itself.

-Colab Annual Report 1982

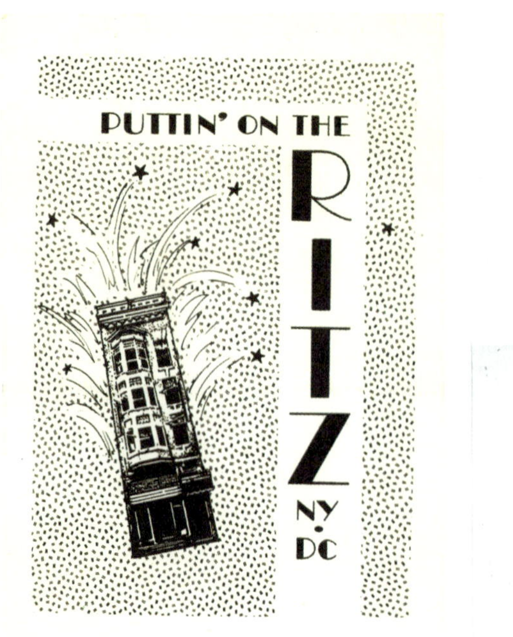

Unknown. *Puttin' on the Ritz*, 1983. Offset printed card, 17.5 × 13 cm. Invitation for The Ritz exhibition in Washington D.C. Courtesy of Andrea Callard.

Ellen Cooper. *Untitled [Perfectly ordinary working class scum]*, 1983. Photocopy, 28 × 21.5 cm. Back cover of press packet for *The Ritz* exhibition in Washington D.C. Courtesy of Becky Howland.

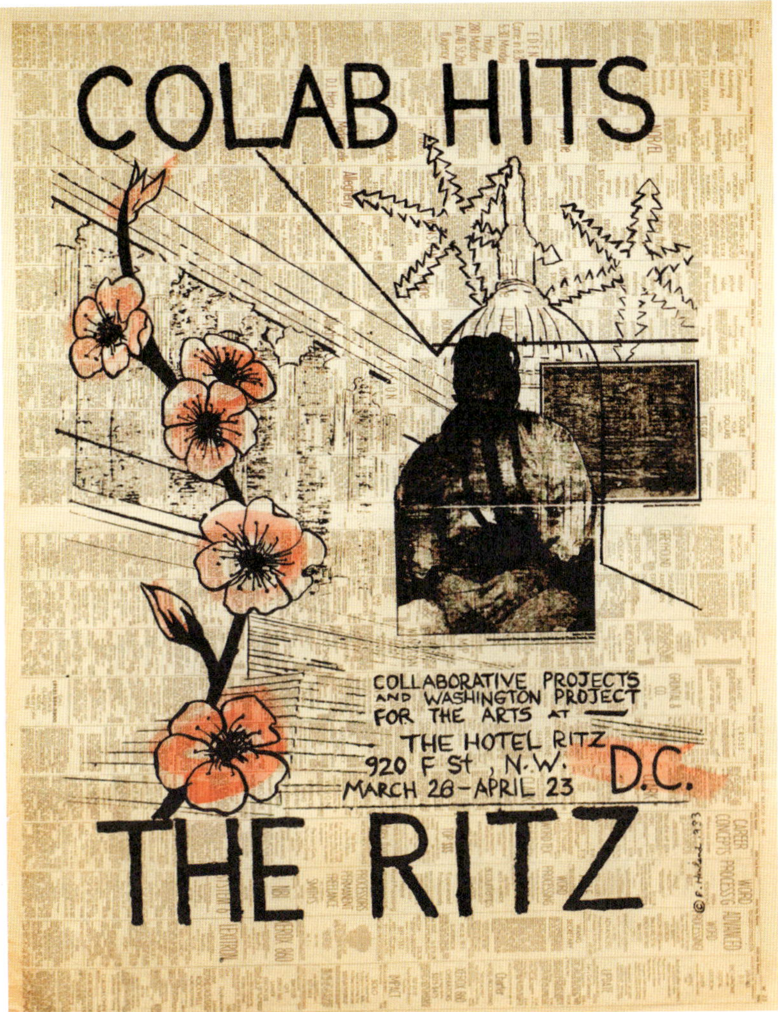

Becky Howland. *Colab Hits the Ritz*. New York: R. Howland, 1983. Screenprint and hand-painting on newspaper, 71 × 56 cm. Poster from *The Ritz* exhibition in Washington D.C. Courtesy of Alan Moore.

Continuing the tradition of traveling shows throughout the US, Colab went to Hallwalls in Buffalo, and it scored a big success. True to its participatory philosophy, it sent out by advance press and open invitation to all Buffalo artists to exhibit in most of the gallery—and 150 artists came with work. The opening was heavily-attended, and all the entering artists voted on the five best (or favorite) works. In the rest of the gallery, Colab exhibited its first definitive edition of Colab Photo Prints: 51 30"x40" black-and-white blow-ups of work, one by each artist. The photo-prints show a common aesthetic to all Colab work: the straight-forward, plain-spoken statement, the cartoon-like comment, the simple, strong graphic, which depicts popular aspects of American Life. Is Colab art a sort of pop art with a social conscience? The critical response is just pouring in.

–Colab Annual Report 1983

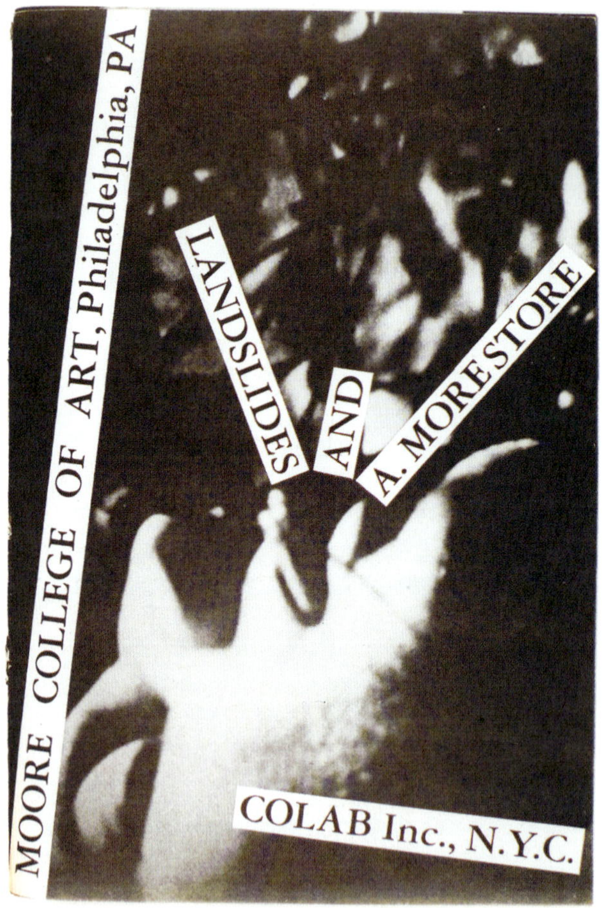

This page and facing:

Collaborative Projects Inc, Christof Kohlhöfer (design). *Landslides and A. More Store*. Philadelphia: Moore College of Art, 1983. Offset printed, pbk, staple-bound, 38 pp, 27 × 18 cm. Cover and interiors.
Courtesy of the Collaborative Projects Archive.

NO ONE OWNS LIFE, BUT ANYONE WHO CAN
PICK UP A FRYING PAN OWNS DEATH

William S. Burroughs

IF WE WANT THINGS TO STAY AS THEY ARE,
THINGS WILL HAVE TO CHANGE.
DO YOU KNOW ?

Giuseppe Di Lampedusa

THOSE WHO EAT THEIR FILL SPEAK TO THE HUNGRY
OF WONDERFUL TIMES TO COME

Bertold Brecht

THE SYMBOL FOR "CRISES" IN CHINESE IS MADE
UP OF TWO CHARACTERS WHOSE MEANINGS ARE
"DANGER" AND "OPPORTUNITY". TO ME, THAT
PRECISELY DESCRIBES THE PRESENT SITUATION

John D. Rockefeller III

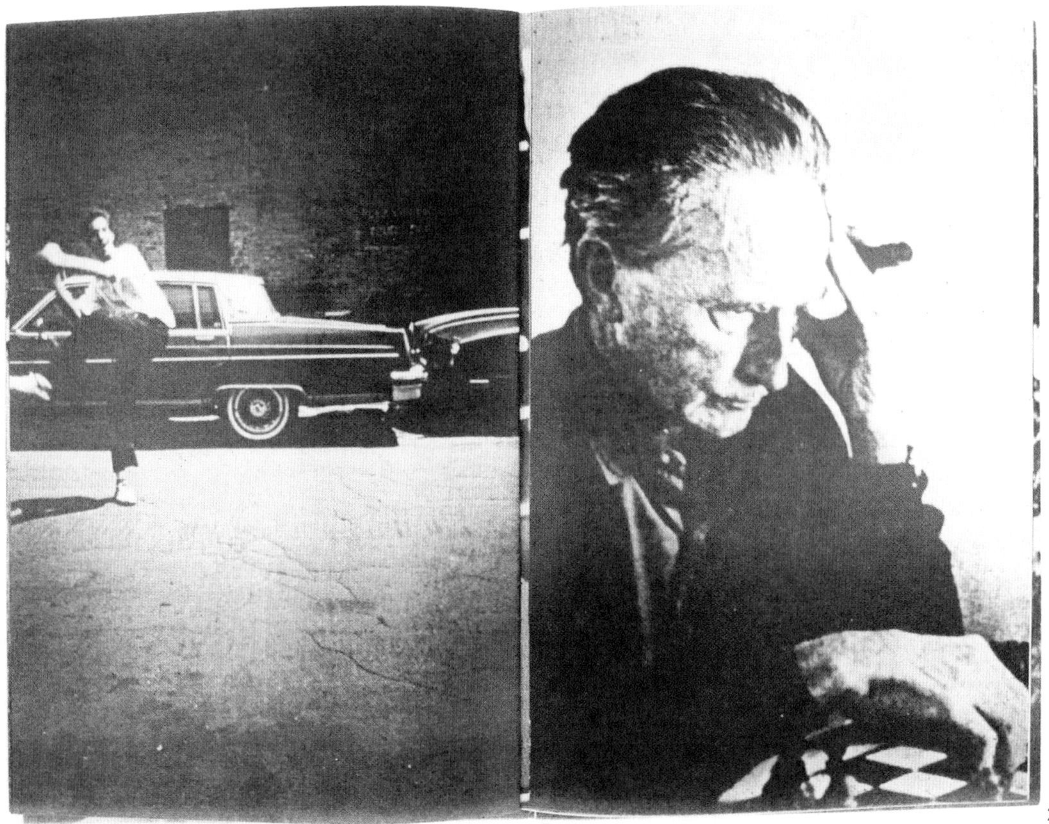

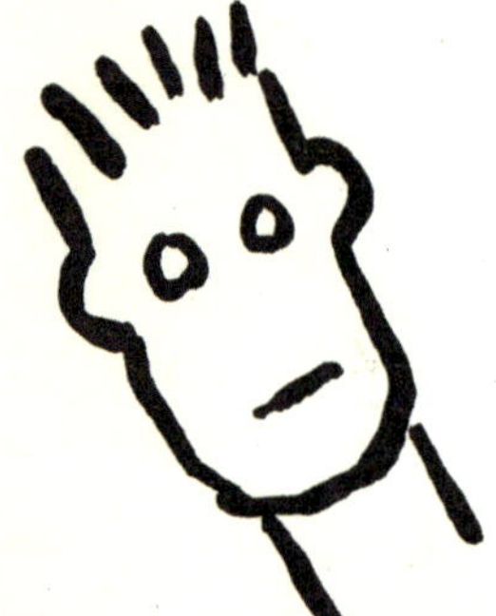
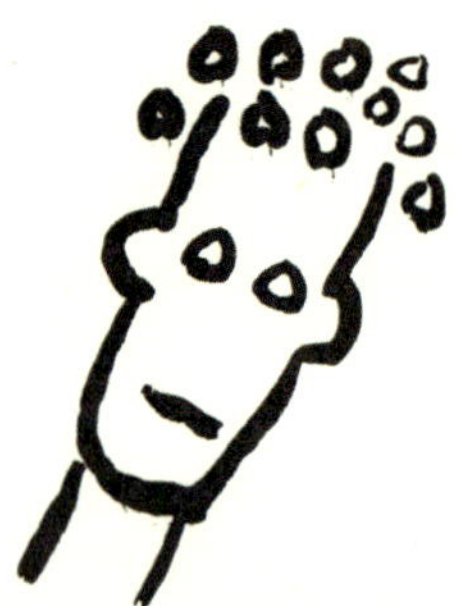

John Morton. *The Colab Story*, 1983. Photocopy poster, 28 × 21.5 cm. From an artists' talk on Colab at SMFA Boston. Courtesy of Becky Howland.

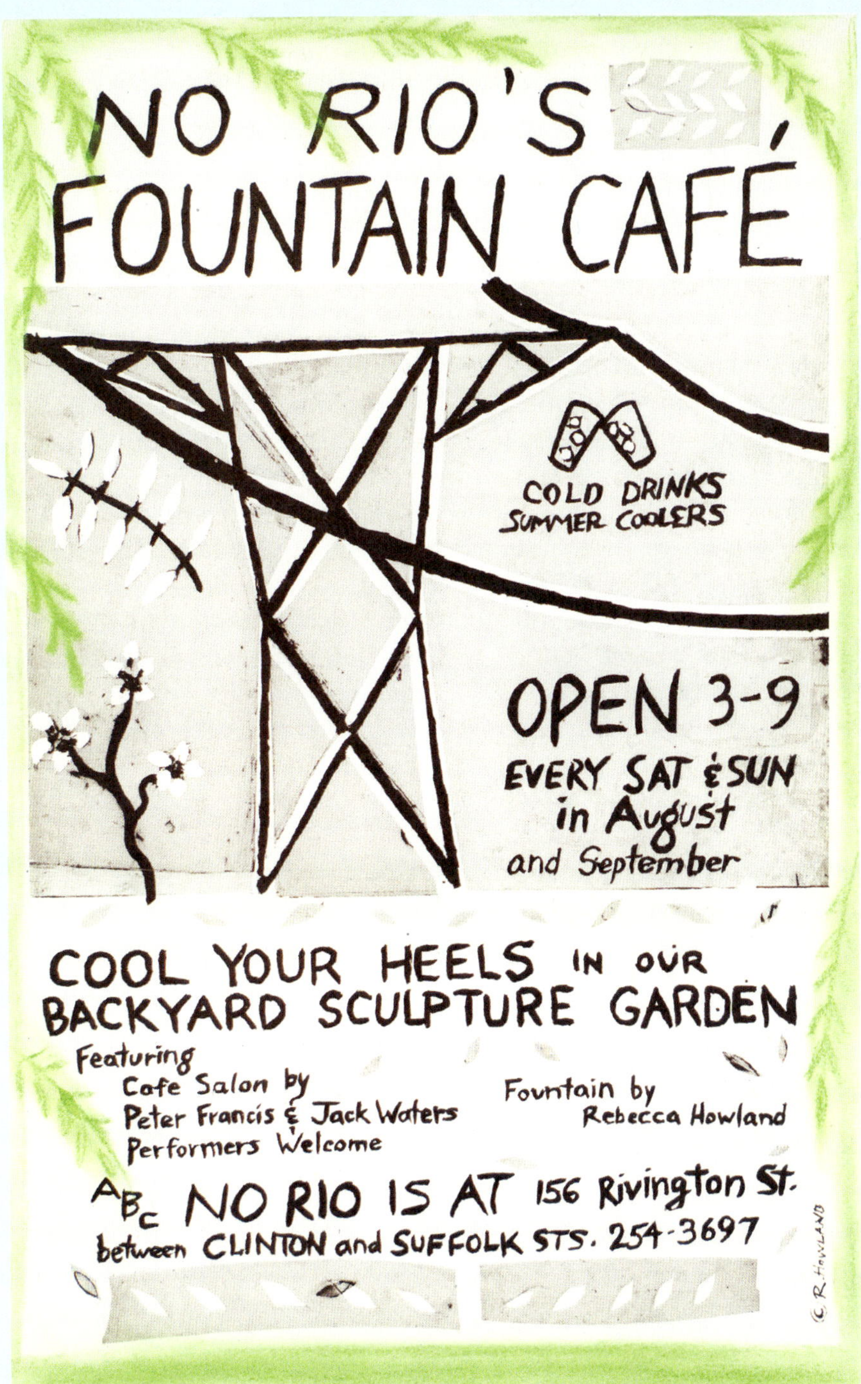

Becky Howland. *No Rio's Fountain Café*, 1983. Hand-painted, offset printed poster, 43 × 28 cm. For ABC No Rio's backyard café. Courtesy of Becky Howland.

My life partner and professional collaborator Peter Cramer and I discovered Colab in the Spring of 1983 when we were established as the second generation of ABC No Rio's co-directors. Almost immediately upon No Rio's inception Colab strategically positioned itself as legally distinct from the newly founded venue. But No Rio had already been cited in the press as the "unofficial museum of Colab." By Colab's loose rules, membership only required attendance of three meetings. Having done so we were officially recognized. Our first Colab activity was to inherit Colab's slot on Creative Time's Art On The Beach project on the pre-constructed Battery City Park landfill. POOL, the performance collective that Peter and I were members of, was morphing from a concert dance troupe into doing whatever site-specific actions would avail, including cabaret acts on the club circuit. Our second official gig for Colab was to curate performances based on the theme "religion" at Limelight, the deconsecrated Episcopal church on 23rd Street and 6th Avenue.

Gay identity for me at the time was decidedly apolitical. At the time we still espoused the oft quoted Gore Vidal contention that *"There is no such thing as a homosexual or a heterosexual person. There are only homo—or heterosexual acts…"*

I think I was in a closet without fully realizing it. I hadn't yet developed a sense of my sexual orientation as something that should distinguish me from the countercultural status quo. It was by no means a secret that Peter and I were gay as were Carl George, Gordon Kurtti, Tony Pinotti, Brad Taylor, and my other queer family in "the new No Rio," as I remember being inaugurated by Kiki Smith at an East Village Colab dinner party in the summer of 1983. Brad Taylor was largely responsible for introducing our circle to No Rio. By that time our group had firmly bonded in the club scene, particularly at our home base The Pyramid Club on Avenue A. With No Rio as a second base, our group would soon bring a greater emphasis on performance, film and inter-arts with an unconcealed, though as yet apolitical faggotry to this sphere. By extension our mere presence was an unpronounced queering of Colab.

I always felt supported by the Colab milieu in general, and I never heard a derogatory reference or felt a homophobic gesture directed at me, Peter, or anyone else who identified as queer. But I can't remember a single overt expression of queer solidarity — let alone any other self referenced queer identity besides ours coming from the ranks of Colab — whether as a political group, an art enclave, or as a social community. I remember the straightest of cis-presenting guys in the tightest of jeans at meetings and events setting off my gaydar. Was this a flirty androgynous unisex come-on, a vestigial remnant of the '60s, or just the fashion of the day?

If there was any overt queering of Colab it was definitely coming from us.

A distinctly unpronounced shroud of silence on homosexuality contrasted the women of Colab's overt expression of feminist politics. Again, is it my queer imagination that flirts with the lesbian allure of Kiki Smith's career as an electrician and Rebecca Howland's group of lady plumbers? Am I grasping at straws?

The only really specific openly homophobic utterance I remember from the period was when an artists retreat in Lexington, NY was established by a group of women in Colab. An artist that was not invited was frustrated by what she thought to be a select clique. At a particularly contentious meeting she challenged that the first residency group was an insular circle of girl friends. She called the residency project a "lesbo art camp." Oops.

I cant help feeling that being on the outer periphery of these circles prohibits me from shedding more light than wishful thinking, speculation. I'm left with sense-memories that propagate the vaguest of insinuations. How homophobic is that?

Were there any openly queer members of Colab besides me and Peter? That I even pose this question is telling.

—Jack Waters

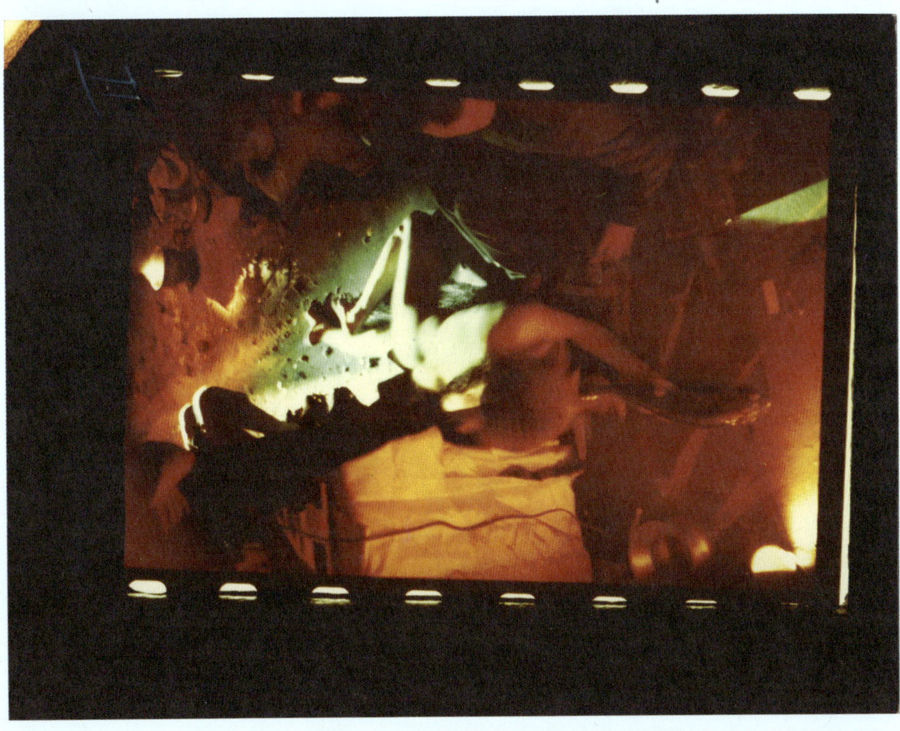

Erotic Psyche (Bradley Eros and Aline Mare). *Fetish is a Fertile Boat*, c. 1983. C-print photograph, 28 × 21.5 cm. Performance held during *The Erotic Psyche Show*. Courtesy of Bradley Eros. Photo: Plauto.

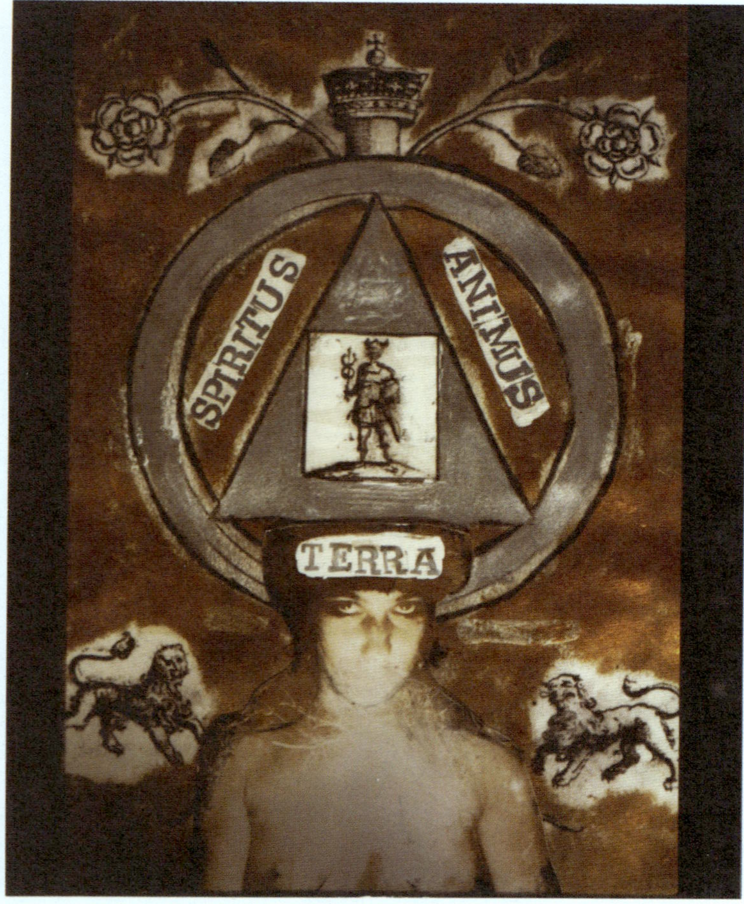

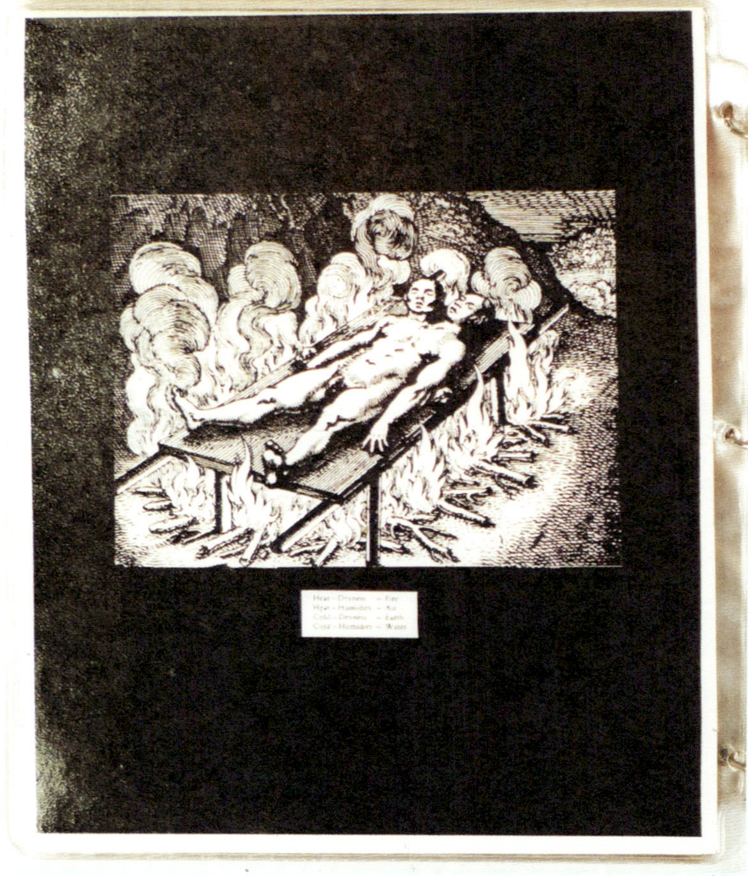

Aline Mare. *Spiritus Animus Terra*, 1982. Color photograph, 25.5 × 20 cm. Courtesy of Bradley Eros.

Erotic Psyche (Bradley Eros and Aline Mare). *Untitled*. New York: Erotic Psyche, c. 1983. Photocopy, in plastic slipcovers, ring-bound, 36 pp, 29 × 23.5 cm, edition of two.
Courtesy of Bradley Eros. Photo: Nancy Linn.

I first encountered *The Time Square Show* in 1980 when driving around in the back of a pick up truck that summer and then later met Colab artists thru our friend Brad Taylor that knew Aline Mare and Bradley Eros (Erotic Psyche). We (POOL: Performance On One Leg) used to rehearse at Jane Dickson's painting studio on Broadway just below Houston Street. Eventually, Jack Waters and I became co-directors of ABC No Rio in 1983, representing the next generation.

—Peter Cramer

Erotic Psyche (Bradley Eros and Aline Mare). *The Erotic Psyche Show*, 1982. Photocopy flyer, 28 × 21.5 cm. Courtesy of Kiki Smith.

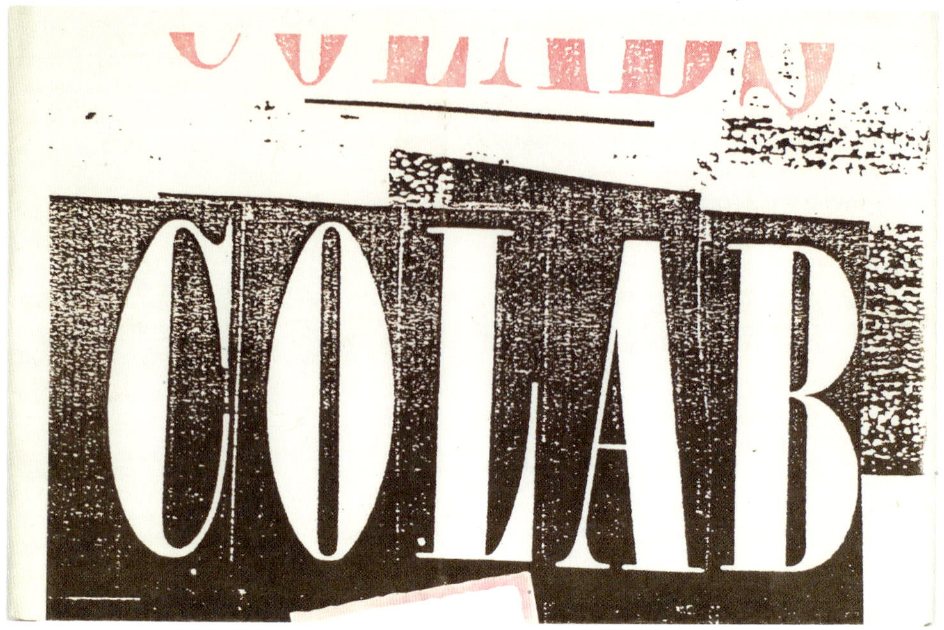

John Hogan and Darryl Turner, editors. *Talk is Cheap*. New York: Collaborative Projects Inc, 1984. Duotone offset printed posters, 43 × 29 cm each (folded) / 86.5 × 58 cm each (open). Set of 28 posters, each a collaboration by Colab artists. Courtesy of the Collaborative Projects Archive. Photo: Nancy Linn.

I'm afraid I was not an 'official' colab member, I don't think I ever actually 'joined' the group. I didn't have the patience for the in-fighting politics & dreary administrative meetings. I did very much enjoy being part of a group of artists who placed freedom of expression above market price. I very much enjoyed being able to express the complexity of being a young woman who embraced sexual freedom as a political statement, while honoring women as independent, intelligent people who could contribute to changing the status quo.

The experience of being part of a group of artists whose interests were varied helped make me the person I am today.

It was an honor to be part of that group, with the fantastic creative energy, energy which was directed at dis-empowering the 'haves' and empowering the 'have nots.'

—Jane Sherry

Colab. Art that goes to the core, peeling away the legitimacy of a hegemony that had taken hold of its exhibition and definition, Colab, a movement toward autonomy of artists. Tom Otterness, Robert Smith-Cooney, Walter Robinson, were in my daily life, Alan Moore, Becky Howland, Robin Winters, Cara Perlman, Matthew Geller, meetings that breathed their own tangible being. Ongoing projects. Collaboration. Colab is home.

—Judy Rifka

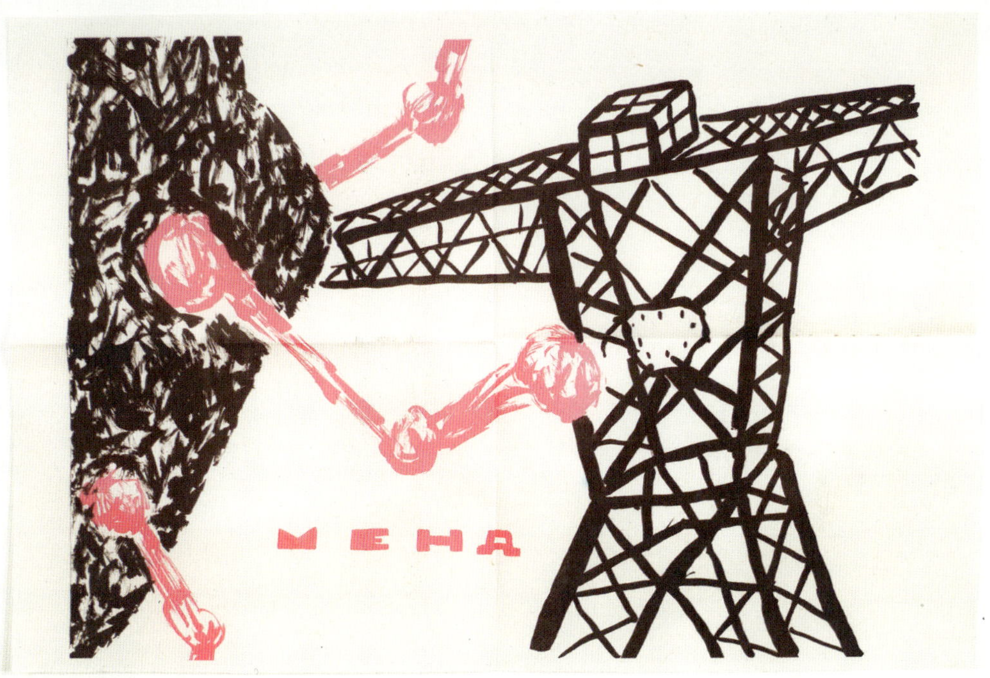

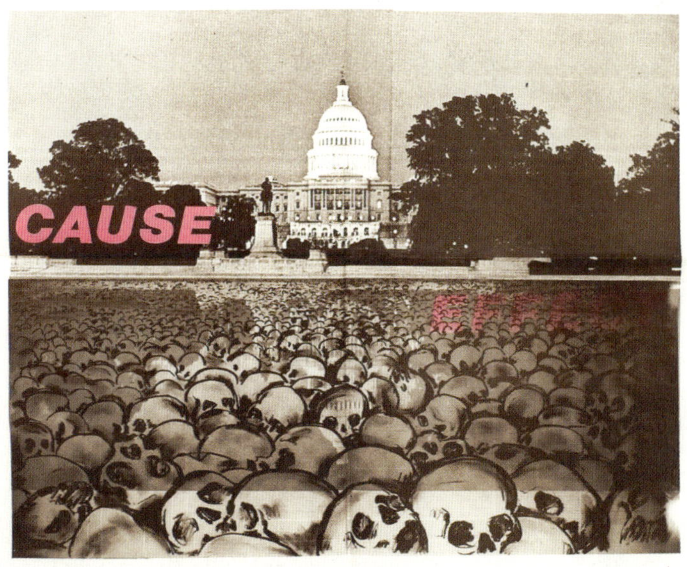

John Morton and Steven Wright (top) and Charlie Ahearn, Jane Dickson and Kiki Smith (bottom) from *Talk is Cheap*, Colab poster publication, 1984. Duotone offset printed, 43 × 29 cm each (folded) / 86.5 × 58 cm each (open). Courtesy of the Collaborative Projects Archive. Photo: Nancy Linn.

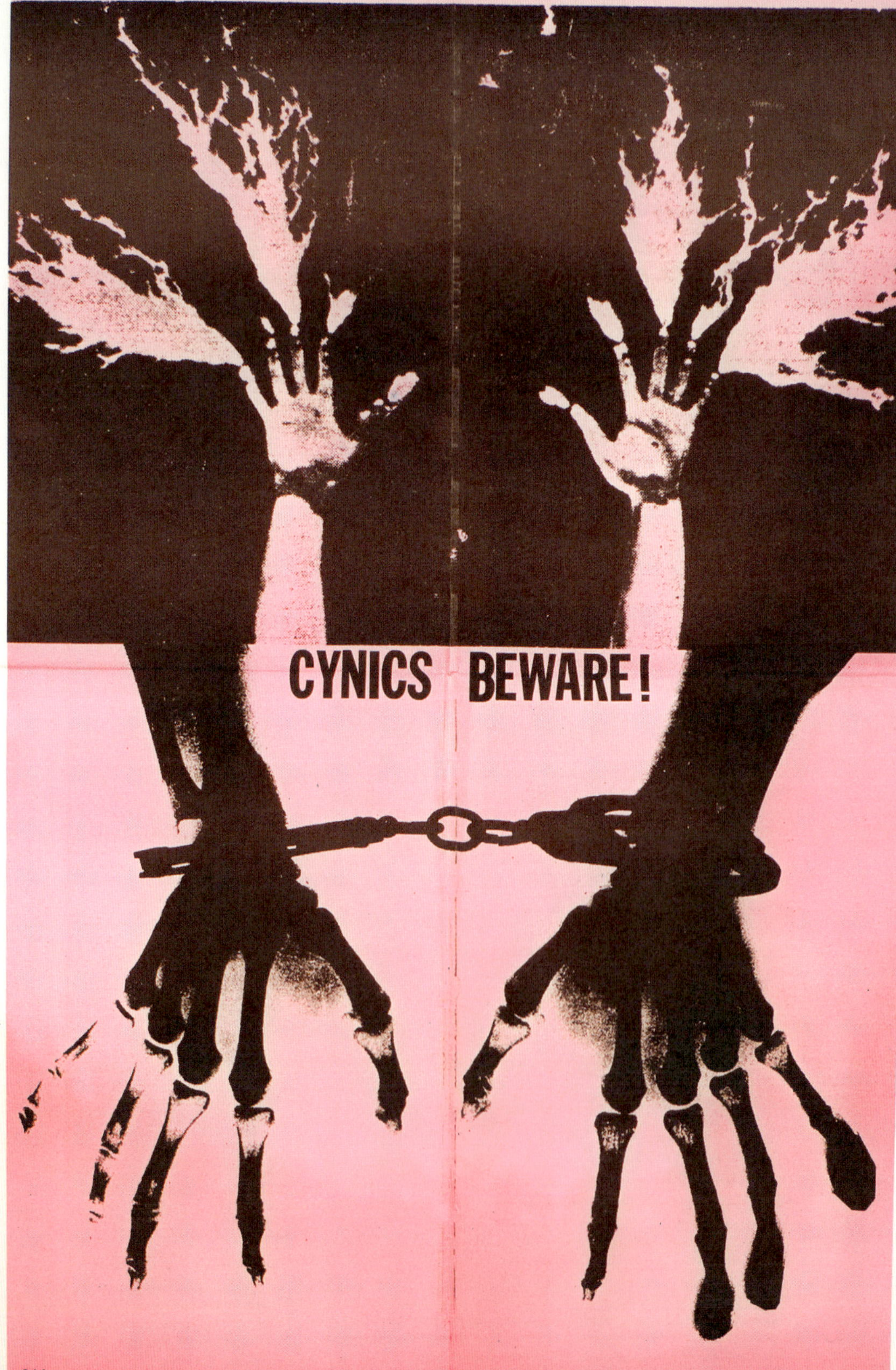
CYNICS BEWARE !

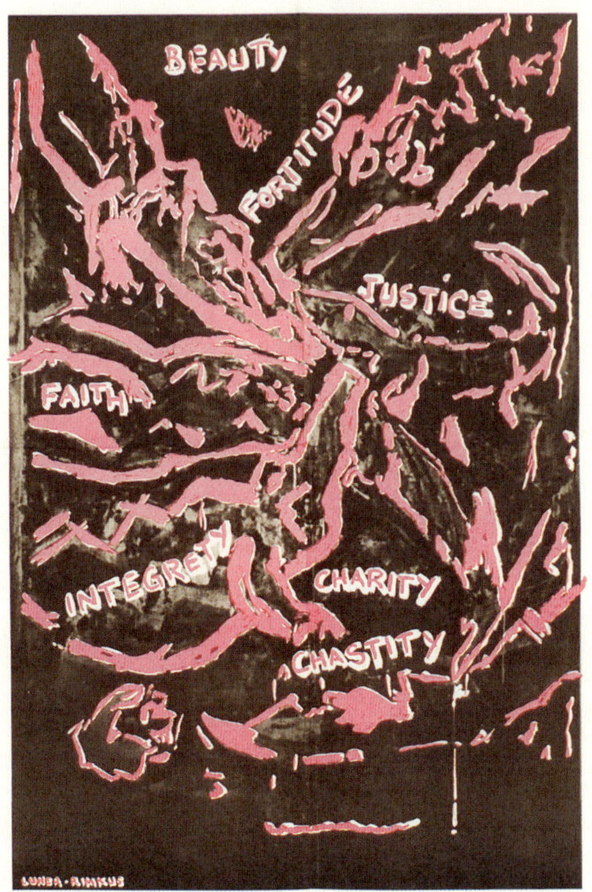

Facing page:

Erotic Psyche (Bradley Eros and Aline Mare) from *Talk is Cheap*, Colab poster publication, 1984.
Duotone offset printed, 43 × 29 cm each (folded) / 86.5 × 58 cm each (open).
Courtesy of the Collaborative Projects Archive. Photo: Nancy Linn.

This page:

Karin Luner and Ulli Rimkus from *Talk is Cheap*, Colab poster publication, 1984.
Duotone offset printed, 43 × 29 cm each (folded) / 86.5 × 58 cm each (open).
Courtesy of the Collaborative Projects Archive. Photo: Nancy Linn.

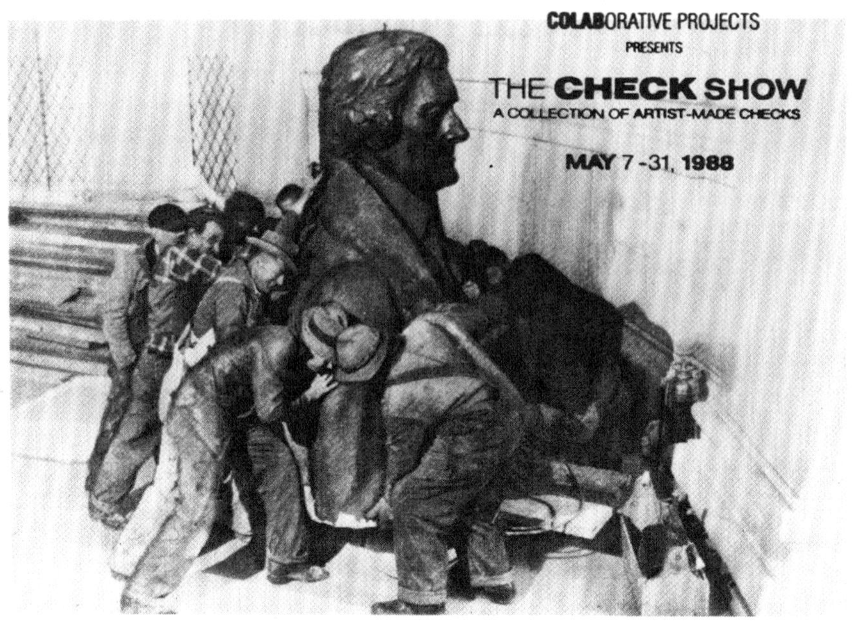

COLABORATIVE PROJECTS

PRESENTS

MAY 7 -31, **1988**

THE **CHECK** SHOW

A COLLECTION OF ARTIST-MADE CHECKS

AT

CITIBANK

55 WALL STREET

LANDMARK BRANCH

MONDAY-FRIDAY 9-3PM

A PROGRAM OF THE CULTURAL COUNCIL FOUNDATION
PARTIALLY FUNDED BY THE NEW YORK STATE COUNCIL ON THE ARTS
AND THE NEW YORK CITY DEPARTMENT OF CULTURAL AFFAIRS

Unknown. *The Check Show* (front and back), 1988. B/W offset printed card, 10.5 × 14.5 cm. Courtesy of Alan Moore.

From Doom to Downtime

*We seem to dip from doom
to downtime...minted...our own·
calculating coins...crash
...cash registers slurs and greedy
gods...dogs of a mean chewing...
undoing a human kind of glue.*

So often with feeling comes death,
but with death comes special breath
...a searching. Could love hum, slummed
in the sampling sum of dumb labor
types who slave to the rhythms
of their warped wills...ill-humored pills?

The banish stands for something lost,
tossed aside...and jiggled, a lithe spike
of heartless darting...targets toughened
in the hit-and-miss of startled
articulation.

—Mitch Corber. "From Doom to Downtime."
(from back cover) Blast. October, 1986.

By 1986 the group's activities waned as artists went their own directions until Colab-related or redux shows made an appearance in 2011, such as *A Show About Colab* (Printed Matter show 2011 and book), *The Times Square Show Revisited* (Hunter College 2012), *XFR STN Show* (New Museum 2013) and *The Real Estate Show* (James Fuentes Gallery, The Lodge Gallery, Cuchifritos/Artists Alliance Gallery, ABC No Rio and Spectacle Theater 2014), *Urban Theater: New York Art in the 1980's* (Modern Art Museum of Fort Worth 2014), as well as the Colab-initiated Wikispaces CollaborativeProjectsArchive and Potato Wolf Colab Projects excerpts on YouTube. How does a round peg fit in a square hole? Colab was that anomaly that didn't quite conform to the larger social geography; it was a crowd of idealist desperados with a horizontal power structure making impermanent thematic work with little or no traditional curation and 50% or more of its members and originators were women. To name some and not all of the participants might be pandering to the elements that Colab was resisting.

—Coleen Fitzgibbon

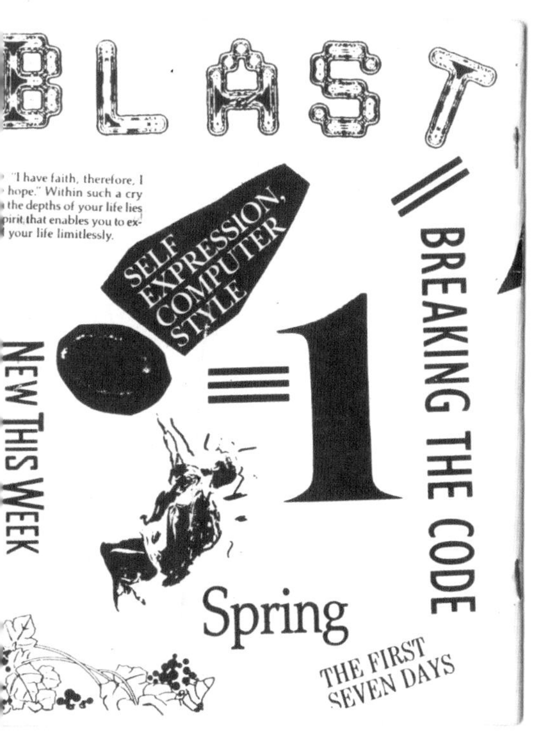

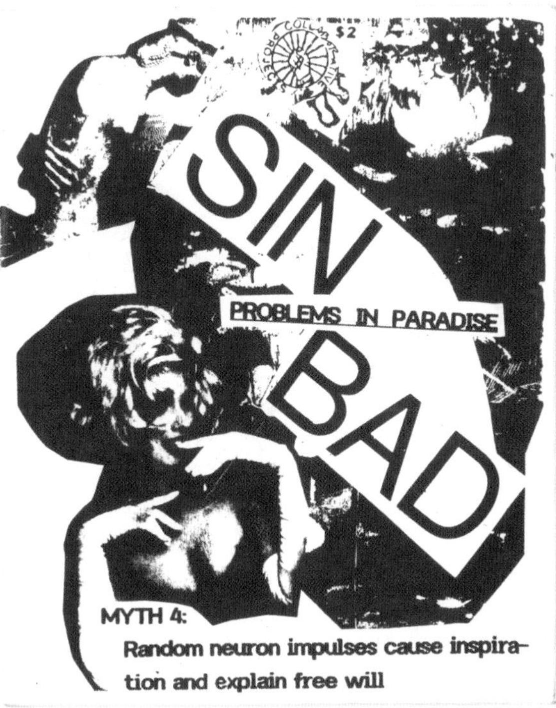

Mitch Corber, editor. *Blast* [Sinbad: Problems in Paradise, Spring '86] New York: Collaborative Projects Inc, 1986. Photocopy, pbk, staple bound, 38 pp, 21.5 × 18 cm. Front and back cover. Courtesy of Mitch Corber.

A Brief History of MWF

During the winter of 1986, a small knot of artists opened a "salon" called the Monday/Wednesday/Friday Video Club in a tiny studio apartment on Houston Street near the Bowery. The apartment was to house a home video rental project. But it was different from the other video stores opening up around town then. We had only artists' tapes—nothing commercial, and nothing that'd ever been on TV…

The twin communications innovations of home video and cable TV were supposed to change everything for artists in the 1980s. Eager to reach a larger audience with more popularly work, visual and performing artists turned to video in ever-increasing numbers.

It was from this moment of hope that the MWF distribution project was launched. It was also a response to art-world conditions. The artists who started MWF had been shut out of the few commercial and institutional outlets for artists' work. The ideology behind the MWF project was populist, and the intentions opportunist. Art should be accessible to as many people as possible, so we elected to sell videos at low prices directly to whoever wanted to buy them.

—Alan Moore. "A Brief History of MWF." Clayton Patterson, editor *Captured: A Film/ Video History of the Lower East Side*. New York: Seven Stories Press, 2005.

Alan Moore. *Wednesdays at Max Fish*, c. 1989–90. Photocopy handbill, 15.5 × 13.5 cm. For screening including MWF Video Club. Courtesy of Alan Moore.

Unknown. *Video Screenings* [Monday Wednesday], 1987. Photocopy handbill, 27 × 6.5 cm. From MWF Video Club. Courtesy of Alan Moore.

Fritz Demmer. *The MWF Video Club Coupon*, c. 1986. Photocopy handbill, 7.5 × 16 cm each. Courtesy of the Collaborative Projects Archive.

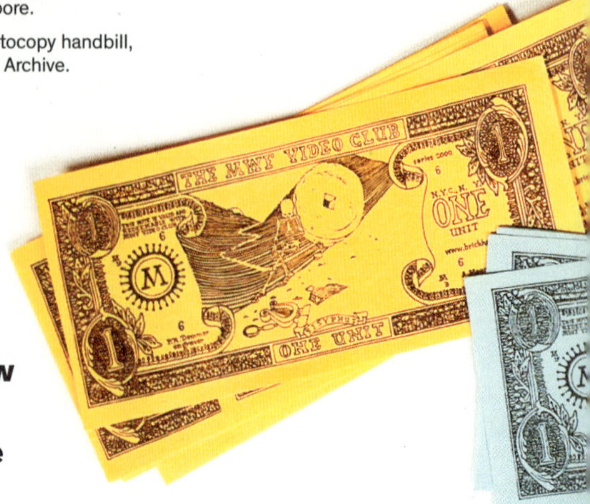

Colab at 80: Tom O proposes we set up a network (retirement!) community in trailorparks in the midwest. This will allow for affordable housing and a degree of flexibility as members migrate during the year from one park to another.

—Ann Messner

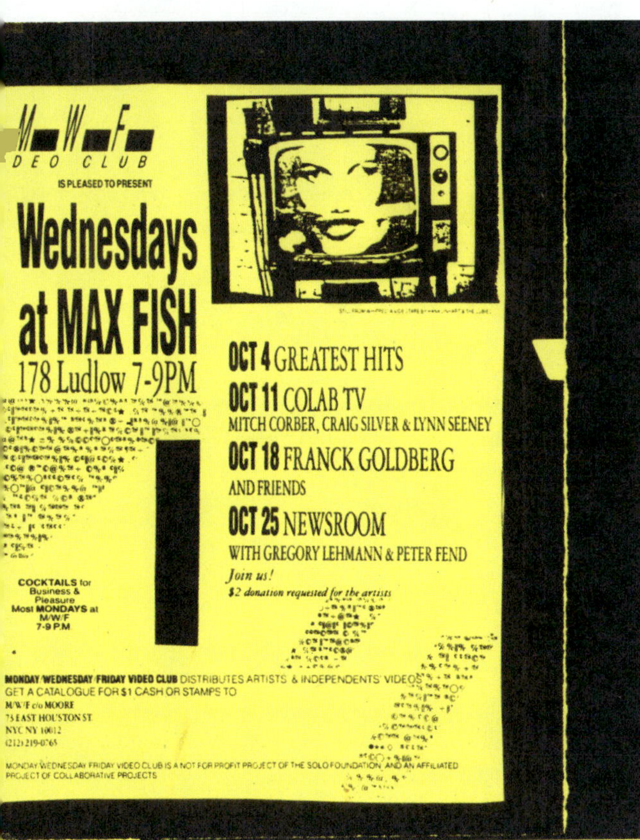
M·W·F·
DEO CLUB
IS PLEASED TO PRESENT

Wednesdays
at MAX FISH
178 Ludlow 7-9PM

OCT 4 GREATEST HITS

OCT 11 COLAB TV
MITCH CORBER, CRAIG SILVER & LYNN SEENEY

OCT 18 FRANCK GOLDBERG
AND FRIENDS

OCT 25 NEWSROOM
WITH GREGORY LEHMANN & PETER FEND
Join us!
$2 donation requested for the artists

COCKTAILS for
Business &
Pleasure
Most MONDAYS at
M/W/F
7-9 P.M.

MONDAY WEDNESDAY FRIDAY VIDEO CLUB DISTRIBUTES ARTISTS & INDEPENDENTS VIDEOS
GET A CATALOGUE FOR $1 CASH OR STAMPS TO
M/W/F c/o MOORE
73 EAST HOUSTON ST
NYC NY 10012
(212) 219-0765

MONDAY WEDNESDAY FRIDAY VIDEO CLUB IS A NOT FOR PROFIT PROJECT OF THE SOLO FOUNDATION, AND AN AFFILIATED
PROJECT OF COLLABORATIVE PROJECTS

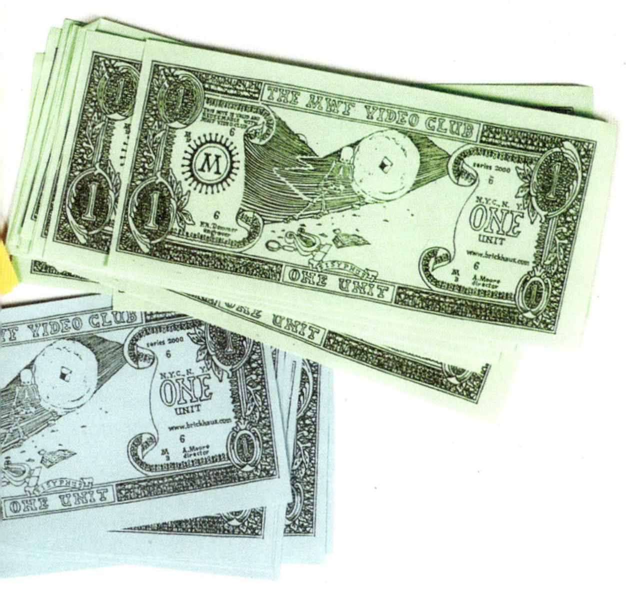
THE MWF VIDEO CLUB
series 2000
ONE UNIT
N.Y.C. N.Y.
A. Moore director
www.brickhaus.com

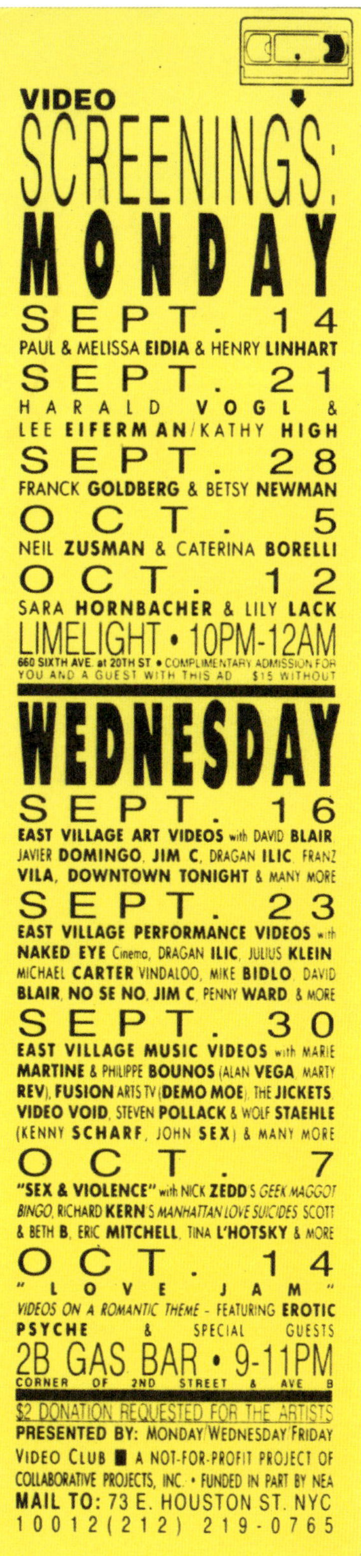
VIDEO
SCREENINGS
MONDAY
SEPT. 14
PAUL & MELISSA EIDIA & HENRY LINHART
SEPT. 21
HARALD VOGL &
LEE EIFERMAN / KATHY HIGH
SEPT. 28
FRANCK GOLDBERG & BETSY NEWMAN
OCT. 5
NEIL ZUSMAN & CATERINA BORELLI
OCT. 12
SARA HORNBACHER & LILY LACK
LIMELIGHT • 10PM-12AM
660 SIXTH AVE. at 20TH ST. • COMPLIMENTARY ADMISSION FOR
YOU AND A GUEST WITH THIS AD $15 WITHOUT

WEDNESDAY
SEPT. 16
EAST VILLAGE ART VIDEOS with DAVID BLAIR,
JAVIER DOMINGO, JIM C, DRAGAN ILIC, FRANZ
VILA, DOWNTOWN TONIGHT & MANY MORE
SEPT. 23
EAST VILLAGE PERFORMANCE VIDEOS with
NAKED EYE Cinema, DRAGAN ILIC, JULIUS KLEIN
MICHAEL CARTER Vindaloo, MIKE BIDLO, DAVID
BLAIR, NO SE NO, JIM C, PENNY WARD & MORE
SEPT. 30
EAST VILLAGE MUSIC VIDEOS with MARIE
MARTINE & PHILIPPE BOUNOS (ALAN VEGA, MARTY
REV), FUSION ARTS TV (DEMO MOE), THE JICKETS
VIDEO VOID, STEVEN POLLACK & WOLF STAEHLE
(KENNY SCHARF, JOHN SEX) & MANY MORE
OCT. 7
"SEX & VIOLENCE" with NICK ZEDD'S GEEK MAGGOT
BINGO, RICHARD KERN'S MANHATTAN LOVE SUICIDES SCOTT
& BETH B, ERIC MITCHELL, TINA L'HOTSKY & MORE
OCT. 14
"LOVE JAM"
VIDEOS ON A ROMANTIC THEME - FEATURING EROTIC
PSYCHE   &   SPECIAL   GUESTS
2B GAS BAR • 9-11PM
CORNER OF 2ND STREET & AVE B
$2 DONATION REQUESTED FOR THE ARTISTS
PRESENTED BY: MONDAY/WEDNESDAY/FRIDAY
VIDEO CLUB ■ A NOT-FOR-PROFIT PROJECT OF
COLLABORATIVE PROJECTS, INC. • FUNDED IN PART BY NEA
MAIL TO: 73 E. HOUSTON ST. NYC
10012 (212) 219-0765

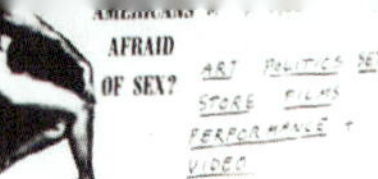
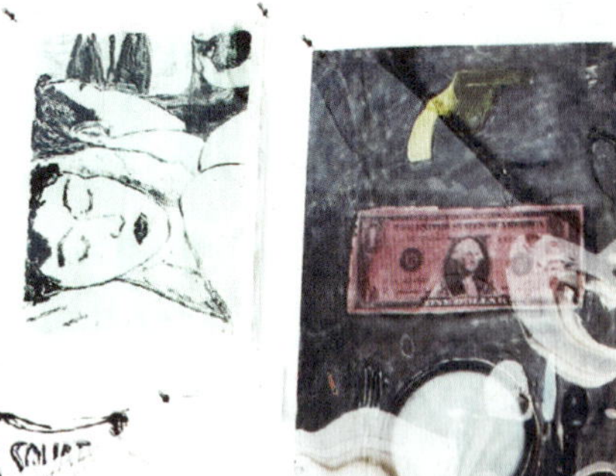
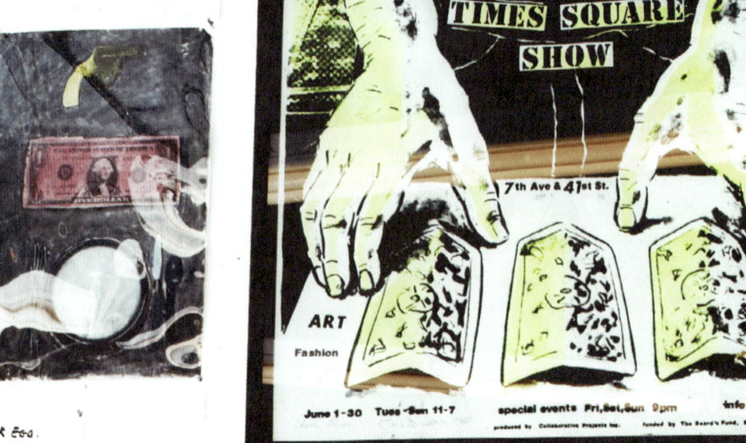
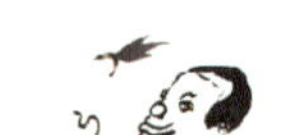
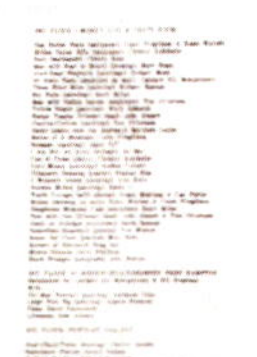
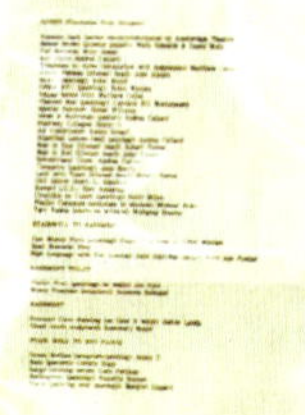
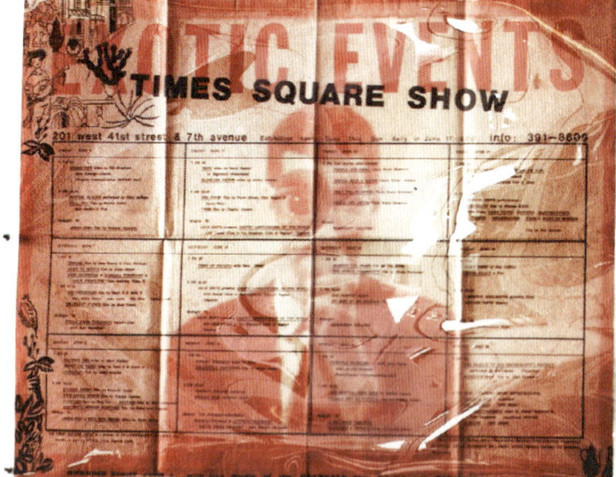
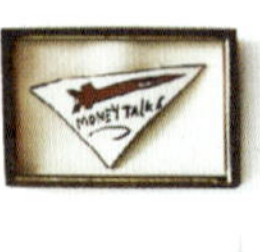
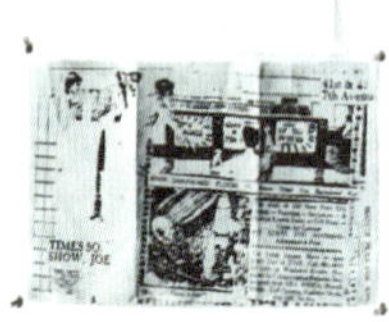
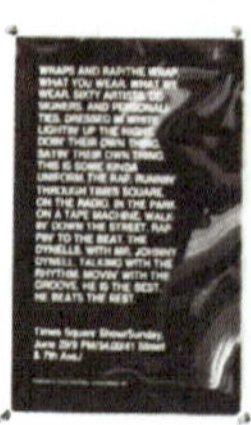
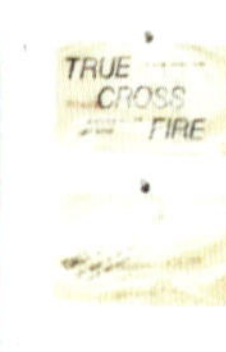
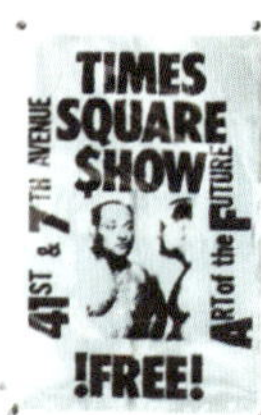
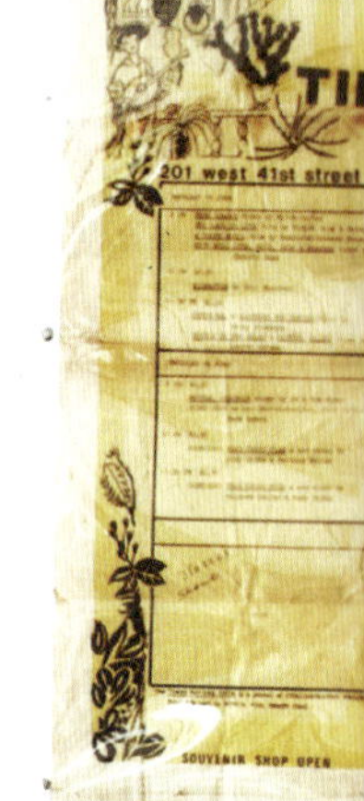
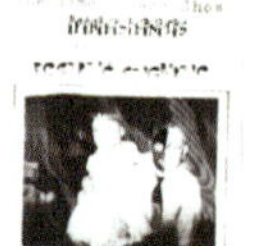
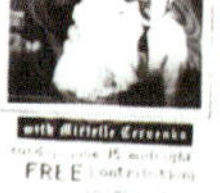

Installation view of *A Show About Colab (and Related Activities)*, October 15–November 30, 2011, at Printed Matter, New York. Photos: John Moeller.

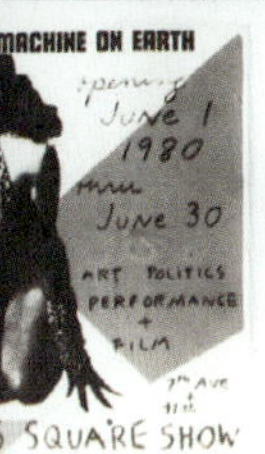
MACHINE ON EARTH
opening
June 1
1980
thru
June 30
ART POLITICS
PERFORMANCE
+
FILM
SQUARE SHOW

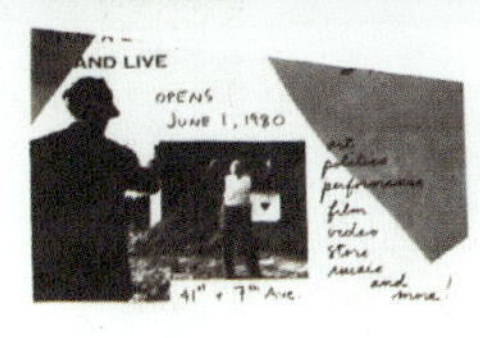
AND LIVE
OPENS
JUNE 1, 1980
41st + 7th Ave.

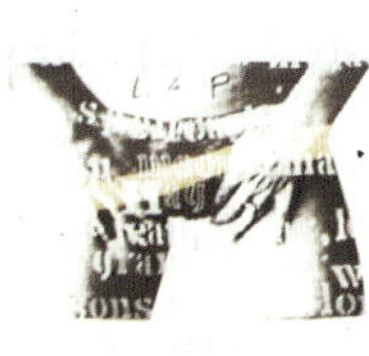
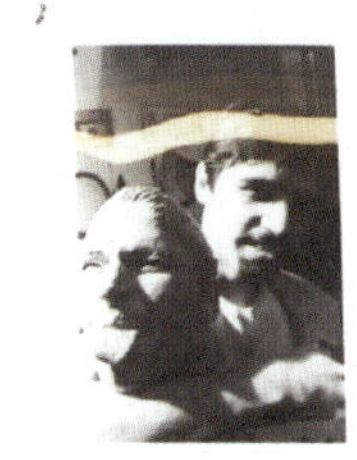
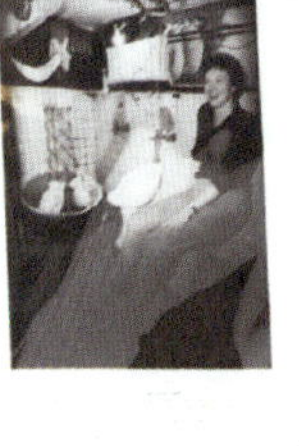
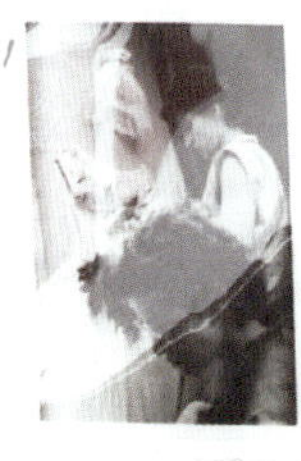

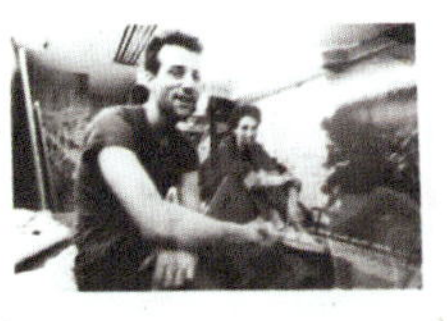
ENTAL BUSINE
ATH ADVICE

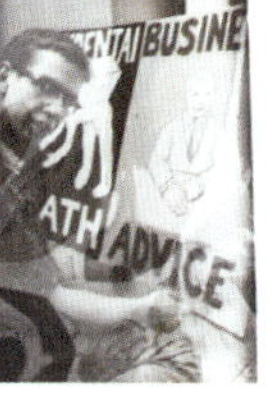
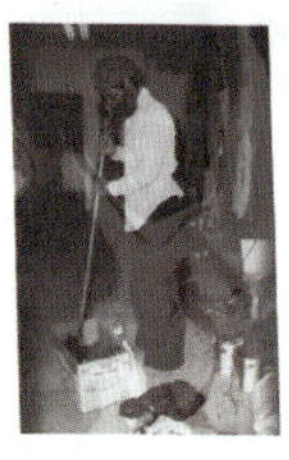
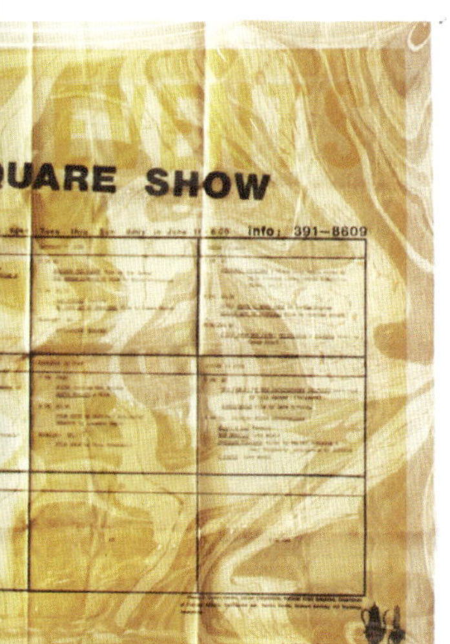
QUARE SHOW
Info: 391-8609
juke box

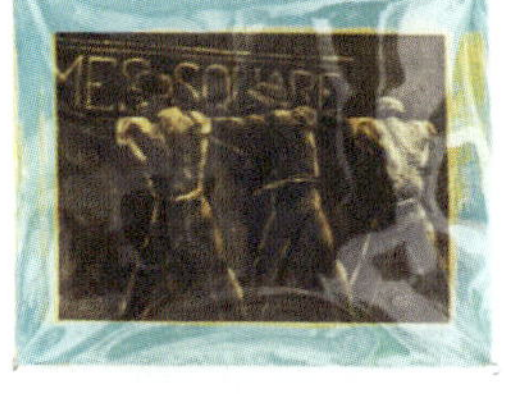
ES SQUARE

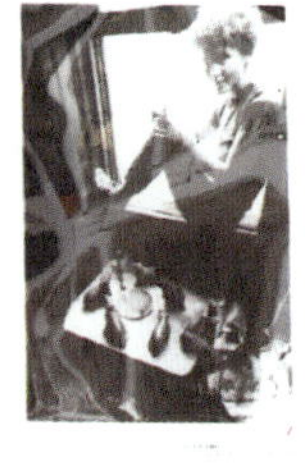
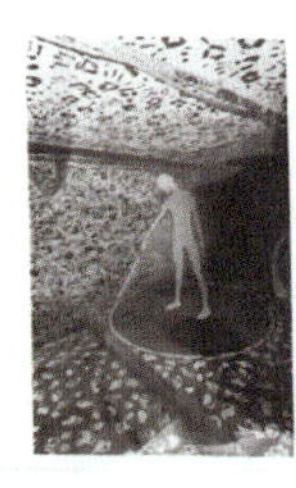
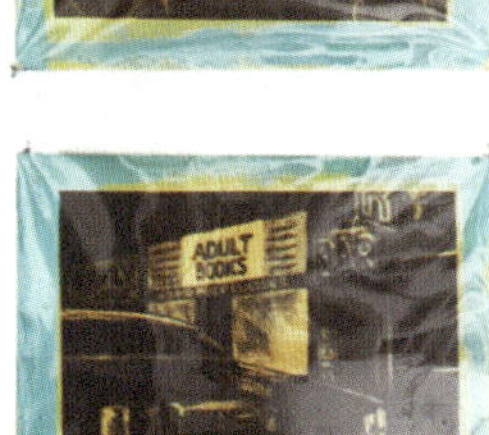
ADULT
BOOKS

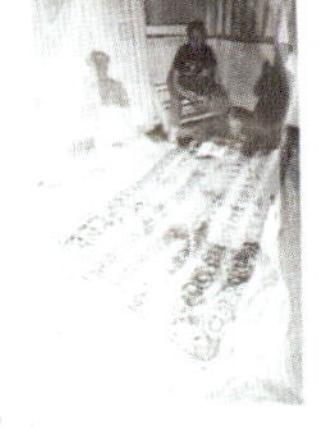
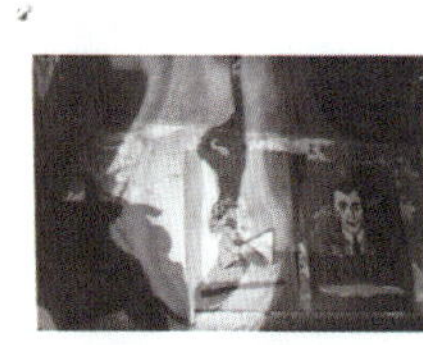
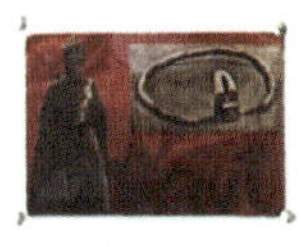
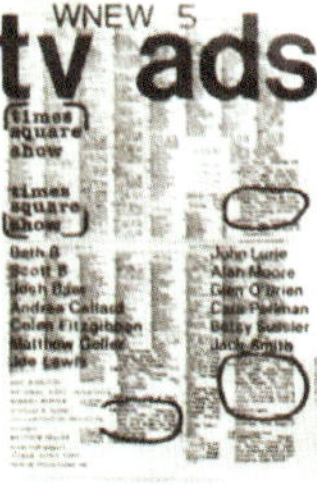
WNEW 5
tv ads
times
square
show
times
square
show
Beth B
Scott B
Josh Baer
Andrea Callard
Colen Fitzgibbon
Matthew Geller
Joe Lewis
John Lurie
Alan Moore
Glenn O'Brien
Cara Perlman
Betsy Sussler
Jack Smith

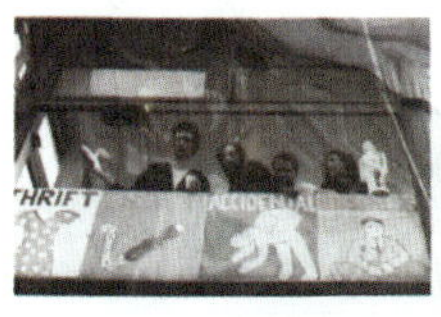
THRIFT
ACCIDENTAL

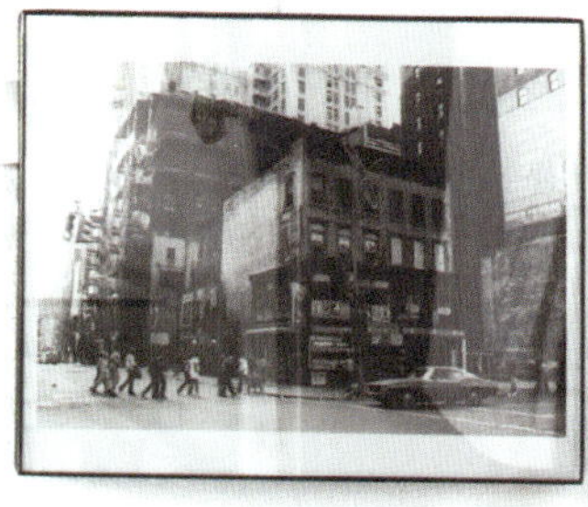
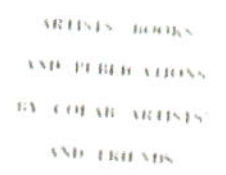
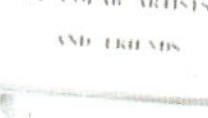
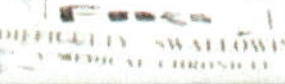
ARTISTS BOOKS
AND PUBLICATIONS
BY COLAB ARTISTS
AND FRIENDS
DIFFICULTY SWALLOWING
A MEDICAL CHRONICLE

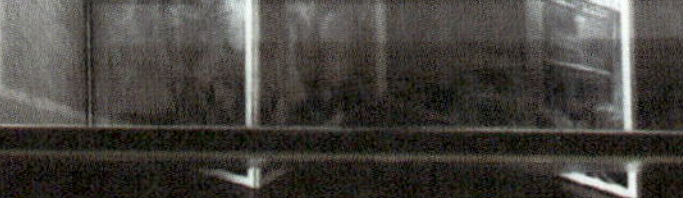

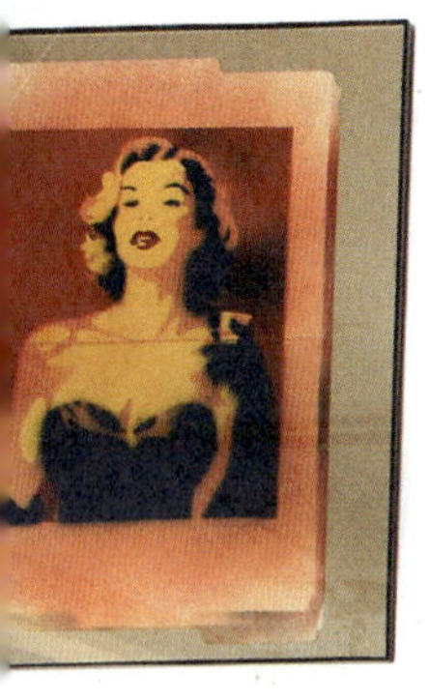
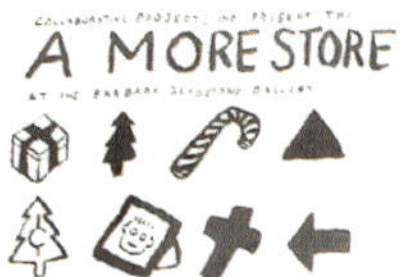

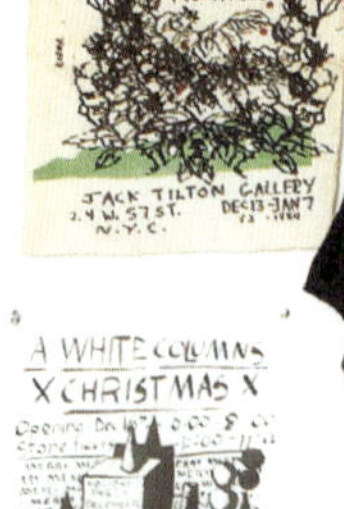

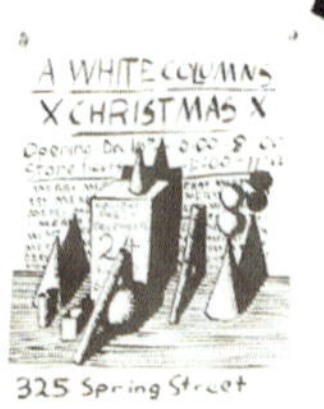

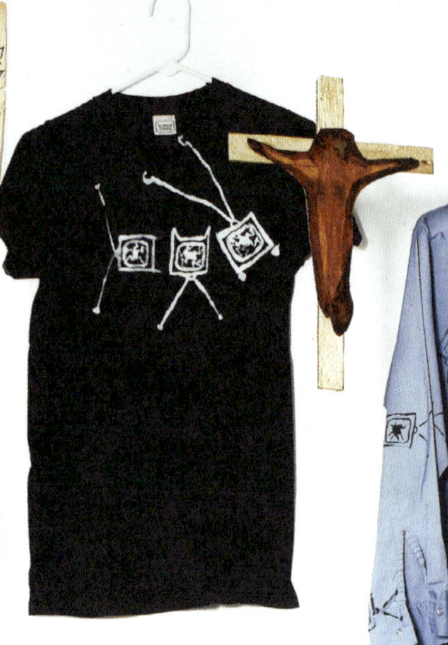
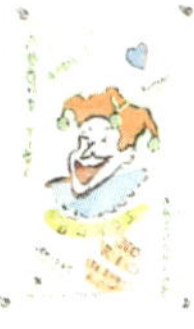
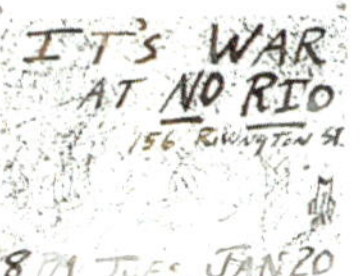

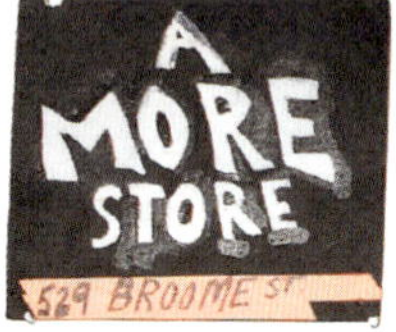

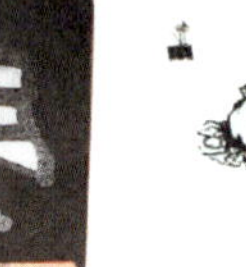
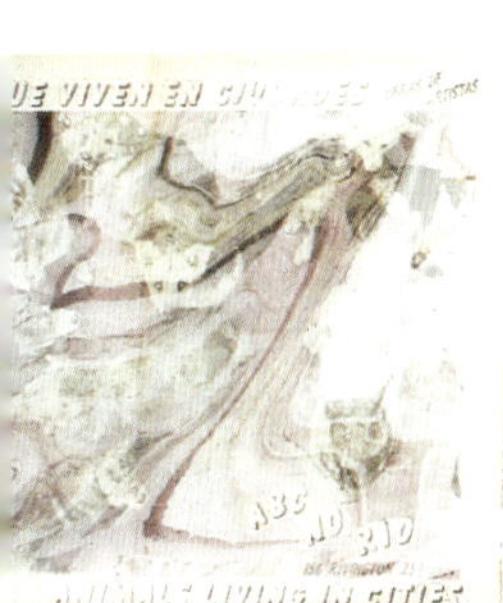

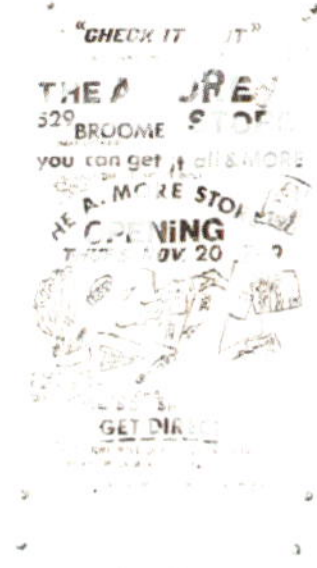

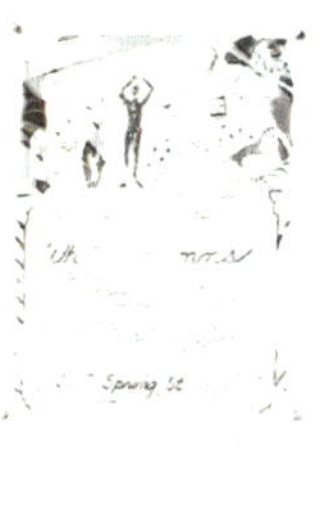

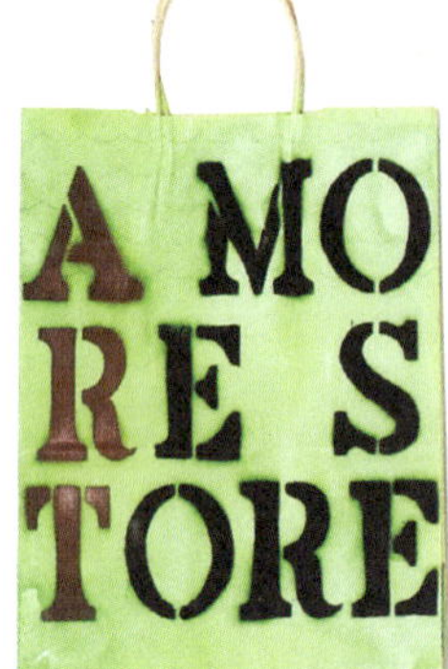

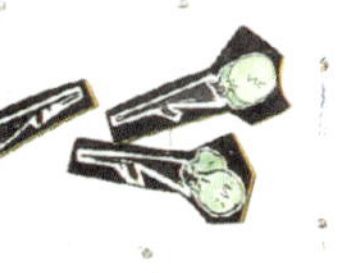
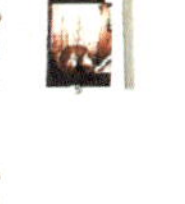

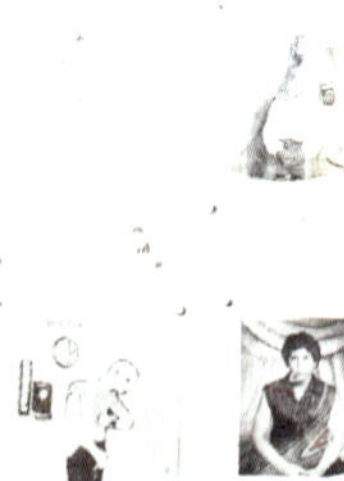
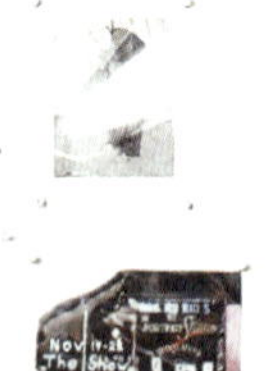
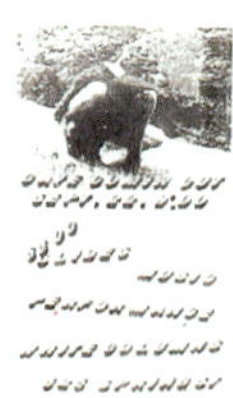
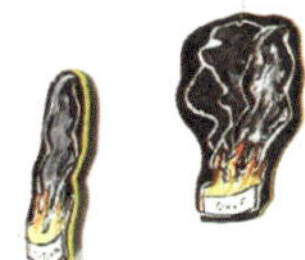

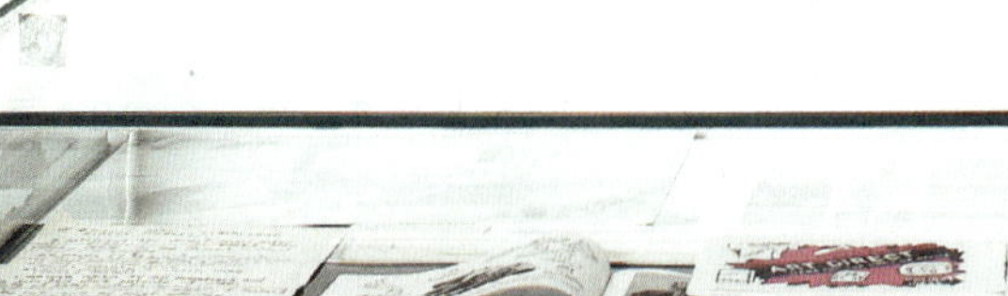

Installation view of *A Show About Colab (and Related Activities)*, October 15–November 30, 2011 at Printed Matter, New York. Photos: John Moeller.

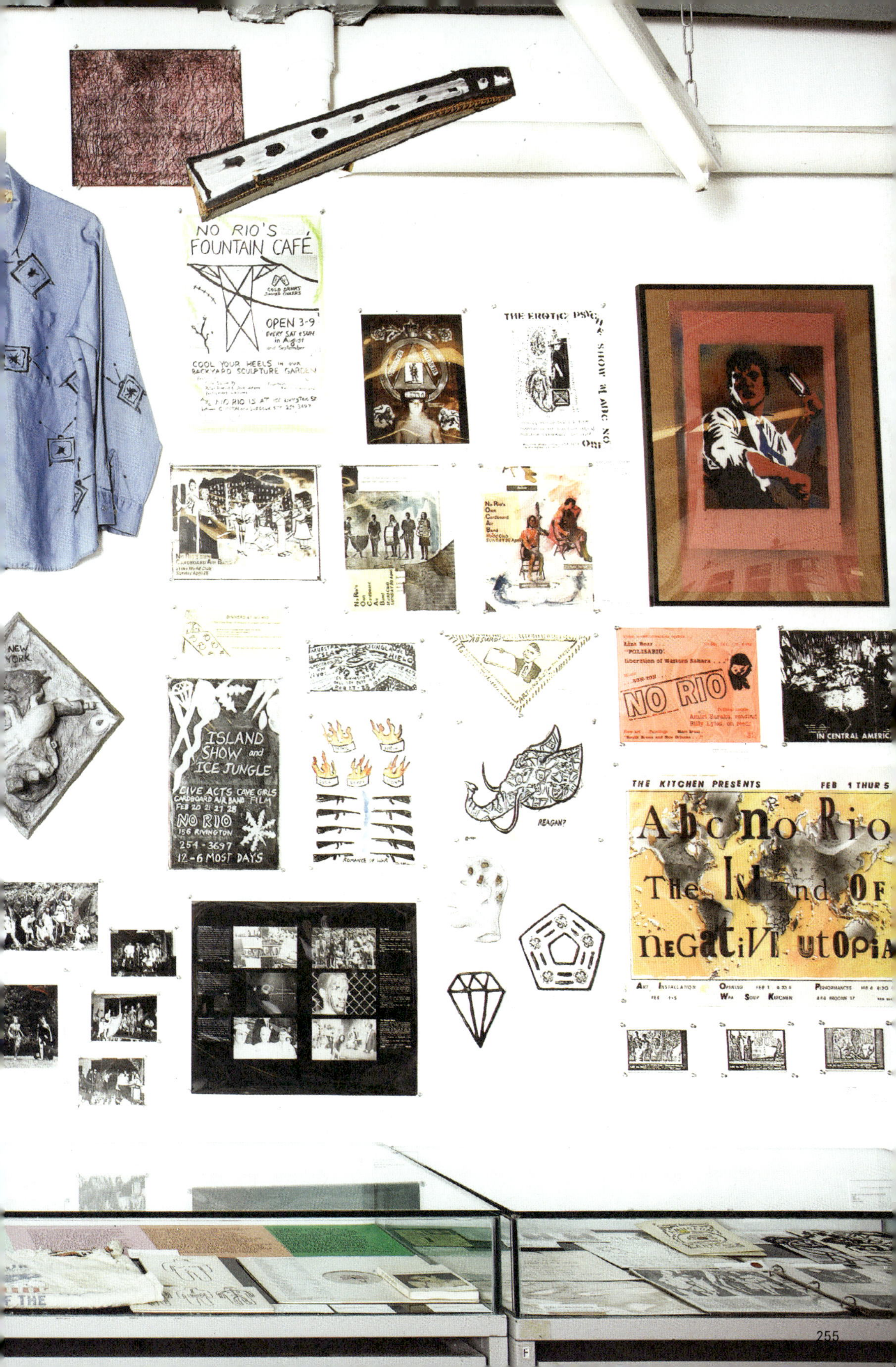

Colab held regular meetings, of course, to scheme and plan and do a little bit of work. The greatest attention was typically focused on allocating grant money for a wide range of projects. Meetings were frequently acrimonious and almost universally considered to be pure torture. In fact, you could say that Colab democracy worked because nobody could stand being in charge for very long. It's an amazing thought: Colab managed to sustain itself as a democratic, collaborative, consensual organization because the meetings were unbearable.

Most Colab members were political in a radical, anarchistic sense. Their politics arose from their own experiences. This bottom-up from-the-streets radicalism is evident in the manifesto for *The Real Estate Show*, which is stirring in its directness. "The action is extralegal—it illuminates no legal issues, calls for no 'rights.' It is pre-emptive and insurrectionary." The statement goes on: "The intention of this action is to show that artists are willing and able to place themselves and their work squarely in a context which shows solidarity with oppressed people [and] a recognition that mercantile and institutional structures oppress and distort artists' lives and works…"

Me, I wasn't so good with politics. My favorite manifestation of ideology was when we put out a list of Colab members with their phone numbers—a contact list—that included Joe Stalin on it. You'll remember that the art world, despite its economic role as a provider of luxury status objects for the rich, always has had groups that take progressive, reformist and even revolutionary positions. Some of our predecessors, like the journals *October* and *The Fox*, which were founded in the 1970s, were almost entirely theoretical and academic—and had little to do with us. Group Material, which was contemporaneous with Colab, was similarly founded by a group of artists, but one with a more theoretical background and practice.

Colab, by contrast, was much more about lived professional and political experience. Few of us taught, and even those who did were hardly academics. We demonstrated a real variety of vocations, and a variety of motives. Peter Fend was into recasting systems on a global scale. Bobby G was firmly rooted in the social dynamics of his Lower East Side neighborhood. I remember Beth B declaring at a meeting that she wanted to launch a project devoted to "human rights." Jenny Holzer was fascinated by the command structures of language, while Kiki Smith was exploring the structures of female carnality. And lots of other members, notably like Coleen Fitzgibbon and Robin Winters, seemed to me to function as born rabble-rousers.

In my more romantic moments, I like to think of Colab as a special homemade kind of socialist commune—from each according to their abilities, to each according to their needs. What did that mean in practice? I would joke that Colab provided a context for both the socially maladept and the stars of tomorrow. It was a perfect utopia of small gestures, the kind of thing that good artists everywhere do every day.

—Walter Robinson, Dec. 16, 2015

I hope the images and first-hand accounts in
this valuable book spark an updated iteration
of Colab — the anarchic group of artists
that lit up the early 1980s. Creators of the
iconic *Real Estate Show*, *Times Square Show*,
Manifesto Show, and much much more, Colab
was wide open to good ideas, good actions,
and good art. Colab lives! Que Viva Colab!

– Lucy R. Lippard

Colab, as an altogether contemporary
collective on the downtown streets of the
NYC artworld in that transitional wonderland
betwixt the late 70s/early 80s, seemed to
exist both welcoming and imperious. Their
pronounced aesthetic, whether it be the
Manifesto Show just up the street from CBGB,
or the abandoned massage parlor real estate
take over of the legendary *Times Square
Show*, the essential tenet of their purpose
was explicit: to be a significant model for the
artist-as-communitarian engaging in activism
as creative impulse.

— Thurston Moore

Colab's innovative members, projects, ideas,
and attitudes were very important inspirations
and encouragements to me as my own artistic
path was just coming into focus. This beautiful
book is an indispensable artifact.

— Jim Jarmusch

Published by:
Printed Matter, Inc.
231 11th Avenue
New York, NY 10001
www.printedmatter.org

First printing of 1,000 copies, 2015
Second printing of 1,500 copies, 2024

ISBN 978-0-89439-085-2

Edited by Max Schumann
Assistant Editors: Dana Kash, Laura Kenner, and Art & Context (Alexis Bhagat and Erin Sickler)

Design direction: Garrick Gott
Design: Yoshié Hozumi
Typeset in Theinhardt, Leitura, and Aperçu Mono

Printed in Canada by The Prolific Group

This publication was made possible with generous support from The Andy Warhol Foundation for the Visual Arts; the New York State Council on the Arts with the support of Governor Kathy Hochul and the New York State Legislature; the Gesso Foundation; and Jenny Holzer & Tom Otterness.

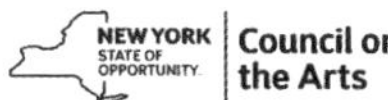
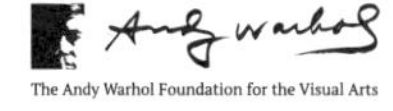

Very special thanks to Keith Gray, Julie Harrison, Jenny Holzer, Yoshié Hozumi, Lisa Kahane, Francene Keery, Nancy Linn, Hannah Marshall, Marc Miller, Tom Otterness, Megan Pai, Greg Pavek, Erin Sickler, Walter Robinson, and all of the many artists and individuals who loaned works, wrote texts, lent advice, fact-checked, and otherwise supported this project.

A Book About Colab (and Related Activities) has been published subsequent to the exhibition *A Show About Colab (and Related Activities)* which took place at Printed Matter October 15–November 30, 2011.

The exhibition and this publication were assembled from publications, documents, ephemera and artwork loaned by:

Philip Aarons and Shelley Fox Aarons, Charlie Ahearn, John Ahearn, Liza Béar, Andrea Callard, the Collaborative Projects Archive, Mitch Corber, Jody Culkin, Jane Dickson, Stefan Eins, Brigitte Engler, Bradley Eros, Barbara Ess, Peter Fend, Coleen Fitzgibbon, Matthew Geller, Mike Glier, Bobby G (Robert Goldman), Ilona Granet, Julie Harrison, Jenny Holzer, Becky Howland, Nancy Linn, Michael McClard, Ann Messner, Eric Mitchell, Terry Mohre, Alan Moore, Barbara Moore, James Nares, Tom Otterness, Cara Perlman, Judy Rifka, Walter Robinson, Christy Rupp, Jane Sherry, Terise Slotkin, Kiki Smith, Jolie Stahl, Franz Vila, Tom Warren, and Robin Winters